# FOURSCORE YEARS AND COUNTING

# FOURSCORE YEARS AND COUNTING

*My Life in Seven Chapters*

Sybil Belle Short Fudge Dewhirst

authorHOUSE®

*AuthorHouse™*
*1663 Liberty Drive*
*Bloomington, IN 47403*
*www.authorhouse.com*
*Phone: 1-800-839-8640*

*Published by AuthorHouse    03/01/2012*

*ISBN: 978-1-4685-5598-1 (sc)*
*ISBN: 978-1-4685-5599-8 (e)*

*Library of Congress Control Number: 2012903163*

# CONTENTS

Part I     AFRICA (January 1923 - December 1940) ........................... 1

Part II    TEXAS (January 1941 - June 1943) ................................ 117

Part III   ALABAMA (July 1943 - February 1976) ......................... 143

Part IV    AFRICA AGAIN (March 1976 - February 1981) ............. 341

Part V     CALIFORNIA (March 1981 - August 1983).................... 431

Part VI    OHIO (September 1983 - January 2005).......................... 465

Part VII   MISSISSIPPI (February 2005 -   )...................................... 585

## CONTENTS

# DEDICATION

To my parents,

Will and Delia Short,

whose lives demonstrated God's will

in word and example.

To God be the glory.

**Will and Delia Short Wedding (1919).**

**Will and Delia Short and children, 1961.**
**Standing (L-R): Bill, Margaret Ann, Beth, Sybil, Foy.**

# Acknowledgements

Looking back on this writing, calling it "done," I gratefully acknowledge the urging and encouragement of my children and grandchildren, with the added enthusiastic boosts from other kinfolks and close friends. The writing of this memoir began about ten years ago as a simple request of my children and grandchildren for the story of my years "growing up in Africa." That did not sound like too much to tackle but when that was done they would not let it rest. They wanted to know about their own growing up years from their mother's viewpoint. Before I knew quite what had happened, I found myself in deep water struggling to tell of my seven completely different lives that my eighty plus years naturally divided itself into.

Heartfelt thanks to my daughter-in-law Sara Faye, who capably edited my writing and patiently put up with my sagging and lagging at times. When I was struggling, searching for the right words to wade through a difficult patch, she had the uncanny ability of putting words to my thoughts. Her loving encouragement and suggestions kept me spurred on to the end and I acknowledge her help with deep appreciation.

THE AUTHOR

# FOREWORD

One of the remarkable women listed in Jesus' genealogy was the Moabite woman named Ruth, the great grandmother of King David. I've been thinking a lot about her lately as I have read the manuscript of the autobiography of my mother-in-law. In some ways I feel a kinship with Ruth as never before. She was drawn to a godly man whom she grew to love, and she was welcomed into a family with strange speech, different customs and a table full of "strangers."

My relationship with Sybil Fudge's son brought us together and I was graciously received and welcomed but marveled at this woman so different from my own mother. Her speech was marked by a decidedly British-sounding flair, she was quiet and reserved, hospitable though not fancy, and busy with a bustling, big family and ever-present friends and neighbors of her six children, even while working full time at the family bookstore in town. I marveled at her efficiency though often feeling intimidated by her wisdom and infinite patience.

For over forty-four years filled with births and deaths and changes, the cords of love have knit us together, her faithful love and support have encouraged me and her godly life has inspired a closer walk with God. But reading this story of her life has opened new vistas in truly understanding and appreciating the multi-faceted jewel she is.

From those early days in Africa emerges the picture of a feisty, curious yet obedient girl who learned the art of homemaking with lessons in sewing and cooking and entertaining even in the primitive conditions of unsettled Northern Rhodesia. From British boarding school to sailing to America for college education, she developed the grit and coping skills she would use all her life, adjusting to new and different environments.

The adventures in mothering six children and running a household on a shoestring budget, the resourcefulness and resilience in business dealings provide insight into the strong and spunky woman she was. Embracing changes and venturing out into new worlds, always carrying her values and principles—this was the widow who would not be bitter or self-pitying, the woman who returned to Africa to care for aging parents, who moved to California and learned to sail, and to an Ohio farm with a second husband who taught her to fish and to use a power saw.

This is the life story of a remarkable woman, whose life fits the profile of the Proverbs 31 worthy woman. It is a sweeping saga which will entertain, inform, amuse, and inspire you. The transformation of this little child of missionaries into the accomplished, active, artistic woman whose life continues to bless so many will be a joy to read and an eye-opening experience to all who see her only as a paragon of godly virtue.

*Sara Faye Locke Fudge*

# INTRODUCTION

FOURSCORE YEARS AND COUNTING is written at the request of my children and grandchildren. It is not a strictly chronological account, nor is it a history book, though some dates are given. My life has been logically divided into seven distinctly different lives. This is a collection of memories of my life: most are my own along with some stories that were told in my hearing enough times that I remember them as though they were my own. My siblings will remember some of the same stories and events in different ways because we were different ages at the time and heard with different perspectives and personalities. Occasionally more than one of us claims the same story as our own; that does not change the facts but some details may differ, depending on who tells it.

I relate memories of family life as my children grew up and tell about other things only as they are connected to that life. My children no doubt will have different memories of some of the same events.

This then is the way it looks to me from where I am now—to the best of my memory.

\*    \*    \*

# Prologue (1894–1922)

William Newton, born December 7, 1894 to James Taylor Short and Flora Ann (Epperson) Short. One sister, Sybil Ann. Two brothers, Clarice and Christie.

Nancy A'Delia (Delia) O'Neal, born January 11, 1896 to Edward O'Neal and Amanda Elizabeth (Phillips) O'Neal. Five brothers, Otto (died in infancy), George, Hershel, Audrey and Joe. Two sisters, Alice Belle and Leota.

William Newton was born in Rome, Kansas. Nancy A'Delia was born in Johnstown, Missouri.

Will and Delia attended Cordell Christian College in Cordell, Oklahoma, where Delia and Sybil (Will's sister) roomed together. Will was drafted into the U.S. Army, sent to Germany just before the end of WWI and remained in army of occupation for some months. Delia taught in a one-room country school for a time and graduated from practical nurses training by the time Will returned from Germany and was discharged.

Will and Delia married August 30, 1919. They lived in Harper, Kansas until they went to Africa.

In Kansas, they heard a missionary from India speak about that work and decided to go to India if possible. Their application for entering the country was denied. About that time they heard through F.B. Shepherd about the work of John Sherriff in Southern Rhodesia, Africa, about the urgent need for workers in the Rhodesias. They felt God was opening a door for them in that field.

Harold Foy was born in Harper, Kansas January 17, 1921. He was eight months old when they sailed from Montreal, Canada to Cape Town, South Africa. Their mothers felt they would never see them again. Will,

Delia and Foy landed at Cape Town November 19, 1921. From there they went by train to Bulawayo, Southern Rhodesia. John and Emma Sherriff took them under their wing and for about eighteen months taught them much about living in Africa.

The Sherriffs had migrated from New Zealand years before, as had close friends, Hadfields and Bowens. John Sherriff earned his living as a master stonemason and many buildings and monuments still in Bulawayo today show his handiwork. African men who worked for him came to Bulawayo from villages of Southern and Northern Rhodesia, Nyasaland and other adjoining countries. Around their evening cook-fires John Sherriff taught them to read and write, using Bibles that he supplied. When those men went home, either to stay or to visit, they taught others what they had learned. These migrant workers took the Gospel of Jesus Christ to people in those countries who in turn taught others. Soon there were many calls for more teachers. It was to find help for these calls that John Sherriff had made the appeal in the U.S.

John Sherriff and Will received permission to work in Northern Rhodesia. They picked a spot about twenty-five miles from Livingstone among some villages where one of the converted men, Peter Mesiya, had been preaching during his visits home. He became Will's friend, helper and interpreter. Sinde Mission was located eight miles from the railroad that ran north from Cape Town through Bulawayo, Livingstone and on to the north. The nearest doctor, hospital and supply stores were in Livingstone.

From a letter written to the U.S. *(Feb. 1926) "Three years ago Brother Sherriff and I came on a freight train to Senkobo Siding, arriving after dark, and camping a few yards from the rails . . . In the morning after a little breakfast, we started west and soon came to a little stream which we followed the remainder of the way. The hills on each side were covered with brush and grass. When almost to the village, Brother Sherriff angled off to the south end of a little ridge and said he thought that was a good place for the building of a mission. This ridge was to become the site of Sinde Mission, and within six months after that visit we had permission to enter here, and I came up to start the work." (W. N. Short)*

\* \* \*

# PART I

## AFRICA

# January 1923–December 1940

## Northern Rhodesia 1923-1928

**Sinde Mission** If the immigration authorities of India had not refused permission for my parents to enter that country as missionaries in 1920, India would likely have been the country of my birth. Instead, I was born in Bulawayo, Southern Rhodesia, January 27, 1923.

When I was six months old, Mother took my brother Foy (2 1/2 years old) and me by train from Bulawayo to join Daddy at Sinde Mission in Northern Rhodesia. Daddy met the train in Livingstone and rode with us to Senkobo Siding, a spot on the railroad eight miles from the mission, where trains stopped on request for loading or unloading. There was a water tank for the trains and one building where Mr. and Mrs. Wilson lived. They handled the mail for the surrounding area and became very good friends with my parents.

Daddy had left instructions at the mission for us to be met at the siding with a borrowed sledge pulled by four yoked oxen tended by a driver and a young lead-boy. The natives cut their sledges from the fork of a tree. It resembled a giant sling-shot to which yoked oxen were hitched—the larger the sledge, the more oxen. A floor of strong sticks across the two branches of the fork kept the load off the ground and loads were secured with rawhide rope. When hauling grain, a large basket was fastened to the floor of the sledge. The one that met us had a basket on it.

For this trip Daddy had lined the sledge basket with quilts and pillows. Foy and I rode in comfort with Daddy and Mother walking alongside. Foy played happily beside the sleeping baby; they could hear him imitating the driver's cattle calls.

The dirt road followed a foot path through the rough country-side. Torrential rains had eroded deep ruts and the sandy soil had become loose sand, sometimes deep enough to bury the runners of a sledge. Travel was slow but steady, the lead-boy and driver carefully keeping to the higher ground. There was no time for getting stuck in the sand; they needed to get to the mission before dark when humans stayed inside their houses, letting wild animals have the outside. But oxen sometimes have a mind of their own. The lead-boy suddenly realized the sledge was too close to the deep rut and tried frantically to pull the oxen away from the edge—he was too late. The driver rushed forward to help him stop the oxen as Daddy struggled in vain to hold the basket upright. Mother watched in horror as the sledge tipped slowly on its side, spilling her babies and luggage into the sand. There were no injuries and while Mother quieted us, Daddy and the driver righted the sledge, got it to level ground and reloaded. The wide-eyed lead boy meanwhile held the oxen in place with a tight rein. There were some shallow spruits (creeks) to be crossed and at one of them the sledge tipped at a dangerous angle but Daddy was able to hold it upright and we reached the mission without further mishap—before dark.

After learning as much as he could about living in the tropics from the Sherriffs in Bulawayo, Daddy had arrived in Northern Rhodesia to begin work from the ground up. He had left Mother and Foy in Bulawayo promising to get them after my birth. He hoped by that time to have a place to live built on the mission. The chosen mission site was registered with the government as Sinde Mission, ground was cleared, temporary housing begun for family and workers and a garden planted.

From Bulawayo Mother brought with her Molly, the Sherriff's grown adopted daughter and two young "colored" girls, Ella and Rhoda, who had been living with the Sherriffs. Ella was about 12, and Rhoda about 9. Their father was a Scotsman, their mother an African; because they were "colored" and wanted by neither their mother's family nor their father's, the girls had been given a home by the Sherriffs. When Mother was ready to go north they asked my parents if the girls could live with us at Sinde Mission. And so they temporarily became part of our family. Mother taught Ella housekeeping and cooking and Rhoda became little nursemaid to Foy and me and later to Beth. This meant she watched us when we were outside and played with us while making sure we always wore our hats and didn't get out of the yard. Mother home-schooled the girls. We loved our "big sisters" and they lived with us until we came to the U.S. on furlough in 1928.

Temporary grass huts housed Daddy and the workers for the first few months. Sunday preaching and communion service was conducted under a big shade tree, unless it was raining when they went into one of the small buildings. Under the same tree was the schoolhouse on weekdays. Their first pupils were a few grown young men who came from the villages to work on the mission and wanted to learn reading and writing. Gradually more came but it was some time before these natives understood the concept of daily school attendance. Many villagers came for medical treatment and Mother and Daddy often went to the village to treat those more seriously ill or injured.

My parents' work had begun and they were not afraid of hard work. They had grown up in the country—Daddy in Kansas, Mother in Oklahoma—accustomed to working. Their physical strength was second only to their unshakeable faith in God. That faith saw them through some unspeakably difficult times and gave us children a sense of confidence and safety.

**Baby Sybil.**

**Peter Mesiya** From the beginning Daddy's right-hand helper was a man named Peter Mesiya, whose home village was near the mission. In the early 1900s he had learned about Christ while working with John Sherriff in the Bulawayo stone yard. He returned to his home in Northern Rhodesia to teach others the Gospel. He announced to the villagers that on the next Sunday he would conduct a service under a tree just outside of the village. No one came and he worshipped alone that Sunday—and the next—and the next. For several months he worshipped alone, all the while talking to the villagers during the week. Finally his mother joined him so there were two who worshipped every Sunday. A year went by before others began to come and very slowly the number increased. Their influence spread into surrounding villages until by 1923, when Daddy arrived, there were more places calling for teachers than Peter Mesiya could serve. He had sent word to John Sherriff for help and my parents had answered that call.

On village trips Peter was Daddy's fellow-preacher, interpreter, guide, protector, advisor and friend. On one trip when Daddy became extremely ill with malaria, Peter, with the help of their carriers, brought Daddy back to the mission in a mashila, (a hammock on a single pole carried between two men) running much of the way. When Mother saw Daddy's condition she knew he must get to the doctor. She could not leave the children so she trusted Peter to get him to the train at Senkobo Siding and from there to take him by train to the hospital in Livingstone. While Daddy was gone a trusted African slept in our kitchen as protection for the family.

About two years after their work together began, Peter Mesiya became ill and died. Soon after that Komboli, another African preacher, became Daddy's life-long friend and advisor. Peter was older than Daddy, Komboli was about Daddy's age. I was too young to remember those men personally but as we grew up, their names were familiar in our household as Daddy told stories of their work and adventures together. They were outstanding examples of faith and steadfast friendship. Even after Daddy and Mother moved to Bulawayo Daddy and Komboli stayed in touch with each other by letter and occasionally visited each other until they were in their eighties.

**Houses** Daddy's first house was a grass hut—a framework of poles, covered with long grass and a straw-strewn dirt floor. There he lived while he built the pole-and-daager (mud) house with two rooms.

Poles about six inches in diameter were set in the ground adjoining each other and topped with a thatched roof. Cracks between the poles were filled with daager, then walls, inside and out were plastered with more daager. When dry the walls were whitewashed, making it lighter inside and making it look good outside; the lime whitewash also discouraged white-ants (termites). A ceiling of cheesecloth was stretched across each room to catch insects, spiders, lizards or anything falling from the grass roof. Windows were small openings left in the walls and covered with screen. During the rainy season wooden shutters kept the rain out.

The floor was clay, gathered from white-ant heaps, leveled and tamped while still damp. All tea leaves were saved and dried. Once a week they were dampened in a pan of water, scattered on the floor, one room at a time, then gently swept up without raising much dust. Grass mats, bought from native women, covered high-traffic areas. Periodically the clay floors were treated with an application of clay thinned down with water to a sloppy consistency. The house worker dipped up handfuls of that mud and spread it and smoothed it by hand over the floors; it filled cracks and settled what would otherwise become a dusty surface. The Africans treated floors in their own huts in the same way.

The kitchen was a separate smaller hut in the back yard; the "stove" was an open fire under a piece of sheet metal that rested on three large stones. During the day a big teakettle was always at the boil on this stove. Skillets, pots and several canvas water bags hung on nails driven into a nearby tree. When a water bag was emptied it was immediately refilled with boiling water from the teakettle. Evaporation cooled the water in the bag. Adults drank cooled boiled water or hot tea. Children drank cooled boiled water and boiled fresh milk or tinned (canned) milk.

Daddy had worked hard to have the two rooms ready by the time we got there. At first their furniture was steamer trunks full of clothing and household goods, wooden boxes of tinned foods and other supplies:

wooden boxes served as seats and a trunk was used for a dining table until Daddy had time to make real ones. Beds were stretchers (camp cots) each with a mosquito net hanging over it. Mother unpacked white linen tablecloth, serviettes (napkins) and silverware to use in that hut. She could handle roughing it, too, but she believed cleanliness and table manners were vital, even for small children to learn. Floors were swept and furniture (trunks and boxes) were dusted regularly.

Native women made mats from long grass about ¼ to ½ inches in diameter split and tied together with fine bark string. They sold some mats but some were kept for their own use. Women spread them on the ground to sit on while men squatted or sat on stools cut from tree stumps. In their huts or around campfires, grass mats were their beds and each person had a blanket they bought or bartered for at the nearest trading store. Fires were kept burning all night and they slept with their heads toward the fire—they preferred to have a toe bitten off by a hyena or a wild dog than to lose an ear or nose.

Some distance from the dwelling Daddy built a toilet (outhouse)—a small hut with thatched roof, erected around a deep hole. Over the hole was a two-hole wooden seat, one large hole, one small. In the corner stood a bucket of lime, with a shovel for sprinkling lime into the pit. We never went to the toilet at night for fear of wild animals; an enamel chamber (pot) and matching bucket with lid (called a slop jar in Alabama) were in the bedroom for night use.

If one of us needed to get up during the night, we called, "Daddy, I need to use the bucket." Daddy lit a candle beside his bed to give us light. During daylight we said, "I need to go to the toilet." No matter how grown we were Mother wanted to know where we were at all times. When we children were old enough to help, the first order of business after dressing in the morning was to empty and wash our bedroom vessels. We did not know what it meant to have indoor plumbing until we went to boarding school at age thirteen, except for the nearly two years we were in the U.S.A. during 1928-1930.

Yards were scraped free of grass and weeds to discourage the approach of wild animals and snakes.

Until children were about five years old parents hired a nurse-maid to always be with them in the yard. As **we** grew old enough to ask permission to play outside, Mother's voice always followed us, "Watch out for snakes!"

Water was hauled from the river in fifty-five-gallon drums on a sledge pulled by oxen. Sundown was the signal for children's baths—in a washtub—with hot water from the big teakettle. After our bath, when we were very young, Mother bandaged our arms, legs and feet to prevent mosquito bites during supper and family devotions. Once in bed, under mosquito nets, bandages were removed and rolled up ready for the next evening. In bed with the mosquito net tucked under the mattress, I felt cozy and safe from mosquitoes and any other creatures that might be crawling or flying around.

In spite of mosquito nets over every bed and screens on the windows and doors, daily doses of quinine were required. I'm not sure at what age they began giving us quinine, but we were still babies, I know. A portion of a quinine tablet (no baby tablets in those days) was mashed in a teaspoon, a little sugar added and water to dissolve it. Daddy or Mother, with the baby in his/her arms held the baby's arms firmly to its side. The other person, holding the spoon in one hand and the baby's nose with the other, poured the medicine into its mouth when it opened for breath, being careful to judge when the baby could swallow. I later saw them give needed medicine to little African babies and they said that was how they gave us quinine to begin with. They must have done it correctly because we all survived!

As soon as we were big enough, they taught us to put the quarter or half pill of quinine at the very back of our tongue and drink a lot of water quickly. Thankfully we all learned to swallow pills well! They believed in a spoonful of sugar making the medicine go down long before Mary Poppins' time—or perhaps those were the times! Even when we had learned to swallow pills they had a spoon with some jam ready for us to eat to help take away the bitterness. Our parents also believed in Cod Liver Oil, that to us was almost but not quite as bad as Castor Oil. As soon as "Cod Liver Oil With Malt Extract" became available they kept it on hand. We thought it was like eating sweets (candy), so they kept the dosage time to a spoonful right after our quinine pill. In fact it was so good that Mother kept the Cod Liver Oil/Malt Extract jar hidden because we would have enjoyed eating it with a spoon any time.

Snugly in bed at night, we went to sleep to the sound of drums in the distant villages and animal sounds, some near and some far away—perhaps yelping of wild dogs fighting each other, grunts of warthogs, the howl of jackals and occasionally the roar of a lion. In the early morning Daddy walked around the yard to see the tracks of what had prowled around the night before. By what he saw he knew what to be on the lookout for during the day.

**Building** A pitsaw was a necessity. A felled tree was barked and set across a pit about six feet deep. One man stood in the pit and another straddled it, pulling and pushing a long large-toothed saw up and down cutting beams and planks. All the while Daddy was making bricks for a more permanent home. He made wooden brick-molds and had workers gather clay from white-ant hills. White ants tunneled below the sandy topsoil, down into clay and brought it up to form their vertical ant-tunnels above ground. Their tunnels were joined wall to wall as they went up in varying heights as much as ten feet, each ant-heap like a many-peaked skyscraper. This clay was also ideal for making floors and tennis courts. With their feet the workers mixed proper amounts of clay and sand to make thick smooth mud; with their hands they slapped that mixture hard into the wet molds to force out air bubbles before dumping the wet bricks onto a flat area to dry in the sun. Sun-dried bricks were used for temporary buildings, burnt bricks for permanent buildings. As the bricks dried, the ones to be burned were stacked in a huge kiln that contained thousands of bricks.

11

The kiln had three horizontal tunnels, called flues, about three feet high and three feet wide, running through the length of the kiln on ground level. Bricks were stacked beside and over the flues and the heat went up through the cracks. When the proper kiln height was reached a coating of very wet clay (called slime) was plastered over the whole kiln to keep in the heat. Kindling topped with firewood was laid on the ground through the tunnels. When the fire was burning well, the openings were sealed with bricks and mud. Periodically the flues were opened, the fire stoked and the flues again sealed to hold the heat. When the fire had burned for a specific number of days it was allowed to die and the kiln sat sealed until the bricks were cool enough to handle. In the building of brick walls thick mud was used as mortar between the bricks. The exterior joints were pointed with cement or real mortar to make them weather-proof.

Roofs of the first buildings were thatched with long grass, windows and door frames were made from planks cut from local hardwood trees. Windows and other building supplies had to be bought in Livingstone and shipped by train to Senkobo Siding where Daddy met the train with a sledge drawn by four or six oxen depending on the size of the load.

Daddy trained bricklayers and as he had time he worked with them to build a substantial brick house. When finished it had pressed tin ceilings, plastered walls and cement floors. The first roof was thatch, later replaced with a corrugated metal roof. Walls throughout were solid brick. Red ochre powder was mixed with the cement for floors and when thoroughly dry the floor was polished with red wax about once a month and buffed daily. Regularly buffed floors were beautiful—also good for children to skate sock-footed on—except for the trouble that followed when the tell-tale red on our socks betrayed us! When we were older Mother taught Beth and me to make braided rag-rugs to put beside our beds—much better than stepping out of a warm bed on to a cold cement floor.

**Home Life** We had candles in the bedrooms and learned early that matches and candles were not to be played with. Lanterns were used on camping trips, in the kitchen and for outside errands at night. Torches (flashlights) were indispensable indoors and outside. Daddy used a headlamp when he needed to carry his gun.

Paraffine (kerosene) lamps with glass chimneys sat on tables or at this stage of our lives could be carried by parents from room to room.

Basic furniture was gradually brought by train from Bulawayo (300 miles away), or bought in Livingstone. The houses had no closets but wardrobes (armoires) were later acquired for the bedrooms. Steamer trunks that came with Daddy and Mother from the States were used for storage. The trunks and anything in the house made of wood had to be moved regularly in case white ants had found a crack somewhere.

No matter what kind of house we lived in, Mother practiced meticulous housekeeping. Serviettes are called napkins in U.S. but in Africa napkins or nappies were worn by European babies on their bottoms. Native babies, for convenience, wore nothing except a string of beads around their middle, or sometimes a short dress or shirt. When old enough, boys wore loincloths and older girls and women wore gathered skirts and sometimes tops gathered on a yoke.

We learned to use a bread-and-butter knife, to hold fork, knife and spoon correctly and to say, "Pass the butter (scones, jam), please"—no reaching across a person or the table for anything. The plates were stacked in front of Daddy at his end of the table, where he carved the meat. He put a serving of meat on a plate, passed it up one side of the table to Mother, who put servings of vegetables on it then passed it down the other side to the person nearest Daddy. This was repeated until everyone was served. A breadboard with bread knife and loaf of bread sat at Daddy's left and he cut slices as requested. Daddy gave thanks before every meal. Loud talk, singing or whistling were not allowed at the table. After breakfast we had family Bible reading and prayer and again after supper. Everyone knelt for prayers then, at home and at church services.

Mail from overseas came by ship to Cape Town and from there by train. Letters sometimes took six or eight weeks to make the trip. Those letters from far away loved ones were like water to thirsty souls. Parcels of clothing often took three months or longer. Cablegrams were possible but used only in emergencies. Ladies in the U.S. sent clothing to missionary children and we learned the excitement of parcels arriving. Incoming mail was sometimes water-stained and stamped "Damaged at sea," and we imagined the storm it might have come through. Parcels were securely wrapped in oilcloth and sewn shut with string and we carefully saved both string and oilcloth. The oilcloth had flowers or designs on it so the missionaries could enjoy pretty tablecloths on the dining tables between meals.

**African School and Work** Molly was the school teacher and helped Mother and Daddy with the "doctoring." Gradually African children came from surrounding villages for school, to be taught Bible lessons, singing, reading, writing and arithmetic. Slates and chalk were provided. The students had no money for fees but at an early age their parents had trained them to work. My parents thought if the African students paid for their schooling by working they would appreciate it more. The students were divided into two groups, one group worked at assigned tasks for a half day in the morning while the other group had school. After lunch they changed places. Mother chose girls to train as helpers in the house and as nurse maids and taught them hygiene, simple housekeeping and childcare. Other girls worked in the vegetable and flower gardens, kept the yard scraped free of weeds and grass and did other outdoor chores. Daddy trained the boys in building, woodwork, gardening and odd jobs around the place. Jobs were suited to age and ability. Native children were accustomed to working for their parents, they herded cattle, tended younger children, hoed crops and like their parents they sang as they worked. Boys learned to carve wood, make bows and arrows and spears. Girls learned to make clay vessels, weave baskets and make grass mats. They made their toys from clay, sticks, wire or whatever their active imaginations taught them.

Adult African men came to the mission to apply for work and there was plenty. Food, clothes, living quarters and a little money was their pay. With those things furnished, they saved their money to buy bicycles or cows. If they had wives and family, the wives stayed in the village to tend the crops and cattle with the help of the children. Most of them went home to their villages on weekends but there was a compound on the mission where employees could live between their visits back to their villages. Some married workers brought their families to live with them on the mission. Individual villages were like large families ruled by a village chief.

When someone applied for housework, Mother taught him or her simple duties: the first task of the day was to come early in the morning to start the fire in the kitchen stove. Most Africans could tell time fairly accurately without a clock so if Mother said, "Come just before light" to start the fire in the stove, that guaranteed the kettle was boiling when Daddy got up at daybreak. Housework included doing dishes, keeping the kitchen and stove clean, the wood box filled, sweeping and buffing floors throughout the house.

**Doctoring** Wherever we lived, the nearest doctor became a good friend and taught Daddy and Mother about treating tropical ailments. As the natives learned what missionaries could do for the sick and injured they lined up in the back yard for treatment of everything from simple itch (scabies) and sore eyes (pink eye) to cough, headache, toothache, minor burns and more serious deep burns and cuts, broken bones, ulcers, malaria, bronchitis, pleurisy, pneumonia and leprosy and many unexpected and unknown ailments and injuries.

Medical supplies were limited but inventiveness and common sense were not. Daddy pulled teeth with sterilized wire pliers and lanced boils with a sterilized kitchen knife or razor blade. Later a retired dentist donated his instruments and a retiring doctor gave them some surgical tools. From the U.S. came old sheets for bandages, either whole or torn into strips and rolled ready to use. A supply of simple medicines was kept on hand: antiseptics, cough syrup, ointment for sore eyes, gargle (foul tasting) and salve called Zambuk for many uses. [Years later, in Alabama, I met "The Raleigh Man" who called on country and small-town housewives with his "rolling store." One of his wares was Raleigh's Salve and its smell reminded me of Zambuk.] Serious infections were treated with wet poultices of permanganate of potash solution. The permanganate came as dark purple powder that Mother mixed with boiled water. A lighter blue powder was used in a weak solution we called "Blue Water" for wet dressings on deep cuts or puncture wounds to prevent and treat infection. Bottles of Hydrogen Peroxide were always on hand.

Permanganate of potash in a solution with cold boiled water was used to disinfect fresh vegetables for eating raw, such as carrots and cabbage. Lettuce was considered too delicate for the permanganate solution and was soaked briefly in very strong salt water. After either one everything was thoroughly rinsed in cold *boiled* water.

**Mwellazuba** Local African women washed their clothes in a river not far from the mission. They worked in groups with loud talking, laughing and singing, sounds that ordinarily kept crocodiles away. But one day a crocodile suddenly appeared and seized the hand of a young woman named Mwellazuba as she was bent over washing her clothes. The nearest woman grabbed her around the waist and the others quickly formed a chain, screaming, holding on to each other in a tug-of-war with the crocodile. The women won and the crocodile retreated leaving Mwellazuba's hand hanging by a tendon. Daddy heard the screams and knew there was trouble. Someone came running to tell him what had happened. He grabbed clean rags and a bottle of Hydrogen Peroxide and ran to meet the women. He applied a tourniquet to her arm and poured peroxide on the wound—and kept pouring as it bubbled—until he had used the whole bottle, then bound up the hand and arm as best he could. She needed to be carried in a mashila to the railroad from where she would be taken by train to the doctor but there were no volunteers so Daddy hired two native men to take her. The doctor couldn't save her hand, but she recovered. The doctor said the peroxide had probably prevented fatal blood poisoning from the crocodile's filthy teeth.

**Fellow Workers** The arrival of other missionaries from the U.S. increased the white population on Sinde Mission. Ray and Zelma Lawyer were the first to join us in 1924 with 3-year old Jeanne and baby George, who had been born in Cape Town. In 1926 little George died of dysentery in the Livingstone hospital and a baby sister, Kathryn was born a few weeks later. Dow and Alice Merritt with Iris and Sterling arrived not long after the Lawyers. Jean and Iris were between Foy's and my ages and Sterling was Beth's age. Now we had playmates. In early 1927 George M. Scott, his wife Ottis and their grown daughter, Helen Pearl, joined us on the mission.

The missionaries' houses were near each other and we children shared yards and a nurse-maid named Vundu. Under her oversight we played outside and got dirty in the sandy, dusty soil. Just before supper it was her job to give us baths in a washtub. One evening when it was Foy's turn for the tub, he decided to run for it and she gave chase. The clothesline was stretched across a side of the back yard. It drooped in the middle but was high enough for children to pass under. Foy ran innocently under it and Vundu, intent on catching him, didn't see the clothesline. It caught her under the chin and she landed on her back on the ground. We thought it was funny but our laughter was cut short when our mothers shamed us for laughing at someone getting hurt.

**Names** The natives were fascinated with English words and many of them added an English word as a second name, whatever sounded good to them. Through my years in Africa I remember knowing of Petunia, Pencil, Candle, Careful, Victory, Matches, Shilling, Sixpence, Tickey, Next, Diamond, Falls, Office, Spider, Bicycle and Vitalis. We were taught by our parents to respectfully call people by their names. Sad to say not all Europeans did so. There was a Bantu tribe in South Africa properly called kaffir but that word was often used in a derogatory sense all over the country, so our parents did not allow us to say the word—ever.

**"Shanks Ponies," Bicycles and Mules** "Shanks Ponies" was Daddy's term for walking and it would be interesting to know how many hundreds of miles he walked in those early years. In Bulawayo he had walked the fourteen miles from Forest Vale Mission to town and back countless times and how many times he walked the sixteen mile round trip between the mission and Senkobo Siding or the many miles he walked on village trips for days at a time, he had no way of knowing. Africans walked or ran. Bicycles were the wheels of all who were able to buy or trade for one, a step up from walking and Daddy rode hundreds of miles on a bicycle. On preaching trips among the villages he rode his bicycle some but other times he preferred to ride his trusty mule—easier on his legs and the mule did not get flat tires from the many thorns along the trails. Possibly when he knew the land was flat he used the bicycle and when the terrain was rough and rocky the mule was more suitable. He said the bicycle's drawback was flat tires and the trouble with mules was their nature!

I recall hearing him bemoan the fact that a mule was undependable because he never knew when it might suddenly decide to baulk. He told of one time he was riding his mule when they came to a stream of water that didn't look deep so he urged the mule forward. As it began wading Daddy thought all was going well. Suddenly the mule planted his front feet firmly in a full stop, sending Daddy head first into the water, his helmet flying off. He said the bottom was muddy and his head stuck in the mud until he got himself situated to sit up and by then his cork helmet was bobbing along downstream and he had to chase it.

On his frequent trips among the villages teaching and preaching, Daddy was often gone for a week or several weeks. Of one such trip with a fellow-missionary, covering more than 200 miles, he wrote of them taking turns riding and walking: *"We had one mule for riding while the other mule carried a load. But the one mule gave us each much rest, except where we had to leave them behind on account of the tsetse fly."*

Mules were also used for pulling light wagons or carts when, for whatever reason best known to Daddy, they were more suited to the job than oxen.

**Thorns** Thorns were a bane and a blessing. Villagers cut branches of thorn trees to make cattle kraals (pens) to put their cattle in at night—the cattle did not try to get out and the thorns protected them from wild animals. Thorn branches were also used to keep cattle and other animals out of the gardens. But thorns could be very painful when they punctured a foot or other part of the body. A thorn bush we learned to watch for and carefully avoid had thorns with hooks on the ends. It was called the "vag n bietjie" thorn (Afrikaans for "wait a little.") If you accidentally ran into one of those bushes, you literally did wait a little—while you painfully extricated yourself from its clutches.

**Birds and Beasts** Meanwhile Foy was learning from his African friends about many birds and animals and at the supper table he had fascinating things to tell the family. Daddy wrote about the honey bird: *"One day as Bro. Lawyer and I were going along the trail from one village to another, a little bird came flying about and calling to us. We followed it for a time and soon found a tree with some bees in it. The little bird told us truly that there was honey there . . ."* The honey bird would lead a person to honey in a tree, then it flew around while the honey was being eaten. The story goes that whoever ate the honey must then leave a portion of a cone containing honey nearby for the bird because, though it liked honey, it could not get it out of the tree hive. If no honey was left for the bird it continued to fly around that person as though leading him to another tree for more honey; however, this time the bird would lead him to a leopard or other wild animal as punishment for failing to leave honey for him.

There was always the underlying awareness of wild animals not far away, though as a rule they didn't come on the mission grounds—in the day time. One day men from a nearby village came asking for help. They said two lions were coming at night and killing their cattle and they wanted the American men to bring guns and help them. They said they had built a platform in a tree near the cattle kraal where the men could wait and be ready when the lions came to eat the dead goat they put under the tree. Daddy, Ray Lawyer and Dow Merritt took their guns and went to sit on the platform and wait. About midnight they saw by moonlight two lions eating the meat. They realized with dismay that their platform was too low, they were much too close to the lions to risk shooting, so they waited quietly until the lions had eaten their fill and gone.

Daddy may have been referring to that when he wrote, *"Each year we have been here we have had lions around in this vicinity. When I heard others talk of seeing lions close to their house, I thought it was wonderfully exciting; but now we have had lions within fifty yards of our house, and the women and children here alone! But the lions passed quietly on . . ."*

About that time Daddy wrote to someone back home, *"The British air machine made the trip to Cape Town from London and back again, the first machine to make that trip. It was marking out the route and making note of the time from one landing to another. In the future an important letter or communication from His Majesty the King can be carried to Cape Town in a few days, instead of weeks."* History was being made.

**"Train Up A Child . . ."** All the missionary parents we knew were strict and we learned early to obey them without hesitation—most of the time. But when I was almost five years old and my friend, Jeanne was six, we deliberately disobeyed my father and it was a major event in my life. There was a pile of dead tree branches not far from the house ready to be cut for stove-wood. All the children were told not to climb on it because snakes could be hiding in it or we could be hurt if the wood shifted. One day Jeanne and I decided it would be fun to climb up that woodpile. Climbing up from branch to branch was easy and the higher we climbed the more exciting it was. But our come-uppance was coming up—or down in this case. A branch moved with our weight and the pile slid. We landed on the ground amidst branches and sticks, scratched, and doubly scared because we knew we had done wrong. Daddy, ever alert for possible danger, heard our cries and came running. We knew exactly what would follow. Jeanne got hers first and went home rubbing her seat and mine followed swiftly. Then while Mother doctored my scratches, she told me she was sure I would not want to disobey again—and I didn't—for four years, but that is a story for later.

**Kabanga Mission** With four American families on Sinde Mission, the couples agreed it was time to begin a new work. They decided on a spot about eighty miles north of Sinde, some forty miles from Kalomo, a small town on the railroad. The Scotts and Shorts remained at Sinde while the Lawyers and Merritts moved to the new place and named it Kabanga Mission. There was no road between Kabanga and Kalomo and the mission was begun from scratch. The two families lived in grass huts while bricks were being made and brick houses built. The Lawyer's hut accidentally caught fire and they lost almost all of their possessions, including their motor car. Fortunately no one was hurt. A few months afterwards tragedy again struck the Lawyer family. Ray was accidentally killed when he stumbled onto a native spear he was carrying. Soon after that Zelma and the two girls moved back to Sinde Mission and our family moved to Kabanga.

The Lawyer's brick house on Kabanga mission was unfinished, no roof, no floors, doors or windows, but we lived in it anyway while Daddy worked on it with the help of native labor and preached among the villages. Until doors and windows were in place fires were kept burning at night to keep away wild animals. Finally each family had a separate brick house with thatched roof and a verandah running most of the way around that shaded the rooms from the direct hot sun. Double windows opened on to the verandah from each room. The living room was called the front room or lounge and had a fireplace. During hot weather, breezes blew through the house. In the winter this central room with a fire in the fireplace was cozy. There were screens at all windows and doors but we still used mosquito nets.

When Foy wasn't playing with us girls, he played with the young African boys whose parents were visiting or who lived in the mission compound. He soon learned enough Chitonga (the local dialect) that he talked as he played and on occasion interpreted for Mother. On Sundays we sang songs in that language. Foy's young friends made little clay oxen and wagons and traded with Foy for clothing or other things that Mother let him have. But the rain could dissolve those clay toys so Foy took a cue from his father burning bricks and his friends from their parents who fired their clay water pots and other vessels. They dug a hole, put the clay animals and wagons down in it, covered them with sand and built a fire over them. Their miniature oven worked and they had weather-proof toys. Foy learned how much his friends wanted empty tins (cans) so he collected them from the kitchen—every kind and size. He washed them, turned under the sharp edges with pliers and traded them for more clay or wire toys or baskets or clay pots.

**A Cake and A Snake** I was nearly six when I asked Mother if I could make a cake. She said, "Poke the fire and put some more wood on it." Mother was at the sewing machine telling me what to do. I had successfully broken three eggs into a bowl and was ready to beat them with a fork, but I wasn't tall enough to work on the table so I held the bowl against my stomach and went to stand in the cool breeze at the kitchen door. As I was beating, a movement on the top step caught my eye and I saw a large snake crawling onto the verandah. I dropped the bowl with a crash and ran screaming to Mother's side. "What's the matter?" "What's the matter?" she kept asking. All I could do was scream but finally got out the word "SNAKE!" She dropped her sewing and hurried to the kitchen door where she saw that the African yard worker had killed the snake with his hoe. I don't know what kind of snake it was nor do I recall whether or not the cake was made that afternoon.

**Daddy and Snakes** Daddy had extremely fast reflexes and had a special way of disposing of poisonous snakes when they appeared too close for comfort. One afternoon the missionaries were having afternoon tea, the ladies inside the house visiting, the men sitting on the verandah talking. A cobra crawled up the steps. Before the other men knew what happened, Daddy had jumped up, planted his heel firmly on the snake's head, grabbed its tail and swung it like cracking a whip and broke its neck. Then its head was chopped off and burned. If there had been no fire handy the head would have been buried in a deep hole, covered with dirt and a big rock put over the place to keep animals from digging it up and eating it. Pythons and green or black mambas were usually seen and shot from a distance. Non-poisonous snakes were not killed unless they were being pests, like chicken snakes in the hen house.

**Furlough 1928-1930** Daddy and Mother had been away from the U.S. seven years and their supporters in the States agreed it was time for a furlough. It took months to make all the necessary preparations: there were funds to be raised in the U.S.; passport pictures to be made; then a wait on the passports to come from the consulate in Johannesburg. Thomas Cook and Sons, travel agents, took care of our train tickets and ship bookings. Finally in November, 1928, our family along with Zelma Lawyer and her two girls, Jeanne and Kathryn, left Northern Rhodesia. It was "going home" to the adults but for the children it was adventuring into a strange country. What a sad time it must have been for Zelma, who in four short years had buried her baby son and her husband, and whose girls had lost their father and little brother.

The train trip to Cape Town was exciting to us children, but we had been on trains before, so the real excitement came when we boarded the ship and sailed out of the harbor bound for America by way of England. Once out to sea, Mother and Daddy had many questions to answer: Why were there two decks above ours where we were not allowed to go? What did they mean by calling each level a Class? First Class was up top, Second Class next and we were Third Class, also known as Tourist Class. But why were tourists and missionaries Third Class? Our parents explained the difference—our tickets were less expensive. We thought that must mean we were poor, but we didn't <u>feel</u> poor. Foy and Jeanne were curious: "What did Second have that Third didn't?" They tried sneaking up the deck stairs to see, but they were caught and that was that, except for complaining—quietly, so Daddy couldn't hear.

The ship stopped briefly at St. Helena Island. I remember Daddy telling us about Napoleon as we stood under a huge tree gazing at his tomb that was surrounded by a wrought iron fence. I have a necklace made of beans from that tree and because of that day Napoleon's history was much more interesting to me in later years.

Our ship docked at the Ascension Islands only long enough to pick up some huge turtles for transport to England. We leaned over the rail watching while they were loaded from boat to ship—men were walking on the turtles' backs as they worked. Daddy explained that the turtles' shells were so thick and hard it didn't hurt them.

Foy asked a sailor what the turtles were for and the sailor said, "They're for the King's soup." Then we were really sorry for the turtles.

We left the ship at Southampton, England, and traveled by train to London for a few days of sightseeing. Nights were spent with the Scotts, who lived in a three-story house. We had heard of "going upstairs" and now we were doing it. But wonder of wonders was the indoor plumbing. A bathtub with hot and cold running water, no carrying teakettles of hot water from the kitchen and buckets of cold water from the well then carrying used water out—here it ran in and out. And the toilet—inside the house—was a wonder; we just pulled a chain after use. Our parents gave us strict orders not to flush the toilet needlessly, nor to keep washing our hands just to stand at the sink watching the water run. Both things were fascinating beyond imagination to children from the wilds of Africa, accustomed to chamber pots and outside toilets and carrying water in buckets. The trains and the ship had such things, but not the houses we knew.

I have no memory of New York or much else connected with our arrival in the U.S.A. Compartments and corridors on trains were familiar to us but here we had to sit still (more or less) in seats while the train took us to Harper, Kansas, where Daddy's family lived. What a thrill to meet our real live Grandpa and Grandma Short. We knew Grandpa O'Neal had died long ago and Grandma O'Neal lived in Oklahoma, but she was there to meet us, too, besides all the uncles and aunts—so many faces to fit the names we had heard Daddy and Mother talk about.

24

Foy went to school, but my parents decided it would be better for me to wait until we got back to Rhodesia. My special playmate there was Betty Williams. She had long brown ringlet curls and I thought she was the prettiest girl I had ever seen—not that I had seen all that many. And there was the wonder of snow, and so much of it. One day our family went to Wichita, Kansas, the nearest city. Plows kept the main road cleared but snow was piled up above the height of our car on both sides of the narrow road. It was like going through a tunnel. Foy asked Daddy, "What happens if we meet a car?" Daddy said, "I expect one of us will have to back up." That sounded bad to us and we watched anxiously for cars.

The most exciting event of all to me was the birth of my little sister, Margaret Ann, on August 27, 1929, in Cordell, Oklahoma. I was old enough to be mother's helper and how I loved to help tend my baby sister. They got the Ann for her name from Daddy's mother and sister, Flora Ann and Sybil Ann but I don't know where the Margaret came from. I was named Sybil Belle after Daddy's sister, Sybil, and Mother's sister, Alice Belle. Beth was named Flora Elizabeth after our grandmothers, Flora Ann and Amanda Elizabeth. Where my brother's names, Harold Foy, came from is a mystery; we failed to record it when Daddy and Mother were living.

Daddy traveled among churches giving reports of his work and raising funds to continue. When he spoke at nearby churches he took the family with him. At some distant church my parents heard that someone said it was fine with them if Will Short came but they didn't want him bringing his "little African savages" with him. Our parents used that in admonishing us to behave well because they knew we didn't want to be known as little savages!

People were interested in hearing the "native language" and when they learned that Foy, Beth and I could sing several songs in Chitonga, they sometimes asked us to sing after Daddy finished speaking. One song we always sang was *Jesus Loves Me, This I Know.* The tune was the same as in English and I remember some of the words: (the letter "i" is pronounced "eee")

First verse:     Jesu u la tu yanda,

Ikuti tuli bana,

Wa tu pa zintu zyonse,

U la tu pa inguzu.

Chorus:       I, u ndi yanda,

I, u ndi yanda,

I, u ndi yanda,

Ambe, nda mu yanda.

Quite often after we sang someone gave us a nickel or a dime each—until one time when no one did and on the way home Foy complained, "They didn't pay us!" That fixed it! Daddy didn't want his children expecting to be paid for singing and after that he told folks not to give us money.

All the while Daddy and Mother were planning our return to Africa. The least expensive route was from Vancouver, British Columbia, across the Pacific Ocean, taking six weeks instead of three weeks across the Atlantic. They bought a 1930 Chevrolet, black 4-door sedan that we named "Sally." Sally didn't know that for the next sixteen years she would take us over and around rocks, through rivers, through the bushveldt, on deep-rutted wagon roads and no roads at all, until she was literally falling apart.

In our new car we crossed the United States to Vancouver, British Columbia, spending nights in cabins. Each cabin had a carport at the side and a kitchenette where we ate supper and breakfast and prepared lunch for the day. We went through the Redwood Forest, marveling. At one place the road was cut through the base of a giant redwood. At a souvenir shop we chose wooden serviette rings, each with a distinctive pattern in the wood and we each had our personal serviette-ring for the rest of our lives.

From Vancouver we sailed to Honolulu, Hawaii for a day; then to Fiji and docked in Suva Bay for a day; from there to Auckland, New Zealand where we spent a day at the Auckland Zoo; then to Sidney, Australia for a night and a day; finally around Australia to Perth and across the Indian Ocean to Durbin, South Africa.

"The Australian Giant" boarded at Perth. He was one of "us" because he had a cabin in Third Class where a special bunk was built to accommodate his length. We have a picture of Daddy standing under the giant's outstretched arm, not nearly touching it. Daddy was 5'9 ½" so we estimated the giant was over seven feet. He took a special liking to five-year-old Beth, who was a talker and happily spent time chatting with him.

On each voyage there was a "Fancy Dress Party" for children of all ages and this time the children from Second Class were invited to join us because they had too few to have their own. We were amazed that they seemed just like us! Mother had made our costumes before we sailed. Foy was dressed as a chef, with a high white chef's hat and big white apron. Since I had won First Prize dressed as an African woman on the way from Africa two years before, Mother dressed me that way again in another long gathered yellow satin skirt, matching top gathered on a yoke, colorful head cloth and a doll strapped on my back. This time instead of brown shoe polish, Mother used a paste of cocoa powder and water to cover my face, neck and arms because it would wash off easier. It worked well until it dried, then it cracked when I talked or laughed and felt awful. Beth was dressed as Little Red Riding Hood in a crepe paper outfit that Mother had made. We each won First Prize in our age category; Mother should have been given the prize.

From Durbin all our belongings except the car and personal luggage were shipped by rail to Salisbury. For the long cross country drive the motor car was filled nearly to overflowing with two adults, four children and our luggage. The first night, still in South Africa, we stopped at Lalapanzi Hotel. There were separate thatched pole-and-daager huts, plastered and whitewashed inside and out, very clean, inviting and luxurious. The Dining Room was a larger, nicely furnished hut. Food was delicious and the white-clad waiters tended to our every need. After six weeks on the ship and this night in such luxury, we were spoiled—but not for long.

The next day we crossed the border into Southern Rhodesia and headed north over two hundred miles to Bulawayo where we spent a night with our good friends, the Hadfields. Three hundred miles north of Bulawayo we came to Salisbury, the capital of Southern Rhodesia, then on to Huyuyu Mission eighty-four miles northeast of Salisbury.

## Southern Rhodesia 1930-1940

**Huyuyu Mission** By this time the Sherriffs had been on Huyuyu Mission for a few years. [When they lived there and until some time after we moved from there, the official name was Huyuyu. Later it was changed to Wuyu Wuyu.] The Sherriffs lived in the main residence he had built. We called it "The Big House." The Garretts, with three children, had arrived before we did and were temporarily housed in a three-room brick, while they made arrangements to settle in Salisbury. Not far away was a two-room brick teachers' house where we lived until the Garretts left. Daddy, Mother and Margaret Ann had the bedroom. The other room was lounge and dining room by day. At night two stretchers (camp cots) were set up, one for Foy and one for Beth and me together—our heads at the ends and feet to the middle. Mother didn't complain that the kitchen was a metal lean-to in the back yard with an open fire and three big rocks holding a piece of flat metal for a stove like the one she had had in the early days at Sinde Mission.

**Tarantula** One evening Daddy was reading the Bible aloud, he and Mother in their rocking chairs, children sitting on a grass mat on the floor. Suddenly Mother grabbed up little Margaret Ann and said, "There's a tarantula. Jump on the stretcher quickly." We scrambled up but Daddy was already on his feet and had stomped the huge tarantula. Out from under his shoe spread a mass of tiny, tiny tarantulas—must have been hundreds of them. Daddy grabbed the Flit gun (a small tank with pump handle) and sprayed as many little crawling creatures as he could before

28

they got into cracks and under furniture. Knowing Daddy and Mother and their calmness in any situation, I'm sure we all settled down to finish reading and prayer—not sitting on the floor, however.

**Memories** My favorite memory in that house was my baby sister's bath time. Margaret Ann was about a year old. Every morning after breakfast Mother bathed her in an oblong white enamel wash pan that was big enough for her to sit in and I enjoyed watching her play in the water. When Mother took her out of the water she wrapped her in a big towel and weighed her on a pair of grocery scales that had a pan on top for Margaret Ann to sit in. I enjoyed playing with her and carried her on my back when she was old enough to hold on.

Daddy's rocking chair was black carved wood and Mother's was brown wood with woven reed seat and back. Mother's hair was done up on top of her head during the day and as they sat in their chairs in the evening she let me take the pins out of it. When the pins were all out her hair uncoiled and cascaded over the back of the chair. She had hip length, auburn hair, thick and naturally wavy and I loved to stand behind her chair and brush it before she braided it for the night. Mother was tall and large boned and usually weighed around 170 lbs. but I didn't think of her as fat—she was stately, always neat, with a soft warm lap for cuddling in. I thought she looked like pictures I saw of Queen Mary, wife of King George V. Southern Rhodesia was a Protectorate of England so the Royal Family "belonged" to us as well.

When the Garrett family went to Salisbury we moved into the house they vacated. We had stepped up in the world—now we had three rooms and one of them was a kitchen with a proper stove. Daddy, Mother and Margaret Ann had the bedroom. Foy, Beth and I had our nightly set-up of two stretchers in the lounge. Beth's and my feet were beginning to tangle in the middle but I don't recall any complaining—at an altitude of over 4,000 feet nights were cold and our feet kept each other warm. Kitchen and dining area were combined and on one wall was a bookcase that figured in a vivid dream I had soon after we moved there.

Next to the kitchen, on a back corner of the house, was a storeroom with an outside door. In that storeroom Beth and I learned a valuable lesson. European adults and children wore hats outside—always. The natives seemed impervious to the sun's rays but Europeans were susceptible to sunburn and sun stroke. Daddy, Mother and Foy wore cork helmets like you see in movies of folks in the tropics. For us girls Mother made cloth hats lined with a special material that protected us from the tropical sun; the hats had enough brim in front to shade our faces and wider brims at the back to shield our necks. Beth's and my hats were identical.

One day, early in the year, when I was nine and Beth nearly seven, the noon meal done, we excused ourselves from the table and asked permission to play outdoors. "Get your hats," Mother said. One of us found a hat and claimed it. "That's my hat," the other said, and an argument started. One of the rules in our family was "No arguing," but the heat of the moment outdid our training. We argued. Daddy snapped his fingers at us—usually enough to stop whatever was going on—but this time we had become too heated to care. Another exchange of "That's mine," "No, it's mine," and our doom was sealed. Rising from the table Daddy said, "Come on, girls." We knew exactly what was coming and why. Frantically we both began back-peddling, "I'm sorry, she can have it." "I'll look for the other one." "I promise I won't argue any more." But it was too late. We were marched out to that storeroom where Daddy did what he needed to do to get the lesson across—unforgettably—with a thin board from a soap box. A paddling when I was five and now one at nine—I never needed another (at least never got another.) From then on quiet words from Daddy or Mother were enough to straighten me out.

Daddy and Mother seldom raised their voices at us. Yes, we were afraid to disobey, but we never doubted their love; they bragged on us when we did well and helped us through troubles and we did not hesitate to call for help or sympathy. Even in their strictness, when we were punished we understood why. They had the wonderful ability of making each one of us feel very special. Deep down we knew the others were, too, but it was good to feel so individually special. After either of them corrected me my feelings were hurt and I resolved to do better but I don't remember harboring resentment. Sometimes I felt they were too hard on other children, including my little sister, Margaret Ann. Several years later she was being stubborn and was sent to bed without supper; I was sorry for her and begged her to apologize. She says now she remembers refusing to apologize because she preferred to feel like a martyr!

**Snake And Scorpion** Daddy always checked carefully for snakes when we came into the house after dark, especially under the stove and in the woodbox where they might have come for warmth. Soon after we moved into this house he found a puff adder under the stove and killed it. Not long after that I dreamed I was standing barefoot in the kitchen in front of the bookcase looking for a book when a puff adder came from under the bookcase and bit my big toe. In my dream I felt its bite and fell flat on my back—dead. In the dream I knew when my head hit the cement floor but it didn't hurt because I was dead! Lying there knowing I was dead, it gradually dawned on me that I was on my stretcher, awake in the dark and stiff with cold. At night when the last candle was blown out, unless there was moonlight, it was dark—pitch dark, and this night there was no moon.

With a quavering voice I called, "D-d-a-a-d-d-y.," and his answering "Hmmm?" was most reassuring. "I had a bad dream and I'm scared." "I'm coming," he said as he lighted a candle. He picked my blanket up off the floor and explained, "Your cover fell off and you got cold. I expect that's why you had a bad dream." He shook the blanket to be sure no scorpion, spider or snake had crawled onto it, then tucked me in.

In the kitchen there was a tall cabinet and on top, out of reach of children, a big box of matches was kept for lighting lamps, candles and fire in the stove. One evening Mother reached for the matches to light a lamp and felt a sharp prick. She jerked her hand back with a loud "OUCH!" Daddy grabbed a torch to look and there, as he suspected, was a scorpion with its tail up. He quickly killed it. Mother soaked her finger in paraffine for thirty minutes. Her finger swelled and was painful, but the strike was so fast she didn't get a full dose of venom. We were reminded, "Never pick up anything without looking first to see if there's a scorpion or centipede underneath."

**Christmas Surprise** While we were living in that house Beth and I noticed Mother crocheting busily and soon realized she was making little jerseys (sweaters), caps and booties. When we asked who they were for, she said she had heard of three little babies who had no sweaters and caps so she was making them some. Beth and I decided she was not giving us the real answer and that actually we were about to get a baby brother or sister! Only a few months before that Dollie Garrett had had a baby and I still remembered Margaret Ann's birth.

When Christmas morning came, there at the foot of Daddy and Mother's bed, where our gifts were always set out, were three doll beds, a large one, a middle-sized one and a smaller one, each with mattress, pillow and blanket. Daddy had made the beds in his workshop without our knowing about it, and each bed was strong enough for us to sit on it or curl up and lie down on it. On each bed was a celluloid doll with movable head, arms and legs, and each doll had on a baby dress left over from Margaret Ann's baby days. Over the dresses the dolls were wearing the jerseys, caps and booties we had seen Mother crocheting. How we did enjoy the dolls and beds! Sometimes Margaret Ann was my "little girl" and she would curl up to "sleep" in my doll bed; we pretended her doll was her "little sister" who slept in her doll bed; and Beth borrowed my doll (the same size as hers) so she had twins!

**Short children in garden on Huyuyu Mission.**

**Grandma O'Neal** In 1933 a letter came from Mother's family saying her mother, our Grandma O'Neal, had died of pneumonia in Morrilton, Arkansas, where she was a House Mother of a boys' dormitory. The rainy season was almost on us, we had been to Salisbury for supplies and on the way home we stopped for mail at Mrewa, seventeen miles from the mission. We knew something was wrong when we saw Mother crying and Daddy told us the sad news as we sat in the car at the back of our house. We had known this grandmother only briefly during our visit to the States and from her regular letters. Grandpa O'Neal had died when Mother was sixteen. We children wept for the grandmother we barely knew because she was our own Mother's mother and perhaps because she was no longer there for us to daydream about going to visit.

Before they left the States our parents had told their brothers and sisters if any family member died to write about it in a letter—not send a cablegram because the cablegram would reach us weeks before a letter would arrive telling of their illness preceding their death. Since our parents could not go home anyway, it was more important to know the events leading up to a death than to suddenly get word that someone had died.

**My Baptism** I was nearly ten years old when I decided I wanted to be baptized, I had been thinking about it for some time and had talked to Daddy about it. I remember feeling very strongly that was what Jesus wanted me to do and I knew I wanted to obey Jesus. Daddy felt I was very young to make such a decision, but I was adamant. The rainy season had begun and small streams called spruits were running where there had been dry sandy beds. One of them ran across the bottom of our long driveway and by this time there had been enough rains to wash the parasites from the sandy soil. The water was not deep enough for us to stand for the ceremony so Daddy knelt in the water and I sat on the sandy bottom as he baptized me, and the people sang *"Oh Happy Day That Fixed My Choice On Thee My Savior And My God"*—one of my favorite songs ever since.

**Diphtheria Scare** Not long afterward Beth developed a severe sore throat that would not respond to all the usual home remedies. The doctor at Mrewa thought it could be diphtheria and sent us to the Isolation Hospital. Beth was the only one sick but all of us children were put in the small ward and we had the place to ourselves. Daddy was not allowed in to read to us or tell us stories and we were hard put to entertain ourselves. Books, pads, pencils and crayons helped and Foy read to us some but he grew tired of that and looked around for something more active to do. The ward was a sun-room with screened windows and door and flies managed to get in. Foy watched the nurse swat some every time she came in and finally he offered to kill flies for her if she would pay him a penny per hundred. She agreed, thinking it would not happen but he surprised her. He swatted flies with fervor, gingerly picking up the dead ones by their wings and laying them along the window-sills, keeping careful count. I don't recall his total but the nurse paid him pennies as promised. Beth soon recovered and no one else got sick.

**Rivers** The little town of Mrewa had a post office, two or three general stores, local government offices and police station. To reach Mrewa from Huyuyu Mission we had to drive seventeen miles on a rough dirt (not gravel) road cleared through the bush, and ford two large rivers, the Manukwe and the Nyazikatzi. The Manukwe River, nearest to the mission, was wide and had a sandy gravel bottom. During the dry season it was fairly shallow, easily forded by foot and by wagons and our car crossed without any trouble. The Nyazikatzi River was not as wide, but the banks were steep, the crossing was treacherous and creeping across in low gear was nerve wracking. The driver had to avoid big boulders that could be seen, while watching for rocks and holes that were unseen but recognized by ripples or swirls in the water. During the rainy season both rivers were impassable by car or wagon.

**Roads And Bridges** Mrewa was not on the railroad but was on the main highway between Salisbury (Harare) and Umtali (Mutare). The highway was a "strip road" and on it when going to Salisbury we could relax for the rest of the trip—except for the bridges. A strip road had a gravel roadbed with two paved strips the right distance apart for the wheels of a car. When two cars met, each car moved over to use the strip on the left side, with its outside wheels on the left gravel shoulder (the car's steering wheel was on the right). On strip roads the rivers had bridges that were concrete slabs with no sides and just wide enough for a car to drive over. Crossing those bridges was scary to us children. "Be careful, Daddy, don't run off the side," begged his backseat drivers, and he assured us there was plenty of room and he would not run off the side. He never did, but until we "grew up" we hid our faces behind the front seat when we came to one of them.

Twice each year we made the eighty-four mile trip to Salisbury: just before the wet season began, and six months later, when the rains were over for about six months dry season. Daddy had business in the city that could not be done by mail and things to buy that could not be found in the trading store in Mrewa and that didn't grow on the mission, such as children's shoes and dried fruit.

**Manukwe Adventure** In late November before I turned ten in January, it was time to make a trip to Salisbury. We were on the way home and just leaving Mrewa when Daddy said, "I don't like the looks of the sky up there at the head of the rivers. But I believe we can make it home before that rain gets here."

The Nyazikatzi River crossing was safely behind us but the ominous cloud was much closer as we approached the Manukwe River. Thankfully it was not raining and was not yet dark. As we neared the edge of the water Daddy observed, "I can tell the river is rising. There must have been a really big rain upstream." And Mother asked, "Won't the high water drown the engine?" Daddy said, "I'll put a sack over the radiator to keep some of the water out." The burlap sacks he kept in the boot (trunk) had many uses and this was one. With sack in place on the radiator, Daddy drove slowly into the water. About half way across the engine sputtered and died and Daddy knew there was no time to waste.

As he took Beth up in his arms and instructed Foy and me on either side of him to hold tightly to his belt, he said to Mother, "I'll be back as fast as I can to get you and Margaret Ann. We'll leave all the doors open so the water can go through the motor car and not push it downstream." As we waded to shore, he instructed Foy to go to the village up the road. "They'll know you," he said, "Tell the men the motor car is stuck in the river and ask them to bring oxen to pull it out. As soon as I get Mother and Margaret Ann out I'll carry as much of our stuff to the bank as I can." Beth and I huddled together on the bank, anxiously watching Foy go up the road and Daddy wade back to the motor car. Soon he was carrying Margaret Ann and helping Mother toward us. What a relief to have them standing there with us. We were wet through, but we were out of the river, and we were not cold—rainy season days were hot and the warmth lingered until after dark. Daddy made several trips carrying suitcases, fifty pound bags of sugar and flour and I'm not sure what else, to the bank. We stood there with Mother, watching—I would like to say "bravely," but I remember too well how we were crying. Each time Daddy went back into the water our fear for him brought more tears. Water was high on the fenders and rushing through the open doors of the motor car when Daddy decided not to go back. He had carried perishables to the bank and covered them with a small tarp; tinned goods still in the motor car might lose their labels but their size and shape would help us guess what was in them.

We watched the road for Foy and the oxen and Mother talked to take our minds off our plight. She could always talk but after a while she must have run out of something to say. Her "Guess what's in that suitcase," surprised us. How could we know? We played a guessing game for a while without success, then she asked, "Who's having a birthday soon?" Mine was the next birthday so we knew it must be a birthday present for me. We begged her to tell us more. Finally she said, "What would you think about a glass doll?" Well! A glass doll was the pinnacle of our girlish dreams—a porcelain-headed doll with real hair, eyes that opened and shut, tiny teeth in its smiling mouth, porcelain hands and feet and a stuffed fabric body. Tears dried up in our excitement.

Just before dark Foy came back with the men and yoked oxen. By the time they got the motor car out of the river and reloaded, darkness had fallen. The drowned engine wouldn't start, so the oxen pulled the motor car the three miles to the mission, with much cracking of the whip, yelling at the oxen, loud talk and laughter. We were soaking wet but it didn't matter, seats were soaked too. Daddy thanked the men profusely for their help. He knew that they did not usually venture out after dark in case lions or leopards were roaming and making a noise as they walked helped to protect them. More rain came during the night but next morning the sun shone brightly. Daddy opened the motor car windows and doors, took the seats out and set them up to drain and dry. "Sally" had many more miles yet to go.

For me the few weeks until my birthday dragged by, then the doll was in my hands. How I did love that doll! Years went by before I was too big to play with it and by then its hair was tangled, one shoe was lost and stuffing poked out of its arms and legs. Mother wrapped it carefully and stored it in her steamer trunk. In 1940 I brought the doll to the U.S. with me; her life was not yet over and the rest of her story is in the *Alabama* chapter.

**Proper School** Foy finished Standard IV in November that year, he would turn twelve in January and Standard V would be his final year of home schooling. At the end of Standard V he would sit the Junior Biet Exam that was sent out from England. If he did well on that exam he would receive a sizeable scholarship that would be a big help when he went to the boys' boarding school in Salisbury. The Depression in the U.S. had caused some of the churches to drop their support and our parents were counting on the scholarship to help pay school fees. But Mother wanted to give Foy extra tutoring for that exam.

Arrangements were made with the van der Merwes in Mrewa for Beth and me to attend school with their two girls. They had a governess named Miss Rolff who would teach the four of us. We thought Miss Rolff was old—I have no idea what her age was. We moved into a rented house in Mrewa by the time school started in January, 1933. On weekends we went back to the mission for church services and Daddy preached. Meanwhile on the mission during the week the native teachers conducted school as usual for the village children.

**Walking To School** Daddy and Mother had told us about walking to school when they were young, and Beth and I were excited that now we were walking to school like our parents had done. Of course they had walked two or three miles or more but we were content with the half mile or so that we walked. Margaret Ann wasn't school age yet and she liked to walk a little way with us in the mornings and after school run to meet us when she saw us coming down the road. And Foy studied hard under Mother's tutoring.

The governess taught school in a room separate from the van der Merwe home, a proper (real) school with proper desks, a first for Beth and me. In that one room, Miss Rolff taught her four pupils: Sybil (10), Ella (9), Beth (8) and Suzanne (7). Memories of that school year are vague other than that along with our usual subjects, we sang the British and French national anthems and learned to count in French rhymes. Two other events of that time, however, are unforgettable, one involved a cigarette and the other a snake.

**Cigarette** One afternoon a young couple came in their convertible to visit Daddy and Mother. The top was down and they were all in the house having tea as Beth and I examined the unusual car. We noticed a pack of cigarettes on the front seat—open—with one sticking out. We knew the young woman smoked (shocking to us), but now we wondered what smoking a cigarette would be like and we decided to find out. We took the loose cigarette and went around to the back of the house, got matches from the kitchen and went behind the toilet (outhouse) to try it. After a puff each we thought about the smoke's tell-tale smell—Daddy and Mother would surely notice. Quickly we threw the offensive thing down the toilet hole and covered it with a shovel full of lime from the bucket in the corner. Then we drank lots of water and stood under a tree in the breeze, hoping traces of our wickedness would blow away before supper time! I never had the slightest desire to try another cigarette; the smell may have blown away but the pain of my guilty conscience didn't—we had stolen that cigarette.

**Green Mamba** Across the front of that house in Mrewa was a verandah one step up from the ground. The front door opened onto the verandah and had a screen door. It was summer and all the screened windows and doors were open. The kitchen at the back was connected to the main house by a breezeway and on one side of the breezeway was the bathroom with a bathtub directly in front of the door; there was no plumbing in there and unpacked boxes were stacked along the wall behind the bathroom door. The house had ceilings but the bathroom didn't—the brick wall ended at the overhang of the rafters and formed a ledge.

One day Beth and I were playing "house" on the ground under a huge shade tree in the front yard. We drew rooms in the sand, put twig furniture in the rooms, used leaves for bedspreads and china shards for dishes. Mother called from the door, "Sybil, Beth, time to wash hands for supper." As we started to the house we heard a "plop" behind us and at the same instant Mother shouted, "RUN! SNAKE BEHIND YOU!" We ran and didn't look back. Mother was holding the screen door open as I dashed across the threshold with Beth on my heels. As Mother slammed shut the screen door behind Beth, a long green mamba hit the bottom of the door, turned and went around the house. Daddy was in his office and Mother hurried to tell him, saying, "It went around the house!" But Daddy had heard her say "snake" and was already headed out the back door with his gun.

The worker scraping weeds in the back yard told Daddy he saw the snake go into the bathroom. They looked all around and under the tub, decided it must be hiding behind the boxes, and began pulling them out very carefully one by one. Suddenly the African shouted and pointed up, "LOOK! THERE!" Daddy looked. There was the snake lying along the ledge *above* the bathtub—it had been watching them all the time! Daddy shot it, cut off its head and put it in the always-burning kitchen stove. Over supper we wondered how long the snake had been in the tree watching Beth and me; what if it had decided to drop down on us? Daddy said probably as long as we were sitting there quietly it only watched, but when it saw us stand up it decided to act. We were thankful it had just watched when they were moving boxes.

**Foy's Exam** At the end of the school year in late November, we went to Salisbury and stayed with the Garretts while Foy sat for the exam in an auditorium with other European boys from the area. By the end of November we had moved back to the mission. Exam results were mailed out weeks later—Foy had passed the Biet Exam with excellent marks (grades) in all subjects.

**Budge** When the Sherriffs moved from the mission to Salisbury and then to Cape Town, they left us two dogs, a beautiful white Scotty and a Great Dane named Budge. We loved both dogs and felt safe when they were nearby. At night they were shut up in the workshop to protect them from wild animals. One day the garden worker came running to tell Daddy some baboons from the nearby hills had invaded the garden and he couldn't chase them out. Daddy shut the dogs in the workshop, fastened both the top and bottom halves of the dutch-door and told the workers not to open the door till he got back. He headed to the garden with his gun, intending to shoot into the air and scare the baboons away, but an extra large male decided to argue and Daddy thought it best to shoot him.

Daddy was a good shot but that time he only wounded the animal and it went up into the nearby hill. Daddy followed cautiously, knowing how dangerous a wounded baboon could be. He was too close before he saw the baboon crouching under a bush, about to spring. He raised his gun and fired at the same time the baboon sprang and at the same instant something "whooshed" past Daddy knocking him to one side as Budge hurled himself at the baboon. The bullet killed the baboon but the baboon was already hurtling forward and he and Budge met in mid-air, the baboon's great teeth ripping Budge's jugular vein.

One of the workers had thought the dogs would not get out of the workshop if he left only the *top* of the dutch-door open, but Budge had jumped over the bottom half of the door and raced after his master. Daddy was sure it would have been his own jugular vein had it not been for Budge. Sadly there was nothing he could do for the dog. [Here I am crying as I write this, thinking of how that dog saved our Daddy's life more than 75 years ago.] Foy dug a grave and we gave Budge a tearful funeral. Then Foy cut and sanded a piece of wood, and on it burned the inscription: "*Here Lies Budge, Killed By A Baboon, December 11, 1933.*"

**The Big House** When the Sherriffs had gone, we Shorts moved into the big house that seemed like a mansion to us with its larger rooms. Daddy and Mother had a bedroom, Foy had a bedroom and Margaret Ann, Beth and I shared the third large bedroom. We each had a proper (real) bed with a proper mattress—no more setting up stretchers every night with crackling mealie-shuck mattresses. Instead of Beth and me warming each other's feet, we each had our own hot-water-bottle. No household would think of being without several hot water bottles (plus some spares in case one sprung a leak!) During the winter they were used every night to warm the beds. They were also used for earaches, toothaches, for warming cold feet during malaria attacks or 'flu and for girls' cramps.

The kitchen was a separate building that Daddy had joined to the main house with a long screened verandah running the length of that end house on the dining room side. There was a door opening from the official dining room out to the verandah and we used that end of the verandah for our "every-day-dining-room." The verandah was probably over 20 feet long—an ideal place to play on rainy days. The kitchen end of the verandah was higher than where we ate, but instead of steps down, Daddy had gently sloped the floor and made it level for the table and chairs at the dining end.

**China Calamity** Beth and I learned to do the dishes in the Big House, taking turns washing and drying. One day it was my turn to dry and put away. As I dried five porridge bowls, five bread and butter plates, five big plates for eggs and sausage, I stacked them on the kitchen table; four-year-old Margaret Ann's utensils were enamel and stacked on top of the others. I was ten going on eleven and I was strong; I picked up the whole stack and headed down the verandah to put them in the dish cupboard. I stumbled, perhaps over my own feet. With a resounding crash the dishes hit the cement floor; broken Blue Willow china flew in all directions while Margaret Ann's enamel dishes clattered and rolled down the verandah, chipped but unbroken—and I burst into tears. I had broken half of our supply of dishes! What would we do when we had company?

Mother assured me she knew I didn't do it on purpose, we still had enough to eat out of and we'd get some more dishes next time we went to Salisbury. The Blue Willow pattern was open stock and about the least expensive china to be had in those days. Later I heard Mother telling a friend about the accident and she described it as an "international incident." When her friend asked what she meant, she said, "It was the

42

breaking up of china!" As long as we lived there we girls never lacked pretty Blue Willow china pieces, all shapes and sizes, for play-dishes in our playhouse under the eucalyptus trees!

**Watch Your Head!** Along the verandah, metal framed crank-windows opened from a bedroom and from the dining room. One rainy day Foy was playing under one of the open windows and forgot it was sticking out above him. He raised up quickly and hit the top of his head on the corner of the metal window. At sight of the copious bleeding from the hole in his head, his sisters wailed in a chorus of concern. Daddy cleaned the wound and filled the hole with mercurochrome; it healed and Foy was none the worse for it.

**"Oh, Daddy!"** The well that supplied water for the mission was near the vegetable garden about a quarter of a mile up the side of the hill on a level area. When John Sherriff had dug and blasted the deep well he had installed corrugated metal lining that kept mud and rocks from falling from the sides. That lining had become rusty and Daddy decided it was time to take it out and install new material. He was down in the well taking the sections apart and had workers at the top pulling them out one at a time with the windlass. He pulled on a section with his bare hands, as he had been doing, but this time it cut his hand across the inside of his fingers. He knew at once that the cut was deep. He had the workers pull him up with the windlass and he ran down the hill to the house, holding shut his bleeding hand. He called to Mother to get a pan of paraffine, sat down on the back step and immersed his hand in the paraffine. Mother was beside him and all of us children were gathered around watching anxiously. We saw Daddy sag against the wall and heard him say, "Mother, I'm going!" He knew he was fainting and Mother understood that, but we thought he meant he was dying and we began wailing, "Oh, Daaaddy! Daaaddy! Daaaddy!" Mother took care of the situation. Daddy revived—and so did we—then she bandaged his hand with a "blue-water" poultice. The paraffine soaked poison from rusty metal cut and that with the poultice kept down infection. His hand healed with no permanent lack of use.

**Pig-Killing** Every year when the weather turned cold enough—forty degrees **F** was cold enough—Daddy killed one or more pigs. (We didn't call them hogs until after we came to college in the U.S.) We were glad the mission workers wanted head, feet and some other parts of the pigs they particularly liked. The parts for our use were brought to the big metal-top kitchen table. Layers of fat with the skin were sliced off of the hams and shoulders, cut into chunks, and put into a big iron pot on the stove to render the lard. While the lard was rendering we took turns operating the hand-cranked mince-machine (meat-grinder) and Mother seasoned and mixed large pans of sausage. We stood around the kitchen table rolling the sausage into patties. Two big iron skillets on the wood-burning stove were soon bubbling with cooking sausage patties.

Petrol was bought in five-gallon tins. The empties were saved and washed to use in many different ways after the tops were cut off and sharp edges turned down. Into one clean tin at a time we put a layer of cooked sausage patties, covered them with hot lard, put another layer of sausage, then lard, then sausage, then lard, until the tin was filled and the last layer of sausage completely covered with lard. A cover of cheesecloth was tied over the top of the tin. I don't recall how many tins were usually filled, but enough to last the better part of the year, with sausage any time we wanted it. The lard-covered meat did not spoil. When we wanted sausage for a meal we spooned out the needed number of patties into an enamel colander and set it over a pot of boiling water. The steam melted off the excess fat and softened the sausage.

After the lard was all rendered we had crisp pork rinds. With some of them we made "crackling bread." The leftover cracklings were used to make lye soap outdoors in the big iron wash pot with a fire under it. Lye soap was not used for skin. It was good for dishwashing, floor-scrubbing and for very dirty, greasy work clothes. We used lard for pie crusts, scones (biscuits), frying and seasoning, and for cakes when there was no butter.

We salted lard and used it as butter when butter was scarce. Our parents told us about America's country smoke houses where meat was salted, smoked and stored but said our Rhodesian climate was not cold enough for that process.

**Native Villages** Huyuyu Mission was among the Shona tribe and some villages were not far from the mission. School was going on all the time on the mission for the children of local villagers. Their classes were conducted in the Shona language until they learned English, then in English through about the equivalent of third grade. Later they could go elsewhere to more advanced schools if they wished. The Shonas were a peace-loving, happy and proud people with an organized society. Each village was ruled by a chief and had its own strictly enforced rules. As in any society some chiefs were good and some were not and some people were more peace-loving than others. At night we heard drums beating in the distance and learned that different sounds had different meanings. Sometimes they were sending messages to each other. Dancing, singing and drinking accompanied celebrations for births, marriages or mourning over a death, each with its distinctive sounds. At other times their singing, dancing and drinking had a very different sound and we knew they were partying just for fun. Their drink was a potent fermented beverage made from rupoko, a millet-type grain. Unfermented, the drink was slightly sweet and what we tasted was pretty good! We liked rupoko-meal porridge for breakfast.

**The Show** An annual event in Salisbury was the "Show." The Show Grounds and the Show itself were similar to the old fashioned "Fair" in the States—with cultural differences. If possible our parents planned the necessary trip to Salisbury to include "The Show" and we stayed overnight with the Garretts. There was judging of animals, dairy products, baked goods, woodwork, sewing, art, crafts and much more, with prizes for the three top winners of each category. My mind is hazy about much that went on but two things are still vivid. One was the March Of The Scottish

Highland Regiment in full Scottish dress and playing their bagpipes. The other was The Rhodesian Mounted Police who did amazing things with their horses while their military band played marches. They concluded their exhibition with horse-and-rider musical chairs; the band played *The William Tell Overture* with sudden pauses when the policemen slid off of their horses to sit in the chairs, one less chair than policemen. When the music began again they scrambled back onto their horses to continue until there were only two horses and riders left vying for the last chair. It was exciting fun to watch their antics as the policemen scrambled and sometimes fell in their hurry. Even the horses seemed to enjoy it! Back home we hummed that tune for days afterwards. [Many years later in Alabama I heard *The William Tell Overture* on the radio as theme music for *"The Lone Ranger"* and it stirred memories of Rhodesian Mounted Police!]

**Family Music** The Sherriffs had left most of their furniture including an Edison cabinet phonograph with eleven records. It had a diamond-pointed needle that never needed changing. The records, a quarter of an inch thick, were practically unbreakable and music on them included *The Old Rugged Cross, Under His Wings, Rock of Ages, Humoresque, William Tell Overture, The Blue Danube, Barber of Seville* and *Stop Your Tickling, Jock,* to name just a few. Over the next few years we gradually acquired an attachment that played regular phonograph records and we were able to add other kinds of music.

There was music in our house as we grew up, a choice for every mood. Musical Chairs was a popular game when we had visitors—indoors, not on horses! Mother had never studied music but she could play the piano by ear and whenever there was a piano around we urged her to play for us. A favorite of ours was her playing on the piano and singing a duet with Daddy, *Away Down On The Old Plantation* or *Oh Lorena, Dear Lorena.* Mother could imitate the Irish accent and we loved to hear her with her strong soprano voice sing Irish songs, *I'll Take You Home Again, Kathleen, On The Banks of The Brandywine,* and *When Irish Eyes Are Smiling.* And could she ever play the mouth organ (harmonica)! When she belted out *The Irish Washerwoman* we all jigged along with the music while she grew breathless and red in the face and we laughed hilariously.

**Driving** Early in our lives Daddy taught us to drive the motor car. He started us out in his lap learning to steer, then with our feet on his, we learned when to use the clutch and change gears (stick shift of course). When we were too big to sit between his knees he let us drive on our own with him in the passenger seat. By the time we were teen-age we had learned to dodge big rocks and holes, straddle deep ruts, drive through deep sand and mud and ford rivers. We had experience on every kind of road and some non-roads. He taught Mother to drive and most of her learning was on the road between the mission and Mrewa, over that extremely rough road, fording the two rivers. When she went to the Native Commissioner in Mrewa to get her driver's license he asked her where she had been driving. She told him and he said, "Here's your license! If you've been driving on that road there's no need for me to give you a driving test!"

**Missionary Visits** Every year the American workers at Sinde and Kabanga Missions in Northern Rhodesia and the missionaries in Southern Rhodesia spent a week together to exchange ideas and for encouragement and inspiration in their work. Those visits were highlights of our years. One year I remember in particular when we were living in the big house they came to Huyuyu for several days—many adults and children and we had camp-cots all through the house at night! The children enjoyed Dow Merritt's teasing and Foy wanted to get back at him. He made little mud balls and dipped them in chocolate icing Mother made for him. After dinner that evening Mother announced that Foy had made a surprise for everyone. He came from the kitchen with a plate of sweets (candy) to pass around, beginning with Dow Merritt. Dow was suspicious and told Foy he would take one if Foy had one first, so Foy immediately put one in his mouth, careful to hold it still with his tongue while pretending to chew.

That satisfied Dow. He took a piece and bit down on gritty mud. He ran outside spitting and sputtering to the delight of the children!

Every evening while the missionaries were there, after supper, Bible reading and prayers, we sang hymns. Everyone (including children) was given a chance to request a favorite song. Finally children were told to go to bed. Foy and I put pajamas on then went to sit on the floor in the hallway by the living room door so we could hear the grownups talk. They enjoyed talking about Bible subjects and many different topics, sometimes heartily agreeing and other times with differing opinions. Mother and Mrs. Reese liked to play devil's advocate and that made for lively discussions. Sometimes they sounded very serious but other times they went into peals of laughter. I don't know how long Foy and I sat there but I never forgot the good feeling that came out of that room.

When it was our turn to go to Northern Rhodesia we had two unforgettable halts on the way, Mica Hill and Victoria Falls. Mica Hill was a long steep climb on the gravel road and Daddy carried extra water bags to refill the boiling radiator at frequent stops on the way up. While we waited for the radiator to cool we collected shiny flakes from the ground. We each wanted to find the biggest piece and split it into transparent sheets that looked like glass. Daddy told us it was mica or isinglass that was used for side-curtains for touring-cars.

At the border between Southern and Northern Rhodesia we crossed the Zambezi River on the bridge below Victoria Falls and always stopped to gaze at the spectacular sight. Some distance above the Falls the river was three miles wide during the rainy season and the rim of the Falls was about one-and-a-half miles wide. Millions of gallons of water dropped over the rim, straight down more than three hundred feet to collide at the bottom with a sheer rock cliff that turned the water back into a fiercely whirling pool, appropriately named *The Boiling Pot*. From there the water flowed through an opening between walls of rock into a larger pool inhabited by crocodiles, and called *Crocodile Pool*. Below the Falls the bridge spanned the deep gorge that continued at that depth for miles downstream. Standing on the bridge we could feel the constant mist from the falls. No matter how many times we saw Victoria Falls it never lost its power to excite us and to inspire awe and wonder.

**Trips to the Big City** The semi-annual trips to Salisbury were eagerly anticipated events of our year and the older we got the more we looked forward to them. We knew we would come home with new supplies not available at the general store in Mrewa—things like toothpaste, Morton's Iodized Salt (the umbrella kid on the box), baking powder, spices, flavorings, prunes, raisins, dried apricots, sweetened condensed milk, Lyon's Golden Syrup (in a green can with a lion and honey bees on it—how we loved that syrup!), treacle (similar to molasses), corned beef in tins, tinned salmon, sardines and potted meat, jelly powders (not yet called Jello) and more, besides the box of chocolates that Daddy surely would buy. Most of what we ate was grown on the mission and taken for granted: mealies (corn), monkey nuts (peanuts), Irish potatoes, sweet potatoes, pumpkins and all kinds of other vegetables; also fruit, oranges, grapefruit, lemons, guavas, pawpaws (like papaya but bigger than anything like that in the U.S.), avocados, quinces, loquats, figs, lady finger bananas, plantains, rhubarb, gooseberries, mulberries and strawberries.

More than once Foy, Beth and I stayed awake all night before making the trip to Salisbury. We were in the big house and were to leave about 4:00 a.m. Mother and Daddy gave us permission to stay up *if* we would be quiet so they could sleep. Margaret Ann joined us for games like *Chinese Checkers* and *Snakes and Ladders* then she got sleepy and went to bed. We had recently learned to play *Monopoly* and Foy, Beth and I played that on his bedroom floor. After what seemed like hours we heard roosters crowing and thought it was morning only to find out it was just midnight. We kept playing until it was time to get dressed to go. After those sleepless nights, as much as we enjoyed singing when we traveled, we slept most of the way. The eighty-four mile trip took time and the forty miles per hour speed limit was seldom reached. With four youngsters in the car rest stops now and then were required for us to "go to the bush;" there were no convenient filling stations there but plenty of bushes! More than one flat tire might have to be patched, or a wait for livestock to get out of the road. In the city we went to Haddon and Sly, one of two big department stores, for the annual new shoes for all but Mother—hers were ordered from Montgomery Ward. I enjoyed the smell of new leather. I liked to watch the shoe salesman measure my foot, see him bring out different shoes and expertly fit them on my foot. Daddy felt of the toes to be sure they were roomy enough to last a year. Then we went to other parts of the store for the things on Mother's list that she didn't usually order from Montgomery Ward.

A big Tea Room was on one of the upper floors where we ate lunch or had tea if it was past lunch time. The white clad server with red fez and white cloth over his arm anticipated our every need and served us tea and sandwiches, little cakes and jam tarts. I enjoyed walking beside Daddy on the sidewalk. One of the earlier times when I was beside him, making sure I didn't step on a crack, I was reading out loud the signs in the windows and along the street when I saw "Pedestrian Crossing" printed on the pavement. Proudly I read it aloud as "Pede<u>strain</u> Crossing." Daddy's chuckle warmed my heart as he explained the correct pronunciation.

**"Doctoring"** On the mission, sick and injured natives lined up at the back door for treatment every morning just as they had in Northern Rhodesia and ailments were the same. Ladies in the U.S. still sent old sheets to keep us supplied with bandages and a supply of the same basic medicines were kept on hand, including the trusty Zambuk, iodine, permanganate of potash and "blue water," gargle and cough medicine, sore-eye salve, borax, carbolic acid, Vicks, Mentholatum, that I can recall. To treat a baby's deep cough Mother put a few drops of paraffine (kerosene) on a half-teaspoon-full of sugar and slowly fed it to the baby, then smeared its little chest with Mentholatum and covered it with a heated flannel cloth. Older children were treated the same way only with Vicks instead of Mentholatum. Daddy and Mother could "doctor" most ills and injuries. Trips to the doctor or hospital were for real emergencies. When a friend of Foy's, 13 year-old Aubrey, fell and broke his arm while visiting us, Daddy set, splinted and bandaged it before taking him to the doctor in Mrewa. The doctor said he couldn't improve on Daddy's setting so he only added a Plaster of Paris cast.

**Playtime** From earliest memory we had chores to do but we never lacked things to do for fun. We did not need to "have company" to play. Our parents encouraged us to play with each other and often they took time after work to play with us, though I'm sure there were times they would rather have rested. Everywhere we lived Daddy set up a croquet court; we had family contests when it was just us; when we had company, adults and children played together. Indoors we played *Draughts (Checkers), Snakes and Ladders, Chinese Checkers, Monopoly* and other table games. The only card game allowed was *Old Maid*.

The ash-heap out back was our treasure-trove. Out of the ashes we girls collected little bottles and pretty pieces of glass or china to use for play dishes. One of our favorite play-houses on Huyuyu Mission was under the eucalyptus gum trees John Sherriff had planted on each side of the driveway. Eucalyptus trees took many years to mature and these were fairly young. Their branches grew almost horizontally, the lowest ones close to the ground, and leaves hung down to the ground around the perimeter. Under them we felt enclosed in our own little world where we felt safe. Weeds and grass did not grow under them and for some reason snakes and other creatures did not like them, perhaps the strong eucalyptus smell kept them away. The lower branches were our upstairs rooms and we drew other rooms on the ground. Depending on what we found handy we used sticks for furniture, empty tins for pots and pans and sticks or little stones for people. Old Montgomery Ward Catalogs were saved to use for toilet tissue *after* we cut out anything we wanted to save, like figures for paper dolls and furniture for their house. The arrival of that catalog was a family event and we knew better than to tear or cut it before the new one came.

Beth and I enjoyed climbing trees in the orchard but she was more athletic than I, which brings to mind one particular tree. It was a good climbing tree and she went up ahead of me. Going up was easy. We climbed high enough to feel excited, and enjoyed the sights from our perch. When we decided to get down, she leaned forward, took hold of a branch a lower than our perch, swung herself down and sat on another branch behind her, then forward again to grasp another branch and on down till she dropped to the ground. It looked so easy I knew I could do it. I reached forward and swung down just fine but she was shorter than I was; my bottom was way below the branch she sat on and pull as I might I could not bring myself up enough to sit on it. Hanging there surveying the situation I realized if I let go, my chin would hit the branch in front and below me and if I leaned back my head would bump a different one. I pulled and pulled trying to lift myself to the sitting place but nothing doing. So we did what we did best when in a pickle—we called Daddy loudly.

Daddy was in the workshop but his ears were always listening. He dropped what he was doing, vaulted over the lower half of the dutch-door and came running, expecting to find us being attacked by a leopard or something equally dire. He was relieved to find nothing more serious than the need for a hand-down from the tree. He strongly suggested we not climb higher than our heads in the future. I practiced pull-ups for all I was worth but my body was too heavy for my arm muscles. Beth and Margaret Ann did the splits, turned flips and climbed ropes; somehow I managed to muddle through life without being able to do those things!

**More Learning** Learning to work and to enjoy whatever we were doing was an important part of our training. We girls were taught the regular things, making beds, sweeping, dusting and doing dishes. We learned to use whatever was at hand for many jobs. Most of our cooking vessels were either cast iron or enamel. If something burned in one of them it was an absolute "no-no" to scrape with a spoon or other metal object. The first choice was a piece of wood kept handy for that purpose. If that didn't work, a heaping tablespoon of baking soda was put into the pot, a cup of water added and brought to a boil then set aside to cool. Usually when cold the crusty burned food flaked up and the pot was clean. Cold ashes from the firebox of the kitchen stove made good scouring powder. Ashes were also used to scrub stained or greasy floors. Vinegar and salt mixture was used on *copper* handles of andirons and on the *outside* of our big *copper* kettle (super-sized pot) to make them shine like new. That big copper kettle held about three gallons and was used to make jam when we had a big crop of fruit. But after years of jam-making the kettle sprung a leak. Thereafter it was polished and used to hold fresh flowers in the summer in the dining room fireplace. From the Sherriffs we inherited a big *brass* squat-shaped urn that we kept polished to hold flowers in the living room fireplace during the summer. During winter those two vessels were kept in corners of the rooms with flowers in them. Since they leaked we didn't put water directly in them, a large glass jar was filled with water and put down in them to hold the flowers.

"**. . . Sew A Fine Seam . . .**" There were other things to be learned, too. As soon as we could sit still Mother taught us to knit and crochet and to embroider simple things, to sew our own dresses, beginning with straight petticoats, then every-day dresses and finally Sunday dresses. We embroidered and crocheted edges on tea showers (large net rectangles, tea trays covers to keep flies off). We crocheted with fine yarn and beads around the edges of net circles for jug covers and made tea cozies. She taught us to darn socks smoothly without lumps. Mother taught us to turn worn out collars on Daddy's dress shirts and later on Foy's and our school uniform shirts. We undid the stitching that held the collar to the neckband, removed the collar, turned it over and carefully matched it to the band, then basted and machine-stitched it back in place. The shirt was good for many more months/years of wear. Mother believed in doing things right. If a seam was crooked, we undid it and did it over again, and again and again, if necessary. Mistakes in crocheting or knitting or embroidery meant undoing and doing over. Thank-you, Mother, for your training that has helped us ever after.

Our first sewing machine had a handle on the wheel that was turned by hand. It took practice to guide material with one hand and turn the handle with the other. If two hands were needed to guide material like georgette, voile or satin, one of us turned the handle for the one sewing. We were nearly grown before a treadle machine came into our lives.

**Mother's Hands** In memory I still see my Mother's hands as she showed us how to do things. From earliest memory I watched her hands with fascination, whatever she was doing. She had large hands with long tapering fingers that were deft and nimble, strong and gentle. Many nights after I was in bed I pulled on my fingers trying to make them taper like hers.

All the while she was teaching us Mother was also teaching native women Bible, sewing, knitting, crocheting, hygiene. One of the native mothers had an ingenious way of drying her baby with no towel. In the warm sunshine she gently tossed her baby up in the air and caught it until the baby was dry. We girls really enjoyed watching the African women with their children and especially the babies. Little girls five and six years old carried their infant brothers or sisters strapped to their backs to help their busy mothers and carried water pots or baskets on their heads. My sisters and I tied dolls on our backs and learned to carry books, baskets or pumpkins on our heads. From the time Margaret Ann was old enough I carried her on my back. When I was eleven and she a lanky five-year-old, Mother made me stop carrying her around on my back for fear of injuring my spine.

**Church Building** Daddy wanted the people to have a permanent meeting house on the mission. From John Sherriff, he had learned to work with granite rock and the hills behind the mission were covered with granite—in large flat slabs on the ground and boulders of all sizes. Daddy drew the plans then with rock-chisels, hammers and dynamite, he and his workers cut stones for the foundation, steps, sills and lintels. He used a team of donkeys to pull the heavy pieces down the side of the kopjes, a series of poles under the slabs for runners, and several workers using poles as brakes in the descent. Generally the team of donkeys worked well, pulling the heavy granite pieces to the building site, stopping and starting as instructed—most of the time. But donkeys were known for their stubbornness and now and then they rebelled. When that happened no amount of pushing or pulling or yelling at them made them budge until they were ready.

One hot morning had been extremely trying for Daddy and his workers and "morning tea" time came as a big relief. In the house Daddy exclaimed to Mother, "*Oh,* those *donkeys!*" as he sat and told her about his frustrations. Mother answered with a mischievous lilt in her voice, "Perhaps there's one donkey too many out there!" Daddy was too frustrated to laugh out loud but he went back to work smiling. The more he thought about what Mother had said the more amused he got. Sometime later he related the incident to a neighbor who just smiled and Daddy was disappointed that his joke didn't go over. Later that neighbor saw Daddy again and began laughing. He said he was working in his field thinking about what Daddy had told him when it dawned on him what Mother had meant by her statement. He said he dropped what he was doing and went to tell his wife the joke! Daddy enjoyed that part of the story as much as the first part.

Thousands of bricks were made and burned ready for the building. Long eucalyptus-gum tree poles were cut and fastened together with nuts and bolts for the rafters. When the time came they were raised into place with winch and pulley operated by manpower. When Mother could spare us from the house, Margaret Ann, Beth and I found a good perch at a safe distance from where we could watch the interesting work. The roof was made of long grass put on in a "driven thatch" that was more long-lasting than regular flat thatch. It was a big building, big enough for well over a hundred people—I don't recall the measurements. The seventy-five year old building is still in use and has been re-thatched many times.

**Sundays at Huyuyu** Sunday morning after breakfast we dressed for church service to begin at 11:00. At 10:30 a bell rang loudly. The bell was the rim of an automobile tire fastened by a chain to the branch of a tree and struck hard with a metal bar. The sound carried over the valley below the mission and back into the kopjes behind the mission. It echoed for miles. Villagers heard and came to meeting.

The congregation that gathered there on Sunday mornings had outgrown the early pole-and-daager building and while Daddy was building the larger church house, that took more than two years to finish, we met under big trees on the grounds. Our family sat on rough chairs or benches from the school, native women brought their grass mats to sit on and the men sat on benches from the old building or their own little three-legged stools or squatted on their haunches or stood around in the shade.

When the walls were part of the way up and the rainy season began, no more could be done until the next dry season, but on any Sunday that was not rainy we didn't need a roof to use the building. A packed mud floor and homemade benches were all that was needed. The custom was for women to sit on one side of the aisle and men on the other. The Communion Table was kept in a shelter during the week and brought out on Sunday morning, draped with a white cloth and set in order. At first there was one bread plate and one wine goblet; when the crowd grew large enough, there were two of each. Another white cloth was spread over them to keep the flies off. A basket was passed around for the collection but very few villagers had money; they gave things like eggs, sweet potatoes, mealies (corn), raw monkeynuts (peanuts), honey-in-the-comb in a container or a live chicken with its legs tied together. After the close of the service Daddy estimated the value of the offerings, put the equivalent amount of money from his own funds into the church treasury to be used for buying grape juice, song books or Bibles. The produce was then used for food for the mission school teachers.

Africans loved to sing and so did we. At church the songs were sung in Shona with their own harmony but using basically the same tunes we knew. Words of the songs had been translated and printed and books supplied for those who could read or wanted to hold a book. The song leader sang the first line alone, then with the congregation he sang that line over again, then he sang the second line and so on through the whole song. More familiar songs were memorized and sung straight through with the leader beating time. I remember some of the words of one song in particular and every time we sing it in church I still cannot help but sing the Shona words to myself as I sing the English words out loud: *"There's Not A Friend Like The Lowly Jesus; No, not one; No, not one."* Shona words of that part were:

*Ha-ku-na um-we ku pen-da Jesu, Ha-ku-na-ba, ha-ku-chi-na . . .*

When Daddy preached he used an interpreter; we could understand what he said, but of course it took twice as long. After his sermon we had communion. One of the native preachers then gave another sermon. Time was not an issue, sometimes we got home after 2:00 or 3:00 o'clock. Native mothers with nursing infants had no trouble keeping their little ones content—mothers nursed their babies even as toddlers and brought food for older children.

**Jack Mzirwa** The main African leader of this congregation was a man named Jack Mzirwa. His village was an estimated three miles from the mission. His family, including his one-hundred-year-old mother, walked to meeting every Sunday morning. I thought he was a good preacher. Though I couldn't understand everything he said I got the idea and he was interesting to watch—and perhaps also because he didn't talk too long! The other fairly regular speaker was Tom Mugadza. We girls heaved a resigned sigh when he got up to speak because he did not know when to stop and we could see Sunday dinner being at 3:00 o'clock or later. It might have helped if I had been able to understand more of what he was saying. I am not speaking for Foy who by then could understand and speak the language.

**Sunday dinner** was a special meal with a special feel about it. Our cook was named Noel. He had trained and worked in big hotels in the city where he could have made much more money, but on the mission he could work and keep his wife and baby nearby. We trusted him like one of the family and his wife allowed us to hold and play with their baby. Noel prepared vegetables from the perpetual garden and cooked a delicious mid-day meal (dinner) every day through the week but especially on Sunday—or perhaps it seemed better on Sunday because we were extra hungry by the time we ate. I can almost smell the chicken or venison or beef, oven-roasted with potatoes, carrots and parsnips, gravy, green beans and cabbage salad (slaw). Dessert was usually stewed fruit of some sort with boiled custard.

Noel always had the afternoons off and we did our own supper-fixing and washed the supper dishes. When the Great Depression forced churches in the U.S. to practically stop sending funds to my parents, Noel was dismissed, to our sorrow, and I began to learn more about cooking. As long as he was working for us Mother had more time to teach her own children and the African women. Native teachers who had trained in advanced schools elsewhere came to teach in the school for the African children. When Noel's baby grew up she married one of the mission school teachers.

**Deprived?** The only time I felt in the least deprived while growing up in Africa was when other children talked about visiting their grandparents—ours were across the ocean; or when we read in books, or our parents talked about their own childhood of going fishing and swimming or wading in streams, going barefoot in summertime, playing in the snow or making snowmen—all things very foreign to our lives—we wished we could do those things but we were having such a good time we never spent much time missing them.

**Crocodiles** Several miles from the Mission was a large crocodile-infested river. We were not allowed even to fish from the river bank because crocodiles could come out of the water, grab a person and take them down, never to be seen again. We were told the crocodile took its catch to an underwater crevice in the bank, wedged it tightly in, then left it there to rot before eating it. We certainly did not want to fish, swim or wade in that river!

**Bilharzia** There was a deadly (to white people) parasite called bilharzia. It was in the water of rivers and in the sandy soil, so there was no wading or going barefoot outdoors for us at all during the dry season. After enough heavy rains the fresh water washed the smaller streams, then we could wade or go swimming in select places. During our years at Huyuyu Mission there was one river that was considered safe. It was on the far side of Mrewa from the mission and a few times we and the van der Merwes went there for picnics and wading. The grown-ups sat on the beach-like bank watching while we played in the shallow water. But one of those times almost ended in tragedy. Ella, Beth and I were wading out towards a big rock that Daddy said was the limit of our space. We had no intention of going beyond it but we wanted to get near it. Beth was leading, Ella and I close behind. As we got nearer the rock Beth screamed and went under. I grabbed her hand and pulled but I felt my foot slipping on a rock slab and a current pulling at my legs. I hung on to her and screamed and reached out to Ella with my other hand. She caught my hand and was able to brace herself on an underwater rock. We hung on to each other screaming. Daddy had seen what was happening, jumped into the water, shoes and all, and reached us quickly. He grabbed Beth and pulled us all to safety. The river had imperceptibly been rising from recent rains upstream and the current was becoming stronger every minute around that rock. When we moved to the farm soon afterwards, Mrewa, the van der Merwes and that river were no longer within our sphere of activities.

**Animals in the Kopjes** Huyuyu Mission was on a slope of a range of boulder-covered hills called kopjes not large enough to be called mountains. Boulders were all the way from fist size to as big as a house—all solid granite. Under the boulders were layers of granite with small trees, bushes and grass growing in the cracks wherever soil afforded. Along the tops of the hills were ruins of ancient forts from inter-tribal warfare and within those ruins were some caves where we found some Bushman paintings. Those kopjes were ideal places for young people to clamber, climb, jump and explore.

Baboons and monkeys inhabited the hills most of the time and we could hear them, baboons barking and sometimes fighting with each other and monkeys chattering and squealing. They both liked the trees, rocks and caves of the kopjes. Monkeys found the chicken house on the mission and they liked eggs. Daddy built high fences with the top round of chicken wire bent outward to discourage monkeys from climbing over the top. Unfortunately chickens liked to fly out more often, so he bent the top layer inward to keep the chickens in, taking a chance on dogs barking or chickens squawking to scare the monkeys away.

Baboons liked to invade the mealie field, the orchard and the vegetable garden where usually a garden worker was hoeing or watering and could make enough noise to scare them away. The baboons had an eye for mealies when the ears were full but still tender. The story is told that a baboon walked down the row, reached up and pulled an ear off the stalk with his right hand, stuck it under his left arm and went to the next stalk to repeat the act. As he continued to pull an ear and put it under his arm, the previous ear fell to the ground. At the end of the row he had only the last ear he had pulled—the rest of the ears were lined up along the row on the ground where they had fallen! The moral of this story was, "Don't be greedy!"

We learned that baboon and monkey noises in the hills were a good sign because leopards came through the hills periodically and when the leopards came, the baboons and monkeys left. When all was quiet in the hills we knew better than to climb rocks or picnic up there because it meant there were leopards in the area. When we again heard the baboons and monkeys, we knew the leopards had gone away and the hills were once more safe for us.

**Big Brother** Foy was two years older than I. When he was about ten he built a cart using two wheels from an old wheel-barrow and some scrap boards. He hitched a donkey to the cart and proudly gave his sisters rides in it. As far back as I can remember I tried to do whatever he did: jumping across ditches, throwing rocks at a target, running races or riding a bicycle. He did all those well and I tried, but usually landed in the ditch, missed the target by a mile and lagged way behind in a race. But my failures didn't keep me from trying and Foy put up with me. He did succeed in teaching me to ride a bicycle when I was about ten. The only bike available was a man's bike that Foy had learned on. He put one leg under the bar to reach the opposite pedal and rode, leaning sideways. I thought if he could, I could. He tried to coach me with the leg-through-the-bar method but I couldn't get the hang of it—it was too sideways for me to balance. We decided that if I straddled the bar and sat on the seat, even though my feet didn't reach the pedals, I could coast down the driveway. Foy held the bike beside a retaining wall at the top of the drive while I climbed on. He assured me I could go down the drive after he gave me a push, that I would keep going until the bike came to a stop in the sand bed at the bottom and there I could fall over into the sand without hurting myself. It worked. I learned to balance and before long I was able to straddle the bar, ignore the seat, and stand on the pedals to go. Of course if the tire hit a rock on the way down the gravel drive, which it did several times, I "came a cropper" and claimed it didn't hurt because I wanted to be tough for Foy.

When he wanted to become more athletic he decided to get up early to run and agreed to let me run with him. He woke me up early and we sat on the back steps to put on sox and shoes. We were trained to turn our shoes over and shake them before putting a foot in. One morning when he turned his boot over a little snake fell out and slithered away. That was a powerful reminder to us of the need to shake our shoes first!

Foy acquired a .22 rifle and Daddy taught him to use it, then he went hunting and brought home his first little antelope—venison for the table. I begged him to teach me to shoot. We climbed up to a place on the side of the hill behind the house where the hill rose more steeply behind the designated tree and he put a tin in a fork of the tree; from there, if (when!) I missed the target the bullet would harmlessly go into the hillside behind the tree. Foy showed me how to stand, how to hold the gun, how to aim and how to finger the trigger. He said, "Just *squeeze* the trigger and *don't shut your eyes*." I squeezed and tried to keep my eyes open but they shut in spite of me and the bullet went somewhere, but not near the tin. Foy was patient but after several more tries, he declared, "Oh, you're just hopeless!" and he never offered to teach me again and I never begged him to. We had other streams to cross.

**Mealie Bag Mishap** Adjoining Daddy's workshop was a store room where 200 lb. bags of shelled mealies were stored. The bags were stacked against the back wall nearly to the roof, three or four rows out into the room. But there was still room on the cement floor for us girls to play on rainy days or when it was too hot outside. One day we were playing contentedly, picking up stray kernels of mealies to use as food for our dolls. We found a "gold mine" of kernels where a corner of one of the stacked bags had a little hole in it. A few kernels had fallen out and we could urge more out as needed. Some full-but-not-stacked bags were on the floor in front of that bag with the hole in its corner. I was leaning over one bag and reaching for some kernels when Beth yelled that the bags were falling. I turned to get away—too late. A 200 lb. bag slid down the stack and pinned me to the bag I was leaning across. I remember Daddy came quickly from his workshop and lifted the bag off. I don't recall how I felt other than squashed and scared. After making sure I was not woefully injured, my parents talked about how thankful they were that the bag evidently slid slowly down the pile to land more or less gently on me instead of falling hard from the top, which might have broken my back.

**Tea Times and Meals** "Early morning tea" was a ritual. Daddy rose at daybreak and was always the first one up. By then the kettle was boiling on the kitchen stove. Daddy made the tea and took his and Mother's tea to their bedroom where they talked as they enjoyed it. Then he brought each child a cup of tea. From the time I was old enough to make my bed the wake-up call to each of us girls was, "Here's your tea, sister," and to Foy, "Here's your tea, son." We knew as soon as we drank the tea it was time to get dressed, make our beds and tidy our bedrooms—Foy had outside chores to do so we girls had to do his room.

*Breakfast, dinner* and *supper* were our regular daily meals—*lunch* was taken in a basket on picnics. We had breakfast about 7 a.m. Mother and Daddy drank tea and children had milk. Porridge was a given—mealie-meal (cornmeal) porridge through the week, oatmeal porridge on Sunday. For a few weeks after each trip to the city we had a choice on Sunday mornings of Corn Flakes, Shredded Wheat, Grape Nuts or Puffed Wheat. What a treat!

Sometimes we bought milk from the natives and always boiled it. Cooled overnight, it had its own taste. When that milk was not available we used tinned milk that we "made up" for breakfast from a tin of Sweetened Condensed Milk. The thick sweet milk was poured from the tin into a jug (pitcher) then half a tin of boiling water was poured into the empty tin to dissolve what was still there and that was poured into the jug. After stirring well in the jug, two tins of *cold* water were added—or three if we needed to "stretch" it. With that milk for breakfast no sugar was needed for those who wanted sweet cereal or porridge, though extra sugar was allowed. If we were out of Condensed Milk we used watered down Evaporated Milk—with sugar for those who wanted it sweet—I didn't. To this day if I run out of regular milk I can use either kind of canned milk.

Bread-and-butter-and-jam were staples at every meal. If we didn't have butter we used lard. Sometimes breakfast included sausage and eggs and scones (biscuits) or toast, but more often that was supper fare. We liked toast made over the coals in the kitchen stove grate. Soft boiled eggs were a favorite—boiled exactly three minutes—served in the shell in an egg cup with the small end up. At the table we learned, with Daddy's coaching, how to use our bread-and-butter knife to cut the top half-inch cleanly off of the egg (the trick was to strike it firmly and fast to keep from getting pieces of egg shell in the open egg.) We sprinkled a little salt on the egg and ate it with the small egg-spoon that fit down into the hole—fun and delicious!

About 11 o'clock was "morning tea" time. It was a welcome fifteen minute break for Daddy from his outside work and for all of us from whatever we were doing at the time. The African workers also enjoyed a break. Dinner at 1:00 o'clock was the main meal of the day. With dinner Daddy sometimes had hot tea while the rest of us had cold water if we wanted it. Cold water gave Daddy severe stomach cramps, hot tea or hot water didn't. At dinner we usually had some kind of meat with gravy, potatoes either mashed, roasted or scalloped, vegetables and either cabbage, lettuce or carrot salad with dressing we made from vinegar, sugar and cream.

The vegetable garden produced all the year round so whatever was in season at the time was used. Dessert was called "pudding" no matter what kind it was, often it was ripe fruit from our orchard, like guavas, mangos, quinces and peaches, stewed and served plain or with boiled custard. Pawpaws were eaten raw, never stewed. Fruit salad was made fairly often from thoroughly washed and peeled fruit. We had cake or pie only when visitors came or for birthdays. Granadillas (passion fruit) were grown wherever we lived and were a favorite addition to fruit salads and for making cake fillings by squeezing the juice from the seeds through cheesecloth and adding it to powdered sugar. Sometimes pudding (dessert) was just bread-butter-and-jam. "Afternoon tea" at 4 p.m. was time for another short break from work with hot tea again. Biscuits (cookies) were sometimes served in the afternoon and definitely were if we had visitors.

"Supper" was our evening meal around 6:30-7p.m. when we used up the leftovers from dinner if there were any. We had no refrigerator to keep food overnight except in winter when leftovers kept well in the pantry and Sunday roast was a sure keeper to make meatloaf or stew on Monday. Mother was expert at making leftovers appetizing. When there were no leftovers for supper we had soup or scrambled eggs and sausage with toast or scones (biscuits) or welsh rarebit on toast—unless we were out of cheese when we might have sardines with toast or saltines (crackers). To make toast we allowed the wood in the stove to burn down to red coals. A slice of bread was skewered on a long-handled metal fork and held over the coals at the proper distance to brown without burning. Sometimes the slice fell off and if not grabbed quickly enough it was ruined and the process began over.

**Rhodesian Mounted Policeman** Any time a European visitor showed up, tea was served regardless of the time of day. About once a month a Rhodesian Mounted Policeman on horseback rode a circuit, visiting unannounced the European households in the area to see that all was well. Now and then he ate the midday meal with us but usually only had afternoon tea. If we had no cake or biscuits (cookies) to serve, we split leftover cold scones, or saltines, spread with butter and topped with grated cheese or jam.

One of those unexpected police visits happened on a 4th of July while we were living in the big house. Daddy and Mother had told us about Independence Day celebrations in the U.S. and Foy thought we should celebrate. That morning he found the large American flag some friends had sent in one of the parcels along with several smaller ones and he proudly displayed the big one on our front verandah and the small ones throughout the front rooms. After the midday meal someone was looking down the road and called out, "Here comes the policeman!"

This particular policeman was known to carry his bottle on his rounds and the last time he had been there Mother and Daddy smelled the strong smell of whiskey when he came in for tea. Now Mother called to Foy, "Take down your flags quickly. He may be tipsy and accuse us of treason!" Foy raced around doing her bidding. By the time the policeman arrived at the house no American flag was in sight and for good measure Foy had put a Union Jack out front where the Stars and Stripes had been. Afterwards Daddy laughed at Mother about that episode and Mother said, "Well, you never know!"

At Huyuyu Mission, and later at the farm, the main road ran past at a distance from our house. The road was not paved so when we saw a dust cloud we knew a motor car was on our road and just as surely knew it was coming to our house. That interrupted whatever we were doing at the time. Mother would say to Beth or me, "Be sure the kettle is on and full." If there happened not to be any cake or cookies or leftover scones in the house, she hurried to the kitchen to "stir up a Theodora cake." By the time I was ten years old she could say, "Sybil, go stir up a Theodora cake. Spread guava jelly between the layers and sprinkle icing sugar on the top layer." It was a very simple sponge cake and I still remember the recipe. The batter divided equally into three round tins (cake pans) took barely ten minutes to bake because the oven was always ready; the stove was kept hot all day to fill water bags and for hot tea. Mother entertained the visitor(s) while Daddy, who had heard the car, came to the house, washed his hands, and joined them. Within about twenty minutes of our guest's arrival tea was ready to be served.

**Books** Daily Bible Reading and Prayer were as regular as meal time: after breakfast, three chapters from the New Testament, after supper, three chapters from the Old Testament, then we knelt for the prayer spoken by Daddy. As we learned to read, everyone had a Bible and found the place and Daddy called on us to read a verse or more depending on our ability. He often asked questions to test our comprehension and explained things we did not understand. Memorizing Bible verses was important as well as memorizing poems for our school work. We vied with each other in recitations. Most nights at bedtime Daddy also read to us from a Bible Story book. As long as there was a young child he read first from *First Steps For Little Feet* (a simplified Bible story book), then he asked questions. After that everyone listened as he read from the more advanced *Hurlbut's Story of the Bible* and asked harder questions. He knew how to make questions fun—not like a test.

Our parents encouraged other reading on our own besides the Bible and kept us supplied with books; but Daddy was a master storyteller and

"Daddy, please tell us a story," was heard frequently. We were never quite sure if he was telling something that had actually happened to him or something he made up, but the stories were always interesting. Sometimes when he got to an exciting place, he suddenly stopped, and we chorused, "What happened next?" and he replied with a twinkle in his eye, "My hat blew off and I had to go chase it!"—leaving us to imagine our own end to the story. After enough times like that we learned to add, when asking for a story, "And don't let your hat blow off this time!"

We grew up loving to sing many hymns and other songs our parents taught us. Any time we took a trip in the car we sang. Daddy and Mother sang duets and we often requested *Whispering Hope* and *O, Heart Bowed Down With Sorrow*—beautiful songs, sung in beautiful harmony. Foy learned to sing bass as soon as his voice changed. Daddy sang tenor or bass or lead, Mother sang soprano or alto and we girls sang soprano. Among the many songs they taught us were *Red Wing, When You and I Were Young Maggie, Two Little Girls In Blue, Come All Ye Texas Rangers, The Farmer Boy, Tell Mother I'll Be There.* On trips to town—a long drive—we often sang until we were hoarse.

**Bad Words** In our family, "bad words" (swear words) were not tolerated, neither were words like *liar, cheat, stupid* or *fool.* Because of our sheltered life the definition of "bad words" was somewhat hazy but we had a general idea—we had heard some of the British versions from neighbors. Of course Daddy and Mother never used such words but one time we heard Daddy use a word that shocked us to goose bumps.

We were going somewhere in the motor car over an almost non-road. Daddy had to stop often, to move a rock out of the way, or find a way around a deep rut, or check a tire. In the car, behind his feet, he kept a small empty teakettle for dipping in shallow water to refill the radiator when it boiled over. The first time he opened his door the teakettle fell out, bounced over the running board and rattled to the ground. He picked it up and put it back in. Before long he had to stop again, and again the teakettle tumbled out and he picked it up and replaced it. Having to stop so much was frustrating and the teakettle was not helping. The fourth time he had to stop, the fourth time the teakettle fell out, his frustration had reached its limit. As the kettle again rattled to the ground, he said with strong feeling, "Oh! this *bloomin' teakettle*." We had never heard him use that expression and assumed with shock that our Daddy had said a "bad word." We gasped and shrunk down in the back seat. Then we heard Mother's chuckle as she said, "Why Daddy, I don't see any flowers on that teakettle!"

**Riding Donkeys** Foy learned early to ride donkeys and now and then we girls were allowed to ride with careful supervision because even gentle donkeys could decide to buck or suddenly run away. Daddy picked the proper donkeys to suit our size. One weekend the van der Merwes were visiting and we wanted to ride donkeys. Foy had the largest donkey and led the group. Beth, Ella and I, each on a donkey, followed him single file. Suzanne and Margaret Ann were younger and not allowed to ride. We rode in single file down the sloping driveway then turned and came back up the drive. In front of the house the driveway divided in a Y with a branch on either side of the house. At the division of the Y Foy decided to go up one side and the girls' donkeys took the other side to where our parents were standing.

Farther up the hill the main herd of donkeys was grazing and one of them brayed. Foy's donkey heard it and decided to buck Foy off and go join the others. Foy slid off his donkey's back before he could be thrown. As soon as his feet hit the ground his donkey galloped up the hill, braying. Our donkeys had been going slowly up the other branch of the Y until they heard Foy's donkey bray and saw it running then they began to run, spilling girls in all directions. I landed with a thump on my bottom, unhurt, one of the donkeys stepped on Ella's hand when she landed and Beth fell on her side and hit her head on a rock; she was knocked out briefly. Daddy and Mother quickly assessed the damage, Foy explained why he had turned his donkey loose and Ella's mother cried hysterically,

"I knew I shouldn't have let her ride." Ella's hand was bruised and Beth revived with a knot on her head but we never forgot that donkey ride.

**Creatures Small and Great** Chongololos were crawling creatures enjoyed by children because they were harmless and fun to play with. We called them "chongolos" for short. They had so many legs they were sometimes called "thousand legged"—we never tried to count them. They were easily distinguished from a centipede because their bodies were perfectly round while centipedes were flat. Chongololos came in sizes from as short as an inch with diameter about one tenth of an inch, to as long as ten or eleven inches and were half inch to three-quarter-inch in diameter. The entire length of the body was made up of a fairly hard shell in hundreds of even sections, like joined rings, each section having a pair of legs. At the front was a pair of short antennae and the back end came to a slightly tapered abrupt end. Its many legs moved in progressive waves to propel it across the ground and left two little trails in sand or soft earth. When touched by anything, this creature curled into a tight circle with its legs inward and remained motionless until danger was passed. When we saw one crawling in the yard we grabbed a stick and gently touched it, watched it quickly roll up, then we hunkered down to wait and see it slowly unroll and go on its way.

Army Ants that we knew as Soldier Ants were fearsome things. They were about three fourths to one inch long with pincers that could cut like a knife. They traveled in line formation and woe betide anything that dared to interrupt their marching line. We learned early not to mess with them.

White ants, similar to termites only larger, lived underground but came up through clay tunnels of their own making to feed on such things as wood, grain or cloth. When Daddy built brick houses he laid the foundation up to a certain height above ground then laid a metal "ant-course" on that before he began the brick wall. The ant-course was cut from galvanized metal about four inches wider than the foundation so it had an overhang on each side. If white ants came up through the foundation they could not go past the metal. On the inside of the house the cement floors covered the metal ant-course so the ants could not come into the house, though they were adept at finding a crack to come through. We made constant inspections and moved furniture frequently, to be sure white ants were not working under them. Legs of our beds were set in discarded tins (potted meat or sardine tins) with a small amount of paraffine in the tins to keep ants of any kind and other creepy-crawlies from going up the bed legs—a comforting thought, believe me!

Lizards came in many sizes and colors that looked iridescent in the sun. All the lizards in our area that I knew of were harmless. Chameleons were of the lizard family, harmless creatures, most often about six to twelve inches long from head to tip of tail. When disturbed or frightened they made a puffing sound. We thought they looked like little dragons because of the shape of their head and the ridge along their back. Their eyes were in protruding ball sockets that could move in opposite directions at the same time when stalking or preparing to catch insects. We liked to pick one up and place it somewhere different in texture and color from where we found it, so we could watch it gradually turn to the color of its surroundings. They were useful in the garden where they feasted on grasshoppers and other insects. We enjoyed placing one on the inside window sill where there were flies buzzing around against the panes. If we were motionless long enough we saw the eyes roll first one way then another while the body stayed completely motionless. Suddenly its long tongue flashed out, caught the insect and rolled back into its mouth in one swift movement that always startled us.

Tarantulas came into the house sometimes as did other large spiders and we gave all of them a wide berth. At an early age we learned to always look cautiously under rocks or pieces of wood before picking them up to be sure no scorpion or centipede was hiding there. Scorpions also came in many sizes from tiny to several inches, but no matter what size they were they could cause pain and we were afraid of them.

Mosquitoes were a fact of life that had an effect on our lives from infancy. In spite of all precautions, we did get bites, so daily quinine was a must. In spite of daily quinine we all had several bouts of malaria. Daddy had the worst and most frequent attacks, perhaps because he worked outside and was least protected.

"Watch out for snakes!" were familiar words as we grew up. I don't remember feeling paranoid about snakes, they were just a respected fact of life. Seldom did we see a snake near or in the house but occasionally it happened.

**Home School** While on furlough in the U.S.A. in 1927-1929 Foy attended school. Our parents had decided I would wait until we got back to Africa to begin in the Rhodesian system so I was almost eight years old when I began the equivalent of kindergarten in 1931. The Rhodesian Government's Correspondence School was headquartered in Salisbury and from there supplied lessons from Sub A through Standard V, roughly corresponding to U.S.A.'s kindergarten through sixth grade. A unit called a "Set" arrived in the mail once every two weeks and Mother guided us through the lessons. The completed Set was mailed to Salisbury where it was marked (graded) and returned to us with a new Set on schedule so we always had a Set to be working on while one was in Salisbury. We felt connected to our teachers in Salisbury by their remarks written on our papers and a short personal letter they sent with each returned Set.

Beth and I began Sub A together but Mother explained to us that since I was older I would go faster until I caught up with my age level. She had permission from Salisbury to allow me to send in lessons for marking as fast as I was able to do them. The first year I went through Sub A, Sub B and part of Standard I. When I was nine I finished Standard I and half of II. The next year I finished St. II and did St. III. I was ready for Standard IV by the time I turned eleven and by my twelfth birthday I was beginning Standard V, correct for my age. Mother's one-room school teaching for a year before she married gave her experience in handling multiple ages and grades in the same room. That along with her inherent common sense and knowledge provided us with a good foundation before we went to high school.

Each Set from Standard II on consisted of Mental Arithmetic, Written Arithmetic, Spelling, Grammar, Composition, Transcription, Dictation, Writing, History, Geography and Drawing. The work we sent to Salisbury had to be done in *INK*. We used pen holders with separate nibs and each of us had an ink-well and blotting paper at hand. We first did the work with pencil on "scrap paper." Mother corrected it, making sure we learned what she had corrected and why. Then we copied the assignments over in ink without making any corrections. If we made too big a mess of it she allowed us to throw that away and copy it over again. "Copy it over" was a familiar instruction and I can almost hear my Mother's voice saying the words. The Salisbury teacher graded spelling, writing and neatness in every part of the Set. We printed through Standard I, then began joint-scrip and from there we gradually developed our individual cursive. As I progressed with cursive I tried hard to imitate my mother's handwriting because I thought hers was perfect.

On school days after breakfast at seven followed by Bible reading and prayer, we brushed our teeth. For some time after trips to the city we had toothpaste; when that was gone we used bicarbonate of soda or salt. If our supply of those was running low we used charcoal out of the cook stove—made by easing a red hot coal into a cup of cold water. We chewed the cooled coal, brushed teeth and rinsed. By eight o'clock we were ready for school.

Mother put us in separate rooms so we would not be disturbed when she was working with each one. We never knew when she might appear in our room. Instead of regular desks we had designated spaces—the end of the dining room table for one—a drop-leaf side table in the living room for another—and the third was a bedside table in the master bedroom. By the time Margaret Ann began school, Foy had gone to boarding school.

Mid-morning we had a fifteen minute recess (break) and a snack. Our midday meal was at one o'clock and, unless we were running behind in something or had unusual interruptions that week, school was over for the day. As I recall Mother had us well trained to keep working even when she was out of sight preparing dinner in the kitchen, giving spelling words or dictation to one or the other of us, or being called to give medical attention to someone at the back door. A strong motivation was our being taught from earliest childhood that God sees us all the time, no matter where we are. Our parents did not use that to scare us but presented it as a fact of God's love and care for us. That was an added motivation to obey them even when they were not present.

As 1934 began Foy was ready to go to boarding school in Salisbury and begin Form I (7th Grade). The boys' boarding school was called Prince Edward High School. There were boys there from the age of six through seventeen. At the end of Form V there was another Exam out of England called Matriculation or the Matric. Boarding school meant uniforms and we girls were proud of our big brother in his school uniform. One of the most exiting things about his being at boarding school was his bringing school friends home with him for the midterm holidays. Some students lived as far away as the Belgian Congo, or Tanganyika or Kenya and could not go home on slow trains and have any time left to be worth going for except for the six weeks at Christmas, so they stayed at school unless a friend who lived nearer invited them to his home. Foy invited boys home and we girls invariably had girlish crushes on them. In particular I remember Eric, Aubrey and Ronald and I secretly vowed to some day name a child of mine Eric.

## Southern Rhodesia 1935-1940

**Faroe Farm** Church support from the States had dwindled until it was evident that my parents could no longer keep up the lease of the site and operate the mission. About twenty miles from the mission the government had divided uninhabited land into farms selling for $1.00 per acre with twenty years to pay at no interest. Daddy heard about that and he and Mother thought on the possibilities: if we lived on a farm Daddy could still preach while growing most of our food and he could sell enough mealies to pay for boarding school for us children.

All farms were named and ranged in size from 3,000 to 8,000 acres. Several tobacco farmers were already operating some of the big ones.

Daddy had no intention of growing tobacco so he and Mother looked for the smallest one and chose *Faroe* with 3,000 acres. Some of the neighboring farms were *Maryland, Virginia, Chizanza* and *Springdale*. Our parents thought they surely would be able to pay off the $3,000 in twenty years and they talked about some day giving each child a portion of the land—even talking about which area would be for each one of us—no harm dreaming.

So the big move began. Clearing the farm building site was easy, but moving was not simply a matter of boxing up belongings. Buildings had to be taken apart piece by piece so the material could be used over again. Roof, rafters, ceilings, doors and windows of the big house were taken down carefully and stacked. Bricks were knocked loose and taken off the walls one by one and mortar scraped off. Two big wagons each pulled by sixteen oxen made numerous round trips to the farm. As load after load was hauled to the farm there was no shortage of laborers eager to earn modest wages.

I was fascinated by the knocking loose of bricks and begged Daddy to let me help. When the walls were down to about three feet from the ground he said I could help. He showed me how to stand on the wall and use a small sledge hammer to knock gently on the brick until it was loose and the brick was taken away to be cleaned. I was working steadily and backing up slowly but in my concentration I forgot to watch for the end of the wall behind me. I stepped off into thin air, scraping my leg on the brick wall from ankle to knee.

Iodine was the usual first aid for scrapes after washing them with warm soapy water and patting them dry, but to my relief Daddy decided this one needed Zambuck salve instead. I like to think he took pity on me, knowing that such an expanse of iodine would have been unbearable. He smeared salve on a cloth then laid it gently over the wound and with added padding over that, he firmly bandaged my leg. I was twelve then and I still remember the comfort of that firm bandage.

[Thirty-seven years later when my husband, Bennie Lee, died suddenly, it seemed as though my entire being was scraped and raw. By the time of the funeral I began to feel as though my whole being was firmly wrapped up and the memory of that long ago feeling came strongly to mind. I thought of the scripture that says God binds up the wounds of his children, and I was comforted.]

The move to the farm was not accomplished in a day or two—it took several weeks. I have a letter that Mother wrote January 18, 1935 to her brother Audrey and his wife Edith, describing a little of what was involved in our move: *". . . Will and I left the children with one of our neighbours (Mrs. deWet) and went to the mission for some more things and Will wanted to see to the loading of the two wagons . . . About 5:30 Thursday p.m. we started for home and had not gone two miles when we overtook the wagons, both stuck in the mud. Some natives were ploughing nearby and they and Will helped get the wagons out but it was growing late and raining. When we came to the river and saw it was rising we went back and slept at the mission.*

*"Early next morning we left again and when pulling around the place where the wagons had stuck we went down and had to get a native ploughing nearby to bring six oxen and pull us out. We arrived at the river to find it still rising and we hesitated to try to cross but natives told us more water was coming down and we had better cross quickly. So we drove in and came to the other side safely. The next river was rising too but we were able to cross. Finally we arrived at Mrewa about 10:30 a.m. and stopped with friends to wait for the mail truck from Salisbury . . . Roads were very bad but we reached home safely and went for the children . . .*

*". . . We didn't get to Makuni village last Sunday although we made an effort but car stuck in the mud and we had to send for oxen to pull us out. We sat in the car 2 hrs. or I did. Will went walking around through the veldt and found a road up above the mud holes so we went the new road today and will do so each Sunday . . .*

*". . . We appreciate your love and thoughtfulness for us so far away from home and loved ones. We enjoy the encouragement and prayers of all of you for us. May the Lord abundantly bless you throughout 1935.*

*With much love to all, Will and Delia."*

At the farm we needed somewhere to live while the brick house was being built. Some kind neighbors (deSwartz) put us up while Daddy built a temporary house of corrugated metal roofing fastened to poles for the walls and corrugated roofing laid overhead covered with a thick layer of long grass to keep off some of the heat. The roof metal and grass were held down by more poles. All our furniture and belongings were in the three long rooms and the kitchen was an open fire in a metal lean-to at the back.

When the brick house was almost finished it was time to make the trip to Salisbury for supplies before the rains began in earnest. Shopping done, we were on the way home when an early torrential rain with high wind came sooner than expected and hit the farm. It was dark and still raining when we arrived in front of our temporary house. The car lights showed the roof on the ground. I can hear Mother yet as she said what she usually said when catastrophe happened, "O-o-h-h, *D-a-d-d-y*! What will we *do*?" and Daddy's replying drawl, "W-e-e-l-l, l-e-e-t's s-e-e!" as he got out to assess the damage. Everything was drenched except one end of their bedroom where the roof had not blown off. Their bed and extra bedding was dry and that night they and Margaret Ann slept there. Daddy drove the motor car close to the wall and Foy, Beth and I slept in it. The next day bright sunshine dried things out and before night our temporary house was restored.

We moved into the brick house as soon as Daddy could get the walls up and the roof on. Work continued all around us but now we had real walls and doors and windows with a roof and packed-dirt floors—but no ceilings—which at our ages was a plus. If we had a bad dream or heard Daddy snoring and thought it might be a lion outside, we called, "Daddy!" and he lit his candle and light shone over the wall; or if we needed to get up in the night, we called and he lit his candle so we could see. During the next two years, between other jobs, Daddy worked on the house. He screened the verandahs, plastered walls, put in cement floors, and installed pressed metal ceilings throughout. The ceilings helped the looks and cut down the noise of rain on the metal roof so we could hear each other talk during hard rains.

That part of Southern Rhodesia is a plateau over 4,000 feet above sea level and nights were cool. Our house was built on a ridge and we never tired of the spectacular view from our front yard that overlooked a wide valley with rolling hills in the distance. The bright blue sky, large and empty, gave a sense of openness to everything, with seldom any clouds—jet trails were as yet unheard of.

**Chewing Gum** Daddy's sister, Aunt Sybil, died of 'flu in June that year in Kansas. We missed the joy of living near aunts and uncles and grandparents, but Grandma Short's regular letters that Daddy read aloud helped us feel connected. She knew chewing gum was scarce in our lives and often put a stick of Wrigley's gum in her letter—one stick didn't change the required 3 cents postage. When Daddy sorted the mail on the dining room table, we gathered around watching for an envelope with her handwriting. We could smell the gum before Daddy opened it. "Oh Goody! Chewing gum! Hurry, Daddy! Open it quickly!"

That one stick was cut into four pieces, one piece per child. We chewed our piece until supper time, then carefully saved it until the next day—and the next—and the next—until we accidentally swallowed or lost it. If it dropped on the floor we washed it and chewed it some more. I don't recall sticking our gum *"on the bedpost overnight,"* but years later when I heard that song I could relate to it.

At some point Beth and I decided the scraped yard looked too bare and asked Daddy if we could plant a "lawn." He said we could make a small bed along the front verandah, about six feet long and two feet wide, provided we kept the grass cut short. We transplanted wild creeping grass (similar to Bermuda), and conscientiously carried water in the sprinkler from the well. As the grass grew we trimmed it with old scissors. We were proud of our "lawn!" There was no shrubbery near the house because it might harbor snakes.

To help with family living expenses, Mother taught several white children from neighboring farms, and their mothers were happy to have someone else teach for them. I was twelve, doing Standard V (sixth grade), so while I kept up my own lessons Mother let me help with the younger children. She and Daddy had decided I would not take the Junior Biet Exam as Foy had done, since Mother did not have time for extra tutoring. I was sorry my parents would not have the help of a scholarship with expenses but I was more relieved to escape the exam. I finished Standard V by the end of the year and was ready for boarding school and Form One in January.

**Boarding School** I approached that January date with a mixture of adventurous anticipation and a heavy dread of leaving home. New and different clothes were exciting, but that excitement faded when Daddy, Mother, Beth and Margaret Ann unloaded me at boarding school and drove away. I was so homesick I cried myself to sleep many nights and it didn't help when the House Mistress (Matron) shamed me, telling me there were girls only six years old who were not crying. But after learning the rules and schedules and making some friends I decided boarding school wasn't so bad.

What would be called dormitories in the U.S. were called Houses. Girls High School, otherwise known as G.H.S., had four Houses and one auxiliary House, each one with its grounds taking up about half a city block *Weldon House* was for younger girls, but I was there three months waiting for a vacancy in *Guest House*, where I spent almost two years. I lived in *Forsythe House* my last two years. The other two houses were *Speake House* and *Biet House*.

Each house, except Guest House, had two stories and an open-to-the-sky quadrangle in the center. The House Matron lived in an apartment at one side of the quad downstairs and down the hall from her apartment were four mistresses' rooms and a Mistress Lounge. On another side of the quad was the Prep Room where we did supervised Prep (homework). Upstairs was a sickroom (infirmary) with a nurse living in an adjoining room. On the four sides of the second floor were dormitories identified by color, *Gold, Purple, Blue* and *Green.* Intramural sports went on between the dorms and also between Houses and all girls were fiercely loyal to their own dorm and House. Each dorm was a long room with eight beds on each side and a chest of drawers between every two beds; sixteen beds per dorm. Two girls shared the chest of drawers between their beds. At the foot of each bed was a locker for shoes, extra blanket and books. The four dormitories opened on to a verandah on the inside around the quad. At one corner were washrooms with bathtubs, showers, washbasins and toilets (commodes) for two of the dorms and diagonally across the quad was another set of washrooms for the other two dorms.

Downstairs the dining room seated sixty-four girls: eight tables with a bench for four girls on each side and a chair at each end, one end for a prefect (student officer) and one for a mistress (teacher.) The House Matron had her own small table at the front center of the dining room and we always felt her eyes on us. As soon as girls filed in and were standing in place behind their bench, mistresses followed by the Matron came in to take their places and the Matron rang her little table bell. We bowed our heads and she said, *"For what we are about to receive may the Lord make us truly thankful,"* we all said, *"Amen"* and sat down. The kitchen was connected to the dining room by a breezeway. It was not cafeteria style—we were waited on and good table manners were required.

Breakfast consisted of porridge made from cornmeal or oatmeal or occasionally some other grain. Each girl had a glass of milk at her place. A sugar bowl and milk jug (pitcher) were passed around for the porridge. I liked the pasteurized milk that was very different from the boiled or tinned milk we had at home. After porridge was eaten the bowls were removed by waiters who then brought one piece of toast each. That with a pat of butter and a spoonful of jam usually completed the meal though sometimes a treat of sardine paste on toast was added and on special occasions we had scrambled eggs. We left no food on our plates—"Waste not, Want not!" we were told. With a little practice we learned to all finish about the same time, ready for the Matron to ring her little bell. When she did we all stood up behind our benches with heads bowed while she said, *"For what we have received may the Lord make us truly thankful"* and we all said, *"Amen."*

Then we filed back to our dorms where we made our beds, gathered our books and waited for the next bell when we went downstairs and lined up in twos. With a mistress in front of the line and another at the back, we headed to the classrooms two or three blocks away, arriving just before 8 o'clock. There we filed into the gymnasium/auditorium for "Prayers." We stood in orderly lines (no chairs), the choir to one side at the front. On the stage the mistresses had chairs with the Head-mistress in the center. We sang from hymnals that had words but no musical notes—the tunes had names such as *Old Hundred, Southgate, Evan, Saxby* and *New York*. One of the mistresses read some Bible verses and a prayer from *The Book of Common Prayer,* then we recited *The Lord's Prayer* in unison. Sometimes we had a visiting speaker or the choir gave a program.

At the end of announcements after "Prayers" a bell rang and girls had to be in their classrooms at their assigned desks, standing in silence before the second bell rang and the mistress came in. She looked around to be sure we were all standing at our desks and said, "Good morning girls." We replied in unison, "Good morning Miss Parsons" or McLaughlin, or Sharp, or MacIntosh, or Jones, or McConnell, or Hill, or Silk—I remember face and stature of each. We had a different teacher for each subject. When she called our name we answered, "Present!" and sat down. No slouching was allowed, whether sitting, standing or walking. I recall the faces of classmates, Hilda and Lily Gallanti (identical twins but for a mole on Lily's upper lip), Sarah Sharp, Hilda duToit, Maude Markham, Evelyn Route and my two best friends, Reshea Barry and Iris Reynolds.

At 11:00 o'clock we had a fifteen minute break when we all went out into the open-to-the-sky quad that was surrounded by classrooms. Prefects were assigned to bring out big baskets of half-sandwiches of bread and jam or bread and peanut butter. In single file the girls walked by to take one half-sandwich only. Water fountains were at strategic points around the verandah. At 1:00 o'clock classes were over for the day and we marched in lines back to our Houses.

After our midday (main) meal we went to our dorms for Rest Period. We had to lie on our beds but could read, write or nap. Then came an hour of Prep (homework) in the Prep Room and after that we had Sports—tennis, swimming or hockey, depending on the season. After a light supper we had another hour of Prep. Bells rang to signal all the changes of activities in the classrooms and in the Houses. After evening Prep we went to our dorms to get ready for bed. Shower and bath times were scheduled and posted, some at bedtime and some before breakfast, to accommodate 64 girls. A warning bell rang at 8:45 for silence and a bell for lights out at 9:00. Some of us who loved to read and had a good torch (flashlight) continued reading our book under the covers by torch light. Sometimes the moon shone through the window brightly enough that we could read by moonlight. The Matron made periodic rounds to be sure everyone was in bed and no lights were on.

I did well scholastically but didn't shine in gym or sports, though I enjoyed tennis and field hockey. We had swimming classes in the municipal pool and I had recurring dreams of swimming like a fish although I never got past "dog-paddling" and "belly flops!" Sports Day was an annual event when girls were divided into age groups and participation was compulsory. We had sack races, three-legged races, relay races, wheelbarrow races and egg-and-spoon races, all of which were fun, but the day concluded with a foot race. Someone had to be last and too often that one was me, earning me the nickname "Hippo." Fortunately none of my real friends called me that and my self-confidence got a boost when I made it into the choir and was chosen one of three girls to sing descant.

Weekends had their own distinct rhythms. Saturday mornings there was detention time for unfortunate candidates. But first we had to write a letter home, put it in an *unsealed*, addressed, stamped envelope and pass it to the mistress' desk where she checked to see that it wasn't just blank pages. Sometimes for variety I wrote my entire letter home in rhyming couplets that would not have won a poetry prize! For example:

*"Now I sit me down to write*
*A letter that I think just might*
*Help you smile and more;*
*I only hope it doesn't bore.*
*Today's breakfast was very tasty*
*Though the eggs were somewhat pasty!*
*And now it's time to say adieu,*
*With all my heart, I love you."*

I enjoyed writing letters and during one of our holidays I had written to a pen pal club advertised in a magazine from Canada that a friend of Mother's sent to us. I received 150 responses from many places in the world, from writers of different ages—teens to fifties. I picked out a cross section of fifteen letters that appealed to me the most and took the others to boarding school to divide among my friends. I corresponded and exchanged stamps with those fifteen for the next two years. They were in Canada, U.S.A., England, Germany, Island of Rhodes, Ceylon, Isle of Man and other places. Finally World War II made international mail difficult or impossible and we lost touch.

While we were in boarding school Daddy and Mother faithfully wrote to each of us every week. All through the years as long as they lived, letters were our means of keeping in touch; we couldn't talk to each other in person or by phone but we talked to each other in letters—the more detailed the better.

We studied Shakespeare and other classics in English Literature and had to memorize long passages. Saturday afternoons when we were having "free" time on the grounds, girls might be seen walking around in the yard with a book in hand, learning and reciting out loud, "*To be or not to be . . .*" or "*The boy stood on the burning deck . . .*" If it was Latin it could be grammar "*amo, amas, amat . . .*" or literature, reading and translating Virgil or Homer.

Saturday evenings we had game time in the Prep Room and once a month was required dancing—Foxtrot and Waltzes—girls with each other, taking turns leading. Part of our gym program was Country

Dancing, similar to Square Dancing in the U.S. At the end of term there was a Formal Evening when we all dressed in our special long dresses for the dance in our Prep Room. We were being trained to "go out into the world" some day, but those were the only dances I ever went to—my world did not include dancing.

On Sunday mornings girls were grouped by faiths, each group escorted by a mistress of like faith to march in line to their destinations: The Church of England, Presbyterian, Roman Catholic, Dutch Reformed and so forth. Those of us going elsewhere that were too few to line up by twos to march with a teacher, were picked up by someone from the church we attended. I attended meetings with The Plymouth Brethren and a couple from there picked me up every Sunday morning and often took me to their home for midday Sunday dinner.

Our Sunday uniform was a long-sleeved white dress that reached just below the knees, School tie, long black cotton lisle stockings and black oxfords and a white panama School hat. For cold weather we had a navy wool blazer. On Sunday afternoons Foy came from Prince Edward High School for Visiting Hour. Some girls with friends in the boys' school tried to claim brothers that weren't, but that didn't work more than once.

School-day uniforms, called gyms, were navy blue wool serge jumpers with a square yoke, three box pleats in front and three in the back. They had to be two inches from the floor when kneeling, held in at the waist by a long braided sash. With that we wore a long-sleeved white shirt, School tie, white panama hat with band of School colors, black bloomers, long black cotton lisle stockings fastened with a garter belt, and black oxfords. For tennis we wore short (just above knees) white tennis dresses with white sox and tennis shoes. Saturday mornings if there was no sports class we wore "civilian" dresses within the school grounds.

Clothes were sent to a laundry but we were responsible for keeping our gyms clean by spot-cleaning them with a damp cloth and a little soap if necessary. If they needed pressing we pinned or basted the pleats in place, carefully put the gym under our mattress between two towels. When we took it out the next day it was passably well-pressed.

When I was fifteen I had to have my appendix and tonsils removed. Daddy and Mother came to Salisbury for the event and Mr. Davis (surgeons were called "Mr") did the surgery, removing both appendix and tonsils while I was under the anesthetic (ether). My best friend, Reshea Barry, had hers done the same day and we recuperated in beds next to each other in the long hospital ward. We wrote notes to each other because talking made our throats hurt and hated to laugh because of stitches in our sides. We had to stay in bed until the stitches were removed on the ninth day and were allowed to go back to the school after fourteen days. I left there determined to become a nurse when I finished school.

Adding to our good times for some school holidays I invited Reshea Barry and Evelyn Route home with me. They were both from the Belgian Congo. Reshea's father was a Railroad Engineer and Evelyn's parents were Presbyterian missionaries. Foy invited Francis Route (Evelyn's brother), and Anthony Graham Hornby-Smith III ("Graham" to us), whose father was a "big-shot" in some distant British government post.

Beth began boarding school at thirteen but we were in different Houses and didn't see much of each other except during holidays.

**Heading to boarding school.**
**(Left to right) Francis Route, Beth, Margaret Ann, Sybil, Foy.**

The school year began in January and was divided into three terms with a three weeks holiday between two of them and six weeks at the end of the year. In addition we had a long weekend each mid-term. School had its pleasures but as holidays drew near we marked our calendars and counted the days. A week before we went home a chant could be heard on the grounds where we sat on benches between other activities:

> *"This time next week where will I be?*
> *"Out of the gates of misery!*
> *"No more Latin, no more French*
> *"No more sitting on a hard old bench.*
> *"No more beetles in my tea*
> *"Making googly eyes at me.*
> *"No more spiders in my bath*
> *"Trying hard to make me laugh.*
> *"This time next week where will I be?*
> *"Out of the gates of misery!"*

When the holiday beginning or ending coincided with our parents' semi annual trip to town, they drove to Salisbury to get us or take us back, otherwise we took the train between Salisbury and Macheke. Passenger trains were European style with compartments containing two long seats facing each other. The padded backs could be raised and with the seats, made four beds. At the end were two windows with a table between them. The table top could be raised to reveal a washbasin under it. A sliding door opened into the corridor that ran the length of the car. Our passenger trains usually left Salisbury in the evening and in winter it became dark soon afterward. By "dark" I mean pitch black, total darkness, if there was no moonlight. Foy and I made that trip several times and I always wanted the window shades closed to shut out that darkness. During the summer with longer daylight and countryside to watch such trips were more interesting.

On one trip Foy slept almost the whole way. I was reading *Oliver Twist* and it became so scary to me that I stopped reading, but the damage was done. I became extremely fearful of the dark outside the windows, closed the blinds and locked the compartment door, but that didn't help much. I knew it was black outside and every time I heard someone walking in the corridor I watched the door handle and cringed. I tried to think of other things and tried to sleep but couldn't—it was a long journey to Macheke and it was several years before I finished reading *Oliver Twist.*

**Neighbors** On the farm our nearest neighbors were the deWets whose farm was *Springdale.* It was three miles from our house to theirs. Now and then for a treat, we girls and Mother walked the three miles to spend most of a day with Mrs. deWet and children, and every now and then she and her girl, Caroline, and youngest son, David, came to visit us. Our families exchanged evening visits more often when our men folks could be with us. The oldest deWet girl, Cecelia, was married to John du Preez and lived on another farm. Foy and Francois, Mrs. DeWet's oldest son, were the same age and they became fast friends. Margaret Ann and Caroline were friends for life. Some neighbors on surrounding farms were Johnson, Pemberton, deVilliers, deJaager and deSwartz. Mother joked that sometimes she felt that our name should be deShort! The Wiggills were special friends but it was about eleven miles to their place.

**Measles** We three older ones had chicken pox, mumps and whooping cough in Northern Rhodesia and I'm sure Margaret Ann had them later but I don't know when. At the farm we all took turns having Red Measles and German Measles. By the time we got over them the sickroom had been occupied for a long time. My memory of those weeks is of the room being kept dark and of Daddy sitting in the doorway where there was enough light to read by. Among books he read aloud were *Ben Hur, The Last of the Mohicans, Jock of the Bushveld, The Pony Express Rider, Tom Sawyer, The Harvester, Lorna Doone, and Betty Zane besides chapters from Hurlbut's Story of the Bible and the Bible.* Our home library was limited pretty much to those books and through our teen years we read them over and over. We enjoyed reading and if we were anxious to keep reading a particularly interesting book we girls sometimes tried to get in some extra reading time by sticking the book under our dress when we went to the toilet. But Mother had a sixth sense and more than once said, "Leave your book here, I need you to come on back quickly."

From earliest years convalescent entertainment included playing with Mother's large button collection, sorting, stringing necklaces and bracelets and deciding which buttons were the prettiest for our next new dress. When clothes wore out, all buttons were cut off and saved to re-use; none of our buttons were store-bought for new dresses.

**Malaria, 'Flu** No one in the family escaped malaria or 'flu. Headaches, chills and body-aching that accompanied Malaria were even worse than those we had with 'flu. As teenagers we each had several bouts of malaria and with those chills no amount of cover or hot water bottles helped. Medicated with quinine and aspirin we shivered and ached until the fever broke and the sweating began; soon after that, pajamas and sheets were soaking wet. Then Mother's gentle hands gave me a sponge bath, dressed me in dry pajamas and made the bed with wonderful dry sheets.

While we had fever, sometimes very high, Mother made a drink of barley water or oatmeal gruel for nourishment and to prevent dehydration. She boiled barley or oats in water, strained it then added a bit of sugar. After our fever went down she added milk. Juices were at hand from the orchard and water was plentiful. Then we progressed to milk-toast (toast in a porridge bowl with warm milk on it and sugar if wanted—I didn't want.) Soft boiled egg with toast and potato soup were two welcome delicacies. Mother knew exactly how to make everything taste good to an invalid.

**Farm Sundays** After we moved to the farm our Sundays were very different from those on the mission. Daddy began having services once a month in our home for any of our white neighbors who wanted to come in the afternoon. The other Sundays in the month we drove to villages where the local church leaders had asked Daddy to preach. On those weekends Mother cooked a beef or venison roast on Saturday. Sunday morning she sliced some of it to make sandwiches for a picnic after church. We did not have store-bought mayonnaise, instead we buttered the bread for sandwiches. Hard boiled eggs were often mashed with butter and made into sandwiches. Sometimes we took the eggs in the shells to peel and eat with our meal. We made jam sandwiches for dessert and often took along fruit of some kind. Those picnics were fun—usually under a big shade tree. There was the usual hot tea that had been made at home and brought along in thermos bottles unless we knew we were going where we could build a fire to "boil the teakettle" and make tea. The ever-present canvas water bags were on the motor car, sitting between the front fenders and the radiator, ready for drinking when we wanted cold water. It was amazing how cold the water was in those bags from the process of evaporation on the canvas.

Daddy drove our trusty Chevrolet wherever we needed to go whether there was a road or not. One Sunday he was heading for a village to which there was no road but he knew the direction. He was driving slowly, watching carefully for a possible problem and beside him Mother was also watching for fallen logs, rocks, holes or other hazards among the bushes and grass. All at once Mother saw something ahead in the shoulder-high grass and said, "Daddy, There's a stump!" thinking it was a partially burned tree from a grass fire. Almost immediately she and Daddy recognized it as a black cobra with its head spread for striking. Daddy called out to us, "Roll up your windows quickly," as he tried to run over it. He thought he had hit it and stopped to finish it off with the shovel he always kept in the boot of the motor car. Mother said, "Be careful, Daddy" and a chorus of voices from the back seat echoed, "Be careful, Daddy," as we watched through the closed windows. He didn't see the snake under the car and couldn't find it anywhere around so we went on our way to the village.

**New Friends** More and more white neighbors came to the meetings in our home and began to volunteer their own homes, and we enjoyed the new friends. Sometimes Daddy assigned Beth and me to tell Bible stories to the younger children and Foy was learning to preach short sermons. After the service of preaching and communion, we all had a meal together. Then the grown-ups sat around visiting while the young folks played games outside, or inside if it was raining. Afternoon tea was served about 4:00 p.m. and after tea people began taking their leave.

**Words and Examples** On Sunday morning Daddy was always ready first and while he waited on the rest of us he paced the living room floor with a hymn book in his hand, beating time with the other hand, learning new songs or just singing because he liked to. He could read shaped notes so when he especially liked the words to a new song he practiced it until he could teach it to the rest of us later.

From those days I only recall one specific sermon during a gathering in the farm living room. Daddy's subject was *The Providence of God.* His text was the story of Abraham being commanded by God to sacrifice his son; how Abraham and Isaac were going up the mountain to the designated place, Isaac carrying the wood, when he asked Abraham, "My Father, here is the wood and the fire, but where is the lamb for the sacrifice?" and Abraham replied, "God will provide the lamb, my son." Just as Abraham was about to follow God's command to sacrifice his son, an angel stopped him and he saw a ram caught in the thicket and used it for the sacrifice.

Perhaps my age and the timing of that sermon made it all the more impressive. We were going through extremely difficult financial times, even more than we had been for several years. Over and over our parents told us, and we heard them say to each other, "God will provide. We must work hard and do the best we can with what we've got." I cried then and I cry now as in my mind I see my Daddy standing there telling the story and saying those words to the small assembly, "God will provide the lamb, my son." He believed God would provide and he helped me to believe—then and now.

We learned important lessons from his and Mother's example even more than from sermons. About then someone was angry with Daddy over something and spread among the neighbors a false story about him. We children knew it was untrue and thought Daddy should tell the neighbors that the man was lying. But Daddy said that there was no need to act ugly in return. He said God knew the truth and that the neighbors who knew him would know not to believe the man. With time we realized that the neighbors respected Daddy all the more for not trying to defend himself. It was a powerful lesson to us.

**Nhowe Mission** The W. L. Browns came from Northern Rhodesia to establish Nhowe Mission about fifteen miles away. While buildings were in progress they lived with us for about three months: two adults and four children, Junior 14, Betty 12, David 9 and Bernard 6. Besides having fun we learned from Daddy's and Mother's actions and words how to get along with people.

I admired Junior's ability to throw his knife at a mark and never miss. At one of our gatherings all of us young folks were outside and Junior was demonstrating his ability. He called for a volunteer to hold their foot very still while he threw the knife on one side or the other. No one volunteered so I did, and he threw the knife several times before Daddy came out and stopped the fun—one of the younger kids had tattled!

**"Setting Yeast"** A ritual not to be forgotten was the "setting of the yeast" from starter reserved on Monday and Thursday mornings. Monday was washday—unless it was pouring rain. Beth and I took turns, one at the washtubs with Mother, the other tidying the house and fixing dinner with Margaret Ann's help. The girls in the house also made the bread, saving some of the yeast for a starter for Wednesday evening—six loaves in bread pans, usually whole wheat—mouth-wateringly good. It was baked by supper time and I can remember now and then we finished off a whole loaf for supper with butter and honey or jam.

Even during the rainy season we could usually count on some sunshine part of the day before the clouds rolled up and rain came. At such times we watched carefully, because if the clothes had been on the line even a short time in that sun they would be almost dry and we didn't want them to get wet again. We had some frantic runs to gather in the clothes when we saw a rain coming. We also brought the clothes in as soon as they dried to prevent them being faded by the sun.

**Mother Talks** My Monday washdays with Mother were special. As we talked over the washtubs she told me things from her life—she was the third of nine children. She told of her brothers and sisters, of college days and meeting Daddy, of their plans for marriage being interrupted by World War I, of nursing school, of teaching in the one-room school after college and much more. As I heard of her experiences I confided my thoughts to Mother and listened to her advice. I wish I could remember actual conversations but the impressions sank in even though the actual words didn't stay with me. During one of those times she told me that as a young girl she had vowed that she would not allow a boy/man to kiss her until they were married. I thought that was a noble thing and secretly made that vow for myself. I stuck to it, though I must confess I was sorely tempted to break it a couple of times.

Monday's wash water was drawn from the well with bucket and windlass, heated in a big iron pot over a fire near the wash-house, which was a two-sided shed under a shade tree. There were four oblong washtubs: one about four feet long, the "washing tub" (that was our bathtub on Saturdays); the next size down was the rinsing tub; the blueing tub was smaller; then a still smaller one for starching. All the tubs sat on up-ended boxes. We learned how to make starch without lumps by dissolving starch powder in cold water then adding boiling water, stirring quickly until it was clear then diluting it with cold water to the correct consistency. We starched table cloths, serviettes, doilies, pillowcases, dress shirts, work shirts, dresses and men's cotton trousers.

All men and women's handkerchiefs were cloth and were favorites for birthday gifts or for stocking-stuffers at Christmas. We girls and Mother each had our own stack of pretty "lady's hankies" with embroidery and/ or lace on them and we were delighted any time we received some as gifts.

We had never heard of Kleenex, we used handkerchiefs. On washdays we dunked all soiled handkerchiefs into a bucket of boiling water from the big teakettle on the stove. With a piece of broom handle we stirred and sloshed them, then holding them in the bucket with the stick, we poured that water out on the ground behind the wash shed and poured more boiling water from the teakettle onto the handkerchiefs. After two such treatments they were lifted out of that water and put into the big boiling pot full of soapy water with the rest of the white clothes. Clean, ironed handkerchiefs were a joy to use even if not fun to wash! When we had colds we used Daddy's oldest handkerchiefs because they were big and soft. With colds or fever we often had fever blisters; I never heard of "cold sores" until I came to the U.S. to college. We girls never heard of Kotex or any suchlike disposables until we went to boarding school. Before that we used old rags which were thoroughly washed after use—separately from the clothes—then boiled with the white clothes in the big pot. Mother taught each of us girls to be responsible for our own rags.

They were ironed along with everything else.

The worst soiled clothes were put to soak on Sunday evening and white clothes were put to soak in the big tub before breakfast on Monday. After breakfast the work began. Mother thought that washboards wore the clothes out prematurely so everything was washed with our hands, first the white clothes, which were then put in the big pot to boil while we washed the colored clothes. Colored things were washed with Sunlight Soap that was more gentle than the lye soap used for white things. As soon as some clothes were ready to hang, one of us began that while the other kept washing and rinsing.

As quickly as they dried, clothes were carried to the back porch dining table. Starched things were sprinkled and rolled tightly and wrapped in an old quilt for ironing the next morning and the rest were set aside to wait for dry ironing. At washday's end our badge of domesticity was how raw the backs of our fingers were from scrubbing clothes—if they bled, so much the more to brag about!

"Sunday clothes" were washed separately, and often on another day of the week, using Lux Soap Flakes. Mother taught us careful handling of silk stockings, silk underwear, neckties and silk scarves, silk blouses and silk dresses; they were not wrung or hung out on the line to dry, but squeezed gently then rolled in "Turkish towels" (terry cloth) and set aside to be carefully ironed with the right temperature of the iron. Daddy's and Foy's "Sunday" trousers and our school gyms (all wool serges and flannels) were cleaned in a special way. Sunlight Soap was worked into a lather in a tub of lukewarm water. Into the sudsy water Mother poured a cup full of petrol (gasoline) and immersed the pieces, raising them up and lowering them into the mixture with very gentle rubbing and no wringing or squeezing. When she thought they were clean she rinsed them in clear lukewarm water several times, again with no squeezing or wringing. Because they still smelled of petrol she hung them "inside out" on the clothesline to drip dry—trousers by the waistbands and gyms by the yoke seam. We pressed them under a cloth, never putting the iron directly on them. Our Sunday clothes lasted a long time and always looked nice—the reward for extra work.

**Ironing** Tuesday was ironing day. The large back porch dining table was cleared. Across each end was spread old blankets and/or quilts with an old sheet over them—one end for Beth and one end for me—with space in the middle for the pile that was to be ironed. *Everything* had to be ironed—sheets, towels, washcloths, underwear, sox, everything. There was a big fly that might lay eggs on the clothes as they hung outside and if the egg got on the skin it burrowed in to form a boil-like rising. When it "came to a head" and was opened there was a maggot. It didn't take but one experience of that to convince us that it was well worth all the extra ironing to minimize that possibility.

So we ironed—and ironed—and ironed. Beginners did handkerchiefs, sox, washcloths, underwear, serviettes. With experience we graduated to sheets, pillowcases, doilies, and "everyday clothes," then to shirts, trousers and dresses. We learned to iron ruffles, puffed sleeves and gathered skirts so when done the dress looked as good as new. There was a trick to ironing on a table, keeping the article in shape so the finished job looked good. I never saw an ironing board until I went to boarding school.

Ironing was done with flat irons that were put on the front part of the stove as soon as breakfast was over; we had seven or eight of them. With plenty of good padding, an iron was picked up by its handle, tested with spit-on-finger-and-touch-iron (tricky business), if it sizzled it was ready to use. It was wiped carefully to get all black off then carried to the table to iron. A well padded tin lid was there to rest the iron on. Later we had irons with a removable handle; we took turns with that special one because there was only one handle to three bottoms, and we still used flat irons.

Mother was our inspector. If something that mattered didn't look good enough she told us to re-sprinkle it and do it over again. Mother constantly reminded us, "Be careful not to scorch anything." That was the danger when a cooler iron was exchanged for a hotter one. For things that just needed to be hot enough to kill the maggot eggs, like sox and underwear, she might say, "Just give it a lick and a promise!" We thanked Mother the rest of our lives for teaching us that a job worth doing is worth doing well.

**Never Idle** Wednesday we sewed or made jam or jelly or whatever needed doing. Mother always had something to do herself and could keep us busy. She taught us simple flower-arranging. Twice a week we cut and arranged fresh flowers in vases in most rooms, suiting the flowers to the containers. We cut flowers from the garden winter and summer. Sweet peas, carnations and roses were my favorites and of course we had petunias, zinnias, red, blue and purple salvias, cosmos, several kinds of daisies and lilies, dahlias, snap-dragons, four o'clocks and more. Wild flowers grew abundantly and some were good for cutting, others were not, either because of thorns or their smell. One purple-flowered plant we called stinkweed was beautiful at a distance—but the smell, ugh! Thistle blooms looked beautiful but . . . Flowering shrubs included hibiscus, rose of Sharon, frangipani (rubber plant), syringa, pride of India (crepe myrtle.) We didn't use any for cutting that dripped "milk" like frangipani. Lavender Jacaranda trees in bloom made a beautiful show and so did the red flamboyant trees. Their blooms made a spectacular sight outside but were not good for cut flowers.

**Thursday** was another bread making day using the saved starter that had been "set" the night before. Again six loaves of bread were baked and we enjoyed the aroma of baking bread that filled the house. The rest of the day was busy with whatever else needed doing.

**Friday** without fail was housecleaning day and we had a set ritual. Smaller rugs were taken outside to shake unless they were too heavy, then we hung them on the line and beat the dust out. We set everything off the tops of dressers, chests or whatnots on to the beds or dining table and covered them with a sheet. We cleaned the marble washstand tops and wash basins, filled the jugs (pitchers) with fresh water, swept and mopped, dusted and put everything back in place.

The sitting room or lounge and the dining room had a larger rug in the center, too large to take out every week. On our knees with a whisk broom and dust pan, we brushed up those rugs without stirring up a dust, then picked up threads or whatever didn't whisk up—tedious work but results were rewarding. Once a month those rugs were hung on the line and beaten. Then it was tea time—time to sit down and enjoy the feeling of the clean house. We were thankful the kitchen worker kept the kitchen clean.

**Mail Day** Friday was also mail day. A worker rode his bicycle to Macheke where he exchanged the padlocked Private Bag containing outgoing mail for the Private Bag of incoming mail. Then he picked up listed supplies from the general store where we had a charge account. We eagerly watched for his return in the afternoon to see what might be in the mail bag. During one of the holidays we had a friend visiting, and we asked Daddy if we could go after the mail. Since Foy and his friend

95

were practically grown, Daddy allowed Beth and me to go with them. We borrowed two extra bikes from workers and the four of us set out on the fourteen mile ride to Macheke. Part of the way was through deep sand, around rocks, up and down hills, till we reached the main road where we had paved strips. Two rivers had concrete slabs as bridges wide enough for a motor car, but scary when approaching on a bicycle down a long steep hill. We decided it would be smart to go as fast as we could down the long hill gathering speed to carry us as far as possible up the other side so we wouldn't have to push our bikes as far up hill. When we told our parents about that they were horrified and told us that we could have been killed if our tire had hit a small rock and thrown us onto the concrete. But we were young and invincible!

**Saturday** morning, first thing after breakfast was ladies' hair washing time. Hair was washed with soap, rinsed well with clear water. The final rinse had vinegar or strained lemon juice added to cut the soap residue and leave hair shiny. Mother washed hers first and Beth and I took turns pouring pitchers of water over her long hair. She spread it over her shoulders to be drying while she worked on ours. I admired her thick hip-length hair and looked forward to the day when mine would be like that—but alas! that never happened.

My hair was fine and straight, but every Saturday Mother rolled it on rags to make ringlets for Sunday—provided I slept in the rags that night. Beth and Margaret Ann had thick wavy hair so when their rag-rolled-ringlets got dry they could take them undone to sleep and still have curls on Sunday. We didn't see movies or have TV but we saw magazine pictures of Shirley Temple and admired her ringlets so we were willing to put up with some pain to have ringlets like Shirley Temple. There was a wild bird whose call sounded very much like "Get your H-A-I-R c-u-r-r-l-l-ed!" When Mother was rolling our hair we could usually hear that bird outside calling; if one of us complained about her pulling, she urged us to listen to what that bird was saying.

Occasionally a well beaten raw egg was a good shampoo to promote healthy shiny hair. We took care to wash with barely lukewarm or cool water and to rinse with cold water. If we used hot water with that "shampoo," the egg became "scrambled egg" all through our hair and had to be combed out with the very fine comb that was also used to comb out lice. Lice seldom happened to us but when they did Mother rubbed scalps with paraffine (kerosene), left it on for a certain length of time, used the fine-tooth comb, then washed the head/hair well with several sudsings and several rinses. We felt ashamed, but she comforted us by saying that *finding* them in our hair was not a shame, but *keeping* them would have been.

Saturday mornings without fail we made communion bread for Sunday. Flowers were renewed in the vases and things were prepared for Sunday dinner. Saturday afternoon was bath time. Water was heated in pots and kettles on the kitchen stove and the largest washtub brought in to the "bathroom"—a small room without bathroom fixtures or plumbing. Cold water was drawn from the well and a bucket full poured into the washtub before hot water was added to feel right. Water in the tub was shallow to begin with but with each addition of hot water between baths it got deeper. Baths began with the youngest, Margaret Ann, then Beth, Sybil, Mother, Foy (I don't recall that he complained, after all he got the deepest water!) Sometimes by then Daddy emptied the tub and put a minimum of water in the tub for his own bath—can you blame him? Mother teased him calling it a "bath in a teaspoon of water."

As soon as he could find the time, Daddy built a brick bathtub in the bathroom, with a drain pipe out through the wall. He plastered the tub smoothly with cement and painted it blue. Outside of the bathroom wall he built a brick fireplace that held a 55-gallon drum up over the fire and ran a pipe through the wall from the drum to the tub. A yard worker kept the drum filled from the well. That was our water heater in the winter time; in the summer the sun warmed the tank of water. We were thrilled to have running hot water and a drain, but not as thrilled as Daddy must have been at not having to carry water in and out.

**Our Cobbler** Daddy, ever resourceful, kept all of our shoes in good repair. From somewhere he obtained two metal lasts, a large and a small, and cobbler needles and heavy thread that he pulled through a block of beeswax to water proof and strengthen it. To half-sole shoes he cut pieces to fit from tanned hide. He learned to tan hides in his early years in Africa or bought tanned hides from the natives. He punched holes with an awl and sewed half-soles to the shoes. For worn heels he cut the proper shape from an old motor car tire and nailed the new heel cap to the shoe.

**Available Foods** Mother also used her inventiveness. One year we had a bumper crop of pumpkins. We ate baked pumpkin, stewed pumpkin, fried pumpkin, pumpkin pudding, pumpkin pie and pumpkin jam—and they were all good if you liked pumpkin, and we did. Another year monkey nuts (peanuts) were plentiful enough for us to use and to supply the African workers. We roasted a lot just to eat. We coarsely ground some of those to put in every salad and sprinkle over desserts. We made monkey-nut butter, using the mincer (meat grinder) that had three discs, one for coarse grind, that we used first, then a finer one that we put the nuts through twice. By then the result was dough-like and that was forced several times through the flat disc that mashed it into butter. Mother even made a mock-meatloaf with ground monkey-nuts but that was one invention that did not go over well, though we ate it because it was set before us. We were all happy to hear her say that she would not do that again! Mealies roasted in the shucks in the ash pan under the fire in the kitchen stove were a treat. When cool and shucked we liked to carry a cob around pulling off and eating the deliciously roasted grains one at a time.

The "Theodora Cake" was an easy-to-make three-layer sponge cake, delicious when put together with homemade lemon curd or jam or jelly and sprinkled with powdered sugar on top. For special occasions (company or birthdays), we went all out with a different cake recipe and proper icing. We did not have a refrigerator so we "set" Jelly (Jello) the night before needed and put it on the window of our pantry, inside the screen. The night air was cool enough to set it and we made boiled custard to go with it.

Other desserts were trifle, prune whip, rice pudding, baked custard, rhubarb pie or stewed rhubarb, stewed strawberries, stewed gooseberries, gooseberry pie. Boiled custard went with all stewed fruit and fruit salad. Fruit salad was a regular, made up of whatever was in season, thoroughly washed and peeled: oranges, pawpaws, ladyfinger bananas, guavas, peaches, gooseberries and granadillas (passion fruit). Granadillas were the crowning touch to any fruit salad, and their juice made cake filling or icing delectable.

**Jams and Jellies** Jam-making was interesting and imaginative: we made pumpkin jam, tomato jam (both green and red), grapefruit marmalade, orange marmalade, kumquat marmalade, guava jelly, quince jelly, fig jam, strawberry jam, gooseberry jam, watermelon rind confection called "konfeit." Some kind of fruit grew all the year round so there was no quitting. Rosella florets grew on a bush, bright red, tart, excellent for making jelly and "wine" (not fermented.) Our orchard supplied all those and lemons, plantains, loquats and more. Pompamoosa was like an oversized grapefruit and was used only for bitter marmalade. We enjoyed jam that was accidentally cooked too long and became stiff enough to roll on a spoon. We ate it like sweets (candy) and none was ever wasted. When Mother began to make something, whether cooking or sewing, and didn't have some item that was called for, she substituted what she thought would work just as well. Her results were usually good and sometimes were even better than the original recipe or pattern.

**Milk and Butter** Mother had told us of milking cows as she grew up and we thought it would be an exciting job. But Daddy explained that those were different cows. Here the chore was dangerous because African cows were semi-wild and most were more wild than semi. Before milking these cows, their sharp horns were tied to a tree at the right distance from a second tree to which their back legs were tied; otherwise the poking or kicking could be lethal. Instead of sitting on a stool like our parents did, the milker squatted, holding the bucket with one hand and milking with the other so he could get away in a hurry if the cow decided to lie down on him. A cup to a pint of milk was all that most cows gave, though when our best cow had a new calf she gave a generous quart most days. When that happened Foy came into the kitchen to watch the measuring, saying with pride, "I think I got a whole quart today!" Milking was done only in the morning and was Foy's special project. He grew up helping to handle the cattle.

During early years on the farm, when milk was brought to the kitchen it was strained into large dish-pans kept for that use. When we moved to the farm Daddy had dug a well 60 feet deep and installed a windlass until some years later when we got a windmill. He built a screened shelter surrounding the well with a chest-high shelf around the inside to set the pans of milk on. We saved two jugs of strained milk, one for supper and one for breakfast, and those, with the pans of milk, were set in trays of cold water on the shelf and covered with a cloth. The well water was very cold and we renewed it in the trays later in the day. At our altitude a cool breeze blew nearly all the time and it was cool in the shade. When the milk in the pans was clabbered (soured and thick), we rolled the sour cream off of the top of the thick milk and put it into a large bowl to make butter. We gave the clabbered milk to the workers if they wanted it—they usually did—and fed the rest to the chickens. For some time we used a wooden paddle to churn the sour cream in the bowl. After we acquired a mechanical milk separator and a churn with a crank handle, the whole operation changed.

Butter for family use was lightly salted and kept in the cool pantry. All extra butter was left unsalted and put into a clean petrol tin on the back of the kitchen stove. As it slowly heated, the milk solid settled to the bottom and the fat stayed on top. When all the milk solid was settled firmly in the bottom of the tin, Mother strained the liquid fat off the top through layers of cheesecloth into another petrol tin and set it in the pantry where it became more or less solid. It was now "clarified butter." When the tin was full it was ready for the next motor car trip to the general store in Macheke. The Greek proprietor had a number of customers who did not use lard and were happy to buy clarified butter. They said Mrs. Short's butter was the best—always clean!

**Workers** When the kitchen or yard workers finished whatever job they were doing, they knocked on the back door and said, "Nda pedza," (I have finished.) Then another job that needed doing was assigned to them. If there was nothing more urgent to be done they were told, "Enda ku tema huni" (go cut wood), which was a constant need for a wood-burning cook stove. Another never-ending odd job for any farm workers who had extra time was gathering dead tree limbs from the surrounding bushveldt to keep a supply on the woodpile ready to be chopped for stove wood.

Men from the villages constantly came looking for work, so there was no shortage of laborers for raising crops and tending cattle and doing other farm work—if there was money to hire them. They were paid an agreed-upon amount of cash per month, plus their room, daily food and a suit of heavy khaki clothes every six months. As far as we were from town they didn't have much reason to use their cash, because in the villages they traded and bartered with each other. Most of them bought a bicycle and saved up money to buy cows to increase their village herd.

**A Bricklayer** Daddy heard that experienced bricklayers were needed in Salisbury and the pay was good. He decided to use his bricklaying experience to earn much needed income. For several months he caught the train from Macheke every Sunday afternoon to spend the week in Salisbury laying brick. He came home on the Friday evening train for the weekend with family and to preach on Sunday.

**Cattle** A necessity for every landowner both whites and natives was cattle. The natives measured their wealth to a great extent by how many head of cattle they owned. One bull was enough for most herds. Cows were especially valuable to Africans for perpetuating herds and as dowry for brides. Farmers needed cows for milk and to increase their herds and oxen were used for crops and hauling.

To control foot and mouth disease, spread by tsetse flies, the government installed dipping tanks throughout the village areas and each farm had its own. On the days Daddy announced that he and Foy would be overseeing the dipping, we girls often found a safe place from where we could watch the excitement. The cattle were driven through the dip tank but they did not always want to go where they were supposed to and it took all hands with a lot of yelling and goading to keep them going through the dip. Sometimes calves had to be helped along with a long crook-staff. Oxen were part of everyday life, pulling loads of many kinds, they pulled stumps, ploughs, harrows, wagons, scotch-carts and when needed pulled the motor car out of deep mud or sand when it got stuck.

**Wagons and Carts** Wagons varied in size depending on their intended use. The bed of a big one was perhaps 12-15 feet long. It had four iron-rimmed wheels four or five feet in diameter, and the tongue was nearly as long as the bed of the wagon. Sixteen or eighteen oxen, yoked in pairs, pulled a big wagon. A scotch cart had two iron-rimmed wheels and was about half the size of a medium sized wagon. It was pulled by two or four or six oxen, depending on the load and size of the cart. Big transport ox wagons were always in demand, as were scotch carts. When the bricklaying job ended Daddy decided he could build wagons for sale to farmers. He bought hubs and metal rims for the wheels then made all the rest in his workshop. He carved and fitted spokes into the hub, carved fellies to go on the spokes to form the wheel ready for the rim. He taught me to use an adze to help carve fellies, and how I did enjoy working with him!

When the wheel was ready for the tire he heated the big rim to red hot in a fire outside the workshop. This was a multi-person team job. Several helpers using strong poles lifted the red hot rim out of the fire and dropped it carefully onto the wheel, quickly hammering it down all around at the same time water was poured on to keep from burning the wood too much. The cooled metal shrunk to a tight fit if everything went well. Not often but once in a while things went amiss, fellies got burned too much and the process had to be started over and new fellies carved. It was an exciting process that we girls watched from a distance with bated breath. Daddy built the wagon bed and tongue from wood he shaped and fastened together with metal pieces he forged in his blacksmith shop. I don't know how many wagons and carts he made and sold. He kept one large wagon for use on the farm.

When Foy was not in school he was the official wagon driver. A young African lead boy went in front holding a rawhide rope attached to the lead oxen. The lead oxen were trained to follow him and set the pace for the rest of the team. Foy had his oxen trained so well to his voice commands and the crack of his whip that he seldom touched one with the lash. The oxen were all named and a good driver knew their names so when one was slacking he could call his name and crack his whip above him and the ox usually got the message. Foy enjoyed the work but it had frustrations and we enjoyed hearing his stories.

Whenever I got the chance I worked with Daddy in his workshop. I loved the smell of charcoal smoke from the forge, of wood being chiseled, and of fresh cut leather when he mended shoes. I enjoyed the sounds of metal being hammered on the anvil and of red hot iron sizzling in a bucket of cold water and the sound of sawing.

**Foy's Steam Engine** Behind the workshop was an old Model T lorry (truck) Daddy brought from the mission. After its usefulness as a lorry had run out, many of its parts had been used for different purposes during the years. Foy decided he could use some leftovers to make a steam engine by the plan he had drawn. He worked hard at it in his spare time and after many days announced to the family that he was ready to build a fire under the boiler and see if the steam engine would power the pulley attached to the mealie grinder. When the steam was ready all the family turned out to watch. It worked—the grinder turned and we all cheered proudly.

**Chickens** Every spring Mother ordered day-old baby chicks, 300 of them from the Agricultural Department in Salisbury. They were shipped by mail train to Macheke and picked up by Daddy in the motor car. He built a secure chicken pen and house for them, using small-holed chicken wire all around, including around their house to keep the chickens in and to keep out chicken-loving wild animals, like weasels. We ground mealies for their feed and they thrived on that and clabbered milk and surplus pumpkins. As the chicks grew they were identified as cockerels and hens. A few cockerels were allowed to become full-fledged roosters and we ate the rest of them through the year. Hens were saved to lay eggs and we usually had a plentiful supply of eggs. We sold some to neighbors and to the store in Macheke. Sometimes at night a wild animal got into the chicken house in spite of the wire and what a noise that set off! When that happened Daddy donned his headlamp, took his gun and went out to get rid of whatever it was.

The chicken wire was fastened to poles set in the ground and stretched up about eight or ten feet. At the top the wire was bent inward all the way around to keep chickens from flying out. One day we heard loud cackling and squawking of chickens and found some monkeys had climbed over the top into the pen and were helping themselves to that day's eggs. We had a hilarious time getting the monkeys out while keeping the chickens in.

**Locusts** From Bible reading we knew about plagues of locusts, but growing up in Rhodesia we *experienced* such plagues. In the distance a dark brown cloud would appear—obviously not a rain cloud—we knew it was a swarm of brown locusts. As the cloud came closer it filled the sky and preparations were made to protect what we could from sure destruction. These were not common green grasshoppers.

All the farm workers built smoking fires in and around the orchard to keep the locusts away. The large vegetable garden near the house was territory assigned to us children. Armed with empty petrol tins that gave off reverberating sounds when hit with wooden or metal bars, we were stationed throughout the garden to make as much noise as possible. We had on hats, but occasionally a locust landed on our faces or arms or legs. We hated when that happened and dropped our tins to dance a jig, frantically flapping our hands and arms until the locust flew off. Then we grabbed up our tins and beat all the harder. As the swarm passed over, it stretched so far in all directions the sunlight was completely hidden. Smoke in the orchard and noise in the garden kept most of the locusts from landing there, but in unprotected areas they settled and began to eat voraciously. The sound of their chewing on leaves, twigs and bark was like fire in dry stubble. When evening came they settled down on crop fields, grasslands, bushes and trees until they all drooped with their load of locusts.

During the night Africans from the villages and farms where the locusts had landed, built fires and prepared big pots of boiling water. At the coolest part of the night, just before dawn, they spread blankets under drooping trees, shook the branches and the cold locusts fell onto the blankets. They were carried to the pots and poured into the boiling water. After several minutes they were scooped out of the water and spread on flat rocks to dry in the sunshine. When thoroughly dry they were stored for future eating.

Soon after sunrise the swarm of locusts flew away (minus a few that couldn't be missed) to do their destroying elsewhere, leaving behind no blade of grass, no leaves on bushes or trees, no bark on young trees, no green crops in the fields—all was brown and bare except for the small areas we had been able to protect. During their overnight stay they laid eggs in the soil that hatched within days after the first rain, a few weeks later. While the wings were developing on the newly hatched hoppers, they fed on new tender grass and crops, then flew away, once more leaving no green where they had been. Fortunately locusts didn't come every year.

To prepare the stored locusts for eating, the Africans plucked off the head, wings and legs, leaving the insides. They were eaten as crunchy snacks or cooked for relish. Foy decided we could eat locusts too—with a difference. He jerked the heads off of live locusts and the insides departed along with the heads. (We liked Foy's method best!) Legs and wings were discarded, leaving the empty body which we fried in butter for a tasty and crunchy snack similar to crisply fried fish fins or tails. Other native delicacies, that I never had the nerve to try, were mopani worms and white ants. [I believe they are available, chocolate covered, in *International Foods* stores in the U.S. now if you have a mind to try some!]

**Grassfires** More dangerous than swarms of locusts and just as destructive were grassfires, though unlike the locust scourge, there was some good done—after the dry dead grass of the bushveldt was burned, tender new grass appeared and cattle and all grass-eating animals thrived on the fresh green grass. Grassfires were an annual happening toward the end of the dry season when all grasses, tall and short, most bushes and many trees were dry. Lightning strikes started many fires, some were purposely set by humans, some were started accidentally.

Grassfires were spectacularly beautiful to watch in the distance at night as there was no artificial lighting of any kind to compete with them. But we knew they were not just a picturesque sight. Daddy and all his workers were mindful of the danger of fires when vegetation was dry. Fire guards were kept cleared around the homesteads, orchard and fields. When a fire was approaching Daddy made the rounds of the cleared fire guards to be sure no trash or fallen dead tree might help the fire cross the space. When they saw smoke in the distance they estimated how far away it was, which way the wind was blowing, and how much time there might be before it became dangerous to our place.

When there was no doubt the fire was headed in our direction Daddy and his workers lit backfires at strategic spots and guarded them well. The men were armed with wet burlap sacks, shovels and whatever branches of green leaves they could find handy and some men carried buckets of water to keep the sacks wet. By this time Foy was old enough to be out in the thick of it with Daddy. Nearer the house Daddy allowed us girls to help where the grass was low. We were stationed with bags to beat out any flames that came the wrong direction from a backfire, or that flared up in a burned area. It was exciting hot work.

**Learning About Death** Most grass fires were at least partly beneficial but sometimes they resulted in tragedy. While we were living at Huyuyu two badly burned young African boys were brought to the mission. Daddy and Mother hurried to give first aid as best they could, then Daddy took the back seat out of the motor car, made a bed of quilts and gently laid the boys on it and spread clean old soft sheets over them. He drove to the nearest doctor at the clinic in Mrewa. One of the boys died soon afterwards and we children cried. I don't remember about the second, less-badly-burned boy. They had been out in the grassland herding their father's cattle when a grassfire came roaring toward them. They knew they couldn't outrun the fire and they climbed as high as they could in the nearest tree. The younger boy had gone up first and got higher so he was less badly burned. As I watched them being tenderly cared for by Daddy and Mother and watched as Daddy drove away with them, my body hurt in sympathy. Some memories don't fade.

Death sometimes came closer to home as it did to our nearest farm neighbor, Mr. deWet. He became very ill with malaria that grew worse in spite of the usual medications, then it turned into fatal black-water fever. By then it was too late to get him to the hospital and he died at home. Francois, his seventeen year old son, made the wooden coffin and the family and close neighbors helped with the funeral. The deWets were our dear friends and we wept with them.

**Fun and Games** Daddy made a tennis court of clay, leveled and rolled firm. For a roller he filled a cylinder drum with cement and while the cement was still soft he installed a pipe through the center with a rod through that. He put a handle on the rod so it could be pushed or pulled over the court while the heavy cylinder rolled smoothly on the clay. He marked the court with lime "whitewash." He bought a tennis net and set everything up with regulation measurements. New tennis racquets were too expensive so he found some old ones for almost nothing in a second hand shop. The strings were all broken or gone but he picked sturdy frames and bought cat-gut to restring them. He did such a good job they "pinged" nicely. Foy and I learned to play tennis at boarding school and now we could all play tennis at home, Daddy and Mother included.

There was the usual croquet court and a tennicoit court that was the size and net-height of badminton. It was scored something like badminton but played with a semi-hard solid rubber ring about 10 inches in diameter. The ring was thrown back and forth over the net, Frisbee style. Later we acquired badminton gear also and used the same court. Rounders (similar to Soft Ball) was a favorite game when we had enough friends over to make two teams.

One year the Irish potato crop was too plentiful for our use, even with the help of all the workers who wanted them. The pigs ate the leftovers. When several friends were visiting one evening we got permission from Daddy to use potato for a game we invented. We chose partners and formed a circle, each player with a potato in hand looking at the person opposite in the circle. On the count of three we aimed and threw. Potatoes flew across the circle, some colliding and some getting to the intended person. After some practice we got serious and if someone's potato fell to the ground that person was out. The object was to see how many potatoes could be kept flying the longest. We played until it was too dark to see the flying potatoes. It was an opportunity for boys and girls who had their eye on a certain person to make sure they were throwing to that person!

Wild oranges grew in abundance on large trees out in the wild. The fruit was about the size of regular oranges but the outside had a hard, thick shell, hard as a rock. Ripe ones could be cracked open and were good to eat but stained clothes badly. Sometimes we played a game with them. We each picked a green unbreakable orange and taking turns threw our orange as high into the air as we could to see who could throw the highest, judged by the watchers. One day the sun was shining brightly overhead as we threw them up. I threw mine up with all my might and lost sight of it. I thought I had really scored a high one and was standing looking up into the bright sunlight when that rock-hard wild orange landed with a thud on the bridge of my nose. Believe me, I saw stars in that bright sunlight!

More than once after a big rain, when a group gathered at one or the other of our houses, we young folks put on old clothes, chose sides and built opposing rock forts. Each side made a heap of mud balls before declaring war, and seeing who could capture the other fort. If a mud ball hit a person he/she was out, and whichever side lost all their army first, was declared loser. *Kick the tin* was also a favorite game to play outdoors. Indoors we played ping pong on the large dining table on the back verandah; the cracks between boards were extra challenges. Indoor games were played by adults and young folks together. Mother and Daddy were enthusiastic participants and other adults who had never done it before, learned how to play and enjoy it.

**Christmas** Christmas trees as known in the U.S. did not grow there. On the farm each year we made our own tree. Sometimes we stripped bark off of a small tree and set it up in the living room and decorated its bare branches with crepe paper chains and anything else we could think of. One year we went to the nearby wilds and cut quantities of fern-like vines, finer textured than asparagus fern. We wound that around the bare branches of a small tree we had stripped of its leaves; it made a passable Christmas tree. We decorated it with crepe paper chains, strings of wild red berries, and odds and ends made of foil that we had saved all through the year from the semi-annual chocolate box treat and the foil chewing gum wrappers from Grandma Short.

Every Christmas Mother and we girls made sweets (candy)—the only time of year we did that. Traditionally we made Chocolate Fudge, Monkey Nut Brittle, Butterscotch, Taffy, Divinity and Turkish Delight. We made biscuits (cookies) of different kinds, Plum Pudding (steamed) served with boiled custard, and Fruit Cake. Plum Pudding always had a ring or coin cooked in it so when served there was excitement around the table wondering who would find the prize in their serving. How much and how many of those things we made depended on that year's financial ability to buy ingredients. Christmas Crackers, when they could be afforded, were a special treat—the kind put at each place around the table. Two people pulled one between them and when the cracker popped open with a bang, out fell a party hat and a toy of some kind and everyone donned their hat.

Some years we just had lots of fruit from our orchard and made Monkeynut Brittle from our home-grown monkey nuts (peanuts). No matter how lean the years were, Daddy and Mother tried to give us a book each at Christmas. Some years our gifts were sox or underwear (no joke!) and handkerchiefs for Daddy and Mother. One year when things were especially tight, Mother said, "Let's make things for each other, and they don't have to be serious." We wracked our brains and worked secretly for days; the girls ganged up on Foy's gift. We wrapped a single sweet {piece of candy) in a little box with a small rock to make it heavy, put it in a bigger box and wrapped that, and then another and another. We watched and giggled as Foy unwrapped box after box to at last find the little sweet. Foy had put water and food coloring in a little bottle, labeled it "Guaranteed to grow hair on a doorknob" and gave it to our very bald-headed Daddy. I have forgotten what the other gifts were, but in the end we had laughed so much we unanimously declared it to be one of our best Christmases ever.

**The Lion** School was out for the holidays and we were all at home when one evening Francois deWet came to the house very perturbed. A lion had come to his cattle kraal the night before and taken a calf. Francois shot but only wounded the lion and it had gone off into the bush. He knew it was dangerous to go after a wounded lion so he came to get help from Daddy and Foy and they sent for two neighbors to come also.

Early the next morning the five men and the native tracker went looking for the lion, leaving anxious women at the house. We even imagined the lion coming to the farm and thought it might be outside of our house so we stayed inside until the men returned. When they finally came back late in the day they reported that they had found the lion and killed it. They laughed about the "big kill," because when they found the lion lying under a bush obviously dying and knew they must finish killing it, the younger men said since Mr. Short was the oldest he should have the honor of killing it. Daddy argued that since Francois wounded it he should kill it, but Francois didn't want to take the honor either. They decided to line up and all five of them shoot at the same time; that way all of them equally shared the honor of killing the lion!

**Foy the Transporter** The year after Foy finished high school he worked at home. Foy let it be known to the farmers at a distance from the railroad that he could haul their shelled mealies (corn) in 200 lb. bags to the railroad. For the job he used the big transport wagon that Daddy had built. Sixteen oxen were yoked to the wagon and Foy was gone for several days at a time with his African assistants. When it was time for him to be coming down the road on the way to Macheke, we girls listened for his whip cracking and his voice in the distance shouting to the oxen. We ran to meet him and rode on the wagon back to the house anxious to hear his stories of exciting adventures.

On one of his trips his wagon load of mealies proved too heavy for the oxen to pull across a river and the wagon got stuck in the river. It looked like a rain was coming and they needed to get out of the river and to keep the mealies dry. There was only one thing to do: Foy and his helpers carried the 200 lb. bags of mealies, one bag at a time on their backs, from the wagon to the shore, got the wagon out and reloaded the mealies. They finished reloading and a tarp over the load before the rain came.

**Pioneers** When the slack season came Foy and Francois decided it would be fun to make a covered wagon like the pioneers of South Africa and of the American West had used. Both of our families could go on a camping trip pretending we were pioneers. Our parents agreed to the plan and Foy and Francois set to work turning the big transport wagon into an old fashioned covered wagon. Mother and Mrs. deWet and all the girls made pioneer sun bonnets and divided-pleated skirts—we thought long dresses would be very inconvenient and we girls didn't wear pants in those days.

The date for the trip was during our holidays from boarding school. Beth and I were home and had our friends, Francis and Evelyn Route, brother and sister from the Congo, with us. Mrs. deWet, Francois, Caroline and David, Daddy, Mother, Foy, Beth, Margaret Ann and I with our visitors packed supplies and bedding and loaded the wagon. The wagon was pulled by sixteen oxen with a lead boy and a couple farm workers to take care of the oxen while we were camped. Foy and Francois took turns driving. Our kitchen worker went along to help and seemed to enjoy it as much as we did. We traveled about fifteen miles to a place Foy and Francois had picked ahead of time. A thorn bush kraal (pen) was made to put the oxen in at night, the native helpers would sleep with their fire nearby. In the daytime they herded the grazing cattle.

Camp was set up under a huge tree near some rocky hills where by day we could climb and explore. The wagon was at the edge of the camp under a branch of the large tree. Girls slept inside the wagon, boys under the wagon and adults on camp cots under the tree beside the fire that was kept burning all night to keep wild animals away. Three Wiggill brothers, Kit, Frank and John joined us for the last three days and nights. We climbed the rocky hillside in the daytime and after supper we sang and played games around the fire and listened to Daddy tell stories.

One evening the boys decided to go hunting, they said to get a buck to have roast venison, but we girls were annoyed that they wanted to go off and leave us! While they were gone we tied their pajama arms and legs in knots and put pepper inside their pillowcases—with the amused approval of our parents. Then we went to bed and waited to hear their reaction when they got back from their hunt. We heard one say, "I can't wait to get to bed!" and another, "Me neither," then we heard "Look at what those silly girls have done, now we've got to untie all this!" Finally they settled down. Soon we heard a sneeze, then another, and another. We giggled into our pillows and heard them vowing reprisals come morning. We went to sleep wondering what they would do.

The next day after early morning tea, we heard Daddy singing as he paced the camp site. He sang the same words over and over about a storm at sea and the chorus, ***"Sailor beware, Sailor take care, Danger is near, So beware, Beware!"*** Up in the wagon we were getting dressed and didn't pay much attention at first but as he came closer to the wagon he sang louder on the words **"Beware, Beware!"** We peeped out a hole in the canvas and saw the boys perched on a branch over the flap end of our wagon waiting for us to come out for breakfast, each one holding a pan of water. But we went to the other end and slipped out. Frustrated, they clambered down and threw the water on us anyway. We retaliated with cups and pans of water and there followed a regular water-fight. In the hot sun our hair and wet clothes would soon dry but Daddy told us to carry buckets to the stream and bring up more water for the camp—he enjoyed watching us have fun but would not ask the Africans to carry water for us to throw away.

**Cambridge Exam** At boarding school by the time I finished Form IV the system had changed and *The Cambridge Exam*, a different exam from England, was required at the end of that year. Those who wished to could go a fifth year for the Matric like Foy had done when there was no choice, but I had a choice and didn't want to go the extra year. Cambridge results on my four years of high school were good enough that I was ready to begin college as a Junior when I arrived in the U. S. My four years of boarding school ended December, 1939 and I was happy to spend 1940 at home.

**Grandpa Short** In October 1940 word came from Daddy's brother that their father, our Grandpa Short, had died September 24th. That left Grandma Short our only living grandparent.

**Marriage Matters** My first marriage proposal came when I was sixteen. Eighteen-year-old Francois deWet asked me to marry him. He was like a brother to me and I had my sights on Kit Wiggill. Kit was seven years my senior and worked most of the year in the gold mines in Johannesburg. He came home for his holidays that had sometimes coincided with my school holidays. Tall, dark and handsome, he had wavy black hair, brown eyes and a deep voice, with a laugh that seemed to rumble up from his boots. There was no question the attraction was mutual.

Several times during 1940, after Kit joined the Army, his mother invited me to spend time in their home when Kit was home on leave. It was nearing the end of 1940. Plans were already made for me to travel to the U.S. to go to college and Foy had been gone for some time when Kit came home on leave. His mother invited me to spend a week with them and what a wonderful time that was! At the end of the week Kit took me home in his motor car. On the way he asked me to change my mind about going to the States to college and to marry him. I was tempted but I told him I couldn't do that because by then plans for my leaving were too far along for any change. We agreed to see what the next three years would bring. He said he wanted to kiss me goodbye but I told him of my vow about kissing. He respected that and kissed my hand instead. I left feeling sure I'd be back there within three years to marry him.

A thirty-seven year old farmer, Mr. Thornhill, attended our home church services often. He lived about thirty miles from our farm but came for weekends quite regularly. He usually arrived on Friday or Saturday afternoon and stayed until Monday mid-morning. I was aware of his eyes constantly on me and I tried to stay out of sight. Daddy and Mother also noticed it and were not too happy about it. Well-to-do, with washed-out blue eyes, he was nice but definitely not for me.

It was the custom for everyone to shake hands when meeting and parting. On my final Monday morning at home he had been with us for the weekend but no one told him I was leaving for the U.S. at the end of that week. As he was getting ready to leave I told Mother I wanted to go hide somewhere because when he shook hands with me he would not let go of my hand for a long time. She said, "Go to the kitchen and be kneading the bread so your hands will be covered with flour. If he asks where you are I'll tell him you're busy in the kitchen." Well, I did and she did, but he came to the kitchen anyway. There he stood in the doorway watching me knead dough—flour to my elbows. He said, "I came to tell you goodbye."

I said, "Goodbye!"

He said, "Aren't you going to shake hands with me?"

I said, "I can't, I've got flour all over mine."

He said, "I don't care," and started toward me.

I went around the other side of the big table with him following me and we went round and round several times before he gave up and went out the door with a feeble goodbye. I couldn't help feeling a little sorry for him. I left for the U.S. by train at the end of that week. Mother wrote to me in Cape Town and told me that the next weekend he arrived with a pickup truck full of fruit and vegetables from his farm. He had come to ask Daddy for my hand in marriage and was shocked when he heard I was in Cape Town on my way to the U.S. Mother knew it would cheer me up to hear that I had missed that scene; her letter reached me when I was feeling extremely homesick and forlorn.

**World War II** Time had turned children into adults and the War hastened the changes we saw coming when Germany declared war on Britain in 1939. Southern Rhodesia was a British Protectorate and so was at war, too. That year Francois deWet joined the Royal Air Force and served out of England. The Wiggill brothers, Herbert, Kit, Frank and John joined the Rhodesian Army and by 1941 all four were fighting in North Africa. In late 1940 Foy had come to the U.S. to college and during January 1941 I was crossing the ocean. Six months later Beth followed on the next crossing of the same ship, *The S. S. City of New York*.

The day I left Rhodesia is as clear in memory as if it were yesterday. During preparations I had been conscious of the fact that I was leaving behind, not only my beloved family, but also saying goodbye to what I believed then (and still do) was the happiest childhood anyone could have lived. My trunk and big suitcase were loaded in our motor car along with Daddy, Mother, Beth and Margaret Ann and me. I don't recall anything about the miles we drove to Salisbury to the railroad station. I do remember watching as my things were transferred from the motor car to the train. When Mother saw I was about to cry she reminded me that I would be very busy and three years would pass in a hurry. That day was December 7, 1940, Daddy's 46<sup>th</sup> birthday. On the station platform the temperature was 105 degrees F in the shade. We were all dressed in our Sunday best and I remember I was wearing a navy blue and white voile dress, white hat, silk stockings and white open-toe shoes.

The warning bell rang and after final hugs and kisses I boarded the train, found my compartment and leaned from the open window for a last hand clasp. The whistle sounded and the train began moving. We waved until a bend in the tracks took them out of sight. They were gone and I cried. Being left at boarding school five years before was *nothing* compared to this. When I finally saw them again—it was not *three* years later, but *seven*.

# PART II

## TEXAS

# January 1941–June 1943

**Abilene Christian College** In my mind my college days began on December 7, 1940, on Daddy's forty-sixth birthday, when he and Mother, Beth, and Margaret Ann saw me off on the train from Salisbury to Cape Town. Foy was already in the States. The pain of leaving family was increased by the realization that the childhood I considered ideal in every way, had ended. When I got on that train I expected to see my family again in about three years—with the qualifying "the Lord willing." Three years was bad enough but it turned out to be seven. When I saw them again I had a husband and two children—but I'm jumping ahead.

I cried off and on almost the whole fifteen hundred miles to Cape Town. Kind friends of Daddy and Mother's in Cape Town took me into their home until my ship was ready to sail in January 1941. I don't remember their names and the time in Cape Town is a blur. My mind came alive after I was aboard the American ship, *The S. S. City of New York,* sailing out of Cape Town harbor. The ship was a part cargo vessel with only fifty-one passengers. I shared a cabin with a twenty-two year old single lady named Evelyn and we hit it off from the beginning.

It was late in the day when we sailed and that first evening most of the fifty-one travelers were in the Dining Room ready to enjoy dinner. The ship was rolling gently from side to side and soon by ones and twos, and then threes and more, people were making their way out of the Dining Room, slowly at first, then hurrying. By the end of dinner I was one of only a few left and I wasn't feeling too good. Details of the next three days are not clear. I was seasick and it was not fun. Then things settled down and the rest of the way I enjoyed the meals and the time aboard ship—even a storm later on was enjoyed in a different, exciting way.

119

On the table at every lunch and dinner were hard rolls, pats of butter, green olives and soda biscuits (which I learned to call *crackers,* since this was an American ship). I had never tasted green olives and my American cabin mate taught me to take a tiny bite of olive and a bite of cracker alternately, then chew them together and in that way I learned to really like olives. Enjoying the hard rolls and butter didn't take any practice—with them I had to curb my liking.

The ship was bound for New York City, officially non-stop, but was to anchor for part of a day at Puerto Rico. We had regular lifeboat drills and every evening the ship was blacked out with heavy curtains over all portholes and doorways. Europe was at war with Germany and German U-boats were known to be roaming the Atlantic. The United States had not yet declared war on Germany and theoretically the U Boats would not attack an American ship, but it had happened and our captain was taking no chances. During the day we forgot about such things and enjoyed the swimming pool, ping pong and shuffle board—unless it was raining—then we went to the well-stocked library and enjoyed indoor games or reading.

The Garrett family was on board, coming back to the U.S., and I saw them occasionally. Mother was so sure we would have a *Fancy Dress Party* that she had made a skirt and top in the African women's style for me. With a colorful "duku" on my head, and a doll tied on my back, I used cocoa and water paste to brown my face and won first prize in the "Home Made" division.

The next week we crossed the Equator and a celebration took up most of that day. The *Captain's Dinner* was special for us because Evelyn and I (the only two single ladies on board) were invited to sit one on each side of the Captain. Later came a *Book Dinner.* We were asked to come to dinner representing some book title.

From a magazine I cut out the figure of a man walking, pasted it at the top of a sheet of paper, drew footprints down the page behind him, cut out a picture of a dog and pasted it in the last footprint on the page, as though the dog were stepping in the man's footprints. I printed the title, "In His Master's Steps." I wasn't positive there was such a title but it sounded like something I had heard! I pinned the paper on my chest and went to dinner. To my surprise I won the prize for most original. (I had forgotten about these details until recently looking through memorabilia I found the ribbons and certificates.)

It was winter in the Northern Hemisphere and the farther north of the Equator we got, the colder the weather. Then we ran into a storm. The ship rolled from side to side and pitched up and down. No one was allowed on deck where waves crashed over everything from stem to stern. We watched through the library portholes until conditions got so bad passengers were told to go to their cabins and strap themselves into their bunks. It was not easy going down the corridors clinging to the rails and cabin stewards went along to see everyone safely to their cabins. In our cabin Evelyn and I tried to follow instructions. Her bunk was on the bottom and when the ship rolled sideways the right way she just fell into it and strapped herself in. When I tried to climb up to mine the ship rolled on its side and I found myself lying flat, face down on the floor. After several tries I finally made it into the bunk and strapped myself in. Later they told us the cargo was loaded too much to one side, which made the ship roll more than it should have. It had been exciting but we were mighty glad when the sea calmed.

The sun was shining brightly for our brief stop at Puerto Rico but no one went ashore. As we were leaving there we were informed that the cargo was bound for Boston instead of New York and that Boston was where the ship would dock. Daddy had made arrangements for me to be met when we landed in New York but there was no chance to let anyone know of the change. Too bad! Of course the people who were to meet me would find out from their end, but that wouldn't help me in Boston. However, we were assured that the ship's company would pay our train fare to New York.

It was January and ten degrees below zero Fahrenheit in Boston. I had only a light coat with a sweater under it, and open-toe shoes. The folks who were to meet me in New York planned to help me get winterized when I arrived, so I would just have to do the best I could until I got there. We went ashore into a very large Customs shed—no heat of course, and there we stayed for seven long hours. As I shivered and grew colder I was sure my feet would freeze but I remembered that Daddy had said walking would keep feet from freezing. So I walked and walked, back and forth. Finally we were on the warm train headed for New York.

I was met and treated wonderfully by Homer Reeves and his wife. During the several days I was there, she took me shopping for shoes and gave me a nice hand-me-down coat. Then she took me to her hair-dresser to get a perm in my very straight hair—finally I had curls that didn't sleep out. The Reeves took me sightseeing but because of the European war, precautions were being enforced and we couldn't go up into the Statue of Liberty. We did look at it from the ferry. I felt dazed and don't remember much else about New York City. Then I was on the train bound for Cordell, Oklahoma where I was to be met by Mother's brother and his wife, Uncle George and Aunt Maude.

The two days and a night on the train were a nightmare. In the first place, this train didn't have compartments like African trains; here everyone sat in seats, like on a bus, and I was afraid to move around in case I lost my seat. Twice in the two days I made it to the Dining Car to get something to eat, and watchfully went to the water fountain now and then. I was afraid to drink much because I didn't want to have to go to the restroom. People around me were sleeping in their seats, but I had heard of robbers in America and I was afraid to go to sleep. Finally I put my arm through the handle of my purse, and with the purse under my head, I did sleep some, but I didn't take my shoes off—what if I had to move in a hurry, and besides I was in public.

I know I changed trains at least once, but where and how, I don't recall. We arrived at Cordell about 8:30 at night of the second day and with relief I stepped off the train. It was dark and my feet were so swollen I could hardly walk. I looked anxiously around for my Uncle and Aunt but saw only the empty platform. Inside the Station Master asked if I was looking for someone and I explained.

Fortunately Cordell was a small town and everybody knew everybody. The helpful Station Master told me he knew my Uncle was gone on a trip, but he helped me use the phone to call the house in case my aunt was there—she wasn't. He asked me if I knew anyone else in Cordell and I remembered the name of a good friend Mother and Daddy had often talked about, Delilah Simcox. He called her house for me and I told her who I was and what had happened. She sounded very kind and told me to just stay put and she'd be right there to get me and assured me I could stay at her house until my kinfolks got home. It turned out Uncle George and Aunt Maude were both out of town and had not received the cablegram Daddy sent.

During my few days with Uncle George and Aunt Maude I was introduced to Post Bran Flakes and mayonnaise on bread for sandwiches but I don't recall anything else. From Cordell I rode the bus to Abilene, Texas, where I was overjoyed to be met by Foy. He had visited the two colleges we were considering and had compared expenses at Harding College in Searcy, Arkansas, and Abilene Christian College. He decided Abilene Christian was where we should go.

Daddy had told me to go see Grandma Short as soon as possible and Foy and I decided there would be time for me to make a short visit before the semester began later in January. She was staying with Daddy's brother, Uncle Christie; he and Aunt Virginia lived in Roswell, New Mexico. Foy was already working and couldn't go, but he saw me off on a bus to Roswell.

As much as I have forgotten, there is not much foggy about that trip. I even remember the blue dress I was wearing, with hose and navy blue shoes and carrying a navy blue handbag. And I was beginning to feel braver about traveling in America.

"Pecos! Ten minute rest stop," announced the driver as he stepped down to stand at the bus door. In the restroom my heart sank at sight of the line. How long would ten minutes last? Too soon a voice rattled off words over the loudspeaker that to my ears might as well have been a foreign language. I hurried out of the restroom as soon as I could, wondering if my destination had been called. There was no bus in sight and with a sinking feeling I turned to the man at the ticket window who pointed with his thumb at the bus disappearing around the corner, "There goes your bus," he said, "next bus to Roswell is seven-thirty tomorrow morning."

It was five-thirty in the afternoon! What was I to do? I had only a little money and decided it was enough to make a phone call to my uncle in Roswell; surely he would say he'd drive down to get me. "I'm sorry," he said, "It's too far to drive. I'll meet you at the bus station here in the morning." I couldn't help wondering if it really was too far, or if he was in effect saying a strange niece arriving from a foreign land was a nuisance. I asked the ticket agent how far it was to Roswell and he said about 200 miles. I had come over ten thousand miles from home and two hundred miles didn't sound so far to me, but with gas rationed it may have to my uncle, and he did sound kind, so I decided to give him the benefit of the doubt.

Here I was in a strange country, in a strange bus station, afraid to venture out into a strange city, and besides, what could I do with a few coins? I decided to just sit around watching people until morning. A magazine display looked interesting and after what seemed hours, I worked up courage to ask the man at the café counter if I could look at some of them. He said I could if I'd be careful and put them back where I got them. What did he think I was? By then I was beginning to feel touchy.

Periodically two Texas Border Patrolmen wandered through. I wasn't surprised since this was early 1941 and war had been going on overseas for three years. Every time the patrolmen came through they looked at me and I shrank farther down in my seat. I thought they were looking for possible spies and since I wasn't one, my mind said there was nothing to be afraid of but my inner quivering wouldn't listen. At eleven o'clock here they came again. This time they stopped at the booth where I was sitting and asked why I had been there so long. I explained my predicament, thinking surely that would satisfy them, but they wanted to know more. Probably my Rhodesian accent made them wonder and they asked if I was a U.S. citizen? Could I prove it? Did I have a passport? I told them that Immigration had kept my passport when I landed in Boston, and I began feverishly looking through my handbag, thinking there was no hope there. What would they do? I had heard of concentration camps—would I be sent to one of them?

In my bag I found the envelope in which the American Consul in Johannesburg had mailed my passport to Daddy. I had kept it for my stamp collection and forgotten it was there. Would this do any good? With shaking hand I gave it to the patrolman. He opened the envelope and wonder of wonders inside was the cover letter from the Consul. The patrolmen were satisfied and said I should not leave the bus station—as if there was any danger of that! But my heart began beating again.

When I left Rhodesia a few weeks before, I had felt very mature and ready to face the world. I had finished high school, I was about to turn eighteen, I was going across the ocean to college. When no one met me at the dock in Boston, nor at the train in Cordell, I had handled those situations well enough. But now my self-confidence was being seriously eroded. About midnight four bus drivers came in to eat. They looked around and all but one sat at the counter. That one walked to my booth and asked kindly, "Mind if I sit here?" and my Rhodesian accent sparked conversation for a while. He said he had seen me earlier when he passed through and was wondering why I had been there so long. When he heard I would be there all night he asked if I had eaten and I told him I didn't want anything. "Not even a glass of milk?" He seemed so kind I accepted the milk, but I kept hoping he would go away.

His meal done, he said, "My buddy is driving tonight, so his room is empty. I'll sleep there and you can have my room." I was shocked, but didn't know what to say. I tried, "No thank-you, I don't want to take your room," but he didn't seem to hear me. He stood up, "Come on," he said, "The maid will change the sheets." I found myself following him down the hall. Four years in a British all-girl boarding school had prepared me for many things but not this. In the room the maid changed the linens and left. My back was against the wall across the room from him and I intended to keep it that way. "This is very kind of you. Thank you very much," I said. "Is that all?" he asked, "Don't I get a kiss?" My heart had been in my throat and now it jumped into my mouth. I managed a head shake and a feeble "No!" To my relief he turned toward the door saying, "Well, Goodnight!"

I made sure the door was locked then sat on the side of the bed trying to stop shaking and wondering what to do. Should I try to sleep and trust the locked door—but surely he had a key—what if I didn't wake up in time for the bus—should I just sit up all night in the room? Finally my mind was made up. I eased the door open and looked around but saw no one. I crept down the hall, holding my breath and fearing a creaking floor board. Back in the haven of a booth my heart rate slowed down. If that bus driver came back I planned to shrink out of sight. But he didn't.

The rest of the night is a blur. I do recall my joy at seeing daylight. Finally it was 7:15 and time to board the bus to Roswell and safety. To a frightened, timid, sheltered girl of the nineteen thirties, it seemed to me I had been woefully naive. I thought my guardian angel must have been at work: perhaps a kindhearted gentleman had recognized a frightened foreigner—perhaps obvious ignorance had been my protection—perhaps—but I'll never know. I did know I had done nothing really wrong, but I was so humiliated and embarrassed at my simple-minded greenness that I kept it all buried deep inside for more than sixty years.

A few days in Roswell with Uncle Christie, Aunt Virginia and Grandma Short more than made up for all my misgivings about my welcome and I was sorry when the visit was over. Oddly I don't recall anything at all about the bus trip back to Abilene.

**Parents' Hopes** Our parents had hoped we would go to Harding College because of past association with people they had known there but there were also people they knew at Abilene where the terms for children of foreign missionaries were more generous. I trusted Foy's decision. The Dean of the college, Walter Adams, interviewed us and said our transcripts from high school in Southern Rhodesia qualified us to begin our Junior year. Foy was my big brother and it seemed to me I should not be in the same class with him. The second semester was just beginning so I told the Dean my reason and requested that I be classified as a second semester Sophomore.

As I recall there were between five and six hundred students at ACC then and it seemed to me everyone was friendly on sight, amazing to me, coming from a stiff and proper British boarding school where it took more time to make friends. Part of that attitude could have been the difference between high school and college age students.

Foy was housed in the boys dormitory and worked in the college bookstore in the basement of the Administration Building. Dr. Paul C. Witt, professor of biology and chemistry, and his wife were completing a new home across the street from the college campus with plans to have rooms upstairs for four college girls. It was arranged that I would live with them and do housework for my room and board. Their daughter, Pauline, was a Freshman in college and we became good friends. Their much younger daughter, Dorothy, reminded me of Margaret Ann and became like a younger sister to me.

While the Witt house was being finished I spent about two months in the home of Zelma Lawyer. It was almost like being with kinfolks because thirteen years before, she and her girls had been with us in Northern Rhodesia, and in 1928 we had returned to the States together. Though many years had passed since then they still seemed to understand my Africanisms. Zelma's mother lived with them and three or four college girls, but they generously made temporary room for me. They helped me more than they could have known to settle into this strange new life with its strange accents, strange subjects, strange teachers. It was strange to be in school without uniforms, strange to be in classes with boys—everything around me was strange.

Jeanne Lawyer was a second semester Junior so most of our activities were separate but she took time to help me find my way around and I loved and appreciated her for her kindness. When auditions were announced for the college chorus, Jeanne, who was a voice major, in the chorus, and one of the Sextet singers, insisted that I audition. She ushered me into the process and was a real encouragement. I was accepted in spite of the fact I could not read music. The director, Leonard Burford, said my voice blended well and if I would memorize the songs, I could manage without reading music. I loved to sing and being in the chorus was one of the joys of my college days.

West Texas was similar to Southern Rhodesia in many ways; the sandy soil, rocky landscape, wide open spaces, the big bright blue sky and low-growing scrubby trees all felt familiar. Starting my American life in those surroundings helped me adjust to life in the U.S. in those early days. Gradually over the next several years in other places I learned to tolerate being closed in with trees and clouds.

I moved into the Witt home in March. On April 1st there was a basketball game in the gymnasium—our boys against a rival college team—and Foy asked me to go with him. Fans dressed in "Sunday clothes" in those days, so I had on hose and medium high heels. It wasn't cold so we didn't take coats. We took a shortcut from the Witt's house across the campus grounds. During the game someone came in to say it was snowing. A late snow was not unheard of in that part of West Texas but it was still a surprise.

When we started home, there it was before our eyes—the first snow Foy and I had seen since we were in the States in 1929. We excitedly started walking through the more than ankle deep, still falling, snow, back the way we had come—we thought. I was on Foy's left side as we passed too close to a recently set-out tree, not realizing how far from the tree the ground had been cultivated. My left foot went down into the soft mud way above my ankle and when I pulled my foot up, my shoe stayed down there. We were not dressed for the cold and already shivering, but we laughed as Foy, gallant gentleman that he was, got down on his knees and reached into the hole to pull up my shoe—full of mud. I couldn't walk barefoot because of cockleburs and gravel, so I stuck my foot into the shoe, mud and all. Foy went to his room with a muddy hand and shirt sleeve.

**Sister Room-mate** When Beth arrived from Africa in June the Witts kindly agreed to let her room with me and share the housework. We may have had sisterly tiffs, though I don't recall any, but I do remember being very glad to have my sister to talk to. We didn't have many clothes and we shared about everything except skirts (because we were different heights) and shoes (because she had size 4 ½ feet compared to my size 7). We shared two wool blazers, one red, one camel. We both liked the red one best and we kept up with whose turn it was to wear it. Since Beth was a Freshman, most of her close friends were among her classmates, so we went our separate ways most of the time but at night we compared notes on our day, chatted and confided in each other over homework.

**Odd Jobs** Besides going to classes and working for the Witts, I often had time to baby-sit, iron and houseclean for other faculty wives. My specialty was ironing. I ironed for an elderly professor whose daughter said, when I applied for the job, "He's *very* particular and hard to please." Evidently my ironing pleased him because I ironed his seven white shirts every week of that year.

**Dedicated Teachers** Our teachers impressed me with their dedication to serving God and their friendliness and kindness to their students. This very thing was a big reason Daddy and Mother had wanted us to attend a Christian college. Dr. Witt was Head of the Science Department, honored in the science world, and a godly man in demand for preaching and also for speaking to Scientific gatherings over the country. And he had another unique talent. With his daughter Pauline accompanying him on the piano, he whistled bird imitations and was in demand for parties and programs. He and Mrs. Witt were like adopted parents to me and I felt he was almost as perfect as my own Daddy.

R.C. Bell was a Bible teacher who had been teaching in the Christian college Daddy and Mother had attended. He seemed to me the embodiment of love and spirituality and being in his Bible class was a treat. When we happened to meet on the sidewalk crossing the campus, he always shook hands, and many times left a $10 bill in my hand with the words, "I love your father and mother. God bless you." He did the same for Foy and Beth; Margaret Ann said when she was in college there four years later, he did the same for her.

Without doubt the most unusual character among the teachers was Howard Schug. Like R.C. Bell, he was old and white haired, spiritual, humble and extremely intelligent. He was tall and spindly and cross-eyed, always kind and friendly—woefully absent minded; and everyone who knew him loved him. He spoke seven or more languages fluently and said he even dreamed in different languages. He was in constant demand as interpreter when foreign students arrived in the Dean's office. Naturally he taught foreign languages, and preached often at a Spanish church downtown. When he felt he had infringed on anyone's space he half bowed, nodded his head up and down and said several times, "Pardon me! Pardon me!" He laughed at himself when students poked good natured fun at his absentmindedness. The story was told on him that one morning he accidentally put shaving cream on his toothbrush and when it foamed up in his mouth he looked in the mirror, nodded his head and said, "Pardon me! Pardon me!"

**Bible Major** After my first semester I was so enthusiastic about classes and getting into the swing of college that I signed up for summer school, finished my Sophomore year and that fall began my Junior year. Foy didn't go to summer school as he was preaching in summer meetings. That fall Foy was still one semester ahead of me but I took more hours than he did and by the next year we began our Senior year together. He assured me he didn't mind me being his classmate! He majored in Business Administration. I began majoring in Art, but after one semester decided Art needed to be my hobby instead of a serious major and changed to Children's Literature. I enjoyed that for one semester but when I found out I would not graduate as early as I wanted to if I stayed with that I changed again, this time to a Bible major. I wanted to finish college and go into nurse's training as soon as possible.

There were sixteen "preacher boys" majoring in Bible; I was the only girl in the class. That fact did not sit too well with some of them who felt a Bible major should be only for preachers. But it didn't bother me and I ended my Senior year with the highest grade in the class. Unfortunately the teacher, Charles H. Roberson, held up my final paper as an example. Out of class some of the "preacher boys" let it be known they did not like being outdone by a girl in "their field." I thought it was funny and so did Foy.

**This and That** I needed another credit in Math to graduate and the only one I could fit in was Calculus. I hardly understood anything the teacher was talking about but thanks to evening tutoring I made a "C." Oddly enough, I don't remember the teacher's name, but the tutor's name was Joseph Hampton, Dr. Witt's assistant. My only other "C" was in American Government. It was very different from British Government and the teacher couldn't understand how anyone who was an American citizen could be so ignorant of American Government. In both of those I was relieved to have a "C," and very glad there were no more credits needed.

Chapel was one of my favorite periods of the day and I looked forward to it every morning. I had grown up hearing singing either in a native language or in a small group of white people. I had thought the hymn singing at boarding school was good with the few hundred girls, but here with over five hundred mixed voices singing four part harmony there was no comparison. It was so thrilling it gave me goose bumps. Chapel programs were varied and always interesting. When the week long annual Lectureship was being conducted, there were well over a thousand people in attendance in the evening services and the singing fairly raised the roof; and I had never heard so many different and able speakers.

About that time J. C. Reed asked me for a date. I had seen him around the campus and thought he was nice enough, but I wasn't enthusiastic about going out with him. I don't remember where we went but before going back to the campus he suggested we go up to the top of the big hotel in town and look out over the lighted city—a favorite spot for college kids' inexpensive sightseeing. My dress had a circular skirt and when we stepped out of the stairwell onto the roof the West Texas wind caught my skirt and sent it up over my head—long before Marilyn Monroe and her famous blown skirt and I doubt she was as embarrassed as I was. J. C. gallantly helped me get it down and I was thankful for the semi-darkness that hid my red face.

That fall, along with the arriving Freshmen came upper class transfers from other colleges. Among them, from Athens, Alabama, transferring from David Lipscomb College, was Bennie Lee Fudge. It seemed to me the girls fell all over themselves to attract his attention, and that made me want to avoid him. I didn't see what they were so excited about, he was not good-looking in the conventional way, he wasn't very tall, he was almost skinny and he had a bouncy walk. He did, however, have black wavy hair. I noticed that he dated a lot of different girls only one time each. I thought that meant the girls didn't want another date. But I heard girls talk and found out it was his choice and not theirs. He told me later he was checking out the girls hoping to find one that appealed to him—he was twenty-eight years old and seriously searching for a possible wife while getting his BA degree.

**Pearl Harbor** On December 7th 1941, I was eating breakfast with the Witts and mentioned that it was Daddy's birthday. Mrs. Witt asked if I would like to bake a birthday cake and we could celebrate. The radio was on in the kitchen where I was making the cake when suddenly the program was interrupted and the announcement made of the Japanese attack on Pearl Harbor. Life changed for everyone.

What we had thought of as "college boys" were now young men, some being drafted into the armed forces and others volunteering for the branch of their choice. The college population was diminished drastically.

Registration for the draft had been going on for some time and Foy, Bennie Lee and a number of others had registered as conscientious objectors. Some of them went into medical training and those who had been actively preaching for some years, like Foy and Bennie Lee, were deferred as ministers.

**Fortuitous Meeting** Foy was still working in the college bookstore in the basement of the ad building. One day after the second semester began in January, 1942, I was in the area and decided to drop in for a little visit with him. While we were talking, Bennie Lee came in with a bucket full of chalky erasers he was going outside to clean. He was head janitor and besides overseeing a crew he did many jobs himself. He and Foy knew each other from life in the boys' dorm and he had stopped by to pass the time of day with him.

Foy introduced us and we eyed each other warily. All of a sudden Bennie Lee picked up two chalky erasers, stepped toward me and said, "I believe I'll dust your face!" I dodged and stepped away saying, "I believe you won't!" He stopped short and looked at me in surprise. Afterwards he told me he had seen me on the campus and thought I was a meek, mousy sort of person. He was testing me with that challenge and at my response, he decided I had spunk after all!

Soon after that Bennie Lee asked me to go with him on Monday night to a country church where Foy was preaching that week and I went. Very few students had cars and a school bus ran for those who wanted to go hear Foy. We rode the bus and talked the twenty miles there and again all the way back, much of our talk about Africa. Most of the time he asked questions and I talked. When he took me back to the Witt's house that night he asked me to go with him on Wednesday night, and I agreed to go, thinking to myself that I was one up on those girls who didn't get asked the second time! And as they say, "The rest is history!" Like Foy, Bennie Lee preached most Sundays in small churches around the area and many times after that he invited me to go with him, and I went. Bennie Lee's roommate at that time was Leon Locke, who told Foy, "You better watch Fudge and your sister. When he got back Monday night he announced to me, 'If Miss Short wasn't determined to go to Africa when she finishes here, I would marry that girl!'"

**Working Summer** The second summer I spent six weeks with my mother's sister, Aunt Alice and family in Stephenville, Texas. She worked in a laundry as seamstress and alteration lady and got me a job as a mangle operator. Two of us girls fed sheets and tablecloths into the huge rollers and a cloud of steam rose into our faces. It was summer and no air conditioning, not even a fan blowing on us, because that would dry out the material. It was hot, hot work, but I had a job and I was paid 17 cents an hour. Best of all it allowed me to be with Aunt Alice and my cousins, Bob, Marjy and Missy. Aunt Alice was two years younger than Mother and looked a lot like her. Besides looks, she had expressions and tone of voice that made me feel I was with Mother; it was a good feeling.

That six weeks included July 4th and we cousins went swimming in a nearby lake. The clouds were thick that day. We ignorantly assumed we would not sunburn with the sun behind clouds and we played in the water for nearly four hours. The next morning I went to work as usual but I hadn't been standing in the steam very long until my shoulders were hurting badly. I asked Aunt Alice to look at my back and she exclaimed, "Why *SYBIL*! Your back is all big blisters." Clothes hurt me and the steam made it worse so I was excused and went home to shed my blouse. Two days were spent on the bed where Aunt Alice turned a chair over to make a sloping foundation for pillows and I semi-reclined with nothing touching my shoulders. Three times a day Aunt Alice slathered chamomile lotion on my back. Ever since then I have had a back full of freckles.

Then it was time to go back to Abilene and look for work there. An army base, Camp Barkley, was just outside the city and laundries in town served the men. I tried out for a job in a laundry that specialized in officers' uniforms, where they divided the work between trouser-ironers and shirt-ironers. I told them I preferred ironing shirts. Pay was 17 ½ cents per hour and I was glad to get that much more than I had made in Stephenville, but every evening I looked in the newspaper for a more lucrative possibility.

Jody Hawkins was living at the Witt's house and we heard about a plant that made egg powder for the troops so we applied and were hired to break eggs. Girls in white uniforms stood at long tables, each with a bucket of candled eggs on one side and an empty sterilized bucket on the other. In front of us was a little sterilized tray with a blade between two sterilized metal cups. We picked up two eggs with one hand, broke them into the cups, picked up a cup in each hand and passed them under our nose. If there was no smell, we poured the eggs into the bucket on our other side. Good eggs didn't smell at all, so if we smelled anything, we took our little tray with its two cups containing the smelling egg(s) to a central station and exchanged them for clean, sterilized tray and cups. We had competitions to see who could break the most dozens of eggs per day. The man supplying the buckets of eggs to us complained that we were breaking his back making him lift so many buckets of eggs to keep us busy! Every night we washed and ironed our eggy uniforms as we happily made 25 cents an hour. We were sorry when it was time for school to start and we had to quit.

Beth had been working somewhere else and saving her money, too. She and I both needed winter coats and as fall came on we went shopping. Mrs. Witt knew of a place having a sale and we each bought a coat for $15. Now we could discard the hand-me-downs that had served their purpose. That night, as we lay in bed talking, we agreed it was a good feeling to own a new coat, paid for with our own money, and Beth said, "Now I don't feel so much like a church mouse!" We had a good laugh, though we both knew that we truly appreciated all the hand-me-downs we had received.

All that summer I had exchanged letters with Bennie Lee. He was preaching ("holding meetings") in churches in Louisiana, Oklahoma, Tennessee and Alabama. By the time school began again in the fall we had learned a lot about each other and were well and truly in love. He told me of his dream to establish a Christian high school in his home town of Athens, Alabama. He said he was all for going to Africa some day but needed to get the school going first and I agreed to postpone my dream for the five years he predicted it would take.

During our Senior year Foy and Bennie Lee were roommates. They had private nicknames for each other derived from their initials. Foy's full name is Harold Foy so Bennie Lee called him "Horse Face" and Foy called Bennie Lee "Bird Legs." It made me happy that they were such good friends.

One of the unusual things to me was how many students were called by double names. For example there was Mary Belle, Martha Faye, Edna Earl, Ona Faye, Mary Helen, Ruth Ellen, Clara Sue, Jim Bob, Bobby Joe, Billy Ray, and I would later marry one of them, Bennie Lee. Occasionally for weekend holidays I went home with one or another close friend: Mary Belle Manor, whose folks lived on a farm near Brownwood, Texas, where I actually milked an American cow; Ona Faye Speck from San Antonio, where we visited the Alamo and the Japanese Sunken Gardens; Helen and Hazel Smith, sisters from Levelland, Texas, where on a very cold weekend the new metal stove in our bedroom burned off acrid smoke that had us opening windows wide in spite of the icy wind.

**Beth And Henry** During school one of the many activities going on was a Sunday evening favorite for a group of us. The Witts invited fifteen or more young people to come to their home for singing after church service. Witts attended Highland Church of Christ across town and Beth and I attended the College Church, so there were folks from both places. One Sunday evening a newcomer was Henry Ewing, an Army Sergeant out of Camp Barkley, who attended church at Highland. He was tall, dark and handsome and girls fairly swooned over him. Clara Sue Shepherd, who roomed across the hall from Beth and me, claimed him at first, then Beth caught his eye and a whirlwind courtship followed. Henry's time away from camp was limited, but he and Beth and Bennie Lee and I enjoyed some hilarious double dates.

One Saturday we rented bicycles and went out into the unpaved countryside to ride. The men, experienced bicycle riders, thought they would show us how well they could ride, but they were used to riding on pavement and Beth and I had ridden through sand and mud and gravel, and very little on pavement. They were amazed at us and we made fun of their wobbling around on rough ground and falling in the sand. When we got home she and I agreed they could have been putting on a show for our benefit; it would have been just like either one of them.

As Juniors and then Seniors, Foy and Bennie Lee had Preacher Training Class, Debate Club and A Club (men's honor society) in which they were leaders and officers. I had a turn as Leader of Girls Training Class, and was in the W Club (women's honor society). We were all three in Who's Who In American Colleges and Universities.

**Piano And Typing** Mabel Burford was the blind sister of our blind Chorus Director, Leonard Burford, who was also Head of the Music Department. She gave private piano and violin lessons and three days a week had pupils who had lessons at the Witt's house. She had some spare time between pupils and asked me if I would like to learn to play the piano. I was thrilled at the prospect and she taught me for six months. Because time was limited she took short cuts so I could cover more material faster than her usual beginners. As a result I learned to read music fairly well and in later years when I had a chance, I could pick my way through a piece, learning it one hand at a time, then put the two hands together and play for my own enjoyment. Almost the same thing happened with typing. I had only one semester available to take typing, but decided some would be better than none. What I learned then stood me in good stead years later when I had a chance to practice on my own and then to work at jobs that required typing.

Meanwhile I had not forgotten Kit. We had corresponded regularly—as regularly as letters could be processed to and from where he was stationed in North Africa. It was a hard letter to write when I had to tell him that Bennie Lee and I were planning to marry when we finished college. He said he was disappointed but was not too surprised since I had been raised in a missionary family and he thought it only proper that I should find a preacher husband. Bennie Lee gave me an engagement ring in early January and my closest friends surprised me with a cedar chest as a birthday gift.

They said every bride-to-be needed a "hope chest"—which I had never heard of.

Toward the end of February 1943, Foy received a cablegram from Daddy that read: *"William Newton, Jr. arrived February 23rd. Mother and baby doing well."* Foy and Bennie Lee knew Beth and I would be on our way from the post office to the Witt's house and they intercepted us in the middle of the campus where Foy read the cablegram to us. It was a complete surprise, Mother was 47 years old and we had not known she was expecting a baby. We were so shocked we just stood there a few minutes then began to cry. Foy couldn't understand that and said, "I thought you'd be happy." We replied tearfully that we were happy, we were just so shocked we didn't know how to act. Margaret Ann was fourteen years old, still in Africa in boarding school. It took some getting used to and Beth and I had a lot to talk about.

College life ended in a frenzy of programs, final exams and banquets: W Club Banquet, A Club Banquet, Junior-Senior Banquet. I made a formal of pale blue and white floral organdy and wore it to all of them with a different color of corsage each time! Naturally Bennie Lee and I went together to all of them.

**Surprise Shower** In between all of those events the ladies of the College Church and college friends gave me a bridal shower—the first time I had ever heard of that kind of shower! They planned it secretly and prepared it for one afternoon in the Parlor of Girls Dormitory. Ladies and girls were dressed suitably for the occasion as they all assembled ready to have me brought in unsuspecting. I was practicing archery out in a field when the emissary came for me. She would answer no questions, just said I was wanted immediately in the Parlor of Girls Dorm. So in bobby sox and oxfords, very causal dress, and with thoroughly West Texas-wind-blown hair, I went to the Parlor to be greeted by all those dressed up ladies and girls. As much as I sincerely appreciated the ladies and the shower, I was embarrassed almost to tears and never wanted to be surprised like that again.

**Wedding Bells** Graduation was Monday evening, May 31; Bennie Lee's and my wedding was set for the following evening, June 1, 1943. Sixty-six years later I wrote this letter to my children:

*June 1, 2009*

*Dear children all,*

*This morning I changed the page on my calendar to June and thought about this time sixty-six years ago which was a Tuesday. On May 31, Monday evening, Foy, Bennie Lee and I graduated from then ACC (now ACU). Bennie Lee graduated Summa Cum Laude; I, Magna Cum Laude; and Foy, Cum Laude. I don't often remember that, or see it spelled out, so I thought I'd look at it in print! Foy was as proud of me as I had been of him when he won the Rhodes Junior Biet Scholarship ten years before. That Monday evening was a momentous occasion, but I don't remember who spoke or anything about the graduation ceremony. My mind was whirling in anticipation of what was to happen the next evening.*

*My girlhood dream had been of marrying a tall, dark and handsome man like the friend I'd left in Africa three years before, fully expecting to go back after college and do that. But Bennie Lee Fudge came into my life with his magnetic, charismatic personality, coupled with all the qualities I wanted in a husband—and he did have wavy black hair and long black eyelashes! It didn't matter that he was only 1 ½ inches taller than I, and weighed only 128 pounds; and he didn't seem to care that I weighed a whopping 140 when I agreed to marry him in January 1943. At that time I secretly vowed I would not marry someone smaller than I was, and I went to work to remedy the situation.*

*Daddy had sent me $10 to buy material for my wedding dress and whatever else I could manage. Home EC that*

139

*semester was Sewing and the teacher said I could make my dress in class. It would be long-waisted with covered buttons down the front, sweetheart neck line, long sleeves pointed over the hand and buttoned up the back of the arm with covered button. The back gores of the skirt extended into a train.*

*But I had a problem. I wanted it to fit what I planned to be by June 1. The pattern I used was for that size, and how was I to fit it as I sewed? Fortunately my best friend, Mary Belle, was in the class and she was the size I intended to be so she was my model. By May 20th the dress fit me and I weighed 125 lbs to Bennie Lee's 128. I was ready to marry him! The $10 had been enough for dress, slip and veil materials and pattern. I had enough savings for shoes ($1.50), and bridal bouquet of white gladioli ($3.00).*

*Dr. Paul C. Witt performed the ceremony in the living room of the Witt house with about fifteen close friends invited, and Reception in the dining room. Pauline Witt played the piano and her fiance, who had a beautiful baritone voice, sang our requests, "O Promise Me," and "I'll Walk Beside You." Mother had told me they were sung at her and Daddy's wedding and I planned for years to have them at mine. Bennie Lee was happy with whatever I chose. Mrs. Witt and the girls who lived there had gone all out with suitable decorations and she made a beautiful cake and pink punch. Beth was Maid of Honor and Foy gave me away and was Bennie Lee's Best Man.*

*Beth and I dressed for the wedding upstairs and she went down first. I well remember Foy's reaction as I started down the stairs and he looked up. To this day I can see his face and hear his voice exclaiming, "Ohhh, **Sybil**!" He put my arm in his and said, "You are beautiful!" The mirror had told me I looked O.K. but his voice and look made me feel indescribably more beautiful than I had ever imagined*

*I could feel. Foy did not know that was the best wedding present he could have given me. I had always admired my two beautiful sisters, and he had made me feel beautiful.*

*Beth and Henry married the following Sunday. She wore the same dress after simply turning up about an inch of hem across the front. The following year Foy and Margaret married and Margaret wore the same dress, after letting that hem out. Thirty-two years later Nancy was planning her wedding and wanted to wear the dress. I washed and ironed it, and it shrank just enough to fit her perfectly. After Joe and I married and took my cedar chest to Ohio, I pulled out that wedding dress, tried it on, and lo and behold, after forty years, it fit me—until I developed farm-work muscles!*

*That's enough reminiscing for one day.*

*Lots of love, Mother/Mom/Sybil*

**Wedding picture of Sybil and Bennie Lee on June 1, 1943 in Abilene, Texas.**

141

**Back to June 1943** We were to take the bus on Wednesday morning. After buying our tickets Bennie Lee had exactly 67 cents left and I didn't have much more. We could not possibly stay in a hotel Tuesday night. One of the faculty families I had done housecleaning for was going to be out of town that week and insisted we stay in their house Tuesday night. But how would we get there from the Witts without our well meaning friends following us? I had done regular baby sitting for an Army doctor and his wife who lived in town, Dr. and Mrs. Sienknecht, and at my last baby-sitting job I told them about our wedding plans. They said they wanted to help any way they could and to call them if I thought of something they could do. I called them and they offered a solution for that night.

When the reception was winding down and I had changed clothes, a strange car pulled into the Witt's driveway and around to the back. Our suitcases had been put behind the back door earlier and the doctor had them in his trunk by the time Bennie Lee and I came through the kitchen and out the door without anyone noticing. The doctor drove away with us hunkered down in the back seat, out of sight of possible watchers from the house. None of our friends knew the doctor, nor where he lived. We just disappeared and they couldn't follow us. Mrs. Witt was the only one who knew our get-away plans and had guarded the door from the dining room to the kitchen.

We were off on the adventure of our lives.

# PART III

## ALABAMA

# 1943–1975

**A New Life** For Bennie Lee, leaving Abilene, Texas on June 2, 1943, following our graduation and our wedding was more or less a continuation of his previous life, only now he had graduated from college and had a wife. He had been preaching for several years and was accustomed to being treated as "the preacher," but for me it was the beginning of a whole new life. I had graduated from college and I was in a new position as "preacher's wife," in what was still to me a strange country. I needed to learn and understand different and sometimes strange customs, words, idioms and environments. My Rhodesian accent was slow to wear off and that, plus the fact that I was born and raised in Africa, made me a curiosity to people who were meeting me for the first time. I felt like a foreigner and the people I met felt like I was one—most of them had never met anyone born and raised in a different country. But the future was an exciting and daunting prospect to me; Bennie Lee was my bridge connecting where I had come from to where I was going—from the known to the unknown.

Now we were on the way to the first two-weeks revival of three he would hold before we went to Athens, Alabama, the county seat of Limestone County where he was born and raised. Two-week summer meetings or revivals were an accepted part of church life, and after these three he had several more scheduled in Limestone County and southern Tennessee.

But Bennie Lee was not just a preacher. He had been corresponding with key people among the church elders in Limestone County, who would help him with his dream of establishing North Alabama Bible School. He and I spent many of our evening dates at the Witt's kitchen table where he wrote letters by hand while I addressed, stuffed, sealed and stamped the envelopes for him. He had been laying the groundwork for many months for the Bible School—a Christian high school that was a new concept to everyone, and he was asking these men to encourage folks to talk about it and to plan to send their high school age children to the school. Classes were to begin in the fall and he had "worked on" fellow graduates he thought would make good teachers in the new school. The school would begin with grades seven through twelve, hoping to add elementary school as soon as possible. Foy was among those coming to teach while he was waiting for the war to be over so he could go back to Africa as a missionary.

**Winfield, Louisiana** Bennie Lee and I were on the Greyhound bus bound for Winfield, Louisiana. Each revival would last two weeks and we stayed in someone's home at each place except the first one. Our hosts in Winfield were J. D. Boyd and his motherly wife who reminded me of my mother. J. D. had been suffering for many years with M.S. but his deep faith and loving heart shone so brightly in spite of his limitations, that he was an effective and much loved preacher, helped by his wonderful wife whose sense of humor matched his. Their daughter had been in David Lipscomb College with Bennie Lee and he had visited in their home when they lived in Tennessee.

**Honeymoon Cottage** They welcomed us with open arms and explained that they had prepared a "honeymoon cottage" for us in their backyard. The "cottage" was a one-room house originally for a hired hand, then used for storage, which they had cleaned out and painted white inside and out. Across the front of the cottage were huge hydrangea bushes in full bloom, and they had placed a big bouquet of those blooms on the table inside. A blue curtain, the color of the hydrangeas, hung across the corner where the commode and sink were—we went to their house for baths. A fan and a cross-breeze at night made the summer heat comfortably bearable. A bride and groom could not have been more cordially welcomed and suitably situated.

One morning Bennie Lee was sitting at the table studying on his sermon while I was making the bed. As I passed behind his chair I leaned over and kissed him on the cheek. He swung around and asked in a surprised voice, "What was that for?" I was taken aback at his question and said, "Because I love you. Don't you want me to do that any more?" His answer thrilled me. "Please don't stop. It's just that I come from an undemonstrative family and never knew anything like that, but I like it. Don't stop, just help me learn to do it too." I kept teaching him along that line as he taught me self-confidence and decisiveness, qualities I felt that I lacked.

We ate breakfast with our hosts in their cozy kitchen and for all other meals we were invited to homes of church members. We fared sumptuously and I knew I would have to be careful or my clothes would soon be too tight. And Bennie Lee preached morning and evening.

**Turkey Creek** From Winfield we went to Turkey Creek where I learned a little about southern Louisiana where drinking water was dipped out of a bayou. We were housed with a kind elderly man and his wife and the wife's bachelor brother, in an unpainted-siding house with bed bugs in a dense pine woods. It was July and in spite of the shade it was hot back in those woods where almost no breezes blew. We ate breakfast with our hosts each day and the Louisiana coffee was memorably strong and sweet. The brother had a bushy, long mustache that got soaked when he drank coffee from his saucer. He used his forefinger to squeegee it down, slurping it into his mouth. It was funny-entertainment I could have done without as I ate my breakfast—but we had to wait until we were in private to laugh about it!

Housewives went all out to "feed the preacher" fried chicken, pies and cakes, and all the good things from their gardens—and they were excellent cooks. For most of the women it was canning time and when there was opportunity I enjoyed helping snap beans, hull peas and cut up squash or okra.

Bennie Lee preached morning and evening—until the second Wednesday night. Early in the second week one of the elders asked him to preach Wednesday night about the Second Coming of Christ and the thousand year reign on earth. The year before, folks from this congregation had heard Bennie Lee preach in a neighboring church and invited him to Turkey Creek. He knew how they had been taught on that subject and had told me he planned to avoid that topic and preach on other subjects because he did not see the need to stir up dissension.

Now he had been asked by one of the elders to do that, so that night he began preaching on the subject as he understood it. He had only preached a few minutes when a man walked into the building and down to the center front row to take a seat. Bennie Lee knew him as a well known and very vocal preacher who disagreed with him on that subject. About half way through his sermon the elder who had asked him to preach on it stood up and said, "That's enough, Brother Fudge. We believe you are teaching false doctrine and we invited Brother Mullens here tonight to take care of you." Bennie Lee calmly said, "I have been giving Bible reasons for what I am saying and will respectfully listen if he wants to point out by the Bible where I am wrong." To which the elder replied, "We are ready for you to leave *right now* and Brother Mullens will finish the rest of the meeting." So we walked out and our apologetic hosts took us home to pack and catch the bus next morning.

Bennie Lee's being challenged on what he believed the Bible to teach was not new to me, though I didn't like it and never got used to it. It had happened while we were in college when he published a booklet on a Christian killing in warfare, giving reasons for his belief based on his understanding of Bible teaching. Naturally at the time that was a highly controversial subject and I knew then that he would stand firmly on his convictions, whatever the subject. I also knew that he was conscientious about having an open mind and kept studying a subject even when he thought he understood it. He was a peace lover and would not stir up contention if it could be avoided with good conscience.

He told me that as a child one of his favorite pastimes was pretending that he was a general of armies, setting up battles between opposing armies in the sand with sticks and stones as men. He was the general of one side then the general of the other side as he planned strategies for both. He said that if he had not come to the conclusions that led him to be a Conscientious Objector he would likely have become a career soldier aspiring to lead an army. That much I had learned about him in the two years we had known each other. He believed that as a Christian he should not be involved in the civil government other than paying taxes, so he did not vote. My own upbringing by a father who believed the same way made it easy for me to understand Bennie Lee's views.

**Olney, Oklahoma** With that meeting cut short for our part, we took advantage of the three days before time for the next one (in Oklahoma) to visit H. L. and Juanita O'Neal in Bunkie, Louisiana. They were good friends of Bennie Lee's from previous years and were anxious to meet his new wife. Three days with them passed pleasantly and rapidly. It was mid-July when we went on by Greyhound bus to Olney in west Oklahoma—hot Oklahoma—dry Oklahoma—dusty Oklahoma—where even the wind was hot—and dry—and dusty. I don't remember the house, except the shower, and a big fan with straw behind it in one window. The straw was kept wet so the air drawn through it into the house was cooled, but the fan was only turned on in late afternoons. I don't remember any of the people, though I know there were people, and a church, and they were kind, and they fed us.

What I do remember is being hot. When I stepped out of the shower and tried to dry myself I was sweating—not perspiring. By the time we were ready to go to church, my voile dress, that I had carefully washed, starched and ironed, was as limp as a rag. By the time the two weeks was up *I* was as limp as a rag, too. And I'm sure Bennie Lee preached morning and evening, I just don't remember.

**Alabama Bound** Then we were on the Greyhound bus bound for Athens, Alabama and more adventures—more new people to meet and things to learn. I was learning that Bennie Lee thrived in hot weather—in fact, he thrived in every kind of weather, but especially in hot weather. He often said, "Hot weather makes me feel *invigorated, ready for action!*"

During those three meetings, when Bennie Lee had a few minutes to spare, he wrote letters to the servicemen he knew from Limestone County. He wrote by hand to each one as often as he could and kept it up until the war ended, trying to encourage and cheer them, no matter where in the world they were. Some of those men never came home but the ones who did told him how much his letters helped them.

When we arrived in Athens, Bennie Lee hit the ground running. Jack Rollings preached for the downtown Church of Christ in Athens and he and his wife, Alene, and three children lived in an small apartment, but they made room for us to spend the first several nights with them.

**North Alabama Bible School** Irven Lee lived in town but preached for a country church and worked with Jack and Bennie Lee getting the school ready to go. They raised money, arranged for conversion of a big old farm house (with minor changes) into a school house, all the while encouraging parents to send their children to the new school. Irven and Bennie Lee did most of the money raising as they traveled around the county talking up the school. Jack talked to anyone who would listen about what good the school would do, but he would not ask anyone for money. If they gave him some for the school without his asking, he put it in "the pot." Many parents who heard about it were enthusiastic about the idea of their children being taught the Bible and Christian principles every day while they learned regular school subjects.

At the same time the three men were preaching every morning and evening in revival meetings among the county churches. When Bennie Lee began preaching at eighteen, most folks in the country either walked or rode in wagons the miles to a church. He had a dream of there being a church of Christ within three miles (considered walking distance) of everyone who lived in Limestone County. If I remember correctly in 1943 there were fifteen congregations of the churches of Christ in Limestone county—in less than twenty years there were fifty-something. By then of course, people had cars, but Bennie Lee's dream had been realized. Much of that growth was attributed to the enthusiasm and spiritual growth of the children attending the Bible School and generated to their parents and grandparents; and to the influence of more preaching in every congregation, done by men who were teaching in the school. Until 1943 preaching in country churches was by once-a-month circuit preachers and the usual two-week summer meetings.

**Meeting In-Laws** As soon as Bennie Lee could tear himself away from the pressing matters of the school, he found someone to take us in a car to see his parents. They lived about eight miles out of Athens and we didn't yet have a car and no bus ran near them. Bennie Lee had already been preaching in the county for ten years, and knew so many people he could always find someone going out that way on Saturday—the day country folks came to town and would be going home about noon.

His father's name was Edward Benjamin Lee Fudge, affectionately known to the family as Papa, Uncle Eddy to other kinfolks and Ed to the neighbors. When I met him he was seventy-nine years old, bald headed with a long beard. He had been suffering from dementia for several years and because of a bad back had not been able to work since Bennie Lee was fourteen. Papa spent his days sitting in his rocking chair—in the living room in the winter—on the porch in the summer—with occasional strolls around the yard or on the dirt road that ran past the house. His wife, Susie, tended him like a child and made sure he began every day neat and clean. When Bennie Lee introduced me to him he looked me over and didn't seem to know what to make of me or of what Bennie Lee was saying about being married.

**Origins** Bennie Lee was born in 1914 at Gypsy, Alabama, west of Athens. The family lived over the combination post office/country-store/

gristmill that his father operated. His mother, Susie (Smith), was twenty-one when he was born, his father was fifty. She was born and raised in south west Tennessee and at ten was taken out of school and put to work in a cotton mill where she worked until nineteen when she and Ed Fudge met. They were married when she was twenty and he forty-nine.

At the age of six Bennie Lee was ready for first grade but the family lived too far away from any school for him to attend (there were no school buses then.) Fanny Rainey, wife of Ed Fudge's nephew Bennie Lee Rainey, was a school teacher. They lived across the county and she offered to have him board with them each week while he attended the school where she taught. Every Sunday Susie packed a small wooden trunk with Bennie Lee's clothes for the week and his father took him in a wagon to the Rainey home and went to get him on Friday afternoons. [One of my children has that little trunk.]

Not long after that the post office at Gypsy was closed and Gypsy went off the map. The Fudges moved across the county to become sharecroppers. Ed's sister, Betty, was the mother of Bennie Lee Rainey who ran a country store in the Ephesus community and was an elder in the Ephesus Church of Christ. Since he was a cousin to the Fudge children, his wife Fanny was known as "Cousin Fanny," though for some reason her husband was not called "cousin"—he was simply "Bennie Lee Rainey" to them and to everyone else.

Bennie Lee Fudge and his siblings grew up in typical sharecropper's unpainted clap-board houses; though theirs were not typical in some ways because wherever they lived their mother kept the house and children as clean as possible. She taught her children early in life that "Just 'cause we're poor we don't have to smell like it 'long as there's soap an' water!" There were cracks in the floors and when she mopped, as she did regularly, she used plenty of water from the well and didn't have to worry about sopping it up—it ran out the cracks. When she swept after meals the crumbs from the table fell between the cracks and the chickens scratched around on the ground under the floor eating them. By the time I met them, however, there was linoleum on the floors.

At one of the churches where Bennie Lee preached after we married, we were invited to Sunday dinner at the home of one of the elders. Our host asked me, "Would you like to hear how I first met this man?" Of course I said, "Yes!"

"Well, it was dead of winter," he began, "even the ground was frozen hard. I was driving down the road in my wagon. Up ahead of me I saw someone crouched in the road picking something up, so I stopped to see what was going on. It was a teenage boy in ragged overalls and holes in his jacket and he was picking up grains of corn off the frozen ground with his bare hands and putting them into the bag he had by him. So I asked him why he was taking time to pick up the grains when he still had most of the sack full. He said that sack of corn was the last they had and he wasn't going to waste any on the ground. He said he was on his way to the mill to have it ground and while he was walking with the bag on his shoulder the corner came loose and corn ran out so he stopped to pick it up.

"Then I said to him, 'Don't you know your fingers are gonna freeze?' and Bennie Lee said to me, 'But I have to save all the corn.' So I got down there and helped him. While we picked up corn I asked him, 'Do you live around here? Haven't seen you at church.' And he answered me that he wanted to go, but he didn't have clothes fit to wear to church. And I said to him, 'You have clothes on now; they're plenty good enough. Don't you know the Lord looks at your heart, not your clothes?' Then I had him to get up in the wagon and we went to the mill to get his corn ground. And pretty soon the whole family started coming to church. And pretty soon Bennie Lee was preaching for us."

Bennie Lee told me the rest of the story—he took his sack of meal home and told his mother about the kind man, and said, "I want us to go to church like we used to." His mother promised to make sure the best clothes they had were patched and clean and the family began attending Jennings Chapel, where the kind man was an elder. From then on he was a great encourager of Bennie Lee's in his preaching and in the school work. At the time I met them the elder's youngest children were attending the Bible School and later graduated there.

As Bennie Lee worked the crops in those earlier days he was "studying to preach" and during the spring plowing seasons he practiced sermons on the mules as he plowed. Neighbors spoke of hearing him when they passed by the field where he was plowing and preaching. While he worked in the fields, Bennie Lee kept his Bible on a stump at the edge of the field so that when the mules needed to rest he could read it. When he began preaching at eighteen he wore his best overalls. In the country many of the men wore overalls to church and were still doing so when I first arrived there ten years later, though by then Bennie Lee and most preachers wore suits. When the Fudge family moved to the Ephesus community to share-crop they attended the Ephesus Church of Christ and the younger children grew up attending there.

Susie had only gone to school through the third grade but she was determined to learn more. As Bennie Lee went to school she studied with him through every grade. Together they made short work of his school books then they spent hours reading the Bible and Webster's Dictionary. Bennie Lee had a photographic memory and his mother must have been not far behind him. Through the years Susie became proficient in arithmetic and an avid reader of books on many subjects as the children brought them from the school libraries for her. When I met her she was enjoying the Nancy Drew series and her children made sure she was kept supplied.

From the time Bennie Lee's father became disabled Bennie Lee was in charge of raising the crops for the landowner. All of the children worked in the fields and helped Susie raise a big garden but he and his mother made sure all the children went to school regularly. Because his work with the crops conflicted with school he went for a week at the first of the school year, explained to his teacher that he would be out a lot and asked for books and assignments. She told him what they would cover before the first test and said she would send word by one of his family before major tests. He studied at home at night, worked crops in the daytime and went to school only to take the tests and the final exam at the end of the year. He finished high school at twenty-one as Salutatorian—"beat by a girl" as he expressed it to me. When he finished his second year at David Lipscomb College and again when he graduated from Abilene Christian College, it was the same story. He said, "I guess I was destined to always be second to a girl!" I assured him he was "Number One" with me and he replied, "And that's what really matters to me!"

The next son in the Fudge family was Roy, six years younger than Bennie Lee. When Bennie Lee finished high school he worked the crops long enough to let Roy finish high school, then they worked out a plan where they alternated going to college—Bennie Lee to David Lipscomb College in Nashville, Tennessee and Roy to Dasher Bible School in Valdosta, Georgia. When Bennie Lee was twenty-seven years old he transferred to Abilene Christian College for two years where our paths converged in our junior and senior years.

The Fudges owned a cow that kept them supplied with milk and butter. A favorite supper was leftover cornbread from the midday meal crumbled into buttermilk—new to me but I liked buttermilk and cornbread so why not together? In my family we had grown up on "bread-and-milk" but in our case it was light bread and sweet milk.

In the winters of the early days before I knew them, the Fudge kitchen was warmed from the cook stove and the rest of the house was cold. By the time I met them they had a Warm Morning Heater in the combination living room/bedroom that kept that room reasonably warm. The kitchen stove warmed the kitchen, but the rest of the house was very cold. When they could afford it they bought coal and to supplement that supply, members of the family took turns walking along the nearby railroad tracks with a bucket or bag, picking up the stray pieces of coal that fell off the regular coal trains that ran by. Bennie Lee told me of his and Roy's bedroom in the attic and waking up on snowy mornings to shake the snow off of their cover before getting up. He said because it was too cold up there for the snow to melt it actually helped keep them warm from the cold wind coming through the cracks.

Later when we spent the night there in winter with our babies, Edward and Henry, we put them in the middle of our double bed (not in the attic!)

with one of us on each side, to keep them warm, along with the baby's bottle of formula for the midnight or early morning feeding.

Bennie Lee's mother was fifty years old when I met her. She had a lovely grandmotherly face and hip-length snowy white hair done up in a bun on top of her head. She was a little shorter than I was. She was welcoming and friendly but I could tell she felt strange having a foreigner as a daughter-in-law, especially one who didn't talk plain English. She made wonderful biscuits for breakfast every morning—one per person—I could have eaten more along with her delicious pear preserves that were made from pears that grew in their yard. Every year she dried peaches and apples from their two trees and during the winter often made fried pies for dessert at mid-day dinner. I had never eaten anything quite like them and I wanted to learn how. She showed me how she did it but mine were never as good as hers.

The two youngest boys, Curtis (9th grade) and Clarence (7th grade) were still at home and rode the school bus to the new Bible School. Next in age to Bennie Lee was Edith, at that time a nanny in the home of a judge in Athens. The next, Leacy lived in Nashville, Tennessee, married to Philip Copeland who was in the navy. Roy was next and then Irma, who were both attending Dasher Bible School in Valdosta, Georgia. Lucy was in secretarial school in Nashville. Bennie Lee's siblings called him "Bubba," all their lives—a common name for the oldest son in a family.

During one of our early visits, Clarence (13) did something his mother strongly disapproved of and she was about to give him a switching. I had seen what happened and thought it was not his fault so I interceded on his behalf as tactfully as I knew how and she relented. Many times during the following years he reminded me of that and we had a special bond beginning with that incident.

**Nurse, Housekeeper, Cook, Nanny** When we first arrived in Athens, Otha Lowe Lee, Irven's wife, was in the hospital recovering from a miscarriage with complications. The doctor said she could go home if there was someone to care for her for several weeks. Bennie Lee and I did not yet have a home and Irven suggested that we stay with them where I could care for Otha Lowe and their girls, Judy (5), and Sandra (3).

At first Otha Lowe was too weak to even raise her head. I was nurse, housekeeper, cook, laundress and nanny. I had a busy schedule every day, seven days a week. Cooking was easy because folks where Bennie Lee and Irven were preaching invited them to their homes for the noon and evening meals and often sent food from those meals home with them. Washing and ironing were a different matter. It was summer with no air conditioners; the men were preaching morning and evening and each needed two white shirts a day. Weekly laundry included twenty-eight white shirts, besides Judy and Sandra's little cotton dresses with puffed sleeves and ruffles, and daily linens for the invalid's bed, along with the usual household laundry. Bennie Lee had a cotton cord summer suit that was cool for him in the hot weather. He wore it often and it had to be washed and ironed often—a labor of love.

During those weeks there was hardly a day that the men didn't bring in fresh produce given to them by members of the churches where they were preaching. When Otha Lowe grew stronger, we spent many hours chatting as we snapped beans, shelled peas, cut up okra, peeled peaches and apples. The supply was often more than we could eat and I learned to use their pressure cooker for canning. I learned about many new things to eat, among them poke sallat (pronounced like that, perhaps not spelled like that!) It consisted of greens picked very young from the top growth of a weed that grew in barn lots in early spring and required a lot of washing. It was par-boiled and that water, said to be poisonous, was poured out and the drained greens were cooked in an iron skillet until most of the liquid had boiled away. Then three or four eggs were scrambled in the greens. It was good to me—but I liked spinach! I learned to fry okra and green tomatoes, several kinds of squash and other things that were strange to me—not the vegetable but the way of cooking.

Judy and Sandra were well behaved little girls and played well together most of the time, playing dolls, coloring with crayons, with occasional actions typical of their ages. They liked for me to read to them and we grew close during the eight weeks I was there.

I still "talked funny" and I was still a stranger and an outsider to the close-knit country families of north Alabama, where everyone had known everyone else all their lives. In spite of that, wherever Bennie Lee preached and I was able to go with him, folks could not have been more welcoming.

By the end of eight weeks Otha Lowe was ready to resume her role as mother and homemaker and we moved to Rogersville where Bennie Lee was already preaching every Sunday.

**Preachers** Bennie Lee was well known in the county where he had been preaching for different congregations since 1932—in summer meetings and monthly circuit-preaching. It was his practice from the beginning of his preaching to memorize the scriptures he used in his sermons but he did not depend on his phenomenal memory. As he prepared a sermon and memorized the verses he planned to use, he marked the places in his Bible with little pieces of paper that stuck out at the top to turn to as he referred to each one. He felt strongly that his audience should see that he was reading out of the Bible; his memorizing was for his own benefit in learning the Bible.

As a result through the years as long as he lived, he was ready and able at a moment's notice to preach a sermon any time anywhere he was called on. I saw it happen many times that a scheduled preacher was prevented from appearing and in the moments of apparent panic among the leaders of the congregation over what to do, he would tell one of them that he would preach if they wanted him to. Soon his reputation was established; instead of panic in such a situation, if Bennie Lee was in the audience, the leader of the congregation quietly asked him if he would fill in. In the same way he could teach a Bible class on any given subject from the Bible without prior notice. He was not a song leader, however. [I jump ahead to say that our sons and son-in-law are able to do that same type of filling in and in their cases to lead singing also.]

In addition to preaching in North Alabama, Louisiana and Oklahoma, Bennie Lee had preached in meetings in rural East Tennessee and South

Carolina where country churches and people in general were even more isolated than they were in North Alabama. But primitive conditions and unconventional people were not the only challenges endured by young preachers. Baptisms could also be hazardous.

**Baptisms** In the early days, almost no country church had a baptistery. Baptisms were done in the nearest creek, river or pond, immediately after a person expressed the desire. If it was after a day-time service the congregation walked to the water to carry out the baptizing. If after an evening service the congregation walked with the candidate(s) and carried lanterns from the church to hold near the water. If some had cars they drove them to the bank as near as possible to shine the car lights on the water.

Bennie Lee told of occasions when there was ice on the water that was broken and hand-scraped away to make an opening for the preacher and candidate. He told of other times at night when it was known that water moccasins were prevalent, men went into the water to form a circle around the preacher and candidate, the men facing outward so they could see any snake approaching and chase it away.

"Baptismal garments" were unknown. A person planning such a move when he/she left home took a change of clothes along. If the action was spontaneous the candidate was baptized in whatever he/she had on and went home wet in summer; in winter a coat was put on over wet clothes. By 1943 many of the churches had baptisteries. Ones that didn't sometimes went to a neighboring church, either a church of Christ or a Baptist church, and borrowed theirs. If one or the other's building burned or was blown away by a tornado, they shared the remaining building, one congregation meeting in the morning and the other in the afternoon until a new one was built. Most buildings were small and tent meetings were popular for summer revivals—they held more people and were cooler. Benches were taken to the tent out of whichever church was holding the revival and people from all nearby churches regardless of denomination, usually attended.

Conditions for preachers had improved considerably by the time Bennie Lee began recruiting teachers/preachers for the new school, most of whom were from our graduating class at Abilene Christian College. These preachers could serve a congregation for their main income and donate their time to the school until the school could afford to pay them. Any one of those preacher/teachers could have gone from college to work in other jobs where they would have been paid many times over what they would get in this situation but they and their wives were sold on the ideal of Christian education for children of all ages and brought vigorous enthusiasm and energy with them.

Bennie Lee personally knew these available preachers, he knew the people in the country churches and he introduced each to the place he thought was most suitable. With that introduction they made their own decisions after a trial sermon or two. Bennie Lee, thereafter, was teasingly called the "bishop of Limestone County" by those preachers/teachers. In addition to the money they were paid for preaching, they were generously blessed with garden produce from the home-gardens of church members besides sharing lavish Sunday dinners.

One of the couples was Charles and Mildred Chumley with baby Judy. Charles had already proved himself an exceptionally talented and capable preacher and radio announcer, but he gave up some lucrative prospects in order to work with the school for several years. Years later he told of an earlier conversation regarding the school that he had had with a prominent preacher from another state who knew him well. Charles remembered their question and answer session:

"How much money do you have?"—"None."

"What kind of building do you have?"—"Just an old two-story residence."

"How much tuition are you going to charge?"—"A dollar a week per student for those who can afford it."

"How much are you going to pay your faculty?"—"One hundred fifty dollars a month, most of it earned by preaching in the county, the difference to be made up by the school at the end of the month."

"That's impossible. The whole idea is completely unrealistic. It can't be done!"

Charles said the only trouble with that brother's assessment was that the people starting the school didn't know that it was impossible—they believed in the dream and were enjoying themselves. [As I write this in 2011, that school is still operating K-12 in Athens, Alabama, having served thousands of students during its sixty-eight years of existence.]

**Rogersville 1943-1947** Rogersville in Lauderdale County west of Limestone County and about nineteen miles from Athens became our first home. The church in Rogersville, membership at that time around 150, was looking for a preacher. Bennie Lee "tried out" there and was hired—at $150 per month. Many smaller congregations did not hire full-time preachers and Bennie Lee was not the only one of the men from the school who circulated among smaller churches in addition to their regular places. Four sermons and two adult Bible classes per Sunday was usual along with two or three mid-week evening Bible classes.

For several months Bennie Lee preached four or five times on Sundays: 10 o'clock at Oliver (six miles east of Rogersville); 11 o'clock at Rogersville; 2 o'clock at Killen (16 miles west of Rogersville); 4 o'clock at Elgin (9 miles east of Killen); then back to Rogersville for evening service at 6:30. Midweek Bible classes were Wednesday evening at Rogersville, Tuesday and Thursday evenings at country churches in the county.

The Bible School teacher/preachers at these extra places were paid whatever was in the collection plate that Sunday, ranging from $2.00 to $10.00. Wherever he preached, Bennie Lee urged the churches to send money to missionaries, locally, nationally and abroad and when it was time for announcements, he read from letters and reports of missionaries in various parts of the world. Many times I heard him say, "The brethren will do more when they know more," and they did. As they did, their Sunday contributions grew also—the more they gave the more they were able to give.

**Church Contribution** When we married, Bennie Lee and I resolved to deposit his pay check in the bank plus whatever uncommitted amounts had been given to him by the extra churches he served, along with any money I might earn. We agreed to give at least 15% "off the top" to the church. Bennie Lee's reasoning, that I agreed with, was that since God required the people in the Old Testament to give a tenth, surely, because of what God did for us in giving His Son to die for our sins, our gratitude to Him would make us want to give more. The first checks we wrote for the month were to the church, one for each Sunday of the month to be put in the collection each week. After that came our monthly bills, then it was up to us to "make do" as best we could with any left over. Sometimes when an emergency arose, we were forced to ask someone to hold a check until the next payday or to ask for credit at the grocery store where it was readily granted. Quite often the extra churches Bennie Lee served handed him more than usual because the contribution was more that Sunday, or we received a gift and were able to catch up.

I was glad to find out that Bennie Lee and I agreed that the amount given to the Lord should be mutually decided by husband and wife and the children should be taught to give out of their allowances. We agreed that contribution should be given without attracting attention. My parents had taught us to put our piece(s) of money in the basket very quietly so as not to attract attention. Daddy believed all citizens of a country should pay required taxes and he paid all Rhodesian taxes, but at that time missionaries were not required to pay income taxes there or in the U.S. When I.R.S. laws changed Daddy began writing checks to have a record for the I.R.S.

When Bennie Lee and I married, we filed and paid Income Tax and I understood the need for writing checks to the church. Some years later we were audited because our claim for Contribution was more than the national average and I was glad we could produce the cancelled checks. As far as I was concerned it was still a private matter between us and God and I cringed at the idea of it being known by the church treasurer, our tax preparer and the I.R.S.

We had no car and volunteers out of the Rogersville church provided transportation to the extra churches. Mannon and Mittie Mae Pate were regular transporters and those Sunday rides with them were enjoyable and enriching. He was a CPA, she taught school and their two young daughters were in middle school. In their forties they seemed elderly to me. Mittie Mae was a poised and gracious lady, wise in manner and speech, a living example of what I hoped to become.

**First Home** Our first home was a furnished apartment across the street behind the church building, two rooms in one side of the McMeans' home. I don't recall her given name but his was Codie and he was a mailman with a country route. He owned coon dogs, summoned them with a horn and enjoyed coon-hunting. Some of Edward's earliest words when he heard the horn were, "Means blow horn!" The McMeans were in their fifties, generous and kind and she was like a mother to me.

Our rent was $15 per month plus half the utilities. We shared a shower-only bathroom and a refrigerator on the back porch. The front room was our bedroom with a coal burning fireplace. A tiny hallway, once a closet, joined our two rooms with a curtain dividing it into a passage way on one side and a curtained closet on the other. We hung our clothes in half of that curtained off space, the other half was taken up with a stack of orange crates that was our linen closet. In the kitchen a "monkey stove" heated the room in the winter better than the built-in fireplace. It was a small pot-belly stove on four legs with a flat top. A lid on its one eye was lifted to put coal in. Its stovepipe went up from the stove-top with a right-angled turn taking it into a hole in the chimney wall. In the winter a teakettle full of water sat on the stove to add humidity and in the summer a vase of fresh flowers from the garden took its place.

I had to learn how to cook on an oil burning cook-stove with four burners, two for regular cooking and two under the removable oven. I remember the first biscuits I made there—their failure not the stove's fault.

All oven-ware given to us in showers was Pyrex because the war was going on and metal was being used to build ships and airplanes. I didn't know you could put a Pyrex (glass) baking dish into a hot oven. I was proud of the light-feeling biscuit dough that I rolled out. I carefully laid the biscuits in the greased Pyrex baking dish and put it in the cold oven, then lighted the burners. By the time the biscuits browned they had been in there so long they were too hard to cut with a knife much less to bite with our teeth. Bennie Lee teasingly said not to worry they would make good ammunition for rabbit hunting!

We found a second-hand old fashioned cabinet for $6 that was a marvel of utility. It had two separate tin-lined bins that tilted out from the base for easy reach; one held about twenty-five pounds of flour and the other ten pounds of sugar; above the sugar bin was a flat-ware drawer. Over them at waist height was a heavy enameled shelf that pulled out for work space. When not in use it could be pushed back out of the way with only about twelve inches still showing for smaller workspace. Over that was a bread shelf with sliding door, and shelves for dishes and condiments. Pots and pans were in the pantry.

Instead of a sink we had a small table with rickety legs that held the water bucket and dishpan. We brought water in the bucket from the back porch faucet and kept a dipper in the bucket. We didn't drink from the dipper (though many country folks drank from theirs). The pantry was a small closet with three stacks of empty orange crates for shelves. Our friendly grocer freely gave the crates to anyone who asked for them. One touch of luxury was the small square dining table with two chairs in the center of the room. It had a leaf for extension and when we had company for meals we borrowed more chairs from our landlady.

Mrs. McMeans had a cow in their two or three acre back pasture and when the cow gave enough she sold raw milk to the neighbors. We bought a quart of milk every other day when she had it. Wild onions grew prolifically in pastures and sometimes the milk tasted horribly oniony. When it did I preferred to use canned evaporated milk, but Bennie Lee said the onion flavor didn't bother him. He still weighed 128 pounds and I thought of a way to help him gain weight. I skimmed the cream off the top of our quart of milk and saved it up until there was enough to make a special banana pudding just for him. I whipped the cream, added sugar and vanilla and layered the mixture alternately with vanilla wafers and sliced bananas. He thoroughly enjoyed the treat but didn't gain any weight—I didn't eat any of it but gained weight!

On washday I brought our round washtub into the kitchen, set it on two chairs, carried clean water in the bucket from the back porch and washed all the clothes by hand. I wrung them by hand and put them in a pan while I carried the dirty water in a different bucket from the tub to the back yard, then refilled the tub with rinse water. I hung clothes on the clothesline in the back yard unless it was raining, in which case I hung them on a line that zig-zagged back and forth in the kitchen. In very cold weather I took my bath in the washtub beside the little heater in the kitchen instead of taking a shower in the very cold bathroom on the back porch. Bennie Lee said he enjoyed the invigorating cold.

Before he went to Abilene Christian College, Bennie Lee had preached often for the church at Tanner, south of Athens. When he brought his bride to Limestone County the ladies there gave us a shower (while we were living with the Lees). What they gave us, along with what had been given to us in Abilene, supplied us with all we needed for housekeeping. In fact, we were given so many sets of pillow cases and so many sheets and towels that I used some of them for local bridal gifts knowing that the givers lived far away. It was ten years before any of our linens began to wear out. The Rogersville folks gave us a "pounding," the old term for a grocery shower, our pantry was well stocked with flour, sugar, meal—all the way down to salt, baking soda, baking powder and spices besides home canned vegetables and fruit.

**North Alabama Bible School** (as it was known for the first several years) was about ready to begin, but they were short a teacher. Bennie Lee wanted me to take that position and I said absolutely not. I had planned on being a nurse but never in all my imagining did I aspire to being a teacher. He was getting desperate and when Bennie Lee was determined to get someone to do something, that someone might as well do it because he would not take no for an answer. He knew how to make that someone *want* to do it and feel good about it—well, almost good. So I found myself, two days before school started, looking through text books wondering how I could teach Seventh Grade Science and English, Eighth Grade Science and English and Eleventh Grade English Grammar.

I know I studied harder every night that semester than any student in my classes. My Seventh Graders were good kids except for one mischievous disrupter, but he was so adorably cute it was hard to be too hard on him. The Eighth Graders were pets—I could not have asked for better cooperation and participation. The Eleventh Graders were a pleasure and a pain—especially one of them who constantly made remarks to make the others laugh, seemingly trying to prove that no greenhorn teacher near his own age could teach him anything.

[One day about eight years later, a strange car turned into our driveway in Athens. A man I didn't recognize got out with a large bag of oranges and grapefruit. I met him at the door and he asked, "Do you remember me?" When he saw that I wasn't sure, he said, "I'm J. W. Andrews. You taught me Eleventh Grade English the first year of the Bible School and I gave you a hard time. I'm ashamed of how I behaved and I've come with a peace offering. Please forgive me!" He was living in Florida and had been married and preaching for several years.]

**Dean Fudge** Telling of the beginning and early years of the Bible school could take up a whole book. The school's board of directors had been chosen and appointed by Bennie Lee, Irven and Jack, and in turn the board appointed Irven Lee, *President*; Jack Rollings, *Vice President*; and Bennie Lee, *Dean*. That arrangement was made after the three men mutually and privately evaluated their own various abilities, and informed the board members! They divided the work among themselves and made all major decisions unanimously. The board was glad to leave the hiring and firing of teachers and day-to-day routine to them, giving them moral support and advice. As different as Bennie Lee, Irven and Jack were in personality, three men could not have been more firmly united in principles and goals, nor have had more profound admiration and respect for each other than they did. When they differed on a subject they had heart-to-heart discussions, each willing to look at the question from all angles to reach a unanimous decision and present a united front vital to the running of the school.

The school was approved for accreditation in February, 1944, while I was still teaching. The day the examiners came to spend time in each class room, I was scared so badly that I didn't trust myself to do anything except ask questions of my pupils and they rose to the occasion. After all classes had been visited, the examiners told the three administrators that they were very impressed with the quality of the teaching that was being done. They said they thought the one lady teacher in particular was doing an exceptional job. They said "Mrs. Fudge evokes class participation and responses from her pupils that show they are interested and involved in what they are learning," and added, "We can tell that all you men teachers are used to being in your pulpits; you lecture your classes too much!" Needless to say my sagging confidence was upped several notches when Bennie Lee told me that.

As Dean, Bennie Lee handled the day by day administration and discipline, where his understanding of the young people, his knowledge of their families and backgrounds, and his sense of humor, stood him in good stead. He knew when to make a big deal of an incident and when not to. He had his own way of handling offenders, suiting the punishment to the deed and personality of the child.

Since Bennie Lee had never learned to drive, a twelfth grade boy drove the bus that Bennie Lee rode as overseer. Two tenth grade boys, much bigger and stronger than he, rode the bus and were usually respectful.

Bennie Lee wore a white shirt and tie every day, rotating the ties from his limited supply. On the way to school one day one of the boys told him they were tired of the tie he was wearing and while the two big boys pinned Bennie Lee's arms to his side, another boy cut his tie off about half way down. Bennie Lee just let them, without struggling or saying a word. The other students on the bus watched, wondering. As the students exited the bus at school Bennie Lee told the three boys to wait. When they were alone he said, "I don't blame you for being tired of that tie; I was tired of it, too. So I'll be looking forward to seeing what tie you buy for me at lunch time today." During lunch time they got permission to go to town and bought him a new tie.

When a student misbehaved and was sent to his office, he greeted the student politely and had him/her sit in the chair across the desk from him. Then as the student squirmed and fidgeted, Bennie Lee went on with his work. After a while, without looking up, he asked quietly, "What are you here for?" The student told what he/she had done and Bennie Lee inquired, "What do you think should to be done to help you remember not to do that again?" One boy said, "I guess six licks with the paddle will do it." Another said, "Having to come in here is enough to make me remember!" Many of them pleaded, "Give me a paddling, but *please* don't tell my daddy I had to come to you!" Those were old fashioned days when parents expected their children to behave at home and at school.

Punishments varied: one might be to scrape chewing gum off the bottoms of chairs in the auditorium, or pick up papers around the grounds, or write fifty or a hundred times on the blackboard a sentence that suited the crime. The worst repeat offender might be given six licks with the paddle as a last resort. Discipline might be for chewing gum in class, or "sassing" a teacher, sneaking out of an upstairs classroom window to slide down the roof, or shooting spit balls with a rubber band, or going to town without permission. Cheating was much more serious and received the most severe punishment.

Bennie Lee's ride to school left home at 6 a.m. and wound through the west side of Limestone County covering about thirty miles as it picked up about 20 pupils. For this route an old rolling store was turned into a "bus" by removing the shelves and fastening benches along the windowless sides. The students named it "The Chicken Coop."

I didn't have to leave until 6:45 a.m. My route was more direct to pick up fewer students who lived along U.S. Highway 72. I drove a dark green pickup truck that had a cab fitted with benches. It was called "The Green Hornet." There was no cafeteria at the school—everyone carried a sack lunch every day. Each morning I made two bologna sandwiches and two peanut butter/grape or apple jelly sandwiches—the least expensive meat and jelly available. If bologna was scarce we had Spam. When we occasionally had scrambled eggs for breakfast I made sandwiches for lunch from leftover eggs. During the next several years the school gradually acquired real school buses and a cafeteria.

**Sunday Dinner** Among the people we knew almost no one "ate out," certainly not families with several children. Sunday dinner was an important event in family life and almost every Sunday, as a matter of course, the preacher and his wife and family were invited to share the meal with a different church family. We made some wonderful friends over Sunday dinners.

Electricity had not yet reached much of the county. In some country households water from the well kept milk and butter cool, other homes had a screened box in the nearby spring-house. Country folk were early risers and Sunday dinner was cooked early in the morning and left on the back of the wood-burning stove to stay warm until after church. Cakes and pies were usually made on Saturday. Windows and doors had screens but flies got in, and during every meal a battle went on to keep flies shooed off the food while we ate. Where flies were especially bad, the older children took turns standing in the dining area and waving a small willow branch back and forth over the dining table as the grown ups ate. Nearly all country homes had big kitchens where the eating was done. When the grown ups had eaten, children were fed unless there was a side table where they could eat at the same time. Of course babies and small children were fed first.

After the meal the hostess and helpers washed and dried the dishes and reset the table, then an extra tablecloth was spread over the top of food and clean plates. Before leaving for evening service anyone who wanted "supper" could remove the cloth and eat leftovers. In the winter, bowls of vegetables and meat were put back in the "warming oven" of the stove after dinner, where they stayed until supper time; salads remained on the table. Tea and lemonade were cooled at the spring or in closed jars put in the bucket and let down into the well.

**Aprons** I always offered to help the lady of the house in the kitchen. The first thing she did was to hand me an apron as she put one on herself to keep our Sunday dresses clean, ready to wear to church that evening. I had been raised with aprons and knew how to make and wear them. My father's mother, Grandma Short, wore bibbed aprons with the lower part gathered on to a band that tied like a sash in the back. Everyday or work aprons were made of gingham or other cotton plain or print material. Sunday aprons or "company aprons" were usually solid broadcloth or linen with embroidery on them and often had wide, fine crocheted edges, ruffles or additions at the bottom. Among my keepsakes is an apron that was my Grandma Short's Sunday apron and I treasure some that my mother wore. All the time my children were growing up I wore an apron at home every Sunday. When we had company for a meal my apron was color-coordinated with the dress I was wearing.

Pretty aprons made ideal gifts. I wonder if many kids now know what an apron is, unless it is a butcher's or baker's apron, but in the old days they were a necessary part of a woman's wardrobe. There were bibbed aprons that covered almost the entire front of the dress to protect it as the lady did her housework; some had a strap to hang over the neck from the bib and ties fastening the gathered waist; some looked more like a jumper covering all the front with wide straps crossing in the back; others were only from the waist down and gathered on a sash to tie at the back. Bennie Lee's mother wore an apron every day and this description of grandma's apron sounds just like hers:

170

*Grandma's apron was to protect the dress underneath, a potholder for removing hot pans from the oven, wonderful for drying children's tears, and on occasion was even used for cleaning out dirty ears. The apron was used for carrying eggs from the chicken coop, or to bring in fussy chicks, or half-hatched eggs to be finished in the warming oven. When company came those aprons were hiding places for shy kids; Aprons wiped many a perspiring brow bent over the hot wood stove and when the weather was cold, grandma wrapped it around her arms. Chips and kindling wood were brought into the kitchen in that apron; from the garden it carried in vegetables, then carried out the hulls and shells. It was used to bring in apples in the fall. When company drove up the road, it was surprising how much furniture that apron could dust in a few seconds. When dinner was ready, Grandma waved her apron from the porch and the men in the field knew it was time to eat. It will be a long time before someone invents something as useful as that old-time apron. -Author Unknown*

**First Dinner Guests** Our limited budget and small apartment didn't keep us from having company. Thanks to generous country folks where Bennie Lee preached, our larder was usually well supplied with fresh produce and home-canned goods. Wayne Mickey and wife Callie were our very first dinner guests. We knew each other from college where Callie was one of my best friends and Wayne was one of the "preacher boys" in my Bible major class and Bennie Lee had known both of them.

I was excited about setting a pretty table and for the first time using china the ladies had given us in Texas. It was winter and flower beds were bare so for a center piece I picked a few wild miniature daisies from the pasture out back and put them in a pair of little porcelain wedding present vases. When we sat down to eat, Wayne looked at the table and said,

"That's the first time I ever saw *weeds* used for flowers." From then on every time I looked at those little vases I thought about weeds!

**Extra Curricular Activities** Bennie Lee found a willing teacher from Texas, Loveta Fulfer, also a college friend of ours. She moved to Athens the end of February and to my relief, took over my job as teacher in the school. I was further relieved when a grown man from Rogersville wanted to take Bible classes at the school and drove the "Green Hornet" route.

Church people in the area served by the preacher/teachers sent their news to Bennie Lee and he edited a mimeographed weekly church news bulletin. He distributed it by mail to all the churches who asked for it. Included in each issue, besides news from those churches, was a report or letter from some missionary either in the U.S. or in a foreign country. Bennie Lee asked me to cut the stencils, operate the mimeograph machine and do the addressing. My willingness was not in question but after only a semester of typing in college, my typing speed was slow and cutting stencils and operating the mimeograph machine were skills to be learned. I was thankful when Loveta occasionally volunteered to do some of the typing for me. The mimeograph machine was the easy part—when it behaved. I addressed them by hand.

Most of that work was done after school on Fridays, sometimes spilling over into Saturday morning. As a rule I rode the bus from Rogersville on Friday afternoon then Bennie Lee and I took either the late evening bus home on Friday or a noon bus on Saturday. From the school and from home the bus stations were about a mile away and we walked it in every kind of weather. The teachers and their wives were like one big family and times together were good for serious discussions as well as for fun. Bennie Lee and I had standing invitations to spend Friday nights with all of them and if we didn't have a pressing need to be in Rogersville early on Saturday, we spent enjoyable times in their homes and in homes of other close friends in Athens.

One memorable Friday evening we were to spend the night with Charles and Mildred Chumley who lived in Tanner, about ten miles south of Athens, where he preached, and from where he drove another ancient oddity full of students to school. This vehicle was called "The Cracker Box;" a van of sorts with benches for seats but it did have windows. We took the Greyhound bus to the Tanner crossroads, then walked about a mile to where they lived in one side of Miss Lily McKee's three story antebellum white clap-board farmhouse.

It was dark when we stepped off the bus into the face of an icy wind blowing hard out of the west. It was misting and almost at once the mist turned into fine sleet hitting us in the face. My coat was heavy enough, but it reached just a little below my knees and soon not only was my face freezing but my legs, too. Bennie Lee's overcoat was long and he told me to walk close up behind him where I would be shielded from the worst of the wind and sleet. I did and it helped. That was a long mile but then we were in the house, enjoying Mildred's delicious supper and being with good friends—the weather forgotten. [Thirty years later, April 1974, while the owners were at church, the upstairs of that old house was blown away by a tornado. An hour later the ground floor was clean-down-to-the-ground blown away by a second tornado.]

**Spend-the-night-guests** There were times when we hosted our own overnight guests. One such time Doyle Banta, J. C. Reed, former classmates from ACC, and my brother Foy, all as yet unmarried teachers at the Bible School, came for dinner and spent the night. When bedtime approached, one of them asked how we were going to manage beds. We decided the three men would have our bedroom with the double bed and we would open the daybed in the kitchen. That sounded good to them, it was cold and they would keep each other warm. I borrowed extra quilts from Mrs. McMeans and we settled down.

Doyle weighed about 300 lbs. so they agreed he should sleep in the middle with Foy on one side and J. C. on the other—that antique bed was stout! I think they had a miserable night in spite of the pile of quilts. By the time the cover went up over Doyle it barely reached to the sides of the bed over the other two. Every time Doyle moved it pulled the cover off of one or the other of them. The next morning they joked that when one wanted to turn over he had to wake the other two and give the word for all three to turn at the same time!

I had finally learned to use Pyrex with a hot oven and to my joy my fresh baked biscuits rounded out a good breakfast to cheer them on their way.

**Young People** Bennie Lee was a "people person" no matter the age. He was a master story teller and could keep little ones and older ones spellbound with stories. In fact, much of his preaching involved telling stories from the Bible. He felt that adult's and children's classes seemed to have better teachers as a rule and he was especially concerned with keeping teenagers interested, so he volunteered to teach them in most places. In our Rogersville work Friday evenings were designated Game Evenings for ages six through eleven and Saturday evenings for ages twelve through seventeen. Parents took turns volunteering their homes and supplying refreshments. It was new to the young folks and at first their parents had to make them attend, but soon they were bringing their friends from the community.

These young people had never played games nor played in groups like this outside of organized sports at school, and they enjoyed it. Bennie Lee had done no game-playing in his life so he asked me to be in charge. I taught them many of the games I played while growing up in Africa: *"Who? Sir, Me? Sir." "Poor Kitty"* and other "parlor games" indoors in bad weather; when the weather was good we played such outdoor group games as *"Kick the Can,"* and *"Drop the Handkerchief."* Our crowds increased and the attendance of young people grew at church, too, where they learned to read Scripture and lead singing in public.

**Baby Number One** Bennie Lee and I were excited beyond words when I became pregnant but we were not prepared for what followed. I had heard of morning sickness but I was sick all day—from the time I stepped out of bed until I lay down at night. I managed to keep doing all the regular things except eat—certainly not if I cooked it. I cooked supper for Bennie Lee but after a few bites I left him at the table and I went into the other room away from the smell of food. I could drink Nehi grape drink and eat soda crackers and I enjoyed a few bites of foods that I had not cooked.

In March, along with continual nausea, severe pain in my left lower back compelled me to go to a doctor in Athens (I remember his name but I won't call it!) He confirmed that I was pregnant and said the nausea was all in my head and the pain was just a passing thing. He told me to go home and take some aspirin. When I told Bennie Lee what the doctor had said he was so angry he wanted to go immediately and talk to him. Fortunately it was Friday afternoon and by then too late in the day.

Sunday afternoon went from bad to worse and after evening preaching, Bennie Lee returned to the apartment to find me fairly gasping with pain and burning with fever. I did not want to go back to the Athens doctor and Mrs. McMeans told us about Dr. Jackson and his clinic sixteen miles out in the country. She and her husband offered to take us there immediately. As we turned in at the clinic driveway the doctor was leaving but he turned around and came back; it was 10 o'clock and he assumed at that hour it was an emergency.

Dr. Jackson said I had a toxic kidney and was on the verge of a miscarriage. He took care of the emergency and kept me there three days then allowed me to go home with orders to "take it easy." Two days later I had to go back. After the third return trip he decided the only way to keep me from losing the baby was for me to lie flat on my back—no sitting up—no pillow—not even raising my head. The only place I could be cared for while doing that was in his clinic. One of the three patient rooms of his little clinic in the cotton fields of west Limestone County became my home for the next three and a half months.

Dr. Jackson's wife, Evelyn, and her sister, Marie, the clinic's R.N., and Bennie Lee had known each other in high school. It was almost like being with family. The clinic was usually a beehive of activity from early morning till late at night, as people heard about the doctor and came from near and far. Dr. Jackson had grown up in that area and seeing the need for a doctor, vowed to come back and start a clinic when he finished medical training. He was diagnostician, internist, surgeon and gynecologist, and he made house calls! Every year he went away for refresher courses to keep up with medical advances.

While I was there, three more regular rooms and a Delivery Room were added on and the waiting room enlarged. I saw many women rolled down the short hall past my room to the new Delivery Room and heard the first cries of their babies while waiting for mine to arrive. Visitors passing by looked into each room, sometimes stopping to chat whether they knew the patient or not. They asked each one, "What are *you* in for?" Return visitors usually said to me, "I see you're still here?" and often, "You don't *look* sick!" To which I sometimes replied, "I don't *feel* sick!" I didn't explain my reason for being there, only sometimes saying I had back trouble and other times, "I'm just having a rest!" When I said that, the visitor looked shocked and said, "I wish I could afford to lie up in bed like that for a rest!" Finally a nurse told the doctor she thought visitors were getting on my nerves and he said, "Put a NO VISITORS sign on her door and half close it during visiting hours." After that I didn't have to answer questions. My personal visitors knew to ignore the sign.

Doyle Banta was a conscientious hospital visitor and came at least once a week, always with a funny story to tell, after he caught me up on the latest news. It was 1944 and World War II was still raging. There were hopes that the war in Europe might end soon and that did happen on June 6th (D-Day) while I was still there. But fighting continued against the Japanese in the Pacific and daily news from there was grim.

In my flat position I could pass the time crocheting some and reading for short periods, so Bennie Lee kept me supplied with Readers Digests. During slack times nurses stopped by to chat and were soon confiding in me, asking advice about boy friends or other life problems. They called me their "mother confessor!" In strawberry season the nurses brought fresh strawberries with whipping cream to the clinic kitchen for their own nightly eleven o'clock snack. They gathered in my room to share the delicacy with me when they had time. After Doctor Jackson's final rounds about 10:00 p.m., he often stopped in to "sit a spell" and chat.

Bennie Lee was busy with school and church work but four afternoons a week he found someone to bring him to visit. On the Sundays that he did not have a preaching engagement in the afternoon, Rogersville friends brought him. One of those ladies had a spectacular flower garden and always brought a bouquet. I especially remember a huge bouquet of tulips that I enjoyed tremendously, almost changing my favorite flower from gladiola to tulip.

Foy lived and preached in Decatur and brought a load of children to the Bible School every day. The converted "bus" he drove was called "Noah's Ark" because of its odd shape. Occasionally he made arrangements for a substitute bus driver and came with Bennie Lee to see me, then spent the night with Bennie Lee in Rogersville. Meantime Bennie Lee knew he needed to get a car of some kind and learn to drive as soon as possible; and he kept his eyes open for something we could afford.

During that confinement I wanted to be patient but did not always succeed. Occasionally I felt sorry for myself and during one of those times I accused Bennie Lee of not coming enough. It hurt him and he tried to come more often. But when I found out there were people criticizing him for "neglecting" me I was angry at their false accusations and tried harder not to complain. He said those critics did not know the whole situation and their criticism helped "keep him on his toes." Whenever he came, Bennie Lee's visits were a pleasure that I never wanted to end—he was an ideal sick-room visitor with a way of cheering patients no matter how low they felt.

**Edward William Fudge** entered the world **July 13, 1944.** He weighed five pounds, had no hair, or eyelashes, or fingernails or toenails, otherwise he was a perfect specimen. He was officially due September 9 but in early July Dr. Jackson was concerned that the prolonged bed-rest might be harmful to the baby and/or to me and said he wanted to induce labor. Bennie Lee and I agreed and it was tried, but after twelve hours of hard labor nothing happened and I was given a sedative. Fearing the hours of labor could be dangerous for the baby, Dr. Jackson then performed a C-section.

While I was coming out from under the ether Bennie Lee was sitting beside me. My upper right shoulder was itching unbearably and I groggily asked Bennie Lee to "Please scratch my back." He asked, "Where?" and I replied, "Up in the Amen Corner where Brother Pate sits on Sunday morning!" He knew exactly where to scratch my back because in the church building at Rogersville there were two short pews on each side of the pulpit platform where the main leaders of the church sat. It was called the "Amen Corner" and Brother Pate always sat on the right side nearest the pulpit!

When it was time to take the stitches out it was late July and I had perspired freely during the hot days. The incision was all the way down my abdomen; adhesive tape covered the dressing from center back around my body and met again in the back—solid. Now I was turned on my side and with both hands the doctor took hold of the whole width of tape ends in the back and quickly pulled it up and toward the front—and I "whooped!" Then from the other side the same thing, and I gave another more intense "whoop!" Under all that tape I had broken out with heat rash and taking the tape off peeled the top off all the rash—I was raw from front to back. The doctor removed the stitches then produced the Merthiolate bottle and I cringed at the sight. He said apologetically, "Now this is going to sting a little but we must put it on to prevent infection." I questioned his "sting a little" as he painted my whole midsection front and back with Merthiolate and I behaved more like a bucking bronco than a patient!

Patients were kept in the hospital fourteen days after major surgery and only allowed to walk around after stitches were removed the ninth day. During the first week I enjoyed holding Edward every day but he was not eating much nor gaining weight—he was actually losing weight. The doctor said he was having muscle spasms of the stomach—not unusual in adults and there was medication for it, but nothing that he had been able to find for an infant so young. When Edward was three weeks old he weighed three pounds and the doctor told Bennie Lee that he would die if he didn't find something to help immediately. He asked permission to try using the adult medication in a dose relative to the baby's weight. Of course Bennie Lee and I agreed at once and a tiny amount was diluted and given to Edward.

All that night Bennie Lee sat beside my bed praying, at times out loud and at times silently if he thought I was asleep. He pleaded with the Lord to spare our son, promising that we would do everything in our power to raise him to be a dedicated servant of God; that regardless of outcome asking that He would help us to be strong and faithful. By early morning the tiny stomach muscles had relaxed and Edward began retaining formula. In a few days he was taking regular feedings and gaining weight. When he was four weeks old Dr. Jackson told me to go home to regain my own strength. He said that just as soon as Edward weighed six pounds we could take him home. School was out for the summer and Foy let us keep his car temporarily so we could visit Edward every afternoon. When he was six weeks old he weighed six pounds and we carried him home. Bennie Lee's sister, Edith, came to help me for two weeks. We proudly took Edward to church on his first Sunday out of the hospital.

When Edward was eight weeks old Bennie Lee went to preach in a meeting out of state. Charles and Mildred Chumley were living in Athens then and invited me to stay with them while Bennie Lee was gone. Their son Buddy was also eight weeks old and their Judy was two. While I was there Maurice Barksdale, home on leave from the Navy, and Donna Hudson came one afternoon and asked Charles to marry them in his home. Bennie Lee knew the Barksdales and the Hudsons from his work among the county churches, but that was my first meeting with Maurice and Donna. We were destined to become very close friends.

Mildred was to be a witness at the ceremony and I planned to stay in the back of the house with the children but another witness was needed. I was asked to join them and Judy was left to her own devices. During the ceremony, as we stood in the living room, Judy decided to play the piano in the dining room and Mildred was horribly embarrassed; fortunately Edward and Buddy slept through the entire event.

About that time Bennie Lee found a very used car. I don't recall the make or model, but I remember it was an old two-door and it cost $75. He set about learning to drive on back country roads on our way to churches, so we always left home with extra time. If we had a flat tire he changed it as quickly as possible; then if time was getting short he asked me to drive the rest of the way.

**Him and Me and Baby Makes Three** When Bennie Lee came home he would take Edward in his arms and talk to him. He told him the day's news and a Bible story and recited to him the Greek alphabet with a great deal of expression in his face and voice and Edward watched, fascinated. Edward loved books as early as he could hold them. He didn't tear them and listened intently as we read to him. He was easy to manage with tone of voice. When he was not yet two years old, Children's Bible Stories came out in Comic Book form. Bennie Lee brought one home about the birth and early childhood of Jesus and read it to Edward, explaining the pictures as he read. Edward was soon identifying the people in the pictures and to each other we congratulated ourselves on being good parents!

Everett and Eulalia Prestridge were among our good friends in Rogersville. They had a boy a little older than Edward and James was a major handful. We visited often in each other's homes where the contrast of behavior between James and Edward was painful—especially to Eulalia. She repeatedly said, "I hope when we have our second babies *you'll* have one like James and *I'll* have one like Edward!"

**Cloth Diapers** A baby in the house meant washing cloth diapers. We kept a solution of bleach in a bucket in the bathroom to hold diapers between washings (the diaper was pre-rinsed in the commode if it had number two in it.) Every day the round washtub was in the kitchen and diapers were washed by hand in suds and rinsed thoroughly. On freezing days, with my coat on and the clothespin bag tied around my waist, I stood in the kitchen and shook out one diaper at a time, took two corners in my left hand, held them as I shook and cornered the next, until I had about ten diapers held by the corners in my left hand. I ran to the clothesline to hang those ten as fast as I could. By the time they were hung, they were frozen stiff. Back in the kitchen I warmed myself while getting the next handful ready. When it was snowing or raining they were hung inside on a rope line that zigzagged across the kitchen and we ducked and dodged until they were dry.

**Beth's Stay** When Edward was five months old I was to have my fallen kidney tied up to prevent a repeat of history if/when I became pregnant again. But who would take care of Edward while I was in the hospital and recuperating? Beth was living with her in-laws in Texas while Henry, still in the Army, was overseas. She and I had corresponded regularly since college and we decided that she would bring her five-month-old Betty and stay several weeks. Bennie Lee and I moved Edward's crib to the kitchen where we slept on the daybed; we put Beth in the bedroom with a borrowed crib for Betty. I recall more about things we did together than I do about having the surgery—except for one incident at Dr. Jackson's Clinic.

On the day before surgery I checked into the clinic and the same day Mildred Chumley checked in to have thyroid surgery. We asked to be in the same room so we could encourage each other. We took with us our prettiest gowns and bed-jackets and by mutual agreement we each took pale pink lipstick and nail polish, though we ordinarily never used either one. We thought that would help us feel cheery as we recuperated! We applied the nail polish that afternoon, laughing about our foolishness. As the evening wore on she took hers off, saying, "What if I die and there in the coffin lies the *preacher's wife* with nail polish on!" I was not going to think like that, but before going to sleep I took mine off, too! Both our surgeries went well and we recuperated with good morale without nail polish or lipstick!

The doctor told me he tied the kidney up securely and said, "The other kidney could *possibly* fall, but *that one* never will." Through five later pregnancies and all the years since I have seldom given that kidney another thought.

**Foy's Wedding** Foy met Margaret Hall at church in Decatur. She was a native of north Alabama working in the telephone company. Foy brought her to Rogersville to meet us and we heartily approved of his choice. They set the date for a December 1944 wedding and Beth was with us for our brother's wedding.

Bennie Lee was Foy's Best Man and Margaret wore the dress that Beth and I had each worn for our weddings. After Foy and Margaret had pictures made she changed into her "going away" outfit. I put on the wedding dress and Bennie Lee and I had a picture made; our wedding snapshot in Texas had not turned out well and I wanted a good picture of the dress I had made that was making history with its third bride. Then Beth put it on for a picture because she and Henry did not have any wedding pictures at all. She got a real kick out of sending a picture of herself in her wedding dress to her husband of nearly two years who was in the Philippines! Foy and Margaret continued to live in Decatur after they were married. The next year Harold was born and when he was about a year old they went to Africa.

I'm not sure how long Beth stayed with us but we were busy. We never ran out of things to talk about as we washed diapers in the kitchen and took turns running to the clothesline in freezing weather. By the time I had recuperated enough to lift babies, the days were warmer. While our babies napped and weather permitting, we sat in the swing on the front porch, talking, hand-stitching and embroidering colorful flowers all around the necks and sleeves of the peasant blouses we made for ourselves. We went shopping in Athens, carrying our babies as we walked around the square. By then Betty weighed eighteen pounds and Edward weighed fifteen and we exchanged babies often to rest our aching arms.

**A Shocking Event** It was the 1940s and segregation of the races in the South was a fact of life that I thought unjust, but in the area where we lived at least, the majority of folks of both races were church-going and believed in treating their neighbors right no matter the color—though we all knew that was not the case everywhere and that there were exceptions close to home.

One evening when Bennie Lee came home after working late in Athens I could tell he was upset about something. His office was on the east side of town and he had to drive through downtown Athens to come west to Rogersville. He said when he approached the square he saw a big crowd milling around and had to make a detour of a few blocks. He had stopped on the edge of the crowd and asked a bystander what was going on.

What he was told made him feel sick. He did not know what triggered it, but some known white racists had stirred up a mob and had beaten a colored man to death on the sidewalk opposite the courthouse. The police had arrested the white men but Bennie Lee said he was afraid they would not get their just deserts. People who lived in Athens knew the man who had been killed as a "retarded," quiet and gentle person, a fixture around the square where people greeted him by name, and often gave him change to buy food. They all knew he would not have hurt anyone. Bennie Lee said he never thought he would ever see such a heinous crime in Athens; it was frightening how quickly mob mentality could be stirred up. The shock could be felt in the air for weeks and a dark shadow of shame lay over our quiet little town.

**The Reeds** J. C. Reed, a single teacher at the Bible School, had been corresponding with his college girl friend in Texas. He returned to Texas for their wedding, then they came to Athens to wait until they could go to Africa as missionaries. Bennie Lee helped them raise funds and J. C. continued teaching at the Bible School. They stayed with us for several weeks—they in the front room and we in the kitchen until they found a small apartment.

**The Hooks** It's a wonder Mrs. McMeans didn't charge us extra rent. Not long after the Reeds moved out of our front room, George and Margaret Hook and small son, Foy, were with us for three months before they found an apartment in Rogersville. They were in Alabama also waiting to go to Africa as missionaries and Bennie Lee helped them raise funds and George taught at the Bible School. Edward, by now a toddler, and their Foy a little older, played well together. Margaret and I had known each other in college and enjoyed our time together.

One Friday night following the Faculty-Family pot-luck in Athens, the three of them and the three of us boarded one of the school buses (very old but a real bus) and headed for Rogersville with George driving. On the way we had one flat after another—nine in nineteen miles. The men had to patch the inner tube each time and pump up each tire when they got it back on the bus. Margaret and I spent the time quieting the little ones, who were wakened every time a tire went flat and the bus came to a bumping stop. By the time we pulled into Rogersville, morning was dawning—it had taken more than eight hours to go nineteen miles! The men managed to find second hand inner tubes the next day. It was 1945 and World War II had ended the 3$^{rd}$ of September but many things were still scarce and expensive.

**Ladies' Hats** Our limited budget made me want to help. I decided to take a millinery course and make and remodel ladies' hats. Ladies in the States had sent hats to us as teenagers in Africa—old ladies' felt hats that I remodeled for Mother, Beth, Margaret Ann and me and that experience spurred me on. Felt material was supplied with the course. I learned to make matching hats and handbags and had no trouble selling them. When ladies found out I could also refurbish out-of-date hats, they pulled hats from their closets; some for me to renew and some for me to keep for material that could be reused. I don't recall how much money I made but it was enough to make it worthwhile and I enjoyed it. I quit when I became nauseated to the point I could hardly look at a hat or stand the smell of felt.

**Baby Number Two** My determination not to be nauseated should have prevented it—but it didn't and Dr. Jackson did not tell me it was all in my head. But this time there were no complications. Edward had been named after his Fudge and Short grandfathers and in anticipation of a second son we chose *Henry Lee*—*Henry* after Bennie Lee's grandfather and *Lee* after Bennie Lee's father and himself. *A'Delia Sue*, honoring our mothers, was held over in case it was a girl.

**A Second Car** Bennie Lee found a car to take the place of the first one that had been nothing but trouble. This was a well used 1931 Chevrolet, black four-door sedan that reminded me of the family car we had in Africa. It cost $150 and was better than the first one but often needed repairs and we seldom went anywhere without having a flat. Tires and inner tubes were still scarce and expensive.

**Margaret Ann** In the summer of 1946 Margaret Ann came to the U.S. What a joy it was to see my little sister after six years, only now she was all grown up and taller than I. One day she and I drove to Decatur to do some shopping. On our way back to Athens, soon after crossing the Tennessee River, we had a flat and pulled off on the side of the road not far from a house, but I had no idea who lived there.

Margaret Ann and I knew how to change a tire. I was largely pregnant by that time and we agreed that I would advise while she did the bending over. But while she was searching for the proper place to put the jack under the car, a Greyhound bus passed, slowed down, then stopped. A soldier stepped off, and the bus went on. As he came toward us, he said, "You look like you need help. I'll change the tire for you." And he did—in practically no time.

We thanked him profusely and I offered to pay him, but he refused and said he only wanted a ride to Athens. I told him that I was in a quandary because I had promised my husband I would *never* give a ride to a stranger. (Bennie Lee gave rides to anyone he saw needing one, but women were constantly warned against it and I had to keep my promise.) I was apologizing and he was almost begging when we saw a woman coming from the house calling to me, "Mrs. Fudge, I didn't know it was you out here. I kept looking and finally recognized you—I didn't know you were expecting a baby." She had moved from Rogersville several months before. She had seen the soldier change the tire and invited all of us to the house for a cup of coffee. The soldier declined and said he would thumb a ride. Margaret Ann and I followed her and watched through a window to see what happened next. We were relieved to see a car stop almost immediately to give him a ride.

Margaret Ann's allotted two weeks were over too soon and it was time for her to go on to Abilene, Texas to visit Beth and Henry and to enter college.

**Another Flat** One Sunday morning in mid-August, we were on our way to a country church about fifteen miles from home where Bennie Lee was to preach. A single-lane dirt road wound its way to the church and we left home early enough to allow for a flat. Not unexpectedly it happened and Bennie Lee got out to repair it. The car was in the sun so Edward and I watched from under a nearby shade tree.

The dirt road was soft and the jack could not raise the car high enough to get the wheel off. Bennie Lee let the jack down, put a flat rock under the jack, and tried again. That was better but it still lacked a little being high enough and he looked around for an idea. He spotted a long pole in the edge of the field and a small boulder nearby. With the jack on the flat rock as high as it would go, he used the pole as a lever under the axle (or somewhere) and the boulder for a fulcrum. When he pushed down on the end of the pole he could tell the car raised just enough, but he couldn't hold the pole down and take the wheel off at the same time so he gently let go of the pole and turned to look at me, his eight months pregnant wife.

He said, "I think if you sit on the end of this pole it will give the needed uppage and I can get the wheel off." I did and it did and he did. When the flat was patched and he was ready to put the wheel back on the car, we repeated the procedure. Then as he pumped up the tire we laughed till tears rolled down, thinking of the spectacle it must have made—after I got over the fact that my Sunday dress got dirty on the way to church. And yes, we were late, but since Bennie Lee was the preacher they waited for us.

**Henry Lee** arrived Friday, **September 13, 1946,** with a minimum of trouble, weighing seven pounds, with lusty lungs that needed no help getting started. Two weeks later we installed him in his bassinet at home and introduced him to Edward, "This is your tiny bitty baby brother!" For months Edward called him, "Tinybittybabybruer" as if all one word. With two-year-old Edward leaning against his knee, Bennie Lee held Henry and told them Bible stories and the news and recited the Greek alphabet and Edward recited along with him. It was soon evident that Henry would listen intently for a little while but didn't want to be still for too much of it. The Prestridges had their second child, also a boy, about the same time and Eulalia got her wish—Doyle had a personality the opposite of James and Henry was the opposite of Edward. As the months went by Bennie Lee and I revised our self-congratulations about being good parents but not our determination to keep trying.

**First Washing Machine** When Henry was a baby we bought a second-hand electric washing machine with wringer attached on one side. As clothes were fed into it one piece at a time, they dropped into the washtub on a chair beside the machine. On washdays I rolled the washing machine from the back porch into the kitchen, filled it with water from the back porch faucet, then emptied it by carrying the used water to the back yard. One day as I was feeding something into the wringer I saw dirt on it. I tried to pull the article back and hung on too long. My fingers got caught in the wringer and there was no stopping it; the cord was plugged into the wall socket across the kitchen; I couldn't reach to unplug it. By the time I thought to jerk the cord from the wall, my arm had gone through up to my elbow. Words might be "taken back" but don't ever try to take back something that has started through the wringer!

**Fashion Frocks** During the last five months before Henry arrived I decided to try a different way of making a little extra income. Home sales of "Fashion Frocks" were the rage for women who seldom had a chance to go to city department stores. The company supplied 8 ½ x 11 inch colored pictures of suits and dresses with attached swatches of the material. I showed them, took orders, and besides commission, earned bonus clothes for myself. I took Edward and went from house to house and sales were good. After Henry was born I took him and Edward both with me and continued selling Fashion Frocks for some time.

**Many Grandmothers** In every congregation where Bennie Lee preached families practically "adopted" him and his family. Invariably there was at least one older lady (sometimes more than one) who was like a mother to us and a grandmother to our children. In Rogersville, besides our landlady, Mrs. McMeans, there was Mrs. Madge Whitehead and her sister, Mrs. Howard. Those two always sat together in church near where I sat and were a great help with Edward when I had to take Henry out. Mrs. Whitehead was a seamstress with an electric sewing machine. When she found out I could sew for myself and baby, but didn't have a sewing machine, she insisted that I come to her house to spend the day sewing whenever possible. Her sister usually spent the day with us and the three of us shared tasks as we sewed, chatted and tended Edward and Henry. With their expect help I made sun-suits and shirts, pants and jackets for the boys and dresses for myself.

Farm women saved the cloth sacks in which their fifty pound lots of flour, sugar and chicken-feed came. The bags were stitched shut with string that was unraveled and saved for many uses. The bags were made of color-fast print material and much prized for dresses, aprons, quilt pieces and kitchen and bathroom curtains. It was up to the imagination of the seamstress how they were trimmed with lace, crocheted edges or ruffles. Cloth salt bags were saved for dish cloths, dust cloths and such like.

**Baptistery Murals** As new church buildings were built with baptisteries included, more and more river scenes on the back wall of the baptisteries were seen. When the Rogersville folks found out I painted some of the pictures hanging in our apartment, they asked me to paint a scene for the church baptistery. I had never done anything of that magnitude before but asked myself "Why not?" and did it.

**Changes in The Offing** In Athens there was a church of Christ downtown and a new one recently started in north town. The Bible School was on the east edge of town. What had been farmland around the school was fast becoming a residential area. The Earl Chandler family had moved from the country and lived across the street from the school; Carl Richter, a businessman in town, and his family lived a few blocks away. Both men were leaders in the churches they attended in the country and both were on the board of directors of the school. They talked to Bennie Lee about starting a congregation on the east side of town, temporarily using the school auditorium as a meeting place.

The Rogersville church had grown and the elders were thinking of building a preacher's home and hiring a full-time preacher. Bennie Lee resigned there and agreed to preach for the new congregation in Athens.

When the new preacher arrived in Rogersville one of the first things he wanted to do was to remodel the baptistery and have a professional artist paint a new scene on the back wall. My close friends were not happy about it and talked to me. I told them in my opinion the change should be put down to progress and the finished job looked a lot better to me. But Bennie Lee grieved over that painting and impractically wished he could have moved it. I assured him that when we got into a house with a big enough wall I would paint one specifically for the spot and do a better job after having practiced in Rogersville.

**My Parents' First Visit** Just before we moved from Rogersville, Daddy, Mother and Bill came from Africa on furlough. It had been seven years since that day in Salisbury when I said goodbye to Daddy and Mother, Beth and Margaret Ann. They had not met Bennie Lee or the boys, and I would meet my little brother, Bill, for the first time. Bennie Lee wanted Edward to "look like a boy" to meet his grandparents and took him to the barbershop for his first haircut the day before they arrived. The barber was elderly and thought all boys should have burr haircuts. He practically scalped Edward and I cried when I saw him looking so peeled. But the world didn't come to an end, and with time his hair grew!

After too short a visit my parents and Bill went on to Texas to see Beth and family, to meet another unseen son-in-law and two more unseen grandchildren. And within a few weeks we moved to Athens.

## Athens 1947-1975

**Little House on the Corner 1947-1950** Chandler Drive was a short street one block from the school. The Rollings and Chumleys each owned half of the west side of Chandler Drive. Unbeknownst to us, they agreed with each other to cut 25ft x 100ft off of each of their lots, moving their lines accordingly to make one small lot at the end. They surprised us with an offer to sell us that lot, 50 feet wide and 100 feet deep, for $1.00 (to make it legal). There we built a small house, Number 500, Chandler Drive.

Two of our good friends in Rogersville were carpenters and built the house in their spare time. We paid for the material with a bank loan and our monthly payments were $49.17. Small was the word for that house of about 600 square feet. It included a living room, bedroom, kitchen and bathroom (shower only), and a tiny central hall with an oil heater in it—literally "central heat." We were excited to have a house and it served our needs for three years. There was no blank wall suitable for a mural for Bennie Lee so that idea was shelved for the time being.

In the bedroom was a small closet. The double bed, an old chest of drawers from Bennie Lee's parents' attic and the third-hand crib for Henry, left just enough room to get around in. The living room had the daybed where Edward slept, a small square table and a cane-bottom chair from Bennie Lee's parents, and later a rocker from there. In the kitchen the old fashioned cabinet brought from Rogersville filled most of the wall between the back door and the new apartment-size electric stove (that I

190

liked much better than the oil one.) A drop-leaf table with four chairs (a bargain from an auction barn), a small ice chest and the rolling washing machine filled the kitchen to overflowing.

When we wanted to seat four people, we first put a chair with its back against the sink, the table next with a chair on each side of the opened leaves, and finally the last chair at the end. If we needed anything from behind anyone, that person had to turn in their chair and reach it. We had dinner guests fairly often. If there were more than four we moved the table to the living room, added the little table as extension that made room for six or eight and used the daybed for seats on one side. We kept some empty orange crates around for extra seats when needed.

Daddy, Mother and Bill came back from Texas in February. The three Shorts used the very small bedroom and the four Fudges slept in the living room. While they were with us we had the biggest snow North Alabama had seen in many years and it paralyzed about everything. For three days we were snowed in with no school and snow too deep to move cars and part of the time no electricity. Our water came from a well at the corner of our lot, with the pump inside of a small concrete block shelter; when the pipes froze in the house we carried water from there. (That well furnished water for all the houses on our side of the street until city water came out that far.) While we were snowed in we had good visiting time and my parents and Bennie Lee had a chance to get acquainted—time they would not have had if he had been going to school and work.

**Texas Trip** Daddy had bought a used car and he, Mother and Bill were going back to Texas for Margaret Ann's wedding. They invited me to take Edward and Henry and go with them. Bennie Lee would go by bus later to attend the wedding and the annual Lectureship at ACC, then he and I with the boys would come home by bus. In Abilene we all stayed with Beth and Henry and their two children in their small, two bedroom duplex near the ACC campus. What a crowd in that small space and what fun we had! Fortunately they had a sleep-sofa in their living room.

Their Pat and our Henry were about seven/eight months old; Edward and Betty were going on three, and Bill nearly four. While we were there a West Texas dust storm came up and in spite of closed doors and windows, everything was soon covered with fine red dust. We mopped the floors twice a day, but Pat and Henry were crawling and soon looked like little rust-colored creatures from another planet. On washdays the usual West Texas wind challenged Beth and me as we hung on to sheets for dear life, joking that if we let go, they might fly all the way to Alabama.

George Ewing's wife, Melissa, in the other side of the duplex, offered to let Margaret Ann borrow her gorgeous wedding dress and the fit was perfect. Margaret Ann and Don Mansur were married in a beautiful ceremony. Daddy gave her away and Bill was ring bearer. My little sister, who was eleven when I left her in Africa, was now married.

**Texas to Alabama by Bus—Again** For Bennie Lee and me, going home on the bus with two little ones was a far different experience from the ride four years before. In Arkansas a stretch of road-work with its slow downs and detours, delayed us so that we missed our connection in Memphis. We were scheduled to be home Saturday afternoon for Bennie Lee to preach on Sunday morning, but Sunday morning we were still in the Memphis bus station. The next bus was not until 2 p.m. and Bennie Lee decided we could take a taxi to Union Avenue Church of Christ and get back to the bus station by that time.

Bennie Lee was in khaki pants and shirt that he had worn from Abilene and I was in the suit I had worn all that time—and my hair was a mess; we did have clean clothes for the boys. Bennie Lee picked that church from the phone book because he knew their preacher was away in a meeting. No one else there knew us. He thought I would feel better about that—had he been alone he wouldn't have cared! We dressed the boys and I did what I could with my hair while he called a taxi. Unfortunately Union Avenue traffic was congested. When we got to the building the congregation was singing and the usher took us all the way down to the second row from the front. In a few minutes Henry began fretting, his bottle didn't quiet him, and I was sure he had fever. There was nothing to do but walk red-faced out that long aisle with him crying and people turning to look. Obviously they had a nursery somewhere because he was the only baby in the auditorium. I hadn't asked about a nursery when we came in—there were none in the country churches we attended. The usher at the back *then* told me about the nursery, but I was afraid I would miss Bennie Lee in the crowd afterwards so I quieted Henry by walking in the lobby.

The service ended, the big outside doors were opened and people began pouring out into the lobby. I stood just inside the outer doors where I thought Bennie Lee could easily find me. I saw him coming but there were people still between us when I heard a bombastic voice over the chatter of the crowd, "WELL! *BENNIE LEE FUDGE*, IMAGINE MEETING *YOU* HERE!" A big Texas preacher with a big Texas voice happened to be visiting, too! I hastily turned my back on the lobby crowd and went to stand on the outside top step lest Bennie Lee get the bright idea of introducing me. But he knew we had a bus to catch and was soon beside me. In spite of typical taxi driving we missed the 2 o'clock bus and the next one wasn't until 5 o'clock.

We hadn't counted on being on the road so long and were almost out of money. Bennie Lee said he had enough to get something for Edward to eat and there was an unopened can of milk in the diaper bag that would be enough for Henry. We drank water and waited, taking turns walking the floor with a feverish Henry. On the bus the boys slept—until we stopped for a rest stop. I stayed on the bus with Henry while Bennie Lee took Edward to the restroom and to get a drink of water.

At the counter getting the glass of water, Edward said, "I'm hungry," and fellow passengers eating their snacks heard him. Bennie Lee thought he had fifty cents in his pocket so he ordered a hamburger for Edward but when he reached into his pocket to pay, he found only a quarter. He pushed the hamburger back and told the waiter he was sorry he didn't have enough money. Naturally Edward didn't understand and said, "But, Daddy, I'm hungry," and in a low voice Bennie Lee tried to explain to him. A man next to them put fifty cents on the counter saying, "Here, give the boy the hamburger," and before Bennie Lee could say anything others put down quarters and fifty cent pieces. Bennie Lee urged them to take the money back, thanking them for their kindness, but nobody would take any back. So Edward got his hamburger and Bennie Lee came to the bus with two more, one for him and one for me. It was his turn to have a red face.

To top the trip off, when we finally got home, my suitcase did not arrive with us—nor ever after. My wardrobe of Fashion Frock bonuses was lost. But the world didn't come to an end over that either, and the next day Henry had two new teeth!

**Alabama Clay** As the children grew old enough to play outside I learned to contend with red clay. Where we grew up in Africa our "dirt" had always been sandy soil, easily washed from body and clothes but not so with red clay which was hard to wash out of clothes and hard to mop off the floors. I learned to keep special "mud clothes" for the children to wear when they played outside after rains. In Athens wash days were much easier than they had been in Rogersville—I rolled the washing machine up close to the sink to transfer water—clean and dirty—no more bucket-carrying. In bad weather we had lines zigzagged in living room, bedroom and hallway and Bennie Lee grew accustomed to ducking and dodging diapers when he came home, but he didn't complain—he was too happy to have little ones in the house.

Our small ice-chest was a luxury. Twice a week an open-bed truck delivered 25, 50 or 100 lb. blocks of ice from the Athens ice-plant. If people didn't have standing orders they could hail the truck as it slowly passed down a street and the iceman brought the block into the house and put it into the ice chest. Our chest held a 25 pound block that lasted three or four days, depending on how much we chipped off for iced tea. The trick was remembering every day to empty the water pan under the icebox, otherwise water ran out in the floor and the kitchen got an extra mopping. We could have pasteurized milk delivered or buy it raw by the half gallon from a neighbor with a cow.

Bennie Lee's erratic schedule made it hard to have a regular family devotions time but we decided that as soon as we finished eating supper, before leaving the table, was a good time, except during the summers.

Gospel meetings were going on in the county churches and we went to preaching somewhere nearly every night all summer.

**Home Perms** About the time we moved to Athens from Rogersville "home permanents" arrived on the scene and I began giving myself one every few months. Some of the neighbor ladies asked me to perm their hair for them, which I did, becoming more or less the neighborhood no-charge hairdresser—even trimming mine and theirs at times. When the "Toni" brand became available requests increased—until a former hairdresser moved into the neighborhood and we all went to her for our perms at a small charge. Years later when I went to work at the Bookstore, I became a customer at "Kay's House of Beauty." My favorite operator was Donna Barksdale, the same Donna whose wedding I witnessed in 1944. She gave me perms and later did my hair every Friday for seven years.

**The Tricycle** Bennie Lee remembered how much he longed for a tricycle when he was little and was determined to get one for his boys. On Edward's fourth Christmas a little red tricycle appeared among his gifts and he rode it around and around in the living room—so much the first day that his little legs ached that night and Bennie Lee sat on the side of his bed rubbing them. When spring came, Edward rode in the small front yard and Henry rode on the back of the trike holding on to Edward. Soon Henry was climbing onto the seat trying to pedal for himself.

From early days Henry was determined to have his own way. We wanted to encourage determination but we had to set limits, and limits were hard for him to take. Not yet three, he was riding the tricycle in the yard and got too close to the ditch along the front. It was just deep enough for the trike to turn over and dump him. He got up crying loudly and pulling mightily on the trike. Bennie Lee and I were watching from the living room window and we could tell he was crying with frustration, not hurt. I wanted to go help him but Bennie Lee said, "He's not hurt. Let's wait and see what he does." Still crying, Henry struggled until he got the trike upright and kept struggling and yelling at the top of his voice until he had it up in the yard then instantly his crying stopped and he climbed on to ride again. Bennie Lee said proudly, "That's my boy! He's got determination and he'll be a good one when he grows up if we can help him channel his stubbornness!" And I remarked, "Judging from stories your mother tells of *your* childhood, he's a real chip off the old block!"

**Thanksgiving and Christmas** Every Thanksgiving and Christmas we went to Bennie Lee's parents' house. All his siblings tried to be there. The first year I made chocolate fudge and divinity candies and cookies and sacked them up for the bus ride from Rogersville to Athens. In Athens Bennie Lee found someone to give us a lift to Bennie Lee Rainey's country store where we unloaded. We borrowed a round wash tub from Cousin Fanny, put the food and overnight bag into the tub, and taking a handle each, walked to the Fudge house—about a half mile short-cut across a field. A road ran past their house but that way was about three miles.

The next year Edward was a baby and we wrapped him warmly, put him in the tub with the baby things and foodstuff, and taking a handle each, we walked. The next year was a repeat with Edward in snowsuit, cap and mittens, sitting up enjoying the ride. The following year we had baby Henry and a car, and our travel mode changed. However, my chocolate fudge, divinity and cookies had become a tradition.

Grandpa Fudge died when Edward was about three. Edward had been fascinated by him and at the same time deathly afraid of his whiskers. Soon after his death Grandma Fudge, Curtis and Clarence moved to a house made of concrete blocks—smaller and much warmer in the winter than their clap-board houses had been.

**Expecting Number Three** Before we married Bennie Lee and I agreed that we would like to have a large family. He was one of eight, I was one of five and we agreed that if God was willing, six would make a good sized family. Henry was sixteen months old and I was not surprised when it became evident number three was on the way. I discovered plain saltine crackers with Dr. Pepper settled well and that was my standby fare for four months. Another helpful trick was not to allow myself to get too hungry. When the four months passed, I again enjoyed regular food and I again told myself, "Next time I'll not be sick."

**Little House Wedding** There came a teacher/preacher from Texas to the Bible School named Alfred Meeks. He courted Bennie Lee's sister, Irma, and in the course of time they wanted Bennie Lee to marry them in our living room with a few family members present. I was seven months pregnant by then but I wanted to make punch and a wedding cake for the reception. The day before the wedding, the cake layers turned out well and I made the icing while Edward and Henry played happily in the living room. I spread icing on the cake and was ready to begin decorating when the phone rang in the hallway. I laid the knife down and went to answer the phone.

While I was talking I heard a chair scraping across the kitchen floor and hurried to get off the phone and back to the kitchen. Henry (2) had pulled a chair up to the cabinet, climbed up, picked up the knife and swiped it all the way across the cake making a trench in the icing. I lost my cool, as they say these days. Edward (4) was standing nearby in awe at what Henry had done and, I imagine, wondering what I would do. I put Henry down on the floor, saying in no uncertain terms, "Henry Fudge, get down from there! Get out of here and don't come back!" I didn't say "go to the living room," which is what I had in mind. Edward took Henry's hand and led him out of the kitchen and I repaired the icing and decorated the cake.

Then I realized with a jolt that I had not heard the boys since they went out of the kitchen. I called and looked through the house but there was no sign of them. I went around the yard, front and back calling them, still no boys and I was worried. The three vacant lots between our house and the Rollings house at the top of Chandler Drive were a solid field of soybeans almost mature and I looked up and down the rows calling their names. Finally I looked across the bean tops and saw Jack Rollings working in his garden and saw the top of Edward's very blond head and Henry beside him. I was so relieved I was crying as I went up the street. When I got there, Jack was leaning on his hoe grinning.

He said Edward came out of the bean field leading Henry by the hand and asked seriously, "Brother Rollings, can we stay with you?" Jack asked, "Where's your mother?" and Edward replied, "She's fixing a wedding cake for Aunt Irma and Henry messed it up and she told us to get out and never come back!" Jack assured him that I was upset over the messed up cake and didn't mean *not ever* and he was sure I would be there to get them very soon. My heart ached at the idea of my little boys pushing their way through those beans higher than their heads, Edward thinking they had been banished forever. I resolved to be very careful in the future what I said and how I said it.

**Robert Clarence** Robert Clarence Fudge arrived on **October 23, 1948.** He was a veritable butter ball at 8 lbs. 3 ozs. *Robert* was a family name on both sides and Bennie Lee's brother was *Clarence*. When Bennie Lee told his mother the news she said, "What? Another boy? Seems like you could have managed a girl by now!" We were still holding on to *A'Delia Sue* for a possible future girl's name.

In those times some men felt "manhood" was measured by how many sons a man had. Because Bennie Lee was not big and tall he was considered by some to be "scrawny and not much of a man." Now besides our natural pride at having three boys, Bennie Lee admitted to me that it secretly did him good to have three sons and no more sly remarks.

We had wonderful friends who took turns keeping Edward and Henry during the daytime for the fourteen days I was in the hospital. Bennie Lee picked them up after work and took care of them overnight. He didn't worry about cooking—neighbors generously supplied cooked meals and he had to tell them "no more" while he and the boys ate up the plentiful leftovers.

The Monday Bennie Lee brought Robert and me home I felt good and thought I could handle the two boys—and the baby—and the meals—if not, why not? After a few days it all caught up with me. That day started well. I cooked breakfast, Edward and Henry were fed and playing, Bennie Lee had gone to work, Robert was crying and it was time to give him a bath and feed him, then sterilize bottles and prepare formula. Suddenly I felt completely overwhelmed. I sat on the side of the unmade bed and cried, wishing for my mother, who was 10,000 miles away—wishing she was near enough to call on for help, or at least for encouragement.

I had gained so much weight that I couldn't wear any of my regular clothes and had to wear maternity dresses—even to church the first Sunday—that had not happened after Edward or Henry. After lunch that day Bennie Lee said he would stay with the children while I went to buy a new dress for the next Sunday. It was not a fun shopping trip—I had to buy a size I hoped fervently would soon be too big (and it was) but I kept it in the back of my closet, just in case.

I had felt very mature in Rogersville; I hadn't realized until now, with a new baby in a house all to myself, how much help it had been to have a motherly Mrs. McMeans in the other side of the house. But we were in Athens, near to Bennie Lee's work and I could call him when necessary. As I think back on our children's growing up years, I realize how often I phoned Bennie Lee to ask his advice or opinion. I trusted his wisdom and ability to size up *any* situation and make the best decision. I was thankful all those years that his cheerful and helpful voice was available to my calls, though I tried to keep calls to a minimum. With the passing years my confidence grew but I always depended on Bennie Lee's help if he was anywhere within reach. Our private talking time was at night after the children were asleep and through the years there were many nights we talked for several hours. We knew our confidences were safe with each other and I felt honored when he told me that he knew he could talk to me about anything or anyone and know I would not talk about it to anybody else.

Robert inherited the crib in our bedroom and Henry shared the daybed with Edward in the living room. Robert was a good baby but he had the same trouble Edward had had after feedings. Until they were about three months old, both babies had trouble keeping milk down if they became the least bit excited after a feeding. With each of them I would think all was well after a bottle at church, then he would begin fretting and I knew what was coming—usually before I could get him off my shoulder. This was way beyond "spitting up." Several times the whole back of my outfit was bathed in milk, and if he was in my lap, we both got the benefit of it. I learned to sit on the back row so nobody else caught it so if I didn't get out in time—and I learned to get out quickly. Fortunately when Edward was in that phase we lived across the street from the Rogersville church and I could go home and change—him and me. With Robert we lived just one block from church so I went home to change as soon as I could get him and Henry (2) out, unless Henry was happy to stay with a helpful lady friend. I didn't worry about Edward—he was sitting on the front row listening to his Daddy preach.

Most women worked at home, taking care of the house and children, raising a garden, canning, making jam, and hobnobbing with each other. Among my close neighbor-friends were some who sewed and owned sewing machines, which as yet I didn't own. While we visited I took sewing to do; when we had hand-hemming or buttons ready to sew on they came to my house. Finally we found a used electric Singer sewing machine and I could sew at home. I made clothes for the boys, embroidered on the bibs of sun-suits and on collars and pockets of white shirts to go with their summer short pants; I even smocked across the yokes of their Sunday shirts—because I wanted to smock! As they grew, their Sunday suits were made from old suits of Bennie Lee's that I ripped up, turned inside out and had enough new looking material to make long pants and matching "battle jackets" that were in style then. At a used clothing store in town I found extra large long men's suits for 50 cents and from them had enough material to make stylish suits for myself.

**A False Accusation** Now and then something happened to disrupt our usually peaceful life. Bennie Lee took turns with other preachers fifteen minutes a day on a daily radio program called *Spiritual Guidance.* Listeners began writing in questions that he answered and soon the other preachers turned the program over to him to do six days a week. A woman listener didn't like what he said in one of his answers and decided she would "fix that preacher." She wrote a letter to him accusing him of raping her teenage daughter and said she was telling it to anyone who would listen to her.

Bennie Lee showed the letter to an elder at the church downtown who was a good friend and highly respected for his wisdom. The elder said, "We need to go see the woman and talk to her." When they knocked on her door and told her they had come to talk to her about the letter she had written to Bennie Lee, she was obviously taken aback. The elder told her that he had known Bennie Lee almost all his life and did not believe the story. "But," he said, "If it *is* true, then the thing for you to do is to bring your daughter to the church downtown to talk to all the elders and tell them exactly when and where this deed happened, so we can do something about it."

She backed down immediately and said she made it up because she was angry at what Bennie Lee said on the radio. The elder asked her if Bennie Lee gave a Bible reason for what he said and she admitted that he did because she had looked it up and that had made her all the more angry. The elder told her to get busy and tell all the people she had misinformed that she had lied and she promised to do so. Nothing further was ever heard about it. Bennie Lee's reputation grew for knowing the Bible and being able to give Bible answers for everyday Christian living. He answered written questions for eleven years on that program and his name became a household word.

**Christmas Tree or Not** Christmas of 1948 was nearly on us. We had not had a Christmas tree since we married and I thought we should have one for our children to enjoy—but our budget did not include the cost of a tree and besides, Bennie Lee had grown up without Christmas trees and couldn't understand why I thought it necessary.

The Chumleys had built a house on Chandler Drive between us and the Rollings. Charles was preaching in the county and someone gave them a big evergreen for a Christmas tree that was too tall for their ceiling. I saw Charles outside sawing off about two feet from the bottom. When I realized that green branches were still attached to that piece of trunk, an idea hit me. At lunch that day I asked Bennie Lee if it was O.K. with him for me to make a tree that would cost us nothing. I explained my idea and he was agreeable. Charles was glad to have the cut-off bottom of the tree taken out of his yard! My philosophy was "If you can't buy it—make it." I took that piece of tree home, pulled up the branches to meet over the trunk and wired them securely together. We had a passable five foot Christmas tree ready to be decorated, just the right height for our living room.

We managed to buy a string of lights and a few baubles and the tree looked good. The boys were ecstatic. Every evening Edward watched us plug in the lights for the evening and then unplug them at bedtime, and we explained why we were doing it. On Christmas Eve the lights were unplugged and the boys were asleep on the daybed as I wrapped gifts in the kitchen and tiptoed in to put them under the tree. In the wee hours of the night I was wakened by a rustling sound and a faint glow from the living room. My first thought was *fire*, but almost as quickly I realized it was not, and went to the door to look. The Christmas tree lights were on. Edward was sitting cross-legged on the floor by the tree picking up one present at a time, shaking it near his ear then laying it down and going to the next one without disturbing the wrapping. He didn't know I was there and I didn't say anything. After a while he got up, unplugged the lights and crawled back into bed. A precious memory! After that we had some kind of Christmas tree every year; usually from friends in the country who allowed us to cut a small fir tree that grew wild on their property.

**Santa Claus** From the beginning with our children we didn't try to disguise the fact that their Daddy was really their "Santa Claus" but we

202

fostered feelings of mystery and excitement. On Christmas morning when the children had all gathered with me in front of the tree, Bennie Lee, in his big old brown bathrobe, came out of the bedroom with a hearty, "HO! HO! HO!" He played the Santa part to the hilt. As far as the children were concerned, how he was dressed detracted nothing from the excitement and fun. I think they actually grew to love that old brown bathrobe that was never replaced and Christmas morning was about the only time he wore it. From that day on we had our own family Christmas early in the morning and went to Grandma Fudge's house about noon, where all her children gathered.

After high school Curtis joined the Army and two years later Clarence finished high school and joined the Air Force. That left Grandma Fudge alone. We invited her to live with us but she said she liked her independence and did not want to live with any of her children. She had vowed that when she had children she would make sure they all graduated from high school and when Clarence, youngest of eight, graduated, her dream was fulfilled and she was happy. The next year she died in October following gallbladder surgery. It was 1949 and she was only 56.

Her six grandchildren, Leacy and Philip's oldest three and our oldest three, were too young to remember much about her or their Grandpa Fudge. Our children would grow up without close grandparents, just as Bennie Lee and I had done, but at least they saw their Short grand-parents when they came from Africa on furlough every five or six years.

**Growing Neighborhood** Houses were being built on both sides of Chandler Drive and vacant lots were disappearing. The Elam Kuykendalls built a house on our side of the street and for a while there was a vacant lot between us. Their boy, Kenneth (5) and Edward (4) enjoyed playing together in one or the other yards.

Bennie Lee bought a desk globe of the world and showed Edward Southern Rhodesia where I was born and told him that I lived there until I was eighteen years old. He pointed out Alabama where we were now living. Edward was fascinated and during several sessions I told him, while pointing on the globe, how my family came in a big ship to the U.S. when I was five years old, then when I was seven we had crossed the U. S. in our car and at Vancouver got into another ship and crossed the Pacific and the Indian Oceans. When I was eighteen I had come across the Atlantic again to go to college. I concluded, "So I have been all the way around the world once and half-way again."

He was so impressed that he told his friend, Kenneth, "My mother has been around the world!" Kenneth said, "I don't believe you." I overheard them and wondered how it would go from there. Kenneth went running home to tell his mother. She told him I was probably just teasing and he came running back to tell Edward what his mother said. Edward brought him into the house and asked me to show him! I took the globe and pointed it out to them, explaining what I had told Edward. Kenneth, now a believer, ran home to tell his mother; she wasn't convinced and came down to ask me about it.

Edward and Kenneth generally got along well though now and then I heard them arguing. They never came to blows but one argument got loud and fierce. One of them said, "My daddy's poorer than your daddy!" the other disputed, "No he's not. Mine's poorer than yours!" Their proof to each other was the age of the cars their daddies drove! They didn't come to me about that one and I never let on that I heard them.

Henry and Robert were unconcerned about such deep subjects—much too busy with their nonstop activities; the only time they were still was when they were asleep. They were a lot alike in temperament and didn't take any nonsense from each other. I tried to let them settle their own differences as much as possible but life was never dull in our house. Edward pretty much ignored their squabbles but there were times when I told him not to give in to them. Chandler Drive was a short street and a popular playground with no lack of children under twelve—fifteen in all—plus several boys from two blocks away who joined them in play.

As their playmates multiplied, our children had to be taught which words we did not say even though they heard other children say them.

Besides real "bad words" that were forbidden, we explained about some other words they were not to say—such as *nigger, stupid, dumb* and *cheat.* Bennie Lee told them, "You can do anything you see me do and you can say anything you hear me say." That was a bold declaration, but he meant it sincerely and lived up to it. It was fairly easy to teach our own children to begin with, but we found that not all parents shared our list of banned words and with the years the task became harder to enforce.

**Childhood Diseases** When Robert was about six months old whooping cough shots were introduced and we took the boys to get theirs so that was one thing we didn't have to deal with. But during the next eighteen months our house was like a hospital with the three of them taking turns having mumps, chicken pox and measles. Robert was eight months old when they were going through measles (shots for measles were not yet available). I thought Edward and Henry were sick, but Robert, the last to have them, had the worst case and developed pneumonia. There was no official quarantine for childhood diseases but there might as well have been because no neighbor with children wanted to go near any house where they were. Of course we kept our children at home and it seemed like we were housebound for ages. Bennie Lee was helpful taking longer lunch and evening times at home. If we needed groceries or medicine, I went and he stayed with the children to give me a break. He read to them a lot and told them his *Jippy, The Little Black Monkey* stories that he had made up for his young brothers and sisters.

When Edward and Henry were sick they wanted me to sit in the rocking chair holding them, which I did as much as possible; but Robert, except when he had pneumonia, did not want to be held, he just stood in his crib crying pitifully. When I held out my arms offering to take him, he shook his head, "no" and turned away, then stood wailing, "B-a-d! B-a-d! B-a-d!" and that made me s-a-d! s-a-d! s-a-d! Fortunately the pain and itch of chicken pox was soothed by Carbolated Vaseline and I thanked Dr. Jackson for recommending it.

**Bigger House 1950-1975** As though on schedule, when Robert was sixteen months old, once again I was eating crackers and drinking Dr. Pepper. Our little house had not grown with the family—it had filled up—and the time had come to do something about a bigger house. The vacant lot on the corner across the street was a large irregular rectangle that belonged to Earl Chandler, one of the elders at the Eastside church where Bennie Lee was preaching. He was still preaching for other churches on Sunday afternoons and those churches had grown in numbers and in contributions and paid their circuit preachers more than in the earlier years. We were able to buy the lot and have a house built about twice the size of the little house. So **503 Chandler Drive** became our home where we lived until all of the children were grown.

Elementary grades were added at Athens Bible School in the fall of 1948 and Edward started first grade there in the fall of 1950. The new house was finished by the first of November that year and we moved about three weeks before our baby was due. In the new house we hardly knew what to do with all the space!

**Benjamin Newton** Benjamin was born, **November 20, 1950.** He weighed 8 lbs.13 ozs. and I thought if they kept getting bigger every time, numbers five and six would be whoppers! Baby *Benjamin* was given his father's and his grandfather Fudge's first name, and his grandfather Short's middle name, *Newton.* We had decided earlier that if this one was a girl we would name her Nancy Sue, a slight change, though still keeping our mothers' names. Once again we reserved the girl's name for possible later use.

Benjamin was a contented, happy baby and all the family enjoyed him. Every day when Bennie Lee came home for lunch and supper he went straight to Benjamin's crib to get his "dose of sunshine." Someone gave us a much-used stroller and even before he could sit alone, it was Benjamin's favorite place to spend time. When his feet barely touched the floor he could give a little push with his toes and make it go. The axles were rusty and squeaked in spite of oiling and the front wheels were stuck at an angle that made the stroller go around in a circle as Benjamin pushed on the floor. When I was in another room and heard the squeaking I knew he was going round and round. If it stopped I went to see about him and often found him sound asleep with his head on the tray, never even waking when I transferred him to his crib.

We settled into our new house and I kept my promise to Bennie Lee to paint a mural on the living room wall. We framed it with left-over molding nailed directly on the wall around the painting. That wall seemed to need a piece of furniture under the picture, so using the old quilt box that had been Bennie Lee's mother's as a base, I made a pleated striped skirt, a padded top and a couple of throw cushions, and we had a "couch"! Best of all, Bennie Lee was pleased with the whole thing!

**Room for Guests** When we had overnight adult guests, Bennie Lee and I gave them our bedroom with its private half-bath. He and I slept in Edward and Henry's room and Edward and Henry slept on a pallet or on the later-acquired sofa bed in the living room—a plan that was put to use many times.

Shortly after we moved into the new house Bennie Lee's brother, Roy, and wife, Mary Ella, with eleven month old Raymond, came to Athens for Roy to preach in the county and teach at the Bible School. While they were looking for a place to live they stayed with us. Raymond was accustomed to a quiet house when he was napping and had a hard time getting enough sleep with the constant noise of children talking and doors slamming. I had read somewhere of a mother with multiple children keeping the radio on all day to have consistent noise so little ones could get used to it and sleep soundly in spite of noise. We tried it and it did help.

Our children were allowed to invite school friends from the country to "spend the night" as long as they consulted with me ahead of time to be sure we had a spare spot for them to sleep—often on the couch in the living room. After one eight-week period we realized we had had one or more "spend-the-nighters" every night of that eight weeks!

**Smokey Mountain Trip** Roy and Mary Ella found a place to live just out of town. When Benjamin was about nine months old we left him and Robert (3) with them for a few days while we took Edward (7) and Henry (5) to the Smokey Mountains on a camping trip. We had no tent—we slept on quilts on the ground with Bennie Lee on one side, me on the other, boys in the middle. Bears roamed freely and we were careful to lock food in the car at night. There were only a few campers in the grounds and on the trails—that was before the area was commercialized and filled with tourists.

The boys had the time of their lives, helping gather dead wood, building the fire, roasting wieners over their very own fire to make hotdogs and then roasting marshmallows for dessert. Even putting out the fire for safety was exciting to them. If anyone was still hungry they had canned peaches and cookies. We all woke up at the crack of dawn but it was chilly up in the mountains and we kept the boys snuggled under the covers until the sun peeped through the treetops. Then they jumped up to help Bennie Lee build a new fire. We breakfasted on bacon, scrambled eggs and bread toasted over the coals. For lunch we opened a can of Spam or Vienna Sausages to eat with crackers—simplicity was the name of the game. Carrying our sack lunches, we climbed part of the way up Mt. LeConte. When we got back down there was still some daylight and much to the boys' delight we visited the Cherokee Village where they each bought a souvenir. The next day they "explored"—climbing around on the rocks and wading in the clear water while Bennie Lee told them about various rocks, trees, lichen and nature in general.

On the last morning, while I was packing up, Bennie Lee took them for a final wade in the cold mountain stream. When he knew we needed to get on the road, he said, "O.K. boys, time to go." Edward started toward the car but Henry jumped up and down yelling. We thought he had hurt himself on a rock, but when Bennie Lee asked him what was wrong, he said, "I don't want to stop! I don't want to go home!"

We drove from there to the Carolina coast to show them the ocean and Bennie Lee went into the water with them. Up to his knees was as far

208

out as he let them go. They waded, splashed and played and then it was time to go on our way. Bennie Lee said, "O.K. boys, time to go!" The same story; Henry jumped up and down yelling. We thought he had stepped on glass or been stung by a jelly fish, but he said, "I don't want to stop! I don't want to go home!"

Soon after we got home Beth and Henry with their four children spent a night with us on their way to Africa as missionaries. The ages of our children parallel each other and adults and children had a great time together. Too soon they were gone and after that our visits with them were even fewer.

**Monkey Bars** Our new house was a block from the Bible School, Eastside church was still meeting in the school auditorium and Bennie Lee still preaching there. On Sundays after church the boys went to the school playground. Henry was only five but he felt every bit as big as the rest of them and tried to do everything they did. He saw boys jump up to reach the monkey-bars, swing their legs up and hang by their knees. He was too short to reach the bars but he was not about to give up. He saw a concrete block at the side of the yard, pulled it under the bars, climbed on it and was soon hanging by his knees—until his knees got tired and he fell on his head on the block. He came home across the back lot calling to me, holding his head with blood running down the side of his face. He explained that he cried because blood got on his white Sunday shirt—but he had hung by his knees and could hardly wait to tell his Daddy and brothers about that.

**Budding Actors** When Edward and Buddy Chumley were both in their 2nd Grade class play, Bennie Lee and Charles took time from their busy schedules to be there. As we stood around talking afterwards, I heard them jokingly brag to each other about their boys' amazing public speaking ability and agree that this was surely an early indication of two outstanding preachers of the future!

**Daddy's Bible** Robert was three-years-old when he dragged a chair from the dining table to the nearby bookcase, pulled out a book, turned and laid it on the table. For some reason he had picked Bennie Lee's preaching Bible and before I knew what was happening, still on the chair, he opened up the Bible, picked up a pencil off the table, and marked on a page—a lot. As soon as I saw it I stopped him and explained why you don't mark in books and this was Daddy's preaching Bible that was to be left up on the shelf—always. I gave him some legitimate paper to mark on and put the Bible back in place, hoping it would be a long time before Bennie Lee opened it at that certain spot. But fate was against me. The next Sunday morning when Bennie Lee got ready to brush up his memorizing of verses for his sermon, he opened that Bible—at that very page.

With horrified unbelief in his voice said, "*Who* has been marking in my *Bible?*" I said quietly, "Robert climbed up and pulled it out and marked it before I knew what was going on." Bennie Lee asked, "Why in the *world* did you *let* him *do* that?" And I explained, "It wasn't a matter of *letting* him."

A few weeks later we had days of rain. All week long I was shut in with four boys who couldn't get outside to play. By Saturday I was worn to a frazzle. When Bennie Lee came home for lunch he could tell it. Instead of taking the list to go for groceries later as he usually did, he asked, "Would you like for me to stay with the boys while you go for groceries?" I jumped at the chance. Earlier in the day I had been ironing; planning to iron again later, I had made sure the iron was unplugged; it was cool and I set it flat on the ironing board so it wouldn't fall off if someone bumped against it.

When I returned an hour or more later, I smelled burnt cloth and said, "I smell something burning!" Bennie Lee said, "Nothing's burning now. Robert found the iron chord hanging down and plugged it in without me knowing it until I smelled it." That was my chance—I said, "Why in the *world* did you *let* him *do* that?" He said, "It wasn't a matter of *letting* him!" And we laughed.

**Danda** About that time Mrs. Little, a retired teacher from Chattanooga, Tennessee, came to the Bible School. She rented the little house we had vacated, right across the street from where we now lived. She was a little lady in her late sixties whom we all loved dearly. She missed her grandchildren in Chattanooga who called her *Danda* and very soon our children were calling her *Danda*—she was the perfect substitute grandmother. Robert would do anything for her and she adopted him as her special boy. With her attention on Robert at church I could concentrate on twelve-months old Benjamin and keep an eye on Henry, who sat up front with Edward while their Daddy preached—a good arrangement most of the time.

An elderly man regularly sat near us and always kneeled for prayer. Robert watched him with interest. One Sunday when the man kneeled, Robert climbed down from his chair and Danda thought he was getting down to go to me. She tried urging him back to his seat then realized he was getting down on his knees beside her. When the prayer was over Robert said "Amen" out loud and climbed back up beside Danda. From then on when that man was there, Robert watched and imitated him. In the early days we kneeled for prayers at home but the custom among the churches we attended was fading as the older people passed on.

Mrs. Little was *Danda* to our children, but at school she was *Mrs. Little*, Librarian, English teacher, and instructor of Distributive Education (business behavior) all the while trying to instill good manners and good grammar where it was lacking in many students. We enjoyed her wit and wisdom and were more than pleased to have her influence in the lives of our children who loved her dearly.

She welcomed any children any time they went to see her. Ours wanted to "go see Danda" more often than we allowed for fear of them being a nuisance, though she declared she reveled in their company. She loved to cook and bake and often brought something over for us, or phoned asking Edward to come to get it—cooked roast or three-fourths of a fried or roasted chicken, a bowl of beans, greens or other vegetable, hot yeast rolls, two thirds of an iced cake or a pile of cookies. Her excuse was that she liked to make whole recipes—she also enjoyed sharing.

211

**Daddy's Little Angels** One evening after supper and evening devotions, with eighteen-month-old Benjamin in his lap and the others gathered around sitting on the floor, Bennie Lee told them one of his original *Jippy, The Little Black Monkey* stories with his usual enthusiasm and excitement. Then while he read the newspaper Edward and Henry went to take their baths and were soon engrossed with water toys in the tub. Robert and Benjamin were happy with toys in the middle of their bedroom floor next to the kitchen. I cleared the table, poured semi-cooled grease from the skillet into an empty shortening can and set it at the back of the stove to finish cooling while I washed dishes.

Bennie Lee finished reading the paper and came through the house. He looked in on the two playing in the bathtub and said, "Goodbye boys, I'm going to work;" through the room where Robert and Benjamin were playing, told them "bye," and on to the kitchen. He was exuding love and pride as he said, "You know, we have some mighty fine boys, don't we?" I agreed with him. Then he said goodbye to me and went to work.

Soon after he left, I heard a ruckus in the bathroom and went to settle Edward and Henry. While I was taking time to calm them and help them get dried, I heard a crash in the kitchen and hurried to check on it. Benjamin had pulled his highchair over to the stove, climbed up, leaned across the stove and pulled the can of still liquid (but not hot) grease toward him. The can turned over and grease ran all over the top of the stove, into the burner pans, down the front into the drawer and onto Benjamin's clothes, arms, legs and shoes with plenty on the floor.

I lifted him down and was wiping the grease off of him when I realized I had not heard or seen Robert since I went through their room to the bathroom. I settled Benjamin with toys, told him to stay right there. I called Robert and looked around just as he came through the door holding the children's paper scissors, saying, "I cut my hair!" And he had, starting at the front and making a path as far back as he could reach. The scissors were labeled "for children"—I found out they would cut children's hair.

Here it was Saturday night, no barber shop open and we had no clippers. I decided there was nothing to do but cut all his hair to match the path he had made. After I finished, he rubbed his head and said, "It feels scratchy!" I said, "Now you have a burr haircut like the big boys," but didn't add, "only shorter!" As soon as he and Benjamin were bathed and safely in bed, I phoned Bennie Lee and said, "I just want to tell you what your little *angels* have been doing since you left!"

The next morning Robert wanted to wear a cap to church so nobody could see his head. He had to take his cap off in the building and we told him it looked good but he scooted down in his chair to get his head below the back of his seat. Once again, the world didn't end, his hair grew, and we bought some clippers very soon.

**Cotton Picking Days** School life was becoming busier all the time and that meant so was our home life—programs, candy sales, sports days and such like. Summers were welcome breaks from that schedule but our summers were short. School started six weeks early, then dismissed for six weeks for children to help their families pick cotton.

That fall Edward and Henry got their first taste of cotton picking. There was a cotton field not far from our house that had been picked over the first time and was ready for bolls to be pulled. Before the days of the mechanical cotton picker, workers were usually paid $5 or $6 per 100 lbs. when they picked the prime cotton in a field. After that there was still some cotton stuck in the bolls and pickers went back over the field the second time, this time pulling off the bolls which weighed more and pay was less, usually $1.50-$2 per 100 lbs. The second picking was not mixed with the first but was taken separately to the cotton gin where the gin separated the cotton from the bolls and baled it separately from the high quality cotton of the earlier picking. Good pickers like Bennie Lee's sister, Edith, could pick 500-600 pounds a day on the first round and such pickers felt they were wasting their time pulling bolls. They were glad to see children come to pull bolls so they could move on to a prime field. The farmers were glad because it helped get the crops in sooner.

Edward and Henry had friends going to pull bolls for a farmer who was paying $3.00 per 100 lbs and begged to go with them. Bennie Lee didn't want them to be a nuisance so he talked to the farmer. He generously said, "There has to be a first time for everyone. Let them come on and see what they can do. They'll be paid for what they pick and if they get tired, they can go home." Edward and Henry went off in a run, carrying their sack-lunches—sacks for picking were supplied at the weighing truck.

The boys persevered longer than I expected and it was nearing sundown when I saw Edward coming across the back lot. He had pulled about 50 lbs. and proudly showed me his $1.50. Then we heard and saw Henry coming into sight, jumping up and down waving something in the air and yelling at the top of his considerable lungs, "LOOK, MOTHER, LOOK! I MADE A DOLLAR BILL! I MADE A DOLLAR BILL!" It was the first time in his life that he had earned or owned a dollar bill! They picked cotton nearly every fall after that. Robert and Benjamin wanted to join them but I wasn't ready to turn them loose yet.

Later on, when Paul was a baby I took all of them to a field where women I knew were picking with their children. It was October and cold when we left home before sunrise. At the field we each took a sack (approximately 2ft.x6ft.) from the stack on the truck-bed and went to work. Following the example of other mothers, I set Paul on the end of my sack where he played with toys and later took a bottle and slept, while I picked cotton and pulled the sack and him behind me. By 9:30 we had shed our sweaters and by noon we had peeled off long-sleeved shirts and were down to summer clothes and wiping away sweat. Benjamin and I thought we were picking a lot but Edward, Henry and Robert left us behind.

We were not pulling bolls this time—even so I thought my sack surely weighed fifty pounds by lunch time when I took it to be weighed. To my disappointment and Benjamin's our combined picking only weighed 35 pounds. We divided the proceeds and he was happy. There was water to drink with a tin cup from a barrel on the truck and we had our sack lunches. After we ate, Edward and Henry wanted to keep picking and I took Robert, Benjamin and Paul home promising to return for Edward and Henry at sundown.

As they got older Robert and Benjamin were allowed to go with Edward and Henry. The next time I picked cotton Nancy was a baby able to sit alone. I made a small sack for Paul, and Nancy sat on the long end of my sack. She played or napped while I pulled her along—again we were picking cotton—not pulling bolls. One of the fields where we picked was near a country store where workers who didn't bring their lunches could buy something to eat. That sounded more exciting to the boys so I gave them each a quarter. Bologna was sliced from a big roll with a large knife on a huge butcher block and cost a nickel a slice; with a nickel's worth of soda crackers from the big jar, a Moon Pie for a nickel and a cold drink for a nickel, it made a satisfying lunch and left them with a nickel each to put in their piggy banks when they got home. Now and then they splurged on a can of Vienna Sausages for a dime instead of the bologna.

Every fall the older boys picked, until mechanical pickers took their jobs and schools did away with the "cotton picking time." What they earned that way along with what they made on their paper routes, was enough to buy most of their own school clothes each year.

It was no secret that the boys were helping the family finances by buying most of their own clothes. They were proud of themselves and enjoyed shopping for their own clothes. We were proud that they were learning to work and getting satisfaction from it. But that fact was used against Bennie Lee when the school needed a new President and he was being considered for the opening. His name was put forward at the board meeting and one of the board members said Bennie Lee was scripturally disqualified because he made his children work to buy their own clothes and everyone knew the Bible said "If a man does not provide for his own he is worse than an infidel." The other board members did not think that scripture applied in this way but one objection prevented the required unanimous vote for approval.

Aside from thinking the objector's use of that scripture was invalid, I felt Bennie Lee did not need another full time job, but it was not my decision to make. While he was being considered for the job, he was torn between wanting to serve the school in that office and feeling that his other many jobs needed his fuller concentration. He prayed that the Lord would show him what he should do. He felt that this was his answer and he was content with the decision. One of the most important qualities I had looked for in a husband, learned from my parents, was complete dependence on God's providence to lead in what was right. From the time I met Bennie Lee it was evident that he, too, lived by that standard and to my mind this incident and his response to it demonstrated that attitude. My admiration and respect for him grew.

In south Athens there was a congregation of colored people (as they preferred to be called in those days) where Bennie Lee had preached quite often and had attended their summer revivals. In that congregation were many listeners to his daily radio program. One night Bennie Lee was working late at the bookstore when there was a knock on the side door. He did not recognize the gray-haired colored man at the door, who said, "Brother Fudge, you don't know me but I've heard you preach at Lucas Street church and I've heard people talk about you. I know you are a man of God and I'm asking you to pray for me. I'm in bad trouble and tonight I was driving around because I didn't know what else to do. When I saw your light, I knew I could talk to you and ask you to pray for me and I know your prayer will be heard because the Bible says God will listen to the prayer of a righteous man."

He went on to say that some weeks before, he had been driving and at an intersection he had the green light but as he drove under the light a car driven by a white man, came from the side and didn't stop and ran into him. No one was hurt but when they were giving the report to the policeman, the white man told the policeman that the colored man ran the red light. About that time another white man came up and said he saw the accident and knew that the colored man ran the red light. The man told Bennie Lee, "Tomorrow I have to go to court about it and I know the judge will not believe me. I'm asking you to pray for me. I need a miracle to happen because I *know* the light was green—I did *not* run a red light. *God knows* I'm telling you the truth." Bennie Lee prayed with him right then and promised to keep praying.

When we had family prayer Bennie Lee prayed for him and asked the rest of us to be praying about it. The next evening was Wednesday so we were at church and Bennie Lee did not work late, but Thursday night there was again a knock at the bookstore side door. It was the same man and this time he was smiling. He said when he stood before the judge and was accused by the man who hit his car, the man's witness was not there, but a different white man stood up and said he saw the accident and he knew the colored man was telling the truth—and the judge believed him. The colored man told Bennie Lee he believed it was a miracle that happened because of his prayers. Bennie Lee told him he was sure it was because of all the prayers and right there they offered another prayer together—one of thanksgiving.

**Addressing Envelopes** Edward was in the third grade and Henry started to school in the fall of 1952. My home brood was down to Robert and Benjamin during school hours and I had time to do something extra. Bennie Lee was working day and night; part of the time with school matters, and the rest of the time with the book business and writing, and preaching, and teaching Bible classes. From the bookstore he was sending out advertising mailings periodically, and I offered to address envelopes at home. The alphabetized customer mailing list was on index file cards in trays that I could bring home. I didn't feel bad about being slow because the pay was twenty-five cents per hundred.

I addressed envelopes on a portable Royal typewriter and it was the ideal work to do without neglecting children or home duties because addresses could be interrupted without frustration. It was also a chance to improve my limited typing skill. After a while Virginia Dale, the bookstore secretary, acquired a new typewriter and I inherited her old Royal upright and my speed improved dramatically. By the time the bookstore got an addressograph machine I had addressed thousands of envelopes at home and my typing speed and accuracy had improved considerably.

**If You Can't Buy It, Make It** Edward and Henry were sharing a 9'x10' bedroom. They had a double bed and said they wanted bunk beds to give them more space but we could not afford to buy them right then. So—we made them. We had been given a second hand couch for the living room and we moved the old quilt box into their room to make the bottom bunk. Our friend at the lumber company cut boards that we put together like an old-fashioned door for the top bunk. From the old double bed mattress we were ready to discard, I made mattresses to fit the box and the top-bunk. Bennie Lee helped screw strong hinges to the two-by-fours in the wall at the right distance over the box so that the top bunk could swing against the wall. On each of the two front corners of the top bunk he screwed in a big eye-screw and fastened them by chains to two giant hook screws in the ceiling—behold, a bunk bed! When the boys wanted to use the bottom bunk for a couch they undid the chains from the top bunk and let it swing down against the wall and used the extra mattress as the couch back. In a growing, changing household, however, that invention only lasted a couple of years before it was time for the next one.

**Baby Number Five** In July of 1953 I was pregnant again and thankful that the intermission from nausea had been a little longer this time. With the help once more of Dr. Pepper and crackers, things went along normally. During the nausea time with each pregnancy, without my asking him to, Bennie Lee made a point of being more available. He stayed longer at lunch time if possible and at night he oversaw the boys' baths, read to them and settled them in bed before going back to work; when a call came from their room in the night he got up. His helpfulness in all of those things made me feel cherished and I wished that those who accused him of having no feelings could have seen him in that role. When he was at work of course I took care of it all, often being sick in that process and while cooking supper. The nearest thing to "ordering in" a meal in those days was the bringing of food by neighbors if the mother was very sick or if there was a death in the family.

218

**Thanksgiving Day** After the death of their mother, every October Bennie Lee sent personal letters to his siblings inviting them to our house for Thanksgiving Day. That year I was thankful the four months were well over before time for the Thanksgiving Family Reunion. Some who lived far away didn't make it every year. Besides enjoying the association with adult kin, we all enjoyed each other's children, rejoicing in the fact that our own children could know their cousins, aunts and uncles—something we had not known growing up.

Each family brought something for the meal, and after a few years we knew what to expect from each other. Everyone seemed happy as long as I cooked the hen or turkey and made the old fashioned cornbread dressing. I always made pecan pies, pumpkin pies and sometimes German Chocolate or Strawberry Cake; others brought their favorite desserts. Duplicates and leftovers didn't matter because everyone took some home with them. When I was growing up Minced Meat Pies were regular holiday treats, but the first time I made one for Thanksgiving I was the only one who ate any so that tradition died for our family.

**Paul Curtis Fudge** In February1954 Bennie Lee was to speak on the Florida College Lectures and the same week in February our baby was due. Otha Lowe Lee said if Bennie Lee was not back in time she would go with me to the hospital. The boys could stay at their house with Judy and Sandra who were now old enough to oversee them. Bennie Lee was not back in time and **Paul Curtis was born February 25, 1954.** To my relief he weighed exactly seven pounds—breaking the ascending weight pattern of the first four. He was named *Paul* in honor of our dear friend, Paul Witt of Abilene Christian College, in whose home I had lived for three years and who performed our wedding ceremony; *Curtis* was after Bennie Lee's brother, Curtis. *Nancy Sue* was the girl name still in reserve for when and if. Paul was a solemn, contented baby and a joy to care for. Bennie Lee and I congratulated ourselves on having the five finest boys in the world! As Jack Rollings used to say, "To every mama crow, her little crow is the blackest!"

While the boys were staying at the Lee's house, Benjamin fell down the steps at the back door and knocked out a front tooth. They never found it and decided he must have swallowed it! In spite of no tooth he was visited by the tooth-fairy and happy. Not yet four years old, he was snaggle-toothed longer than usual.

**Evelyn Blanton** In early spring of 1954, a Tennessee preacher came to talk to Bennie Lee about his cousin, Evelyn Blanton, who lived in Florida. She was anxious to leave the environment where she was and wanted to attend the Bible School for her last two years of high school. But she needed somewhere to live and he wondered if we would give her a place in our home. He said she was willing to help with housework and baby-sitting.

We discussed it with the boys and thought and prayed about all that would be involved. Making room for her was easy enough if we bought another set of bunk beds. We could give Evelyn the 9x10 room that had been Edward and Henry's and put all five boys in the 10x11 room. Two sets of bunk beds with the crib in there with a low chest under the double window left just enough space in the center of the room to turn around in! After all it would only be for two years and everyone agreed that we could make it work for that long. Evelyn was a big help to me and the boys soon got used to having a big sister in the house; she was one of eight children and didn't mind all the activity and noise. The "full house" didn't hinder our children from inviting school friends from the country to spend the night; we just scheduled more carefully. When we had adult overnight guests we gave them our room and Bennie Lee and I used the sleep-sofa in the living room.

Days were still hot and nights didn't cool down much until after midnight. At bedtime, fresh out of their baths, the boys went to sleep well enough but by 10:30 or 11:00 they were sweating and became restless. When I heard one of them stirring, knowing they would wake each other up, I grabbed my two pieces of cardboard (cut from the sides of a big box), stood in the center of their little room and fanned until they were cool and sound asleep again. After a time we splurged and installed a big window-fan in the dining room window. It sucked hot air out of the house and cooler air in through the partially open other windows throughout the house.

**A Grandmother in Town** It was still spring of 1954 when Daddy, Mother and Bill came to the U.S. on furlough. Daddy needed to travel among supporting churches from Oregon to Georgia and in between. After they visited kinfolks in Kansas they wanted more time with Grandma Short, who was getting along in years. They decided to bring her with them to Athens, where they would rent a furnished house for several months while Bill attended the Bible School. Between travels Daddy would be with them. The house they rented was 101 E. Lee Street, between our house and town. The railroad ran right beside the yard but Mother said they could get used to the noise and besides, the house was clean and fully furnished and the landlord was willing to rent it for less than a year. For about seven months our family enjoyed grandparents in town where we could go see them when we wanted to and have them visit us often.

Bill attended the Bible School for the remainder of fifth grade that spring and the first part of sixth grade in the fall. He rode the Bible School bus that passed within a block of their house. His first teacher was Mrs. Givens, an older, experienced teacher, unfamiliar with the British school system. Later, Bill told me she was shocked that he didn't know decimals and "Mother was a little miffed that she made such a deal about it in front of the whole class!" When he went into the sixth grade that fall, Mrs. Whitehead was his teacher, also older and, Bill said, "somewhat kinder, but when Daddy visited the class one day *he* thought she was too kind because there was a lot of talking in class!" (unheard of in Rhodesian schools.)

Paul was a few months old when they came to Athens. All the children enjoyed Great-Grandmother who told them stories or read to them when they sat still long enough. Mother was "Granny Short" to our children and she made the most of the few months, living up to what grandmothers were noted for. She kept home-made cookies on hand and she talked to them like they were grown ups and listened intently to their talk. She had a special way with Robert and Henry, who were six and eight years old and very active and independent. Henry was her yard "supervisor" and Robert was her self-appointed helper at whatever she wanted done. Bill, Edward and Henry helped pick up sticks and rake leaves and keep the yard mowed with our reel push-mower that we took over for them to use. Somehow she made Robert feel it was his "job" and the others were just helping with it! Mother bragged on all of them and they enjoyed working for her.

As soon as we arrived at her house, Robert marched in and asked Mother what she wanted him to do and she was always ready with something. One time I heard her ask him if he ever ran out of anything to talk about and he said, "hardly ever!" When cold weather came she appointed Robert caretaker of the "Warm Morning" heater, the large upright, coal-burning heater in the center of the house. When closed up at night it held live coals ready for chunks of coal to be added the next morning. When the damper was opened flames quickly rose up and the house was soon warm. His special job was to take the ashes out. He put a bucket in front of the heater, scraped the ashes from under the grate into the bucket and emptied them near the back yard fence. The dirtier he got the better he liked it.

In the back yard was a huge old tree with branches at different heights going in many directions—a perfect climbing tree for Bill, Edward and Henry to enjoy. Paul, five or six months old, was always happy with Edward carrying him around and one day I asked Edward to take care of Paul while Mother helped me cut out a dress. After a time I went to see how they were doing. I didn't see them anywhere in the yard and when I called, Edward answered from above me. I looked up and up there in the tree were Edward and Bill sitting on a branch talking, Edward holding Paul in his lap. My heart did a triple summersault.

"*Edward!*" I exclaimed, "How in the world did you get Paul up there?"

"We passed him to each other as we came up. It's O.K. Mother, we're taking good care of him!"

"Well, pass him to each other and come back down, and please be careful!"

My mother came out when she heard me calling them, and she and I silently watched their every move, putting ourselves under where Paul might fall as they slowly passed him down. When they were safely on the ground, I said, "*Please* don't ever take a baby up in a tree like that again—unless you're escaping from a wild animal!"

In October Mother noticed that I wasn't eating much and, as she put it, "You look peak-ed." And I felt that way but assured her it would pass in a few weeks. In spite of that we enjoyed every minute of our time together. She took pleasure in grocery shopping and cooking "American style." Knowing cooking was not my favorite thing at that time, she invited the family for Sunday dinner often. By winter Daddy had completed his travels among supporting churches, so we were all together for Thanksgiving and Christmas. By then I could once more enjoy cooking and had them over to our house for meals more often. We were sorry to see the time passing so quickly because it meant that they would soon be gone but we were having more time with them than during any of their furloughs.

All too soon they were at our house telling us goodbye. They would take Grandma Short to Kansas on their way back to Africa. Robert was sorry to know they were going and had told Mother several times when they talked about it that he wanted to go with them. Mother said jokingly that she could pack him in her suitcase and take him along. But now they were actually saying goodbye and while we were talking in the living room, Robert disappeared. Mother hugged and kissed all of us in the room then looked around for Robert. We found him under his bed. He said he didn't want to come out because he didn't want to be packed in a suitcase. She assured him that she had been teasing so he emerged to tell them goodbye.

When my parents were in Africa we wrote frequent letters to each other. I had learned from Mother to give many details that are not always given in letters, describing a new dress I made, how I rearranged the furniture in a room, or what I served for a company meal. All of that, plus details of the children's growth and clever, unusual or cute sayings and activities, helped us feel closer to each other. When we met again every five or six years we didn't feel the need to get reacquainted after the long separation. For a long time after Mother died, when something happened that I wanted her to know about, I found myself thinking, "I must tell Mother about that in my next letter."

**Robert's Dickie Birds** Robert was to start school in the fall. He had imaginary "dickie birds" that he kept in his pocket in the daytime and at night put them in "their house." The chest beside his bed had a drawer on one side and a door on the side next to his head. When he undressed for his bath he took the dickie birds out of his pocket, said "goodnight little dickie birds," put them inside the door, closed it and said, "tick-a-lock."

The next morning he "unlocked" the door, talked to them, then put them in his pocket for the day. We wondered what he would do when he started to school, but didn't say anything. The first morning of school he said, "Good-bye, little dickie birds, I'm going to school now." He left them in the cupboard and never again mentioned them to us, that I recall.

**"I Don't Want To Go To School?"** Robert was nearly seven when he started to school because his birthday was in October and the rule was "6 years old by September 30." He insisted he didn't want to go to school. When we asked him why not, he said, "Because I already know everything!"—and he almost did know everything that would be taught in the first two grades. He had been taking in what Henry was learning just as Henry had learned from Edward. His and Henry's inexperienced young teachers in first and second grades were sometimes in desperation over them because they were never still and their report cards invariably said, "Talks too much." In the third grade Henry responded to the more experienced Miss Holt and began to like school better.

But it was when Robert started the fourth grade and had Mrs. Givens, that his attitude changed. On the first day he went into the classroom and sat down at the back, as was his custom, Mrs. Givens said, "Robert, I need you to come sit on the front row and be my assistant." And she gave him real jobs that helped her and kept him busy. He came home the first day and announced proudly, "I'm Mrs. Givens' assistant!" He felt useful and liked her and did better with her than with any other elementary teacher he had.

**Camp Wyldewood** Edward joined the Boy Scouts and advanced rapidly in the different levels. When he was twelve he wanted to go to Scout Camp. Bennie Lee had recently heard about Camp Wyldewood, a Christian camp near Searcy, Arkansas, and had some brochures describing it that he gave to Edward to look at. Bennie Lee thought it would be a better place for him to go, though it was about three hundred miles away.

Edward agreed to go there and enjoyed it so much that every summer after that he went until he was too old, and then he went for a summer as a counselor, not only there but in other camps, too.

With Edward going off to camp, Henry wanted badly to go camping, too, but he was only ten and we wanted to see how it went for Edward before letting him go. In a phone conversation with Lucy, Bennie Lee's sister in Nashville, I mentioned that Edward had gone to Wyldewood and that Henry felt left behind. She said, "Let him come spend a week with us. We would love to have him and we'll make sure he has a good time. Robert (her husband) and I would really enjoy having a child in the house and you know how we feel about all your boys and about Henry in particular." So Henry spent a memorable week in Nashville being treated royally.

We were so pleased with Edward's experience that beginning the next year Henry went, too, and from then on all our children went to Camp Wyldewood when they reached the minimum age of ten. We had to leave home very early Sunday morning to be in Searcy in time to attend church in town, have lunch and get out to the camp by the official opening at 3:00 p.m. There we unloaded their things and as soon as we had seen their cabin(s), we left the happy camper(s) in good company and headed back to Athens, arriving home around midnight.

Our boys wanted to attend different sessions from each other and we understood that. Sometimes we shared trips and kids with parents of other campers from Athens, but one time I couldn't go and no one else was making the trip so we sent Henry by train. Searcy, Arkansas was one of those places you can't get to! His train missed its connection in Memphis and Henry called collect to tell us. Bennie Lee encouraged him the best he could and comforted me saying, "He's eleven years old." We found out later that when he finally arrived in Searcy late at night no one met his train and I remembered what it felt like to arrive at a strange place and not be met, and I had been eighteen. When we heard what a time he had getting to camp, my heart ached for "my little boy" and we never sent anyone to Searcy by train again.

The camping season of 1961 was so memorable that I wrote a description of some of it in a letter to my parents . . . "*Edward had gone to Abilene with Bennie Lee and would be dropped off at Wyldewood on the return journey in two weeks. A friend, Freddy Richter, was going to Wyldewood that session and his brother-in-law volunteered to take Freddie, Robert and Benjamin from Athens. He said he and Freddie would be by to pick our boys up at 2:30 Sunday morning. Saturday night my boys were packed and we went to bed at 8:30. At 10:00 p.m. the doorbell woke me up—it was Samuel (Filipino boy) and one of his friends on their way to Huntsville to sell Bibles and wanted to sleep at our house. They had had supper so I made beds for them and we all got to sleep about 10:45. I was up at 2:00 and had Robert and Benjamin fed and ready but they didn't leave till 3:15—the brother-in-law was late! My alarm went off again at 4:30 for me to rouse Henry (who never heard an alarm) for him to take his and Robert's paper routes. Back to bed I went and slept until 7:30 by mistake (mine)! We went to church close to home rather than be late out at Pleasant Valley—also I had to attend Bennie Lee's aunt's funeral that afternoon.*

"*All that week was odd with just three children in the house. Henry took care of paper routes until the next week when he went with some other paperboys to Birmingham for a free trip they had won. Sammy Fain, a neighbor boy, helped me run the paper routes, in the car, but when Henry got home I told him not to win any more trips! Bennie Lee arrived home, having dropped Edward off at Wyldewood on the way. He was to go back to Wyldewood that Friday to take Henry and bring home Robert, Benjamin and Freddy. A letter from Bill* (my brother) *said he would be with us two weeks—the weeks Edward and Henry would be gone, sorry to say. And so the summer went!"*

**Paperboys** Athens was served with two newspapers out of Birmingham—The Birmingham News and The Birmingham Post. Edward took a paper route and soon Henry and Robert had routes. When they had an afternoon route, as soon as they got out of school they went to the "paper house" where their bundles of papers had been dumped by a truck from Birmingham. There they rolled their papers, put rubber bands on them and filled their canvas paper-bag, hoisted that into the basket on the front of their bicycle and delivered to their memorized routes. If it was raining they had to insert the papers into plastic bags as they rolled them. Sometimes they had a morning route and left the house about 3:30 or 4:00.

Most of the time they rode bicycles and I was comfortable with that, but for a while an older Henry had a motorcycle. I felt motorcycles were extremely dangerous and spent some anxious early mornings listening for his return, imagining him lying in a ditch somewhere and I heaved a sigh of relief when I heard his motorcycle roar up the driveway at just about my getting-up time. Paper route experience was good for the boys: they learned to be dependable deliverers, responsible bill collectors and good record keepers. Like the proverbial postman they delivered papers rain or shine, snow or sleet. I admired their zeal, though at times they were less than enthusiastic, especially in the winter when it took willpower for me to deny their requests to take them in the car—unless they were sick and really needed the help. When they needed a substitute for a good reason, they substituted for each other if they could but if not, Benjamin and I (in the car) did the runs for them. There were dogs in many of the yards and after a bad experience with one dog, Benjamin was deathly afraid of all dogs for a long time, though he learned their routes and on occasion substituted for them on a bicycle, braving the chance of an unchained dog.

When Paul was old enough he had paper routes, too. His last one was the most unusual I had seen. Sewell Hall's son, Gardner, was about Paul's age and when they were sixteen, both with paper routes, they formed a working partnership. Gardner had his driver's license and a VW with a sun-roof, so he drove while Paul stood up, head and shoulders through the roof, throwing rolled papers on to the proper yards as Gardner drove slowly along their combined routes.

**Which Arm?** The children had school insurance, paperboys had insurance, the family had family insurance. When Henry was about ten he went with other students on a school bus as spectators to a track/field day in another town. While on that school's grounds he and a friend were jumping from one gatepost pillar across the driveway to the other pillar. Henry fell and broke his forearm. For the prescribed number of weeks his arm was in a cast and the school insurance paid the doctor cost, his paper route insurance paid the doctor cost, plus the cost of his substitute, our family insurance paid the doctor cost—there were no stipulations otherwise. When it was all over he had $50 above his cost. The week after his cast was taken off I was in the kitchen when he came out of his bedroom looking at his arms, first one then the other. I asked if his arm was hurting. He answered with a grin, "No, Ma'm, I was just trying to decide which arm to break next and make another $50!"

**"It's A Girl!"** In those days mothers did not know what sex a baby would be until it arrived. It was time for number six and Bennie Lee and I went to the hospital, prepared for another boy, while thinking just maybe this would be a girl. We had changed the girl name to *Nancy Elizabeth:* Bennie Lee said that since his mother was long dead and his favorite Aunt Betty (Elizabeth) was still living, he would like to honor her by using her name as one of our girl's. Of course we had a boy's name ready just in case, but we didn't need it. **Nancy Elizabeth** was born **May 13, 1955,**

weighing 6 lbs. 13 ozs. There was great excitement in family, school and bookstore when word spread that "Fudges have a girl!" She was the third one of our children to be born on the 13$^{th}$—Edward July 13$^{th}$, Henry September 13$^{th}$, Nancy May 13$^{th}$.

While Bennie Lee went to get me and the new baby from Dr. Jackson's Clinic, two teenage girls who lived on our street, Judith Rollings and Judy Davis, made a banner that stretched the length of our front porch with big letters proclaiming, "IT'S A GIRL!" When we walked in the door they greeted us playing the piano and singing, *"The Lovely Lady of Chandler Drive"* that they had paraphrased to the tune of a popular song.

During the fourteen days I was gone Bennie Lee and the boys managed well with the help of Evelyn and a daytime baby sitter for Benjamin and Paul. The first morning at home I intended to go to the kitchen to help with breakfast but they insisted I stay in bed while they treated me with breakfast-in-bed. Fifteen-month-old Paul climbed up on the bed with me and watched every move I made and asked for bites, while the others hovered by the bedside watching and telling me, "I put the bread in the toaster,"—"I buttered your toast,"—"I folded the napkin for you,"—"I put the flower in the vase," whatever each one had contributed to the breakfast. What mother could have asked for a better welcome home?

With the imminent arrival of each of Henry, Robert and Benjamin, when the doctor said the baby could arrive any day and I was still home with no signs of anything happening, I energetically rearranged heavy furniture and vigorously cleaned house, hoping it would hasten the process. But it didn't make any difference that I could tell. So when Paul's and Nancy's arrivals were "any day," I tried something different. At night after all the children were asleep and Bennie Lee was back at work, I went to the back porch where the floor was concrete (so it wouldn't shake the house) and jumped a rope! That didn't seem to help either and I decided babies had minds of their own, even before they were born.

We had six children and we were happy with our fulfilled dream. My memories of the total twenty-four months of nausea out of the last eleven years were completely dimmed by the joy each child brought to our lives.

We delighted in the daily changes as the babies grew and developed their own differences and personalities. We were excited over each first tooth, first step and first word. No two were alike and each presented thrills and challenges. Daily we fervently thanked God for the blessings they were to us. When Nancy arrived Bennie Lee told me, "I think I know something about raising boys, but I can tell you right now, I have no idea what to do with a girl—except to spoil her and leave the rest up to you!" Paul and Nancy being only fifteen months apart, were "our babies!" From her first day I reveled in dressing our girl in girly clothes.

**Sundays And Babies** Every one of the babies was taken to church the first Sunday after coming home from Dr. Jackson's clinic. Going to church wasn't something we decided on each week—it was as much a part of our weekly schedule as eating and going to bed, unless someone was sick enough to stay home. Then depending on which child was sick and how sick they were, either I or one of the older boys stayed with them.

On Nancy's first Sunday I asked Edward to dress Paul while I got myself and Nancy ready. Other than Paul, the boys could dress themselves in clothes I laid out for them the night before. At that time Bennie Lee was again preaching at Eastside church and we were still meeting in the Bible School auditorium. Edward and Henry usually took the shortcut across the back lot while the rest of us went by car when Bennie Lee came from studying his sermon at the bookstore. That day when we got out of the car in the parking lot I looked down at my feet—I was still wearing my bedroom slippers! I told the others to go ahead and with Nancy on the seat beside me I drove home to put on my shoes!

My usual Sunday morning routine was to get up at 5:30 or 6:00 depending on whether I was starting dinner before church or not. I dressed myself ready to go—all but my hat and Sunday shoes—and put an apron on to protect my dress. I woke the boys beginning at the oldest, giving each one a certain amount of time in the bathroom before calling the next one. I tried to keep plenty of their favorite cereals for Sunday morning breakfasts and each one ate before getting dressed for church.

Some Sundays I grabbed a spare minute and put my hat on before making the final check to be sure the boys were properly clad. More than once when we were all settled in the car and backing out of the driveway, one of them said, "Mother, did you know you still have your apron on?"

**"Word"** Edward was eleven years old when Nancy was born. Fifteen-months-old Paul called Edward "Word" and obviously thought there was no one like his big brother. One Sunday morning I dressed Paul ready for church and turned him loose while I was getting Nancy ready. I heard water running in the boys' bathroom and knowing there should be no one taking a bath I hurried to see what was going on. Paul had climbed into the tub and was standing under the faucet with water running over his pants legs, white sox and just-polished white shoes—cold water fortunately. I put dry clothes on him and wiped his every-day shoes as clean as I could. Edward was always ready first so after that incident it was his responsibility to watch Paul and Paul loved it. In memory I see Edward walking around the house with a happy Paul astride his shoulders saying, "Turn wight here, Word!" or "Doh stwaight, Word!" Paul loved to be proved right about something and we invented as many occasions as we could just to hear him say, "I was wight and you was wong!"

**Fur Trimmed Red Velvet** Finally I was able to make frilly dresses and a girl's coat with matching bonnet; the first outfit was light blue when Nancy was one year old. For years I had daydreamed of making a red velvet coat and bonnet trimmed with white rabbit fur. Sears Roebuck had such material and I made that for Nancy when she was two years old. I was sorry when she outgrew it after two years.

All the family enjoyed Paul and Nancy and Paul and Nancy enjoyed each other. They always shared. If I gave Nancy a piece of apple, cracker or cheese, she held out her other hand saying, "For Paul," and he did the same for her. When Bennie Lee took Paul to Gadsden with him one day, he gave Paul a pack of peanuts to eat as they drove. He noticed Paul ate a few then folded the top down and put the packet in his pocket. Bennie

Lee asked him if he wasn't going to eat them, Paul said he was saving half for Nancy and he gave them to her when he got home. On trips with his Daddy Paul enjoyed learning the Greek alphabet and that pleased Bennie Lee.

**Alexander's Six Girls** One of the early teacher/preachers who came to the Bible School was Everette Alexander with his wife, Nan, and their one-year old Nancy. For about twelve years he taught at the school and preached in the county. Edward's birth in 1944 set the two couples of us off in an interesting sequence of children. During the next eleven years Nan and I approximately alternated, she having girls and me having boys, until our Nancy broke the record. The year after we had Edward they had Barbara, the next year we had Henry; then we had Robert and the next year they had Frances; then we had Benjamin and were ahead; they caught up with Virginia, then took the lead with Phyllis. Paul's birth tied us, each with five children of the same gender. In February 1955 their sixth and last girl, Rachel, arrived and the same year in May we ended the one-gender-only run by having Nancy.

With the two fathers preaching in different churches through the years, our two families lived in different communities and only saw each other on school occasions; consequently our children didn't know each other well. But Nan and I made a pact that at least once she would leave her six with me for a few days while she went with Everette to one of his out-of-town meetings and I would leave my six with her on a similar occasion—not too close to the same time! Their Nancy was 13 and Edward was 12 the year we carried out the plan. We never had a chance to do it again. After that experience Nan and I agreed that "cheaper by the dozen" might be true in some ways but we had no desire to prove it personally, half a dozen suited us just fine!

**A Run-Away** One day Henry, at a young age I don't recall, came from his room and announced, "I'm running away." I was in the kitchen preparing supper. I asked why and he said Robert made him mad and no one loved him. I had recently read some hints on mothering and decided to try one of them. I said, "Well, I'll miss you. Good-bye!" He looked at me in surprise, picked up a cold biscuit off of the counter and stuck it in his pocket as he walked out. If the article was right he would soon be back—I hoped before dark. It was getting near dusk when he came in the door. I greeted him and he said that it was getting dark in the woods, he was getting hungry and that it wasn't the same in the woods as when they went camping so he decided to come back. I told him I was glad to see him and supper was almost ready. All was well that ended well but I fervently hoped there would be no more runaways.

**Kites** Kite-flying was a spring and fall event for our household as soon as Edward got big enough to help fly one. Very seldom could we afford to buy ready-made kites or rolls of string but we watched for any sticks suitable for making a kite, saved any string that came around, and hoarded usable paper. Bennie Lee's suits came from the drycleaner in paper covers thin enough to make good kite paper. Until the boys could do it themselves, I helped them make the kites and fly them and I must have untangled *miles* of kite string. Most of that time there were vacant lots close by—good places for flying kites. I can still see boys running with kites flying high over their heads and kites nose-diving to the ground to be picked up and tried again. In Henry's case his dog ran along with him or sat on its haunches watching him.

**Dogs** From the time he was in third grade Henry had a dog, sometimes a grown stray or sometimes a puppy dropped in the grass beside our house, and he loved every one. An indelible memory is of Henry running home from school to be met by his bouncing, tail-wagging dog; of Henry dropping books and jacket on the porch steps, sitting down to hug and pet his dog then jumping up to run and tumble with it. Chandler Drive was not a busy street and cars drove slowly on it but the main street on the other side of our lot was busier. At least two of his dogs suffered untimely deaths by running out in front of cars.

I had forgotten Henry's essay about one of them until going through some keepsakes recently. The essay, in his own handwriting was not dated but he remembers the dog featured and said he thinks the essay was written when he was in third grade. He gave me permission to include it here unchanged:

> *The Dog*
> *I am a dog. I lived in the woods until Henry Fudge got me. I was very happy until I died. Now I am dead. I have been dead about six days. I have no calendar to keep up with the date so I do not know just when I died but I remember about when it was. I am about to get buried so I have to get ready to go to the funeral.*
>
> *—Henry Fudge*

Henry's mother says, "Priceless!"

At some point Henry asked if we could have a dog house and I thought, "If you can't afford to buy it, make it," and told him we could. Our friend in the lumber yard cut boards for us for uprights and sides according to the plan I gave him. Henry, Robert and I put it together, shingle roof and all. It was so heavy there was no danger of it blowing away and it lasted for years, serving all the dogs the boys had.

**Books** We tried to keep a good supply of books for all ages in the house to encourage the children to read. Birthdays and Christmases were not complete without new books for each one. The living room and every bedroom had bookcases in them, and finally the wall of the long hall had full bookshelves, too. When their friends came, if it was a first visit, they asked, "What in the world do you have so many books for?" and our child said, "To read, of course!" Henry and Robert were so busy with outdoor activities I thought they were not reading much but I found out later they read more than I knew about and remembered what they read. They were a challenge to their teachers throughout their school days.

Many of our neighbors were getting televisions but Bennie Lee and I felt that television-watching would keep the children from reading as much as we wanted them to. We did not forbid the children watching a limited amount of television if they happened to be visiting a friend's home where there was one; but when friends visited our children, after the initial question, "You mean you don't have a TV?" they always found plenty to do without it.

**Linda Reynolds** We had known the Reynolds family for years and their children attended the Bible School. Linda was finishing her junior year when the family was about to move away from the county. She wanted to finish her senior year at the Bible School and they asked if she could live with us for that year. Linda and Evelyn were already good friends and both would be seniors. They agreed they could manage in the little bedroom where the double bed, chest of drawers and small desk left little room to spare. They said with all their senior year activities, sleeping was about all they would do in that room anyway. So Linda came to live with us.

The house was full and humming with life. Every morning Bennie Lee walked his mile to work; two girls and three boys headed for school in rapid succession across the vacant back lot; and I was left with only Benjamin, Paul and Nancy. There was plenty to keep me busy until the school bunch came pouring back in bursting with tales of school happenings. Bennie Lee usually came home for lunch so the younger ones had some Daddy-time to themselves. At supper all ten of us sat around the big round dinner table (with two leaves in it) and everyone was heard—I think! The two girls helped with house-work and baby-sitting as they had time, and I was able to sew for Nancy and some for them and enjoyed every minute of it.

**A Forced Vacation** One night I was wakened by the phone and noticed it was nearly two o'clock. Bennie Lee had gone back to work after supper and I realized he wasn't home yet. When I answered the phone a man identified himself as the policeman on night duty who patrolled around town. He said when he passed the C.E.I. Store door he noticed the light in Bennie Lee's office and could see the legs of a man lying on the floor. I told him I would bring a key immediately. My heart was racing as I looked up our street to where I knew Elam Kuykendall sometimes worked late in his print shop. His light was still on so I phoned and asked him to go with me to the bookstore.

We found Bennie Lee sitting at his desk. He said he must have blacked out—that he had come to on the floor. The next day he willingly went with me to see Dr. Jackson. The doctor said his blood sugar was dangerously low and asked him how many hours of sleep he was getting. When Bennie Lee said "Oh, four or five," the doctor said, "And you work seven days a week, don't you? Are you trying to kill yourself? I want you to take off for at least two weeks, go somewhere clear away from all your work where nobody knows you and no one will phone you. Get lots of sleep and eat a candy bar—preferably with peanuts in it—every two or three hours, and let Sybil do all the driving." Bennie Lee said, "I don't have time to take off like that." Dr. Jackson said, "Do you have time to die?" Bennie Lee asked him if he was really serious about that and the doctor said he was dead serious.

We went home and got ready to leave the next day. Evelyn, Linda and the boys could manage before and after school; Wilma Curtis, a dear friend, offered to keep Benjamin and Paul during school hours and we took Nancy with us. Paul was only two but he loved Wilma and would do fine having Benjamin with him.

We put our luggage on the floor between front and back seats and made a pallet of quilts over it so Nancy had room to roll around and play and sleep. (Before the days of baby seats.) We drove to Florida, stopping at motels when we were tired. All the highways were two-lane and a vivid memory of that trip is of driving down a long hill with a big semi-truck in front of us and another big one barreling down behind us and I had visions of being squashed between them!

I don't recall where we went other than somewhere in northern Florida. Bennie Lee slept day and night as we drove and when we stopped. When

I called home each evening, Evelyn and the boys assured me they were doing fine. After one week Bennie Lee felt so much better he decided we would go home. From then on he put lots of sugar on his cereal in the morning, ate a nutty candy bar twice a day, got about two hours more of sleep most nights and once again went full steam ahead.

**Full House Less Full** In the spring Evelyn and Linda needed formals for their Junior-Senior Banquet but neither one could afford to buy a ready-made dress. I told them if they were willing to risk my sewing I would make their formals. They gladly shopped for material and did extra chores and baby-sitting to help me while I sewed. After they graduated we all missed the girls but agreed it was good to once again be "just us."

**Redecorating** We had been in the house about six years when we decided with so much traffic the hardwood floors were badly in need of refinishing and the walls and woodwork needed a coat or two of paint. Hiring it done would cost too much and that meant we would do it ourselves—meaning me, mostly. I blithely rented a sander and went to work on the floors of the dining room, living room and foyer. I was not prepared for the power that machine would unleash. It jerked me hither and thither unmercifully and I vowed "Never again!"

By the time I had wrestled with it through those rooms on the first round I wasn't sure I could go on for the second round with the fine sanding—but it had to be done before the finish could be applied. Someone had told me to use Gym Finish for a tougher, longer lasting shine and for good measure I put three coats on. By then I had decided that the bedrooms didn't really need their floors refinished! After the floor job, painting the walls and woodwork was a breeze, though my arms and shoulders ached from fighting with the sander.

**Company And More Company** While the girls were with us the full house had not hindered our having frequent overnight guests and mealtime visitors. In fact there was so much coming and going around our place that the neighbors called it "Grand Central Station." Preachers who held meetings where Bennie Lee was preacher at the time usually stayed with us. Members of the congregation invited the preacher to midday and evening meals so I only fixed breakfasts for him. Bennie Lee was always invited to go along with the preacher and went, unless he was unavoidably tied up with school or bookstore work. Our whole family was usually invited and I went with the younger boys if the older ones had too much homework or a school activity to attend. Occasionally I left all of them in the care of Evelyn and Edward and went with Bennie Lee.

Leonard Tyler, preacher and good friend, whose company we always enjoyed, was staying with us during a meeting at Eastside. On Monday morning I made biscuits and accidentally left them in the oven too long and the tops were almost black! I apologized and Leonard gallantly replied, "That's O.K. I like black biscuits!" Of course I knew he was joking but that evening we were invited along with him to have dinner with a couple who had never "had the preacher" before. The hostess had insisted that I be sure to come to help her feel more at ease so I took Paul and Nancy and went with the preachers. While I helped her put things on the table she was very nervous and I tried to reassure her. She turned the oven off but left the rolls in to stay warm. When she opened the door to take them out—they were very dark brown on top and she was horrified. I said reassuringly, "Don't worry, they're just dark brown—that's how my biscuits looked this morning and he likes them that way!" She took me literally and after that told other women preparing meals that he liked his bread almost black on top!

I was not with him at every meal from then on but at the end of the meeting when he was telling our family goodbye, he said, "Sybil, I believe I have you to thank for the burned bread I was served at every meal. Several women said they understood from you that I liked it that way!" I replied with a grin, "I'm sorry! Did I misquote you? I promise next time you stay with us I'll make sure you don't get burned bread!"

One early summer Saturday evening Bennie Lee called from the bookstore to say he had four young men on their way to Georgia to sell

Bibles for the summer. They were hungry and broke until they could make their first sales, and they planned to drive on to Georgia that night. I thought about the big pot of spaghetti-sauce cooling on the back of the stove, that I had made for Sunday dinner—expecting to have leftovers on Monday night. I told Bennie Lee to bring them on. I hastily prepared a pound of spaghetti, salad and toast. They devoured it all and we had something else for dinner on Sunday.

Several times Bennie Lee called late in the afternoon to say, "There's a family here on their way to _____ and I wonder if you could fix a bite of supper for them before they go on?" Sometimes they had from one to five children and more often than not, all I could scare up on that short notice was canned soup, cheese and crackers, and/or bologna sandwiches. Bennie Lee often knew the preachers from previous contacts in other places. Years later when Bennie Lee and I visited distant churches or attended out-of-town lectureships, more than once we met someone I didn't recognize, who said, "We met you in 19__ when we came through Athens on our way to ___with hungry children. You fed us soup and sandwiches—and soup and sandwiches never tasted so good!" Two of those preachers and families, the Sewell Halls and the Sam Binkleys later moved to Athens and our families became close friends.

**Our Guest Book** Early in our marriage Bennie Lee and I realized how frequently we had out-of-town visitors, besides missionaries and other preachers, and began keeping a Guest Book on our coffee table for them to sign. Here is the list of visitors from *overseas* who signed the Guest Book 1950-1975 (many forgot to sign. Some of these only "had tea" or ate a meal, others spent from one night to three weeks or more.

*W.N. and Delia Short and Bill, Bulawayo, Southern Rhodesia (my parents);*
*J. C. Bailey, Canada and Madras, India;*
*Samuel Belo, Cotabato, Philippines; Abilene Christian College*
*Jack Belo (Samuel's brother), Cotabato, Philippines*

*Ronnie P. Sadorra, Cotabato, Philippines; Abilene Christian College*

*Felix A. Bravo, Cotabato, Philippines; Abilene Christian College*

*S. K. Dong, Korea*

*Mr. & Mrs. Gene Tope w/three girls, South Africa*

*C. H. & Sara Bankston, Alabama; Southern Rhodesia*

*Dan & Jeanie Clendening and family, Germany, Austria, England, Saudi Arabia; (moved to Athens, AL and became close friends)*

*Henry P. & Beth Ewing and family, Floydada, TX; Southern Rhodesia, Botswana (my sister and family)*

*Harold F. Short, Jr., Southern Rhodesia (nephew)*

*James L. Short, Southern Rhodesia (nephew)*

*Ellen Short, Southern Rhodesia (niece)*

*Mason Harris, Norway*

*Bob Nichols, Osaka, Japan*

*Ralph F. Brashears, Baguio City, Philippines*

*Samuel Miao, Singapore, Malaya*

*Peet & Andre Joubert and Zarida South Africa (Florida College)*

*Carl & Ruth McCullough, Texas; Northern Ireland*

*Andy & Lily de Klerk, Lynette, Lee-Ann and Lauren, South Africa*

*Brett Clendening, Brussels, Belgium, Florida Collage, Athens*

*David & Debbie Hanson and family, Air Force—Okinawa and Philippines*

*Stephen A. Canfield, Belgium*

*Bob & Marian Tuten, Norway*

*Kim Wahlberg, Sweden (Ambassadors for Friendship tour)*

*Helge Evaret, Germany (Ambassadors for Friendship tour)*

*Jolly Karuhanga, Uganda (Ambassadors for Friendship tour)*

*Anne Grethe, Bergen, Norway (Ambassadors for Friendship tour)*

*Greetje Rol, Holland (Ambassadors for Friendship tour)*

*Ronnie & June Sadorra, Jacky and Macky, Manila, Philippines*

*Johnny Chin, Malaysia*

*Edna Pendergrass, Donnie and Larry, Germany, Athens*

*Pat Kendall-Ball, Southern Rhodesia and Bern, Switzerland*

*Marv Nerland, Alberta, Canada*

*Thomas A. Thornhill & son, Bergen, Norway*

*Felix Bassey, Uyo, Nigeria*

*Douglas Nerland, Alberta, Canada*

*Leslie Maydell, South Africa*

*Norman & Joyce Flynn, Rhodesia **

*George & Gwen Massey, Rhodesia*

*Herb Wilson, Rhodesia*

*Fred & Ann Melton and son Bonnie, Texas; England*

*Jim Schneider, U.S. Navy (Raymond's Best Man)*

(Besides the 346 from many U.S. States who signed the guest book during 1950-1975)

There is a story connected with each name and their telling would make a whole other book. But I'll tell one. Norman and Joyce Flynn from Rhodesia (now Zimbabwe) were long-time friends of my parents and the rest of my family in Africa though we had not met them before they came to our house. They were originally from South Africa and spoke Afrikaans fluently. When they learned that I had studied Afrikaans in high school and we had had several Afrikaans neighbors, Norman spoke to me in Afrikaans and I answered him in that language. He jumped up excitedly, "Do you remember the song, Sarie Marais?" (pronounced *sorry maray)* I did remember and with his wife we sang it, to his great delight and that of my family.

241

**Not For The Faint of Heart** Edward wanted a CB Radio and set about to install wires and antenna. He drilled a hole through the ceiling, crawled into the attic, ran the wire from his bedroom out through the louvered attic window and up to the roof where he set up the antenna. He used a ladder leaning against the side roof and when he came down he left the ladder in place to use later. Paul was about two years old, playing busily in the floor while I was in the kitchen. I did not realize Edward had left the screen door unlatched or that Paul had gone out until the phone rang and my neighbor across the street said, "Did you know Paul is on your roof?" I called to Edward and hurried to the back to stand under the eaves in line with Paul in case he fell while Edward climbed up and coaxed him down.

I constantly reminded boys to let me know when they went out a screen door so I could latch it behind them but sometimes they forgot. When Nancy was not yet two, one day I answered a knock on the front door. There stood a strange man with Nancy in his arms. "Is this your child? She was standing in the middle of the street!" Needless to say I was startled, worried and embarrassed. I thanked the man profusely and tried to think of more ways to keep the little ones safe, thankful that we lived in a slow moving little town and have guardian angels.

**Left Behind** When Robert was about six he went to sleep at church and was left at Eastside in the school auditorium after Sunday morning worship. No one saw him asleep on the front row when everyone went home and the building was locked. By then we were accustomed to him walking home ahead of us with Edward and Henry. The school janitor lived directly across the street from the school and when his wife called him to dinner he happened to glance over at the school. He saw a child on the inside of the glass door frantically waving his arms and hurried over to let Robert out. A tearful boy came across the empty lot behind our house and through the door wailing, "Why did you leave me there all by myself?" I was glad it was daylight.

One night during the summer meeting at Jennings Chapel we all went to hear the preaching. I sat on the second row with Nancy, still a baby, and Bennie Lee sat on the front row with Paul, who went to sleep on the pew beside him. As usual, when the service was over Bennie Lee talked to people all over the building. I took sleeping Nancy to the car to wait for the rest of the family. The lights were all turned off and when the boys saw Bennie Lee come out they piled into the back of the station wagon.

Three or four miles down the road the boys began singing the "Isaac-a-zumba" song. Paul always joined in and I noticed his voice was missing. I asked if he was asleep. We were horrified when they said Paul wasn't there. Bennie Lee said, "He was asleep on the pew so I left him there and I assumed he woke up and was with all of you." By then he had the car turned around and was speeding back to the church building. Fortunately Paul was still sound asleep on the pew and I was very thankful he had not waked up in the dark building with everybody gone. Friends good-naturedly teased us about having so many children we couldn't keep up with them!

**Six in a bunch at ages 12, 10, 8, 6, 3-1/2, 1-1/2.**

**Accidents Happen . . .** Besides the usual mishaps and minor injuries to be expected with a bunch of children there were a few accidents that stand out in my memory:

1. The barbershop that Bennie Lee and the boys used was just off the town square. One day I loaded up Robert, Benjamin, Paul and Nancy and headed to town for Robert (7) and Benjamin (5) to have haircuts. I was going on to take care of other business while they were there so I parked across the street from the barbershop to let them out. Robert was in charge and waited with Benjamin while a car went by, then Robert, knowing it was clear, ran across the street thinking Benjamin was with him. But Benjamin had hesitated and saw a car coming the other direction and waited on it, then ran, forgetting to look back the other way again; from that direction the oncoming driver braked to stop, but his car hit Benjamin.

I saw his head hit the radiator and saw him fly through the air and land on the pavement. My heart was pounding as I quickly got out of my car, watching for him to move. But he didn't move. Dr. Blue's office was in the building opposite the barbershop and I heard someone say, "Get Dr. Blue." As I knelt beside Benjamin I was conscious that a man knelt on the other side and began to turn him over. I said emphatically, *"Don't move him till the doctor comes."* I hadn't looked at the man until he said, "Mrs. Fudge, I'm Dr. Blue. I saw it happen and I think he wasn't hit very hard; in fact I think he's coming to now and he'll be all right. But I'll take him in my car to the Emergency Room to check him over. Follow me and don't worry." As I got back into my car I realized that when I got out leaving Paul and Nancy inside, from habit I had turned off the ignition and taken the keys with me. I was thankful for that habit because Paul, at two, was known for wanting to "turn keys."

No bones were broken and Benjamin seemed O.K. Dr. Blue told me to keep him awake for a while and to wake him up every two hours all night. When I got home I could not rest and called Dr. Jackson (our family doctor who had brought all of our children into the world) to tell him what had happened. He said he agreed with Dr. Blue's instructions but if I was still worried he would come as soon as he finished at the clinic—and be sure to call him again if I wanted to. I didn't call him again but about an hour later there was a knock at the door and Dr. Jackson was standing there. He said he couldn't relax without taking a look at Benjamin for himself. I was reassured and Benjamin was fine the next day with a knot on his head.

2. Almost three-year-old Paul's fascination with car keys led to another memorable accident when Paul ran over himself! It was just after lunch and Bennie Lee was still at home when Burl Grubb's car pulled into our driveway. He got out to "just say a word to Bennie" about something urgent and left his car motor running and the door open. After he disappeared into the house, Paul, playing on the front porch, saw the open car door and went to investigate. Standing on the ground he looked inside and saw the keys hanging in the ignition.

He explained his actions later, saying he knew Daddy always took the keys out so he climbed up in the car to get the keys and take them to Brother Grubb. Apparently as he held on to the steering wheel and reached for the keys he accidentally bumped the gear shift out of Park into Neutral and the car began rolling back down the sloping drive. In his fright he let go of the steering wheel, we supposed to climb out, but he fell out. His cries brought us all outside. He was curled up at the side of the drive crying, "He forgot his keys; I was getting his keys for him." He said his leg hurt and we saw black marks down the side where the tire had rubbed, thankfully not run over, his leg. The car stopped undamaged in the shallow ditch on the opposite side of Chandler Drive.

3. When Nancy was about two, Paul three and a half, Benjamin seven, Robert nine, Henry eleven and Edward thirteen, Bennie Lee was preaching for the Pleasant Valley church, sixteen miles from home. The electric lights at the church building had been installed when electricity came to the county some time after 1943. Four fixtures with two long fluorescent tubes in each fixture hung on chains from the ceiling; one on each side near the front of the auditorium and one on each side near the back. I always sat in the second row from the front where I could keep the little ones quieter if they did not see other children around them;

Benjamin and Robert sat on the row with me. Edward and Henry were allowed to sit with their friends farther back.

One Sunday night when we all stood to sing the invitation song—I'll never forget the song: *"Prepare to Meet Thy God"*—we had begun the second verse when there was a "CRASH" behind me and sounds of breaking glass and screams. The chain on one end of a fixture had come loose at the ceiling and the end of the long fixture had swung down. It hit a teenage girl on the top of her head, knocked her out, then swung on across a row of people before it stopped. In that row Henry was sitting in line with the swinging fixture and as he looked up to see what was happening, it hit him on his forehead. One of the men picked up the unconscious girl and ran to his car to take her to the hospital, his wife holding a cloth on her bleeding head. I turned around to see where my boys were in all the confusion and saw Henry in the outside aisle coming toward me holding his head—blood dripping through his fingers. I grabbed a clean cloth diaper to hold on the cut as we loaded up the family and headed for the hospital.

Bennie Lee took Henry into the Emergency Room while I waited in the car with the others. When the doctor looked up from stitching the girl's head and saw Bennie Lee ushering in Henry with his bloody head, he said, "Well, Brother Fudge, you must have preached a real hellfire and brimstone sermon tonight to make the lights fall! Any more casualties?"

4. Paul at nine, loved to ride the little old bicycle the boys had bought from a friend for $5.00. They painted it black and named it "Tar Baby." Bennie Lee was on a traveling sales trip to other Christian bookstores and Paul and Nancy were with me at the bookstore after school one evening as I worked late. Their homework done, Paul was riding Tar Baby on the deserted sidewalk out front, Nancy watching him. Suddenly the door opened and Nancy came rushing in looking frantic. "Mama! Paul had a wreck on the bicycle and he's bleeding." I was already at the door by then and hurried out to meet Paul. He was holding up a bleeding hand and blood was running from his nose.

"What happened?" I asked, leading him into the store. "I was pretending I was riding a bull," he explained, "And I put my head down like a bull to bellow and go fast and ran into a parking meter and my thumb got caught in the chain." (Not long before I had taken the children to the annual visiting rodeo). I cleaned Paul up as best I could and got him to the ER a few blocks away. Dr. Pennington said his nose was broken and he would tend to it as soon as he did some patchwork stitching on his thumb that was "pretty thoroughly chewed up." The doctor talked to Paul as he worked, explaining what he was doing while Paul watched intently. He proudly told me, "The doctor showed me my thumb bone!" Then the doctor put an insertion in Paul's nose to help keep it straight. On the way home Paul bemoaned the fact that his thumb was all stitched and bandaged up, "I'll have to just tell my brothers I've seen something they haven't seen—I've seen my thumb bone, but now I can't show them!"

5. A teenaged Henry took off on his motorcycle to deliver papers one rainy afternoon. He hadn't been gone very long when the phone rang. It was Bennie Lee calling from the Emergency Room and my heart began pounding. "I'm here with Henry, but don't worry, he's not hurt bad!" And my heart calmed down. The pavement was wet and as Henry rounded a corner his motorcycle skidded, turning the bike on its side with Henry's leg pinned under it. The motor was still running in gear which made the vehicle and Henry with it, go round and round scattering rolled papers as it turned and scrubbing his back on the pavement through his new leather jacket. He had no broken bones but his back was skinned and painful. I think he mourned his ruined jacket more than he moaned over the pain!

6. When Robert was in the eleventh grade, playing touch football with a bunch of boys, he and one of them collided. Robert's collar bone was broken. The players around him said they heard it snap and were impressed, which gave Robert pleasure! The coach called Bennie Lee, who took Robert to the E. R. and the doctor said he needed surgery to have temporary screws and a permanent wire put in to keep the bone in line. Robert was in the hospital a few days and thoroughly enjoyed being the center of attention of his visiting classmates—especially the girls!

Henry, Robert, Paul and Nancy still carry the scars of having had their chins stitched at different stages, but somehow Edward and Benjamin escaped that.

All these recounted together sound like a lot of accidents but considering the sum total of six childhoods of eighteen years each, totaling 108 years, it doesn't sound quite so bad! There were a good many close calls through those years—some I knew about and perhaps some they never told their parents about! We felt blessed and thankful that none were worse.

**The Bible School Bookstore** In 1943 when the Bible school began, there was no Christian bookstore in Athens and parents and visitors to the school often asked in the school office how they could get a Bible. So beginning in the very early days of the school Bennie Lee kept a supply of Bibles on a shelf in his office. Soon he added Cruden's Concordance and Peloubet's Bible Dictionary. The demand grew and he decided to begin a small bookstore, gradually adding commentaries, Sunday School material, communion supplies and baptismal garments. A mail order business developed. It operated out of one side of the building behind the Bible School that housed the Print Shop where Elam Kuykendall taught printing classes. From that beginning the Bible School Bookstore took off. Bennie Lee also began editing a little monthly magazine he called The Gospel Digest, a collection of inspirational religious articles, patterned after Readers Digest. Elam Kuykendall printed it.

Mamie Brackeen graduated from high school there where she had taken bookkeeping and she was hired as the bookstore's accountant. Soon after that Virginia Dale Bailey finished secretarial school and Bennie Lee hired her as his secretary. Her birthday was on Valentine's Day and *that* date Bennie Lee never forgot, but she had to remind him of *my* birthday that he couldn't remember! I secretly resented that fact but managed to excuse it because mine wasn't on a holiday!

Before long it was decided to officially separate the bookstore business from the school. Bennie Lee bought the inventory and began *Christian Enterprises International.* In the 1950s the bookstore was thriving. It had outgrown its original space and was moved from behind the school to a corner on the square in town where the retail section was called *The C.E.I. Store*. The building had been a funeral home for over a hundred years but when the funeral company moved, the building was completely remodeled by the owner. *The C. E. I. Store* became a fixture on the square with Fudges running it for twenty-five years. (It's still there but since 1974 has had no connection with the B. L. Fudges.)

**Family business on the Courthouse Square.**

**Bennie Lee The Person** Bennie Lee walked the almost mile to work regardless of weather. On rainy days he wore a hooded, brown, heavy plastic poncho that reached nearly to his ankles. He liked it because it protected him better than a conventional raincoat. I thought it looked tacky but he didn't care. The boys told him he looked like an Elizabethan monk, but he didn't care about that either! He had a long torso and short legs and took long steps that caused him to walk with a bounce. One very rainy day he was going to work with his bouncing stride in the pouring rain, when a friend, Calvin Tidwell, stopped to offer him a ride. Bennie

Lee and Calvin constantly exchanged good-natured banter and to the offer Bennie Lee said, "No thank you. I'm walking for my health and my looks!" To which Calvin retorted with a grin, "Well, if it's not doing your health any more good than it's doing your looks you're wasting your time!"

On the way to the bookstore the sidewalk passed through an old residential area with large trees in the yards of a variety of large older houses, some of them antebellum homes with fascinating histories. Many were occupied by elderly folks who had lived there all their lives. When anyone was in the yard, tending flowers or raking leaves, Bennie Lee stopped briefly to pass the time of day and became well acquainted with the residents. The big old trees were teeming with birds of all kinds and Bennie Lee could identify most of them by their calls. At the supper table in the evenings he often told us the names of different birds he had seen or heard and told the children interesting facts and stories from his childhood that involved many of them.

He said his walks were his time for meditation and communing with God and praising Him for His glorious creation so that when he walked in the door of the bookstore he was primed for the day's work and ready to deal with people and business. His days were so filled with phone calls, either about business or someone in the county wanting to ask a Bible question or to get his opinion on some matter, that often by the end of the workday he had found very little time to do his own work. When the other workers clocked out, the doors were locked and he settled down to what he considered his work, opening his morning mail, answering correspondence on his Dictaphone for Virginia Dale to type the next morning, or writing copy for the upcoming catalog and making necessary plans for running the business with five to eleven employees.

The bookstore was open to the public and customers were frequent. Bennie Lee's office was behind the scenes but he was constantly called out to acknowledge someone who asked specifically for him. He was known for his honesty and fairness as a counselor and Bible student. Athens, Alabama was at the crossroads of East-West U.S. Highway 72 between

Huntsville and Memphis and North-South U.S. Highway 31 between Birmingham and Nashville. The C.E.I. Store in Athens became a stopping place for travelers as well as local people. His days were never long enough to get it all done yet he seemed never to lack time to give to others.

Bennie Lee tried not to neglect his family, though sometimes the children and I felt we were getting the short end of the stick. He never acted like it was a nuisance when I needed to talk to him; by the same token I tried not to bother him unless absolutely necessary. He wished and I wished that he could spend more time with the children and it was one of his deep regrets that it didn't seem to happen. He tried again and again to spend more time at home in the evenings and would succeed for a time until some rush work again took over.

When the children needed to talk to their Daddy at work, he usually took time to listen without acting impatient, but Robert tells of one time as a teenager when he wanted to talk to his Daddy about something at an especially busy time. After several unsuccessful tries in person in the store, Robert went across the street to use a pay phone and called him collect! When Bennie Lee asked him why he phoned instead of talking in person, Robert told him he had tried to talk in person to no avail. Bennie Lee apologized to Robert and tried harder to be more available to his children.

As I came to know Bennie Lee more intimately I changed my mind from thinking of him as just naïve, to believing that actually he was a man as completely without guile as a human could be. Ever since then when John 1:37 is read, where Jesus says of Nathanael, ". . . *Behold, an Israelite indeed in whom is no guile . . .*" I think of Bennie Lee and his transparent honesty in every facet of his life. That quality in him I wanted to imitate. He was one who practiced what he preached, he exemplified his sermons.

**Life In A Fish Bowl** I learned soon after we married, and our children learned fast, that a preacher's family was subject to constant scrutiny and was expected to be on a higher plane than anyone else. We were watched by everyone, some looking for an example to follow and others to find fault, all of them expecting perfection. Many were quick to criticize when they thought a mistake was made by anyone in the family. All seemed to have their own definition of exactly what a preacher and his family should do and be and they differed with each other over the specifics. If we traded an old car for a later model (much less a new one), or went on a little vacation, or built a modest house, or one of us came to church in a new suit or dress, we heard rumblings from some quarters about the preacher spending too much money—perhaps he was being paid too much—where did he get it all when they couldn't afford to do that? Certainly not everyone was like that but enough were to keep us on our toes.

We had rules of behavior for ourselves and for our children that we tried to teach and enforce, recognizing there would not be perfection in us or our children. As they grew up we prayed that any mischief they were involved in would be harmless. Our children banded together with other preachers' children in the neighborhood calling themselves "WPKs"—*Wicked Preacher Kids*—they felt that was how other people saw them. It was not unusual to get a phone call on Monday morning from some lady not hesitant to identify herself because after all she was telling the truth and it was her duty to inform me about something she had seen one or more of our boys doing. It happened more often as the boys got older and Bennie Lee taught me to answer, "Thank you for your information. I'll see that it is taken care of." He said we needed to make allowances for the good intentions of the tale bearers who sincerely thought they were doing their duty.

One Friday night Henry and Robert wanted to go alone for the first time to a football game at the city high school. After family discussion and urging good behavior, Bennie Lee said they could go. Monday morning when the phone rang I hoped for the best. A lady's voice began talking and I steeled myself for whatever would come. She said, "Mrs. Fudge, this is Joyce, I was sitting behind Henry and Robert at the football game Friday night and I must tell you . . ." and I thought, here it comes, what did Henry and Robert do? She continued, "I have never seen two teenage boys behave so well at a ball game. They didn't get up and down and run in and out like others were doing around them, and in general they acted like gentlemen, even saying 'excuse me' when they walked in front of someone. I know how people are quick to find fault with preachers' kids and I thought you could use some good words." Joyce was among the earliest students of the Bible School and I knew she was married and lived in town but we never saw each other. Her call "made my day." As parents, we had sense enough to know our kids would not always do so well but it was a good start.

**Discipline Matters** Those were still the times when many parents, including us, believed *"train up a child in the way he should go and when he is old he will not leave it"* and *"spare the rod and spoil the child."* We didn't want spoiled children—for their own good as well as for the good of those who lived around them. We believed chastisement was for the best when done correctly—*positively not to be administered in anger,* and the reason for any punishment was to be made plain to the child. Corporal punishment was kept to a minimum and used only as a last resort. Though I'm sure the child at that moment didn't believe it, I knew that it did hurt me more than it did him and more than once I cried along with them.

Henry and Robert experienced more of that philosophy than the others but since then they have assured me that they appreciate what I did and said, "Who knows what I might have turned out to be if you hadn't used that firm hand when I was young?" They had hard times with their tempers and I tried alternative measures first, but when they went beyond a reasonable decibel, sterner action was needed. When they got some older I tried sitting the two combatants in chairs facing one another close up and made them take turns reading the following to each other:

> *Let dogs delight to bark and bite, for God has made them so.*
> *Let bears and tigers growl and fight, for 'tis their nature to.*
> *But children, you should never let such angry passions rise;*
> *Your little hands were not made to scratch out each others*
> *eyes! (Unknown Author)*

It wasn't easy keeping them reading it but they usually ended laughing! After the first time it was enough just to pull out chairs and papers. But that was not always a cure. At a still later time I told them when they felt their temper rising beyond control to go to the garage and pound on the wall instead of on each other; out there they could yell as loudly as they wanted to and I wouldn't hear them! Henry tried it once and came in very soon looking sheepish and saying it made him feel stupid!

As my last resort on Henry and Robert I used a flexible leather "pointer" that my father had brought from Africa for Bennie Lee to use at blackboards. I tried it on myself first and knew how hard to administer five or six licks to get the lesson across without going too far. After some use it disappeared and I wasn't sorry. Fortunately by then the boys were more responsive to talk. A few years later when we were remodeling that part of the house and unloaded the books out of the shelves in the study, we found the "pointer" behind the books and Robert confessed having hidden it there!

I felt it was positively wrong for me to threaten a child that I would tell their father when he came home. I believed Daddy's homecoming at the end of the day should be a happy time. When they were older, a few times I thought something was too serious for me to handle and I sent the offender immediately to see his Daddy at the bookstore with instructions to tell him why he was sent. I was confident Bennie Lee would handle it wisely.

A serious talk was harder on Edward, Benjamin and Paul than a spanking would have been. I recall only once that I felt the need to do more than talk to Paul. For Nancy a small green switch used on her legs a few times when she was about two, cured her of going into the street when she found the screen door unlatched. With so much coming and going it was next to impossible to keep the door always latched and she learned to stay in the yard if she did go out.

Paul's one time came when he had just started school. All our children had strict instructions to come home as soon as school was out. Then, if they had no homework and wanted to go back to the playground sometimes, they got permission. After the first several days of excitement over hurrying home to tell me about school, Paul discovered that as soon as school was out he enjoyed playing with other children first. Several times I went to look for him and admonished him of the need to come home first and each time he said he forgot and promised to remember. Finally I told him if he forgot again, I didn't want to, but I would have to spank him to help him remember. The next day it was a good forty-five minutes after school was out when he came slowly into the kitchen. I said, "Paul, did you come straight home when school was out?" He looked up at me with his big eyes and said "No, Ma'm, I guess my *remembery* didn't work." He looked so penitent and sad it was all I could do to administer a few whacks—not very hard ones at that, but he never forgot again.

**Use Your Bible Workbooks** From the time Bennie Lee began teaching in Sunday Schools, even before he began preaching, he had felt strongly that there should be class material for churches that taught the pupils to study the Bible itself instead of quarterlies that they could look through and complete their lesson without even opening their Bibles. Since there was nothing available like that then, in the late 1940s he set out to write a series himself. He called the series *The Use Your Bible Workbooks.* He began with Primary and to familiarize himself with that level of vocabulary he collected and studied second and third grade level school books. He wrote the *Primary Use Your Bible Workbooks* first, followed by *Junior* and *Intermediate*—twelve workbooks in each age group, advancing in vocabulary and Bible knowledge.

He soon realized he could not get all the workbooks written quickly enough in his few minutes a day of spare time. To concentrate on writing them he would have to get away for periods of time, away from the phone, away from all the other interruptions of his days. He delegated the work in the bookstore and disappeared for five days at a time as often as he could. I was the only one who knew where he was and had his phone number. He called me every night and Virginia Dale relayed any bookstore message through me. He called it "holing up" in a motel room at some distance where no one would recognize him when he ate in a café or went for his daily walk. By the end of the week he had copy written in longhand for one or more workbooks. Virginia Dale then typed it ready for the typesetter and printer.

Otha Lowe Lee wrote a hardback preschool Bible story book called *Mrs. Lee's Stories About Jesus*. It was published by The C.E.I. Publishing Company and I illustrated it. She gave us permission to use stories from her book for the *Preschool* age in the workbook series. For each week's story I drew a picture to color as part of the workbook. When Bennie Lee saw how long it was taking him to write the workbooks he asked R. L. Andrews to write the twelve workbooks for *Senior* high school age—though he wished he could do them all himself. When the series was completed there were workbooks to cover four quarters each year for three years so that students who began with *Primary* and went through the whole series till they graduated from high school would have studied the Bible all the way through three times at each level, progressing according to age. As the workbooks were written I designed the covers. It took several years to get the whole series into print.

The *Use Your Bible Workbooks* became popular and their sale was not limited to churches of Christ. They were used in almost every State in the U.S. and in many foreign countries for many years. In 1980 Maggie and I were coming back from Africa to the U.S. through England and spent a night in Tunbridge Wells, Kent. At church on Sunday morning, to our surprise we saw a *Junior Use Your Bible Workbook* in the song book rack in front of us—they were being used in the Sunday School there.

Years later after I married Joe and lived in Ohio, I found them being used in two country churches we attended and later when attending Mason Church of Christ, in our Sunday morning class of retired folks was a man who had worked as traveling salesman for Standard Publishing Company (very familiar to me). He told me that as he called on Christian bookstores over the country during his years of selling and had taken many orders for *Use Your Bible Workbooks* and *Mrs. Lee's Stories About Jesus* and the name

Bennie Lee Fudge was familiar to him as author, publisher and salesman. Several of the old folks I met there said they went through Sunday School studying *Use Your Bible Workbooks*.

A separate company was set up for publishing called *The C.E.I. Publishing Company*. In addition to the *Use Your Bible Workbooks*, Bennie Lee wrote a series of workbooks for adults called *A Student's Guide to The New Testament*. Besides his own sermon outlines he published sermon outline books by other writers, various workbooks by other authors and several hardback books. Some of our publications were translated into several languages including Spanish, Norwegian and dialects of Africa and the Philippines. Most of our printing was done by Decatur Printing Company in Decatur, Alabama, and hardback binding was done in Nashville, Tennessee.

As workbooks and paperback sermon outlines were printed, they were picked up from the printer in Decatur and brought to the bookstore in flat boxes that held about 1,000 workbooks each. The books had to be counted into bundles of twenty-five and tied with string for ease of shelving and order filling. At first Bennie Lee and other bookstore workers did that chore whenever they had a few spare minutes but sometimes the boxes of uncounted books piled up and Bennie Lee spent his evenings counting and tying. After Evelyn came to live with us, when the little ones were in bed and she and Edward and Henry had homework to do, I left them to it and went to help Bennie Lee count and tie workbooks.

It was a good time for us to catch up with our private talking that was hard to do a lot of the time. I had to get up early to get children off to school and Bennie Lee could sleep later if he had worked late the night before, which happened most of the time, so if I was asleep when he came home he didn't wake me. Some nights he worked until one o'clock or later, but if I woke up we talked till all hours catching up on each other's day or sharing deeper subjects for which there was little time when we were surrounded by children. It was my strength-gathering time—my growing time—well worth the loss of sleep.

**To Work At The Bookstore** From the time Bennie Lee began feeling the need to go back to work after supper every evening, he had promised that in about five years he should have things shaped up so he could get his work done during the day and stay home in the evening. Years went by, the business grew and so did his goals. Our long range plan made before we married, that we would go to Africa as missionaries "when the Bible School was well established," had become "when the business could be managed by someone else," then had faded into the distant future. After nearly fifteen years he admitted he was not likely to be able to cut out night work. We were feeling the need of being together more and after a great deal of talking and praying, we decided if we found a good baby-sitter/housekeeper, I would go to work at the bookstore. He felt there were jobs I could do that no one else had time or was qualified for and we could feel more together as we worked and went out to lunch together. Mrs. Bates, a widow with three boys in the Bible School, was looking for work during school hours. She became our housekeeper and baby-sitter for Paul and Nancy and I was home by the time school was out in the afternoons.

My first job was to illustrate *Mrs. Lee's Stories About Jesus* that Bennie Lee had agreed to publish. I did not want to draw people but tackled the job anyway and worked at it for months until the book was published. I am admittedly a perfectionist in some things and I struggled over drawing the people for the illustrations. I developed a stomach ulcer that Dr. Jackson said was likely due to constant stress. When finally the illustrations were all done and the book was with the printers, the stomach ulcer gradually disappeared.

My improved typing skill qualified me for my next assignment. Blanche Seal Hunt had written the *Little Brown Koko* books and contacted Bennie Lee about publishing two of them. In spite of the popularity of her first two published ones which they had seen, the NAACP insisted we could not publish these without changes. In all her books she had consistently described her little hero as *black*, with *kinky* hair and called his mother *Mammy*. In order to publish the delightful stories, the spokesman for the NAACP insisted all references to black had to be changed to *brown, kinky* had to be changed to *curly* and *Mammy* to *Mommy* and in the illustrations none were to have thick lips. My job was to retype her manuscripts making those changes before they were sent to the typesetter. The stories were such a delight I enjoyed that assignment, by turn wiping away tears and chuckling out loud as I typed.

When the manuscripts were completed and approved by the author, she wanted three or four artists to illustrate a story and submit their work, incognito, for her to choose the one she preferred. We contacted my good friend from college days, Jody Hawkins, and she and I were two of the four who sent our work to the author. The author chose my work. Here I was again faced with drawing people but this time I had a plan. Jody liked to draw people and was especially good at putting dramatic action into her characters; she took the manuscripts first and illustrated the stories in pencil and sent them to me. I prepared them for the printer, making the people's faces look more like what the author wanted. Jody and I thoroughly enjoyed our collaboration and Blanche was happy. *Little Brown Koko at Work and Play* and *Little Brown Koko's Pets and Playmates* by *Blanche Seale Hunt* were published, *Illustrated by Sybil Fudge and Jody Hawkins.*

Blanche Hunt and her husband had no children but she asked me to do a 30"x36" water color picture of Little Brown Koko kneeling at his bedside saying his prayers to put in the "Little Brown Koko Room" in her home. She was delighted with the result and I am glad I took a photo of the picture for myself before sending the original to her.

**This And That** I gradually worked my way through almost every job in our business, helping anyone who was behind and filling in for anyone sick or on vacation. I filed, transcribed from the Dictaphone, waited on customers, dressed the show-windows, checked inventory and ordered from publishers for the retail bookstore, addressed labels and laid out mail orders to be shipped, wrapped books and church materials for mailing, invoiced mail orders, counted and tied workbooks, stocked shelves in the retail store, operated addressograph, graphotype, offset press, folding machine, assembled/ stuffed/sorted advertising mailings and catalogs, proof-read publications as galley-proofs came from printer, designed book covers and jackets, helped Bennie Lee plan and paste-up pages for the catalogs we sent out—about everything except official bookkeeping, though I was familiar enough with accounts that I could check on complaints. Later on when long time secretary and assistant manager, Virginia Dale (Bailey) Holder was at home with two preschool children, I served as acting secretary and as assistant manager when Bennie Lee was away.

**Boys Work** On Saturdays and any afternoon after school that the boys did not have ball practice, they came to the bookstore workroom to count and tie workbooks and were paid by the thousand. They had fun competing with each other to see who could count and tie the bundles of twenty-five the fastest. They learned to wrap packages for mailing and to operate the addressograph and the graphotype machines. On Saturdays when mailings were being assembled, envelopes stuffed and sorted for the post office, I could almost always find a trusted teenage girl willing to baby sit Paul and Nancy and do light housework while I was at the bookstore keeping boys busy addressing envelopes, stuffing mailings or counting and tying workbooks. Sorting stuffed envelopes by States and major cities became a game of watching for the most unusual names of people or towns.

One day Mamie and I were working on a mailing of catalogs in the back room and Robert (about 8 or 9) was helping. As usual he was talking non-stop and after a while Mamie jokingly said, "Robert, if you will sit on that stool over there and say nothing for <u>five</u> minutes, I'll give you a <u>nickel</u>." He promptly said, "Will you give me a <u>dime</u> if I don't say anything for <u>ten</u> minutes?" She said yes, and he didn't say a word for ten minutes, and she paid. Then he offered to do it again any time!

**House Add-On 1959** The business was prospering, children were growing and the house was getting worn. We decided to remodel, adding bedrooms that would allow the children to spread out. When it was done we had four big bedrooms and one small one and two and a half bathrooms. Paul was five and Nancy four—the youngest at home. A while before that our first housekeeper/ baby sitter had resigned for health reasons. She was replaced by Mrs. Romine who was our invaluable sitter and efficient housekeeper until Nancy started to school. The children loved her even though (or because) she was strict along with her love. Her special treat for the family was the cake she made every Friday—a two-layer, white or yellow cake that she covered with made-from-scratch chocolate fudge icing or caramel fudge icing. It had a "No touching until Sunday" sign on it and was our Sunday dessert as long as she was with us. When Nancy started to school and she "retired," we all sorely missed Mrs. Romine—and her cakes!

**"Jesus Is The Head Of This House And The Unseen Guest At Every Meal"** were the words on a plaque that hung in a prominent place in the dining area of our kitchen. I brought it from the bookstore when we moved into the house in 1950 and we took it down when we moved out in 1975. I think Edward now has it in his home office. On the wall of that same area facing the back entrance was another fixture, a 24"x30" "blackboard"—only it was green. Every morning when all the children were gone to school and I was leaving for work at the bookstore, I left messages for the children to see when they came in after school. When they had activities after school they left messages for me to see when I got home. We wanted them to feel free to call us at the store if they felt it necessary—and they did—often. Ours was a family business relationally and organizationally, and along with free use of the telephone, that green 'blackboard' communication helped us feel close.

**Play Times** Christmas Day was our main "family day" of the year—the one holiday that Bennie Lee did not go to work. All other official holidays, when all the employees stayed home, were prime opportunities for him to get his own work done without interruptions of telephone calls, visiting preachers, customers and employees' questions.

261

Christmas Day we had our early morning Santa Claus time. When everyone else had gathered around the Christmas tree, Bennie Lee in his old brown robe emerged "HO! HO!"-ing from the bedroom to act like Santa Claus. When the excitement had quieted down we had a special breakfast. Then dishes were left in the sink and we played table games around the big round dining table—Monopoly, Parcheesi, Checkers, Chinese Checkers, Old Maids, and such like. Each year a new game was added to the supply. Edward was the most unenthusiastic about the games but he played, too—until he was allowed to retire to read his new book. By that time Henry and Robert had usually reached the end of their indoors tolerance and were ready to go outside to play with neighborhood boys. The younger ones played with their new toys while Bennie Lee helped me in the kitchen and we talked as we prepared our Christmas dinner to eat about four o'clock. After evening devotions, depending on ages, we played more games or read books. I was as sorry as the children were for the day to end!

**Home Playground** At some stage all the kids up and down our street had roller skates. Since our street was short and not busy it was used as the neighborhood skating "rink." The kids kept asking me to skate with them and finally one day I agreed to try. It had been so long since I skated that I didn't do so well but they got a kick out of it—and so did some of their mothers along the street who came to their doors to watch.

Our yard was big and during those years of growing children we had no real lawn, though the older boys mowed the weedy grass with our old fashioned reel mower—for 25 cents. Ours was about the only yard large enough for softball games where it didn't matter what happened to the grass. One day boys of the neighborhood gathered with Henry, Robert and Benjamin for a soft ball game. They needed another player to make two teams and one of my boys came in begging me to fill the need. I had never played soft ball and told them I probably couldn't hit the ball, but they said it didn't matter and insisted that I try. I joined them—in my housedress of course, I didn't wear slacks in those days.

When it was my turn to bat, I whaled away at the ball and to my surprise made contact. The ball went down the yard past the infielder and I heard my team yelling, "Run, Mother!" and "Run, Mrs. Fudge!" so I ran.

When I neared First Base they hollered at me to keep running for Second. The baseman didn't catch the ball from the infielder and the yelling was louder: "Run for Third! Run for Third!" I ran for Third. The ground was wet from a recent rain and just before I got there, without my knowing what was happening, my feet slid out from under me and I sat down—on Third! How my team cheered as the other team looked on in amazement! That Sunday at church several mothers said, "I heard you slid in on Third! I didn't know you could play ball!" I didn't know it either and that was the nearest I ever came to it!

**Birthdays** Birthdays were celebrated with cake and candles at supper time and Bennie Lee tried extra hard on those days not to be late for supper. On Benjamin's third birthday, supper was ready, the cake with candles sitting in the center of the table waiting for Daddy. Benjamin was so excited I promised that we would have candle blowing first thing when Daddy got home. Bennie Lee tried, but someone delayed him as he was leaving the store. I was in the living room answering his call when I heard a chair scraping across the kitchen floor. I found Benjamin already up in his highchair at the table, cake pulled toward him. He was looking at it singing, "Happy Birthday to MEEE!"

When he was in about fourth grade he asked me if he could have a birthday party with decorations and invite some of his friends. I told him I was very sorry but I absolutely did not have time to do anything but the cake for supper. He asked if he could do it himself and I told him he could, provided he cleaned up after it was over. He promised. I made cupcakes instead of the usual cake and furnished ice cream and canned Hawaiian Punch, paper cups and paper bowls. He did such a good job that every year after that it was his own birthday tradition and well attended by his friends.

**Picnics** The children thought it was awful that their Daddy didn't take days off so we could go for a picnic now and then. One time I suggested that we have a watermelon feast on our back patio and invite their Daddy to join them and he took an hour off mid-afternoon. The watermelon was good and everyone had fun. Another time he managed to get away from work a little earlier than usual, I packed our supper and we went to a neighborhood park to have a picnic—short but sweet before the mosquitoes chased us away.

With permission from Bennie Lee, Henry, Robert and Benjamin dug a hole in the vacant back lot with much talk about digging all the way to China! One day when they complained we never had picnics like other people I thought about the hole they had been digging and asked if they would like to have a family wiener and marshmallow roast over a fire in that pit. They loved to build fires and it was a great success. One Sunday when Bennie Lee didn't have to preach in the afternoon, we loaded Sunday dinner into the car and drove to the picnic area on Monte Sano northeast of Huntsville. They couldn't say we "never did" but could say "seldom!"

**Trips With Daddy** All through their childhood years, Bennie Lee took one of the children on a trip with him when his business permitted, to Decatur Printing Company, to publishing companies in Nashville, Tennessee, to Abilene, Texas, to Gadsden, Alabama and to Birmingham. It was a treat to the child to have his/her Daddy all to himself/herself and their Daddy said he enjoyed it as much as they did.

On long trips Henry's favorite meal was a hamburger and chocolate milk—breakfast, lunch or supper. He came home excited from a summer trip to Abilene with his Daddy telling about finding a place to eat named "Henry's Hamburgers;" and about then O'Henry candy bars were a favorite, too. When the older ones began driving and had their learner permits, Bennie Lee took them one at a time to the Abilene Christian College Lectureships, allowing them to drive (before Interstates) and learn to maneuver through traffic in Memphis, Little Rock, Dallas and Fort

Worth. Lectureships were in February and not the least of their joy then was missing a week of school!

Occasionally when he needed to go to Nashville taking some of our publications to stores there and bringing a load back from publishing companies there, if the children were all in school, he asked me to go along and when I could I did. The business owned a dark green panel truck we called "Joseph"—why, I don't know but all our vehicles had names. One day with our load of workbooks we headed for Nashville, talking a blue streak as we usually did when we had a chance. Somewhere up the road in southern Tennessee, the highway wound around the side of a very high hill. The passenger side was on the outer edge overlooking the steep drop to the valley below where there was a fence running along beside a small creek and across the creek was a pasture.

Suddenly a tire went flat. There was barely room to pull over with very little space left for changing the tire. It was so narrow I didn't want to get out on that edge so I moved over to the driver's side to let Bennie Lee get the spare out of the back. As he upended the tire in the back and rolled it toward the door I had a mental vision of it getting loose, rolling out the door and down the steep hill. I was about to say, "Don't let go of it!" but before I got the words out he let go and it did exactly what I had pictured. It bounced out of the truck, went bounding down the rocky slope to the bottom, jumped *over* the fence, *across* the creek and came to a stop in the pasture on the other side. Bennie Lee just stood there watching it in unbelief. I wanted to laugh but I smothered it because I was sorry for him. He clambered down the steep slope, slipping and sliding on the grass and rocks, retrieved the tire, and laboriously pulled it back up the hill, sweating profusely—there he laid it down flat! By that time I could not contain myself and began laughing out loud. He said, "I don't see what's so funny!" But when the job was done and we were once more on our way, he laughed with me.

**Conventions And Lectureships** Christian Booksellers Association Conventions were an annual business event which we attended for many years. We had a booth exhibiting our own publications among the other publishers and the mingling was enriching, inspiring and invaluable. During those years we met and listened to many famous writers and speakers, including Gene Autry, Pat Boone, Dale Evans, Corrie Ten Boom, George Beverly Shea, Albert Schweitzer, Billy and Ruth Graham, Elizabeth Elliott, Maria vonTrapp, Vance Havner, Francis and Edith Schaeffer, Catherine Marshall, and many more. We attended conventions in St. Louis, Chicago, Philadelphia, Minneapolis, San Diego, Miami Beach, Atlanta, Cincinnati, Washington D. C., and several of those cities more than once.

Every year Bennie Lee attended Lectureships at Abilene Christian College and at Florida College. In both places he had a book booth under a big tent along with many other publishers. In Abilene we expected, and . usually experienced, extreme cold. In Florida—well, it was Florida where people went to get away from the cold. In the earlier years Bennie Lee hired someone to work shifts with him in the booth while he attended as many of the lectures as he could. Once or twice we divided the children among willing friends for the week and I went with him to help in the booth. As the boys reached their teens he alternated years taking one of them to be his helper. They liked it for a lot of reasons, not the least of which were the daughters of some other publishers who helped in their fathers' booths.

**Staff Meetings** Every Monday morning at the bookstore we had a staff meeting and on Bennie Lee's first Monday morning back home the bookstore staff was treated to an inspiring report on the Convention or Lectureship he had just attended. He could make us feel we had almost been there. His effervescent enthusiasm inspired and motivated the employees, not only on those occasions but every Monday morning, giving the week a good start. We had a brief devotional after which Bennie Lee introduced new books or gave demonstrations on "how to handle and sell Bibles." When the boys were older one of them asked me, "How come every new Family Bible that comes in, Daddy says it's the best one he has ever seen, when that's what he said about the last new one that came in?" The truth was that he carefully studied each one and each of them in some way was in his opinion an improvement over the last one.

Bennie Lee was a fast reader and read every new book that came in before he demonstrated it to us and put it on the shelf to sell. Besides learning about books, we learned about the first printing press and of the many Bible translations through the years; we learned Bible Geography and History and about pioneer Bible students and preachers—not just in the United States. Each Monday morning was an inspiring hour-long seminar. He urged all of us who waited on customers in the retail store (which was all of us except the two accountants) to read as many of the new books as we could to familiarize ourselves with them to be able to help customers better. Over the years, while under the dryer at the hairdresser or a little at a time at night, I read many books on a wide variety of subjects.

**Daily Home Devotions** Whether at home or at school, for the whole family, Bible reading and memorizing was not just for head knowledge, it was our practical guide for life in our attitudes and actions whether religious, social or business, and it influenced every decision we made. When Bennie Lee was not away on business or preaching trips he came home for supper. Afterwards we sat around the table and had Bible reading. We each read aloud sections from a different version of the Bible and then we often talked about what we read and the notable differences in the versions.

During one period of time Bennie Lee fastened a long piece of plain paper on the dining room wall. At the left end he wrote *Creation,* at the right end he wrote *Return of Christ* and in between at approximately appropriate distances from each other, *The Flood, Mt Sinai, The Cross.* Allowing Nancy to go first, we took turns, called out the name of a Bible character beginning with A and fit that person to the time line on the chart and if possible told something about him/her. When we had exhausted all the A s we could think of we went to B. If one couldn't answer, the next age up had a chance to answer. Every one enjoyed it and over time we went all the way through the alphabet. One by one the boys became more involved with school activities in the evenings—ball practice, play practice, annual-staff meetings and such like—our after-supper group decreased and we did well to have evening meals together most of the time.

**Bill Returns** My brother Bill came to the U.S. for college in 1960. He spent the summer with us before enrolling in Harding College in Searcy, Arkansas. In a letter he wrote a brief summary of that time: *"Those first few weeks at your house, before going off to Harding were truly memorable . . . The Jim Reeves records ("Turn the Jukebox Way Down L-o-o-o-w") . . . Edward and I driving your salmon pink Rambler station wagon. The little grocery store down at the corner where Edward liked to listen to a cranky "old man" radio personality . . . Helping at the bookstore—I had never seen a dust mop and Bennie Lee thought he was never going to get me to quit using sweeping motions with it! Mamie, Virginia Dale et al . . . Great cooking at your house! Occasionally eating lunch at Athens Café and getting acquainted with Thousand Island dressing, and leaving uneaten rolls on the table—we paid for them, we should have eaten them! And going with you to clothing stores as you set me up with American-college-appropriate clothes. Grandmother Short died April 23, 1961 and you and Bennie Lee picked me up from Harding and took me to her funeral, in Harper, Kansas. Beth and Henry, Margaret Ann and Don were there, and grandmother had left instructions for us to enjoy being together and not mope around. Our cousin Howard had a go-cart course and several go-carts, so we drove go-carts till dark and sang hymns after supper. Uncle Clarice said my singing voice sounded just like his father's."*

Soon Bill, in Arkansas, was busy working his way through college in the college print shop and preaching at nearby churches on Sundays. He returned to us for the three weeks Christmas Holidays that year but we didn't see much of him in the years that followed. He finished at Harding College and went to Abilene to work on his next degree. He married Marilyn and some months later they moved to the northeast.

A massive snow storm (for north Alabama) had Athens deep in its grip, schools closed, cars stuck in driveways and our family was enjoying a "holiday" at home. We were sound asleep when I realized someone was knocking on our bedroom window and got up to look out. There stood Bill deep in snow. He and Marilyn were on their way north in a loaded station wagon and had made it to our house about 1:30 in the morning. We got them warmed, fed and bedded and next day melting snow allowed the roads to be passable and they went on their way.

The deep snow also "socked in" a visiting basketball team from Montgomery, Alabama. They played the Bible School team and the out-of-town boys were divided among families for the nights, two of them in our house. During the snow paralysis, boys staying with other families heard from our guests that "Fudges have a big house and kids galore" so boys and girls trudged through the snow to gather at our house during the day.

One noon I was in the kitchen preparing a meal for the crowd and overheard them talking about lighting fireworks. I called to Henry and Robert and said firmly, "No lighting fireworks in the house!" So they opened the front door, lit cherry-bombs and quickly threw them out into the snow—except one of the bombs missed the open door and exploded *inside*. I had heard Robert's voice a lot and called loudly, "ROBERT! I SAID NOT IN THE HOUSE!" But I had falsely accused Robert and apologized to him when one of the guests came to the kitchen and said, "Mrs. Fudge, that wasn't Robert—I was the one that threw and missed. I'm sorry." He tried to scrub the black circle off the wall where it exploded but it wouldn't scrub off and I was glad it was behind the door. I heard him telling the boys he hoped no one would tell his dad about it!

**The C.E.I. Companies** As the business had grown we had opened a retail store in Abilene, Texas and then one in Gadsden, Alabama and a smaller branch in Birmingham, Alabama. The retail stores were incorporated as The C.E. I. Stores, Inc. The C. E. I. Publishing Company was a separate corporation handling the publishing end of the business.

The C.E.I. Sales Company was established to train and send out college boys who wanted to sell Bibles and other books to help with their college expenses.

I felt strongly that the addition of the Sales Company, operating out of Abilene alongside the retail store there, was spreading things too thin, but I did not feel qualified to question the decision of more experienced personnel. It didn't become apparent for some times but it turned out the enthusiasm and dreams of the young men running things in Abilene exceeded their wisdom. When it did become obvious in late 1960, Bennie Lee spent a lot of time out there trying to analyze and rectify. He said he had no one to blame but himself for turning it over to inexperienced men without proper supervision.

**Filipino Boys** As the business had prospered, things looked rosy and we enjoyed being able to be more generous as the many opportunities came along. In 1957 while the business was at its zenith, three Filipino young men wanted to come from the Philippines to attend a Christian College. They needed a sponsor and Bennie Lee had been recommended to them by Samuel's father, L. N. Belo, with whom Bennie Lee had corresponded for several years. Bennie Lee sponsored the boys and we were able to pay part of their college expenses. Samuel Belo, Felix Bravo and Ronnie Sadorra became "our boys" while they attended Harding, Lipscomb and Abilene Christian College. They spent some Christmas Holidays with us and time during several summers when they weren't selling Bibles. They were a joy to have in our home and were like older brothers to our children. We rejoiced at being able to help them attend college and talked of the time when we would do the same for our own children.

When publishing company salesmen from out of state called on our retail store and quite often visiting preachers, Bennie Lee took them to lunch at downtown Athens Café. Our family never gave a second thought to having dark-skinned Filipino boys in our home but the first time Bennie Lee took one of them with him to have lunch at Athens Café, as soon as they stepped inside the door they were stopped by a waiter and told, "The colored entrance is at the back." Bennie Lee said quietly, "This man is a guest in my home and he eats where I eat. If he is not welcome here then neither am I." The manager had overheard what was going on and stepped forward immediately to tell Bennie Lee that any guest of his was welcome there.

**Mumps Again** It had been so many years since the three older boys had the mumps that we were shocked when Paul got sick and his jaws swelled up. He was not too sick otherwise and being naturally quiet, he understood and obeyed our rule of "quiet play" while getting over the mumps. After the first two days he amused all of us with the fun he had looking in the mirror and laughing at himself. He asked Edward to take his picture to show his teacher later! But not so with Benjamin and Nancy, who developed the ailment soon afterward. They were very sick for about four days, and though they didn't swell up as much as Paul did, it was enough to make them cover their faces with their sheets when anyone went into their room.

When they felt better, Benjamin, who was eleven, was an invaluable help reading to Paul and Nancy and playing with them while they recuperated. He was artistic and inventive and enjoyed making things with them from paper and cardboard. I have a memory picture of the three of them in the double bed, Benjamin in the middle, while he read to them, or all three coloring with crayons. I took extra reading material and coloring books home from the bookstore for their entertainment. After Paul was cleared and went back to school, Benjamin designed and hand-stitched doll clothes for Nancy's dolls. They had me show them how to knit and they each knitted a scarf. Mrs. Romine was still with us during school hours and I was with them on Saturdays and Sundays.

**"Nearly Forty"** In January that year I turned thirty-eight and my children teased me about being "nearly forty!" I told them not to judge me by themselves—Edward had been "nearly sixteen" for two years before he got there and the others were almost as bad! I informed them that I'd be "nearly forty" when I reached thirty-nine and three fourths!

**Short Family Reunion** During 1961-1962 Foy and Margaret and family, and Beth and Henry and family were in the U.S.A. on furlough from Africa. Bennie Lee and I thought it a shame that Daddy and Mother could not have been in the U.S. too and perhaps all the family could have been together. Bill had been born in Africa after we three older ones had come to the U.S. for college and Mother and Daddy had never had all their children together. Bennie Lee felt so strongly about it that he began contacting people in several states who knew Daddy and Mother, telling them the situation and asking them to help raise funds for them to come—it had been about six years since their last furlough. There was good response. Bennie Lee sent a cablegram to Daddy telling him that only a few hundred dollars was lacking to pay their way and he felt sure it would come and for Daddy to be making arrangements for the trip.

Daddy sold his car in Bulawayo which supplied what was needed and they made arrangements to fly over. It was their first time ever to fly—all previous trans-ocean trips had been by ship. When they arrived in New York, Daddy called us and said when they got to Atlanta he would call again to give time of arrival in Huntsville, Alabama. I waited anxiously for that phone call. When it came, Daddy said their layover in Atlanta was short and they would arrive at the Huntsville airport in twenty-five minutes. I nearly panicked—how could we get to the airport in time to greet them as they came off the plane? At the airport just as Bennie Lee found a parking place, we saw their plane landing and we were in time to meet them coming out of their gate. Daddy said it was a weird feeling when they realized they would arrive in Huntsville *before* they left Atlanta! They had experienced time changes many times before but never so quickly. When we got to our house and they were unloaded, he paced the floor in our living room, hands behind his back, saying over and over, "I caahn't believe it! Yesterday we were in Bulawayo! I just caahn't believe it!"

Meanwhile Bennie Lee had been busy making sure the rest of the family would all be at our house at the same time between Christmas 1961 and the New Year. It would be the first time in all our lives that my parents had all their children under the same roof at the same time and as it turned out it was the *only* time in their lives that it happened. Samuel Belo, one of our Filipino boys was spending Christmas with us and was included in the family gathering—making thirty-three in all.

Foy and Margaret and family were visiting her sisters around Huntsville and didn't have far to come.

Beth, Henry and family drove from Floydada, Texas, and Margaret Ann and Don and family drove from California. We gave Mother and Daddy the master bedroom; Foy and Margaret with their youngest, Kay, had Nancy's room; Henry and Beth with their youngest, Linda, had Benjamin and Paul's room; Margaret Ann and Don with their two youngest, Greg and Tim, had Henry and Robert's larger room; Bennie Lee and I with Nancy, had Edward's room. I borrowed extra quilts and blankets from neighbors to make pallets. The big girls, Betty, Sharon, Ellen, Vonnie, Genie, Bonne slept on the floor in the living room. The big boys, Samuel, Bill, Edward, Harold, Henry, Pat and Robert, were on the floor in a line down the traffic side of the kitchen while the younger boys, Jimmy, Benjamin, Mike, Paul and George were on the kitchen floor between the refrigerator and stove. Before we mothers could fix breakfast we had to get all of the floor-sleepers up and bedding folded, but there was so much excitement it wasn't hard to do.

We had three days of talking, laughing and constant activity. Adding to the fun—it snowed and there were snowball fights and snow-cream. There were impromptu piano tunes as different ones passed the piano and stopped to play something. With a heater in the garage the ping-pong table was kept busy. Henry had a motorcycle at the time and gave the teenage girls rides—that they speak of to this day! The women were in the kitchen a big part of the time, talking all the while we prepared meals out of the big chest freezer we had stocked for the occasion. The men were in the living room talking and the younger children were all over the place. Every day ended with Bible reading, prayers and singing.

The allotted three days and four nights passed before anyone was ready for them to and too soon all were gone except Daddy and Mother. They visited with us a while longer before going on west to see other kinfolks and report to their supporting churches. As it turned out it was literally a "once-in-a-lifetime" event and the joy of being together for the first and only time in our lives far outweighed the pain of belt-tightening we all had to do to carry it off.

During the 1961-1962 school year Edward was in the twelfth grade and Nancy was a first grader—for one year all six of our children were in the Bible School.

**Costume Parties** Comings and goings, school functions and activities, visitors, both adults and children's school friends, kept our household like a beehive. Every year at the end of October there was a Costume Party for all the school, including parents. Our older boys didn't care much about dressing up for that, but Benjamin, Paul and Nancy enjoyed it and we worked hard on their costumes. When Paul was a First Grader we dressed him as a knight in armor and Nancy went with him as a court lady of the same period. I had saved cardboard from Bennie Lee's laundered shirts and cut them to form sections of body armor and helmet with visor. I fastened the sections together with paper fasteners then sprayed it all with silver paint. We made Nancy a silver cone-shaped head piece with a sheer scarf flowing from the tip, matching her long dress tied at the waist with a silver rope. As a pair they won First Prize for most original. The next year in something equally imaginative they won First Prize again. When they didn't win a third year they were disappointed but reluctantly agreed that it was someone else's turn to win!

**What Makes It Work?** Paul had an inquisitive mind, wanting to "look inside to see what makes it work" from the time he was a toddler. No doubt that is why when a toddler, he stuck a screwdriver into a wall socket because the socket looked like a "screwing place." I have a clear memory of the Christmas he was three—almost four—when he was given a tricycle. Bennie Lee had not had time to assemble it the night before and after breakfast on Christmas Day he and Paul went to the front porch to do that. Paul squatted on his haunches watching intently as his Daddy fit the pieces together one by one. I heard Paul say, "But Daddy that doesn't go there, it goes over here!" He was right and Bennie Lee remarked to me, "I think I better let him put the thing together!"

That inquisitiveness got Paul in trouble when he was about 7. While everyone was busy here and there in the bookstore, Paul with screwdriver in hand, pulled a chair up to the old fashioned cash register and unscrewed one of the top plates to see what made it work underneath. Bennie Lee saw him at work and verbally chastised him—then Bennie Lee had to take Paul's advice on where a screw went to restore it to working order! A few years later Paul said he wanted to be an inventor but he couldn't because everything had already been invented!

**Family Music** Our radio was in the kitchen, turned on constantly. I enjoyed working to the sounds of music and hoped my children would feel the same way. For some time I had been talking up the idea of having a stereo at home and Edward's enthusiasm over Pat Boone's songs worked with my idea. Buying a stereo at that time was out of the question but in his room Edward made a turntable, buying a piece at a time.

There he played his several Pat Boone 45 RPM records. We couldn't hear his music in the rest of the house and with permission from his Daddy to make holes in the walls for speakers, ran a connecting wire up into the attic and down to the speakers—one in the long hall between the bedrooms and one in the hall near the kitchen. When he was done we had music throughout the house from his room. For some time it was almost all Pat Boone and we liked it.

Then Edward got very busy with school and we were needing some variety of music. I recounted to Bennie Lee how much music had influenced my home life and how important it could be for our children. We ordered a stereo LP player from Sears for the children's Christmas and invested in a variety of 78 LP records—two records each of *50 Favorites of the Masters*, some Western Music, *Tennessee Ernie Ford Hymns*, two recordings by the *Robert Shaw Chorale*, three of *Mennonite Hymns* and Mary Poppins songs. Over time we gradually added others. When the children were in bed at night I stacked L.P.s on the stereo beginning with a Mary Poppins record (the youngest children would go to sleep first) then cowboy songs, and progressed with samples of each kind ending with the orchestra classics.

On Sunday mornings I stacked sacred songs, Tennessee Ernie Ford, Robert Shaw Chorale, Mennonite Hymns. I turned them on loudly when it was time for everyone to be waking up. When I began that practice there was much less fussing as they got themselves ready for church—instead of shouts from the bedrooms, "Mother, I can't find my socks!" "Mother, where's my blue shirt!" "Mother, he got *my* belt?" the person who had something to say came to where I was in the kitchen or bedroom to ask the question in a calmer voice—most of the time!

Gradually the boys brought in records of their own choosing to add to the mix. I recall a few of the singers: *Peter, Paul and Mary, Jim Reeves, Johnny Cash, The Kingston Trio* and *The Riflemen.* Who brought in which I don't remember. Robert succeeded in getting his daddy's permission to bring in a selection of *Beatles* and *Elvis Presley* records (to the surprise of the rest of the family). At first Bennie Lee had said "No" to Robert's pleas on both counts but one evening Robert heard a Beatles song on the kitchen radio that gave him an idea. He turned up the volume and asked Bennie Lee to listen. He listened and said, "Now that's all right. I don't mind that kind," and Robert exuberantly declared, "That's the Beatles!" So we heard some of their music after that, along with some Elvis. Robert had pictures of Elvis in his room and let his hair grow as long as he could get by with and combed it into "ducktails" like Elvis, and in imitation of Elvis went around with his eyes half shut! Bennie Lee and I consoled ourselves with "this too will pass" and it did!

We certainly had variety—something for every mood. Paul and Nancy had grown up on all of that mix and had their favorites among them but if they had an individual "idol" I don't know who it was. To my mind it is no accident that the children as adults all enjoy good music.

**Donna Barksdale** The bookstore walk-in customers had increased and Donna Barksdale came to work with us in 1963. She and Maurice lived with their three children between our house and town and attended Eastside Church of Christ when Bennie Lee was preaching there. Their daughter Terry Jo and our Benjamin were classmates in the Bible School for twelve years. Donna worked as a hairdresser for many years but had resigned a couple of years before she came to the bookstore. She was excellent with customers of all dispositions and very soon became a valuable asset in keeping the retail store ship-shape. Children loved her—in fact, my children sometimes asked me why I wasn't more like Donna and came nearer wanting to do something when she suggested it than when I did.

She and I had known each other since 1944 but it was not until she began working in the bookstore that we became very close friends—with a friendship that deepened through the years and at this writing is still one of my most cherished treasures. Donna worked in the store for twenty-five years, some of that time after we Fudges were gone.

Though Donna had not been with the business as long as Virginia Dale and Mamie, she soon became the third "pillar" as far as Bennie Lee and I were concerned—each in their own sphere. They could be depended on to efficiently and cheerfully do whatever needed doing, always willing to go the second mile. With their dedication to the Lord, their work ethic and loyalty, their wholehearted support of the concept of spreading the Gospel through the printed page, they were lights in the business and in the communities where they lived.

When they answered the phone and it was one of our children calling for their daddy or me, not once did I ever know of them speaking impatiently to them—knowing the frequency of the calls it must have sometimes been a temptation.

In our family life Virginia Dale, Mamie and Donna were like sisters to me and favorite aunts to our children. They acted thrilled over each new baby and were as proud of every child's accomplishment as any favorite aunt would be. No major event in our lives from births through school years, or later showers and weddings, ever went unnoticed by them. Mamie and Virginia Dale have passed on but at this writing Donna is ninety and still being an encouragement and an example of love and faith to all who know her.

**The Hummingbird** In the 1950s and 1960s, besides the many, often very long freight trains and twice-a-day slow passenger trains that ran through Athens, there was a fast passenger train called *The Hummingbird* that streaked through from south to north and on alternate days from north to south without stopping unless someone had a ticket to get on or was on board and needed off in Athens.

Smiths Grove, Kentucky, was on the Hummingbird line and the Roy Fudges had recently moved there. At the time of the grand idea, Robert and Benjamin were nearly 14 and 12, and in their minds—and in the mind of their daddy—were old enough to escort Paul 8, and Nancy 7, on the train to visit their cousins. Robert and Benjamin were to return the next day on the Hummingbird's flight south. It was agreed that Roy would bring Paul and Nancy home by car after a week.

In my memory I see Robert and Benjamin in their new matching boat-neck, three-quarter-length sleeves, blue/green/white striped knit shirts and newly popular calf-length pants, Robert's blue and Benjamin's green. I thought they looked very summery and well-dressed. I don't recall what Paul and Nancy were wearing but I do recall how uneasy I felt about sending them off like that with such young escorts. Bennie Lee said no one learns responsibility without being made responsible for something and this would be a good experience for all.

With many admonitions we watched them excitedly climb on board and the train zoomed away. Robert and Benjamin returned on the Hummingbird the next day reporting a good trip and I hoped they were not exaggerating. Roy brought Paul and Nancy home the next week. They said they had a good time for the week;

Nancy said, "only coming home I was car-sick and stuck my head out the window so it went all over the side of Uncle Roy's car." At least it was outside!

**Calls for Help** Calls for help came often, some to Bennie Lee at the bookstore and others to him at home. He evaluated them and referred some to the church's benevolent action. We took care of others ourselves, at times asking friends to join us if we knew they were interested. Sometimes the calls were for food, other times for clothing and often for both. If the person asking for help said he was on the way somewhere with a hungry family and needed money, Bennie Lee escorted them to a café and bought food for them. If they asked for money to buy gas he escorted them to a filling station and paid for a fill-up. When they said they needed money for car repairs he told them to go to a certain garage where the car would be fixed, and he called his friend, the manager, asked him to fix the car and promised to pay the bill. In the first instances the food and gas were accepted and the person(s) went on their way. When Bennie Lee went to pay the garage owner he often said nothing was owed.

In the case of local calls for food and clothing, I served as collector and deliverer in most cases. As often as possible I tried to time deliveries when one or more of the boys could go with me as helpers. Almost every time on the way home they commented that seeing the needy situation made them really appreciate what we had and made them ashamed to complain that some of their friends had better clothes or house than we did. One time after Edward went with me, when we walked into our front door, he looked around and commented, "I never thought I'd be *ashamed* of having shiny hardwood floors!"

One evening when Nancy was about eight, we had some things that needed to be taken to a family who lived about ten miles out in the county. We were working late getting Bennie Lee ready to leave for the Florida College Lectureship the next morning and Paul and Nancy were with us at the bookstore. Cold weather was coming and the things needed to be taken so I told Bennie Lee I would take Nancy with me and deliver them. He asked, "Do you know the way?" I was sure that I did because I'd been there several times before.

Many roads fan out from Athens into the county and I took the one I was sure was right. Several miles out I saw landmarks that I didn't think were supposed to be there and finally came to a country store I knew was not on the road I was supposed to be on. I stopped to ask directions. The storekeeper told me which road I should have taken and I was about to

279

head back to town to start over, when he said there was a shortcut that would take me almost to the spot where I was going. He said, "It's a one lane blacktop road and it crosses a creek. There's no bridge but cars ford it all the time. People from back in there come out that way going to work every day." It was getting late but not yet dark and I left feeling confident—I had forded rivers in Africa.

We came to the creek and across the fairly wide expanse of water we saw the road continue up the hill on the other side. I headed straight toward that road. I had only gone about the car's length when I felt a back wheel drop into a hole. I tried reversing but the wheel just spun. I tried forward and quickly back but that didn't work either. I thought of how in Africa sometimes we used bush branches to help. I pulled off my shoes and waded to the bank we had just left to get branches. The branches didn't help and it was getting dark. I pulled one of the heavy coats from the box of clothing and put it over the branches hoping that might add traction, but it didn't. So I wrung out the coat, put it in a plastic bag in the car and climbed back in.

The water was icy cold and in between those tries I sat in the car warming my feet, blowing the horn and flashing the lights. We could see lights of a farmhouse up the road but I told Nancy we would just have to wait. To save the battery I turned the lights off. Every few minutes I turned on the lights and blew the horn some more. She began to cry, "What if nobody comes?" I reassured her that her daddy would get worried and come to look for us when he thought we had been gone too long. How long we were there I don't know but it seemed like ages even to me, when to our relief we saw lights coming toward us from the house.

A pickup truck stopped on the other bank and a man got out and called to me, "I know your back wheel's in a hole. I'll go to the house and get my tractor to pull you out. Just sit tight!" We sat tight, but I knew by that time we should have been back in Athens and Bennie Lee would be wondering where we were. The man came back on a tractor and drove it across the creek, turned around and headed back, stopping in front of our car. I noticed that he crossed in an arc and when he stopped to hitch the chain on to the car, he explained that everyone who crossed that creek regularly knew to drive in that curve to avoid the very hole I was in.

He explained that he had just gotten home from work and was about to sit down to supper when his wife said, "I keep hearing a car horn, there must be kids playing awful late down at the creek," and he said, "But they never stay this late, maybe someone's in trouble." He walked out onto his back porch to look down that way and the lights were on and the horn was blowing at that very moment. He would not accept any pay and kindly reassured me it was not far to where I was going. We delivered the clothes and groceries and headed back to Athens. Bennie Lee was surprised to see us walk into the store. He had assumed that we went on home and had not given us a second thought! But that experience did not entirely cure me of taking shortcuts—even in my eighties, as Robert or Beth could tell you!

**Sam Robinson** Sam lived in a room in the old Athens hotel and operated a concession stand to eke out a living. He was very independent. After he operated for many years on a corner one block off the square in Athens, he was ejected from that spot to make room for progress. Bennie Lee had known him since high school and helped him get a permit to operate his stand on the corner of the square beside our bookstore. He had been crippled from childhood and had developed a polite but defensive attitude. When I met him he had straggly whiskers, was practically toothless and chewed tobacco, but he ran his clean, well-stocked concession stand with integrity and care. It was his life's work and he put himself wholeheartedly into it. He was accustomed to children making fun of him so when our children treated him respectfully he was cautiously appreciative. Every Thanksgiving and Christmas Day we filled a large dinner plate with food before we sat down to eat and Bennie Lee delighted in taking it to Sam. When Bennie Lee died, Sam, dressed in his suit, hobbled on his cane the mile and a half in freezing mist to the Eastside church building to attend the funeral.

**Time For Redecoration** It had been about five years since the addition to the house when everyone decided they were ready for some redecorating. The boys had their own ideas and wanted to redo their rooms themselves for a change. I gladly turned them loose to choose their paint and do the work, including cleaning up their messes. They opted for simple—walls and wood trim the same colors except for the special closet doors that Benjamin was inspired to do in his and Paul's room. He painted the sliding double doors of one closet sky blue with a sun at one top corner and flowers and grass across the bottom of both doors. The other closet's sliding doors had a moon and stars on a black background.

Henry was a senior and he and Robert were so busy with basket ball and other school activities that they chose the fastest way. Edward was home from college for a year working in the bookstore and during evenings and weekends redid his small room. He painted three walls white, the other red, and hung a large U.S. Flag on one white wall. He painted the chest of drawers red with white knobs and the small desk red, to go under the flag.

Nancy's heart was set on a canopied bed high enough up to use steps. The quilt box of Bennie Lee's mother, that had been a couch in the living room then the bottom bunk in Edward and Henry's room, was now used again. It was set on a platform of 2"x8" boards, cut by our friend at the lumber company, who also made the movable two-steps to climb into bed. At the Mill Ends store I found chintz, white background with small royal blue roses rambling over it and royal blue corduroy both @ 15 cents a yard. With Bennie Lee's help we nailed 1"x2" strips on the ceiling to hold curtain rods for the chintz canopy curtains that were held back in the daytime with royal blue ropes. A bed skirt of blue corduroy with chintz bedspread completed the picture-perfect "canopy bed" Nancy had dreamed about. The window drapes were made of royal blue corduroy with rope tiebacks. We painted the formerly pink walls white.

Interestingly through the years the boys exchanged in different combinations brother-best-friends with each other. When they changed they switched rooms and roommates. Bennie Lee and I enjoyed watching the inter-play of "best friends" between them.

**Ladies Bible Class** About 1963 I began leading a Ladies Bible Class at Ephesus that lasted for eleven years with good participation. During that time I studied a lot and learned a lot. I came to the conclusion that my thinking and attitude was more Pharisaical than Christ-like and I was consumed with shame. I prayed earnestly that God would forgive me and help me change. While we were doing a study through the Bible book by book, I worked up thirteen lessons in workbook form on the book of Isaiah. Bennie Lee felt there was a need for that workbook and published it. I have no idea how many were sold but over the next fifteen years it was reprinted several times—2,000 at a time. There were many requests for a teacher manual and for a follow-up workbook on Jeremiah. When he saw the demand for the workbook on Isaiah Bennie Lee wanted me to do the workbook and teacher manual on Jeremiah but the time never seemed available. I taught other ladies classes but none that lasted so long with such interest. Wherever Bennie Lee preached I usually taught classes of either primary or preschool children.

**The Glass Doll** When Nancy was ten years old, a few months before Christmas, I decided it was time to revive the doll I had brought from Africa. In the Mill Ends store I found green satin to make a long dress with long sleeves and a matching bonnet, all trimmed with antique-looking lace. From a hair-piece no longer in use, I made a wig for her; sewed up the split places on the doll's body and replaced her long-lost shoes by fashioning imitation leather shoes from scraps of a coat I had made for myself. I found a suitable box to lay her in and wrapped it up for Nancy's Christmas with a letter telling the doll's story. Nancy was as thrilled as I had hoped she would be. She displayed the doll on her bed every day after that and it was a real incentive to her to make her bed in the mornings!

**Overflow** Speaking of beds reminds me of the time multiple requests among the boys for having friends spend the night resulted in all the beds in the house being full. Everyone was asleep when there was a knock on the front door and I looked at the clock—it was 2:00 a.m. and Bennie Lee went to the door. He recognized the young woman standing there—she had baby-sat for us some years before. She was on her way from Ohio to see her mother who was ill but it got too late and she needed a place to sleep with her two-year old and six-week old baby. Bennie Lee invited her in and helped her carry the sleeping babies in. We moved a couple boys off the couch and put them in bed with other boys. She said she needed something for the baby to sleep in because she was afraid of putting her in the bed with her and the two-year old. Bennie Lee and I looked at each other trying to think what, and he said, "How about a drawer out of our chest of drawers?" We emptied a big drawer, put it on two chairs and lined it with pillows and blanket. The next morning they went on their way and our house returned to "normal" full occupancy.

**Growing Years Miscellany** Bennie Lee's time to attend the children's school functions was limited and I tried to make up for his absences as much as possible. There were PTO (Parent Teachers Organization) regular meetings, class plays, ball games and much more to attend. With four, five and six children in school, depending on which years, the children were busy with homework, science projects, candy sales, magazine sales, class plays, and so on. Henry, Robert and Paul played basketball during their high school years, which meant constant ball practice for them. I attended many games, though not all. I was noted for not being a loud fan, but at one of Henry's games I embarrassed myself.

Henry and his team were playing against some very tall boys who snatched every rebound and the score was mounting in the wrong direction. Late in the seemingly hopeless game, Henry dribbled the ball down the court, looked around and saw all the tall boys waiting near the basket ready to grab the ball again. He suddenly stopped at almost mid-court and aimed. He was so far away I thought there was no way he could make it and in my consternation I yelled, "HENRY! NO!" just as he turned the ball loose and a hush fell over the crowd. My yell was heard loud and clear—the ball went into the basket and thunderous cheers rose.

People around me turned and laughingly said, "Did you say 'No Henry'? He fooled you didn't he?"

Henry and Robert were captains of their basketball teams and as such, in their senior years, they each proudly escorted the Homecoming Queen of that year. They objected to wearing their first "man's suit," and new shirt and tie, but I got the feeling they secretly enjoyed it. In Robert's case the queen was Dianne whom he later married.

Toward the end of each year the pace grew quite frantic with special elections for things like Beta Club, Outstanding Teenagers honored by Lions Club, Escorts of Homecoming Queen and her court, being voted on for Most Athletic, Most Studious, All Star Club to name a few. I am not fitting boys' names to each activity and achievement nor to their later achievements in college for fear of mixing them up. There is no danger of getting the wrong name when I say Nancy was *Miss Merry Christmas* in the Athens Christmas Parade! She represented Athens Bible School on the float with girls from all the county high schools. Attached to every one of those activities and more are tender, proud, embarrassing, amusing and altogether precious memories.

Edward won a speech contest that I did not know he had entered until the day before it was to be delivered in the county finals. Since Bennie Lee and I could not attend the finals, Edward delivered his speech to us in the back of the bookstore and I was astonished at his ability. He began preaching when invited and by the time he was a senior in high school he was preaching fairly regularly, but since I went where Bennie Lee preached I didn't hear him until one stretch of six weeks when he substituted at Pleasant Valley in Bennie Lee's absence. I was gratified at his ability and the depth of his understanding of scripture and of people. Edward, however, was not satisfied.

As we were leaving church on Sunday at the end of the six weeks when Bennie Lee was again preaching, Edward announced, "I'm not going to preach any more." Bennie Lee asked him why not and he said, "Because nobody changed. I preached all the things they needed to hear and after six weeks nobody changed." Bennie Lee told him, "It's not the preacher's place to change people. We do the preaching and God does the changing." But Edward said he was done with it. Some weeks later I was in the kitchen when he came from his room and said that he had just found a passage of Scripture that he believed applied to him. When Jeremiah was fed up because the people did not change after he told them over and over what God wanted them to do, Jeremiah said he would tell them no more, but later said he felt a burning in his bones and couldn't be quiet any longer. Edward said he was feeling God's Word burning in his bones and he would not be able to stop preaching.

Nancy recalls saying on one of our Sunday trips home from a country church where Bennie Lee was preaching, "Daddy preaches at church and Mama preaches in the car going home!" No doubt I was guilty as charged. I remember times on the way home when I made a comment about some point in the sermon, one of the children would say, "Here comes Mother's sermon!" and we all laughed. I tried not to get into a "preaching voice" too often.

Edward and Bennie Lee often sat at the table after supper discussing Bible subjects, questioning and looking for answers together. I was busy in the kitchen but enjoyed listening to them and learned a lot from their frank give and take on many subjects. My heart recognized their conclusions as what I too believed but had not put into words as they were doing. Less comforting were their discussions following recent debates on the current "issues." I resented that expression as it came to be used by the general "brotherhood" and applied to how/when orphan homes and foreign missions should be supported by the church and over which supposed-to-be-brethren were arguing and dividing. I was thankful to hear Bennie Lee and Edward say they believed all immersed believers were brethren in Christ and should behave with love toward each other even when their opinions differed.

In his senior year Edward won the typing contest and his typing expertise helped him earn pocket money at Florida College when he typed term papers for other students. I missed him from home for many reasons and one of them was that typing ability—he had typed Henry's hand-written term papers when he couldn't stand to see Henry struggling with his "hunt-and-peck" typing. After Edward left I took pity on Henry sometimes. Henry may have taken advantage of this to get out of doing what others would do for him more easily—or perhaps it was a foretaste of his delegating ability that he used well when he was elected president of his college class.

**Of Kitchens And Counters** One of the after-dinner chores assigned to the boys and Nancy was to take turns—one clearing the table, another washing dishes, the other drying and putting them away. Sometimes they agreed among themselves to exchange duties and that was up to them so long as they didn't get too vocal about it. As they each became busier in their final year of high school they were excused more often.

The door from the back porch opened into the kitchen and traffic passed through to a door into the hall going to bedrooms and another door to the dining room/living room. At one side of the traffic path was a table and chairs and under the windows beside the back door was a large chest freezer. The kitchen proper was divided from the traffic area by a long counter with cabinets over and below it. The counter was table-height on the traffic side and chairs from the table could be used there; that was where we ate breakfast and other meals when the whole family was not sitting down together around the kitchen table or at the dining table.

My usual weekday rising time was 5:30. I dressed for work first thing then ate my breakfast, to be free for the rush as the others got up. While eating I read daily devotional material and highlighted parts that especially impressed me, then left the book open on the counter. One by one as the family came through to eat, they often read what I left open. Whether they read it or not was their choice—I never quizzed them on it, but often later, one or the other commented on something they read and it sparked further discussion.

I was not the only one who left reading material on the counter. From Henry and Robert's talk and their magazines, *Popular Mechanics, Hot Rod* and *Motor Trend,* I heard and read about the Daytona 500, the Indianapolis

500 and the drivers in those races. I recall such names as Earnhardt, Foyt and Petty. To this day I often watch those races on TV and hear their sons' or grandsons' names. I heard a lot about cams and shocks and other mechanical words I have since forgotten. In one of those magazines I read about the first automobile trip from London to Cape Town in the 1920s. It was an amazing feat that included hair-raising adventures across the Sahara Desert and through the jungles of central Africa, finally passing very near to where we lived when I was a child. I could imagine their feelings when they had flat tires in unfriendly territory or had to make long detours and ran out of gas and had to walk miles to find some.

That counter was also a favorite homework place and from there the day's happenings were talked about and memory work recited to me. By the time six of them had gone through twelve years of school each, I had listened to untold varieties of recitations, most of the time because they wanted out-loud practice, but sometimes I think, to show me how much they were learning. For whatever reason, as a result, my own knowledge of Bible verses was enhanced and I heard uncounted poems—from first grade simple to twelfth grade *Thanatopsis, Gray's Elegy, The Raven* and many, many others, until I could quote most of them myself. They recited their parts in class plays and I have never forgotten Henry's very first part in a Thanksgiving Play. He had to announce in a strong voice, *"Me big chief Squanto!"* He was so excited he wanted to have it memorized perfectly and practiced that line over and over with such feeling that the others teased him.

There were times when they had something private to say that seemed to come out easier in that setting—telling it to Mother's back while she worked in the kitchen triggered confidences and confessions. Those times across the kitchen counter were well-spent times that helped cement our relationships—whether they realized it or not.

**Different theories** As they reached the age of being allowed to use the car to go somewhere on their own or with friends, each one had a different theory about asking permission. Edward did not ask for anything unless he was pretty sure it would be allowed. He had a discerning mind and said he didn't see any use asking for anything that might be refused. Henry said he had a good idea what he would or wouldn't be allowed to do, too, so he asked when he thought it would be allowed, but if he was sure it would be denied he went ahead and did what he wanted to without asking and took the consequences; at least that way he'd had the enjoyment and could handle being grounded for two weeks or more, depending on how bad it was! Robert asked for a lot—and often; if refused the first few times, then he waited a while and asked again, and again, and again. His theory was that the more things he asked for and the more times he asked, the more he would be allowed to do—it was the law of averages! By the time Benjamin reached that age, he knew what was allowed and what wasn't, so he chose well what to ask for and was almost never refused. Paul and Nancy were friends with young people who did many things as a group and that made it easier for them to get permission. As a result the three older ones accused us of spoiling the three younger ones!

**"Enjoy Your Children . . ."** Those were hectic years, a combination of family home life mixed with church, business and school. To my mind now they resemble a crowded collage of memories—some wonderfully happy memories—some extremely trying ones—all incredibly busy ones. Every day was a new adventure in the unpredictable unfolding of lives. We were very proud of our children and enjoyed them as they grew through all the various stages and phases, though some of those phases we were thankful to know would pass and glad when they did! Occasionally while the children were young someone of the many people who were watching us all the time and had grown children, said, "You better enjoy your children while they're little because when they get older you'll be wishing they were little again."

But over the years from babies, through elementary school age, junior high, senior high, through college, and into married lives, Bennie Lee and I agreed that we enjoyed every age and every stage and what made it even more fun was having at any given time one or more of them in each of

289

several different stages. Fun bubbled over in our daily lives and I wish I had made notes of things that at the time I thought I would never forget. Now I can't recall many specifics, I just remember we had a joyful household along with the accidents, problems and troubles. I thanked God many times for giving us all a good sense of humor to oil the wheels of daily life. At some point when the children were young I became conscious of waking in the mornings wondering what adventure would be ours that day. Best of all we all loved God and each other and wanted to do what was right.

One by one at different ages, as they were each convicted in their own heart that they wanted to obey their Lord in baptism, they took that step. I don't recall exact dates—I do remember we rejoiced over each—one by one.

Besides our family prayers, private prayers went up to God daily. One night Bennie Lee was preparing for bed while I was still in the kitchen. As I went through Nancy's room into the shared bathroom between our two bedrooms, I heard Bennie Lee's voice coming from our room and thought he was talking on the phone then realized he was praying aloud. I heard him pray for each of our children, individually by name and circumstance, praying that they would not be tempted beyond their faith to resist, that the Lord would give them strength and wisdom in whatever situation they found themselves.

The next day Edward was leaving for Florida and before he left I told him about the prayer I had overheard. Henry was in Florida attending college and working a night shift in a chemistry lab. When Edward saw him, because the prayer had meant so much to him, he told Henry about it and they shed tears together. When Edward told me about that, I thanked God for letting me overhear Bennie Lee's prayer.

**Irons In The Fire** From the very beginning of the *school* Bennie Lee was involved with it in some way: as cofounder, Dean, teacher or board member, some years as President, always a staunch supporter. The *business operation* was full time. *Preaching* was full time. *Mission Work* was always on his heart and he corresponded regularly with missionaries in many different lands and in the U.S.A. to encourage them. As much as possible Bennie Lee used Sunday afternoons to visit sick folk in the hospital or in their home. His visits included chatting with them about various things of interest and ending the visit with a brief scripture reading and a prayer. Sometimes after the children were older I was able to go with him. I remember elderly Mrs. Jarrett who was bed-fast, often asked him to read 2 Corinthians 4:16 . . . *Therefore we do not lose heart. Even though our outward man is perishing, yet the inward man is being renewed day by day* . . . Many times Bennie Lee said he went to such visits to encourage the shut-in and came away feeling that he had been encouraged.

**Business Failure** When the C.E.I. Stores, Inc. and The C.E.I. Publishing Company were going well and things looked very rosy, The C.E.I. Sales Company had been set in motion to recruit, train and send out salesmen of Bibles and related books. During the summer after graduating from high school Edward sold Bibles as far away as Oregon. Henry sold during a summer or two especially in Mississippi and southern Alabama and when Paul reached that stage he also sold Bibles. Bennie Lee could see potential in each one of those companies for immeasurable service and unlimited growth and their growth was exciting for several years.

But trouble was ahead. Churches were dividing over "issues," many times, in my opinion, provoked by preachers. Bennie Lee believed he could differ with people in matters of opinion and still maintain love and brotherhood but many others felt that if they differed they had to cut off all association and bad-mouth the opposition. Because of the influence of some who differed on "the issues," preachers and churches were branded and many churches and customers from the over 200,000 we had been serving, stopped ordering from us. In a relatively short time our business dropped drastically. We trimmed expenses every way we could and tried everything we knew to save the companies but it became obvious that more drastic measures had to be taken.

The Sales Company was dissolved and the Abilene, Texas and Gadsden, Alabama retail stores were closed. When Bennie Lee was in Abilene seeing to the closing of that store he called home one evening urgently asking our bookkeeper to go to certain men who might be willing to lend $1,000 each because $5,000 had to be in the Athens bank by noon the next day to avoid very drastic action. He said he could not possibly get back in time to take care of it himself. The bookkeeper refused, saying it would be embarrassing to him. Bennie Lee asked Virginia Dale to do it as secretary of the corporation, but she told him she had never done anything like that and she absolutely could not do it. He phoned me and said he knew I had never done anything like that but he was desperate. He explained the situation to me and told me who to go see and how to ask them and said he would call me later that night. I was literally scared sick.

It was evening and the children were fed, little ones in bed and the others settled with homework when I told Edward I had to go out on business and for him to take care of things at home. Before I left I fell down on my knees by my bed and prayed from the depths of my heart asking God for courage to say the right words and to soften the hearts of the men I was going to see. They were good friends and if possible that made it even worse, but as I visited with each one in their home and explained the need as Bennie Lee instructed me, they each wrote a check and I thanked God all the way home. The deposit was made the next day before noon.

Meanwhile Bennie Lee was on his way driving home from Abilene and stopped to get some sleep in a motel, and called me. He said he had been without sleep for so long it was dangerous for him to drive but he would get on the road early the next morning. The next day he told me that in the motel he still could not sleep and had prayed and read Psalms 37 and 38 and prayed and read the psalms and other passages several times over, asking God to show him where he was going wrong and if he was not wrong to give him strength and wisdom to carry on as he should. He said he was finally at peace and slept a few hours.

The drop in business had been so drastic and so swift that bills could not be met. After struggling for some time we reached the point that our attorney advised Chapter 11 arrangement and it was set up with a judge in Decatur overseeing it. Under that protective arrangement business increased and we were making regular payments, whittling down debts. The judge, with whom Bennie Lee met regularly to discuss everything, was pleased with our progress and we became hopeful of climbing out of the hole. When the Chapter 11 arrangement had been going for two years an inspector out of Washington D. C., who did not know the situation as the Decatur judge did, and obviously did not care, inspected the books in Decatur and told the judge to throw the whole thing out of Chapter 11 and into Bankruptcy. The judge told him progress was being made only more time was needed, but the man said two years was long enough. So the C.E.I. Stores, Inc. was thrown into Involuntary Bankruptcy. The Publishing Company was a completely separate corporation along with the company Bennie Lee had set up some two years before to be a retail outlet called B.L. Fudge Book Company.

In the bankruptcy sale the inventory of the retail store was bought by Kregel Publishers, a Michigan publisher we knew from The Christian Booksellers Conventions. When Bob Kregel came with a U-Haul truck to load the store inventory, Bennie Lee asked him to wait until closing time and we would help him pack and load. We invited him to our house for supper but he refused, wanting us to eat out with him. I needed to go home to feed the family but Bennie Lee went with him. Then Bennie Lee and I, with our children, helped him pack and load everything that was to go. He said he felt very bad about the failure of our business and was amazed that we were willing to help him like that. All along he had been a good friend and one of our most lenient creditors.

By about ten o'clock he was gone and we went to work moving books from the back of the building where the stock belonged to The C. E. I. Publishing Company and B. L. Fudge Book Company. We spread books flat to take up space over the shelves in the store so that it did not look emptied and the next morning we opened for business as usual—as far as the public could tell—only we knew how depleted the stock really was. When customers asked for books we did not have we ordered them and in addition were able to gradually build up stock of the most popular items. We continued to operate on a cash-with-order basis with all our publisher-suppliers as we had been doing for the past several years.

Herman Baker, head of Baker Book House, came soon afterwards to pay a personal visit and see for himself how we were weathering the storm. Through the years we had stocked and sold many commentaries and other books from Baker Book House and they had published hardback books for us. We were deeply in debt to them and they had been patient in our time of trouble. We invited Mr. Baker to family dinner in our unpretentious home and felt it was a mutually beneficial visit. We were encouraged by his expression of appreciation for what he saw in the business and at home—that we were truly economizing, trying to do right and make the best of a bad situation.

Within the business, of the eleven employees we had formerly had, the only ones left were Virginia Dale, Mamie, Donna, Curtis, the bookkeeper and Bennie Lee and me. Our children worked with us when they were not in school or at school activities. As they got old enough they had each learned the store inventory and waited on customers, filled mail orders, wrapped them for shipping, besides working in the stock room; they were a helpful and valuable part of our business.

When the Involuntary Bankruptcy was announced in the newspaper I felt completely humiliated. The first Sunday after that, on the way to church, I told Bennie Lee that I wanted to be almost late, sit on the back row and leave as soon as "AMEN" was said. But he said, "We have tried to deal honestly with everyone and have done nothing wrong that I know of. The Lord knows our hearts and is our judge no matter what men may think or say. You hold your head up high and walk right down to your regular seat and after church greet people with your usual smile. God will help us through all this. It may be hard, but you can do it." And I did.

A few days after the contents of the retail store were bought by Kregel Publishers, Bennie Lee got a phone call from Sam Moore, the head man at Royal Publishing Company, a branch of Thomas Nelson Publishing Company, saying that he wanted to talk to Bennie Lee when he next came to Nashville. We needed Bibles and other books from Nashville to replenish our depleted store so very soon Bennie Lee went to Nashville and made a point of seeing Mr. Moore. He and Bennie Lee had become friends during the past several years as Bennie Lee featured and sold many of their Bibles, especially their Royal Bible. To Bennie Lee's surprise Mr. Moore offered him the job of sales manager of Royal Bibles and named a very generous salary. If Bennie Lee took the job it would require that he work full time out of Nashville and preferably live in Nashville. Bennie Lee asked him to give him some time to consider it.

We talked about the pros and cons and prayed earnestly about it. It would mean considerable financial relief but it would mean uprooting our family and taking the children out of the Bible School. It would mean that Bennie Lee would let go of the vision he was already working on of making a go of what we had left of our business with dreams of building it back up to more than it had ever been. In Bennie Lee's mind there was no question about what he *wanted* to do but even more strongly he wanted to follow God's leading. He said if I strongly urged him to take the job he would feel that was an indication of the Lord's will. I told him it was strictly up to him and that I would stand with him either way. He contacted Mr. Moore, expressed sincere appreciation for the offer and declined.

**God's Provision** During those stressful lean years many times those of us in the bookstore did not get paychecks. There were times when an urgent payment was due in the business and no money available and we wrote letters asking for leniency on a deadline; I hoped fervently for the day to come when I would never have to write another letter like that. Sometimes at the very last minute of a deadline an unexpected check arrived in the mail or a creditor extended time or took some of our own publications in payment. We deeply appreciated every word and act of encouragement and there were many; we felt that God was using them to buoy our spirits and to help us face each new day with enthusiasm, patience and grace. Some gave (not loaned) unexpected monetary help from a $5.00 bill to a few hundred dollars, each one specifying whether for the business or for personal use. The money helped, to be sure, but the accompanying expressions of confidence in us personally and in what we were doing, were truly God-sends. For both we thanked God and the persons.

In our family affairs we skimped and did without as much as we could. I had told my parents the business was struggling but I never told them to what extent nor had I gone into details regarding our personal finances. At one time of desperation when we had not been able to cash several salary checks and did not know what we would do, we unexpectedly received a check from Daddy. His letter said when we were children he planned to give us small allowances but was not able; also when he had cattle on the farm he had pledged to himself that a percentage of newborn calves would be allotted to each of us in turn. He had kept track of the allowance money and how many calves belonged to each one of us. He sold the cattle when they moved from the farm to Northern Rhodesia in 1946 but he had debts to pay and was not able to send any money at that time. The check could not have arrived at a more opportune moment.

Later on having no salary checks for some time, our personal affairs had again reached the point of desperation and we were threatened with foreclosure on our house. Bennie Lee explained to our children that we might need to leave our house and although we did not know what we would do, we would keep praying about it and something would work out. Bennie Lee's brother, Clarence, and his family lived in a fairly new modest home in the county and he had a good job in Huntsville. Whether through Curtis, who worked in the bookstore, or some other way, learning of our situation, Clarence came to Bennie Lee and told him that he and his wife, Barbara, had agreed that they wanted us to have their house rent-free for as long as we needed it and they would rent a house for themselves. Bennie Lee objected but Clarence said he would not listen to such talk because Bennie Lee had sacrificed and done for all of his brothers and sisters in years past and it was time someone did something for him. As it turned out we did not have to take Clarence up on his generous offer because about that time there came a letter from my parents with a check for enough to catch up the house payments. Daddy said they had sold the farm that they homesteaded in the 1930s and had divided what he and Mother wanted to share with their children. Those were not the only God-sends that kept us and the business going during those times but they are among the most memorable, and we thanked God constantly for His care.

Bennie Lee made many sales trips to bookstores all over the Midwest, Central and Southern states, to promote our books while we struggled to keep the business going. He was able to be gone with confidence knowing that Virginia Dale, Mamie, Donna and I could keep the business going at home—helped along by the momentum he generated when he was at home between trips and with his nightly phone calls to me.

**The Nest Empties** One by one the children graduated from high school. Bennie Lee took Edward to Florida College, a two-year college in Temple Terrace, Florida. Because he found it almost impossible to express emotion, after he had helped Edward unload at Florida College, he gave him the few dollars he had, shook his hand and left. When Bennie Lee got home he told me leaving Edward like that was one of the hardest things he ever did in his life. It hurt all the more knowing he could not help Edward financially and that he would have to fend for himself. Bennie Lee had fended for himself when he went to college and knew what it meant, and he wished he could have done better for his own children. All five of the boys made us proud by making their own way through college without complaints.

**Emotions** Bennie Lee did not show his feelings as much as we might have wished but it didn't mean he didn't have deep emotions. We had agreed when we married that we would keep our disagreements private and the same with our demonstrations of love for each other. Perhaps it would have been good for our children if we had shown more of both in front of them. But we felt it was unseemly to "moon around over each other" in public. I never knew all the words to the song, "Behind Closed Doors," but the ones I knew, fit—unfortunately I did not have enough hair to let it "hang down low!" Behind closed doors there was no lack of demonstration of love between us. At times behind closed doors we worked out some heated (for us) disagreements. When he was on overnight trips Bennie Lee wrote a letter to me every night, in addition to his phone calls and I saved all of the letters. After he died, when I was emptying the house for sale in 1975, I took time to read every one. I have kept them in a suitcase in case my children ever want to read them after I'm gone—except for a few that I felt were so private they were for my eyes only—I burned them.

Bennie Lee had battled with a hot temper all his life and kept it under control most of the time. When something got the better of him at work or at home, rather than let an employee or one of the children have the brunt of it, he tended to turn it on me and after that happened I usually found a place to hide and shed a few tears. I didn't enjoy it but I understood it and he always apologized to me later in private. The business was in such distress I knew he was overloaded almost beyond human endurance and I was determined to understand. I could tell that the long-time trusted employees also understood.

At home I only remember one time that he lost control. We were at the dinner table and he said some hard things to me in front of the children. I knew he was pressed beyond measure at work and I didn't answer, but gathered up some dishes and went to the kitchen to have a little cry over the sink. Edward, who was home from college, followed me and said, "Mother, why do you let him talk to you like that?" I explained to Edward that I was sure he didn't really mean to hurt me and told him of some of the stress his daddy was handling at work and that I knew his explosion was really about that.

**Goings and Comings** Edward's leaving made a big hole in our family. After one year at Florida College he stayed home a year and worked in the bookstore, then went back for his second and third years. He was working at the bookstore when President John F. Kennedy was assassinated—I was in the kitchen ironing when Edward came home for lunch and burst excitedly in the door to tell me about hearing it on his car radio.

When he went back to Florida College he met Sara Faye Locke. They were both in the college chorus and made trips around the country. On one of their rounds they stopped overnight for a program in Athens and Edward invited Sara Faye to spend the night at our house. They arrived late at night and she sat in the living room waiting as we hastily prepared Nancy's room for her to sleep in. I thought she was the most beautiful young woman I had ever seen. She was an only child and I wondered how she would react to being thrust into the midst of the boisterous Fudge household. I'm sure it took great effort on her part but she valiantly weathered it. Edward went on to Abilene Christian for a year to get his BA degree while Sara Faye was getting hers at Peabody in Nashville. She grew up in Franklin, Tennessee, in a house her father built just a block or two off of old U. S. Highway 31, the main road from Athens to Nashville. Her parents were delightfully steeped in "southern hospitality" and stopping by the Locke's house became almost routine when we sent one of our boys to Nashville with a load of books. Mrs. Locke always brought out something delicious to go along with Mr. Locke's interesting stories and the boys enjoyed being the center of attention.

**"I Against Me"** Paul was enough younger than the other boys that much of the time he was left to his own devices. During one of our big snows Paul went out to play. I looked out the kitchen window and saw him in the snowy back yard. He threw a football then ran like crazy to where he threw it, grabbed the ball and threw it back, at times throwing himself at it as though tackling. I called Bennie Lee to the window to watch. After a while Bennie Lee went out and asked Paul what he was playing. He said it was football and said, "*I* am playing against *Me* and since there's only one of me I have to be both sides!" We admired his inventiveness at the same time feeling sad that he had no one to play with. He explained that he did that sort of thing quite a lot.

**Another Off To College** Henry was an extrovert, bubbling with enthusiasm over whatever he was doing at the time. When in 1964 it was his turn to graduate from the Bible School and go to Florida there was another big hole left behind and we marveled at how quiet the house became. In Florida he worked night shift in a chemical lab for some time and I was concerned that he might not be getting enough sleep to keep up his health and grades. He especially like German Chocolate cake and I tried to send one to him for birthdays and occasionally in between. At the end of two years he came home to live and teach at the Bible School and what a joy it was to have him effervescing at home once more. At the same time Jack Smith came to teach in the Bible School and lived with us for a time. He shared a room with Henry and we enjoyed having him in the mix.

During the summer between Robert's Junior and Senior years of high school he worked with a construction company on the new courthouse in Huntsville. When he told me about it I empathized with his horror of heights and having to work on scaffolding without side rails. When that job ended he did roadwork and came in at the end of the day sunburned and with tar on his clothes and boots. But he was proud of the paychecks he earned. After his final day of work at the end of the summer he came into the kitchen carrying a 15"x12" wooden spinning wheel entwined with artificial morning glories. He presented it to me saying, "Mother, this is a small token of apology for all the trouble I gave you growing up!" His mother cried and stored away a precious memory.

Very soon after school opened for Robert's senior year he came to the bookstore ushering in a tall good-looking blonde. Beaming broadly he introduced her to Bennie Lee and me, "This is Dianne Gravitt. She's a new girl in our senior class and I'm going to marry her!" or words to that effect. She had transferred for her senior year from Parrish, Alabama and was boarding with a family across the street from us. The rest of the year she and Robert were a pair and we saw a lot of her. Being the youngest of nine children she was undaunted by the constant hubbub at our house.

**Unforgettable Year** The years were unfolding like roller coasters, each unforgettable with so much activity and so many people. Even so 1967 stands out in my mind. There were multiple graduations coming up in the spring: Nancy from the sixth grade, Robert and Dianne from high school, Edward with his BA Degree from Abilene Christian College and Sara Faye from Peabody with her BA Degree.

Bennie Lee was to deliver the address at Nancy's graduation and needed to stay with the business as much as possible and that fact made the decision for us as to who would stay and who would go to Abilene to be with Edward. I didn't want to drive the approximately 1,000 miles alone and invited Barbara, Clarence's wife, to go with me. We left Athens at 4:00 a.m. and drove to Fort Worth, Texas the first day. As we drove we talked so much there was no danger of getting sleepy. But in the motel I slept soundly. Barbara woke up before I did and when she saw I was in the same position I had been in when she went to sleep she thought I had died in my sleep!

After the graduation ceremonies Edward loaded all his belongings into his and our cars and we drove back to Athens to prepare for his and Sara Faye's wedding. They were married June 23rd in Franklin, Tennessee. The wedding and reception went off beautifully and the bride and groom left for Abilene, Texas, where she would teach school while Edward worked on his Masters.

In the business we felt that things were looking up, though we knew we still had to keep our noses to the grindstone. At home we were busy preparing for Robert and Dianne's wedding July 10th in the Buchanans' beautiful back yard, with the reception to be held in our house. Before the wedding they found an apartment across town and moved their things into it. The day before the wedding, as Robert was leaving our house with a load of his belongings, I met him in the hallway and he said, "There's no way I can get all my stuff out of here in time for the wedding." I tried to calm him by saying, "That's O.K., you can always come back after the wedding and get the rest of it." His reply sent my heart plummeting—as very emphatically he said, *"When I go out of here to get married I'm not setting foot back in here for at least . . ."* by then I thought he was going to say *years* and I wondered if I had been too hard on him as he grew up and this was my pay-back. I was hugely relieved when he finished, *". . . at least three weeks!"*

After the reception they borrowed our car and drove to Nashville for a mini-honeymoon in a hotel bridal suite they had reserved for one night. The next afternoon when I got home from work, I prepared supper of pinto beans that had slow cooked during the day, cornbread and cabbage slaw. An elderly county preacher, John Hayes, had brought a bucket of apples from his tree the day before; most of them had worms in them but I managed to salvage enough to make Apple Crumble for dessert.

Bennie Lee, Benjamin, Paul, Nancy and I had just sat down to eat when the phone rang. It was Robert. In a sheepish voice he said without taking a breath, "Can we come and eat supper with you we're at our apartment but we found the place in a terrible mess our friends broke in and put salt in our slippers and peeled all the labels off our canned food and to make matters worse we both feel sick because the car battery burned up and the smell was awful and we had to get a new one what are you having?" I took a deep breath for him and said, "We're having pinto beans and slaw and cornbread and Apple Crumble. We'll be happy to have you join us." His declared three week absence had turned into overnight and we had to laugh.

**San Diego** That summer the Christian Booksellers Convention was held in San Diego. The trip would take almost two weeks and Bennie Lee said there was no way he could leave the business for that long but he felt it was important that one of us put in an appearance as it would show our various publisher suppliers that we were still in business. He wanted me to go. Benjamin had his learner's permit so he could help drive and Paul and Nancy would go with us. After the convention we would spend a night with Margaret Ann in Simi Valley and go on north to spend a night with Roy and Mary Ella in Clovis, California, then head home from there by way of Fort Worth, Texas to see Irma and Al Meeks.

On the way west through New Mexico we stopped for gas. Like dummies we all went to the restrooms at the same time, leaving the car locked while it was being filled with gas. When we came out the attendant told us a back tire had a gash in it probably from glass in the road. It did look bad and we had seen a lot of glass along the road-side but we didn't have a good spare, only a makeshift in case of short emergency. I phoned Bennie Lee and he said even though we could ill afford it, the only thing to do was to get a new tire. Naturally that station had tires for sale. Benjamin and I chastised ourselves for leaving the car unattended—we had read about scams and this surely looked like one.

In spite of that, the trip with my three children was a good experience. While Benjamin and I took turns driving, Paul and Nancy took turns being sign-watcher and journalist. The sign-watcher made sure we stayed on the right road and told us how many miles to the next town. In a big scrapbook the journalist wrote interesting things about the trip. We played different games as we drove, one I recall we each chewed a whole pack of bubblegum then tried to blow the largest bubble! While driving through the desert in our air-conditioned station wagon, looking out at the vast expanse of undulating sand, Nancy said, "I wish I was on a horse riding out there"—then she thought about the heat and added—"if it was air-conditioned!" We teased her about her "air-conditioned horse" until she wished she had never said it!

At the Convention we visited publishers' booths but skipped the lunches and dinners that cost extra. However, we did visit the famous San Diego Zoo one afternoon. Our time was so limited we only spent one night with Margaret Ann and Sharon in Simi Valley (Vonnie was away at the time), then on to Clovis. The evening of our arrival, Roy, Mary Ella and I were talking in the living room and the children were in another room. Soon Raymond, Philip, Paul and Benjamin came to us with a plan. They proposed that Raymond and Philip return to Alabama to live with us and finish high school at the Bible School. Benjamin and Paul were agreeable to the plan and promised to share rooms with them. They and our boys had been good friends all their lives. Raymond would be a senior that fall, Philip a sophomore.

**Two More Fudges** I phoned Bennie Lee for his opinion. He said if I thought I could handle it then he would agree to the plan. There was some hurried packing that night for our early morning departure. They didn't have much money and neither did we, so we agreed to drive all night taking turns and we were glad that we had Raymond to help drive. While we were stopped for supper at a fast-food place in Reno, Nevada, it rained. That was the first rain the California boys had seen in over a year and Philip ran out into the parking lot jumping up and down whooping with excitement.

We took three-hour driving shifts during daylight but after dark we cut it to two hours. By eleven o'clock Benjamin and Raymond said they couldn't keep their eyes open any longer. I told them to sleep while I drove and I'd wake one of them to relieve me in about three hours if I could last that long. About two in the morning my eyes wouldn't stay open so I tried calling first one of them then the other but they couldn't be roused, so I pulled into a rest stop. By then it was cool outside. Doors were locked and I made sure all the windows were closed except for a tiny crack at the top for air, then I slumped behind the steering wheel and slept. It seemed only minutes later when the surrounding eighteen-wheelers began cranking up and revving their motors and woke us up. It was only five o'clock but the nap had helped and we got on the road again. That night we reached Fort Worth about ten o'clock—too late to go to Irma's house. I hadn't told them we were coming since I wasn't sure we'd make it. We checked into a motel—all in one room—and slept like logs. Strangely, I don't recall anything else about the rest of that drive home!

The two new boys fit right into our home and added to the busy-ness and fun—after all they were Fudges, too! Paul and Philip really enjoyed being friends and rooming together, even becoming "business partners." They decided to make a big birdcage in the garage and raise parakeets for sale. They worked on it every spare minute and it was big. Besides the parakeets they had starlings in a separate cage, and even a spider monkey at one time. Though they didn't make much money, Bennie Lee and I rejoiced that at last Paul had someone near his own age to enjoy.

**Shock!** But a bolt from the blue had hit the business while we were gone. One of the creditors who had accepted the copyright of the *Use Your Bible Workbooks* as collateral on a large loan decided to foreclose without notice; that it was a trusted friend made it seem all the worse. That event stands out as an extreme low of that year (1967) because it set everything back from what little progress we thought was made. True to his forgiving nature, Bennie Lee made allowances for the friend and never showed any resentment that I could tell, though I know it hurt him badly, emotionally and financially.

**June 1, 1968** That date was our 25th Wedding Anniversary. Raymond graduated in May and had gone and Philip was visiting his family for the summer. As soon as school was out Bennie Lee took Benjamin and Paul on a long-promised five-day trip to the Smoky Mountains. Our children had informed us that they were giving us a 25th Wedding Anniversary Reception in our house on Sunday June 2nd. I thought they should wait until the 50th but they said they had thought about the fact their daddy was older when we married and who knew if we would get to a 50th? Who indeed? So plans were under way for the afternoon of Sunday, the second day of June.

**A Sunday To Remember** That was a Sunday to remember in many more ways than one. At the worship hour that morning Edward preached in Kirkwood, Missouri, where he and Sara Faye were living, Henry, Robert and Paul each preached a sermon in three different county churches and Benjamin taught a teenage class at another; in addition we knew that all the boys were able song leaders and Bible class teachers. Bennie Lee and I felt our hearts near to bursting with joy and thankfulness to God.

On Saturday before the big day, Dianne came to help me clean house. We were on hands and knees in the kitchen floor scrubbing at built-up wax when Nancy came from her cleaning in another room to say there was a strange station wagon full of girls in the driveway. I hurried to the door. It was a load of *Ambassadors For Friendship*. Months before we had signed up as a host home if they wanted to bring girls from foreign countries to spend a night on their way around the country showing them a cross-section of family life in the United States of America. Part of their plan was to give no advance notice other than the fact that we had signed up for it. So here we were with supper to fix for eight more. About that time Bennie Lee, Benjamin and Paul pulled into the driveway from their camping trip. I hurried to the back door and urged them to unload their dirty clothes and camping equipment into the garage.

Then while Bennie Lee and the boys entertained the strangers, Nancy and Dianne finished cleaning in the kitchen and began supper. I made a quick grocery store run and with their help a meal for fifteen was on the table by supper time. As we finished eating it was getting dark. We cleared the table and when the dishwasher was turned on the major fuse blew. It was hot weather. Now there was no air-conditioner, no dishwasher, no lights. Bennie Lee called an electrician friend who happened to have a fuse at his house and came to our rescue.

We could take care of some of the girls but not all and during the afternoon I had called neighbors I thought might take a girl or two for the night. We had an interesting evening visiting with everyone together, then we escorted some to their places for the night. They were on the road early next morning—whether before or after breakfast I don't recall, but after they were gone we made it to church on time!

Sunday afternoon the 25th Anniversary Reception went off as planned with the efficient help of Donna Barksdale and Mamie Brackeen assisted by Dianne and Jo Ann, Terry Jo Barksdale and Brenda Birdwell. Many friends came to celebrate with us and in spite of the "No gifts" stipulation, there were gifts galore.

**Eventful Furlough** Late in the year Daddy and Mother arrived from Africa and visited with us a few days before going on to Amarillo where Beth's husband, Henry, was dying of cancer. He had become ill while they were living in Botswana (South West Africa) and they had returned to Amarillo, Texas some months before he died. A short time after Henry's death, Bill and Marilyn's two year old Mark was accidentally killed when he ran in front of a car. As much as I wanted to be with my sister and brother on those occasions it was impossible for me to make the trip and I was doubly thankful that our parents were with them.

In early 1968 Mother had cataract surgery in Dallas—the old fashioned kind—ten days in hospital for each eye with her head between sand bags to keep it from moving. She recovered well and they came for a visit later in the year. When it was time for them to go to New York and return to Africa, Bennie Lee and I took them to Birmingham to catch the train. Daddy told us that they did not expect to come back to the States any more but would spend the rest of their lives in Africa. It was a sad leave-taking thinking as they boarded the train that we would probably never meet again in this life.

**Beulah and Pleasant Valley** For two years Henry preached at Beulah in west Limestone County and another two years at Pleasant Valley while teaching and coaching at the Bible School and working part time in the bookstore. I heard him during his time at Pleasant Valley (while Bennie Lee was traveling a lot) and I was thrilled at his depth of Bible knowledge and ability to communicate. During that time, in 1968, he and Jo Ann Humphrey planned an August wedding. We had known Jo Ann since she was a fourth grader—now she was a grown-up almost seventeen, and a most welcome addition to the family, another good-looking blond. They had a church wedding and the reception followed in our house. They set up housekeeping in a mobile home east of Athens. After two years they moved ten miles north of Athens onto a few acres where Henry raised purebred Duroc hogs in addition to preaching, coaching at the Bible School, working in the bookstore and selling Bibles by appointment.

**Daughters-in-law** Our three oldest sons were now married and to his delight Bennie Lee had officiated at all three weddings. We congratulated ourselves on the excellent daughters-in-law our sons had chosen. Many have been the times in the years since that I have given God thanks for my wonderful daughters-in-law and prayed that I might be a good mother-in-law. About the only verbal coaching I did in preparing my sons for marriage was to urge them "Never, ever, tell your wife something she cooked or did was not like your mother did—that is a positive NO-NO for new husbands and don't forget it!" I'm not sure how well the boys followed that advice and as the years passed some amusing stories came to light.

One of them was about banana pudding. I frequently made banana pudding for Sunday dessert and as with all my cooking, I took shortcuts whenever possible. I found that Instant Vanilla Pudding prepared with my own slight variations from the package directions made a satisfactory pudding to pour over sliced bananas and vanilla wafers. Refrigerating it overnight allowed the pudding to soak into the cookies. My children didn't know any other kind of banana pudding in their growing up years—except when they visited a friend and came home saying, "Their banana pudding tasted funny!" My daughters-in-law had all grown up with made-from-scratch banana pudding—boiled custard poured hot over sliced bananas and vanilla wafers, which was the recipe book way to make it. They knew the boys liked banana pudding and proudly set it before them made-from-scratch. One by one the boys let their wives know that the pudding they made was somehow different from what Mother made. One Christmas we were all together and the girls asked me how I made banana pudding, expecting to hear some exotic recipe unknown to them. They were surprised and we all enjoyed a good laugh when I confessed to my shortcut recipe using Instant Pudding!

**African Kinfolks** Foy and Margaret came to see us every time they were home on furlough from Africa. Their oldest three children were Harold, Ellen and Jimmy, roughly the ages of our oldest three. On one visit Jimmy was just three-and-a-half and our boys liked to ask him how old he was just to hear his deep voice and Rhodesian accent when he answered, "Ah free an' a haahf!" I'm sure he got tired of it but he always answered and laughed with them. Margaret worked for a while at the Bible school and I kept Jimmy, who was a little older than Paul. They and Nancy played well together. Later Kay arrived in their family and the next time I specifically remember seeing them was at our Short family reunion in December, 1961.

When Harold finished high school in Rhodesia he made a trip to the States and came to see us. He was seventeen and we all thoroughly enjoyed his visit but he did not stay in the States. A grown Jimmy came by on his way to Florida College and was also an instant hit in our family. For the next few years he was a frequent visitor and always welcome. Two years later Ellen arrived to go to college and our home became her home away from home while she attended Florida College and Western Kentucky University. She met her future husband in Nashville, Tennessee. Her mother came from Rhodesia for the wedding but Foy was not able to come and Bennie Lee gave the bride away, in the absence of her father.

In 2007 Ellen wrote . . . *I have always felt blessed that I was able to look on your home as my American home because I knew you understood what it was like . . . I had someone on this side of the Atlantic who could understand what it was like being a teenager so far from parents . . . you have and will always have a special place in my heart because you took me in, treated me like one of your own, and put up with my teenage foolishness . . . You and Uncle Bennie Lee were a part of my life from my earliest memories . . . whenever we needed help from someone in the States, dad would call/write you . . .*

One of the strengths of Ellen's and my relationship was how much alike our thoughts were about being foreign born. Though I was Rhodesian born, my parents were citizens of the United States of America. I was both a citizen of Rhodesia and a citizen of the U.S.A.—until Robert Mugabe took control of Zimbabwe and did away with dual citizenships there. When I went to boarding school I was an oddity, being an American—when I came to live in the U.S.A. I was an oddity, being a Rhodesian. That was enough to cause mixed feelings in me as a child and as an adult. After living there from birth until the age of eighteen I felt more Rhodesian than American and if I had been given a choice of where to live then, there is no doubt in my mind I would have chosen Rhodesia.

I love America—I also loved Rhodesia. My dual cultural background affected my life and I'm sure the lives of my children in unimaginable ways. I know that living in such different cultures helped me grow in tolerance and understanding of differences in people no matter where they were born or live. I am thankful that my parents taught me that spiritual citizenship is the important thing and when I have felt like a stranger on earth, I remember that as God's child I am truly a stranger and pilgrim in this life looking forward to an eternal home-country.

**1969** Benjamin had graduated from the Bible School that spring and in the fall went to Florida College and how we missed him. With him gone, Raymond gone and Henry and Jack gone, the house was empty feeling—but still busy. Philip returned for another year and he and Paul resumed their friendship and activities at school and at home; and all the time Nancy was growing up.

Henry and Jo Ann presented us with our first grandchild, Henry Lee II, born November 16th. Bennie Lee was so proud to have a grandson that I wished all his children could have seen him "near-to-bursting" with pride over it. Then began for me the joys of occasional evenings of baby-sitting helped by an enthusiastic Aunt Nancy.

**1970** When school was out that spring Philip went to live with his parents and Paul missed his companionship. We all missed him and his sense of humor. Before Philip left Paul acquired a German Shepherd puppy. He named her Penny and Penny was a joy to him. The sturdy doghouse we had built for Henry's dogs was still good and Paul put up a wire fence across the back yard to keep Penny from going into the street. But Penny dug under the wire to get out and run. She loved to run and ran to her ultimate demise—in the street. It was a sad day for Paul and we all mourned with him.

After a year in Florida College Benjamin went to New Jersey to work in a bakery for the summer of 1970. In July Paul went to Washington, D.C. with some friends from Pleasant Valley, the oldest of the four taking them in his new car—and I breathed a huge sigh of relief when they arrived home safely. That week Bennie Lee left for the North American Christian Convention in St. Louis, Missouri, and took Paul to Camp Wyldewood on his way. While in St. Louis Bennie Lee stayed with Edward and Sara Faye and I was sorry I couldn't be there, too.

Since Nancy was not able to go to camp, Bennie Lee promised her that we would do something special with her and her best friend, Marsha. Our Income Tax Refund came in the nick of time. We had heard of *Six Flags Over Georgia,* a new park near Atlanta, and decided we could use a weekend plus Monday and take them for a treat—a leisurely drive over there and back with two nights in motels, eating in little cafes—all rare treats to the girls. For once we didn't have to be somewhere by a certain time and leisurely driving was such a novelty it was fun for all of us.

The fact that once we paid our way in we could ride anything we wanted to, as many times as we wanted to, made the day in the park a huge success—but I resolved to never again get caught on a *"Run-away Mine Train!"* The girls loved that *Mine Train* and rode at least five times! Bennie Lee and I enjoyed *The Logs* going over a waterfall, the bumper cars, riding in a boat through the *Okefeenokee Swamps* and *Jean Ribot's Adventure.* Best of all we enjoyed watching the girls enjoy themselves on the multitude of rides.

October 6th Henry and Jo Ann's second boy, Eric William, was born and Bennie Lee beamed some more, and baby-sitting joy doubled for Nancy and me. Most of the opportunities came when Henry and Jo Ann left the babies with us while they went to evening ball games—Henry was still coaching at the Bible School. I was amused at Henry when at work one morning he asked, "Mother, where were you last night?" I told him, "Nancy and I went to Huntsville. Why?" He said, "Jo Ann and I decided to take the boys with us to the ball game but on the way we drove by your house. There were no lights on and I thought 'grandmother is always supposed to be at home in case we want to leave the babies with her!'" I knew he was joking but it gave me a warm fuzzy feeling!

Robert and Dianne's son, Robert Clarence II was born November 13th. And Bennie Lee's chest swelled noticeably. We were sorry they lived too far away for us to see them more often and to baby-sit with Bobby.

Thanksgiving Day that year all of Bennie Lee's brothers and sisters with their families were able to be at our house—the first time in years that all eight siblings were together—and the last time.

**Business Merger** *The Gospel Guardian* was a publishing company in Texas that Bennie Lee always called on and he and the owner were good friends. They had similar ideas of changing the controversial nature of the magazine published by that name, into an inspirational family magazine and decided to merge the companies. The owner with his wife and daughter moved to Athens along with their inventory of books and the magazine and businesses were integrated. I deplore mentioning the politics of it all but some of it is necessary in order to understand the unfolding of later events. For now I will say that the merger was extremely unpopular with the more contentious element of the "brotherhood" who voiced their uncomplimentary opinions about that change in other magazines, in their church bulletins and by word of mouth.

**Mini Skirts And Rules** It was 1971, mini skirts came on the scene about then and Nancy's friends came to school with their's shorter and shorter. Of course Nancy wanted hers shorter, too. Bennie Lee firmly set the limit for her at one inch above her knees. Considering how some girls acted over it with their parents I felt we had it fairly easy with Nancy, though not without some complaining and self pity on her part.

We had good reason to be proud of our children's behavior and about that time Nancy made us even more proud. Our rule for her was "No single dating until you are seventeen—only double-dates or in a group."

One evening after a ball game in the Bible School gymnasium she came to the house with a boy. She came in the front door leaving him standing on the porch because he didn't want to come in. She said he wanted her to go with him to Dairy Queen and she came to ask me, though she had told him she was sure the answer would be no. She was standing with the opened door between her and the boy—she and I could see each other and I could see him. When she asked out loud if she could go with him to the Dairy Queen, I asked, "Just the two of you?" and she said yes. Then, where only I could see her, she shook her head emphatically and mouthed, "Say NO, Mother! Say NO!" I was trying hard to think of a nice way to refuse her in the first place but she had made it easy for me. I told the boy, "Sorry, but we have a rule and must stick to it." She explained to me later that she really didn't want to go with him but he wouldn't take her "No" for an answer.

**A Big July 4ᵗʰ** That year Benjamin graduated from Florida College in May. As the kids were packing to leave their dorm rooms, Benjamin invited some of his closest friends to come to our house for a party on the 4ᵗʰ of July. In no time word spread that "Benjamin is having a 4ᵗʰ of July Party," and boys came to his room—"Can I come too?"—"I want to come too!" He had planned to limit the number to a special few but they were all good friends and he didn't want to refuse any one. I was helping him with final packing and loading and was amused at his predicament but knew with his experience hosting parties at home, he could handle it. Benjamin and Terry Jo organized and spearheaded the event and prepared the house for the day's influx. The day before, I cooked six chickens and two big beef roasts. Another mother furnished a ham. July 4ᵗʰ arrived and young people poured in. Boys brought watermelons and drinks and girls supplied other eats. Bennie Lee and I went on to work as usual. When they had cleaned up after eating, they sat around on the living room/ dining room floor to sing from books Benjamin had brought ahead of time from the church. Their singing was so thrilling to him that he called Bennie Lee and me at work and asked us to come hear them. We went to listen and it was like a heavenly choir. Their harmonized voices poured out their hearts in song after song and it truly was a feast for the ears—and hearts. That was their farewell to each other as they parted to go their separate ways into their chosen fields, many of them never to see each other again. Before they said goodbye they eagerly signed the Guest Book—all 68 of them!

**A Get-Away** In the summer of 1971 Bennie Lee said he needed to get away to write a workbook completing the *Student's Guide To The New Testament* series. We decided it would be a good time for me to work on the Jeremiah workbook and it would give us much desired time together. With Bibles, writing pads and pencils in hand we spent five days in a small motel in the pine woods near Moulton, Alabama. We ate breakfast and lunch in a little neighborhood café and kept fruit in the room for our evening meal. We studied and wrote morning, afternoon and evening. When the four-hour afternoon writing was done we walked a mile, ate fruit, and were ready to write more. By Friday afternoon Bennie Lee had finished his assignment but I was only about a third way through Jeremiah—doing the Workbook and Teacher Manual simultaneously. At home I put the work away and didn't have time or inclination to look at it again for 35 years.

**Last Picnic** One Sunday morning in November, 1971, Paul went to a different congregation while Nancy, Bennie Lee and I went to Pleasant Valley where Bennie Lee was again preaching regularly. Before we left home Nancy said, "Daddy, it's a beautiful day and Mother has dinner all ready, why don't we pack it up and have a picnic on the way home?" He queried, "You mean just the three of us?" "Why not?" she asked. After church we drove to the Elk River Park and ate among the pine trees. I'm glad Nancy took her camera and we have pictures.

That year Eric and Bobby had their first birthdays and Lee had his second. Bennie Lee was determined that he would be the one to give his first grandchild a tricycle and couldn't wait for Lee to be big enough. He found a small red tricycle and presented it to Lee for his second birthday.

In December Bennie Lee was invited to speak Sunday evening at a church in Cullman on *The Holy Spirit.* Paul and Nancy, the only ones at home then, were with their friends at church and for the evening afterwards, so I went with Bennie Lee. We left Athens early—he had forgotten to ask the time of the evening service. When we got to Cullman he called someone and found out we had time to spare so we went to a restaurant to have pie and coffee. I remember our conversation, the pecan pie and much of the sermon he preached.

**First in Four Years** Christmas that year was a real treat for the family: Edward and Sara Faye came from Kirkwood, Missouri; Henry, Jo Ann and boys were living just north of Athens and joined us; Robert, Dianne and Bobby came from Hueytown, Alabama; Benjamin was home for the holiday from Western Kentucky University; Paul and Nancy were still at home. It was the first time in four years that all the family was able to be together and it was a joyful time. Little did we know that it would be Bennie Lee's last Christmas with us.

At the end-of-year business meeting of *The B. L. Fudge Book Company,* a family corporation, after he gave the required business report, Bennie Lee announced, "I have compiled a list of the ten most important things in life and I am delighted to tell you today that I have nine of those ten. What is more, the only one I lack is money—and it is at the bottom of my list!"

**Christmas 1971 at 503 Chandler Drive in Athens.**
**(Left to right) Benjamin, Bennie Lee, Sybil, Edward, Sara Faye, Dianne,**
**Robert (holding Bobby), Jo Ann, Henry (holding Lee), Paul, Nancy.**

**1972** The last week of January Bennie Lee loaded the company van with books for a booth at the Florida College Lectureship. A week later, Saturday 29th he arrived back at the bookstore. When he came in the door we could tell that he was ill, and when he asked Curtis to please unload for him, we knew he felt bad—he always wanted to unload and put the books away himself. He said he must have caught the flu that was going around at the lectures and was going home to eat oranges and sleep—his cure-all when he felt under the weather. I offered to go with him but he said no because he didn't feel like talking and just wanted to sleep. Monday he was no better and I urged him to go to the doctor but he said all he needed was the juice and soup I was giving him and sleep. But Wednesday he was no better and agreed to go to the doctor. (Dr. Jackson had died of a heart attack a few years before and Dr. Waddell was our family doctor). He said Bennie Lee definitely had the flu and gave him a shot. Thursday Bennie Lee said he felt worse and I called the doctor. He wanted him to come to his office but Bennie Lee said he didn't feel like it and the doctor allowed our friend, an LPN, to come by and give him another injection.

When he said he thought he felt better on Friday I was encouraged. I sat in the room with him Thursday and Friday and he wanted to talk off and on. He had had a good visit with Homer Hailey at the lectures and said, "He told me that he has the utmost respect for my integrity and his opinion means more to me than he could know. He has been one of my best friends and encouragers ever since our days in Abilene Christian College when he was my Bible Teacher. I'm glad he is at Florida College to teach our children. He used to tell us in Bible class that 'One man plus God is a majority!'"

Saturday morning Bennie Lee's skin had a grayish look and I told him I was taking him to the E.R. He didn't object but he was not able to walk to the car. I called Sewell Hall, a friend indeed, who lived nearby. He came immediately and after one look he said, "I'm calling an ambulance to take him." Dr. Pennington was on duty in the E.R. and after a brief examination said Bennie Lee had double pneumonia. In no time he was in a room under oxygen. I called Henry to let him know where we were; he came at once and we sat watching Bennie Lee. He seemed to be sleeping and breathing easier so after Henry stayed a while, he went home to finish feeding his hogs and to shower and said he would come right back.

A short time later Bennie Lee seemed to rouse some and told me there was a cigarette vending machine on the wall opposite him and he knew it was the devil trying to tempt him to smoke. He said, "He thinks that's a vice of mine but I've never smoked and I'm not tempted. He doesn't know I only have one addiction and that's you. Did you know you are my only addiction?" He didn't say any more and I thought he was sleeping, but soon after that he stopped breathing and I hit the emergency button. Code Blue activity followed but to no avail. It was February 5, 1972. He would have turned 58 in April.

I blamed myself for not persuading Bennie Lee to go to the doctor sooner but he had been sick so seldom in his life that neither he nor I realized how sick he was. Dr. Waddell said when people have been so seldom sick it is hard for them or their family to recognize how sick they are; but I blamed myself anyway.

I called Henry and Sewell Hall. Paul was at ball practice and Nancy at her friend Marsha's house when Sewell told them. When Paul walked into the house by way of the kitchen he wrote on our bulletin board, "The Lord giveth and the Lord taketh away, blessed be the name of the Lord."— Job 1:21. Henry came to me at the hospital at once and I left everything up to him. How thankful I was that he was there to take the sad load of calling his out-of-town brothers, and making all other necessary calls and arrangements.

My mind is unclear about details from the time Henry walked into the hospital chapel where I was. I vaguely remember people coming to the house Saturday evening, but not who. I remember being thankful the children were all there but don't remember them arriving. I recall very little about being at the funeral home with them, making arrangements—the funeral was set for Monday. I remember Edward standing with me beside the casket looking down at Bennie Lee's body—when, I'm not sure. Edward and Sara Faye were living in Kirkwood, Missouri, where Edward was preaching for a church; Robert and Dianne were living in Hueytown, Alabama, where Robert was working as a car salesman and preaching; Benjamin was in Western Kentucky University in Bowling Green, Kentucky. As soon as possible they had all come home.

My mind is a jumble about most of the next two days. I do remember we went to church Sunday morning at Eastside and that we didn't tarry after the service. Visitation was at McConnell Funeral Home Sunday afternoon and evening. Some time before that Benjamin had remarked to me, regarding a friend's visitation, that he thought visitations were pagan and useless, but after seeing and experiencing the outpouring of sympathy from so many who came to the visitation for Bennie Lee, he told me afterwards that he had changed his mind. He said he realized that it helped the family beyond words and seemed to do good also to the people who came.

Donna, Mamie and Virginia Dale automatically took over at the house and I don't know what we would have done without them. We asked Sewell Hall and R. L. Andrews, two of Bennie Lee' most like-minded and closest preacher friends, to speak at the funeral. *The Gospel Guardian* magazine dated *March 2, 1972* carried Sewell Hall's article repeating what he said at the funeral.

## BENNIE LEE FUDGE
### Sewell Hall

The minister of the First Baptist Church in Athens, Alabama, opened services last Sunday morning with these words: "I'm stunned this morning by the loss of a real friend, Bennie Lee Fudge." This well expressed the feeling of thousands of citizens of Athens and Limestone County. Those who counted him their brother felt an even greater sense of loss. One said it this way: "When I go to town, it is as though the courthouse were missing from the square."

The respect in which he was held was indicated by the hundreds who came to the funeral home on Sunday afternoon in an almost solid stream over a period of several hours; by an assembly of over 700 for funeral services on Monday; and by the banks of flowers and scores of calls that came in from all over the nation. So many who came had stories to tell of kindnesses shown and services rendered, that we could not but remember Dorcas whose mourners, on the occasion of her death, stood by "weeping and showing the coats and garments which Dorcas made."

THOSE WHO CAME An older generation remembers a young man of unusually sober mind, who very early in life accepted a large share of responsibility for the rearing of seven younger brothers and sisters. They remember the limitations this placed upon his efforts to attend school regularly; but happily they recall his success in both endeavors and his very high standing in every graduating class of which he was a part, first in Athens, than at David Lipscomb and finally at Abilene Christian. They recall his return to the county which all his life he called home, and his tireless efforts to see Christ preached in every community of it.

Here another generation joins in the reminiscence, recalling his dreams for Athens Bible School, his major role in the initiation of it, and his uninterrupted contributions to its success over a period of twenty-nine years. Widely remembered, too, is his work of broadcasting the gospel by radio, six days a week, for eleven years hardly missing a broadcast. Most of this time he was simply answering the questions mailed in by listeners. When others took the broadcast, people used the phone or stopped by the bookstore to get answers *in person from Bennie Lee. They appreciated the simple Bible answers he gave and marveled at the breadth of Bible knowledge that made them possible.*

*A younger generation, many of whom attended the funeral services, do not remember those things. But they think of him as the father of Edward, Henry, Robert, Benjamin, Paul and Nancy—a father who was always concerned for his children, yet eager for them to form their own convictions and stand on their own two feet. They remember seeing him bounding along East Washington Street toward the bookstore with a bounce that suggested there were springs in his knees, refusing all offers of transportation, communing instead with every bird or flower along the way. They remember his light burning far into the night as they passed his place of business. They remember one who always counted his young friends among his favorite friends, who was always excited by an opportunity to study with them the way of the Lord.*

*THOSE WHO COULD NOT COME But as we sat among the large assembly of those who came to pay respects, we could not help but feel that there was a host of others present in spirit. We thought of men scattered across the world preaching Christ—men who always found at the Fudge's home an open door and a welcome for a meal, for a night's lodging, or for a week's visit—men who were always encouraged in their work and assisted in finding support. He and his family knew well how to "set (them) forward on their journey worthily of God," and without ever leaving this country they were genuine "fellow-helpers for the truth."*

*During the service we thought of those who knew him only through his publications, as author and publisher of the "Use Your Bible" workbooks and of other similar series which have attained wide usage among churches of Christ and in some denominational bodies. The Gospel Digest, of which he served as editor and associate editor for several years, is still favorably mentioned, though the last issue was printed eleven years ago. Numerous other booklets and pamphlets which he published have edified many whom he never met.*

*Nor can we forget those who were influenced by his personal correspondence. This writer especially recalls a journey of 1,000 miles from Eastern Nigeria to Ghana in 1958. There were no known Christians after the New Testament order in that country at that time. From Accra we traveled the fifty miles into* the heart of Ghana to the town of Swedru, then eight miles to the little village of Nkum. There in the typical African mud house, we found J. O. Gaidoo, a Ghanian who had only recently resigned his post as a Major in the Salvation Army. Instrumental in that resignation were the well-read and carefully marked pamphlets and letters which we saw in a stack on a table. They were from Bennie Lee Fudge. It was, of course, with Bennie Lee's encouragement and assistance that we were in Ghana to meet him. And we found his heart well prepared for reception of the truth which he eventually obeyed. This godly man converted some fifty-five souls before his untimely death. Thus the work was launched in Ghana, due entirely to the initiative of a man who never saw Africa. Years later, a visit to the Philippines revealed his widespread influence among brethren there, many of whom he had assisted in numerous ways. Present at the service, were these men from the Philippines, along with Ghanians, Rhodesians and Nigerians, and a host of others who may not know of his passing for weeks to come.

THE SERVICE Funeral services were conducted at the building of the Eastside church in Athens, a church which he served as evangelist for eleven years. The service was planned by the family. Opening prayer and remarks were by Doyle Banta, long-time friend and co-worker. Clinton Brackeen, who had worked with him in many meetings, led inspirational congregational singing. Other longtime associates participated in the remainder of the service: Irven Lee reading the scripture, A. J. Rollings leading prayer, and R. L. Andrews speaking. It was the privilege of this writer to also participate.

Those who participated felt keenly the incompleteness of their tribute to a good man. Yet this was not their prime purpose. They were asked by the family to honor Bennie Lee's desire that at such a service, Christ be glorified as the source and inspiration of whatever he had accomplished and that the grace of God be cited as the basis for all their hope. It is hoped that this was accomplished. The service was climaxed by the singing of the following hymn—a favorite of the deceased and a request of the family:

## MY HOPE IS BUILT ON NOTHING LESS

*My hope is built on nothing less*
*Than Jesus' blood and righteousness;*
*I dare not trust the sweetest frame,*
*But wholly lean on Jesus' name.*

*When darkness veils His lovely face,*
*I rest on His unchanging grace;*
*In ev'ry high and stormy gale,*
*My anchor holds within the veil.*

*His oath, His covenant, His blood,*
*Support me in the whelming flood;*
*When all around my soul gives way,*
*He then is all my hope and stay.*

*When He shall come with trumpet sound,*
*O may I then in Him be found;*
*Dressed in His righteousness alone,*
*Faultless to stand before the throne.*

*On Christ, the solid Rock, I stand,*
*All other ground is sinking sand,*
*All other ground is sinking sand.*

Bennie Lee's body was laid to rest in Athens Cemetery not far from the Eastside church building. We had requested "no flowers" and suggested donations to favorite charities or other good works but there were many beautiful flowers anyway.

When I left the hospital following his death I felt dazed. At the funeral home before people began arriving for the visitation, the children and I were there and as I gazed down at his body the realization that he was actually gone became real to me. I felt as though my whole being had been cut in half and was raw and bleeding and I wept. After that torrent of tears to my surprise I did not cry so easily again.

When we were back in the house from the cemetery there was food brought in by neighbors for everyone and I sat down with the children and families to eat. I felt "firmly bound up" and thought of that long ago experience when my Daddy had bandaged my badly skinned leg. I realized it was the same sort of feeling only now it was my whole being that felt bandaged and it was almost as physical a feeling as that had been. As we sat at the table one of my sons said, "How can we all sit down to eat like this when we have just come from burying Daddy?" I reminded them of the familiar story of David who after the death of his infant son, ate food for the first time in days and his servants asked him why and his reply was, "Before he was dead I fasted and prayed that he would live, but now he is dead I know he will not return to me but I shall go to him." As we ate we talked about Bennie Lee and of some day meeting him again.

All my life I had cried too easily. I dreaded going back to work where I would be constantly facing sympathetic workers and visitors. I especially dreaded the preachers who would be passing through town and would want to speak to me. I thought my old tearfulness would rise up in spite of everything, but to my relief it didn't happen. I believe the Lord, with that firm binding was holding me together through it all.

In an article I read during that time there was a description of a man that I thought fit Bennie Lee so perfectly I copied it to carry in my billfold—it is there still and I share it here:

*". . . The extraordinary sense he gave of being alive—such vitality of personality—a vitality so superbly disciplined that it sometimes left the impression of cool detachment, but imbuing everything he thought or did with intense concentration and power. When he entered a room, the temperature changed and he quickened the sensibilities of everyone around him. His curiosity was unlimited. The restless thrust of his mind never abated. He noticed everything, forgot nothing. He lived his life so intensely that in retrospect it almost seems as if he must have known it would be short and that he had no time to waste."—Author Unknown*

**Carrying On** The Board of Directors of the business corporation elected me President and we pressed on for nearly three years, carried forward in a large part, I believed, on the momentum that Bennie Lee had generated. The .business did well and we steadily paid down what debts were left after paying all possible with the insurance Bennie Lee had carried for that purpose.

Henry and Jo Ann were still living near Athens and helping in the bookstore as he continued to preach, coach and raise hogs. Benjamin came home from Western Kentucky University to live at home and work in the store. How I did appreciate having him at home once more with Paul and Nancy. Paul would be graduating from high school in a few months and had many school activities. Edward and Sara Faye moved from Kirkwood, to Athens so that Edward could help in the business and they stayed with us for five months while their house was being built.

I was surrounded by loving children; I wanted to be strong for my children but it seemed to me that I leaned on them for strength instead. When Edward or Henry was busy at something else and books needed to be picked up from Decatur Printing Company, I took the chance to have time to myself. Going and coming I crossed the Tennessee River drawbridge. On one of the trips as I got to the bridge I thought how easy it would be to drive off into the deep water and I would be with Bennie Lee, but no sooner had the thought hit my mind than it was replaced with how wrong it would be to do that, and what I would be doing to my children and I prayed for strength to carry on.

I found myself working all hours at the bookstore as Bennie Lee had done, putting in 12-14 hour days. Paul and Nancy often kept me company in the evenings doing their homework at the store if they weren't busy at school. They were very patient with me and it was a great help. Winter was on us and it was after dark when I stopped work at the bookstore. On one of those evenings I had letters ready for the post office. Paul said he would run around the block to drop them off and I could pick him up at the corner on the way home. I looked at him, "But, Paul, you don't have a jacket!" "I'll run to stay warm!" he assured me. Nancy and I locked up, got in the car and I drove blithely all the way home in the windy, freezing mist.

I was in the kitchen fixing supper when Paul walked in the door in his shirtsleeves, shivering from the cold, red-faced, hair wet and windblown. He had practically run all the way home. His words cut me to the heart, "Did you forget something, Mother?" I threw my arms around him, hugging him tightly trying to warm him, filled with shame and remorse at my forgetfulness and his obvious suffering from the cold. What else could I say but "OH, PAUL, I'M SO SORRY!"

Work seemed automatic but it took time for me to personally feel like I knew what I was doing. I read something Joan Didion wrote that made sense to me regarding grief after the death of a loved one:

*"Healing (from grief) is not a fait accompli. You don't actually get over things. They become part of everything you are. This does not mean you walk around crying all the time. But you change."* My life had changed and I had changed and continued to change. I had depended on Bennie Lee's wisdom, judgment and decision making—as though riding on his coattails—but now I had to think for myself. I resolved with the Lord's help to be stronger in every way.

**"Young Athenian To Rhodesia"** Those were the words in the local newspaper. Paul turned eighteen in February of 1972, just twenty days after the death of his Daddy. He graduated from the Bible School that spring and during the summer he went to Rhodesia for six weeks to spend time with his grandparents and with Foy and Margaret. It was his first venture abroad and excitement was keen as he prepared to go. My feelings were mixed—this was my youngest son, just eighteen, going 10,000 miles away—and yet I had done that when I was eighteen during the days of World War II—and an ocean voyage instead of a two-day airplane flight—but still . . . Six weeks later he arrived home safely, an experienced traveler. It was a foretaste of what he would be doing some three years later.

**Paul to F.C.** What was left of that summer was spent getting him ready to go to Florida College in the fall and we missed him sorely. Edward and Sara Faye moved into their new house and it was a good thing Benjamin was at home to keep Nancy and me from feeling that the house had become completely hollow. Benjamin had brought some L.P.s home with him and we listened to them a lot; one in particular, *Bridge Over Troubled Waters*, I almost wore out, though we did listen to more cheerful music a lot, too.

Lee and Eric were joys to all of us as they grew. When Lee was nearly three he spent the weekend with us. We were having some work done on the dining room end of the house where carpenter ants had done considerable damage. As the men took out faulty wood they threw it out into the driveway with nails still in it. In spare minutes on Saturday I hammered out nails and stacked the boards to use for kindling in the new fireplace they had installed. Lee was fascinated with the hammer and wanted to help. I gave him a hammer and he worked beside me with concentration and serious energy. Eric was two and wanted his turn to come to my house so Jo Ann left him with me for a little visit all by himself and that pleased both of us.

It was a joy to me to have Edward working in the business as advertising manager and head of our publishing division. The editor of *The Gospel Guardian* magazine asked him to be an Associate Editor—causing more criticism from the opposing forces when they saw Edward's name on the masthead. Soon after Edward and Sara Faye moved to their new house, on January 17, 1973 Melanie Ann was born, my first granddaughter. I had more baby-sitting to enjoy. That January 27ᵗʰ I turned fifty. Nancy and her friends, with one of their mothers, thought such a notable milestone deserved a special treat. They took me bowling for the only time in my life. My first try was a strike and the two teams each wanted me on their side—after that every single ball went into the gutter. So ended my bowling career!

**Nancy to F.C.** Nancy graduated from the Bible School in 1973 and our summer was busy getting her ready and packed for college and helping Paul repack for his second year. I was proud and yet my heart ached as I helped them unload into their dorm rooms at Florida College and said goodbye—my "babies" had grown up!

Ahead of time I had thought of the 700 mile drive home and asked a young friend at church, Nathan Brackeen, to go with us to keep me company and share the driving on the way home. It was my turn driving as we approached the brightly lighted Interstate Bypass around Atlanta. Rain was coming down, street lights, traffic lights and car lights mixed with lighted signs and building lights along the sides, all reflected on the eight lanes of wet pavement. I couldn't tell what was on the ground and what was up in the air. When I told Nathan that, he said, "You better pull over first chance and let me drive. I think I know which is right side up!" I gladly turned the wheel over to him.

Nancy soon found out the girls in college were wearing mini skirts but instead of begging to shorten hers, she was ready for the new style that came in about then of ankle-length dresses. She sent me an SOS for a long dress. The Mill Ends store was still operating so I found material and got busy making a long dress for her. I told her I'd work on a second one as soon as possible. Another popular item that had come out in girls' wear was the man's light-weight blue denim work-shirt with lavish embroidery on the back. Without embroidery the shirt was inexpensive so I bought one and set to work in my evenings embroidering it for her. I enjoyed using all the stitches I had learned to do so long ago, and for good measure satin-stitched a design on the cuffs and her initials on the breast-pocket lapel. It made such a hit with her college mates that she said she was afraid it might be stolen!

A combination of things made Nancy decide that she did not want to go back after her first semester and I was glad to have her home. She tried again the next year but one more semester was enough. I told her not everyone had to go to college and it was her decision to make, so she came home and worked in a lingerie company in town. She was grown up and we developed a close relationship that I enjoyed and have treasured through the years in spite of our being separated by many miles most of those years.

Benjamin had been working in the bookstore ever since his daddy had died. In late 1973 he took some vacation and with three of his Florida College friends, Herby Hinely, Reatha Jackson and Marilyn Lake, backpacked through Europe on 50 cents a day. There were no cell phones then and I'm glad Benjamin took the time to write of their adventures. He mailed a long letter to me each week recounting their days and that collection would make an interesting book.

**1974** Leslie Ann arrived September 17th to make three for Henry and Jo Ann and a second granddaughter for me. The next year they moved to Missouri to live on a farm and raise hogs and Henry preached in a nearby church. We missed them beyond words.

In early November I was sitting at my desk reading a letter from my father that told about him and my mother being very sick with flu. When Benjamin came in I told him about it. He said, "Why don't you go see them?" I told him there was no way I could afford it. He said, "If your refrigerator quit working you would get a new one on credit and pay it off gradually wouldn't you? Why not do the same with a ticket to go see your parents? That's more important than a refrigerator!" I got a passport in record time and bought a roundtrip ticket on TWA—my first time ever to fly. After all the overtime I had put in I had no qualms about taking a three week vacation and the business was in the good hands of Edward, Benjamin and my "three pillars," Virginia Dale, Mamie and Donna. The visit with my parents was good for them and for me and I was re-acquainted with my birthplace, Bulawayo, where they lived.

I was gone over Thanksgiving and Benjamin and Nancy hosted the Fudge Family get-together of their uncles and aunts and cousins at our house.

**Paul and Janis** Paul did well in Florida College his two years. He and Janis Boulnois from Orlando, Florida, found each other and by graduation time they were making plans to marry and go to Rhodesia as missionaries. They were married December 23, 1974. Janis' family came from Florida and the wedding took place in the Ephesus church building. Edward performed the ceremony for his youngest brother.

**Business Changes** The business was growing well but more major changes were coming to our lives. At that time an offer to buy the business was made to me and after consulting with the boys and Nancy, with many prayers, the business was sold—in good faith on our part that its profits would be given to a Christian college. It was only later that I learned the approach to prospective investors in that purchase was in essence, "Sybil is a pitiful widow struggling with that business she inherited and she deserves our help!" I did not know I was "struggling"—we were making a profit and paying off debts. When someone approached me about selling the company it seemed logical they could want to buy a going business that was making a profit and our family decision was made with that understanding.

I never aspired to being a "business woman" in my wildest dreams, just as I never aspired to being a "school teacher" (in 1943), but when each one was thrust upon me I believe the Lord helped me meet the challenges with the wonderful support of a loving husband in 1943, and loyal co-workers and children in 1972-1974.

A complicated combination of events over more than a year after that initial sale culminated in the resale of the business and the firing of Edward by the new owners because of his stand for what he believed. The profits never to my knowledge went to the college. Too much of what happened seemed underhanded and I prefer to put it out of my mind. It took five years on my part of praying earnestly for grace to forgive the wrongs which, in my perception, were done to us and especially to Edward. I thank the Lord the five years I was in Africa helping my parents enabled me to effectively call those events buried with no ill-will toward the perpetrators.

I continued as manager for a time to ease the transition, with the understanding that it was only temporary. By early 1975 all of the Fudges were gone from the business except Curtis who stayed on as shipping clerk. Longtime employees Donna, Mamie and Virginia Dale also continued working there for several years, conscientiously doing their jobs regardless of who their employers were.

In some ways, it was the end of an era, the end of Bennie Lee's dream. And yet that dream lives on even now in the lives and hearts of all who ever worked in the business with joy and pride; in the untold number of Christians who walked into the CEI bookstore to purchase a Bible or a reference book for Bible study; it lives on in the minds and memories of all who ever studied a *Use Your Bible Workbook* or a *Student's Guide* or one of the many other publications we produced. God allowed me to participate in Bennie Lee's dreams—the Bible school, the Bookstore, the many publications that were aimed at spreading God's message throughout the world. I cherish my memories of those good works.

**Clearing Out** In the big storage space upstairs at the back of the store offices were hundreds of boxes of files and records from years before, much of it personal material that was of no concern to the new owners. I did not want to dispose of the boxes without looking through them in case there was something important that needed to be saved. Benjamin used the panel truck to take load after load to our house. At first he lined the halls

331

with the boxes and when there was no more room there, he stacked them in the foyer and living room. Then began for me the monumental task of looking through them one box at a time, one piece of paper at a time. As I finished with them Benjamin hauled the discards to the city incinerator when he came home from work each evening. It took many weeks to clear it all out.

**Africa Calls** Beth's son, George, working in Florida, was critically injured in a motor cycle accident. When it happened, Beth, with her youngest, Linda (16), were in Africa helping Daddy take care of our ailing Mother. Beth sent an S.O.S. to me because she needed to come to the States to be with George and our parents needed someone there. My children were all grown and independent, all of them settled in their own homes and didn't want to live in the family house, so we decided to sell it. The proceeds would pay my way to Rhodesia to take Beth's place helping Daddy and Mother.

**The Day Off** During that time Paul and Janis, who had been in Florida with her family, came to our house to finalize preparations for going to Rhodesia. By the time I had wound up my affairs at the bookstore I felt stretched almost to my limit and they suggested the three of us go to *Six Flags Over Georgia* for a day of relaxing—the change might do us all good.

When we entered the park, one of the first things we saw was new—*The Great American Scream Machine.* Jokingly I said, "I feel like I could do with a good scream." And they said, "Do it!" A few years before that I had ridden a run-away train and had vowed "never again," but the sign said this lasted only three minutes and that didn't sound long. So we climbed on. Immediately there was a sharp dip and I decided to scream just for the fun of it. To my horror after that I couldn't stop screaming and up and down we went and scream I did—the whole three minutes! When we stopped, a young boy seated in front of me turned and said, "Boy! You sure did scream!" and I admitted, "I sure did!" As I climbed off of that machine my legs were like jelly and Paul and Janis helped me to a bench. I told them to go do whatever they wanted to and come back for me when they were done! That day and that screaming relieved my feelings amazingly and I went home ready to tackle whatever might come my way—and plenty was coming.

**Nancy and Raymond** Raymond had ended six years in the U.S. Navy during which time he and Nancy had corresponded regularly. He was in Missouri working with Henry and hogs when Nancy went to visit Henry and Jo Ann. By the time Nancy was ready to come home she and Raymond had decided to marry. They planned an August wedding and it was already June. Nancy was uneasy—how could they have a wedding in our living room with boxes still there? I told her "It will be fine, we need seating for the guests. We can line up the boxes in rows like pews and drape sheets over them!" I hastened to assure her I was teasing when her horrified, "MOTHER!" let me know she thought I was serious. I promised to have those offending boxes out of there all in good time.

**Another Grandson** Edward and Sara Faye's Jeremy Locke arrived June 25, 1975. When he was a few weeks old I went to sit with him and Melanie one evening while their parents were out and Melanie furnished me with a story I have since told many times. It began on Sunday afternoon when Benjamin "borrowed" two-year-old Melanie for a project for his Child Psychology class. He was to follow her around for fifteen minutes taking notes on everything she did and said. He thought it would be a good time to help her learn to pronounce "f" because she called herself, "Menny Ann Budge," she called me "Bammo Budge" and the fish in our aquarium were "bishes." Benjamin pointed to the fish and said, "Fish," she said, "Bish." He said, "F-F-F" and she repeated it correctly then he said, "F-F-F-fish" and she said, "F-F-F-bish." She did the same with other "f" sounds he tried.

The next evening I baby-sat her and Jeremy. I was tired and lay on the couch while Jeremy slept in his bassinet and Melanie played in the floor.

She picked up a toy and I asked her what it was. She said "Big Bird," and another was "Cookie Monster" and so on, all ones I recognized. Then she picked up one that I didn't recognize. When I asked what it was she said, "Quessamy Queet." I said, "I'm sorry, Melanie, I don't know that one" so she repeated it. After about the fourth time of me apologizing but not knowing what she was saying, she was exasperated and said very emphatically, "*You* know, **F-F-F**-*Quessamee Queet!*" I still didn't know but we went on to other things. When her parents returned they explained that she was saying "Sesame Street." That became one of many favorite grandmother-stories!

**Home Wedding** Nancy and Raymond's wedding preparations were in full swing. She wanted to wear the wedding dress that I had made and worn, that Beth had worn and Foy's wife, Margaret, had worn. It fit Nancy but it had been in the cedar chest for thirty-one years and had turned yellow. I assured her that it could be washed and ironed and if that didn't work we still had time to make a dress. After soaking it in Lux suds for several hours it washed clean and back to its original off-white. I rolled it in a big towel for a little while, then began ironing. The dress was floor length in front with back panels that extended to form the train, but when it was wet it drew up to about thirty inches total length, train and all. Nancy saw it and nearly panicked, but I assured her that during World War II we had washed and ironed the rayon crepe of those days and knew it just had to be ironed until it was dry, beginning while it was more wet than damp. It took five hours to do, but when it was done it looked good and fit Nancy perfectly. The original veil had deteriorated so I made a new one.

She and Raymond were married August 29th and the wedding and reception were in our house with a number of guests seated in chairs—not on boxes! Raymond's father, Roy, performed the ceremony. They loaded their belongings in a U-Haul trailer attached to their car and drove away to Missouri to live near Henry and Jo Ann.

Events had been happening in such rapid succession there was hardly time to feel forlorn over the fact that my two youngest children were now married and scattering far and wide. Benjamin was the only one left and I was very thankful to still have one at home. He was teaching in a county school and planned on moving into an apartment when we emptied the house.

**This, That And All Kinds of Other** Paul and Janis were staying in our house finalizing their preparations for leaving the end of August 1975. A returned foreign missionary knew Paul and Janis would need footlockers for shipping their personal belongings and offered to give them eight or ten footlockers he had stored after his return to the States. The lockers had been stored in a damp basement or crawl space where the metal outsides had rusted and Paul set about sanding and painting them. After he had sanded most of them he developed a bad cough and fever. He finally went to the doctor who said he had pneumonia, probably from breathing the sanding dust. Fortunately the job was about done by then. As fast as the paint dried, Janis and I packed. Then name and address had to be painted on each one and the three of us worked on what seemed like an endless task.

They were faced with a deadline to get their stuff to the coast to be shipped and to be ready for their flight. The night before Paul and Edward were to leave with the trunks and lockers in a U-Haul at 5:00 a.m., and we were still painting addresses—at 2:00 a.m. Janis and I were still painting addresses. We had persuaded Paul to sleep some so he could stay awake driving. Our eyes and hands were getting so tired we felt we could hardly go on but we encouraged each other one letter at a time. I said, "Just think, we *know* by 5 o'clock we'll be *done* because by then Edward and Paul will be gone!"—and they were—then we slept. Very shortly after that Paul and Janis were gone to Africa, their departure made easier knowing I was soon going to the same country.

In November Foy was preaching in a meeting in the county and staying with us. Fred and Ann Melton had gone to England to work and their son, Bonny, was staying with us until the end of the year. Benjamin's birthday, November 20, was at hand and I wanted to make his favorite cake. He had brought the recipe when he returned from his European trip and I had made it once before—it was, as the kids said, "Out of this world!"

Foy was in his room studying his evening sermon and there was constant traffic through the kitchen as I assembled the ingredients for the cake. Thinking I had succeeded, I put the three layers in the oven. When I opened the door to take them out I was shocked to see they had not risen one iota—if anything they were flatter than they had been to start with! I turned them out on a cooling rack and wondered—surely I must have forgotten something. I pinched a tiny piece off to taste—there was no sugar in it! Benjamin came through the kitchen as I was "woe-is-me-ing" and said, "That's O.K., Mother, they'll be like pancakes, just go ahead and make the icing and put them together—we'll eat it." Well, I did, and we tried, but it was no good. The icing was cream cheese, coconut and pecans and delicious, so the rest of the afternoon whoever came through the kitchen and liked icing, ate some off with a spoon until most of it was gone. We threw the cake part away—even the dog wouldn't eat that! I think there was no birthday cake that day. [I recently came across the recipe and sent it to Benjamin, hoping Susan will want to make it someday. It really is good with sugar in it!]

**So Much Stuff!** I cleared out drawers, closets and stored boxes, preparing to sell the house. Each of my children went through the house taking what they wanted, then we had a yard sale. While waiting for the house to sell I set out to spend two weeks with each family beginning as a guest of Benjamin's in his apartment. I thought he had done a wonderful job of arranging and decorating his furnished apartment and I enjoyed being his guest.

My next visit was in Missouri for two weeks with Henry and Jo Ann. Lee was in kindergarten and rode the school bus every day. It was fun to see Eric and Leslie's excitement when we walked to the bus stop to meet him, to see him eagerly get off the bus and run to greet us, breathlessly telling about school. The pond where the livestock drank was frozen over from the extreme cold. One day Henry had to be gone and Jo Ann went to the pond with an axe to break the ice so the animals could drink. I stayed with the children and we anxiously watched her through the window, hoping the ice wouldn't break with her on it. But it was thick and she returned safely to us. Their Collie had five or six furry, playful puppies, and a precious memory is of four-year-old Eric rolling and romping with them.

One evening when Eric had stubbornly misbehaved Henry paddled him. After supper and family devotions, Henry said, "O.K. Boys, it's bedtime!" We three adults had been taking turns going upstairs to tuck them in. It was Henry's turn that night but as Lee got up to go, Eric said, "I want Grandma to go with us."

Henry looked a question at me and I said it was fine with me and went up with them. Lee got himself ready while I was standing over Eric helping him pull his pajamas on. Looking up into my face he said woefully, "My Daddy spanked me." I said, "You know, God gave boys and girls mommies and daddies to help them learn to be good and sometimes they have to spank to help you remember . . ." He was looking into my face so intently I thought, *he is really taking all this in.* When I paused for breath, he said, "Grandma, did you know you have hair in your nose?" Another favorite grandmother story!

When I told Lee and Eric I was going way off to Africa and would not see them for a long time, Eric asked how long. I told him he would be much bigger when I saw him and he said, "When you see me at the airport you'll say, 'Who are you?' and I'll say, 'I'm Eric!'" Sure enough, when I saw them next it was at the airport and he was ten years old. Remembering his words five years before, I said, "Who are you?" and he said, "I'm Eric!"

Raymond and Nancy were living not far from Henry and Jo Ann at the time and I spent two good weeks with them. Nancy was working in a shoe factory so we didn't get a lot of time together but we made the most of what time we had. She gave me a guided tour of the shoe production.

Coming out of their post office one day, I did not notice there was a small step-down and landed hard on my hands and knees. It was 15 degrees cold that day and how it hurt! A few days later my feet were as blue as my knees—I learned that bruises travel down. They were living in a rented mobile home and since I wanted to stay busy while they were at work I asked Nancy's permission to do their ironing and clean their stove which helped her and gave me pleasure.

Next I drove to Jacksonville, Florida to see Robert and Dianne. Bobby was almost five. We played games with their friends and one of them was called *Lie, Cheat and Steal.* I thought it was a terrible name for a game! After a few rounds they said I was not a good partner because I couldn't lie without my face showing it—a compliment as far as I was concerned! During my visit five year old Bobby gave me a grandmother memory. He had misbehaved and was sent to his room. After the prescribed time Dianne called to him from the living room, telling him he could come out. When his door opened we looked up to see him coming down the hall wearing dark glasses, carrying his big guitar and singing the John Denver song, *Take Me Home Country Road.* Favorite grandmother stories were piling up—I never hear that song without thinking of Bobby coming down that hall.

While in Jacksonville I traded my 1972 Chevrolet for a little 1975 Honda Civic that I took to Africa.

I drove back to Athens to finalize my preparations for leaving at the end of February. I spent two weeks with Edward and Sara Faye preparing my mind and my affairs to be gone an indefinite number of years. Sara Faye hosted a farewell tea in my honor, attended by many of my lady friends of the area. The ladies of my long standing Ladies Class at Ephesus gave me a farewell party in one of their homes.

Every visit had been a joyful experience as I crammed my mind full of good memories of my children and grandchildren. As each two-week visit with my children ended I thought of a quote I had read one time about a teacher and his student that fit perfectly my thoughts about my grown children: *"A teacher's greatest triumph comes when his student leaves him behind."* My children had left me behind in many ways that made me feel triumphant. We told each other good-bye not knowing when we would meet again; I was going to help Daddy take care of Mother with no set time table in mind.

The 503 Chandler Drive house was sold. I packed the few things I felt I would need in a small wooden crate and a steamer trunk to ship along with the Honda from New Orleans to Cape Town. Arrangements were made by Thomas Cook and Sons Travel Agency. The day came to leave for New Orleans. Edward drove his car pulling a U-Haul trailer with the crate and trunk and I followed driving the Honda. We spent a night in a motel in New Orleans and I was very thankful to have Edward with me as we finalized the shipping arrangements.

March 5, 1976, a few days after we got back from New Orleans, I flew from Huntsville, Alabama on my way to Salisbury, Rhodesia. I had an overnight lay-over in Atlanta, Georgia and the Sewell Halls, who lived near the airport, met me and took me to their home for the night; then saw me off early next morning.

As my plane flew over the expanse of clouds, 37,000 feet above the earth, I couldn't help thinking about how I had rid myself of almost all my earthly belongings, I had told my children good-bye and I felt nearer to heaven at that moment than ever before in my life. I thought if we crashed I would be with Bennie Lee. I thought about my Daddy and Mother needing me and prayed to God to give me a safe journey to be a help to them and someday return to see my children.

On March 6, 1976 I arrived in Salisbury, Rhodesia (as it was then.) Paul and Janis, Jim and Becky Short met me at the airport. Of course my passport had my birthplace as Bulawayo, Southern Rhodesia, 1923. The Immigration Officer looked at it, then looked up at me and said, "Welcome home!" Thirty-six years had gone by since I boarded that train out of Salisbury on my way to America.

The book of my life had turned the page to another chapter.

# PART IV

## AFRICA AGAIN

# 1976–1980

Thirty-five years earlier I had boarded the train out of Salisbury on my way to Cape Town and thence by ship to America to attend college—a young girl, naïve and untested. Now it was March 6, 1976. My modern-day plane taxied to a stop at the Salisbury airport bringing home a widow and mother of six adult children. I joyfully spotted Paul and Janis, Jim and Becky among the sea of faces on the open balcony of the one-story building from where people saw planes arrive and leave. They watched me descend the plane steps and waited for me to go through customs and immigration.

The Immigration Officer's warm "Welcome home!" had surprised me, then I walked quickly down the short hall to be enveloped in even warmer hugs. Janis and Becky hadn't changed since I told them goodbye in the States some months before but Paul and Jim looked very Rhodesian, dressed in khaki safari suits and sporting newly grown beards.

Salisbury was a large beautiful modern city. Jacaranda and flamboyant trees in full bloom lined the streets and surrounded businesses and homes, shedding lavender and flaming red blossoms like a carpet. Flowers bloomed in every possible place. On the way to Jim and Becky's flat we drove by Girl's High School, my alma mater of boarding school days. After so many years it looked only vaguely familiar—buildings looked smaller and trees looked huge.

The young folks were anxious to hear about "back home" and said it only took a few months away from it all to be ignorant of most of what was going on back there. Their cook had prepared a delicious roast-chicken meal that we ate as we talked. Then Paul, Janis and I drove to Gwelo, a smaller city about 200 miles south of Salisbury. Their second-story flat was in a complex on a terraced hillside covered with flower beds and blooming shrubs. The beauty of the surroundings made up for the almost stark simplicity of the interior but the plastered white walls and sparse furniture provided a cool haven from the heat. Paul and Janis worked with the small church in Gwelo and on Sunday morning after church services we drove approximately 125 miles south to Bulawayo, a larger city than Gwelo and another beautiful city of flowers.

Mother and Daddy were anxiously watching for us in their home at No. 8, Bamboo Road, Newton West, where I would live with them for the next five years. In what seemed like only a few hours I was over 10,000 miles from what had been my home in Alabama, ready to settle into a new and very different life.

Beth had been living with our parents but had gone to the States to be with her son George after his accident. Her daughter, Linda, stayed on to finish high school and became like a daughter to me. She rode her bicycle six miles every day to *Evelyn High School* in town. I remembered my *Girl's High School* hockey team playing in the annual tournament against *Evelyn's* team in the 1930s.

**My New Home** I was born in Bulawayo but had never lived there. In 1960 Daddy and Mother moved to Bulawayo from Namwianga Mission in Northern Rhodesia (Zambia) where Daddy was in charge of buildings. When he blacked out, fell off a roof, and injured his back, he and Mother decided it was time for him to stop climbing on buildings. It was also a good time for Mother to stop running a dormitory for twelve white boys ages six through twelve in their home while she taught school. The Shewmakers housed twelve girls but a few years later they also resigned and moved to Bulawayo to live across back yards from Daddy and Mother. My younger brother Bill went through that mission school and had gone on to high school in Lusaka, the capitol of Northern Rhodesia, before going to college in the U.S. in 1960.

By now my parents had been living in Bulawayo sixteen years. Daddy was a spry 81 year-old and Mother was 79 but not so spry. Their spacious house was in the outer edge of the city, two blocks from "the Bush," beyond the last row of houses there were no buildings or lights of any kind. Daddy's office, library and print shop were in a separate building close behind the main dwelling. Attached to the office was the laundry room which contained an automatic washer and dryer—the dryer used only during prolonged bad weather.

Vegetables grew abundantly in the small garden tended by Wilson, their faithful house servant for sixteen years. Aaron, the yard worker, took care of the large front lawn and croquet court and flower beds. Wilson and Aaron lived in a small house behind the vegetable garden. At the back of the half acre lot was a quarter-acre orchard where grew oranges, lemons, guavas, grapefruit, pawpaws and a big mulberry tree. The house had city water but grounds and gardens were watered from a borehole in the back yard.

My bedroom had a large window overlooking the front yard from where I enjoyed a continual show in a nearby acacia tree, home to dozens of weaver birds. They were about the size of American goldfinches and their nests hung from branches like round balls with long tunnel entrances near the bottom. The male built the nest while the female watched—if she didn't like it she tore it apart and he had to begin again. I noticed that they took turns sitting on the eggs, feeding their babies and teaching them to fly.

**Snake Fright** A few days after arriving I went out to gather a bouquet of roses for Mother. Concentrating on cutting, I stepped backward without looking and felt something hit the top of my foot at the same instant that I heard a puffing sound. I froze, thinking *"Puff Adder!"* and almost died of snake-fright on the spot. Forcing myself to look down I saw a harmless big chameleon high-stepping away as fast as it could; apparently when I stepped on its tail it had flopped over onto my foot. In the house Mother looked hard at me and said, "You look pale, are you all right?" When Daddy heard the story he said the puffing sound of a chameleon was just like that of the puff adder. That made me feel less foolish, but I resolved to look before stepping in the future.

**Cape Town Trip** Two weeks later word came that my Honda was in Cape Town. Paul, Janis and I took the train to go fetch it. The European style train was not crowded and for two days and nights we had a compartment to ourselves. Unfortunately the train compartments were not heated. During the day sunshine warmed us nicely but by sundown it was bitterly cold. We spent two miserable nights in spite of the heavy wool blankets that were furnished. We were so cold that Paul and Janis crowded into one narrow bunk and gave me their other blanket. Even with socks on, my feet were like blocks of ice all night. Before daybreak we were wakened by a loud knock on the door and a man's voice called loudly, "Passports please!" We were crossing the border into Botswana. We passed our passports through the barely opened door. At daybreak there was another knock and a more welcome voice announced, "Morning Tea!"

After tea we dressed in several layers of clothes and paced the corridor trying to get warm while we waited for the Dining Car to open. We were eagerly looking forward to hot coffee and looked at each other in shock when we were served something in tiny cups very different from any coffee we had known—so strong it was almost thick enough to hold up the spoon. We asked the surprised waiter for pots of hot water to dilute it and used all the cream on the table. With our eggs we expected crisp bacon but it was thick and floppy, but it tasted good and we were thankful for delicious toast and marmalade.

Saturday night in a Cape Town hotel we reveled in hot baths and slept warmly in beds that didn't sway and jerk. At church Sunday morning we were surprised to meet some Americans who were with Shell Oil Company and we were even more surprised to find we had mutual acquaintances in the States.

Thomas Cook and Son Travel Agency and The Rhodesian Automobile Association had cleared my motor car from the ship and with Paul's help it was an easy matter to get through the rest of the red tape. Our luggage fit nicely in the small Honda hatchback and with the four spare tires in the back seat we set out on the long drive back to Bulawayo. We chose the direct route through the mountains and across the middle country instead of the seacoast "Garden Route" that might have been more beautiful but was farther to drive.

Once out of the verdant valley around Cape Town we came into the mountains—rocky, barren, beautiful and awe-inspiring—part of the Drakensberg Range—South Africa's own version of the Rocky Mountains. Then we passed through flat, barren country that looked like southern New Mexico and Arizona, then crossed the wide Orange River and saw occasional farm houses.

The first night we stopped in a small town where the hotel desk clerk told us to take everything out of our motor car or it would all be gone next morning—locks or no locks. Paul carried the suitcases while Janis and I hoisted a spare tire in each hand, laughing at each other as we took the small elevator to our second floor room.

Approaching Johannesburg the next day was a lot like coming into any large U.S. city—highways, traffic, expressways, industries, sky-scrapers and people, though naturally here the majority of the people were black. We spent a night with the Votaws, longtime missionaries in South Africa who had visited us in Athens, Alabama. The next day was spent shopping for things friends and relatives in Rhodesia had asked us to bring back.

It was almost unbelievable what we managed to cram into that little Honda. Tins (cans) of food filled the inside of the four stacked tires and the center well; every nook and cranny imaginable (and some you would never imagine) were filled—around the luggage, in the floor, on the seat around the tires and between the seats. Paul had mailed his books from the States to the Votaws to save exorbitant Customs in Rhodesia. These he unwrapped and slid under the seats and floor mats. There was barely room for one of us on the back seat; every stop or so we rotated seats and driver.

About nightfall we reached Lalla Panzi Hotel, where in 1930 my family had spent a night on the way from Durbin to Huyuyu Mission. Thatched cottages, whitewashed inside and out, bougainvillea blooming on trellises around the doors, white wicker furniture, metal beds and mosquito nets, were just as I remembered. To our relief the desk clerk told us a watchman patrolled the fenced grounds all night so we could safely leave things in the locked motor car.

Welcome tea was served in our room as we relaxed. After dinner and a stroll on the grounds we were sitting in our room talking when we heard a strange sound coming from the corner behind my armchair. Paul investigated and found the biggest frog we had ever seen. He urged it into a wastebasket and released it in the yard. When I pulled my bed-covers back a huge spider crawled across my pillow. I stripped the bed, shook everything thoroughly, and generously used the can of insect spray—supplied in each room. I remade my bed, crawled in and slept like a log—I was back in Africa!

The scrumptious breakfast in the Dining Room—coffee served in larger cups—was a good send-off on our way. Heading north we reached the Limpopo River which was the border between South Africa and Rhodesia. There we had to go through immigration and customs on each side of the river/border.

The South Africa Customs official asked for a list of what we were taking out of the country, then went outside with us to verify it. He said he usually asked people to put everything onto the grass where he could check it with the list, but when he looked inside and saw how we were packed he decided to take our word for it! The official on the Rhodesian side also took our word for it. Evidently we didn't look like smugglers!

As we neared Bulawayo we saw people along the sides of the road selling curios and produce. One of them had good looking watermelons for 25 cents each. Janis said excitedly, "Paul, we haven't had a watermelon since we got to Africa. Let's get one." "Where do you think we'd put it?" he asked, and I volunteered to hold it in my lap. Paul said, "O.K. And when we get to town I'll stop on a street corner and call out, 'Come buy this cheap watermelon so I can find my mother!'" At their house Daddy and Mother enjoyed helping us eat the watermelon.

**Getting Settled** Petrol (gasoline) was rationed in Rhodesia. My Honda got 50 miles to the U.S. gallon and my allotment was Four Units

348

per month (approximately 5 U.S. gallons, though we bought petrol by the *litre*). Because of Daddy's ministerial work and larger vehicle he was allowed Eight Units. Sharing was allowed and with careful planning we were able to make all necessary trips. Occasionally friends saw at the end of the month that they had ration coupons extra and gave them to us. That allowed me to drive to Gwelo once in a while to visit Paul and Janis.

The biggest surprise to me was coming back to a thriving, independent, manufacturing and industrial country that had been barely out of the pioneer stage when I left more than thirty-five years before. Now cotton materials were manufactured, clothing made, goods canned and packaged. Even Dunlop tires and machinery of many kinds were manufactured—just about every commodity necessary except petrol and that was imported from South Africa. Necessary raw materials that Rhodesia didn't have could be imported from Japan, Switzerland and South Africa, three countries that paid no heed to the sanctions put on Rhodesia years before. Tea, coffee, cheeses, copper and other things produced in Rhodesia were exported to those open countries.

**To Get A Job Or Not** I had no income and intended to get a part-time job but Daddy asked me not to. He said he would give me $100 a month for my personal expenses so that I could help them with many things he had been doing, or friends were doing for them, or were left undone, and things Mother wanted done that she would not ask anyone else to do. He said besides the *doing* there was the *being* company for Mother while he worked in his office studying, writing, talking to visitors who came constantly for advice or encouragement, all of which he had neglected in order to take care of Mother after Beth left.

**Getting Mother ready for the day, 1978.**

Daddy was gradually relinquishing the publishing of *Rays of Light*, the little monthly magazine he had been editing and printing for many years. However, he still translated and printed tracts. He preached part time, taught classes and served as an elder in the Hillside congregation where we attended. He was highly regarded by all (black and white) who knew him personally and by reputation. Hardly a day passed without someone coming to ask him Bible questions or to seek advice. And he was still able to repair almost anything that needed it (except the roof) and kept fruit trees and roses pruned.

My stay-at-home job kept me busier than I had imagined possible. Mother could do no physical work; she spent her days in her chair crocheting granny squares between naps. I sewed them together for her and after just six weeks she had made five afghans. I had put up eighteen pints of guava jam, made a dress for Mother and one for Linda, besides cooking, serving tea, helping pick and process fruit, and as time permitted, tidied cupboards with Mother's oversight.

Mother and I had wonderful talks even with her loss of short term memory and reasoning power. But if there was not someone in the room with her she felt deserted and afraid. When Daddy asked her what she was afraid of, she said of us leaving her behind if terrorists came. No amount of reassuring helped and Daddy thought that was perhaps because she could not think it through or get around by herself. In the house she could stand and push a straight chair ahead of her like a walker and every afternoon Daddy and I supported her as we took a short walk on the driveway.

Two or three men from church took turns coming on Saturday afternoons to try to beat Daddy at chess—which seldom happened. Their afternoon often ended with a croquet match. Other evenings Daddy and I played croquet and Mother sat on the sideline watching and coaching. It was interesting to me that we could be so busy yet life seemed relaxed with time to play.

**Out Of The Past** Ella and Rhoda were frequent visitors for afternoon tea. They had lived with us at Sinde Mission in Northern Rhodesia when they were young girls. They were with us long enough then to weld a lifelong relationship that was kept up through the years. They had good husbands, had raised several children, among them school teachers and businessmen, and each had several grandchildren. Also among my acquaintances were some renewed from our childhoods: Alan Hadfield, grandson of the Hadfields so familiar from the 1920s and 1930s; his wife Verna, granddaughter of the Bowens of those days; Gladys Claasen, her daughter Rona (my age), and son Freddie (Beth's age).

One day after I had been there a few weeks, Daddy answered the telephone and I heard him greet someone warmly. He chatted for a while then called, "Sybil, here's someone who wants to talk to you." It was Kit Wiggill, who featured prominently in the last few years of my teens. His voice had not changed and memories flooded my mind. He said my voice sounded the same except for the American accent! He told me briefly of his life after we stopped writing to each other in 1942. When the North African Campaign was over he was sent to England where he met and married a young widow with two little girls. After the war ended they came to Rhodesia and had a daughter. He and his family lived on a farm not far from Gwelo and their three girls were grown.

**My New Life** Daddy decided his driving was getting dangerous and handed his motor car keys to me. The steering wheel on the right side made it easier for me to stay on the left of the road but I had to learn different road signs: *Give Way* meant Yield, *Filter* was Merge and Traffic Lights were *Robots*—but *STOP* did mean STOP! Four-way stops were common and I had my first experience with a *Round About* at an intersection. When Daddy had bought his car in the U.S. in 1968 he had the steering wheel changed to the right side but the odometer was not changed to metric. The posted speed limit in town was 60 but the fine print under that said *kph* and I learned that roughly translated was 35 mph. Driving out of town for the first time I saw the posted speed limit of 100 and said, "Wow!" I didn't see the fine print on the sign and had to remember that it was kilometers per hour not miles.

I learned to always sift flour, sugar and meal (bought in 4-kilogram bags) to remove sticks, leaves, gravel or insect legs (hopefully of grasshoppers.) The first time I opened the giblet package inside a dressed hen, to my surprise I found two whole feet (nice and clean of course!) We always gave some of the hen to Wilson and Aaron and since Wilson said he liked the feet, I was happy to put them with his and Aaron's third of the hen. They also appreciated the fat cut off of beef—roasts or steaks. To my surprise chicken was much more expensive than steak.

**Bicycles** Bicycles were everywhere. Mail was delivered on bicycles morning and afternoon. Five mornings a week African men loaded their three-wheeled cycles with boxes or baskets on the front and from downtown fanned out through the suburbs. A bicycle bell near the back door could signal the milkman with his insulated box containing milk in glass bottles or one-litre plastic bags packed in ice. (Bags took up less room in the refrigerator; we clipped a corner off and stood the bag upright in a special wire rack.) Or the bell could be the vegetable man, or egg man. Twice a week it was the bread man with loaves of white and brown bread fresh from the bakery—unwrapped, unsliced. If he accidentally spilled a load on the ground he picked up the loaves, blew them off, repacked and went on his way! Beth was an eyewitness to this unhappy event one day! Six days a week ice cream carts roamed the residential streets, ringing little bells, selling chocolate and vanilla ice cream in small cups, chocolate covered ice cream popcicles and fruit flavored popcicles.

Quite often an African woman came to the door and called out, "Goh! Goh!" (the equivalent of "Knock! Knock!") She was selling crocheted doilies, tablecloths, shawls and beaded jug covers and did excellent work. If we wanted some of her wares but were short of cash she gladly traded for used clothing—what she couldn't use herself she could sell.

**Routine** Our usual day began with early morning tea at 5:30. Breakfast at 6:00 a.m. was bacon or sausage, eggs, toast and marmalade or jam, and coffee. Afterwards we sat at the table for morning Bible reading and prayer. Our main meal, called lunch, was at 1:00 p.m. after which my parents took 15 to 20 minute naps. Supper was cereal at 6:00 then dishes were cleared away for evening devotions and hymn singing. Daddy sang bass or tenor, Mother sang alto, Linda and I soprano. Then we played games for about an hour. Mother enjoyed playing Rack-O and Rummikube but her favorite was Dominoes. She studied the layout and liked to tell us what our score would be if we had such and such a domino. Daddy and Mother went to bed at 9:00 o'clock. Linda and I played or read or knitted for a while longer—she did homework as soon as she came home from school.

Wilson kept the kitchen clean and did the floors throughout the house, hung out clothes, folded them and ironed what needed it. He kept the vegetable garden yielding all year round by rotating crops according to the growing season best suited to them. Occasionally he got caught up with his work and helped Aaron who never got caught up. Aaron had learned to cycle the flower-growing according to the seasons to keep the yard filled with blooms. Lining both sides of the long driveway, depending on the season, were lavender-blue agapanthus, multicolored dahlias or fragrant banks of sweet peas, making the entrance a joy to behold. At first it was hard for me to adjust mentally to having servants but I soon realized that if I did all of the work they were doing I could not do all of the things I was doing. It didn't take long to get my guilt feeling under control!

**One Never Knows** A very English lady we knew told this story about an African she employed to do washing and ironing. He did such a good job on her husband's white starched collars and cuffs that her friends noticed and remarked about it. She decided to watch unseen to discover his secret. She saw him fill a large tumbler with water, put it to his mouth and she thought he must be thirsty. When his mouth was full he spewed a fine spray over the shirt and ironed between spews. Ignorance can be bliss!

**A Week During School Holidays** I had barely been there a month when it was time for the first school holidays of the year. For four weeks we enjoyed 15 minutes extra sleep before early morning tea. During that time Wilson went home for a three weeks holiday to the Tribal Trust Lands and I realized I was already spoiled to having him around, though having Linda home from school most of those weeks helped a lot.

Monday, the first day of holidays, about 9:00 a.m., our dear friend, Mabel Bailey, with her mother and sister who were visiting from Canada, came for a visit. After tea Mabel and her sister went with Daddy and me to the orchard to pick guavas while her mother visited Mother. We picked five big dishpans full and gave them one to take home. By then it was nearly 1:00 p.m. and time to warm leftovers from Sunday. We had roast beef, carrots, onions, potato salad, green beans and pureed guavas with boiled custard. Then Daddy and Mother took naps and I wrote letters. Later Daddy went to his office, Mother crocheted and I kept writing as we talked. Afternoon tea was at 4:00; and afterwards Daddy sat reading to Mother while I worked on Linda's dress that she wanted for the Young Folks gathering in Umtali that weekend.

After breakfast on <u>Tuesday</u> Mother, Daddy and I sat at the kitchen table talking, as we peeled and cut up guavas to stew for puree. For lunch we had kraut and wieners, mashed potatoes, green beans and guavas. While Daddy and Mother napped I finished Linda's dress and kept an eye on the cooking guavas. Some men came after supper for a meeting with Daddy. Mother crocheted, Linda and I hemmed her dress and sewed on buttons.

<u>Wednesday</u> Linda and her friend, Valda rode their bicycles to town to shop and I finished getting Linda's things ready to pack. In the afternoon a couple came to visit. I served tea and hand-sewed as we visited. After supper we went to church, Linda carrying her packed bag to go home with a friend—to leave early next morning.

<u>Thursday</u> morning Ladies Bible Class was to meet in our Living Room; I left breakfast dishes in the sink (no Linda!) and had just finished brushing the rugs and arranging chairs for class when a motor car drove up. A family from Zambia (who had been farm-neighbors to the mission when Mother and Daddy lived there) were on their way home after getting their children from boarding school. They were in a hurry, refused tea and left just in time for me to go for two ladies who needed a ride to class.

There were eleven ladies that time, ages ranging thirty to sixty. Volunteers took turns leading the weekly class a month at a time. Sometimes we studied Bible texts and other times topical study books. After class we had tea and ladies went home, except the two I had picked up; Daddy and Mother went with me to deliver them. While we were out we went to the bank, grocery store, chemist, and back by *Eskimo Hut* (like Dairy Queen) to buy ice cream for home and a cone each. Daddy joked that his motor car automatically turned in at Eskimo Hut—they had stopped there so much, and I saw no reason to object to that! At home we had a quick lunch. While parents napped I went to Daddy's office to use his typewriter for my newsletter to family and friends. Then I put stewed guavas, that had been in the fridge since the day before, through the crank-sieve to make puree.

355

Friday—More guavas through the sieve, this time to make jam and guava butter (like apple butter.) While that was cooking I baked a chiffon cake. We didn't know who—but we expected company for afternoon tea. After parents' naps, sure enough, friends came. We had tea and chiffon cake, ladies crocheted and knitted, men played croquet.

Saturday Mother wanted to play Scrabble. Daddy played with us and I cooked the midday meal while we played. Naps were barely over when the phone rang. Fred Bowen from New Zealand with his brother were visiting kinfolks in Bulawayo. He and his wife, Theodora Sherriff, as children had known Daddy and Mother in the 1920s. Wanting to pay their respects, Fred and his brother came for afternoon tea and the last of the chiffon cake. After they left, Daddy said he would read in the living room while Mother crocheted and I went to the office to cut the stencil and mimeograph my letter. Soon it was 6:10 and the news was off—time to put cereal on the table. After supper I put a roast out of the freezer to thaw for Sunday and made Jello and boiled custard. (I made a quart of custard every week—Daddy liked it on his Jello or guavas; Mother preferred ice cream on hers; I took mine plain.)

Sunday morning, with Linda and Wilson both away, Daddy washed breakfast dishes, I cooked dinner while Mother got ready. We left for church at 9:00. There we met two visiting couples from Zambia. Don Simmons, his wife Bertie, and their two little boys were in Bulawayo waiting for their third child to arrive any time. Don said he was at Camp Wyldewood in 1956 or '57 in the same cabin with a Fudge boy (Edward was there then). Sam Ezell and wife, who looked very frail, had been in Zambia about eight months and she was to have tests of some kind. Zambia had regressed since its independence and many white people went to Rhodesia or South Africa for doctors and hospitals and to have babies. We invited both couples to dinner and they stayed until about 3 p.m. While Daddy and Mother napped I cleaned up the kitchen. By then it was tea time, then time to leave for evening service.

The second Monday of the holidays Mother said she would dress suitably for company—she felt in her bones we would have some! I was cleaning the kitchen when she came pushing her straight chair, bringing a dress she wanted to wear but wanted the hem let out first. I was drying my hands to do her bidding when a motor car drove up. It was Herbie and Rene Wilson, dear friends of many years. At the same time J.C. Shewmakers came across our adjoining back yards and through the kitchen door.

Mother put on a different dress and I served tea. While they talked I hung out two loads of wash Daddy had put through the machine earlier. Visitors left and I hemmed Mother's dress. I had just gone to the kitchen to get the guavas out of the fridge when another motor car came. It was Genie (Beth's daughter) and Ed from Gwelo with their two girls. They had been visiting his parents in Bulawayo, were in a hurry and wouldn't stay for lunch, so we had tea again. After they left we had lunch of broiled fish with white sauce, slaw, green beans, toasted leftover scones and guavas. During parents' naps I finished addressing the newsletters and took them to the mailbox at the end of our long driveway, did the dishes and tea things from the morning and worked on more guavas.

That was a fairly typical week during school holidays, the rest of the time things were a little calmer though it was not unusual to have callers nearly every day. Each Tuesday evening during the school terms we had dinner and Bible Study with George and Gwen Massey, dear friends of many years, alternating houses with them until it became too difficult for Mother to go out and they came to our house every week.

Before I left the States a friend said, "I hope you don't get over there and bury your talents!" I liked to think, if anything, talents were being developed. Certainly I was learning patience on a different level. When possible I did what Mother asked me to do along with whatever necessary job I might already be doing. If I said "As soon as I finish this," it sounded to her as though I didn't want to do what she was asking of me and it hurt her feelings. No wonder Daddy had asked me not to take an outside job.

**To Do and Not to Do** Our clothes line was near the kitchen but if Wilson and Aaron happened to be gone we did not leave clothes on the line, even for a quick run to our local post office branch a few blocks away: the clothes could disappear. Stealing was a way of life and most Africans did not trust their fellow-Africans, though there were some very trustworthy ones. They often wore jerseys no matter how warm the day. A friend gave her servant one of her husband's brightly striped jerseys and when the servant came to work in the yard wearing it on a very hot day she asked if he was sick. "No, madam," he replied, "I want to be a shining light to the neighbors!" Another worker said, "I want people to know that I have one!" Some wore jerseys all the year round and explained that there was no other safe place to keep them from being stolen. Some wore several layers of clothes to work rather than leave their extras in their houses for the same reason. No one left an unlocked bicycle anywhere—even for a few minutes. Stealing, in their culture, was not wrong—getting caught was!

In towns most Europeans lived in houses built either of solid brick or of stucco over concrete blocks. Their roofs were corrugated metal or Spanish tile and they had steel-framed windows and doors. Windows and many doors had bars and yards were fenced, sometimes with a dense hedge covering the fence. There were no back alleys or back gates; the only way in or out was through the front gate, making it harder for an intruder to escape. Such measures only slightly deterred the efforts of determined thieves, however. Thinking the household was asleep or gone, a thief fished through the bars of an open window with a hook on the end of a long bamboo fishing pole, pulling out anything close enough to reach: clothing, bedspread, blankets, sheets or whatever could be pulled through the bars. One man woke up to realize someone was fishing through his bedroom window bars, he grabbed the pole and pulled the thief to the window, where he held his arm until the police came. Thieves overcame that danger by embedding a razor blade in the end of the pole.

In hot weather we left windows open during the day while Aaron worked in the yard but closed them at night. Many people kept watch dogs in their fenced grounds and some people had geese or peacocks in a backyard pen—good alarm systems. Motor cars left unattended on the side of the street or road for any reason (even if locked) were stripped of tires, battery and other parts.

The Health Department sprayed the city regularly for mosquitoes so we didn't need mosquito nets or screens on doors and windows. Doors stood open during the day for air to circulate and I hoped that a friendly snake wouldn't come in. I hadn't been there too long when our washing machine ran hot and was taken to the shop for repair. When the repair man brought it back he said he found a dead cobra inside the casing! We kept a sharp lookout for its mate but never saw another one.

**Bible Correspondence Courses** Daddy asked me to relieve him of the two Bible Correspondence Courses, one more advanced than the other. About a thousand pupils were enrolled, including several nationalities but mostly Africans from all over the southern part of Africa: Rhodesia, Botswana, Malawi, Zambia, South Africa and more. Weekly mail totaled from 25 to 60 to be "marked" (graded) and returned along with a new lesson. Many of the pupils asked questions. Copied here are a few examples:

1. *If Eternal God made everything perfectly, why do our bodies grow old and die?*
2. *God told Noah exactly when the flood would happen. Why does he not tell us exactly when judgment will happen?*
3. *How may I become a priest in the Church of Christ?*
4. *Since all peoples on earth came from Noah why is there difference of skin?*
5. *What kind of sin was Adam and Eve making? Why is it they began to bear children after the sin, but not before?*
6. *I would like to know if God our Lord is male or female?*
7. *Which is the best way of baptizing a person:*
   *(1) sprinkling the face with water,*
   *(2) taking a bucket of water and pouring over the person,*
   *(3) taking a person under the water and making him to rise again?*
   *Please explain.*

Some lessons were returned with short letter, here are some excerpts:

*"May you kindly send me the forms which will be having*
*some questions. So would you be very politely sending me*
*these papers. I hope you shall be very merry to enroll a new*
*student and I shall be very merry too to receive your reply.*
*Yours faithfully, Stanley Stanslous Chivasa."*

*"How is life down there? Here it is flowing like milk in*
*a river."*

*"Since I began these lessons I have been converted to*
*the last atom. May God bless you and fill your place with*
*tranquility."*

To anyone who asked for a Bible we mailed one along with their first lesson. During my first two years I mailed 233 requested Bibles. Interested friends in the Athens, Alabama area gave money to Donna Barksdale and she ordered King James Bibles from the American Bible Society for me to send out. Daddy ordered Bibles in the Zulu language from the British Bible Society for those who specified that language.

**Terrorists** Not long after I arrived, Daddy talked to me about a decision he and Mother had made several years before when the terrorists first became a very real threat. On the missions Daddy had kept a gun for protection against wild animals and to kill for food, but when they moved into town in 1960 he disposed of his guns. People asked him why he didn't keep one in case of terrorist attack. He said he would not kill a human being. He told me that while Mother was still able to understand, they had agreed that if terrorists came into the house and threatened them he would ask them to let him pray for them before they shot. If they allowed it then the terrorists might leave without doing anything. "But if they shoot us we will be with the Lord." He asked for my thoughts and I told him I agreed wholeheartedly with his decision. Our daily prayers were that God would give us strength to carry out the resolve if that time should come.

At the time most terrorist attacks were along the country's borders, on isolated European farms and among African villages. Overseas news reports claimed that the terrorists were actually "freedom fighters liberating the black people from white rule," but everyone inside the country knew they were killing hundreds of black people who refused to harbor them or to hand over cattle, radios, blankets and food when they raided a village and committed unspeakable atrocities on the villagers. It was no secret that terrorists were coming into the country from camps in Zambia and Mozambique, equipped with weapons from China and Russia. They abducted children from the villages, took them to the camps where they were brainwashed, trained and equipped to fight against their own people.

The terrorist-harassed Africans in the Rhodesian Tribal Trust Lands had asked the government for help. Consolidated villages were organized for their protection and a related benefit was better schools and medical clinics for the villagers. However, as the terrorists gained ground throughout the country they destroyed schools and clinics and abducted many more children.

**Beth's Return** In the U.S. toward the end of April Beth's son George was moved to a rehab center and she returned to Rhodesia to stay until Linda finished high school in November. Beth and I shared a bedroom and thoroughly enjoyed being together. Since college we had seen each other only briefly five or six times. We shared many jobs around the home but Beth liked teaching in the schools and I enjoyed what I was already doing.

The city elementary schools invited Bible teachers from the different churches in town to teach once a week Bible classes in each grade level. Beth taught several classes a week. They were divided by denominations and the children were allowed to choose which one they wanted to attend. There were black, colored and European elementary schools and black, colored and European churches. Volunteer Bible teachers from each church worked out their schedules with each other. "Colored" meant those of mixed races and Asian, East Indian and any other brown-skinned people. Following Beth's return I was able to go to Gwelo for a weekend with Paul and Janis.

**Ladies Bible Class** Ladies volunteered their homes for our Thursday morning Bible Classes. After Bible study the hostess served tea and we visited while we crocheted or knitted jerseys and afghans for needy families. Tom Brown, an elder at the Paddonhurst congregation and an accountant in a men's clothing factory, asked us if we could make use of 12"x16" sample swatches of men's suiting, polyester and wool blend of different weights and colors. We said yes and he gave us three huge boxes full. Three of us with sewing machines at home sorted them by weights and sewed them together for quilt tops. We lined them with inexpensive heavy unbleached sheeting and took them to the group. There, instead of "quilting" we "tied" the backs to the fronts with colored yarn. Sixteen finished covers were given to needy families we learned about who welcomed the heavy thickness for the winter's cold nights.

The constant knitting and crocheting by most women was from necessity, not just to keep their hands busy. Early mornings and evenings, even in summer, were cool and jerseys were worn year round. Different qualities of yarns were available from expensive fine wools, cottons and acrylics to very inexpensive acrylic, wool or silk yarns. For many people it was cheaper to make jerseys than to buy them ready made. Most housewives did not work away from home and saved money by knitting sweaters for their household. When going anywhere a knitting-bag was as much a part of a woman's wardrobe as her handbag. When visiting each other all the women I knew took their knitting or crocheting to work on as they talked. I saw African women knitting as they slowly walked to or from bus stops or waited for a bus, or went to the store. I revived my own crocheting and knitting abilities and during my time there crocheted several afghans to give away. I learned from Beth how to do knitted fair-isle and other designs and knitted gifts for each of my children and grandchildren.

**"A Slow Boat To China"** In this case to Rhodesia. My wooden crate and steamer trunk finally arrived by train from Durbin—months after they were shipped from New Orleans. It was exciting to have some of my own things, among them my commentaries and a small metal typing table and an upright Royal typewriter that I could use in my own room.

**Winter** June, July and August were winter months. Houses had many windows for cross ventilation that were open during the day but closed at night—summer and winter. Most of the windows had a narrow horizontal section at the top that could be closed and locked on the inside and could be safely opened at night during hot weather. But, being over 4,000 feet above sea level, once the sun went down even in summer it was cool.

At the interior top of an outside wall in each room was an "airbrick." It was a screened concrete block turned on its side to let hot air out and cool air in. The block was not covered or closed any time even when the night temperature was 39-45 degrees Fahrenheit—at least other people didn't. But when it became that cold I taped plastic over the one in the bathroom and promised Daddy I would take it off when the weather warmed! We had frost several nights and a few mornings there was a thin crust of ice on the birdbath. The house didn't have central heat; we relied on the back-to-back fireplace in the dividing wall between living room and dining room to warm both rooms. There was a small space heater in the bathroom. Cold bedrooms were healthy! When I wrote home about having cold feet after the usual hot water bottle lost its heat at night, my children sent an electric blanket that I could keep on low all night. During the days when the sun wasn't shining I wore a jersey as a camisole or blouse and kept a cardigan over my shoulders, all the while trying to think it wasn't really cold!

Both Europeans and Africans wore interesting assortments of clothing during the winter. Many Europeans had immigrated to Rhodesia from colder climes, bringing their winter wardrobes with them and wore them in winter regardless of temperature. I attended a winter wedding one afternoon when the temperature was about 85 degrees F. One lady was wearing a fur coat, hose and boots. At the same event I saw among the guests a lady in a bare-backed sundress, bare-legged and wearing sandals.

By the end of August winter was gone and I looked forward to hot weather with mixed feelings. It would be good to have warm feet all day and I was resolved not to complain about the heat! Eight months out of twelve people were so concerned with staying cool in hot weather, they tried to ignore the other four months of cold nights and early mornings which was easier to do because during that time the days were almost always sunny and warm.

**Khami Ruins** One Monday morning, on a school holiday, teenagers from the four white congregations in town, who had bikes, left town in early morning and cycled thirteen miles to Khami Ruins Picnic Area. Five of us "young older ladies" went in motor cars, taking loaded lunch baskets and the teens who didn't have cycles. Soon we were all climbing around on rocky hills and exploring ancient ruins. Beth and I noticed that our minds climbed the rocks faster and more easily than our legs did! Findings of early excavators were in the small museum. There were artifacts from three levels: the Chinese Ming period, the 15th century Portuguese era and some even more ancient undated items.

After lunch the women knitted while the young folks played volleyball and cricket. Following afternoon tea and tinned biscuits (cookies), the cyclists left for home in time to get there before sundown and those of us in motor cars followed slowly to be sure all arrived safely.

**Eating Out** Two big department stores had "Tea Rooms" practically unchanged since the 1930s. Once in a while Beth and I enjoyed having tea there between errands. The two good restaurants in town were very expensive but before Beth left for the States in December that year our close friends, Norman and Joyce Flynn, took us to eat in one of them.

Less "elegant" were several small cafes and a fast-food place similar to McDonald's called *Wimpy's*. Occasionally on trips to town with Daddy and Mother, one or the other of them suggested we take home "fish-and-chips" for lunch from the *Fish and Chips Café*. A serving was one or two large whole fried fish and thick wedges of fried potatoes (giant French fries.) Each serving was wrapped in layers of newspaper to soak up the grease and then wrapped in butcher paper for greaseless carrying.

**School holidays** In September school was out for four weeks before the last term of the year. With no Scripture classes Beth relieved me at home and I spent a weekend in Gwelo with Paul and Janis. That Saturday we attended a small-town wedding in QueQue about thirty miles from Gwelo. In contrast the next Saturday in Bulawayo, Beth and I attended a wedding in the Anglican Cathedral—our first time in that impressive building.

**Victoria Falls Trip** Late in September Daddy and Mother were feeling well and said they thought their children should have some get-better-acquainted time before Beth and Linda went back to the States, since we had been together very little during our adult years. They assured us they would manage at home quite well for the few days. It would be a break for Foy, Jim and Paul, who were on 24-hour-a-day, seven-days-a-week call with their work—not to mention us women. Beth and I left cooked meals in the freezer and friends from church said they would check on our parents every day.

Early Monday morning we set off north to Victoria Falls and Wankie Game Park about 240 miles away. Foy and Margaret in their motor car with Jim and Becky led the excursion; Paul, Janis, Beth, Linda and I followed in Paul's VW Golf. About 120 miles up the road was *Halfway Hotel and Garage* where we stopped at 8:30 for breakfast and petrol fill-up. While we ate Foy entertained us with stories from early Rhodesian pioneer history of that area and some of his own experiences during earlier years.

We reached the little town of Victoria Falls about one-thirty, checked into chalets and unloaded the motor cars. Our lunch was hot tea and sandwiches at a *Wimpy's* before we went to see the magnificent Victoria Falls. Neither Janis nor Becky had ever seen the Falls; Paul had been there while on a summer trip in 1972; Linda, Beth and I were born in Rhodesia and had seen it several times as children. (The Falls is described in detail in Part I of this book.)

The border between Zambia and Rhodesia was the middle of the Zambezi River and the middle of the bridge across the deep gorge below the Falls. On the Zambian side soldiers guarded their end of the bridge keeping Rhodesians away and Rhodesian soldiers were on guard at their end to keep possible terrorists from coming into the country from Zambia. Legitimate travelers between the two countries crossed the river upstream on a ferry.

While we were having afternoon tea on the front terrace of the Victoria Falls Hotel we watched an interesting event take place on the bridge. Zambia, a land-locked country, had plentiful copper to export and needed to get it through Rhodesia by rail to South Africa. As we watched, it became evident that an agreement had been worked out for getting the copper across the border without a person crossing it either way. A Zambian train loaded with copper approached from the north and stopped before it reached the bridge. The engine was switched from the front to the back of the train and the loaded cars were *pushed* onto the bridge. It stopped with the south end of the loaded car exactly half way across the bridge. A Rhodesian engine *backed* on to the bridge, hitched on to the end of the copper-laden train and *pulled* it into Rhodesia from where it could be taken to South Africa by Rhodesian personnel. In that maneuver no Zambian crossed the border into Rhodesia and no Rhodesian crossed the border into Zambia!

**Game Viewing** Inside the game park we spent a night in each of three different camps. Each camp had a number of cabins and each cabin had two bedrooms with single cots, clean linens and mosquito nets, a furnished lounge, screens on the windows and small screened verandahs. We cooked on outdoor rock fireplaces—utensils furnished. We brought our own food and we all ate together. In the center of the camp was a block of toilets and showers with hot and cold running water. It was "roughing it" enough to suit me. The camps were surrounded with sturdy high fences and park rangers patrolled at night.

Every day we took sack-lunches to eat as we drove around in the park watching for wild animals. We saw giraffe, zebra, warthogs, baboons, monkeys, wildebeest, waterbuck, reedbuck, steinbok (tiny antelope), duiker (small antelope), impala (beautiful leaping antelope) and larger antelope—kudu, sable, roan antelope and eland. We saw black-backed jackals, mongooses, elephants, hippos, crocodiles and exotic birds. As a rule the animals paid no attention to motor cars unless there was some unusual noise or action. The park curfew was sunset and back in camp we cooked supper and sat around talking and singing.

One day we were winding slowly here and there when up ahead Foy waved his arm for us to stop. A large herd of elephants was wandering through the bush toward the road, munching on trees and bush-tops as they came. We had been told to give them the right of way so we waited and watched as they slowly crossed the road some distance ahead of us. When we thought the herd was gone, Foy drove slowly on but Paul had barely started moving when Janis called out, "LOOK!" A huge bull elephant had lagged behind the herd and was coming out of the trees. We waited for him to cross in front of us and follow the others but he stopped right in the middle of the road and slowly turned to face us. Paul had the motor idling and gently slipped it into Reverse ready for a hasty retreat if necessary. We understood any movement might be seen as a challenge and we had no intention of challenging that monster. Suddenly the elephant stomped a foot and snorted loudly. We all jumped and someone said, "Don't look him in the eye in case he doesn't like it!" So we waited with eyes averted! After what seemed a long time he slowly turned and ambled off into the bush in the direction of the herd and we caught up with Foy waiting around a bend in the road.

Foy and Margaret had been on many of these trips and planned the drives. They asked a ranger to mark extra points of interest. Jim and Becky were with them. The rest of us, in Paul's motor car were following, keeping them in sight in spite of the cloud of dust their vehicle stirred up. About 5 p.m. Foy began to circle back to be in camp before the curfew but somewhere he missed a turn. He sped up and so did Paul and the road got rougher, then it narrowed to two tracks and ended in a clearing at a fire tower. Foy said, "Sorry, folks, we'll try the other turn." By then it was getting dark and instead of 15 mph we were going about 30 mph hurrying back to camp regardless of bumps. Part of the time the road was so washed out we were straddling a ditch driving along the middle ridge and outside edge. At times bushes hit the sides of the motor cars and stubby scrub slapped the undersides, making so much noise we couldn't hear each other. Dust was so thick we couldn't see anything except Foy's tail lights and we could hardly breathe, but Paul was not about to let Foy out of sight.

We came to another fork in the road and Foy chose the left. Just as we thought the road was getting a little better we hit a spot that had been an elephant stomping-ground during the rainy season but now was dried and hard as concrete. It was so unexpected we just hit the high spots as we bounced across it. Fortunately Foy recognized two more such places in time to slow down. But then the tracks faded and we were in bushy grass with no road at all so it was back to the last fork to take the other one. Obviously the ranger had marked the map wrong. At least we didn't hit any more dried elephant tracks but by now it was nearly seven o'clock.

Beth, Linda, Janis and I began singing and Paul said he would like to join in but needed to concentrate on seeing through the dust, dodging rocks and stumps, missing holes and making the curves while keeping up with Foy. But he wanted us to keep singing and we sang on. Janis and Linda were already nervous and Paul, Beth and I didn't want to alarm them further so we didn't mention that if we didn't reach camp soon we would run out of petrol and might have to spend the night in the motor car unless a ranger found us. With lions, elephants, leopards, snakes and other dangerous creatures around it was not a happy thought. We also knew we were near the edge of the Park nearest the border from where terrorists were known to be coming into Rhodesia. We took comfort in the thought that they would not want to risk wild animals at night any more than we did. Foy had his hunting rifle and Jim his revolver in case of emergency with animals and Paul had a pellet gun loaded with blanks—he said in case we needed to make a noise!

All at once the tracks opened out into a road and we saw a sign pointing to the camp. Just as we saw the lights of the camp we met a ranger in a land rover coming to look for us. He said we were one hour late—it seemed like more than that to us. We were fined $9.00(R) ($13.50 U.S) per head but no one complained. We were so hungry we only washed our hands and hurried to cook supper. We ate with heartfelt thanksgiving and laughed at the sight of our faces and hair that were covered thick with dust in shades of red and brown. By then the wash house hot water was all gone but we made do with cold water.

We didn't ask a ranger to mark anything after that and very carefully kept to roads with clear signs. The last evening we enjoyed a fabulous five-course dinner in the restaurant with first class service—in the "wilds of Africa."

Foy and Jim were to preach in little churches on Sunday on their way home, so on Saturday we left their group at Victoria Falls. We stopped for lunch and petrol at *Halfway Hotel* and reached Bulawayo in time for afternoon tea with Daddy and Mother before Paul and Janis went on to Gwelo.

**The Political Situation** I had been in Rhodesia only nine months but the political situation was changing rapidly. Terrorists continued coming in from neighboring countries. Villages and farms were being raided, cattle rustled, crops destroyed and village children abducted from homes and schools. When their teachers or parents tried to stop the abductors they were either shot or locked in their huts and the huts burned down over them. That was the mildest of the atrocities that were beyond imagination—so terrible they made my skin crawl and I will not tell about them here. The Security Forces included men out of every ethnic group who trained and served with the regulars. During the whole period of terrorist warfare men from businesses and many occupations served year after year alternating six or eight weeks in the bush and six or eight weeks at home in their jobs. Many farmers had hundreds of black employees who were loyal to them and were sheltered within compounds near the farm houses, surrounded by high security fences with guards on patrol day and night.

I previously wrote of the Wiggill family, our friends during the Faroe Farm days. The five brothers had two sisters, Grace and Alice. They had all stayed in touch with Daddy, Mother and Foy through the years. Alice, now a widow, had one child, a daughter, who with her husband and five children lived on a farm some distance from Gwelo. One evening while eating dinner, the entire family was machine-gunned and the house burned over them. Their farm had the usual security fence, shortwave radio and helicopter pad, but a traitor among the employees had left the gate unlocked for terrorists to come in and they had no chance to radio for help.

Naturally Alice was devastated and moved into town from her small chicken farm outside Gwelo and later sold her farm. She found a house near her sister, Grace, also a widow. Alice and I corresponded regularly until I came back to the States in 1980.

**Precautions** All through the bush country terrorists planted land mines that maimed and killed many among blacks and whites. Regular daily buses served the outlying country. Soon terrorists posing as villagers came into towns on the buses and by night they planted landmines on some streets and roads. Radio warnings were broadcasted telling residents to never run over what looked like a pothole or patch of gravel, nor over any paper, even if it looked like a harmless sweet (candy) wrapper—a landmine could be under it.

We were told to keep several gallons of fresh water in jugs and a stock of tinned (canned) goods in our houses in case of a prolonged attack. Beds were to be placed on inner walls in case a grenade was tossed in a window during the night. If attacked we were to move into an inner hall until police arrived. With no American Consulate in Rhodesia, the one in Johannesburg, South Africa promised U.S. citizens they would be notified by radio if it became necessary to be evacuated. We were to keep passports and legal papers in a briefcase in the hall at all times, ready to leave at a moment's notice; no other luggage was to be taken with us to the airport where a plane from South Africa would be waiting to evacuate U.S. citizens. The airport was twenty-three miles from our house. In spite of those warnings, which we obeyed, daily life went on about as usual in the towns.

**Bus To Town** An interesting sight to a newcomer like me was the loaded buses that transported people into town from the outlying country. There may have been an official passenger limit but if so it was ignored as people crowded on, seats ran over and people stood in every space possible. A large luggage carrier on top was piled high with everything imaginable: suitcases, boxes, bundles—even live chickens in woven cages. Some passengers inside carried a live chicken under their arm.

One day a man came to town on the bus. He had never seen or tasted ice cream. Someone persuaded him to try a cone and he liked it so much he wanted to take some home to his family. He bought a half gallon and since it was solid he put it in his suitcase. The suitcase was put up in the luggage carrier on top of the bus where the temperature was over 90 degrees F. Soon melted ice cream was running down the outside of the bus. How disappointed he must have been! A true story.

**Home and Church Activities** The first week of December Mother was ill in the hospital and bedfast at home for another two weeks. During that time a lectureship at church with four services a day for four days went on with different speakers from around Rhodesia. Daddy, Beth and I

371

took turns going and staying with Mother. Every evening after the service we had people in for coffee. Foy, Margaret, Jim, Becky, Paul and Janis were among our welcome visitors.

**Christmas** The day after the lectures ended Foy, Margaret, Jim, Becky, Paul, Janis, Genie, Ed and girls came for midday dinner. That was our "Christmas" get-together since they could not all come back at Christmas. On Christmas Day Paul and Janis, Genie and Ed and girls came back and we had a lovely day in spite of the 90 degree heat. Our Christmas Dinner was roasted chicken, ham, green salad, vegetables, mashed potatoes and gravy, apple pie, pumpkin pie, mincemeat pie and traditional Christmas Pudding with lemon sauce. Christmas Pudding was like fruitcake only steamed instead of baked. Beth and I boiled small coins to sterilize them, then mixed them in the pudding batter before steaming it. A highlight of the meal was carefully eating the pudding, wondering who would find a coin in their serving. We had traditional Christmas crackers to pull and pop. Each one contained a small prize and a funny hat that we all wore. Some of those antics were strange to the "fresh from America" younger generation in the group but brought back many memories to the rest of us.

**Beth and Linda** December 27th Beth and Linda left on their way back to the States. Planes were crowded so they flew separately to Johannesburg then together from there to London and on to Miami. We missed them every way we turned! We especially missed Linda's daily practicing of advanced piano music.

**January 1977** The new school year began in January but with Linda gone we had no school girl in the house. Late in January Sewell Hall spent time in Rhodesia and preached in a meeting at Hillside. We were able to attend every night. He spent three nights in our home and what a treat that was, but not nearly enough time to talk about everything.

**Bible Classes** The classes Beth and others had been teaching in the public schools needed teachers and I volunteered to take some of them, as long as Mother was well enough for Daddy to take care of her the few hours a week that I was gone. The shortage of teacher volunteers forced us to combine some classes and at one time I had as many as four classes a week in four different elementary schools.

**People** Every Wednesday morning on my way to class at one of the schools, I passed through part of the industrial section at the time laborers were gathering at the gates. Most were employees of those plants and others were there in case of job openings. It reminded me of the parable Jesus told of the men in the market place waiting to be hired. Thousands of Africans, men and women, some on bicycles, some on foot, swarmed along the sidewalks and sides of the streets and in overloaded buses and motor cars. Some were dressed in suits, heading to office jobs, others were in every possible variety of clothing ready for many kinds of work.

The African women going to work wore brightly colored modern dresses—no slacks. Some were bareheaded with "Afros," many wore brightly colored crocheted or knitted caps or scarves—bouffant or head-fitting—others wore traditional *dukus* (brightly colored head scarves wrapped around the head and tied tightly with ends tucked in). Many women, especially younger ones, wore high platform shoes. It was not unusual to see a woman walking along the sidewalk up town in high heels or platform shoes, modern short dress, often with a baby on her back, wearing either a cap or wide-brimmed summer hat and on top of that sat a bulging suitcase or a plastic bag filled with fire-wood, or an overstuffed string-tied cardboard box.

Africans always wore something on their heads when walking or working in the sun. One of many interesting things to me was the originality and inventiveness of the men's head gear. We saw the flagman on a road-working crew wearing one of the cone-shaped orange road markers for his hat. One day I saw an African walking jauntily down the street wearing on his head what looked like an inverted small canoe. It was a rectangular piece of cardboard about twenty-four inches long wound front and back over the top of his head with toilet tissue that held the ends together, then wound around the back of his head to keep it on—an effective sun-shade. Some pulled off their shirt or coat and tied them over their heads. Of course there were all types of regular hats and caps, too.

**Disparate Population** The population of Rhodesia consisted of African, European and Colored people with distinct educational and cultural levels. Each of those levels, regardless of ethnicity, generally had the same education, lived in the same types of houses, furnished their houses alike, talked and dressed similarly. Many of them spoke their own languages at home and English at work.

As in any society or culture there were the affluent, middle class and poor among all ethnic groups no matter where they lived in the country. The more affluent were in government positions, managers in offices, banks, post offices and businesses of all kinds. Many of them owned their own businesses; some were heads of schools, or teachers, clergymen, doctors and nurses; some operated large farms with hundreds of employees; there were dentists, lawyers, electricians, engineers, architects, plant managers and more. Within that group were degrees of affluence from government officials all the way down to "everyday" people who all employed African house servants, garden workers and nannies for their children.

Most of them, whether African, Greek, East Indian, Jewish, Italian, Chinese or European, shopped in the same department stores, super markets, bookstores, bakeries, and so on, though many preferred their own ethnic food and clothing and there were specialty shops that they frequented. No one was barred from any business or gathering that I knew of, though they tended to gather within their ethnic groups for most social functions.

Urban laborers worked in factories and throughout the white suburbs and in city centers as yard workers, house-servants, Red Cross nurse aids, nannies, janitors, waiters, and peddlers. They lived in the "townships"—a city within the city with African-run businesses of every kind. They dressed in uniforms while at work or in clothes supplied by their employers and lived in small houses or rooms in the townships or in little houses provided for them in the back yards of their employers. Their food was a combination of traditional African and European. Some had their wives and children with them; others periodically went home to visit their families in the Tribal Trust Lands where their wives and children cared for their livestock on small parcels of land.

By far the largest segment of the more than seven million Africans in Rhodesia lived in villages in the Tribal Trust Lands, raising cattle and crops much as their ancestors had done—but wearing more clothes—having access to district schools through the third grade, medical clinics and general stores, operated by Africans. Each village had a chief who ruled his village. Witch-doctors still wielded an influence, even on some of the more educated.

**March 1977** Hard as it was to believe, I had been there a whole year and the rainy season was winding down, nights were becoming cooler but days were still very warm.

**Abductions** At that time two incidents in Rhodesia made the national news. Some Roman Catholic missionaries were killed in the north-eastern part of the country about 350 miles from Bulawayo. Nearly seventy-five miles south of us 400 children were abducted from a mission school in a Tribal Trust Land near the Mozambique border; it was the biggest, boldest raid terrorists had made. Some of the children escaped, found their way home and said they were all threatened that if they went home, the terrorists would come to their villages to kill them. Not making the national news was the abduction about the same time of a group near the Zambian border from which an escapee reported that 15 of the children had refused to take the training and were promptly shot. South of Bulawayo our garden worker's younger brother was taken in a group of about 35 when their village was raided.

**Social Events** Even in a country with such frightening barbarity taking place, there still was civilized culture to be enjoyed. The Bulawayo Philharmonic Orchestra had first rate musicians and often had distinguished guests from other countries. One week my friend, Joyce Tulip, and I attended a Violin Concert by the First Master Violinist of the Berlin Philharmonic Orchestra and his pianist of equal renown. We thrilled to Mozart, Bartok and Brahms and thoroughly enjoyed our evening out.

Twenty-first birthdays were occasions for coming-of-age celebrations. A young woman, Ann Gray, who attended Hillside church, turned twenty-one. Ann had suffered brain damage at birth and though she was twenty-one she was more like a twelve year old in many ways. She and her parents appreciated the young people at church including her in their activities. Her father was a government man of some standing and he and Ann's mother gave her an elaborate, catered birthday party in a suitably decorated rented hall. Ann's friends from church as well as acquaintances of her parents attended with all the expected merry-making. It was my first time to attend such a festive occasion. There were other twenty-first birthday celebrations during my time there but none so elaborate.

**Benjamin Dennis** June 3, 1977 my seventh grandchild, Benjamin Dennis, was born to Paul and Janis in Gwelo. Janis was in the hospital the whole month of June battling chemical pneumonia caused from accidentally inhaling anesthetic during her C-section. After three weeks little Benji, still in the Nursing Home (Maternity Hospital), was doing well and would have been at home but Paul needed to spend as much time as possible with Janis. Twice a day he visited and cuddled Benji, but clearly help was needed.

Foy and Margaret had partially moved from Gwelo to spend weekends in Bulawayo working with the Queens Park congregation across town from us. They agreed to sleep at our parents' house on week-ends and I made arrangements with friends from church to check on my parents during the first part of each week. I went to Gwelo to take Benji home and tend the house for Paul. Janis was able to come home June 30th, still very weak. Benji thrived and Janis grew stronger and Paul was able to do his work. But now I needed to get back to my parents. Paul hired an African woman to do the housework and July 13ᵗʰ I went back to Bulawayo.

**Trade Show** The Rhodesian Industrial Trade Show was held in Bulawayo that year. Unofficial attendance for the nine days was over 120,000. I went with Joyce and Norman Flynn on the last Saturday evening and was impressed anew at the number and variety of things manufactured, produced, mined and grown in that little country. The largest item on display was a rail freight car made of Rhodesian aluminum for use in that country and for sale to South Africa. Its extreme light weight allowed for a heavier load of freight.

Since Japan, Switzerland and South Africa did not recognize the sanctions and so much was produced within Rhodesia, the sanctions did not hurt as much on the importing as they did by preventing exporting that would have brought in revenue. True, there was not the multiplicity of brands per item as seen on store shelves in the U.S. or in South Africa—there were one or two brands each of such things as pickles, mayonnaise, peanut butter, canned fruits and vegetables and only four or five kinds of ready-to-eat dry cereals. On the plus side that made shopping much easier!

**Fazo Shandavu** Fazo Shandavu, a six-foot, gentlemanly, former schoolteacher visited Daddy in his office often and I enjoyed serving them tea and biscuits. Fazo was a preacher among the Africans and in a letter to my father he wrote of a revival he conducted. I quote it here in his own words to give an idea of some of his work. (Sikhoveni, Insukamini and Magwegwe were names of localities of the churches involved in this revival.)

*"I write to converse about the Bible Revival Meeting held during Easter Holidays at Church of Christ Sikhoveni. I with the Insukamini and Magwegwe brethren and sisters left Bulawayo at 12:30 p.m. Friday. The Bible Revival Meeting*

started at 3 o'clock p.m. Songs were sung and the prayers prayed. The attendance was 95 people present on Friday afternoon.

"On Saturday at 8 a.m. the whole brethren and sisters left the church building went to the villages. It was a long and tiresome walk going up and down the hills. We walked to village to village singing, praying and preaching the gospel to those fallen from grace and to those who did not like to hear the gospel being preached to them. Then we returned to the church building at 3 o'clock p.m. with many people with us to the church. The attendance was 113 people present.

"After 2 hours services on Sunday in the morning we left again the church building. The time was 8 a.m. We walked to village to village then returned to the church building at 12 o'clock p.m. Shortly we had arrived we began the Holy Communion Service which only took one and one half hours. Then at 1:30 p.m. we had the gospel meeting (preaching). There was good discipline. People worshipped the Lord Jesus Christ with whole of their hearts filled with good heavenly spirit.

"There were many people. The church packed to its capacity. The word has been sown. The Father and the Son shall water. Then the seed shall germinate. The meeting lasted for a few more hours then dismissed. (Curfew was at dark)

"We went to and from Sikhoveni without coming across to any difficulty or trouble. We prayed and thanked God and the Son Jesus Christ of their mercy to us.

"Pass my best wishes to sister Mrs. W. N. Short and the young sister and wish you the Lord's blessings.

Yours in Christ, Fazo Shandavu"

**Conviction** One Thursday after ladies Bible class a young woman was baptized at the church building. She had been attending Bible studies with her sister and brother-in-law in their home and came to ladies class on Thursday mornings while her husband was at work. He had forbidden her to come on Sunday and told her to stay away from "that junk." She wanted to be baptized anyway and take the consequences, that turned out to be a resounding row when he came home from work and guessed the truth; their five-year-old girl had volunteered her own deduction, "Mummy fell in the swimming pool at church this morning." We hoped his rage would subside with time but I never heard the rest of the story.

**Mother's Continued Decline** Mother had gradually declined since my arrival though she had improved from her most recent lengthy illness. She was able to crochet and read again but her legs never recovered strength and it took two of us to help her around in the house. We used a wheelchair when going to church services or visiting. After so many years of seeing my parents only for brief visits every five to seven years, to say I enjoyed being with them from day to day would be a gross understatement. Daddy and I had wonderful talks on many different subjects.

At that time a friend of ours told us of her two visitors from Ireland traveling together, a Catholic and a Protestant. She asked how they could be such good friends in Ireland with Protestants and Catholic fighting each other. They laughingly replied, "*All* the Irish are not fighting!" Perhaps *you* thought that *all* of the black people in Rhodesia were fighting against *all* of the white people—not so. Of the nearly 7 million black people and about 800,000 Europeans in Rhodesia the majority were not antagonistic toward each other.

That fact was noticeably illustrated by the mutual trust of the majority of employers and employees. An example was seen on school days when servants (African men and women) took young European children to schools, some "lifting" them on bicycles, some walking, leading them by the hand. At one school where I had a weekly scripture class I saw a little European boy brought in a large vegetable basket on the front of the African's bike. Many European babies were almost wholly cared for by African nannies and there were numerous trusted employees like our Wilson and Aaron.

**From My Window** Sitting in my bedroom one morning, I wrote:

> *"The sun is shining, birds are singing, humming birds are flitting among the yellow cannas blooming outside my window. From here I can see blue agapanthus lining both sides of the driveway and behind them orange chrysanthemums and red salvia. Bushes full of red hibiscus blooms brighten the landscape. Near the croquet court a jacaranda tree is covered in lavender blooms and flowering agapanthus circle its trunk. Near the front gate the flamboyant tree is bursting into bright red blossoms and on the pillars of the front verandah bougainvillea are in full burgundy and while colors—not to mention daisies, nasturtiums, petunias and zinnias around the yard. Roses are blooming prolifically in our rose garden. Flowers are everywhere and going to town today will be a pleasure drive through a showplace of flowers."*

In early September my father suffered what the doctor called a "coronary spasm" and spent three days in hospital. Two weeks later he had "a small coronary" and was in the hospital for three weeks. During that time I managed my mother with the help of a walker and a wheelchair. We wanted to go see Daddy every afternoon and managed to get her in and out of the motor car "with main force and awkwardness," as she would have said many years ago. On Thursdays through Sundays Foy was in town for his work at Queens Park and met us at the hospital entrance and did the heavy lifting.

We brought Daddy home October 3rd so shrunken and weak he could not walk alone or dress himself. He gained a little strength each day and gradually improved. I never saw him fail to be patient and kind. One night during that time Mother took sick suddenly and she and I had a midnight ambulance ride, leaving my father at home in bed. I saw her safely admitted in the hospital and talked to the attending doctor before I took a taxi home at 2:30 a.m. where Daddy was awake listening for me to come in. She was in hospital just over a week. At home once more she was not able to help herself nearly as much as before. Her doctor said he thought she had suffered a mini stroke—probably not the first.

**Red Cross Nurse Aides** Foy and I decided drastic measures were in order and made arrangements to have day and night Red Cross Nurse Aides. We signed up for two nurses with twelve hour shifts each. What had been Linda's room was now the nurses' room where the night nurse could sleep so long as she heard Daddy's call if she was needed. They had three years of training and were a great help in caring for Mother. The nurse and I could help Mother from wheelchair to armchair and Daddy, in his weakened condition, could watch without feeling so useless. Now there would be someone always with them when I needed to go to town. We invited the Nurses to eat at the table with us but they said they were not allowed to, but would accept a tray that we dished up for them to eat in their room. They gladly joined us for Bible reading, hymn-singing and games. Early in my time there Daddy brought to the table four different hymnals that he said they had been alternating using in their singing. We decided to pick one hymnal, begin with No. 1 and sing several songs per evening. We kept count of how many we *didn't* know in that book before going to the next one. Many hymns were in all four books and we sang them again when we came to them. If we didn't know one, Daddy read the music and we practiced until it became familiar. Four years later we had sung through all four books and counted 150 songs total that we didn't know or learn out of approximately 2,000 in the books.

**A Furlough and A Holiday** Paul and Janis with baby Benji went to the States on six months furlough. I surely missed knowing they were near enough to visit. Christmas came and went quietly for us and before we knew it we were into 1978.

In March Mother's sister Alice's daughter, Mary Batchelor, arrived for a two week visit. I had last seen her in the States when she was 12 and I was 18. Daddy decided it was time for me to take a little holiday and enjoy Rhodesia with her. Mary and I made reservations for a five-day flying-package-tour of Rhodesia's three main attractions: Victoria Falls, Wankie Game Park and Kariba Dam. We were to leave the following week.

On Thursday and Friday Mary visited with Mother and Daddy while I cooked dinners for five days to put in the freezer. Saturday she and I packed a picnic lunch and drove 30 miles to Matopos National Park. The Security hot line said it was safe to go after 8:30 a.m. and return by 3:30 p.m. On our way we had morning tea on the front verandah of the hill-top Matopo Hotel overlooking magnificent scenery. We scheduled ourselves to be back there for afternoon tea—Mary was beginning to like tea as much as I did! We arranged for two Red Cross Aides each shift and Daddy asked our close friend, Mabel Bailey, to come for a while every day.

**The Matopo Hills** A road wound among the granite boulder-strewn hills. The hills were made up of great piles of multi-sized rocks that looked as though they had been dumped there from a giant wheelbarrow. Here and there gigantic boulders were doing balancing acts on top of unbelievably smaller ones. We drove around exclaiming to each other, "*Look* over there!" and "Would you just look at *that!*" We ate lunch sitting on a big flat rock near the road and heard baboons barking. They sounded close and when they began fighting each other we got back into the motor car in case they thought we were taking sides! The grave of Cecil Rhodes was carved into the solid granite dome that topped a hill he had named "World's View." The tomb was carved and engraved by the late John Sherriff, the missionary stone mason I had known long ago as "Grandpa Sherriff."

We parked the motor car at the foot of the hill and climbed to the top of World's View, saw Rhodes' grave and those of several other famous pioneers and soldiers whose names were engraved in granite. While we were there the Park Ranger said it was time for the lizards to eat their daily handout of mealie-meal bread crumbs. He made sounds like calling pet dogs: lizards came from all directions, running from under rocks, jumping from tops of rocks, many shapes and sizes from tiny to foot long ones, blue, yellow, orange, green, gray, brown and black ones. They kept coming until we counted 37 in all. That evening Daddy listened with a happy smile to Mary's exuberant description of our day's adventures.

Tuesday noon Mary and I took a bus to the airport. We were sitting in the twin-engine prop plane waiting to take off when we were told there was engine trouble. We disembarked and waited two hours for the needed part to be flown from Salisbury. Finally we took off in a spiral fashion to 10,000 feet over the city before leveling off. This action was to avoid flying over the nearby bush country where terrorists were known to have heat-seeking missiles waiting for low flying planes. We flew above 10,000 feet until we arrived over Victoria Falls airport at 4 p.m. There the plane did its corkscrew descent to land. The perimeter of the airport was guarded by military vehicles with mounted guns. A bus took us ten miles to the hotel area that was surrounded by a security fence and patrolled day and night. On the bus a man with a rifle rode "shot gun" beside the driver and two military jeeps with mounted guns and men with rifles escorted us. Mary was so excited she could hardly sit still.

The year before, Zambians had fired mortars across the Zambezi River hitting two hotels that had burned. Security had been tightened, the hotels were rebuilt, and it hadn't happened again. Tourist places were still popular; people were determined not to let the terrorist war disrupt their lives. We met visitors from Australia, England, Greece, Israel, South Africa and Rhodesia, all enjoying their holidays.

In a picturesque thatched-roof motel on the banks of the river we reveled in first class rooms and five-course dinners—part of our "package tour." The choice of entertainment after dinner was pool or ping-pong. We played ping-pong—no one else seemed so energetic. The next day we viewed Victoria Falls in all its glory but we were not allowed on the bridge over the deep gorge. In the afternoon we took a cruise up the Zambezi River on the top deck of a double-decker launch. An armed patrol boat zipped up and down between our launch and the Zambian side. Both cruise launch and patrol boat kept well to the Rhodesian half of the river. The next day we visited Crocodile Ranch where we saw literally thousands of crocs from just-hatched babies the length of a man's hand to 15-foot granddaddies. They were raised for sale of skins as well as to restock rivers and lakes.

With the same military protection as the previous day we flew that afternoon to Wankie Game Park and were safely escorted to the Safari Lodge with its 300 rustically modern rooms. It was on the edge of the bush and for fear of wild animals we didn't walk at night in the lighted, well-kept grounds. Roasted pheasant was the highlight of the excellent dinner where the Italian manager strolled around chatting with guests. We took three game-viewing drives in a mini-bus through the parts of the park kept patrolled and considered safe from terrorist landmines and ambushes. Mary could hardly contain herself as she spotted wild animals: giraffe, zebra, warthogs, baboons, monkeys, wildebeest, waterbuck, reedbuck, steinbok, duiker, impala, kudu, sable and eland, besides black-backed jackals, a mongoose, elephants, hippos, crocodiles and beautiful birds. Lunch each day was a *braivleis* (cook-out) in the hotel grounds under big shade trees—a cool breeze blowing.

Friday afternoon we flew to Kariba with the same safety procedures and were escorted to "The Cutty Sark Motel" on the shore of the lake. The heat was oppressive, mosquitoes were thick even in the daytime and we were happy our room was air conditioned. On the wall inside, facing us as we walked in was a sign in bold letters: "In case of terrorist attack alarm will sound. Extinguish all lights. Lie flat on the floor under the bed. Do NOT come out until the all clear is sounded." We read it aloud and Mary said, "Humph! *Come out?* They'll have to *sweep* me out if that happens!"

Kariba Dam was built on the Zambezi River gorge, miles below Victoria Falls. It formed a lake over 90 feet deep and 165 miles long. We were taken on a cruise but our launch stayed close to the Rhodesian side—a few days before Zambians had fired on a launch, saying it got too close to their water. The huge power plant was owned and operated by a foreign neutral corporation and generated electricity for both Rhodesia and Zambia.

That evening two men were watching our ping-pong game and we challenged them to play. At first we beat them but after they saw we meant business, they showed us real ping-pong. They said they were on military duty in the area and had been the two "riding guns" in our escort jeep that afternoon. They wanted to hear about America and asked one question after another to keep us talking so they could listen to our accent! Saturday afternoon we flew to Salisbury—50 minutes by air. Becky and Jim Short met us and we visited in the airport until time for my flight to Bulawayo. Mary spent the weekend with them to get acquainted with her cousins and to see Salisbury.

**To South Africa** For months I had planned to go to Johannesburg for a Bible College Lectureship in March and my visa and export-import license were ready for leaving the country temporarily. Rene Wilson, friend and retired R.N., came to stay with the folks while I was gone—her company and cooking would surely be a pleasant change for them. Her husband, Herbie and Daddy enjoyed talking and challenging each other at chess whenever they had the chance.

Monday Mary came from Salisbury by train. Early Wednesday morning in my Honda we picked up Alan and Don Hadfield, father and son, and joined the group of motor cars that formed the convoy headed south with military escort. Foy and Margaret with their passenger were also in the group of 54 motor cars going the 200 plus miles to the border. Two convoys each way per day were escorted with a dozen to a hundred motor cars per convoy.

I asked Alan to drive at least to the border. The drivers were called into a huddle and given instructions in case of a terrorist ambush and they in turn instructed their passengers. Three armed vehicles with four armed men in each vehicle did the escorting—one in front, one in centre and one at the rear of the convoy. About 120 miles down the road the convoy halted at Midway Hotel and garage for a rest stop to have tea and fill our petrol tanks before going on to the border.

The Limpopo River was the Rhodesia/South African border. There were Immigration and Customs Offices to go through on each side. Foy and Margaret had an appointment and once through, they hurried on their way; no convoys was necessary in South Africa. We relaxed when we crossed the river and began looking for a picnic spot. We found it under a gigantic spreading baobab tree. Its huge trunk was hollowed out like a room, large enough for a family of walking natives to build their fire and spend the night—a wayfarer's inn. We spread our picnic in the shade of that tree.

Big-city traffic in Johannesburg took some getting used to after two years in slow-moving Bulawayo but I soon adjusted to it. Lectures were inspiring, five a day plus an hour of singing. The women of the area brought food each day and everyone was invited for lunch and supper; from thirty to fifty people ate each meal together.

Alan and Don stayed with special friends of theirs. Foy, Margaret and I stayed with Ray and Thena Votaw. Mary had booked her room earlier in a city hotel in order to sightsee. She saved special sights for the two of us to do together as I joined her during Saturday and Sunday afternoon breaks. We climbed to the top of the Carollin Tower where we met and talked with two young men from Waxahachie, Texas, Mary's birthplace.

We toured the Carlton Centre that was a marvel even to Mary as familiar with U.S skyscrapers as she was. It was 50 stories high and covered four downtown city blocks. There were three levels underground, all shops, surrounding a sky-lighted courtyard landscaped with gorgeous potted plants. From the shops to the top were floors of offices. The 50th floor had its own non-stop elevator that went up and down at incredible speed—two floors per second. On that floor were restaurant and gifts shops along with an aerial view of the city.

Monday morning Mary left on a six-day bus tour of South Africa ending in Durbin from where she would sail back to the U.S. in a freighter as she had come. I had spent the night with her to see her off and since

Monday was a holiday I was foot loose and fancy free! I went to Carlton Centre to window-shop and found a huge bookstore open among the many closed-for-the-holiday shops. Six happy browsing hours later I thought I remembered the way back to Votaw's house but missed the turn and instead of 35 miles, I drove 50 before finding it.

Tuesday morning Alan, Don and I went to the French *Hypermarket* to shop for needed things too expensive or unavailable in Rhodesia. Compared to our limited "super markets" in Bulawayo, the *Hypermarket* was mind-boggling. Of course I bought a box of Cadbury Chocolates for my parents and a toaster to replace ours that had died of old age—the same type that would have cost three times as much in Bulawayo.

We left Johannesburg by 1 o'clock but we knew we could not get to the border in time to catch the last convoy of the day so we stopped at a motel about 80 miles south of the border. On the road at 4:30 next morning, we made it through both sides of Immigration and Customs only to be told the convoy had been gone about five minutes. The official told us to hurry and catch up with it. With Alan driving we joined it not far up the road and by noon we were in Bulawayo. My parents listened with smiles to my stories. There were piles of letters to answer, correspondence course lessons to attend to and soon I was back in my regular routine.

**Painting And Other Amusements** As I became more house-bound with Mother I began landscape painting with oils and spent more time practicing on the piano. The next Trade Show came to Bulawayo after I had done a number of oil paintings. I entered four of them in the Art Show and was gratified with two Second Place awards and one Third. One of the Seconds was a 14"x16" seascape. A lady phoned saying that she had seen it and wanted to buy it—my first sale. Then a friend of a friend offered to pay me to paint a 14"x24" picture of her husband's old home place from a small black and white photo. I used my imagination for the colors and added a couple trees and some shrubs that I thought it needed. It was an anniversary gift and she was overjoyed with the result and asked, "How did you know there was a tree and those bushes growing there?" She gladly paid what I asked for it—my first commissioned painting. I sold a few more of the thirty-seven I painted while there and gave the rest to family and friends when I left the country.

When Mother thought I wasn't playing the piano enough she said, "We need some music around here!" and I gladly obliged; she didn't mind that I was not an accomplished pianist like Linda. A small neighborhood bookstore had second hand books for a pittance that could be traded in after reading. I read a lot at night and discovered Douglas Reeman's books. He was a veteran of the World War II British Navy and survivor of many battles that he wrote about in a series. Under the pen name of Alexander Kent he also wrote a series about England's naval battles of the 1800s and I read all of them I could find. I had read several of his books when I wrote to tell him how much I appreciated his writing, especially the fact that he made the action real without wallowing in gore like others I had tried to read. To my surprise he replied with questions about life in Rhodesia and began a correspondence that lasted for the next eight years as he continued writing books and I continued reading. His books were translated into multiple languages and sold worldwide.

Late in April Paul, Janis and baby Benjamin arrived back from their furlough in the U.S. and after they found a house in Gwelo and settled down I visited them one weekend. To conserve precious daytime visiting hours I chose to go by train. I left Bulawayo about 7:45 p.m. to arrive in Gwelo "round about" 1:30 a.m. Paul said he didn't mind meeting me at that unearthly hour. Two days later I left Gwelo "round about" 12:45 a.m. to be in Bulawayo "round about" 7:30 a.m. We called it "the round-about-train" because the Station Master, when asked the time of a train's arrival or departure, always said, "Round about . . ."

Then it was winter again. In my unheated bedroom, getting out of my warm bed each morning in the 38-50 degrees F. cold (Brrrr!) I thought of my family in the States sweltering through hot July; but I was reading a book about Siberia and actually almost felt warm!

Daddy was again teaching and preaching occasionally. He had just finished typing his version of the book of Matthew that he had been compiling in handwriting over many months. He used what he considered the best wording from 30 translations he studied from among the 67 different translations of the New Testament that he had collected over the years. He said he was doing it for his own satisfaction, not for publication.

**Common Ties** Mother's legs were becoming gradually more useless but we still took her in the wheelchair to church and some visiting. One week Martin and Marty Broadwell (father and son) whom I had known in the States, were speaking over the weekend at Queens Park where Foy worked, and came to see us. The week after that Jim Lovell from Durbin, South Africa, was preaching in Bulawayo and we went every night to hear him. He was from Ohio and had attended Florida College with Edward and Henry. If you have never been separated from family by years and thousands of miles, you cannot imagine what it meant to us to see folks with common ties back in the States.

**Tonya Suzanne** About that time word came from the U.S. that my eighth grandchild, Tonya Suzanne, was born to Nancy and Raymond July 14, 1978. She was the twenty-fourth great-grandchild for my parents.

**Scarcity Of Men** At church services we were having only the disabled men and those over 55. White missionaries among the Africans in the outlying country were asked by the natives to leave and let them carry on their own church work so that terrorists would be less likely to kill them for meeting with white people. Those white missionaries went back to the U.S or moved from their missions into towns. In the towns, at the request of the black brethren, white teachers stopped going to the African townships to visit or conduct services, not only because of danger to the whites, but also because of very real danger to the black Christians; either they or their families might be persecuted or killed by terrorists for associating with white people.

In the townships terrorists recruited informers from among employees throughout the city. The employees were instructed to listen carefully for anything their employers said that could be used by the "liberating forces" against the employers, with threats of what would happen to informer's families if they failed to report what they heard. Loyal employees like Wilson asked their employers to refrain from talking politics of any kind in their hearing so they could say truthfully that they hadn't heard anything. Adding to their pleas were the government warnings to everyone (white and black) to be very careful what they said at any time because they could not know who might be informers. That reminded me of posters I saw during World War II that said, "Loose Lips Sink Ships."

Over the next years several of our African preachers in the Tribal Trust Lands were killed for refusing to stop preaching. Other villagers who refused to help the terrorists suffered unspeakable atrocities and died. Such atrocities were being perpetrated over and over again. Our daily prayers were that each of us, regardless of color of skin, would be true to God if such a test came to us. To encourage each other we talked and prayed about it in our homes, over dinner and tea times, in church services and in meetings of all kinds.

**August-October 1978** Summer was approaching. Winter had been 115 consecutive days of bright sunshine and blue, blue skies, with the last rain in mid-May. During that time the countryside turned shades of brown; many trees and shrubs lost their leaves. Grassfires swept the country during August and September and into October. They made the atmosphere along the lower horizon smoky while overhead the sub-tropical sky was an almost unreal blue. Now nights became warmer, days hotter. Without a drop of rain suddenly bare trees burst into lush green or into their spring covering of flowers; land blackened by grassfires was carpeted with new green grass. The change was even more spectacular than usual because of record rains the year before that had left the water table higher than in fifty years we were told.

Standing at the kitchen counter making early morning tea I watched sunrises on clear mornings. At times the pink eastern sky turned gradually to lavender-blue and the sun came up in a blaze of gold. At other times puffballs of bright pink clouds against grayish blue sky gradually changed through varying shades of gilt-edged pink as the sun slowly crept up from their edges. On days when the air was smoky the sun came up like a big orange ball—not blinding at all until it was high in the sky. There was a different show to watch every morning. I tried my camera but photographs didn't do justice to the sights.

**Good-bye Little Honda** One Friday I came out of the bank to find a note on my Honda windscreen. Thinking it was a parking ticket I hurried to see why and was relieved to read, *"If you are interested in selling this motor car call David Levy at this number—."* He was the well-to-do proprietor of a dry goods store in town. With Daddy's help I decided on an asking price and called the man. Within ten minutes I had sold my Honda. To be sure he dickered me down some but I was prepared for that! He and his wife were immigrating to Israel, he said. They wanted a small motor car with the steering wheel on the left and he thought there was no harm in asking.

**59<sup>th</sup> Anniversary** On Thursday, August 30 my parents celebrated their 59th wedding anniversary. On Sunday eight families of the Hillside congregation brought their lunches to eat with us on folding tables set up in the yard. Afterwards we sang while the little children played hide-and-seek in the big yard. Thursday evening three families of our closest friends and Foy surprised us after supper with cake and ice cream and we sang some more. Almost all get-togethers ended in hymn singing with no lack of four part harmony.

**Tennis Time** Three ladies invited me to make a fourth at tennis on Saturday mornings and at the time the home front was such that I could be gone a couple of hours. Surprisingly I could still play a fair game after all the years of not touching a racquet. We were out for the fun and exercise so no one got upset over missed balls but after six Saturdays my tennis career came to an abrupt end with a painful case of tennis-elbow.

**Daddy's Gentleness** Daddy's health improved but the doctor told him "no heavy lifting," so the Red Cross Aides were a continued necessity. Daddy could still be very firm but I marveled daily at his kind, patient and gentle handling of Mother. In my memory he had always been that way and as she became more and more difficult to handle it was beautiful to see. One morning at breakfast she jerked the bib off that he always tied around her neck. He calmly tied it back, saying gently, "Leave it on, Mother," but she pulled it off again. After the third time he spoke sternly, *"Mother, I said leave it on."* She looked up at him with eyes of wounded surprise but left it on and he sat down. When he said grace he asked the Lord to forgive him for speaking harshly to Mother. The memory of it brings tears to my eyes again.

**A Mugging** Saturday afternoons and Sundays were Wilson's time off. He usually went to town, always returning to his house before dark. One Saturday evening during devotions at the kitchen table there was a knock on the back door. Wilson stood there bent over, holding his hand to his chest, blood running down his arm. I told him to come inside where it was warm but he refused; he didn't want to get blood inside, he said, and sat down on the step. I hurried to put a blanket around him and he objected, "I don't want to get blood on it." I assured him it would wash out. Daddy gave him a clean towel to hold over the wound in his chest then called the police with their ambulance.

Wilson said he was walking toward our house along a deserted street when about a quarter of a mile away, four black boys jumped him, probably thinking he was old and easy prey, he said. He was stronger than he looked and fought them off, but in the struggle one of them stabbed him in the chest. The police took him to the hospital where Daddy and I visited him every day of his four day stay. The doctor told Daddy the knife missed vital organs but the wound was deep and he needed IV medication to prevent infection. When Daddy told Wilson we would come to get him when he was dismissed, he argued and insisted he would walk home but we didn't listen. The injury left him weaker than he had expected and Daddy insisted he take the month off.

**Traumatic Trip** Paul, Janis and Benji drove down to visit us for a couple of days then Paul returned to work, leaving Janis and Benji for a few days extra. I was to take them home the next weekend. Verna Hadfield's son Don and family lived in Gwelo so I asked her if she would like to go with me to visit them. We invited Gwen Massey, a mutual friend, to go along. The highway to Salisbury went through Gwelo and was so busy during the day that no military-escorted convoys were considered necessary.

Friday morning we set out in Daddy's station wagon at 8:00 o'clock, the earliest that travel was permitted. The speed limit sign said "100 K or as fast as safe. Do not stop for any reason." Our planned rest stop was a garage-filling station about half way between Bulawayo and Gwelo. We had gone less than 40 miles when the motor began to slow down gradually from 60 mph and no amount of pumping the accelerator did any good. Before long we were creeping along at 20 mph. Our hearts were beating fast when at 10 mph we finally sighted the garage and rolled to a stop. The mechanic worked on the petrol line, said it had water in it, blew air through it, thought it was fixed and took it for a trial run. He decided it was good to go and off we went, zooming along at 60 mph. About a mile and a half up the road, without warning, the motor died and there was no restarting it.

I told the others I would walk back to the garage and if a motor car stopped to inquire the trouble to tell them I was walking to the garage and they would surely hurry to give me a lift. Our feelings were not helped any by knowing that the previous evening a band of terrorists had surrounded a local farm house where the people were having a cookout and had shot all of them. But we reassured each other that it was still morning and that incident had happened at sundown. I didn't have to tell the ladies to be praying and I prayed as I walked. I was barely out of sight over a ridge when a motor car caught up with me and stopped to give me a lift.

As soon as the mechanic saw me, he dropped what he was doing, jumped into his truck with his assistant and hurried off. They pulled our motor car back to the station and worked on it again. He said there was again water in the petrol line and this time he felt sure he had blown it all out. After a longer test run we set off again and this time made it into Gwelo—very slowly the last few miles. Paul's mechanic and personal friend sacrificed his weekend to work on the problem which he found and corrected. Monday morning after a good weekend visit, Verna, Gwen and I practically held our breath all the way back to Bulawayo.

**Radios** Everyone listened to the daily news with dread of hearing names of friends or family killed in action. A popular morning program allowed family members to send special messages of a personal nature to their men in the Security Forces. Knowing the terrorists were also listening, messages were carefully censored for the protection of the men out in the bush.

Mother kept the radio on a big part of every day and we heard the same songs several times a day. One of the popular songs at the time was *By The Rivers of Babylon.* The words were from Psalm 137: *By the rivers of Babylon, there we sat down, and there we wept as we remembered Zion. Those who carried us away into captivity required of us a song. How can we sing the Lord's song in a strange land?* As I heard that song over and over I thought how wonderful it was that God's children could sing His song in any land, any time. When I came back to the States I tried to find that cassette but never did.

The changeover to black government was due in December and it was now October. We heard of terrorist activity happening in town and getting closer all the time to our neighborhood. In spite of their leaders' claims to be "freedom fighters" against "white oppression" the majority of their victims were other blacks, especially the ones in the Tribal Trust Lands and in the townships. By late 1978 more than 8,000 natives had been killed by terrorists compared to only a few hundred Europeans. Because of military call-ups there was hardly a European household in the country that did not have one or more of its family members in the armed services. Out of our four European congregations in Bulawayo totaling approximately 400 people, there were more than sixty men serving their various times in about every branch of the forces. With the small size of the country and the involvement of families, everyone was well informed about what was going on all over the country.

Terrorists infiltrated the African townships where most of their activity was robbing stores and throwing grenades into crowds at beer halls or bus stops. Some European homes were broken into and guns and radios stolen. Knowing of the terrorists in the towns and expecting more action as election time drew nearer, many families who did not already have guns bought them. Daddy was urged by friends to do so as well. But he would not buy a gun and refused the offers of men in the congregation to take turns bringing their gun to spend the night at our house. He told them we appreciated their concern but God being his helper, he would not kill a human. "But what will you do if they break into your house?" he was asked. Daddy replied, "In the first place *what if* may never happen at all, and my answer is the same as before, I will pray for them."

We talked often with Foy and Margaret, Paul and Janis and Jim and Becky as well as other Americans. Collectively and individually we asked God for wisdom to know what we should do about staying in Rhodesia or leaving. The need seemed more urgent than ever to stay to encourage the Christians who lived there. Some American workers were leaving when their U.S. sponsoring churches told them their support was ending. We saw Rhodesians, black and white, move to South Africa. Many European families moved to Canada, Australia, England and other overseas countries, some because their jobs were lost when places of work closed, some trying to get away from the tensions in the country. Even so at that time there were still more than 250,000 Europeans in Rhodesia. With many preachers and teachers gone, all the help and encouragement we could give was badly needed. One troubled couple asked Foy, "What will we do when Mugabe and his crowd get into power?" Foy replied, "We will keep on being Christians."

As available to us as the inside information on military and terrorist activities was, we were confident there would be ample warning if a battle were shaping up and getting out of the country was imperative. The American Consulate in Johannesburg frequently updated its registration of American citizens in Rhodesia in case the need for evacuation should arise. They promised that if that happened an evacuation plane would be sent immediately.

There were now even more wide open Bible teaching opportunities. In Bulawayo and Gwelo Foy, Paul, Donald Hadfield and Leonard Cluely, fulltime workers whose schedules I happened to know, had as many classes and home studies as they could handle and there were openings for many more. Many of the Scripture classes in the public schools that had been taught by wives of missionaries and older Christians were left without teachers. I had to give up the classes I was teaching because Mother needed me at home.

I was studying with a lady and her married daughter every Friday on my way home from my weekly business trip to town and after the hour of study they always asked if I could stay longer. There were three other women who asked me to study with them but I could not be away from home that much.

With Daddy's maturity and background of fifty-seven plus years in that country he was advisor, encourager and stabilizer to many Christians, white and black. Even now not a day passed without one or several men coming to his office to consult with him and it was my pleasure to serve them hot tea and biscuits while they talked.

That month I ended my letter to family and friends in the U. S. with these words: *"Let me assure you again that life goes on here in a calm daily routine and we sleep soundly at night. Please don't worry about us, just join us in believing God is in control and pray for us as we do for you."*

**Friendship Renewed** In November Foy received a letter from Iris (Reynolds) Smith, asking for my whereabouts. She had seen his name in the newspaper and remembered he was my brother. She was one of my boarding school "best friends" when we attended *Girls High School* in Salisbury where our "crew" consisted of four girls: Iris Reynolds, Reshea Barry, Sarah Sharp and Sybil Short. Among other things, we shared a conscientious desire to be Christ-like in attitudes and behavior even though we attended different church services on Sundays: Iris to Church of England, Reshea to Presbyterian, Sarah to Dutch Reformed and Sybil to Plymouth Brethren. When I left Rhodesia in 1940, World War II was raging and we lost touch with each other. Hearing from Iris was exciting and I immediately wrote, telling her of my situation and inviting her to come for a visit. She couldn't get away then, she said, but urged me to visit her. She was a widow and Matron of *Forsyth House* at *Girls High School*, the very house where she and I had lived our last two years of high school.

Daddy thought I should go visit her and hired extra nurses for the week. I took the 7 a.m. train Tuesday. As I was buying my ticket the Rail Road agent said, "This train is supposed to get to Salisbury at 7:35 p.m.—that is if they (terrorists) have left enough track for us to get through. They have blown up tracks twice but so far no train damage!" I was glad to see 15 of our soldiers boarding the same train. Trains had four classes and were not segregated. Two coaches of First Class with European style compartments; two cars of Second Class, which I took, also had compartments; Third Class was less expensive and had seats like the day trains in U.S.; Fourth Class consisted of box cars with open floor space and was the least expensive. The Dining Car was between First and Second Classes.

It was only about 300 miles to Salisbury from Bulawayo but the trip took from twelve to sixteen hours because of frequent stops. I made a list of all the stops where I saw a sign: Mpopoma, Cement, Heany Junction, Ntabazinduna, Bembezi, Lochard, Kombo, Insiza, Shangani, Gado, Que Que, Nalatale, Daisyfleld, Somabula, Willoughby, Dabuka, Gwelo, Manyama, Samwari, Sherwood, Umniati, Battlefields, Ngwena,

Gatooma, Hartley, and Norton. There were other signs I didn't see in time to copy. During a thirty minute stop at Gwelo, Paul, Janis and Benji met me for tea at the *Rail Road Café*. Sixteen month old Benji was learning to be excited about trains.

In Salisbury I luxuriated with Iris in her lovely flat. Meals sent up from the house kitchen were served in her dining room by a waiter in white uniform and red fez. Iris was able to be off duty several hours each day and showed me around town. We window-shopped one day and had tea in a "posh" department store Tea Room. We talked nonstop—thirty-eight years of catching up. Thursday Jim and Becky invited us to afternoon tea. My return was booked for that night to be in Bulawayo early Friday morning. However, on Wednesday the Rhodesian Rail Roads had announced over the radio that for security reasons there were no more night trains so I left the next morning. Returning home on Friday, the Gwelo stop was short but Paul, Janis and Benji met me for a brief visit bringing a refill of tea for my thermos.

Several Hillside members had made a special point of visiting the folks while I was gone and all was well. During the past year such visits had been cut back as petrol became more expensive and scarce for civilians because of the growing needs of the Security Forces.

Hot dry days of September and October had left us sapped and we welcomed rains in early November. Snow in the Cape sent a cool spell sweeping up our way with the rain, and bed-socks felt good for a few nights!

**Christmas 1978** We had two weeks of celebration. Foy and Margaret were to be in Salisbury over Christmas so they came to visit us December17th. Paul, Janis and Benji were with us 22nd through 26th. Genie and girls came half days on 24th and 25th. while spending the week with her in-laws in Bulawayo (Ed was in the bush with Security Forces.) We always enjoyed Genie and her girls. A tall blond, with vivacious, laughing ways, she reminded me a lot of my daughter-in-law Jo Ann as we tended children and talked about what our dear ones in the States were probably doing at Christmas.

**1979** The year began calmly—the national election had again been moved forward, from December to April, so we were kept wondering what would happen. In the meantime desegregation was making rapid progress; on city buses blacks took the front seats and whites went to the back without noise or demonstrations of any kind.

**Squashed!** Mother's legs were becoming less able to hold her up. One Saturday morning after Daddy went to his office to write letters, the nurse and I were helping Mother get settled in the living room. We had her up out of her wheelchair and were backing up to the armchair when I realized her leg on my side was giving way. I tried to hold her up but we both went down. I landed with my left ribs across the metal edge of the sofa with Mother on top of me—all 230 pounds of her. She slid off to a sitting position on the floor and the nurse landed across the arm of the chair. I had not been so completely deflated since as a teen I took a header over the handlebars of my bicycle. Mother wasn't hurt and we were laughing, though my laugh was between whoops of trying to get my breath. We called Daddy from the office and Wilson from the kitchen, and between us all we got Mother up and into her chair.

But I was not just winded—my chest hurt—every breath was a gasp and every move was agony—surely all my ribs were broken and poking me! I phoned Ann Roberts who drove me to the doctor. He said the x-ray showed my left lung was severely bruised and punctured at one spot and he thought some ribs were cracked. He put a deadening shot where it hurt the worst so after a while I could stand almost upright. He prescribed some powerful pain pills and told me to "take it easy," and to come back immediately if I coughed up blood.

We called for double nurses, two for days and two for nights. I managed to do the cooking and very little else for the next two weeks except sit with Mother, reading, knitting and practicing piano. The worst torture was getting in and out of bed; otherwise everything was just fine as long as I didn't move—or breathe—or laugh—or cough—or worst of all, sneeze!

At that time Paul and Janis were temporarily living in Jim and Becky's house in Salisbury. Paul was substituting in Jim's church work while they were in the U.S. on furlough. Daddy decided I needed to fly to Salisbury for recuperation time with my children. He let the word out at church and good friends, Max and Gwen Taylor, volunteered to stay with them while I was gone. Gwen would cook—relieving me of planning and freezing meals in advance. Max and Daddy could read, talk and play some chess!

I flew to Salisbury on Monday evening and back Friday morning. The flight took 40 minutes—quite a contrast to the12-16 hours by train of my last trip to Salisbury. I couldn't pick Benji up but he showed off for me in a very gratifying way. He would be two in June when a brother or sister was due.

By the time I got home it had been three weeks since the accident and more x-rays showed three ribs had been broken and were healing, somewhat justifying my grunting. I asked the doctor if lifting Mother would help to strengthen the muscles and he replied with an emphatic "NO! You need more healing time."

January 27th was my 56th birthday. Ann Roberts visited over morning tea, Foy and Margaret came for lunch and Paul and Janis phoned. It was a good day. After supper we were sitting with the nurses at the kitchen table singing when a motor car drove up—then another—and another—and another. "What in the world is going on?" I asked on my way to the door. Masseys, Stevenses, Baileys, Burgesses and Hadfields had come with cake, ice cream and song books for a surprise birthday party. What beautiful singing and what fun!

During the party the phone rang. Reshea Barry, one of my "crew-mates" from high school days, who lived in Australia, was visiting her daughter near Bulawayo. We hadn't seen each other in forty years and planned a get-together for the next week. In the 1930s she had gone home with me several times for school holidays because she lived too far away to go home (the Belgian Congo) except for the six weeks Christmas holidays.

It was guava time again and the trees tried to outdo themselves. I can almost smell guavas cooking even now! I put up eight half-gallons of puree and made uncounted pints of jam. We ate guavas stewed, pureed and raw for weeks and enjoyed every bite. Somewhat less offensive than boiling cabbage, the strong pungent odor of cooking guavas made me thankful for warm weather with windows and doors wide open. One day I was oil-painting at the same time guavas were cooking—what a combination—turpentine and boiling guavas!

**Deteriorating Conditions** Daddy was again preaching twice a month. Mother was becoming harder to move around and the doctor said he was sure she was having more small strokes. She still liked to go in the motor car and we managed to get her to all church services, though she slept through most of them. But I had to cut out all other going except to ladies class and the business trip to town once a week. Either Daddy or I stayed in the room with her when she was in the living room as she had decided the black nurses were not to be trusted. There was no way to reason with her so we tried to keep her pacified.

She still tried to crochet granny squares. More than once when she was about to put her work away in the evening she asked for the scissors and cut some threads. The next morning she saw the cut thread and asked, "Who cut my crocheting?" I tried to tell her she did it the night before but she said she knew she didn't and "Somebody is guilty." She told the two nurses and me to sit in chairs opposite her and stay there until one of us confessed. We sat like that until she forgot why we were there and told us to "Get to work!"

One morning when Barbara, a nurse with very dark skin who had been her favorite, was about to bathe her, Mother shouted, "Get away from me, you old black thing." Cordelia, the other nurse on duty, had lighter brown skin and she allowed her to bathe her. When I apologized to the nurses they assured me they understood that she was not responsible and her words didn't bother them. We knew she was not mentally responsible but it made us sad to see this change in her after the many years of her loving the native people.

**Other Changes** I had been there three years and could see many changes in the country. Groceries had gone up more than 12%. Sales tax had gone from 6% to 15% to help finance the anti-terrorist war that was costing over $900,000 (U. S.) per day in that small country. Income Tax for Europeans was 20% across the board plus 10% surcharge. Fifteen years of sanctions, the increasing shortage of foreign currency along with the high cost of the terrorist war had slowed industry. Factories were forced to cut back or close down. Unemployment rose sharply. The continued rise in cost of living made housewives who formerly employed 3-5 servants cut back to one or two and many who had had one or two let one or both go. Wilson told Daddy he did not want his accustomed annual raise because he understood the situation and was content with his wages.

**Holiday Bible School** For several years the Bellevue and Hillside congregations had together conducted a week's Holiday Bible School during the April-May school holidays. With many of our members gone to South Africa or overseas and almost all the remaining men on national call-ups, we wondered what to do. The Hillside elders told our ladies if we conducted it we would have the school—even if only a few came. Ann Roberts was organizer and I helped select and order the material and substituted for teachers when needed. Several teachers came from the other congregations bringing a number of children. The elders thought we would do well to have 25 to 30 present but to everyone's surprise there were 79 present the first day. Gastric flu hit town that week and illness kept some away who had planned to be there, even so, the number never went under 70 the rest of the week.

**National Elections** From the 12th of April 1979 until some time after the elections ended the 24th, every man in the country of military age was on duty. The Security Forces were spread throughout farm areas and the Tribal Trust Lands to protect people, black and white. Men over 50 were trained for reserve duty in the cities and towns, patrolling the streets to help the regular police. Daddy's health and age (85) kept him from patrolling the streets but he volunteered to do whatever he could. He was asked to be on watch for unusual activity and report anything suspicious. Night meetings of every kind were cancelled. We had Sunday evening services before dark.

Gwelo's regular volunteer fire fighters were all on military duty and the call went out for reserve volunteers. Paul joined them and went through the training process. Most of their alarms were for grass fires that were more frequent in the town's vacant lots than house fires since all houses were brick or concrete.

Elections went off more smoothly than was expected. Three candidates were running for President. *Abel Muzorewa,* a Bishop in the Methodist Church, had become a nationalist leader who worked within the system without resorting to any violence. *Joshua Nkomo,* a Kalanga (Shonas who had been absorbed by the Ndebele) whose terrorist faction called ZAPU was aligned with the Soviets, armed and trained by them in Zambia, fought primarily in the western part of the country. *Robert Mugabe* was leader of the Shona terrorist organization known as ZANU, which was aligned with the Chinese and Frelimo of Mozambique, who trained and armed volunteers and abductees in Mozambique; they terrorized eastern Rhodesia. Both ZANU and ZAPU claimed to be "freedom fighters" but they were bitter enemies of each other.

The country was saturated with black and white Security Forces to give people protection to and from the polls. Extra buses were added to be sure everyone who wanted to vote had a way to travel. In one of the Tribal Trust Lands a bus load of 126 voters was blown up by a land mine; terrorists had filled the land with landmines during the past 15 years. But even that did not stop the flow of people going to vote. There was no violence connected with it in any of the cities or towns; it was more like a city-wide boisterous picnic—and why not? They were off work for a day with pay to go stand in queues to talk and joke, sing and laugh as Africans did at every gathering.

Some, including our two servants, and the nurses who told us of others, wanted to vote for Ian Smith to stay in power because they could believe what he said. He was unlike the "big-talking" black leaders of the terrorist factions, they said, who would say anything to please whoever they wanted to impress. But Ian Smith's name was not on the ballot, and Daddy urged any who talked to him like that to vote anyway. Ian Smith and others made speeches over the radio and TV, urging all to go out and vote for a black leader for the long term good of the country. A majority of them did—but not for the terrorist leaders: Abel Muzorewa won by a landslide.

**A New Country** June 1, 1979 the country was renamed "Zimbabwe-Rhodesia" and Abel Muzorewa became Prime Minister. He appointed Ian Smith, the former Prime Minister of Rhodesia, "Prime Minister without Portfolio." Muzorewa tried, with limited success, to include other African parties in the government departments. Robert Mugabe and Joshua Nkomo were so angry about losing the election they refused to cooperate and the terrorist war escalated.

The communist-backed terrorist war went on. Daytime travel was still with military-escorted convoys through many areas. There was no travel at night anywhere outside of cities; so many land mines had been planted by terrorists that all dirt and gravel roads were dangerous. In spite of all those things there was an atmosphere of optimism that sanctions would soon be lifted, that the country would be recognized and that the terrorists would either surrender or go away. The number of terrorists who gave themselves up every day increased as they heard that their objective of a black government had been achieved, but most had been too brainwashed to accept the change. Abduction of children and intimidation with atrocities still went on among the villages.

The big blow came when Britain and U.S.A. refused to recognize the new government and to lift sanctions. President Carter's reasons for the refusal (as quoted in our newspapers) were totally inaccurate and to us sounded positively stupid. Meanwhile under the new government, blacks who could afford to do so began moving into formerly all white areas, buying or renting. Everyone seemed to take it much more calmly than I remembered it happening in the U.S. in the 1960s when segregation became illegal. Available jobs had already been going to blacks as they qualified for them but now the closing of businesses for lack of money put many, both white and black, out of work.

**Taking For Granted** Some things I thought I would never take for granted were: driving on the left side of the road; jay walking; bicycles so thick I was afraid to drive for fear of hitting one; light switches pushed down for ON—up for OFF; loaves of bread sold unsliced and unwrapped; fresh pasteurized milk in plastic bags; always sifting meal, sugar, flour and custard powder to remove weevils, insect legs and wings, small sticks, rocks and other foreign objects; potatoes sold by weight encased in thick layers of mud, so expensive we used more flakes than fresh; harmless wall spiders whose lives I spared because I was told they ate mosquitoes! People felt hot or cold by Celsius degrees, though I and the American thermometer in my room still thought in Fahrenheit degrees!

I was proud of Janis and Becky for doing so well at adjusting in what to them was a very strange country. I had the advantage of having lived there my first eighteen years and I took for granted Paul would adjust since his mother was born there! Beautiful scenery, ideal climate, friendly people, slower pace of life, all combined to make it a delightful place to live—if only the terrorists had not been ruining the country for everyone, black and white. The price of petrol, groceries and everything else went up more each week. I decided one could save a lot by not eating or going anywhere!

Foy and Margaret sold their home in Gwelo to an African school teacher. They bought a place across town from us in Queens Park suburb where Foy worked with the church and we looked forward to seeing them more often as petrol allowed.

Paul and Janis's second child arrived on June 15, 1979. He was named Douglas James and was my ninth grandchild. Janis had no complications with her C-Section this time. I felt one week was about all I should be away from my parents so Paul asked me to wait until Janis was ready to go home from the hospital. He said he and Benji were doing well; friends invited them to their homes for meals and their African servant kept house and did laundry. In the meantime I filled the freezer with pre-cooked meals and Daddy assured me they would do fine with the nurses for a week.

**The Law Of The Gun** About that time we saw a headline from U.S. newspapers, "It's The Law Of The Gun At U.S. Fuel Stations." The article described how people in the States brandished guns and pistols, forcing their way to the fuel pumps. I wrote to family and friends and urged them to be very careful when they went to fill up with gas in that dangerous country!

In August of 1979 Paul and Janis moved into a smaller house with lower rent to help counter the rising cost of living. Then Paul went to the Salisbury hospital for surgery on his nose. The ENT specialist thought surgery would help the breathing problem that had plagued him for years. I borrowed a motor car from Foy and went to Gwelo Sunday afternoon to stay with Janis and babies until Paul got home Tuesday. The few days I was gone Foy and Margaret kept an eye on our parents.

Daddy was doing well but still under orders not to lift. Mother was becoming less able to help us lift her and it was becoming nearly impossible for the one nurse and me to move her. Then much to my disgust I tore a muscle in my chest wall. The doctor said heavy lifting probably did it. We hired two nurses per shift. After it was healed he told me if I resumed heavy lifting it could easily cause another, perhaps worse tear. Foy built a hoist beside Mother's bed to help lift her to her wheelchair and with that two nurses per shift were able to manage.

**A Different Ladies' Class** Early that year the ladies of our Thursday a.m. Bible class had asked me to teach the class using *The Challenge of*

*Being a Good Wife* by Ruth Hazelwood. Interest and participation were extremely good. A neighbor of Verna Hadfield's attended all the lessons and asked me to conduct the same class in her home with six of her friends. It turned out to be eleven friends and a very rewarding class with a full hour for discussion. All the ladies were Anglicans, including the local minister's wife. Following class we had visits over tea. The husbands of these women came from a variety of occupations including a dentist, an army officer, a medical doctor, a city official, a tanker driver who hauled petrol from South Africa, and a farmer who had moved his family to town because of the terrorists. We prayed constantly for their husbands in their work and as they each served their times in the Security Forces in the bush.

One day the tanker driver's wife said she wanted us to give special thanks for her husband who had just returned safely from South Africa with a tanker full of petrol, prominently labeled "Pet Milk." Terrorists didn't care about milk but wanted all the petrol they could hijack. On the way from the southern border, the convoy was ambushed. Military vehicles and lorry drivers stopped and with their shot-gun riders took to the ditch beside their vehicles, exchanging rifle fire with the ambushers. After a while the terrorists withdrew and drivers assessed the damage. The Pet Milk tank had been hit and petrol was spewing straight out from two bullet holes. The driver hastily chewed a whole pack of gum, plugged the holes with gum that stopped the leaks until they reached town where the petrol was unloaded. His wife said he always kept a good supply of chewing gum with him since he couldn't smoke in that lorry. He was sure his guardian angel had kept the petrol from exploding.

When I returned to the States I corresponded with the farmer's wife. They moved to South Africa where her husband was manager of several farms fairly near the border with Rhodesia. They did well for several years. Then Rhodesian terrorists sneaked across the border and killed him when he was working in the fields. She and their two children moved into the city where she got work. Not long afterwards we lost touch with each other.

**New Daughter-in-law** News from Benjamin in Oregon told of his engagement to Susan Henning from Southern California. They planned a September wedding. It grieved me sorely to miss that occasion but Margaret Ann filled in for me as Benjamin's mother. Meanwhile Susan and I got acquainted by mail.

**Cost Of Living Rises** In January I bought a 600gram tin of cocoa powder for $1.98 (R) or $2.98 U.S. Just seven months later the tin size had been reduced to 300grams that cost $3.95(R) or $5.92 U.S. So we drank more hot tea instead of hot chocolate. The price of beef had soared because of increased cattle rustling by terrorists. The prediction was that by the end of the year beef would be unavailable. When I got there in 1976 steak was much cheaper than chicken but now the price of both had gone up. Farmers were already slaughtering cattle and selling the meat rather than risk the loss of herds to terrorists. Fortunately we liked beans and corn-bread; the price of mealie-meal had also gone up but our vegetable garden still produced beans! Our borehole pump broke down in May. It was the dry season, repair men were scarce and by the time it was fixed the flowers and lawn were dead. For the first time since I arrived there the yard was brown.

**60ᵗʰ Anniversary** Daddy and Mother's 60ᵗʰ Wedding Anniversary arrived. We had a celebration for them complete with decorated cake, ice cream and punch. Mother sat in her wheelchair on the patio beside the decorated table and Daddy sat by her side while friends congratulated them. More than 60 people were present. There were speeches, singing and visiting. Paul and Janis with their boys, Foy and Margaret, Jim and Becky, Ella and Rhoda, church folks from all over Bulawayo, Kit Wiggill from his farm 150 miles away and other folks from near and far came to help celebrate the occasion. Tributes were spoken ending with one that Daddy wrote in honor of Mother. As he read his tribute there was not a dry eye:

# *On Our 60th Wedding Anniversary*

*Do not forget Mother who has stood by me and with me all these years. Mother, who has forgiven me for all my shortcomings and unthoughtfulness—all my failures. Mother, who has endured many long hours while I have been occupied in something which in the end may prove of not much value, the Lord is to be the judge of that. But mother endured those hours for love of me. More than that, mother endured those hours for the Lord, for we both loved the work of the Lord.*

*It was mother who encouraged me in the hour of trial. It was mother who helped me in facing and battling discouragement. And it was mother who gave such good council and advice in times of doubt. I thank God for such a companion through all these many years. Mother has been so good to me.*

*At our wedding reception a song was sung, "I'll Walk Beside You," and truly my love has walked beside me. In sorrow she has sorrowed with me, and comforted me. In joy she has rejoiced with me, and been my joy. She has given me many pleasures. She has given me help and encouragement all the way. She has indeed walked beside me and it has been an honor to me to be her husband.*

\*   \*   \*

September brought the beginning of rains. By then the borehole was repaired, the yard turned green and flowers bloomed again. All over town jacarandas, bougainvillea and other vines, trees, shrubs, flowers and especially roses bloomed in abundance. We rejoiced in the beauty around us and every trip to town or church was a multicolored scenic drive.

**South On Holiday** For some time Paul, Janis and I had planned to take a holiday the last two weeks of September, going south of the border to the edge of the Drakensburg Mountains. I asked Thomas Cook Travel Agency whether a Rhodesian-born American needed a visitor-visa for South Africa. The voice on the phone said, "Definitely not." So we blissfully proceeded with our plans. Foy and Margaret agreed to stay with our parents while we were gone.

On Friday before we were to leave on Monday I took out my passport to go for traveler's checks at the bank. Turning the pages I saw where I did get a visa for South Africa when I went eighteen months before; why hadn't I remembered or looked before? I mailed my passport to the South Africa Diplomatic Mission in Salisbury asking them to hurry with a renewal. We phoned motels and changed our bookings to a week later. Optimistically Paul, Janis and little ones came down on Thursday so we would be ready to leave as soon as my passport came back. It came on Friday—our changed bookings were exactly right.

Saturday morning we were up before 5:00 to catch the 7:30 armed convoy to the border. By 8:30 it was HOT. Paul listened with the other drivers to the instructions from the convoy leader. They were told if the convoy was attacked to keep going as long as the military vehicles did; drivers were to scoot down in their seats as low as possible to keep steering, and passengers were to lie down in the floor. There would be no stopping for a flat tire as long as the 55mph rate was maintained. If a motor car broke down completely one of the three military escort vehicles would stop to help and if possible fix the problem. If at all possible the drivers were to keep going as long as the military vehicles did. If attacked and our escorts stopped, then everyone was to get out of their motor car on the ditch side of the road and lie down as low as possible in the ditch until the attack was over. After Paul relayed all of that to us it was no wonder Janis and I had headaches by the time we started!

The 200 plus miles to the border was through the "low-veldt" and Paul's motor car was not air conditioned—very few were. By the time our convoy arrived at the half-way hotel for a rest stop, Janis and I were ready for a double dose of aspirin. The two little ones couldn't sleep because of the intense heat. By the time we got to the border and through customs and immigration lines on each side of the border, our heads were pounding again. At least from there on we were free from the terrorist threat and a convoy was no longer needed.

In the first little town on the South African side of the border we stopped to drink water and take more aspirin. Janis was pouring ice water from our big thermos jug while I held crying Doug on my lap and the cup in one hand. He kicked the cup and icy water spilled on his leg—he really screamed. Meanwhile Paul was doing what he could for fretting two-year old Benji. After 90 miles through more low veldt we reached Louis Trichardt in mountain foothills. There we had reservations at "Cloud's Inn Motel" for two nights. I cannot remember ever before feeling as weak on a trip. With Paul's help I made it inside to a bed where I lay with a wet cloth on my face. It was only a little cooler in the room but that little helped. While we all had baths we were drinking water like camels. By 4 p.m. a gentle breeze was blowing under big shade trees on the grounds and the round tables set for tea looked inviting. The cool breeze, afternoon tea and little sandwiches served by an attentive waiter worked wonders and things began to look better!

Sunday morning David and Joanne Beckley came by to take Paul and Benji with them to Vendaland for church services with the Africans. They told us the dirt roads through the low veldt were extremely dusty and the heat was unrelenting. Janis and I decided to stay at the motel; she didn't want to take Doug there and I still felt weak. They returned about 4 p.m. Cool baths and clean clothes again revived us all.

We had a communion service in our room and afterwards visited over afternoon tea while their boys and Benji played on the shady lawn. That evening the Beckleys took us to a new Spanish restaurant they wanted to try. Food was good but service was so slow we were there two hours. Fortunately we were not in a hurry and enjoyed visiting while we waited. Monday morning the Beckleys went with us to town to get a few necessitates then we took Kentucky Fried Chicken to their house for lunch. (Yes, KFC in South Africa!) After lunch we told them goodbye and drove on to "Blyde River Canyon Resort" where we had booked a chalet.

**Relaxing In The Mountains** There we spent four days relaxing, reading, studying and talking as we enjoyed the children enjoying the swimming pool during the hot days. We played some tennis with the children enjoying running all over the tennis court. We took turns having time off from the children and when it was my pleasure to baby-sit, Paul and Janis climbed and hiked in the nearby hills. We grilled supper three nights and generally had a lazy good time. On Friday, Natal's school holidays began and the chalets were booked up so we drove across the mountain 45 miles to a guest farm with rooms for only 16 people. It was not fancy but very restful. We could sit on the front verandah and enjoy beautiful mountain and valley scenery without even moving. We were within easy driving distance of any number of water falls, canyons, historical sights and the huge Kruger Game Reserve but we preferred to relax, just taking walks.

We chatted over coffee after dinner with the other guests. Sunday morning Paul, Janis and I had a communion service in our chalet. We left there on Wednesday, spent a night in Pietersburg with more shopping on Thursday. In the stores we walked around marveling at the many brands of items. We were only allowed to take back $50 each of duty-free goods—we couldn't afford more anyway. We bought only things we needed with a tiny bit of splurging on a few food items and chocolates for Daddy and Mother. There was good candy in Rhodesia but it was very expensive and one didn't buy things like that when one was at home! We needed a new electric teakettle again—standard equipment in that tea-drinking country.

After our experience on the way down we were dreading the last lap going home. We took our time leaving Louis Trichart Friday morning; Beckleys had gone to Jo'burg and left the key for us. We ate a picnic lunch in their kitchen while a blinding dust storm raged outside. We didn't dare open any windows, yet the fine red dust got in. Inside it was as hot as an oven but we preferred the heat to the choking red dust. We hurriedly cleaned up the kitchen and left to get away from the dust, reached the border about 3 p.m., passed through immigration and customs on both sides, then checked into a motel in time for afternoon tea. Saturday morning we caught the 7:30 a.m. convoy and drove home in the cool of a cloudy day with sleeping babies, very thankful for the uneventful last lap of a much enjoyed holiday.

Margaret had fixed lunch and after lunch Paul, Janis and boys drove home to Gwelo. A week later it hardly seemed possible we had ever been away but for the glow of pleasant memories.

With the double shift of Red Cross Nurse Aides, Daddy was happy for me to be away from the house for more studies. In addition to the extra ladies class still going on, I added two more home studies with women and joined in various other church gatherings I had missed for many months. Because of the higher cost of living Daddy had stopped the personal allowance he had been giving me each month and by this time he was able to pay for only one set of nurses. When we hired the second set I paid for them with money from the sale of my Honda.

**December 1979** The special ladies class ended in early December. School holidays began and families took their holidays (vacations). The European custom of four to six week annual holidays for employees was used there and many went to Europe or South Africa to visit relatives during that time. At our house excitement knew no bounds on Monday, December 17<sup>th</sup> when Margaret Ann arrived from California to spend three weeks. The same day Janis and two little ones came by bus from Gwelo and Paul motored down on Friday. Words could not express the joy and good time we all had together.

Margaret Ann sat a lot with Mother while Janis and I baked cookies, made candy and watched after two little boys. Doug learned to sit alone while they were there and Benji was a busy little boy. One particular day his independence caused us quite a scare. Janis and I suddenly realized he was out of sight. He was not in the house and within minutes we were all in the yard calling his name and searching frantically for him. Then Janis heard his voice, "Det hammah an' baws" and knew at once he was in Granddaddy's office trying to drag out his favorite play thing—the grown-up's croquet set. He had remembered from previous visits where to look for it. Granddaddy had not noticed Benji in the little side store-room where the croquet set was kept and had gone out locking the door. When he opened the door Benji was struggling to pull the heavy croquet set out, blissfully ignorant of having been locked in.

Ed was in the bush, so Genie and girls came for the day on the 26th, as did Jim and Becky. Foy and Margaret came for part of the day but Foy had a fever and they went home early. We had turkey and cornbread dressing, but no cranberry sauce (none in stores), green beans, corn, hot rolls, gravy, beet pickles, lettuce salad, Christmas Pudding with custard, and mincemeat pies. The weather was very hot but a cool breeze blew through the house most of the day. After dinner we took pictures and played horse-shoes and croquet in the shady yard.

Margaret Ann's childhood friend Caroline (deWet) Allen lived in Salisbury. Margaret Ann contacted her and she and her husband invited Margaret Ann for a weekend. She went up by train and had a wonderful visit. Her return was on the night train—running again by then. About 5 a.m. it was still dark but she knew they should soon be approaching Bulawayo. When the train stopped she looked out the window to see if there was a station but saw only darkness. She asked the conductor who was coming along the corridor, why they had stopped. He said the Bulawayo station-master had radioed word that ZAPU and ZANU (the opposing terrorist organizations) were having a battle in the Bulawayo township, shooting at each other across the railway line. The train had to stop until the battle died down. Margaret Ann curled up in the corner of her compartment to wait.

The train was due in Bulawayo at 7:30 or "round about that time" and I was to meet it. Daddy and I heard the guns and mortars. At first I thought it was thunder but Daddy said, "No, that sounds more like rifle and mortar fire." When I called the Railway Station I was told simply that the train was delayed. About 8:30 it seemed like the firing had died down so I went to town, parked in front of Haddon and Sly (department store) and went inside where quite a crowd was waiting for further developments.

About 9:30 a taxi pulled up and I was relieved to see Margaret Ann get out. She said when she got off the train no taxi would take her. She stood around for some time before a taxi driver, who had seen her waiting said,

"We could be in trouble if we take a white person but you want a ride—I want a fare—I will take you—please sit low down." She sat very low down and gave him an extra large tip.

While she was with us she told of an encounter she had in the Johannesburg airport on her way to Rhodesia-Zimbabwe. She had a long layover so she decided to sit beside a well dressed black man and be friendly. They exchanged greetings and found they were both waiting for the plane to Bulawayo. He learned she was the daughter of missionary parents on her way to visit them. When he heard that her father was W. N. Short, he asked how old he was and if he had traveled among villages long ago. She learned the man was born in a remote village in Rhodesia in the late 1920s or early 1930s. They decided that Daddy was the white man who had come to their village on a bicycle when this man was about eight years old, the first white man he had ever seen; he ran to hide but his father told him not to be afraid because this was a good man. As the boy had grown up he heard often about "Baba Shohti," as they called him. (Baba was a respectful Shona word for father.) After going through high school in Rhodesia this man had gone overseas for higher education and was now on his way to meet up and serve with Mugabe in his mission to free the country of white oppression.

Margaret Ann was eleven when I left home and in the forty years since then we had seen each other only briefly five times. We got reacquainted during her three-week visit and found out that we still liked each other—a lot! She spent time with Daddy asking questions about his boyhood and early life while I typed his answers. But all too soon her time was up and she was gone. The six weeks Christmas holiday ended, school started and everyone was back on schedule. I began home studies with three different ladies and resumed teaching Ladies Bible class on Thursdays.

**Government Unrest** Since the West did not recognize Muzorewa's government, another election was scheduled to take place, again with British and U.S. oversight. In London Lord Carrington was to oversee a conference with the three leaders. A three-way peace treaty was signed by the Muzorewa Government and Mugabe and Nkomo, stipulating that each of them would keep their forces within three widely separated designated camps—there was to be no terrorist activity during the conference. As the conference went on, something of vital importance to Rhodesia-Zimbabwe was left out of foreign news reports, but was factually *known* within the country. While Nkomo and Mugabe were stalling the talks in London, their terrorists within the country did not stay in their designated areas but were mingling among villages and in the townships, intimidating the people. Mugabe's men told villagers Mugabe would know whether they voted for him or not—if they voted for anyone but him they would be killed. Nkomo's faction was spreading terror in the same way. Meanwhile freshly trained young terrorists from Zambia and Mozambique were being equipped with uniforms and arms and put in the camps to look like they were obeying the peace-treaty terms. Only Muzorewa's Government Security Forces were observing the treaty and staying within their designated camp.

Lord Soames, from England, was in the country to oversee the election and he and the Zimbabwe—Rhodesian government and its Security Forces were leaning over backwards trying to make the agreement work out for a peaceful election. But it was being undermined in London by Mugabe's and Nkomo's haggling and stalling. During that time Foy's house-servant was beaten severely in the township one weekend because he failed to give the "Nkomo sign." Muzorewa had been elected by a huge majority in April. If those people stuck to him in spite of intimidation, there was a good chance he could win again. However, with the intimidation and atrocities going on among the villages and townships it seemed unlikely. We took solace knowing Almighty God knew what was in men's hearts and controlled their final destiny.

On a Friday, the last day of the elections, Paul called to say that Janis was very sick with high fever and was being treated by the doctor for mastitis. Little Doug was sick with the "tummy bug" from which Paul had just recovered. That sounded like an S.O.S. to me. I asked Margaret and Foy to take over with our parents, lend me a motor car and let me go to help my children. Within four hours after Paul called I was on the way, praying fervently that the Lord would protect me on the road we had been told to stay off of unless absolutely necessary. The heavy traffic I saw on the highway was reassuring and I arrived at Paul's in time for four o'clock tea.

By the next Wednesday Doug was well and Janis was much improved. With great fortitude I now curb my inclination to tell of cute things two little grandsons did while I was there—but one I must tell! Benji told me about watching with his mother while Paul and his Civil Defense Fire Brigade buddies demonstrated their equipment and training at the municipal swimming pool. With excited voice and expressive hand gestures Benji told me, *"Some men ran and jumped up on the ironing boards* (diving boards) *and the other men turned a big hose on and water whooshed on them and they fell in the swimming pool—SPLASH!"* Not surprisingly Benji spent much of his play time being a fireman with all the sound effects.

The sixth of March 1980 marked the end of my fourth year over there—four years since I had seen my children, grandchildren and friends in the U.S. Daddy told me that he wanted me to go to the States by the end of the year to see them. By that time it would be five years since I had told them goodbye and he felt that five years was long enough to be away from them without a visit. He said he was not sure just how it would be worked out but he was praying to that end and wanted me to plan on it. Little did we know what would happen before the end of the year.

The elections were over and Robert Mugabe, the dreaded terrorist leader, was elected Prime Minister. No one was surprised in view of the atrocious acts his terrorist army had carried out among the villages. As soon as he was in power he began moving ex-guerillas from the assembly points (where they had been since the election and where they were supposed to have been during the conference in London) into empty houses in Salisbury and Bulawayo. They were allowed to retain their weapons and the crime rate in both cities soared.

**Home Changes** As Mother became more disabled she slept later, so Daddy and I had breakfast together at six o'clock. Then I went about my work and he went back to their room to sit on the side of his bed and read his Bible while he waited for Mother to waken. When she began to stir, usually about 9:30, he called the nurses. They bathed her, put her into the wheelchair and took her to the living room to give her breakfast.

June 30 began as usual—my day to go to grocery store, bank, chemist and any other errands that needed doing. I left Daddy sitting on his bed reading and went first to Foy and Margaret's house to tell them goodbye as they were leaving for Salisbury on their way to the U.S. on furlough.

About eleven o'clock, business done, I was driving home and met a motor car whose driver was waving at me to stop. It was a friend of the family. He said without preamble, "Your father is dead." I was so shocked I could only ask, *"What happened?"* He said, "Nothing. He just died as he was sitting on the bed." He said he had gone to visit Daddy and arrived as the ambulance pulled in.

I recognized the doctor's motor car and the Emergency Response Ambulance in our drive. The nurses met me at the door and told me what had happened. They had looked into the room at 9:30 and again at ten, saw Daddy reading and didn't go in. At 10:30 when Daddy hadn't called them, they went to investigate. He was still sitting with his Bible in his lap but when they touched him, he fell over sideways on the bed and they saw that he was dead. They had no way of reaching me and had called our doctor and the medics. The doctor told me there were no sign of struggle or pain and that evidently Daddy's heart just stopped. Edward wrote about his Granddaddy's death, *"It was as if God said to him, 'We're closer to my house than we are to yours: just come on home with me.'"*

Foy and Margaret had already left Bulawayo but I knew they planned to stop in Gwelo so I called Paul with the news. He told Foy and Margaret, who turned around and came back, delaying their furlough until after the funeral. The Memorial Service was held at Hillside church where a large crowd gathered. Ray Votaw was in Rhodesia at the time and spoke at the service expressing his high regard for Daddy, recalling his dedication to the

Lord's work evidenced by his years of work in many parts of the country and the high esteem in which he was held while he lived, as shown by the constant stream of men who visited him seeking his counsel. Foy spoke on behalf of the children; Jim and Paul spoke for the grandchildren, and long-time friends gave talks and led prayers. His ashes were placed in the Memorial Wall in Bulawayo.

Later I was questioned by someone as to why Ray Votaw had a part in the service since it was common knowledge that he and Daddy had disagreed strongly on some doctrinal opinions and at some time in the past had exchanged heated words. I told the questioner that in all my times with them through the years neither Daddy nor Ray had *ever* said anything to me about any of that—*ever*. I told the questioner that what I did know personally was that the previous year when Ray was up from South Africa he had come to see Daddy and they had a long talk in Daddy's office. When they came to the Living Room for tea they said that Ray had come to ask for Daddy's forgiveness for his harsh words of years before and Daddy had confessed his own fault in that and asked for Ray's forgiveness. They had prayed together and agreed that in the future they would disagree with respect and love. They had parted with expressions of appreciation for each other's love of the Lord.

**Mother's Reactions** It seems unthinkable to me that I cannot recall whether we took Mother to the Memorial Service or not, but surely we did. Foy and I tried to tell Mother about Daddy's death but she made no response. As days went by sometimes she looked around the living room and asked me, "Where's Daddy?" When I replied, "He died, Mother, he's gone to be with the Lord," she said, "Oh." That was all she said and in a day or two she asked the same question again.

Margaret Ann knew Foy and Margaret were in the States and she wanted to help. She took a six months leave of absence without pay from her job as Electrical Mechanical Designer at Litton Industries and came over to help us. She arrived in August and what a blessing she was. As the weeks passed, the fact of Daddy's death seemed to gradually become real to Mother. She talked about being the only one left now that he was gone and said she wanted to go home. We asked her where home was and she said with surprise, "Why, Cordell, of course." She enjoyed visitors some of the time but other times she didn't seem to realize they were around and often did not recognize them.

One day Margaret Ann and I were sitting across the room from her so she could see we were with her.

Mother looked hard at Margaret Ann and asked, "Who are you?"

Margaret Ann said, "I'm Margaret Ann, your daughter."

Mother: "How did that happen?"

Margaret Ann looked at me, "What do I say now?"

Pointing at Margaret Ann, I said, "Mother, this is Margaret Ann. She is your *youngest* daughter. I am Sybil, your *oldest* daughter."

"Oh!" Mother replied, seemingly satisfied.

"That was easy!" Margaret Ann commented.

Major decisions needed to be made and I was thankful to have Margaret Ann there to help me. After many prayers and considering all possibilities and circumstances, it seemed best to take Mother back to the States—if at all possible to Cordell Christian Home. On their last furlough in the U.S. she and Daddy had visited her brother, George, in the Cordell nursing home. George by then was bedfast and didn't know anyone and Mother told Daddy that she wanted to go there if she got like George. In the U.S. Foy, Beth and Bill worked to that end.

**Ann Gray** In the midst of all this activity, early one morning the phone rang and I answered. A shaking voice said, "Ahnty Sybil, this is Ann. My mother shot herself." I was shocked almost speechless but I assured her I would come to her at once. When I told Margaret Ann she said, "I'm going with you," and I was glad to have her. Mr. Gray had died from a heart attack the year before and Mrs. Gray had been severely depressed. Ann had seemed to mature amazingly in trying to help her mother. We reached the Gray home right behind the ambulance. Mrs. Gray was not dead but she died a short time after they got her to the hospital. Ann, with the help of her maid, had already called her brother and two sisters in South Africa; they said they would come immediately. As soon as they could after the funeral, they took Ann with them to South Africa.

**Going Home Preparations** Meanwhile Thomas Cook and Sons, Travel Agent, told us that Mother would have to travel as a stretcher patient taking up six or eight first class seats and that the air lines required a medical attendant. Jim's wife Becky was to finish her internship as gynecologist in the Salisbury hospital November 21 and she agreed to attend Mother on the trip. To the best of our ability we estimated costs involved and wrote to the churches that had supported our parents through many years. They promised to raise travel funds and to keep supporting Mother. They and other friends in the U.S. began sending money. The airline needed advance booking with payment up front for that type of flight. Though we didn't have all the necessary money yet, we booked their flight for November 28th and prayed for the money to come by the specified date.

God gave me strength and with Margaret Ann's encouragement, I went to our bank to borrow the needed money for Mother and Becky's expensive tickets. I was ushered into the presence of the Bank Manager. He expressed sympathy over Daddy's death and spoke of his respect for him through the more than twenty years of dealings. He listened intently as I told him the whole story of our need. He was already aware of Mother's deteriorating condition during the past several years.

I told him she was booked to leave November 28th and that the house was to be sold but the transaction could not be expected to be complete by then—it wasn't even in the works yet. The manager looked at me and said, "In other words, you are asking for a loan and have no tangible security?" Before I could answer he went on, "I have done business with your father long enough that I trust the word of his daughter. How much do you want and how long do you want it for?" I asked for the estimated amount needed, that sounded to me too much to expect approval. But without a word he turned to his intercom and gave instructions to have that much put in my account at once. Then he turned to me, "My secretary will have papers ready for you to sign on your way out. It has been my pleasure doing business with you." I could hardly wait to tell Margaret Ann and drove home giving thanks to God.

**Needed Surgery** In Alabama in 1975 I had fallen and jammed my right thumb. I thought it would get better on its own but from the time I had arrived in Rhodesia in 1976 it had given me trouble and was getting worse all the time. I could hardly hold a piece of paper and had trouble typing. The orthopedic surgeon in Bulawayo said he could repair it with surgery. After Margaret Ann settled in, I entered the hospital. If I had known how painful the after-surgery would be, I might have put it off. The surgeon told me the procedure he had done was called a "trapezium carpectomy." He said there was a chip of bone in the joint irritating it and causing considerable arthritis and he had removed all of that. For weeks it hurt more than I can describe and continued painful for three years—but my grip was restored gradually over that time.

**The Future?** One day Margaret Ann said, "What do you intend to do when you get back to the States?" I told her I hadn't decided yet other than to try to find a job in Cordell. She said, "If you don't get that job, why don't you come to California and share my house?" The more we talked about it the more we thought it was a good idea—if I couldn't get a job and live nearer Mother.

Blessed, beautiful, bountiful rains began in November! We had not seen a drop since April. An interesting thing was that the gloriously-colored flowers and trees did not wait for the rains but started showing up as soon as the weather turned warmer in September and especially in October. There were so many blooming trees and shrubs that folks with allergies, including Margaret Ann, had a hard time.

After five years in that country, Paul, Janis and boys returned to the States. The joy of being on the same continent was ended but not the many memories of times shared.

**The Dietrichsens** During the 1960s when the little magazine, *Rays of Light,* was still being edited, printed and mailed to hundreds of subscribers by Daddy, there was a couple at church, about his and Mother's ages, who wanted to help. Every month Daddy went to get Mr. and Mrs. Dietrichsen and the four of them sat at the dining table, stapling, folding and inserting the papers ready for mailing. Afterwards they ate dinner together and visited before Daddy took them home. The Dietrichsens didn't have a car and were picked up for church by volunteer members. When the volunteers left the country Daddy began picking them up on Sunday mornings.

Both Mr. and Mrs. Dietrichsen were retired from the Rhodesian Railroads, having spent most of their active lives on trains. They told some interesting stories during our visits. They said they were very irreligious during that time but after their retirement, when they settled in Bulawayo, they met Christians and turned to the Lord. I think I never met anyone more whole-hearted in their commitment to Christ.

Their health deteriorated and their pension was limited though it did include medical coverage. When I knew them they were living in a small apartment where they both stayed busy. They collected string from anything that came in sewn sacks (potatoes, salt, flour) that neighbors threw away. Mr. Dietrichsen separated the strands of string, spliced the pieces into long fine yarn that he rolled in balls. From the yarn Mrs. D (as we called her) crocheted beautiful, intricate doilies, antimacassars, baby jackets and even a jersey for herself. They had two sewing machines, his was an ancient hand-turned model, hers an antique electric one, both table-top versions. People gave them cast off clothing or scraps from which she made children's shirts and dresses for the needy. From her left over scraps he pieced cushion covers on his sewing machine. Our Ladies Bible Class members found homes for some of the things that they made.

. Then Daddy died and it was up to me to do what I could for the Dietrichsens. Several nights the phone rang after midnight when one or the other of them was suddenly taken ill and needed to go to the E.R. (Taxies, their former way of travel, had become too expensive.) Someone said, "They are using you," and my response was that we would never know and I would rather be "used" than to fail to respond to a real need.

During my last visit Mrs. Dietrichsen told me to look around their living room and pick out something to take as a keepsake. I was reluctant to take anything from them but she insisted and I chose a metal tea-tray with a picture of a South African farmstead on it. She said, "That's not enough, take something else better than that!" I asked her about a pair of candle holders that were obviously hand carved as many of their curios were. They were black and very heavy so I knew they had not been inexpensive but she seemed so genuinely glad for my choice that I took them with many thanks and promises to remember our times together. She and I corresponded regularly until they both died from pneumonia in 1988, within two weeks of each other.

**My Last Newsletter** With my own time in Africa drawing to an end, as I wrote what would be my last newsletter, I thought of how I would miss watching for things to write about. I thought of things I would miss: early morning tea; squeezing the middle of the tough toothpaste tube then using pliers to turn up the end; air-bricks in walls letting in cool air in summer and *cold* air in winter; wall-spiders coming out on bedroom walls at night like peeping-toms; seeing thousand-legged chongololos crawling over the yard after rains; being called "Ahntee Sybil" by all acquaintances under 18; being a minority in a ratio of 20 to one black and white; and hearing "My pleasure!" when thanking anyone. And I would miss getting letters. For five years letters from "home" had done more than any one could know to keep homesickness at bay.

**Gearing Up To Wind Down** Word came that arrangements had been made for Mother to be admitted to Cordell Christian Home. It had been a hard decision for us to make—we all wanted her to be in one of our homes, but we all had to work for our living and she needed full time care for which we would have to hire full time nurses. On the long journey Becky would be Mother's medical attendant. Foy and Margaret would meet them in New York, ready with ambulance to make the change of airports and help during the unavoidable eight-hour layover. Beth and Bill would meet them in Oklahoma City with an ambulance to complete the trip to Cordell and watch over her admission into the Home. We liked to think that Mother might even recognize some old acquaintances there.

I booked my flight for December 5th, trusting that the house would sell and everything else would work out by then. Margaret Ann already had her own return ticket and we booked her on the same flight. The house was up for sale and Margaret Ann and I continued the huge task of sorting and packing things to be put in storage for Foy and Margaret—including Daddy's more than 2,000-book library. Out of what they did not want we picked some sentimental things and packed two steamer trunks and a wooden crate—one trunk shipped to Beth and the others to Margaret Ann's address for us.

November 28th Becky and Mother were taken to the airport by ambulance. Margaret Ann and I with the nurses followed in the motor car to see them off. Becky had Mother's passport, I had her other official papers.

With three weeks to spare our plans were complete. Margaret Ann and I would wind up affairs and take flight December 5th. We would spend a few days in South Africa with childhood friends, John and Cecilia duPreez. After a few days in southern England we would land in Windsor, Ontario, December 20th. From there Margaret Ann would go on to California. The Sewell Halls would meet me and I would spend Saturday and Sunday with them in Michigan, then fly to Huntsville, Alabama Monday 22nd. It all sounded very matter-of-fact in a letter to family and friends but my feelings were far from matter-of-fact. I was leaving Africa again, moving into another major life-change. I would be seeing my children and their families after five years—would we look very different to each other?

**The Lord Provides** The response of our parents' supporting churches and many dear friends was truly amazing. Every day Margaret Ann or I eagerly went to the mailbox to see what had come. The day before my note was due at the bank we totaled and figured and realized that several thousand dollars was still lacking. She said, "What are we going to do?" I told her, "We still have tomorrow morning's mail; we'll keep on praying hard. I believe the Lord will provide—I'm not sure how, but I believe He will." The next morning we watched for the mailman on his bicycle. We saw him put something into our box and she said, "*You* go see what's there!" I opened the lone envelope with shaking hands. There was a letter from our parents' life-long friends I recognized from letters they had exchanged through all our lives. They said they had decided to take an amount out of their savings to help their dear friends and their check for that amount was enclosed. It was the *exact* amount that was lacking! I cried with thanksgiving as I hurried back to show Margaret Ann, then I made a triumphant trip to the bank to repay the loan.

The house and furnishings sold for reasonable prices considering the changed situation in the country. Last of all we sold Daddy's station wagon to an African who said he planned to use it for a taxi—we could imagine the fifteen or more passengers that could be crowded into that Chevrolet Station Wagon. We gave Wilson and Aaron their last pay with a good bonus, thanked them for their loyal service and told them goodbye. Aaron had told us he wanted to buy a cow when he left and Margaret Ann admonished him to be sure he bought a cow and not something to drink out of a bottle! Wilson said he planned to work as a builder and would buy tools. They said they were very sad to see us go.

Dear friends for many years, Fred and Rose Stevens, invited Margaret Ann and me to stay with them the last two weeks. When everything seemed lined up for our leaving we had a few days left and decided to do a mini-tour of Rhodesia (we could not yet bring ourselves to call it Zimbabwe). As an adult Margaret Ann had not seen much of the country. She wanted to see the Matopo Hills and spend a night in the famous five story, semi-circular Manamatopa Hotel in Salisbury. Jim kindly let us borrow his motor car for our tour.

We spent a night in Midlands Hotel in Gwelo and contacted Kit Wiggill and his wife, Mary. They invited us to lunch and we had a pleasant visit. In the front yard of their fortified farm home was a large concrete slab clearly marked as a rescue helicopter pad. What amazed us were the fortifications inside the house: in the living room and in each bedroom, two feet in front of the windows, was a two-bricks-thick wall extending two feet on either side of each window and two feet above it. This wall would help protect the interior of the house from mortar fire or grenades thrown in through the window. Deep within the house was a concrete room equipped with radios to where the family could retreat in case of attack. A high security fence with locked gate surrounded the whole property including the laborers' compound. Their place was typical of the farm homes in those days and to us it was a sad reflection of the country's deteriorated condition.

We thoroughly enjoyed our tour and were back in Bulawayo at the Stevens' home on the 4th. They told us the lady in charge of my travel documents at our bank had phoned, urgently asking that I see her before closing time that day. The bank closed at 1:00 and it was already 11:00. I hurried to town praying for a parking place in front of the bank. The lady said one of my papers had been returned from Salisbury because it needed an affidavit signed by the consul. There was no consul in the country but an attorney was registered to do that and had done papers for Daddy. I rushed (ran!) across the street to his office and met him leaving for the weekend on a fishing trip. He obligingly returned to his office, signed the proper paper and I scooted back to the bank.

The immigration department in Salisbury would send an acknowledgment when they received that paper—but there was no more time. The helpful lady called Salisbury, assured them the needed paper was signed and on its way to them. She then turned to me, "I know everything is now in order even though that paper will not get back in time for your flight tomorrow. I'm stamping your passport *Cleared For Departure*. Now go to the far window and get your money. Don't volunteer anything, just hand the man your passport and tell him how much money you have in your account. He will give it to you. Don't volunteer anything." I did as I was told, received my money, and walked out just as the bank door was being locked. My racing heart took longer than that to slow down!

I had kept Mother's papers with mine—a blue one for money clearance, a green one for some other clearance, a brown one certified Income Tax was paid, and a pink one cleared a widow leaving the country. I had Mother's pink one but unfortunately my pink one was the one held up in Salisbury. I put all our papers together in one large envelope and the next day Fred and Rose took us to the airport. Would immigration stop me because my pink one was missing? I walked up to the Immigration desk, pulled all the papers partly out as I handed the envelope to the Officer saying, "My mother has gone on as a stretcher patient and I'm carrying her papers with mine." He flipped through the papers saying, "Brown, Pink, Green, Blue—good!" and stamped my passport! Whew!! Customs didn't take long—I was cleared to go.

Margaret Ann was ahead of me on the other side of a curtain listening to it all, wondering if I would get through. When I joined her we both breathed easier but it was not until we were up in the air that we finally felt free. Then and there I decided I would never ever try to be an undercover agent!

In South Africa our friends of many years ago on the farm, John and Cecilia (deWet) duPreez, gave us a good time before sending us on our way. In London we hired a motor car that Margaret Ann insisted I drive. It was Saturday. We drove to Tunbridge Wells, Kent, checked into a Bed and Breakfast and scouted for a church to attend the next day. Sunday morning we parked a short distance up the street from the church building to watch people arriving. All the people we saw go into the building were black—no problem—we went in and took a seat about half way down. In a congregation of about 130, besides us there was one white man and his small daughter. The singing and sermon were inspiring and we were welcomed cordially. We went on our way glad to have been there.

For four days we wound our way through the country roads purposely avoiding the main highways. It was December and we could see through the hedged fences to the interesting houses and gardens. We spent one night in a large Manor Hotel that had long, long ago been the Royal summer retreat. That evening we dressed for dinner and pretended to be "royalty" descending the wide winding staircase to the Dining Room where we enjoyed the fabulous dinner that was included with "Bed and Breakfast." At Portsmouth we toured Lord Nelson's ship, *The Victory.* We saw the White Cliffs of Dover, intending to cross the Channel to Calais but the weather was too bad. We visited Canterbury Cathedral then hurried to see Salisbury Cathedral. We drove to a Devonshire Tea Room to fulfill our dream of eating Scones with Devonshire Clotted Cream and Strawberry Jam with cup after cup of tea. Before we knew it our time was up and we were back in Gatwick Airport.

Sewell and Caneta Hall met our plane in Windsor, Ontario, and we saw Maggie off to Los Angeles before going to their home in Michigan for the weekend. What joy to be with them again! At the Huntsville, Alabama airport I saw my group waiting: Edward and Sara Faye, Melanie and Jeremy; Henry and Jo Ann, Lee, Eric and Leslie; Nancy and Raymond, Tonya and Chris. I looked at ten-year-old Eric, remembering our conversation when he was nearly five and had told me that I would not know who he was when I came back. So I asked, "Who are you?" and he said, "I'm Eric!"—just like we had talked about five years before.

During the five years in Africa I ended many letters to family and friends in the States with these two scriptures:

Proverbs 25:25: *As cold water to a weary soul, so is good news from a far country.*

I Thessalonians 1:2, 3: *We give thanks to God always for you all, making mention of you in our prayers, remembering without ceasing your work of faith and labor of love, and patience of hope in our Lord Jesus Christ in the sight of our God and Father.*

My sojourn in that "far country" was ended. I was back on American soil but my life was far from settled. What lay in store for me as I turned the page to another life?

# PART V

## CALIFORNIA

# 1981-1983

Being back in Alabama fresh from five years in Africa took some getting used to. My children looked much like they did when I last saw them, but the grandchildren had been growing all that time and there were some I had not seen before except in pictures. At first the older ones eyed me cautiously then warmed up and began talking to me. The younger ones didn't know what to think of this strange woman who suddenly appeared in their lives wanting to hug them. I spent two weeks with each family, beginning in Alabama with Edward, Sara Faye, Melanie and Jeremy; Henry, Jo Ann, Lee, Eric and Leslie; Nancy, Raymond, Tonya and Chris. Two weeks was much too short a time to get caught up on some of what I had missed during the past five years. When I told them of my plans to live with Margaret Ann in California unless there was a job opening in Cordell, Oklahoma, Nancy asked why I didn't settle near them. I reminded her of their history of moving often and told her if I settled there and they moved across the country somewhere, where would that leave us?

I flew to Florida to visit Robert, Dianne and Bobby in Jacksonville. Robert, a car salesman at the time, sold me a Toyota Corolla and I drove to Longwood near Orlando to visit Paul, Janis, Benji and Doug. Two weeks at each place was far too short a time before I was headed back to Athens to get my belongings and continue westward.

Valdosta, Georgia was on the way north so I stopped at the church there for Wednesday evening service, prepared to spend the night in a motel. That church had helped support Daddy and Mother during their many years in Africa and had promised to continue their support of Mother and I thanked the elders on her behalf. The preacher was much younger and didn't know my parents personally but he invited me to spend the night in his home. At the house he introduced his wife then she disappeared and he showed me to a room. No food was offered and I was glad I had eaten before I got to church—they had probably eaten before church, too. I had the feeling their hospitality was somewhat grudging with no word of what to expect the next morning but perhaps his wife was mad at him or they had never had a "foreign missionary" there before. I was up and ready to leave by 4:30 a.m., left a note on the bed saying "Thanks," and slid out silently before anyone appeared. I drove away thinking that for all they knew I might have been an "angel unaware"—but then decided my thoughts were less than angelic and shamed myself.

**Westward Ho!** At Edward's house in Athens I loaded the car and set out for Cordell, Oklahoma. I divided my route into approximately three-hundred-miles-per-day segments that allowed me to spend a night with dear friends and kin on the way—the Sam Binkleys in Columbus, Mississippi, Ida Andrews in Palestine, Texas and my Uncle Clarice in Harper, Kansas. At each place I enjoyed a refreshing, heartwarming visit. On the fourth day I reached Cordell, Oklahoma to spend the afternoon with Mother in Cordell Christian Home. She did not seem to recognize me but talked a little. I visited a while with her niece, my cousin, Frances Rieter and husband Mac, whose mother was also in the Home. Frances assured me that she visited there nearly every day and would certainly visit Mother and keep an eye out for her welfare. She and Bro. Redwine, Daddy and Mother's special friend for many years, had told me that jobs were scarce and what were available were filled immediately by local people in Cordell and vicinity. Taking their advice to forget about settling there, I drove on to Beth's home in Amarillo, Texas.

Darkness came on soon after I left Cordell and I became dangerously sleepy. I pulled in at a truck stop to get black coffee, a coke and "stay-awake" candy—my recipe for driving alertness. I reached Beth's by midnight. Margaret Ann was already there, having flown from Los Angeles. Our two days with Beth were gone much too quickly. Margaret Ann and I left about 3:30 a.m. to get as far on our way as possible while we were fresh.

With Interstates all the way, a three-week-old car, two drivers taking turns, and never running out of things to talk about, we pulled into her driveway in Newbury Park, California within our estimated twenty-four hours.

Margaret Ann had been divorced for almost twenty years. She had been living in Simi Valley but had sold her house there and recently moved to Newbury Park. She worked at Litton Industries in Guidance and Control Systems as an Electro Mechanical Draftsman, recently promoted to Electro Mechanical Designer.

It was early March, 1981 when we began our life together. This would be a completely different lifestyle from any I had ever lived before. She and I wanted to have an understanding of what we could expect of each other and had a conference laying all our cards on the table. She would be our accountant. We would half the household expenses, including house payments, insurance and taxes. After we had discussed all we thought of, she said, "Just to have a complete understanding from the beginning I'm asking that you not preach to me about my spiritual life." I promised to abide by her wishes. We both knew she would not have invited me to share her home in the first place if she had thought I would do that!

The house plan was perfect for dividing our sleeping quarters, her room opened off the living room, mine was the larger of two rooms off a small hallway that opened into the den and we each had a bathroom. Before spending the first night I was already enjoying my California home.

**Job Hunting And Traffic** The first order of business for me was finding a job. At Margaret Ann's suggestion I signed up with three different temporary agencies. I found that office equipment had drastically evolved over the five years I had been in Africa. When I left The C.E.I. business in 1974 my IBM Selectric was the most up-to-date typewriter available and we had only heard of computers. How could things change so drastically in just five years? Fortunately for me the keyboard on the office machinery was practically the same as a typewriter. I told the temp agencies up front that I could type on a regular typewriter and do general office odd jobs. I pleased them with my speed in assembling papers and stuffing envelopes. Most offices had that kind of work and most applicants didn't want it.

**Maggie and Sybil in their back yard, 1981.**

At each place there were opportunities to learn on the modern machines and in spite of being 58 years old, to the surprise of my supervisors, I learned quickly. One of the employers' office supervisor took time to show me how to work on a computer making thousands of repetitious entries because of an error made by a previous operator. She told me she was tired of putting young girls on that job and them complaining of boredom and she thought perhaps I would have more patience. It was a simple, tedious task and I stuck with it until it was done. As each job drew near the agreed expiration time, some places asked me to stay longer and renewed my contract; others offered full time work which I declined—I didn't enjoy working where language was as foul as any I had ever heard. Margaret Ann said I needed to understand that might be the same everywhere, but I kept working temporary jobs and hoping.

My work required another adjustment—driving on freeways and learning my way around streets in strange areas. At first the frantically busy freeways were extremely intimidating to me. Margaret Ann taught me how to adjust my speed to drive onto and on them. Every day we both had to take a freeway to get to and from work—she to Litton 26 miles away and I to nearer work places—some in Thousand Oaks, others in West Lake Village. Every morning we left home early enough to avoid the big traffic rush and every evening after work I waited in my car in the parking lot reading a book until I felt the worst rush was over.

**Church** Churches of Christ were plentiful. I visited different ones, some only once, some more than once but for some time I didn't find one where I wanted to place membership. I went somewhere every Sunday and Margaret Ann went with me many times, often to show me the way in the strange-to-me area where she had lived so long. Benjamin and Susan lived in an apartment about three miles from us and went with me quite often.

**African Friends** In June 1981 Ian Allen, husband of Caroline deWet, Maggie's close friend since childhood, sent word from New York that he and his friend, Alan Nichols, were in the U.S. Both had lived in Rhodesia (Zimbabwe) all their lives. They had been brought over from Zimbabwe by the U.S. government to take a course in communications at Cornell University in Ithaca, N.Y. Their lecturers were amazed at how much they were already doing in that field in Zimbabwe and had been for more than twenty years and said they wished all of the teachers and pupils of the course could go to Zimbabwe and see for themselves how the things they were teaching were actually being put to use along with some good ideas they did not have. People who talked to the two men had been surprised at how un-racist they were—that "whites were actually friends with and trying to help the blacks." Ian's father had begun the Agricultural Development Program in the 1930s. Ian and Alan said people had been very friendly with them after they found out they were not the "bigoted racists" they had expected of white men coming from Zimbabwe. We gave them my room and our guest room across the hall and I moved in with Maggie for three weeks.

Co-workers of Margaret Ann wanted to meet some "real live Africans" so we invited them to afternoon tea one Saturday. Over tea and talk Margaret Ann and I enjoyed watching the reaction of the Americans. Sunday morning Ian and Alan went with us to church but Alan stayed outside waiting for us. Ian said he really enjoyed the sermon and asked a lot of questions during lunch. He asked if I had called the preacher to tell him to preach on that particular subject! I didn't even know the preacher's name!

We had become acquainted with several ex-Rhodesians living in our area and invited them over for a Sunday afternoon visit while Ian and Alan were with us. Among them were the two school teachers I had met in January at Paul's in Florida. They were staying temporarily with a family of ex-Rhodesians, Jan and Winnie Wennink and their children. Also Winnie's parents were visiting them from Holland. They were formerly Dutch settlers in Indonesia who had been POWs of the Japanese during WWII. Winnie was born in the POW camp and her father had survived the infamous "Death March" in Burma. After the war they immigrated to Rhodesia where Winnie met Jan whose father had settled there after being sent to Rhodesia while in the in the Royal Air Force. Years later Winnie and Jan had moved to California. Now their daughter, Paula was just finishing high school.

Though the folks from Rhodesia had never met before, the afternoon was filled with excited talk as they found out that they knew people each other knew and went to school with, or their kids had. Benjamin and Susan came with Aaron, as did Margaret Ann's sons Tim and Greg with his family and they thoroughly enjoyed hearing the interesting stories and different accents.

Margaret Ann and I were off work that Monday. We went with Ian and Alan to Disney land and Knott's Berry Farm sixty miles from our house. They persuaded us to ride the Matterhorn train which we had said we would not do, or anything *like* it. Afterwards we *knew* we would not do that again nor anything like it! When would I ever learn? While Margaret Ann and I were at work they bought and installed patio lights for us as a "Thank-you." This was exceedingly generous, considering the fact they bought almost all meals and paid our way into everywhere we went that cost anything. We argued but not too much!

**New Wardrobe** Summer was coming on and I didn't have anything to wear to work or on Sunday, having only brought a very few clothes with me from Africa during the winter. For years Margaret Ann had been wearing pants almost all of the time, but she decided she wanted to change her image and wear more skirts and dresses. We shopped sales and outlet stores every weekend until we both had a reasonable wardrobe. Not long after she began wearing her new clothes to work she was asked to host the Manager's Club Evening at Litton—she said it was the first time anything like that had happened in all her nearly twenty years working there and attributed it, in part at least, to her new image.

**Mary Kay Consultants** Margaret Ann was a Mary Kay Consultant on evenings and Saturdays using the name "Maggie." The name stuck and ever since then, she has been Maggie to me. She recruited me as a reluctant consultant and I worked evenings and Saturdays at that for several months. During my C.E.I. days in Athens I had vowed never to be a salesperson other than possibly "clerking" in a retail store, but she convinced me this was not "selling" it was simply "demonstrating" and therewith she "sold" me! She did very well and I did fairly well! It did give me some extra income. The Mary Kay Jamboree was held at Anaheim Convention Center at that time and I worked extra hours at my day job so I could take off two days to attend it with Maggie and Vonnie, also a consultant.

**Sentimental Moments** Toward the end of July our crate and trunk arrived from Africa—eight months after we shipped them from Bulawayo. Maggie and I excitedly unpacked and spread things around the living room and dining room so we could look over them and rehearse the memories they evoked. Then we displayed them throughout the house to keep enjoying. We were relieved to hear from Beth that her trunk had also been received.

**Jolly Nephew** Jim Short, Foy's son, was teaching in a high school in Ojai about fifty miles away. He came to visit fairly often and was always a joy. One notable weekend followed by a holiday Monday, he came on Saturday afternoon and spent two nights with us. Monday at 5 a.m. he took Maggie to LAX to catch her plane to Amarillo, saving me from a scary (to me) trip in L.A. traffic. She could fly very inexpensively since Vonnie was a flight attendant and every few months Maggie flew to Amarillo to go with Beth to visit Mother in Cordell and return the following day.

That evening Jim and I ate supper with Benjamin and Susan and had a "jolly good time!" as we used to say in Rhodesia. The next day Jim went home and that evening there was a message on our answering machine from Andrew Townsend, who was in L.A. from Zimbabwe. He said Jim had told him he was sure we would put him up at our house—nice to have a reputation for hospitality! Andrew was in California looking for work and a place to live, hoping to bring his family over. He had been a farmer in Zimbabwe, living in a fortified farm house and several times had fought off attacking terrorists. He wanted to get his family away from that situation and thought California was a likely place. He was with us only overnight and enjoyed our "den-couch-hospitality."

**Benjamin And Susan** How I did enjoy spending time with Benjamin and Susan, sharing meals, baby-sitting Aaron occasionally, going to church together and just knowing they were near. When Maggie was with her children in Santa Barbara I often spent time with Benjamin and Susan, sometimes at their house, sometimes at mine and other times driving to the coast to "whale watch" or just to see the ocean. There the wind was usually cold and while Susan walked, Benjamin and I sat in the van talking and keeping Aaron. Enjoying Aaron so much made me realize how much

I was missing all my other grandchildren and I was thankful to be near at least one of them.

**Kissing The Ground** One Friday evening Michael and his friend took Maggie and me to dinner at a Benihana Restaurant—a fun meal. Afterwards we decided to walk on the pier. We had to pass through a gate where the pavement had metal teeth that faced outward so cars could drive *out* safely but not *in*. We were walking *in*. As we walked across it my sandal caught on one of the teeth and my *foot* stopped but my body didn't. I executed a painful five-point landing—two hands—two knees—and face. My glasses were shattered. It was dark and for a few seconds my companions didn't even know I had fallen. It seemed a lot more than that to me as I lay there wondering if they would just go off and leave me! Sunday at church and Monday at work I looked decidedly the worse for wear, limping along with a black eye, skinned.

**A Fulltime Job** In October a call came from State Farm Regional Office in Westlake Village wanting me to fill in for an office-worker who was on two months maternity leave. This proved to be what I was looking for—in my initial interview I was told they did not allow profanity in the workplace. In February 1982 after six weeks with them I became a bone fide employee in the Agency Administration Department where we serviced 697 agents. This Regional Office was in a huge building housing all departments with a total of 1700 employees. There was a verandah around the whole building where I walked rapidly for exercise every day after lunch. This was my comfortable work place for eighteen months at which time I resigned to get married (but I'm jumping ahead!) I was number 13 in our office of all women except the boss. My children appreciated the number because our family's "lucky number" had been *thirteen* all through their growing up years with three of them born on the thirteenth.

My next-desk-neighbor was Joel Anderson, a woman about my age, originally from South Alabama. We clicked the first day. The more we found out about each other the more we enjoyed our time together—cemented by the fact that her youngest (a boy) and my youngest (a girl) were born on May 13, 1955 and each weighed 6 lbs.13 ounces at birth!

**New Experiences** In March of 1982 Edward was in L.A. on business and spent nights at our house. Benjamin met him at LAX. After work I picked up Kentucky Fried Chicken and a cherry pie, Maggie brought a salad and we joined them at Benjamin's house for a joyful evening talking, with Aaron providing entertainment. Edward carried one of my paintings back with him—a framed 30"x36" African scene that hangs in their living room to this day.

Pat Edwards, Maggie's friend of many years, was horrified to learn I had never been to a Big Screen Movie and took us to L.A. to see *Raiders of The Lost Ark*. I had to shut my eyes a lot—too much blood and too many snakes! I prefer smaller screens.

Sunday morning Pat went to church with us and the sermon was really thought-provoking on "recognizing eternity in our hearts." Once more I was accused of having called the preacher to tell him what to talk about because it was right down the line that Pat had been talking to us about on Friday evening when he exploded over some wickedness he had witnessed. Of course I had not done that but Pat obviously didn't believe me.

**Painting** Soon after I moved there Maggie had shown me a postcard seascape that she had saved since 1979 when she saw a large painting like it and wanted to buy it. It cost $3,000 so she just kept the postcard, hoping to someday get one painted like it. This was her chance. She asked me to copy it on a 36"x48" canvas to go behind the couch in our living room. By the time it was finished I wanted to continue painting. I gave my Mary Kay customers to Maggie and spent evenings and weekends painting when possible, working toward having enough to put some in an Art Exhibit. When we looked at the winners' entries we decided the judges all went for the Modern and Impressionist types, but it was fun anyway. My co-workers at State Farm threatened that if I didn't take each finished one to show them before disposing of it I would be in trouble! I did not do animals or people and occasionally someone looking at a picture asked where one or the other was. I told them the animals were behind the big rocks, or the horses were out to pasture and the people were behind me when I took the picture!

My second April there, Maggie and I water-colored hard-boiled Easter eggs for our grandchildren and I couldn't resist the temptation to paint pictures on mine. I enjoyed it so much that I painted extras. Maggie took some to her workplace and sold them for $15 each. At work I showed my 14"x16" oil painting of a little boy (back view!) on a pier looking out over the ocean. My supervisor said it looked exactly like her little boy and wanted to buy it for an anniversary gift for her husband. I sold it to her for $25. Maggie and Joel said I was not charging nearly enough for my paintings.

Joel's ex-husband and good friend, asked her what she wanted for her birthday. She told him she wanted a pair of my 14"x16" African scenes to hang over the buffet in her dining room. She instructed me to ask $55 each for them and he happily paid it! Those were just the beginning and I lost count of how many pictures I painted and sold besides the ones I gave away. I mainly painted African landscapes and did enough to give each of my six children one or more.

**Live Paintings** That August the Laguna Beach Art Festival was widely advertised and Joel and I decided to go. (Pat had bought a sail boat in Harbor City and Maggie had gone to help him sail it to the marina where he would keep it.) At the Festival Joel and I looked and walked and looked and walked until we were exhausted but didn't want to overlook anything. We were thankful when it was time for the evening Art Pageant. Fifty paintings of the Great Masters were reproduced on a huge stage with live models made up as the people in the paintings. They looked for the world like huge paintings. Each one was shown for 90 seconds, long enough for us to see it well and during that time the models did not move a muscle. The special lighting dispelled all shadows that might have shown the figures as not belonging to the backgrounds.

**Income Tax Time** Early in the year Maggie took me to her regular tax man who did work in his home so we could conveniently go in the evening. He said since I didn't have any reportable income while in Africa I could average three of those years with my one year in California—so I got a refund of all that was withheld since I had begun work in California. That was a $721 godsend.

**Jim's Work** In Ojai Jim was preaching several sermons before beginning his fulltime work with the church there and that Thursday evening Maggie and I drove to Ojai to hear him and eat supper together afterwards. On Saturday Jim came to spend the afternoon with us and tell us about his recent trip preaching at various churches over the U.S. He said it seemed strange in Athens, Alabama, not to see a bunch of Fudges, but he enjoyed a visit with Henry and Jo Ann. Jim was determined to lose weight before his wife, Rebecca got there in December when she finished her Obstetrics time in Salisbury. He was on the Cambridge liquid diet and wanted to stick to it so Maggie and I bought some for ourselves and we three sat around the table *drinking* our evening meal from cans. It was the easiest "company dinner" we had ever prepared!

**A'sailing We Will Go** Maggie belonged to the Litton Sailing Club and invited me to go with her on two sailing trips. The first was with eleven others in a 50 foot sloop to Catalina Island. John, the captain, had told everyone to take Dramamine before we started and soon we were all lolling around the deck half asleep—one way for him to have a peaceful trip! We enjoyed a walking tour of Catalina and a picnic lunch in a park before time to set sail again. On the return trip we were wide awake and the captain allowed each one to steer. Exciting!

**Sailing.**

About a year later we were ready for another sailing day and Maggie checked at the club for a suitable captain. Our preference, John, was not available and she settled for Larry. We were to sail in a 30 foot sloop this time. Maggie and a co-designer named John, Sharon and her friend Michael, and Sigi (a recently met pen friend of mine) and I made up the "crew" with Captain Larry. We met at Marina Del Ray harbor and were told the 30-footer had gas in the bilge and we were assigned to a 28 foot sloop instead. It started up well and we motored toward the exit of the harbor. As we were passing out of the harbor Larry said, "I think we're about out of gas but since we need it only at the end of the day to get back into harbor it should be O.K." As we set sail for Paradise Cove we looked at each other and wondered about our skipper.

About two miles out he said he needed to go below to pump the bilge and Sigi, who was steering at the time, said he would go with him if someone else would steer. I volunteered to take a turn if Maggie, a seasoned sailor, would stand beside me. As he went below the skipper said, "Keep it on 270 degrees." I saw it was on 280 and just as I began turning it gently toward 270 he stopped and said, "No, put it on 280 so it won't heel so much while we're below." So I turned the wheel just a tad to get back to 280 but it went to 290 and I tried to bring it back but it kept going—to 300. The more I turned it the other way the more it went on to 360 and by then we were swinging around in a full circle. Thinking I was panicking and turning it the wrong way, Maggie pulled on the wheel the opposite way. She saw that I wasn't, and began helping me turn it the other way. The skipper came running up shouting, "What do you think you're doing?" and jerked the wheel out of our hands but the boat kept going in a circle in spite of his frantic turning of the wheel. Maggie and I just looked at each other.

Larry finally realized there was no connection between the wheel and the rudder. He yelled, "You men help me get the sails down!" Maggie knew as much as they did about that and helped them. Sharon and I crouched in a corner out of the way. One of the men looked in the chest for the emergency tiller and tried it but it didn't help. Michael crawled down into the chest where he could see the works and found where something had jammed. He worked it loose and could steer the boat by hand but the wheel still didn't work.

By then the skipper was very upset and not knowing what to do next, he shouted, "All women get below!" Well, Maggie bristled (as I would have expected) and climbed higher up on the deck out of their way to watch and help if she could. Sharon and I got deeper in our corner of the cockpit seat to make ourselves as invisible as possible; we were sure if we went below the gas smell down there, combined with the boat going in a tight circle, would make us seasick; we preferred to take our chances up top. If John, the captain on our other trip, had been our skipper and given that order, we would have obeyed him without question because we would have had confidence in his judgment, but we had lost all respect for Larry.

The order was barely out of Larry's mouth before he changed his mind and began giving everyone orders that didn't make sense to anyone. Fortunately the day was calm and clear and the water smooth. The men helped steer with the emergency gear, no longer going in a circle, and we began going forward on an even keel. The wind died, Larry started the motor and we all wondered if we had enough fuel to get back to harbor. We did—with a little to spare—and we safely tied at the slip. We spread our lunch on deck and enjoyed our picnic even though it wasn't at Paradise Cove, our original destination. To tell the truth we were very thankful we had not reached there under the circumstances because we saw a dark cloud rolling up in the northwest where we might have been. We helped scrub the deck, left everything ship-shape and went our separate ways home, vowing never again to sail with Larry as skipper.

**Home** Maggie's son Michael and daughter Sharon lived in Santa Barbara; Tim, and Greg with Jerri and children lived near us and Vonnie came from Kansas when she could. Benjamin, Susan and baby Aaron, were within a few miles. Maggie and I enjoyed each other's children and grandchildren and were glad they were getting to know each other better. When my children came for a meal I cooked—Maggie cleaned up. When hers came she cooked—I cleaned up. When they all came we all pitched in. When it was just the two of us she usually cooked and I cleaned up—an arrangement we both enjoyed.

**Trips** Occasional holiday weekend trips were highlights for us. On one such trip Joel and Doris Hostler, Sharon's mother-in-law, drove with Maggie and me up the coast in my car. Doris smoked and I told her I would appreciate her not smoking in the car, but that absolutely any time she felt the need of a cigarette she should tell me and I promised to pull off the highway where we would happily wait for her to enjoy her smoke. Good sport that she was, the plan worked and we had fun about it.

We decided on the spur of the moment that with four of us sharing a room and splitting the cost we could spend a night in the much talked about "Madonna Inn" where each room was named for a country and decorated typically of that country. We chose the Swiss or "Water Wheel Room." One wall was all natural big rocks with front porches and roofs of

Swiss Chalets built into them and little china figurines moving around on each porch. Among the rocks was a real waterfall with a waterwheel that turned on and off—we didn't keep it on very long because it splattered the bed. There was a cuckoo clock with little people that came out and circled back in every time it "cuckooed." The closet looked like a small Swiss outhouse and there were two king size beds. After we got over "ooooohhing" and "aaaaaahhing" we decided it was rather funny because then we noticed that the carpet didn't blend or match, the bedspreads were faded and old looking, what wallpaper showed was orange and green stripes and the drapes were a sickly yellow color! In spite of that it was a fun place to spend the night at $36 each.

Sunday morning on our way to Hearst Castle, we stopped in Cambria where we ate breakfast and Joel and I went to church. The singing was real country style and brought back memories of my family's times at Pleasant Valley in Alabama.

We toured Hearst Castle marveling at the contents that ranged in antiquity between 3,200 years and 50 years, including Roman marble and 300-year-old silk brocade from China. As impressive as we agreed the interior of the castle was, it still didn't compare with the natural beauty and wonders of the roses and rhododendrons in full bloom throughout the magnificent grounds. The trip was such a success we vowed to do more like it but everyone was too busy and it never happened.

**Cassette Tapes** All that while I was enjoying the New Testament on cassette tapes, listening to readings each evening while preparing for bed, each morning as I got ready for work and while painting or traveling. Paul and Robert sent me tapes of the Mennonite Choir that added to my enjoyment. My solo trips to Fresno to visit Nancy, Raymond and family were wonderful listening times.

**Carousel And Zoo** In a letter written to my children I found something that made me laugh: *"One Sunday morning Joel and I went to early church service then drove through Malibu Canyon to the ocean. We ate* *brunch overhanging the water . . ."* In the margin I had made a note: *". . . the restaurant was hung over—not us!"* We went on to Santa Monica Pier where we rode on the famous carousel featured in the movie "Sting."

The next day, Monday was a holiday for all of us working people. Benjamin, Susan, Aaron and I made a picnic lunch and in their van we drove to the Zoo down in L.A. somewhere—the directions a friend gave them were not clear and we got lost. We found ourselves in China Town and when Benjamin tried to ask directions with sign language (how do you sign "Zoo?") the person could only point and try to tell us in Chinese. We kept going and hoping. After two hours of wandering Aaron was hungry and so were we, so we ate lunch as we went. After the third try of asking, we finally reached the Zoo. Aaron's excitement at seeing the animals made it all worthwhile—even the getting lost.

**Frank Shirley** Among the many interesting people I met during my time in California was Frank Shirley, friend of Pat Edwards. Maggie and I had invited him and Pat to dinner more than once. He was an R.N. at the State Hospital. Born in England, he joined the British Navy at seventeen, served in the South Pacific during WWII and had lived in New Zealand before he moved to the U.S. and became a U.S. citizen. After twenty years, when I met him, he still had a British accent. He lived in a sailing boat in Ventura Marina and was making plans to sail solo around the world.

For five years he had been training himself, practicing many different conditions by taking trial runs out into the Pacific. He quit his job and spent the last three months working every daylight hour preparing his boat. The *Osiris* was a 34-foot sloop with one mast, a main-sail and a jib-sail. He installed an extra, larger jib-sail, making a "cutter" out of his vessel (he said—I wouldn't know!) Since the wheel was out in the open on the stern, he wanted a way to steer from the inside in stormy weather so he cut a round hole in the forward hatch, installed a fiberglass bubble big enough for his head with a hard-hat on to fit up into the bubble and allow him to see out. He built a seat exactly the right height into which he could firmly strap himself while steering. He installed an extra wheel attached to the steering equipment so he could steer from outside or from inside depending on the weather.

He persuaded companies to supply his special suit for very cold weather and most of his food (the kind used in space ships)—enough to last 300 days. He carried extra sails, survival gear and medical supplies. He installed a rain-catcher so that water could run off the sail through a pipe into the fresh water tank. He planned to stay at least 200 miles from any land except when going around Cape Horn and Cape of Good Hope, and to stay clear of shipping lanes as much as possible.

June 16, 1982 Frank's ex-wife, Stephanie, Pat, Maggie, and I took B-B-Q'd chicken, chips, etc. to eat with him in his cutter and to wish him "bon voyage." He proudly demonstrated to us all the special additions. He was a very quiet man, medium size, strong, healthy, very methodical and thorough in all he did. His "high" was so low-keyed it was almost comical. When we asked if he was excited he quietly said, "This morning I put one sock and shoe on one foot then the other shoe and forgot the sock!"—an odd thing for him to do and we knew it showed his excitement! We watched him sail out of Ventura Island Marina and disappear into the mist.

Many months passed without word of any kind—not that we expected any. About a year later word reached his family that his cutter with his dead body in it had washed up on the shore of a small island in Fiji—no explanation.

**Bicycles** Maggie and I decided it was time to try out our hopefully not-forgotten-ability to ride bicycles. We had heard that was one of the skills that could never be forgotten. We drove north to Camarillo where the roads were fairly flat and rented bikes. We started out well enough only these bikes had the brakes on the handlebars instead of back-pedaling. Since that was the kind of bikes we had learned on in Africa we decided it would be no problem. We were tooling along feeling proud of ourselves when we came to an intersection and had to stop. I back-pedaled but nothing happened, then I remembered to use the handbrakes but I didn't mash hard enough quickly enough and only slowed down. I forgot that before one steps off of the bike one must come to a full stop, I stepped off while still rolling. That threw me off balance and I landed on hands and knees, skinning both. If I ever ride again I will remember to full stop!

**Merle Norman Tower of Beauty** One Saturday morning Maggie and I went with Doris Hostler to the *Merle Norman Tower of Beauty*. It was a museum in which everything operated, ran or worked. In the fabulous show-room were vintage restored Rolls Royces ready to drive that had once belonged to famous people. The show room had floors of green, gray and black marble from three different countries. The huge pillars were made of Rose Marble from the Belgian Congo of long ago. A huge crystal chandelier hung in the center of the frescoed ceiling.

The second floor was called *Cloud Ninety-Nine* because, they said, "Cloud Nine" would have been much too tame! On that floor were one of about every kind of musical instrument that had been made into player types. They were operated in orchestra form by a special instrument called a Vorster, an electronic robot that played the music from rolls. The sound had all the intonations and feeling of the master players—not like the old player-piano sound; and there were four different kinds of orchestrations from the old days before live bands began to play in restaurants of the rich. The instruments were in huge cabinets fitted into alcoves around the walls—listeners stood in the center of the area.

One of the pianos was said to have been given as a gift to Kaiser Joseph I of Austria-Hungary for his Golden Jubilee. It had been smuggled out with the family when he went into exile, later sold for money for them to live on. It was finally found and brought to the U.S. Everything had an interesting history told to us by the curator who conducted the tour and it was concluded with a low key advertising of Merle Norman cosmetics.

On the way home we treated ourselves to lunch at a Marie Callender's, intending to eat some of her famous pie. We were hungry and began with a cup of soup and delicious cornbread but then we were so full we had to skip the pie! We decided next time we would start with the pie and let that be an end in itself.

**This, That And T'other**

Fairly frequent letters from my offspring across the continent kept me feeling up to date on all of the families. Being 2,000 miles from them beat 10,000 miles by a long shot and made telephoning every now and then more do-able.

Early in 1982 Joel began going to church regularly with me. One Sunday we left home early, ate breakfast on the way to Ojai and went to church where Jim preached and took him out to lunch. Afterwards she and I drove to Santa Barbara where every weekend there was a perpetual art show on the board-walk. We looked and looked and vowed to do it again but never did.

**Our Mother's Death** Friday August 13, 1982 we got word that our Mother had died in Cordell Christian Home. We had known her health was failing so it was not a big shock except as the death of a parent is, no matter how expected, and knowing that an era had ended. Maggie and I flew to Amarillo Saturday and drove with Beth to Cordell. Early Sunday morning I phoned the contact person at each church that had been supporting Mother in the Home so they could announce her death at church that day. On Monday afternoon there was a good crowd for the memorial service. Our brother Bill was there from Abilene, Texas, and our father's brother and wife from Harper, Kansas, Mother's two nieces from Stephenville, Texas, besides other kinfolk and friends.

Maggie and I got home Tuesday. We had "Compassionate Leave" until Thursday morning so that afternoon we drove up the coast to Morrow Bay. There we sat on big rocks overlooking the ocean, watching the waves roll in and crash on the rocks below as we talked about our Mother and reminisced about our early life. We had promised Mother after Daddy's death that her ashes would be flown back to Bulawayo to be interred beside his. They had both said they wanted to be buried over there, the home they had chosen sixty-two years before when they dedicated their lives to teaching God's word in that country. I wrote thirty "Thank-you" notes to the eight churches and twenty-two individuals who had continued

452

sending money to our mother while she was in the Home. I remembered then and still remember what a blessing and privilege it was for me to spend five years with Daddy and Mother during the 1970s.

**Another Grandson** Benjamin and Susan's second son, Joshua Dean, arrived October 19. He reminded me of Henry as a baby in size and looks, round face and head and cute as a bug's ear! The folks where they went to church brought a complete dinner each day for two weeks so Benjamin did not have to be concerned over meals. I stopped by after work as often as possible to see the baby and do what I could.

**Fiji Vacation** Maggie and Vonnie used their fall vacation for a trip to the Fiji Islands. It wasn't the first time for me to be alone in the house at night but this time lasted more nights than ever before—enough to get me used to it—somewhat. I was fine until dark but we didn't have blinds on all the windows so I left lights off and went to bed early! Anyway it was summer and I enjoyed getting up extra early. Being in a good neighborhood also helped. Maggie and Vonnie enjoyed their trip, had lots of pictures and plenty to talk about.

**Christmas 1982** was hectic and good. On Friday evening Maggie and I hosted an open house buffet dinner for Greg and Jeri and children, Jim Short and his guests (a couple from Vancouver that he had known in Rhodesia), Winny Wennink, Pat Edwards, Benjamin, Susan and children. We had a lovely evening mainly discussing the various cultures represented.

Saturday morning Benjamin and Susan invited Maggie and me to their house for a 10 a.m. brunch. We had a great time and the two little boys furnished lively entertainment. Then Maggie drove to Santa Barbara for afternoon Christmas dinner with Sharon and family. Joel had invited me to 4:00 p.m. Christmas dinner with her family of two grown sons and a daughter. Their gracious reception of me, practically a stranger among them, was heartwarming and I felt no urge to rush away. I pulled in our driveway right behind Maggie at 8:30 p.m. It was too early for bed so we immediately began knitting on projects for our grandchildren for the next birthdays!

Nancy had told me Monica was extremely allergic to man-made materials so I bought cotton material and made four little dresses for Monica and a couple for Nancy, hoping they would fit. I found out that I was terribly out of practice with sewing.

**Mothers Are For Listening** It seemed like hardly a week passed without one or the other of my children telling of work lay-offs, illnesses and hard times in general. They could empathize with each other because they were all experiencing many of the same trials and I had not forgotten what it felt like from my own past years. I think one of the hardest periods of a mother's life must surely be when such times come to her beloved children and their families. After writing some of that in a letter to my children, Robert's answer was a real comfort to me: *"Mother, don't let it get you feeling down. Kids (even 30-40 year-old kids) still feel deep inside that it helps to tell mama! Don't get down over it; just know that by listening you have lifted a load for us."* My thanks to Robert for that.

**January 1983** The new year took off in a whirl of activities besides regular work. I celebrated my 60th birthday and didn't feel a bit older. Nancy, Raymond and family moved to Fresno and I began making plans to visit them as soon as they were properly settled.

Maggie and I had each invested in a fondue set the year before and hosted several fondue dinners for friends. The previous November I gave Benjamin a birthday rain-check so in January I invited Joel to join us and made a fondue supper in his honor. With two sets we had a pot for hot oil to cook meat and one for melted cheese to coat bread. Then we cleaned the pots and melted chocolate in both, dipped fruit chunks in one and angel food cake cubes in the other. It was delicious and fun. We had so much food left over that Maggie and I enjoyed it again the next night.

Vonnie's husband, Gene, bought two of my paintings for her birthday. The pictures had been hanging in our office at State Farm by request and after they were gone I was urged by fellow-workers to hurry and paint two more to hang in their place.

One Saturday morning in February, in spite of rain predictions, Susan and I with baby Joshua left at 7:30 on our way to visit Nancy and Raymond in Fresno. It had snowed in the lower mountains between us and them and at one place the snow was near the road. It had been several years since Susan had been in snow in Oregon and she asked me to stop so she could feel of it. She gleefully made and threw snow balls. We had a good visit in Fresno and drove home Sunday afternoon. It was 197 miles between our exits and from then on it didn't seem like they lived too far away to visit occasionally.

A pen friend correspondence with a man in Kansas was becoming more interesting all the time and he promised to come for a visit in March. He didn't come and in April he wrote that he was very ill and ended our correspondence. Within a few days we were hit with several more news flashes. We heard that our friend, Ian Allen, now in Africa, when going through an intersection on his motor cycle, was hit by a car that ran a red light; both his legs were broken and several ribs. Benjamin had a flat tire in a very dangerous situation on the Freeway. Sharon's daughter Brandee broke her arm at school. On the other hand, Maggie's son Mike announced his engagement to Paula Wennink. News, good or bad, seemed to come in bunches.

Average annual rainfall in that area was five inches and that year in February and March alone we had 20 inches—Southern California was flooded. We felt sorry for people with houses in the low areas or on slide-prone hillsides. Our house was on a hillside but not a steep one and the ground underneath was solid. Most of the houses that slid had been built on fill dirt, so even though they might have been there a long time, there were hollow places underneath.

Maggie and I were raised by the same mother who taught us to keep our hands busy so we did just that. Every time we had a few free minutes

455

we were either crocheting or knitting, or she was macramé-ing a lampshade and I was painting; or cooking for company, working in flower beds, washing our cars or cleaning house. During the two plus years that I was there we turned out baby sweaters, caps and shawls; children's sweaters; ladies' sweaters; men's sweaters; ladies' shawls and afghans. Those were things within our budgets that we could give away and with as many children and grandchildren as we had we were kept busy.

We and our nearby children visited each other often. Many times we had all of them at once, sometimes only one family at a time and other times various acquaintances were included, many of whom were ex-Rhodesians. The side trips and events I have written about were only a few of many that happened during my almost three years there. And of course we did our "work jobs," she at Litton and I at State Farm.

Finally I had worked long enough at State Farm that I had some paid vacation coming. I could combine that with a couple of personal days and a weekend, making time to fly to Florida to visit Robert, Dianne and Bobby in Orange Park and Paul, Janis, Benji and Doug in Winter Park. By May 26, 1983 I had sold enough paintings to buy my roundtrip ticket and I booked a flight. What joy it was to be with my Florida families a few days each. Soon after I was there Robert, Dianne and Bobby moved to Decatur, Alabama.

Weddings were in the breezes and in all the talk every way we turned. A co-worker from my office had a big church wedding that Joel and I attended. We had word from Beth that her Linda's wedding was in the offing in Amarillo, Texas. Closer to home, Michael and Paula were preparing for their wedding. Maggie made her own dress and Vonnie came to stay with us and be helpful in general. Paula's mother, Winnie, made Paula's wedding dress, a dress for Paula's younger sister, Anita, and one for herself. Not being in the wedding party I could wear a "Sunday dress," but I was constantly called on to hold, measure, pin, or give my opinion!

**God's Open Arms** One Saturday in early 1983 I was at the kitchen counter painting on a big picture while Maggie was making sandwiches for lunch. I don't recall how the conversation began but she asked me if I thought God could forgive someone who had rebelled and thought and said very hard things about Him for a long time. I said I was positive that He would. She asked, "What can I do about it?"

"Tell Him that you want to come back to Him and ask Him to forgive you," I replied.

"Do you think He will?" she wondered.

"I *know* He will," I emphatically assured her.

By then we were both crying and hugging each other. After more than twenty years of constant prayers for her, my prodigal little sister had returned to her Heavenly Father and I was sure heaven's angels rejoiced over it.

Maggie and I did many interesting things together but regardless of what we were doing we enjoyed every minute of our time together, whether working around our home, having company or going places. We both enjoyed doing crossword puzzles and someone told us about the big puzzle in the back of Globe Magazine. After that on our way home from work every Friday we stopped for groceries and bought a Globe to work the puzzle after supper. Naturally we looked through the personal ads in the back pages, too. Life changing events began to take place.

Twenty-six years later I wrote about it for Joe's and my children. Here is a copy of that letter:

*August 1, 2009*

*Dear children all,*

*On this date twenty-six years ago Joe and I were married.*

*Many times during the almost twenty years we shared, we talked about how the providence of God brought us together and blessed our marriage. How we found each other is as fresh in my mind as if it were yesterday. I was sixty, sharing a house with Maggie in Newbury Park, CA, during my second year of working in the State Farm Regional Office in Westlake Village. I had been a widow eleven years.*

One day in early March, Maggie told me she would be going on a date after work and asked me to pick up milk on my way home. In the checkout line I decided the big crossword puzzle in the Globe would be good entertainment for the evening. But before I did the puzzle I read the personal ads in the back. One from a sixty-five year old farmer in southwest Ohio caught my eye. Could be an interesting pen pal, I thought.

It took me three hours to write and re-write a concise introduction of myself. When Maggie came in I asked her to read it and comment. She read it and said, "Sounds good, but he asked specifically for a petite widow with grandchildren. You didn't say you're petite." I said, "Because I'm not!" "Yes you are!" she contradicted, from her towering 5'7 ½" to my 5'5." So I added at the end of the letter, "P.S. Borderline petite!"

The next week I went on a two-week vacation to Florida to visit Paul and Janis near Orlando and Robert and Dianne in Orange Park. When I returned to California there was a letter from Joe Dewhirst—five pages of his big writing on 8-½ x 11 paper. That evening I answered his letter.

Later he told me he had answered my first letter immediately and counted the days to when he thought he should get my reply. When it was two weeks past his expectation date he decided to call one of the local ladies who had answered his ad. He had received seventeen letters in the batch that included mine, he said, and mine was the third one he opened. After he read it he put all the others aside to write to me. (He received 301 letters in all.) He decided the local lady didn't interest him and began writing another letter to me, in case I answered.

His rapid, detailed writing took him three days, then he copied it over, hoping I could read it. When he received *my second letter he was ready with twenty-two pages that he mailed at once. He spent so much time writing that Myrt and Newell were shocked when they went to the farm and the yard wasn't mowed—Joe never let his mowing go. But he was busy writing and mailing a letter every day. Every evening I answered that day's letter, and so it went the rest of May, June and July. We wrote about everything imaginable and much unimaginable. It was like talking to each other without let up for three months. We estimated that if we had dated conventionally it would have taken about three years to tell each other as much.*

*In late June Joe added his phone number, saying, "If you would like to talk by phone give me a call." On July 4ᵗʰ I decided to call. He was at home and we talked. After that he called three times a week and sometimes more often, but we kept writing. Then over the phone he asked me if I'd like for him to come to see me and I said yes. He asked when and I said how about next week! I think he nearly fainted but managed to say he couldn't make it the next week but how about July 21ˢᵗ? And I said fine. I had never been so forward in all my life, but in later years when I learned how Joe habitually procrastinated, we both decided my forwardness was part of God's providence.*

*I told Joel, my best friend at work, that Joe was coming and she said, "When you go to meet him wear the cream colored skirt and blouse with the bronze blazer that you look so good in." So I did. As I left the office I said to her, "Wish me well. This may be the beginning of the rest of my life!"*

*I was at the gate in LAX by 12:45, my heart pounding. Would I recognize him from the picture he sent? Would he look in person like he looked in the pictures? Would he be disappointed when he saw me? How should I greet him? Should I offer to shake hands or what?*

459

*Then he was coming toward me and I knew it was him and he obviously knew it was me. We looked into each other's eyes a moment then hugged and kissed. I liked his eyes, and his smile—and he had thick black wavy hair!*

*We talked as we found the car, we talked as we ate lunch and we talked at the house until time to go to dinner at a restaurant up the coast. We talked all the way there and all during dinner as we ate shark steak and watched otters through the window beside our table. We talked until we were ashamed to sit there longer and went to the car and decided to stay in the parking lot instead of driving more since I wasn't familiar with the highway.*

*At 11:30 he asked me to marry him and I said "Yes."*

*Before I saw Joe I had been planning to ask Henry to go to Ohio to do some investigating for me. But after seeing him in person I was convinced, even more than the letters had convinced me, that Joe was everything he said he was. By 11:30 that evening I was still more sure he was the genuine article and scrapped the idea of asking Henry to be a detective.*

*Joe stayed until the following Tuesday. He was to return 2 ½ weeks later to get married; afterwards we would drive in my car to Ohio, visiting all our kids on the way. We called all our children and nearly shocked their sox off. I gave notice at work and my co-workers gave me a farewell party. Maggie and I found the perfect fuchsia pink suit with cream colored blouse for my wedding outfit.*

*Before he had gone back to Ohio, Joe found out California required a blood test and a waiting period and suggested Reno. I said, "No way! Nevada is O.K. but not Reno." So we settled on Lake Tahoe. And if we married there we could stop in Fresno to see Nancy, Raymond and family on the way back to Newbury Park.*

*Joe arrived on Sunday afternoon, July 31<sup>st</sup>. We were*
sitting in the den talking when he said,
"When do you want to leave?"
I said, "How about this afternoon?"
He said, "How long will it take you to pack?"
I said, "My suitcase is packed!"
So we went north, angling toward Nevada and stopped
in Bishop, California for dinner and the night. While we
were eating supper in the restaurant (lights were bulbs
suspended from the ceiling on cords), the lights began
noticeably swinging back and forth, and we felt vibrations.
Joe said, "What in the world?" Almost three-year veteran of
California that I was, I said, "It's an earthquake!"

The next morning, Monday, August 1, 1983, we bought
the marriage license in Carson City, Nevada. We picked a
Wedding Chapel out of the many in Lake Tahoe, Nevada,
and scheduled a 4:00 p.m. ceremony, then drove the short
distance to South Lake Tahoe, California, where motel prices
were more to our liking. We rested and cooled off, dressed and
went back to be married. The minister's name was Mike
Love. Joe thought it must be for publicity but I told him I
knew a family of Loves in Abilene, Texas, so it could be his
real name. We fervently hoped the marriage certificate was
legal!

It was so hot we were glad to get back to the motel, change
clothes and have a cool drink. By then it was cooler outside
and we climbed up the side of a nearby mountain to sit on a
rock and look out over beautiful Lake Tahoe while we talked.
We treated ourselves to a delicious "wedding dinner" at the
local restaurant, still talking.

The romance of Sybil and Joe continued till he died
almost twenty years later.

With love, Mother/Mom/Sybil

461

**Wedding picture of Sybil and Joe on August 1, 1983 in Lake Tahoe.**

**Back to 1983** The next day we drove to Fresno and knocked on Nancy's door about an hour earlier than she was expecting us. I soon learned it was a habit of Joe's to arrive earlier than expected! Nancy was so shocked she blurted out, "But I wasn't expecting you for another hour!" and I asked jokingly, "Do you want us to go away and come back in an hour?" Of course not, so I helped her get ready for us! We spent the night and had a wonderful time with her, Raymond, Tonya, Chris and Monica, who all took to Joe immediately.

In Newbury Park we visited Benjamin, Susan, Aaron and Joshua. They had already met and approved of Joe. We packed and sent by van all my stuff except what my Toyota would hold. As we said goodbye to Maggie my excitement was mixed with sadness—I was saying goodbye to her and our happily shared time and home on Colonett Street.

By the time we reached Albuquerque it was Saturday evening. Sunday morning we drove south and stopped in Socorro, New Mexico for church. The preacher was from the Dominican Republic. He preached a good sermon and the small congregation welcomed us warmly. There we met a lady who had known my brother Bill at Harding College and was thrilled to meet Bill's sister.

We spent one night with Edward, Sara Faye, Melanie and Jeremy in Katy, Texas, a night in Biloxi, Mississippi, then on to see Paul, Janis, Benji and Doug in Winter Park, Florida. From there we went to Daytona Beach to meet Joe's daughter, Merry Jo, husband Bob, sons Chris and Johnnie, who were on vacation there. We met Joe's sisters-in-law Angie and Mary and husband Ed who kindly treated us to a family "Wedding Reception" in Angie's home.

Robert, Dianne and Bobby had moved to Decatur, Alabama since I saw them last and Joe enjoyed their swimming pool. Henry, Jo Ann, Lee, Eric and Leslie lived in Madison. We spent a night with each family before going on north. Joe and I were thrilled that so far there had been instant rapport all around with each other's children and kin and I looked forward to meeting Scot in person.

A completely new and very different life was waiting for me on the Ohio farm.

# PART VI

## OHIO

# 1983-2004

**A Farmer's Wife** We arrived at the farm sometime in the night of August 23rd. The next-farm-neighbors, Steve and Gail, saw our lights and early the next morning invited us to breakfast. They were a young couple who raised horses and we enjoyed a cordial neighborliness until they moved away a few years later.

Our neighbors on the other side were Bud and Lucretia Whitacre, about our ages. They had been friends with Joe and Grace during the growing up years of their three girls who were in the same schools as Merry and Scot. Lucretia came to welcome me to the neighborhood, bringing a beautiful gladiola in a special antique bottle. Neighbors across the back fields congratulated Joe on his new wife and welcomed me to the community. I soon found out, however, that the only neighbors with whom we would have any kind of social life were the Whitacres.

On my second evening there I met Tiff, Joe's bull mastiff, when the neighbor who had kept her while Joe was gone brought her home. Joe and Tiff greeted each other warmly then Tiff stood beside Joe's chair looking across the room at me. I purposely ignored her to see what she would do. In a few minutes, without any prompting from Joe, she walked over and lay down across my feet. Joe said, "Well, Tiff has adopted you!"

**Crocheting with Tiff.**

I had never owned a dog nor lived in the house with one before. It seemed like a good idea to be friends with Tiff since we would be living in the same house and sharing Joe's attentions. She got no argument from me about that—she weighed 130 lbs. and that was exactly how much I weighed at that time! She was accustomed to sleeping on the floor beside Joe's bed but after a few nights she was content with her new sleeping place in the hall beside our door. The first morning after my arrival when Joe started back to the lake, Tiff followed him as far as the garage then stopped and looked back to where I was standing on the porch. Joe kept walking and Tiff hesitated then turned and came back to stand beside me. I was glad to have her around when strangers came to ask if they could fish in the lake. When a strange car pulled into the drive, Tiff barked and the people took one look at her and did not get out of their car. I went to the door and the driver called out to me, "Will your dog bite?" I said, "Not if I tell her not to!" Then I told the would-be fishermen to park out by the barn and walk back to find Joe for permission to fish.

Joe was apologetic about the dusty house. He had gone to California leaving in progress a major redo of the old bathroom. Drywall dust was thick everywhere. While he had been gone the fields had grown up with grass, ragweed and Queen Ann's Lace. He felt his most pressing need was to crank up his old tractor and bush hog the fields. I knew my most urgent need was to clean house. For the next two weeks he worked outside and I worked inside.

We took late afternoon walks to familiarize me with the layout of the farm. The farm included a five-acre lake, about twenty-five acres of ravines and woods across one end and about eighty acres of cultivated fields in addition to nearly ten acres around the house and barn and the area between that and the lake—over a hundred acres in all.

Fall colors were bursting all around. Our walks along the winding, up hill and down dale back road as the sun was setting were through a tunnel of blazing yellows, oranges and reds of the maples, oaks, sycamore, sassafras and other trees and shrubs that lined the road and spread into the adjoining fields.

One of the first things we did in the evenings was to open and read the letters Joe had received in answer to his ad in the Globe magazine. He had opened only three of the earliest ones received and put the rest in a box unopened. He felt that it was only polite to jot a note on each letter saying, "Position filled. Thanks all the same" and return it. Many women had enclosed pictures that they wanted returned. I asked him, "What if you find one you wish you had opened first?" He said, "There's no danger of that!" But we had a good time reading each one, looking at the pictures and talking about them!

Joe could hardly wait to get me out on the lake in his little boat to fish. My one condition was that he put the worms on the hooks! The first time I caught nine crappies and eight the next time but never that many again. My biggest catch was a five-pound bass that Joe helped me get into the boat. My wildest dreams in the past never included such a life as was unfolding before me every day.

Not long after I arrived it came time for mushrooms. Joe came in one day with two big round white balls that he said were "puff ball mushrooms." I had never heard of such a thing! He wanted me to cook them for dinner and said all I needed to do was wash and slice them like bread, dip the slices in beaten egg and fry. So I did, and set them before him, but didn't take any on my plate.

He said, "Aren't you going to try some?"

My skeptical response was, "No way! They're probably poisonous."

He declared, "I've been eating them for years and I know they're not."

My reply to that was, "Perhaps you built up immunity to the poison!" But after watching him eat several bites with no visible signs of poisoning, I took a slice and began to eat.

"I thought you weren't going to eat any," he said.

"I decided if you were going to die I might as well die with you!"

**New Faces** When I arrived in Ohio I felt as though I knew Merry, Bob and the boys from our meeting and brief time together in Daytona Beach. It seemed to me I already knew Scot, not only from what his father had told me about him, but also from his letter to me in California along with the lovely bouquet of lavender roses he sent welcoming me to the family. We didn't actually meet, however, until Joe and I went to Columbus. Very soon Scot and I were on the same wavelength.

Scot, Merry and Bob invited us to go with them to the Ohio State vs. Michigan football game that fall. It was my first time ever to watch a game other than on TV and a never-to-be-forgotten experience, though I don't recall who won. We spent the night at Merry and Bob's house and met Bob's parents, Bob, Sr. and Rose.

**Newell and Myrt** Joe's half brother and his wife lived about thirty miles away in north Cincinnati. The first Sunday afternoon of my new life, Joe tried to phone Newell but got no answer. He said. "Let's go on anyway and maybe they'll be home when we get there." I was hesitant to go without warning but he said he was sure it would be fine. On the way he told me that it might take a little while for Myrt to warm up to me. They were at home and welcomed us warmly—and immediately I felt accepted as family. From then on we enjoyed a close relationship. They said when they saw Joe's concentrated writing of letters to me before he went to California, they thought anyone that important to him must be a catch! That afternoon when we were leaving Myrt told me that she wanted me to come any time and I did not need to call first. That made me feel good though I usually did call.

**Eldon and Dottie Phelps** The second Sunday afternoon Joe wanted me to meet his dear friends, Eldon and Dottie Phelps. There again, it was instant acceptance and for me the beginning of another enduring friendship. Eldon and Joe had worked at Formica Corporation for years and they and their wives had taken many vacation trips out west for the men to hunt elk and the women to enjoy sight seeing and antiquing. Soon after my first meeting with them Eldon and Dottie both retired and moved to Lake Placid, Florida. From then on we visited them almost every year, usually combined with a visit with my son Paul and family in Florida. The men caught lots of fish and we women did lots of antiquing and sales shopping—almost never buying anything—to the men's amazement. We ate out almost every meal and that suited everyone. The annual deer season in Ohio began the day after Thanksgiving and several years, when Eldon and Dottie came from Florida to visit their many kinfolks and friends in the Cincinnati area, they came to spend a few days with us so he and Joe could hunt. Whether in Ohio or in Florida our times with them were special.

**First Thanksgiving** We invited Scot, Merry, Bob and boys, Chris (10), Johnny (6), Newell and Myrt, to come for Thanksgiving Day and I began planning what I would cook. Paul, Janis and boys flew up to join us. I made my usual kind of southern cornbread dressing, but found out my Ohio folks were accustomed to *light-bread stuffing*, so my southern *cornbread dressing* was not a hit. Neither was the sweet potato casserole, except to Myrt and to me and Paul and Janis. I was learning but had a lot more to learn.

Paul and Janis needed a car and Joe and I didn't need two in addition to Joe's truck, so I sold them my Toyota Corolla and they drove home to Florida in it.

**First Christmas** We invited the Columbus kids and Myrt and Newell to our house for Christmas and I made *light bread stuffing* for the turkey! I made several pies and a Jam Cake from a recipe I had saved since the 1940s. I remembered that it was delicious and thought it couldn't fail to please. It turned out superbly and was as delicious as I remembered—but no one else cared for it because it was too much like fruit cake to them. I froze the cake in serving-sized pieces and enjoyed one piece at a time—for nearly a year! I never bothered to make another. I found out that Scot, unlike the rest of the family, liked regular fruit cake as much as I did and from then on I made sure we had a small fruitcake for our enjoyment every Christmas.

**First Ohio Winter** On Christmas Eve night the temperature dropped to minus 16 degrees F and all our cars froze up except Scot's Vega. It was the beginning of the coldest winter I ever experienced before or since. Throughout January and February the nights were zero or below and the days, mostly with sunshine, were only 20 degrees F. Ice on the lake was so thick when Joe sawed a hole in it to let the fish get oxygen, he measured it as 16" deep.

Every morning after breakfast we donned layers of clothes, two pairs of sox with heavy leather boots, woolen gloves inside of leather work gloves and thick-knit wool caps. We worked outside six to eight hours almost every day. The conditions were ideal for Joe to cut dead trees around the lake. He let them fall onto the ice and it didn't crack. If he let them fall into the woods they would have been harder to work on. On the lake where they fell he cut the trees into fireplace lengths and I stacked the wood on the shore. I dragged the brush out to the middle of the lake where we burned it on the ice. I was afraid it would melt the ice and we might fall through but Joe assured me that wouldn't happen and it didn't.

We built a footbridge across the narrow neck of the lake that was picturesque, if not particularly useful, and we chopped and burned cattails that were clogging the lake edges. By then it was March and though still cold, it was less frigid. We cleared multi-flora roses and other unwanted underbrush to make a "Trail" along the drain ditch that we called "the creek" running to the lake from the culvert under the driveway.

**Building a footbridge on Ohio farm, 1984.**

**Swallows, Bluebirds and Buzzards** On March 15th that year I heard for the first time about the annual return of the buzzards to Hinckley, Ohio. Why would buzzards keep coming back to Hinckley? Tradition said that they took a liking to that area after what was known as "The Great Hinckley Hunt of 1818." The hunt was a roundup of stock-killing wild animals on Judge Hinckley's land in order to end their raids on farms of the surrounding settlers. On December 24, 1818, several hundred hunters surrounded Judge Hinckley's woods and converged upon the encircled animals. The hunters killed a large number of bears, wolves, deer, turkeys, foxes and raccoons. Animal carcasses that were not used for food and/ or furs were left there to freeze over the winter; when they thawed in the spring the buzzards had a feast. The following spring, and every year after that, on March 15th buzzards have converged on that spot.

My thoughts were that England has its *Bluebirds Over The White Cliffs of Dover*, California has the date *When Swallows Come Back To Capistrano* and now I was informed that in Ohio the buzzards return to Hinckley. It was understandable that popular songs were sung about the first two but I could not imagine anyone composing a song about buzzards!

**New Every Day** Every day Joe and I talked as we worked and continued to learn more about each other than our prolific letter writing had revealed, though we thought we had told in them all there was to tell. In our writing we had described Grace and Bennie Lee to each other and expressed admiration for each other's former mate. Without discussing it specifically we evidently came to the same conclusion that we would not compare our present mate to them—our former lives had been very good yet completely different from what we were now living. Joe and Bennie Lee were two of the most admirable men I ever knew. They had outstanding qualities in common—strength of character, integrity, gentleness, strong willpower, self control and the ability to see good in their fellowmen, to name a few. At the same time their physical build, training, capabilities and experiences were about as different as anyone could imagine.

I soon found that Joe had an exceptional ability to judge weight, distance and time. When we caught fish he threw many back in and kept the ones he said weighed enough. We had no scales with us in the boat but when we weighed some after we got home we found his estimation was always within an ounce or two. When he found a big snapping turtle caught in a trench of the spillway, he took it out and told me it weighed 37 pounds—I never doubted him. He estimated distance when we were driving in the car and if we later measured it with the speedometer, his estimate was correct. If he told me it was a certain distance to a point on the farm I knew better than to question it. He didn't need an alarm clock but told me the night before when he would wake up—and he did.

**Spontaneity** Joe's spontaneity took some getting used to but I grew to enjoy it and tried to match it with flexibility in my activities and plans. He liked going to flea markets and I never knew when he might suddenly say on Saturday morning, "Let's go to the Caesar Creek Flea Market this morning!" He didn't tarry long, so with practice on my part, any idea of browsing was forgotten! We walked up and down the sections looking rapidly, then, perhaps because he never liked to leave without buying something, he might buy a bunch of bananas! There was always a booth that sold Funnel Cakes and we shared one to make my enjoyment complete—he could take them or leave them and they didn't count for his buying something! When he suggested going to the flea market he learned to add for my benefit, "We'll get a funnel cake!"

Now and then on Friday evening he said, "I'll call Merry and see if it's O.K. for us to come to Columbus tomorrow! We'll leave about noon." He would tell Merry we'd be at her house about 1:30. I thought that meant I had all morning to get ready to leave by 12:00. But he might come through the house about 11:00 calling to me, "We might as well go now and not have to rush!" I usually said, "But Merry's not expecting us until later." His reply was always, "She won't care!" And if she did, she was always good at hiding it. We spent many nights in Columbus, sometimes at Merry and Bob's house and sometimes at Scot's. At both places we enjoyed wonderful visits with talks, activities and game-playing. We all liked word games and played many different ones together. After a while Scot and I developed an ongoing competition with Scrabble. When the others decided they had had enough in an evening, he and I went for more Scrabble. He kept a running score from visit to visit and we often played until the wee hours of the morning. Even yet on the rare occasions when we are together, we enjoy Scrabble.

Sometimes out of the blue Joe said, "Let's drive over to Waynesville and look around in the shops!" Waynesville was advertised as the *"Antiques Capital of the Mid-West"* and we spent many happy hours browsing through the stores without hurrying. We were constantly amazed at how similar were his and my memories of things we saw from "the old days." It was one place where Joe didn't rush me.

**Bible Reading** Before we met, while we were writing to each other, Joe told me that he had not gone to church regularly since he was grown. I told him going to church every Sunday and daily Bible reading were not options with me, they were a way of life like eating meals. He said he wanted to change his life and have what I had. The first Sunday after we married he got ready for church and never missed after that unless he was too sick to stand up. The first Sunday I noticed him do something that he did every Sunday morning when getting ready—he polished his "Sunday shoes"—just like my Daddy and Bennie Lee had done as long as I knew them. It was a small thing perhaps but somehow touching to me.

We decided to have our regular Bible reading as soon as breakfast was done. We sat at the cleared table where we could spread our Bibles and reference books. After we had read through the entire Bible the first year, with his phenomenal memory Joe remembered many details better than I did after my many years of reading. I wish I had kept a record of how many times we read through the Bible; as soon as we completed it we started over again. We discussed many things as we read, often spending an hour and a half or two hours discussing and looking up references. We also read a chapter every day from the inspirational book by Oswald

Chambers, *My Utmost For His Highest.* The messages never got old and we read it through so many times we wore out two sets of paperback copies. Joe told me how during World War II, when he was in combat in the South Pacific, his mother kept her Bible on her night stand open at Psalm 91. She read it over and over, especially verses 1, 2 and 7. He said he read those verses over and over while he was in the South Pacific, and knowing that his mother was reading the same verses helped him.

**Unconscious Influence** Our breakfast table was beside the window near the outside electric meter and the monthly meter reader passed by while we were reading. One Saturday morning some years later, we were reading when there was a knock on the front door.

A stranger greeted me, "You don't know me but my name is—. As I drove in sight of your house this morning I had a very strong feeling that I should stop and tell you what you have done for me and my family. For years I checked your meter and every time I passed your window I could not help but see that you were reading your Bibles. My wife and I were raised going to church but we stopped going and let our lives slide. After seeing you with your Bibles month after month, I told my wife I was going to church. She said she had been wanting to go too. We have been reading our Bibles regularly and taking our children to church and our lives have changed for the better. We thank God for that and I wanted you to know what you did for us."

**My First Spring** By the middle of March the snow was almost gone, ice was melting fast on the lake and we began to see the very first signs of spring—clumps of snow-flowers blooming in shady places through unmelted snow. We began watching for other signs like spring beauties and wild violets peeping through the early grass; soon there were crocuses, hyacinths, daffodils and tulips. Joe found out I had a soft spot for violets and every spring he watched for the very first ones. He picked some for a little bouquet and brought it to me with his love. That became one of our very special moments each spring. I had a certain little vase that I put them in to enjoy on our kitchen table. Years later when Joe had become too weak to do any of his work and could only walk slowly with a stick, he came in with violets. I was surprised and asked, "How did you reach them?" He said, "I got down on my knees and picked them then crawled to the planter and pulled myself up!" I was touched to tears.

That first spring Joe showed me wild flowers I had never seen, though I had read of them in books like *Anne of Green Gables* and *Girl of The Limberlost*. Besides spring beauties there were wild strawberries, May apples, Dutchman's britches, trillium, jack-in-the-pulpit, Solomon's seal, trout lilies, lady's-slippers, wood anemone, blood root, dog-tooth, pepper plants, wild bluebells and sweet Williams and more. And we reveled in the show of blooming redbud trees and pink and white dogwoods.

Robert, Dianne and Bobby came for a weekend in March and were our first Alabama visitors. We enjoyed showing them around the farm with Joe's enthusiastic running commentary and much to his pleasure they were suitably impressed.

**Joe's Garden And Yard** As soon as the ground was dry enough to plow Joe put out a garden—about a half acre. He thoroughly enjoyed plowing the garden patch and getting it ready. He delighted in the planting of it and watching for everything to come up. He was excited over the first ear of corn mature enough to pick or bean or ripe tomato. However, it wasn't long until he was including me in his statement after breakfast, "We need to weed the beans," or "We need to pick lettuce" or tomatoes or any number of other things related to the garden!

He didn't expect me to mow the yard but I noticed that he hated to trim around the edges and to me that was a necessity. So by my own choice I became the "trimmer." When we were not in the garden we were kept busy in the yard. Besides the regular mowing and trimming we battled weeds, wild grape vines, poison ivy and such like around the perimeter, along the ditch in front of the house, around the milk house and the tractor shed. During the next few years we worked outward from the edge of what had been Joe's approximately one-acre "yard" until we had almost five acres of "yard" surrounding the house. Gradually Joe was persuaded to decrease the size of his massive vegetable garden and incorporate that into the "back yard" until we hardly knew where the yard ended from the house to the lake.

**Horse Radish** In the fall he dug some of the roots of the horse radish plants he had carefully avoided with his bush hog. He brought them into the kitchen and I asked, "What in the world do you want me to do with those crooked knotty roots?" He explained, "That's horse radish to grind up and make horse radish relish. I liked horse radish that came in little packages with Arby's roast beef, so I went to work on the roots. He didn't warn me that putting them through the meat-grinder would be equal to or worse than putting strong onions through it. Tears flowed as I worked but I persevered until a quart was filled, then said, "No more!" On a trial basis I mixed about a half teaspoon of ground horse radish with a half cup of mayonnaise but it was still too strong for our taste and the closed jar was stored in the refrigerator. Some time later Scot was visiting and saw that jar of white stuff and asked what it was. I told him it was home grown horse radish. He opened the jar to take a whiff and it nearly took off the top of his head! We had a good laugh about his shock at its power. But he said if we weren't going to use it he would take it home and mix a little with mayonnaise to use on sandwiches. I gladly gave it to him and I think it lasted several years! He said the trick was to use enough mayonnaise.

**How To STOP!** One day early in my farm life Joe thought it was time I learned to use the riding lawn mower and I climbed on. He started me in the large area behind the garden and away I went—but not too fast! I soon realized I was heading straight toward the lake and decided to turn around—but I couldn't see space to turn around in so I thought I would stop, but Joe had forgotten to show me how to stop! Fortunately he wasn't too far behind and yelled, *"Push the clutch down all the way!"* At first I didn't push hard enough and the lake was coming closer and closer and I pictured myself submerged. He yelled again, *"Harder!"* That time it worked and I stopped—much too close to the water for my comfort—but I had learned how to stop!

**Big Barn Burned** A red-letter day in the farm's history was June 10, 1984. Lee was visiting us when that Sunday the huge antique barn burned to the ground. We had gone to church then to eat at Duff's cafeteria in Wilmington before heading home. As we neared home we saw a sheriff's deputy stopping cars near the little church down the hill from the farm house. The officer told Joe, "Your barn is burning and we wanted you to know before you got in sight of it." We breasted the hill and saw volunteer firemen still spraying the smoking ruins. They told us a passer-by had seen the smoke and called the fire department but the fire was too far gone for them to stop it. They said the flames had gone about 200 feet into the air and if the wind had not been blowing *away* from the house there would have been no way for them to have saved the house and garage. As it was the bushes and trees on that side of the house were severely scorched and took several years to grow out again.

The barn was at least 150 years old with massive forty foot long, hand-hewn oak beams. Joe said the gable ridge was sixty feet from the ground. I would not question that. During the preceding fall strong wind had blown up some of the metal roof on the barn and I had "helped" Joe when he climbed up there to nail it down. He was up top, I was on the ground, but it was a scary job. I planted myself under where he was working as though I thought my 130 lb. body could have broken his 178 lb. fall if he had lost his footing! But he had tied a rope to his belt before he went up and I did help when he threw the other end over the gable. I was able to securely tie the rope to a heavy piece of farm equipment on the ground. Joe was surprised and pleased that I knew how to tie a sailor's knot! When we were kids our Daddy had taught us that.

Bob and Merry had stored some furniture in the loft of the barn as well as many of Joe's mother's things and other antiques saved through the years. A neighbor's combine was parked in the "pass through" to be out of the weather and it burned along with everything else. A road working crew had parked their ton truck near the barn for the weekend—the fire was so hot the windows, windshield and tires melted, and the steering wheel was melted beyond recognition. The fire chief said he was certain the fire began from spontaneous combustion in the bales of hay stacked under shelter at one end of the barn that became damp when rain had blown in on them.

When the ruins finally cooled Joe and I spent days looking through the debris for possible salvage but most of it was beyond saving. Of course nothing of wood had survived and what had been baskets full of Mason fruit jars were shapeless globs of melted glass. It took Joe many days to compile lists of contents for the insurance adjuster. After that process was all settled, Joe hired a man with a bulldozer to dig a huge hole and push all the debris down into it and cover it up, except the pieces of partly burned oak beams. Then Joe observed, "Well, I was about ready to tear the old barn down anyway, though that certainly wasn't the way I would have chosen. But what in the world would I have done with all that stuff that was in it?" At the same time it was sad to think of that antique piece of history gone up in smoke.

**Grandchildren** Joe's grandsons, Chris (11) and Johnny (7), were familiar with the farm from their earliest memories and came often to fish and enjoy the country. As my grandchildren came to visit, one after the other, I teased Joe that he needed to remember how his ad in the Globe magazine had specified ". . . widow with grandchildren!" We wanted the grandchildren who lived in cities to have a taste of country life, too.

June 8th of that year began our first summer of visiting grandchildren. Lee (14) was the first to come. He helped with whatever work we were doing and he and Joe fished often. We took him to Kings Island Amusement Park and that became a given—when grandkids came we went to Kings Island. We joined them on some rides but I drew the line for myself at roller coasters.

After two weeks we took Lee home in Joe's double-cab truck, spent the weekend and brought Dianne, Bobby (13) and my piano that they had been keeping for me. My intentions were to practice on the piano for hours at a time but somehow the time flew by with very little of that happening. After mornings of work Joe and Bobby fished while Dianne and I either watched them or went shopping. The next week Robert came for them and brought Eric (13).

Eric's 4-H Club experience helped him fit into farm life easily and Joe let him drive the tractor. He did such a good job of handling the tractor that the next year Joe let him do scraping and scooping with it as they worked on the drain-ditch between the house and lake. Eric surprised us by opting not to go to Kings Island, saying he would rather work with Joe. How could workaholic Joe not love him for that! Eric was interested in antiques and asked Joe if he could have the cast iron bathtub that had been removed from the old bathroom. The tub was so big and heavy the contractor had enlarged the hole where the window was and with the help of several men lifted the tub out through that hole! They had left the tub in the back yard and Eric helped Joe and me—and the tractor—move it into the back of the tractor shed where it stayed for several years until Henry took it to Alabama.

Leslie (10) came next. She was with us in Columbus to see the public fireworks on July 4th. She was a joy to have and especially enjoyed the small turtle she rescued, fed and played with. Then Melanie (11) and Jeremy (9) flew from Houston for a visit. When we went fishing Joe took Jeremy in one of the flat-bottom-boats while Melanie and I used the other—after Joe first put worms on our hooks! Melanie began dramatically calling to the fish, "Come here, little fishies, here's a juicy feast for you!" Then she thought of the "poor little worms stuck on the hooks," and she thought of a "poor little fishy swallowing the hook." She became so emotionally distraught she didn't want to fish any more. So we just dangled our hook-less lines in the water and pretended we were fishing while the boat floated on the lake. Meanwhile Jeremy caught one fish after another as fast as Joe could take it off of his hook. He announced each catch with a loud cheer that Joe thought would scare away the fish, but they kept biting. All summer each evening was game-playing time. By the end of the summer

Joe had learned to enjoy playing table games—something he said he had never done before.

As the grandchildren grew older their summers became filled with sports of different kinds and not all of them came every summer. However, Bobby came almost every summer for several years, to work with Joe and to fish as much as possible. In the beginning Joe and Bobby had to come to terms with each other. Bobby was about fifteen when one day early in his visit, with Joe's promise of going fishing after lunch, they went to work around an old apple tree on the way to the lake. Joe had visions of clearing the brush, pruning the tree and installing a bench under it. He told Bobby that his dream was to sit on that bench and sing to Grandma Sybil, *"Don't sit under the apple tree with anyone else but me!"* Bobby caught the vision and they worked hard and talked more than usual—the breakthrough had happened. When I rang the dinner-bell I heard them nearing the house, talking and laughing—and my heart sang. Joe said Bobby really worked hard and Bobby said Joe was fun to work with! From then on his annual visits were even more enjoyed than before.

**Combined Families** Our combined family of eight children, seven spouses and sixteen grandchildren supplied joyful happy times through the years as they came to the farm for visits or we went to their homes. Each family was busy making a living and taking care of their own affairs and we understood when they could not come to see us as often as we would have liked. There was a scarcity of grandfathers in the combined family: Bennie Lee was gone and on the in-laws side Jo Ann's, Dianne's and Janis' fathers had died. "Grandpa Joe" filled the gap and became the grandfather they loved and admired. And I rejoiced in the loving relationship that grew between me and my stepchildren and step grandchildren. My loving brood had increased. Our visits with children, whether in our home or theirs, were thoroughly enjoyed, leaving us wishing for more every time.

Among our children and grandchildren as they grew up, was an interesting mix of personalities, interests, employments and accomplishments: fathers, mothers, homemakers, school teachers, coaches, attorneys, preachers, counselors, factory-workers, building contractors, merchants, writers, poets, song writers, fitness directors, computer experts, insurance agents, firemen/paramedics, sign language experts, potters, artists, nannies, caterers, an iron man triathlete. Many of them fit more than one of those categories at the same time.

During their visits we talked, joked, laughed, walked around the farm, cooked out, picnicked, went to Kings Island Amusement Park, visited historical Golden Lamb, toured the Antique Airplane Museum in Dayton, went through Mammoth Cave in Kentucky, watched the Columbus fireworks with 600,000 other people, pruned Scotch Pines into Christmas tree shapes (watching for wasps and hornets), burned piles of brush, laid scraps of sod in bare places of the yard, raked leaves (dropped sun-shades and had a search party), taught girls to crochet and knit, explored the ravines (got stuck in quicksand), rappelled up and down the steep cliff, sprayed yellow-jacket holes in the garden, played in the snow (lost glasses, found the next spring), fished, hit golf balls on the sod field (with strict orders from Joe for retrieval), tore down the old milk house and burned it, all of that and much more, and always played games in the evenings.

Whether they came to visit together or alone, from Ohio or Alabama, Tennessee, Florida, Texas, Oregon or California, from the moment they arrived until the end of their stay, times were a combination of serious, joyous and fun. Joe always had projects on his mind and expected help from visitors when they stayed long enough, but he expected the workers to have at least a half of every day for fun. Thanksgivings and Christmases were always special no matter with whom or where they were spent.

During one ten year period one or more grandchild graduated from high school each year. College graduations with the obtaining of BAs, MAs, MDiv, JDs, Certifications and various extra post-graduate work included sons as well as grandchildren. Trips south or west for graduation ceremonies always included visits with as many branches of families as could be included on the route. We weren't able to attend every graduation but we were proud of each one as they attained that milestone in his/her life.

Weddings began in 1990 and we were able to attend most of the happy occasions as they took place in Ohio, Alabama, Florida, Texas and California. When Joe couldn't go I went alone. Our parent-hearts swelled with pride over our large brood and we thanked God for them every day. Not too long after weddings began happening, great-grandchildren began arriving. By the time Joe died we had six great-grandchildren and when I moved from the farm in February 2005 there were ten. My wedding gift to each grandchild couple was a large crocheted afghan and to each great-grandchild a crocheted baby afghan, each one made with love in every stitch.

**Summer Olympics** For some time Merry, Bob and their boys had planned to attend the 1984 Summer Olympics in Los Angeles. Because of their work Bob and his brother Steve flew west to attend. Merry invited Joe and me to go with her and the boys by car. We left home August 7th and took time to sightsee along the way. Merry, Joe and I took turns driving. Chris was 11 years old and Johnny was 7—fun ages. We bought lunch fixings and stopped to eat in picnic areas where the boys threw balls and ran around. Nights in motels and McDonald's for breakfast were the daily routine. Our evening meals in "real" restaurants were at Joe's insistence—the boys thought McDonald's was the place to eat every chance possible and by the time we got home Joe had had his fill of McDonald's for a while!

We covered hundreds of miles each day but still managed to stop at points of interest. As we were driving down the famous street in Las Vegas, gaping at the magnificent hotels, Johnny's mind wasn't on them. "My back hurts," he complained. I was in the back seat with the boys and offered to rub it for him. As I rubbed, he observed with a huge sigh of satisfaction, "This is the life! Being chauffeured down the main street in Las Vegas with my own personal masseuse!"

In California Maggie put us all up in her house. I felt as though I had come home. Benjamin and Susan were living in a small apartment at Fuller Seminary where he was in school while working at Pepperdine

University Library. I wanted to use what time I had to visit them and Maggie so I skipped the Olympics while Joe attended some of them with the others.

One afternoon Merry with Chris and Johnny, Benjamin and Susan with Aaron, Joshua and three month old Rebekah, Joe and I went to Huntingdon Library for an interesting time looking at the many historical items. An exciting find was the letter (under glass) in George Washington's own handwriting. Among his other occupations he had been a surveyor and this letter described the Virginia Military Land Grant District that included 4,204,800 acres of southwest Ohio, of which Joe's farm was a very small part. The land was reserved by the State of Virginia to satisfy land grants made to veterans of both the French & Indian War and the American Revolution. The letter stated that he, George Washington, was eligible to receive land in the district, but he never applied for the land patent, though he made frequent visits there as a surveyor. We crowded around to see and hear, but it was Joe's phenomenal memory that latched on to details he later enjoyed repeating back home to anyone who would listen.

Bob and Steve flew home and Joe, Merry, the boys and I set off north to see more of the country on our way home. The first stop was in Fresno to visit Nancy, Raymond and children. Joe and I enjoyed introducing our daughters to each other and watching our children get acquainted with their step-cousins. Our weekend with them fit perfectly the expression, "A good time was had by all!"

From there we zig-zagged through various states seeing famous sights as we covered the miles. We arrived home August 23rd exactly a year to the day from when Joe and I had arrived at the farm.

**Garden Bounty** Joe's garden had not been idle in our absence and we returned in time to pull weeds and enjoy fresh vegetables every day. We filled the freezer with corn, zucchini, okra, green beans and tomatoes. I canned 53 quarts of tomato juice and 30 quarts of whole tomatoes to be later made into juice (Joe's favorite beverage). I learned to make zucchini bread and grated and froze zucchini in two-cup bags to use for future bread-making. I tried my hand at making tomato jam like I remembered from growing up in Africa and I enjoyed eating it, though no one else did! That fall we had pumpkins galore to use and to give away. We ate baked pumpkin, pumpkin pies and pumpkin bread and I made pumpkin jam and pumpkin butter—two more things enjoyed only by me!

**Joe's Birdfeeders** Joe loved the birds and kept filled bird-feeders hanging around outside the house. We enjoyed bird-watching as birds of many kinds enjoyed his largess—hummingbirds preferred the flowerbeds. We used his big Bird Book to identify those he didn't recognize and kept a list of the ones we saw anywhere on the farm. Over the next eighteen years we saw cardinals, blue jays, red-headed woodpeckers, downy woodpeckers, pileated woodpeckers, gold finches, purple finches, nuthatches, chickadees, junkos, bluebirds, cowbirds, cedar waxwings, scarlet tanagers, doves, sparrows, Carolina wrens, mocking birds, meadow larks, quail, grouse, bob whites, rufous-sided towhees, indigo buntings, blue herons, fantail hawks, red tail hawks, night hawks, grackles (by the thousands), crows, redwing blackbirds, big owls, barn owls, wild ducks, Canadian geese, wild turkeys, pheasants, a bald eagle and believe it or not, there were more!

**Remodeling** According to Scot's research into courthouse records the farm house was built in 1837. The original house had two large rooms at the front, each with a door facing the road and a window on each side of each door. Behind those rooms was a much larger central room with a porch on each side of it and a walled staircase going up to a landing and bedroom. There was a fireplace and rock chimney in one front room and a wood-burning kitchen stove in the other with its rock chimney on the outside of the house. The central large room also had a fireplace—its chimney on the inside.

Not long after Joe and Grace bought the farm in 1954 Joe began making changes. He, Merry and Scot said from then on there was a constant state of remodeling going on somewhere in the house. By the time I arrived, it only faintly resembled what it had been when they moved there and by the time he and I finished, it was a very different place even from that. From the very beginning it was not a restoration by any means; the materials used in the remodeling were eclectic, which made our work much easier. On one of Merry and Scot's visits I asked if it made them sad that we were changing the house so much from what they had grown up in. They assured me they were happy to see what was being done and looked forward to seeing the progress upon each visit.

In late September 1984, as soon as Joe had bush hogged the fields, he told me details of his plans to extend the upstairs bedroom upward and outward to make a master bedroom and to fashion a bathroom in the adjoining attic. He had obtained a price from a contractor and decided he could do the work himself for a fraction of the cost. That memorable day after breakfast he went upstairs to begin. Without a word to him I donned jeans and work shirt, tied a scarf on my head, and joined him. He was already knocking plaster off the walls and ceiling, exposing the lath underneath. I picked up a hammer and went to work. Thus began my heretofore untried career as assistant demolisher, carpenter, plumber, electrician, brick layer, tool organizer and general "go-fer."

Joe made a chute from the window to his truck below and we shoveled the plaster on to the chute hauled to wherever he needed a hole filled. Lath was tied in bundles, dropped from the window down to the truck and stored in the back of the tractor shed. In the plaster we found little wads of hair—red and black and blonde; Joe explained that it was an old custom to add hair clippings to plaster to hold it together. After finding that hair I joked that all we needed was to find a skeleton! We did find an odd item behind the plaster—the leather high-top of an old fashioned lady's shoe. Joe surmised that it had been brought there by a pack rat—how many years before? But no skeleton! All of the nails were square and various sizes from ¾ inch to 6 inch ones. I saved buckets full of them but sad to say they eventually went the way of the trash dumpster. Many of the beam joints were held together with hand-hewn pegs that we left intact and Joe even carved some like them to install in appropriate places in the antique oak beams.

As we made progress Joe's ideas grew—he always did more than he first planned. What he originally projected as a three month's job kept growing and the ongoing project took the better part of nine years! He could do anything that he saw needed doing, if he had never done it before, he figured it out. That quality reminded me of my Daddy. That quality also made it very difficult for Joe to call a professional for any job because, he said, "I can do it better myself." That was true in most cases but occasionally it was a drawback.

We worked well together and enjoyed the challenges and seeing the work progress. During the winter we worked primarily in the house. When spring arrived we tidied and cleaned the house and concentrated on the outside while the weather was suitable. Both indoors and out, what I had learned in my early years working with my father stood me in good stead and Joe welcomed my presence. Many times he commented that the two of us were able to do—not twice as much—but at least *three times* as much as he could have done alone. And that commendation was reward enough for me.

We exposed large hand-hewn oak beams in the upstairs and cleaned them of more than 150 years of dust and mud dauber nests. We put coat after coat of polyurethane on them until they shone pleasantly and were reasonably smooth to touch but still looked hand-hewn and antique. Joe extended the ceiling upward by three feet and extended the side walls of the bedroom sloping into the attic four feet on each side with knee-walls. The good-sized bathroom in the attic just off the landing was a challenge to his ingenuity but he succeeded in a good way. In it we installed plumbing, electric wiring and duct work and put ceramic tile around the bathtub and on the long counter-vanity beside the washbasin—a first for both of us. He installed a long mirror along the back of the counter to fit the low wall and I found an antique stool to set in front of it.

**War Veterans Meet** Donna and Maurice Barksdale took us up on our invitation and came from Alabama for a few days in October that year. Joe and Maurice found out they had been in the South Pacific at the same time during World War II and as they compared notes, they realized that they were on many of the same islands, Maurice in the Seabees and Joe in the Army but attached to the Marines. They were excited to discover that on Guadalcanal Joe's platoon had guarded the perimeter around Maurice's men while they were building the airstrip; any doubt was dispelled when they remembered some of the same specific incidents during that time. They never ran out of things to talk about and neither did Donna and I. Before they left we made plans to go to Washington, D.C. together the following May.

History and antique lovers, both Donna and Maurice basked in the historical, antique-filled Golden Lamb Restaurant Inn in Lebanon. It is a nationally known Inn where famous people, including some presidents, Mark Twain, Charles Dickens and many others, spent nights after its establishment in 1803. It had been a stagecoach stop on the old main highway between Cincinnati, Columbus and Cleveland. At this writing rooms are still available, still furnished with the original antiques and the three floors are open for interested viewers. There seems to be no lack of top notch chefs for their kitchen that consistently serves first rate meals.

**The Raders** Joe and I had briefly attended two or three different congregations of the Church of Christ, of which there were plenty around. We settled on one in Loveland about 23 miles away where we attended regularly. There we became acquainted in particular with Jim and Helen Rader and our friendship grew with the passing years. Jim and Joe had much in common as veterans of the Pacific Theater of World War II. Our first New Year's Eve at the church, the Raders opened their home for a church pot-luck party and we sang the New Year in.

On July 4th the Raders invited church folks to a picnic in their large shady yard—a perfect setting for such an event. Afterwards while Helen and I were doing dishes in the kitchen, she mentioned that she wished she could know the Bible better. I asked if she would like for us to study together. It was some time before we worked out the *when*. Jim and Joe wanted to study with us and in 1987 we began regular weekly meetings—one week at their house for dinner and study, the next week at ours. We continued that schedule for nearly thirteen years. Then Jim's prostate cancer returned and he became too sick. By the time he died, Joe was battling the same kind of cancer and became too ill for our studies. After Joe's death Helen and I resumed studies at midday on Wednesdays at her house and each time ended our visits with lunch at a nearby Wendy's.

**The Whitacres** We became close friends and frequent companions with Bud and Lucretia Whitacre, our closest neighbors; Bud was also a veteran of World War II. For several years we took turns meeting at each other's house one evening a week for light refreshments, lots of talk and friendly games of Euchre. Serious card players would have been horrified at us because we talked about whatever came to mind while we were playing, at times forgetting whose turn it was to deal or which suit was Trump. Finally Lucretia began keeping notes of those details to help us keep going.

We and the Whitacres went out to eat about once a month using coupons from the *Prestige Dining Club* books each couple bought every year—we liked the "buy one, get one free" offers. The Whitacres enjoyed antiques and flea markets as much as Joe and I did and many Saturdays we explored such places. Other excursions included the County Fairs and special events in Lebanon, such as the Apple Festival, Honey Festival, Onion Festival and Wood Carving Shows. We took in a Quilt Show in the Chatsworth College gym and saw quilts dating from the 1870s to the present day. There were frequent Home Shows in new developments to which Bill Duncan, as building contractor, gave us tickets. We "Oooed and Ahhed" over the big new houses but we returned home glad to have our own smaller, less pretentious abodes.

**A Busy 1985** On January 5th a big snow came and for the next several weeks fresh snow fell. It was March 8th when we again saw the ground. When the snow melted we were able to get back to more clearing of wild unwanted vines and underbrush around the outer yard, cutting, chopping and burning.

Our year was off to a busy beginning on the farm and having company. In April Foy and Margaret came for an overnight visit that left us wishing for more. Soon afterward Alan, Verna and Brian Hadfield came for two nights on their way to Alabama and thence back to Africa. Their visit was a treat too soon ended. Then it was time for our trip to Washington, D.C. with Donna and Maurice Barksdale.

We toured the Smithsonian and the Art Museum where Joe and Maurice tried every trick in their book to hurry Donna and me along—we didn't see nearly all we wanted to. We toured the battlefield at Gettysburg where Maurice's ancestor general was killed, went through the chocolate factory in Hershey, Pennsylvania, and stopped at other interesting places along the way.

When we reached home and opened our back door we were greeted by water running over the threshold. The water was running down from a crack in the sagged ceiling in the hall and into the adjoining bedroom. Joe thought he had turned the water off before we left but a small trickle had been running all that time from the upstairs commode where the bolt that held the tank down had broken. It was a mess to come home to, but as we carried bedding and clothes outside to dry, we couldn't help laughing about our watery welcome, thankful that our remodeling of the downstairs had not already been done.

Soon it was Memorial Day. Our Columbus folks and Newell and Myrt came for a picnic and fishing and much talking. Myrt and I let the rest of them do the fishing while we sat in lawn chairs beside the lake enjoying the shade and the breeze, watching the geese and ducks swimming on the water. Many fond memories are connected with the Memorial Day and Labor Day weekends through the years, usually times for picnics on the farm with Newell and Myrt and our Columbus gang.

**Newell and Myrt** Newell and Myrt were very special people with never ending stories and a never ending sense of humor. Newell, Joe's half brother, was eighteen years his senior and Newell and Myrt had married when Joe was only eleven. Their home was like a second home for Joe when his widowed mother was working. They had no children of their own and Merry and Scot were like children to them. Whenever we had an occasion at the farm we usually invited them to join us. Besides those times, Newell regularly drove to the farm and Myrt came with him when she wasn't too busy. Each spring he liked to put a few rows of butter beans and tomato plants in Joe's garden. Joe cultivated Newell's rows when he did his own but Newell came to pull his own weeds and fish, even when Joe was busy and didn't fish with him. He often stopped at his favorite donut shop on the way and brought a dozen donuts. Sometimes he brought White Castle hamburgers that had been favorites of his and Joe's for years. Before getting to work we sat at the kitchen table talking, eating donuts and drinking coffee or eating White Castles and drinking iced tea. I learned a lot about their lives as Joe and Newell told their stories.

**Maggie** Through all of my years in Ohio, Maggie, my "little sister," was a constant, not only in character but in her welcome visits, whether for a few days or for several weeks. She and I had been close ever since she was born when I was six years old. I left home for college when she was eleven and for many years we were separated by circumstances and miles. The almost three years that I had lived in the same house with her in California had renewed and cemented our relationship and I was thrilled that she came to the farm when she could. She worked with us at whatever we were doing and with her presence even hard or tedious work took on a happy glow. She and Joe got along well though she didn't take any nonsense from him and they often sparred with words, adding to our fun. After one of her visits Joe said, "I enjoy having Maggie here. I love her but I'm glad I'm not married to her!" When I told her what he said she said she felt the same way about him!

When she first came for a visit to the farm in October, 1985, it had been over a year since we had seen her in California. She flew into and out of Columbus and we spent a night at Merry and Bob's house. The next morning Scot treated us all to a fabulous breakfast at Hyatt Hotel. On this visit Maggie helped me pick carpet for the upstairs bedroom. We picked wallpaper for bedroom and bathroom and she helped me apply it—a real challenge on the many-angled walls of the bathroom.

**Upstairs Done** Joe and I had set a goal to finish the upstairs before Christmas and time was flying. We finally called it done in time to clean house before Christmas. Scot, Merry and Bob, with their boys came to celebrate Christmas with us and Merry and Bob were the first to sleep in the new master bedroom. The day after Christmas, Benjamin and Susan, Aaron, Joshua and Rebekah arrived from California. The children were excited over the snow on the ground, something they did not see in southern California except on the distant mountains. We dressed in warm clothes and boots and went for a walk through the snow. Tiff always walked along with us and I have a sweet memory of 3 ½ year-old Joshua walking along beside Tiff with his arm over her neck. Tiff seemed to like it, accommodating her steps to his shorter ones.

We and the California Fudges left by car for Alabama on the 28th to attend a Fudge family get-together at Robert and Dianne's house in Decatur. Mrs. Andrews, close friend for many years, graciously vacated her house so that Benjamin's and Paul's families could use it; Edward's family stayed with good friends, Mark and Phyllis Whitt; Nancy, Raymond and children stayed with Bennie Lee's sister, Edith; Joe and I were at Robert's; Henry and family joined us each day. For several days we were all together from morning till late at night and had a wonderful time. It was the first time since Christmas 1974 that our family had been together—how the family had increased! In 1980 when I first returned from Africa we had gathered at Edward's home in Athens but then Benjamin's and Paul's families had been missing.

**1986 Back To Work** On our way back to Ohio we let Benjamin and family off in Nashville for their flight back to California. At home once more, Joe and I picked up immediately on our remodeling project. We were thrilled to be sleeping in our new master bedroom and before we turned the light out at night we lay in bed looking around at the finished room, recalling from the beginning all we had done. Besides the big bedroom, there was the tiled bathroom, a large landing and a little bedroom under the eaves across the landing from the bathroom. When we stopped for the holidays we had lacked papering the landing walls and Joe helped me do that as soon as we got home. We finished that job by the hardest and agreed that in the future he would do other things while I did the papering—one of very few things we did not enjoy doing together!

**Tiff's Death** Joe's beloved dog Tiff was old and sick and she died January 17, 1986. She had been his constant companion for many years. I asked him if he wanted to get another dog but he said he didn't. He said he was planning on us traveling as much as possible and it was a chore finding a place to leave the dog while we were gone. A very sensible decision, but we missed her.

**Maggie's Call** Late one night in June Maggie called to tell me her youngest son Tim had died. My heart grieved for her. The next day I flew to California. Benjamin met me at LAX and I stayed with him and Susan in their apartment at Fuller Seminary until after the funeral then with Maggie for a few days. Much as I would love to have stayed longer I needed to hurry home to help Joe keep up with summer yard and garden work.

**Downstairs At Last** The day after we declared the upstairs done, we were sitting at the lunch table talking over what would be next. Joe had built a good-sized bedroom within the large room at the foot of the stairs with a hall around that bedroom from the back door to the kitchen. He had been careful not to damage the floors or ceiling. We agreed that that bedroom needed to be removed and the large room opened up. Before I got the lunch dishes washed, I heard banging and squeaking of nails being pulled from wood. Joe was already at it with his hammer and crowbar.

I called to him, "Aren't we going to move the furniture out first?" and he answered, "Simpler this way—where would we put the furniture anyway?" As fast as he pulled the paneled walls apart I carried the pieces to the garage. It wasn't nearly the dusty job I had expected and working around the furniture was certainly the best way.

There had been a large fireplace in that big room that had been bricked up when he had an oil furnace installed in the basement. Joe's heart was set on an old fashioned wood-burning heater/stove and something had to be done about the chimney that he knew was big enough to hold parallel flues. Accomplishing that feat was a challenge and an adventure to remember. It took all four of our hands to install two columns of clay tiles from the basement to the very top of the roof—one flue for the furnace in the basement and one for the stove in the room. That was one of many complicated things Joe figured out how to do and my admiration for his ingenuity grew with every one of them.

**Crooked Stairs** After dismantling the downstairs bedroom, we surveyed the walled stairway and decided we wanted an open stairs—so down that wall came. Joe thought the stairs looked crooked and unstable so he took them completely apart in order to rebuild them. (While work was being done on the stairs we couldn't go up and down and slept in the little side room on a three-quarter size bed.) We wanted the steps to have a natural finish. Joe removed the paint, board by board and was excited to find under the paint that the risers and steps were made of black walnut. He counted fifteen coats of paint on them and each board took a day and a half of hard work with paint stripper and sandpaper.

He fashioned newel posts from 6"x6" oak posts he had taken from the upstairs walls; he made banisters from trimmed down oak 4"x4"s also taken out of the walls. I painted white balusters and risers and polyurethaned everything else with coat after coat so they would not wear out—painting, sanding, painting, sanding, painting—over and over. It was a huge undertaking getting that stairs put back in place, but finally it was done—a job to be proud of. As we worked we named the rooms: the big room at the foot of the stairs became the "Hub Room" because its many doors went to all parts of the house. The little attic bedroom had been Merry's childhood room, where she still slept when she came alone to visit, and was Maggie's room when she came, so naturally it became the "M & M Room."

Each year from early fall until spring for almost six more years, some kind of work was going on in the house—with time out to clear brush and burn it or to do some other urgent project outside. When a trip was planned, we cleaned up our remodeling mess and took time off for the trip. From early spring through summer Joe tended his garden, mowed the yard, all the time constantly busy filling holes to keep the wall of the dam from leaking. I found a plentiful supply of wonderful rocks to make rock-walled flower beds to my heart's content and took pride in beautifying the yard. Our neighbors that had horses gave us a truck load of aged manure and our flowers and vegetables were prizes for the next two or three years.

The garden yielded plentifully and I canned and froze green beans, zucchini and tomatoes by the buckets full. I was glad that Joe enjoyed sitting with me in the shade snapping beans and talking. We had so many tomatoes one year that I finally told Joe that jars and freezer were full and suggested we put a sign by the road: "FREE TOMATOES—PICK FOR YOURSELF." Sure enough someone stopped and asked if we were serious. They said they operated a grill in town and could use all the tomatoes they could get—ripe or green—and they cleared the lot!

**Having Company** Fairly often, when there wasn't too big a mess with our work, we tidied up and invited a couple at a time from church to an evening meal at our house. At first Joe was reluctant, saying he didn't know how to "have company." I assured him it would come easy to him and it did—he was a natural host. After Thanksgiving in Alabama that year, on our way home Joe and I decided to hurry with the downstairs and have more company.

We burned our bridges by immediately issuing invitations for three parties over the holidays: the first party would be December 27 with our Columbus bunch and Bob's parents, his brother Steve, his sister Nancy with her four boys and Newell and Myrt. The second party would be December 30 and to that one we invited Joe's sister, Margaret Denzler, her three sons and wives, Alan and Fran, Bruce and Gloria, Gary and Nancy with their families, and Newell, Myrt, Scot, Merry, Bob and their boys. For the third one, January 2, we invited all of our neighbors whose land joined ours. To make it easier, all invitations specified "Pot-luck." All three occasions were pleasingly successful—even enjoyed by Joe.

**1987 Mountain Tops and Valleys** Immediately after our parties I began painting pictures for the Arts and Crafts Show in May, an annual event at Athens Bible School. Donna had urged me to bring paintings and share a booth with her. To make January all the more hectic Joe had finally agreed to have needed prostate surgery that he had put off for some time. Through no choice of our own it was scheduled for January 27th, my 64th birthday. Joe lamented that it was a poor birthday for me but surgery went well, he recovered nicely and that was present enough for me.

In March Robert, Dianne and Bobby came for a weekend and surprised us with the happy news of Dianne's pregnancy that was progressing well. They had been married twenty years—Bobby was seventeen and there was great excitement.

**Tragedy Strikes** At 5 a.m. on April 24 our phone rang and we wondered who would be calling so early. It was Henry telling us that Eric had died after a motor cycle accident the night before. What a heart-rending shock! We rushed to get ready and left for Alabama as soon as we could. How our hearts ached for Henry and Jo Ann and Lee and Leslie. We spent nights at Robert's house and days with Henry's family. Edward spoke at the funeral that was held in Ardmore High School Gym where a large crowd gathered. Eric, sixteen years old, ready for the eleventh grade, was dearly loved by all who knew him. Words failed to express our sorrow and how we all missed Eric and his bright, sunny disposition.

But we were not done with tragedy. May 23 Robert called to tell us that Dianne was in the hospital for emergency colon surgery. The next day he called to tell us their baby girl, Kristen Nichole, was born prematurely and lived only ten minutes. I wanted to go at once but Robert asked me to wait until Dianne was ready to go home from the hospital, when her need would be greater.

The next day, May 25, Raymond called to say Nancy was in the hospital with double pneumonia and very sick. For the next several days I called her room every day to check on her and visit with her. After about a week she was allowed to go home with orders to rest. She asked the doctor how she could do that when she had three little children. He told her to get someone to take the children for a while, but she decided to try it on her own first.

Dianne went home from the hospital and I flew down to help her and Robert. When Joe came for me, we took Nancy's children, Tonya (9), Chris (7) and Monica (5) home with us for two weeks to let Nancy really rest. She said after the children were gone she slept day and night for a solid week. The children were a joy to us. We kept them busy, mixing play with work, along with afternoon fishing and evening game-playing. At the end of two weeks Nancy was feeling much better so we took the children and a picnic lunch to meet her and Raymond at the Kentucky/Tennessee Welcome Station.

**Bill and Betty** Bill and Betty Duncan lived about fifteen miles from the farm. He was a builder and a farmer and a jack-of-many-trades. The previous year he was passing the farm and saw signs of attempted sod-growing. The year before, a man and his two sons had agreed to grow sod for Joe, but they had other irons in the fire and couldn't find the needed time to keep the grass mowed properly. Bill told Joe he could do it and they worked out an arrangement for him to grow sod on the farm. He went to work rescuing the sod and that July we got the first check just before Joe went to Alabama to get the children and me.

Joe and Bill enjoyed each other's company and formed a solid friendship. When I met his wife Betty, we hit it off immediately and a beautiful friendship was launched. Bill's first wife had died, Betty was divorced; they had been married a year longer than Joe and I. They each had four grown children, who lived close around them. When Bill was busy mowing or working in the sod field, Betty often came with him to visit with me. We spent many happy times sitting on the patio talking or going on shopping trips when we actually did more looking than buying—puzzling to Joe who thought "shopping" meant "buying!"

Every few weeks the four of us went out to eat and as often as possible we played miniature golf afterwards. Nearly every one of our evenings together ended with yogurt cones at our favorite frozen yogurt place. We went to Florida together to spend time with our friends Eldon and Dottie in Lake Placid, where the men went fishing and the women went antiquing. We and the Duncans went to Huntington, West Virginia to see the famous Christmas Lights. We spent three days in the fabulous Grand Ole Opry Hotel in Nashville, Tennessee and took a Dinner Cruise on the Cumberland River. We went to Hawaii and Alaska together. And Bill successfully grew sod on the farm.

**Family Gathering** Between Christmas and New Year we again had a Fudge gathering at Robert and Dianne's house in Decatur—all except Edward's Texas and Benjamin's California families. It was a happy/sad occasion after the loss of Eric and baby Kristen.

In an attempt to put the tumultuous events of the previous year into some sort of perspective, I wrote the following letter to my children:

*January 29, 1988*

*My very dear children,*

*As hard as it is to believe, a new year has already put its foot down. This first month has been for me one of reading inspirational material, meditating and pondering, especially over the events of the past year: what the year may have meant to all of us, each in a unique way, yet with many things in common. I want to share with you some of the thoughts that have filled my mind.*

*The last year could be compared to a journey over a mountain range with its series of heights, valleys and dark tunnels; by faith we knew there was light on the other side and that our God would take us safely over and through, though at times the darkness was almost overwhelming. There were potholes of doubt and fear; our groping steps were nudged on here and there by the angels He sends to minister to His children as we asked and depended on Him for strength and guidance. Angels without wings? Perhaps—only He knows for sure; we may not have recognized them at the time. But true to His promise there has been strength to go on one step at a time, one day at a time, the light growing stronger and brighter after each step.*

*I am grateful for so many things: to be learning more and more of life; for all the wonderful people I have been given to love; for the steadiness of personalities; the constancy of love; the preciousness of the moment; the power of imagination; the strength of the God-given force that enables us to hold each other up when our wings get broken. Learning perhaps above all that pain and joy are inextricably mingled and that out of suffering does come love and hope. He said it would be so.*

*Almost every single day I stand looking for a while at all of your pictures, loving each one of you, praying for you individually. Thank you for being you and for your love and loving ways.*

*Lovingly yours, Mother/Mom/Sybil*

**Bed Dolls Begun** In January I bought patterns, yarn and dolls to make bed-dolls for my five granddaughters for the next Christmas. Almost every evening, sitting beside Joe as he watched ballgames or movies, I crocheted on that project and by the end of September I had finished four of the five to be done.

**Hurry To Downfall** On a day in February when the temperature was 15 degrees and the ground frozen, I hurried to the mailbox. Mail in hand I decided to run back to get out of the cold sooner, stubbed my toe on a rock in the walk and fell on my left hand with my little finger bent backwards. I showed it to Joe and asked him to pull it back into place but he refused to touch it. In agonizing pain, we hurried to an Urgent Care. The upper bone of my little finger was pushed down into the lower section and the knuckle at my hand was shattered. It hurt almost beyond endurance. The doctor took one look at me and at my finger and said, "Oh, my word!" Somehow that was gratifying! The finger healed with a permanent crook in it and I joked that I could hold my teacup in my *left* hand and my little finger would have the socially acceptable crook in it!

**Africa** Joe had been talking about going to Africa to see the country where I grew up. He wanted to go in the fall of that year and it was only by the hardest that I convinced him we needed to begin preparations in April. "What's the hurry?" he asked. We made plans to visit Beth in Tanzania, Foy and Margaret in Zimbabwe, Alan and Verna Hadfield in Johannesburg, and to see Cape Town for a week before going back to Johannesburg to fly home.

We had to get passports, international drivers licenses and inoculations, all of which took time. Our passports were properly stamped with visas for Tanzania and Zimbabwe, but the travel agent told us because of animosity between Tanzania and South Africa it would be a mistake to stamp a visa for South Africa in our passports. She said the South African consul in the U.S. would issue that visa on a separate piece of paper and under no circumstances were we to allow anyone in Tanzania to see it or our return tickets from South Africa. She said to hide them somewhere safe, but not in our carry-on bag, where Tanzanian immigration would be sure to look. I wondered where that safe place would be.

**Oregon Here We Come** With all of that set in motion, we flew to Portland, Oregon for five days with Benjamin, Susan and family whom we hadn't seen in a long time. They were living in Silverton, not far from Salem, where Benjamin was working in a bank. Susan and the children met us in Portland. On Benjamin's day off from work we went for a scenic drive along the coast. That day it rained off and on, the sun shone off and on, and the wind blew on COLD all day. But the sights were truly grand and beautiful. The next day we drove up the mountain to the Christian Renewal Center where Susan had worked and where she and Benjamin had their "first wedding" on September 1, 1979, attended by close friends. Susan knew her mother's heart was set on a beautiful church wedding for her only daughter, so afterwards they went to Agoura, California where her parents lived. There they had a lovely church wedding on September 15. Maggie stood-in for me as mother of the groom since I was in Africa with my parents at that time. We teased them that with two weddings they were surely well married!

We spent our last night in Oregon with John and Wendy Wolfgang in Portland to be near the airport for our early flight the next day. John and Wendy had been classmates with Benjamin at Florida College and had been in our Athens home several times. While in their home Forrest and Elizabeth Moyer came by to see us. She was a daughter of the Dow Merritts, co-missionaries of early Africa days. Maggie and Elizabeth had known each other from childhood and were good friends when as young married women in that area their husbands worked in a lumber camp. Bennie Lee and Forrest knew each other through the book business they each operated.

**Africa Bound** The summer flew by and things were shaping up for our Africa trip. We would be gone eight weeks. Bob Wieland's cousin, Joe

Fisse, agreed to house-sit for us. My mind had been whirling with ideas of how or where to hide our South African papers and return tickets. I decided to make a soft fabric envelope for them and pin it inside my panty-girdle where surely it would be safe from view!

September 27 we flew to Amsterdam. We bought tickets to ride the train to town but to our surprise we never had to show them—going or returning. In the city we walked around, did a boat tour on the canal and were awed by the three and four-story houses so obviously leaning, knowing they were hundreds of years old; and we wondered how much longer they could stand. Joe wanted to eat lunch at a McDonald's but I said, "We can do McDonald's any old time back home, let's be adventurous and eat Amsterdam food!" To our later sorrow he listened to me. What I ate was fine but Joe chose salmon croquettes. After one bite he said they tasted funny and I urged him to send them back and order something else, but he persisted in eating what he had ordered.

Back at the airport we waited for our midnight flight. When they called for boarding Joe said he had to make a quick restroom trip. He was gone so long I was becoming worried, but he got in line at the last minute and told me he was sick. Our flight was supposed to go directly from there to Dar es Salaam but when we got on the plane we were informed our plane "had a package to deliver" at Jeddah, Saudi Arabia. We were not allowed to get off the plane there but we saw the sand through our window and could say we had been to Saudi Arabia. The entire crew changed there and we assumed that was "the package" to be delivered—we heard that the crew from Amsterdam was not allowed to go into Tanzania for some reason.

**Tanzania** At the Dar es Salaam airport, before we were allowed off the plane, all passengers were required to buy $50 U.S. worth of Tanzanian money—hundreds of their paper shillings. Beth was there to meet us and went with us to claim our luggage that wasn't there. We were told our bag had failed to be unloaded and had already gone to Malawi. They said the plane would be coming back through that night but we couldn't wait on it. We promised to call for our bag when we came back the next week on our way to Zimbabwe. So we were without our clothes for the week. Fortunately I had packed night clothes and changes of underwear in our carry-on bags just in case of such a happening.

One of the missionaries had brought Beth the 500 miles from Chimala Mission in his Chevrolet Silverado Station Wagon. We drove half way back that afternoon, but regulations were to get off the road before dark and we spent a night in a Game Park Lodge. While we were eating dinner that evening everyone was excited to see a large elephant walking around the outside of the Lodge. We hoped it would be satisfied to *look* through the big glass windows and not *walk* through them. Joe was sick all night.

On our way the next day we stopped in a small town to have lunch at a little café. After eating, Beth and I went down a small hall to the restroom. Passing the kitchen we saw their "dishwasher" in action—an African girl squatting on her heels leaning over a large pan on the floor. Water in the pan was gray and greasy with particles of food floating on top. She was "washing" the dishes in that and stacking them on a cloth on the floor—no rinsing. We were thankful that we saw her *after* we ate and not before.

Over the next three days Joe slowly improved but to his disappointment he didn't feel well enough to go with the mission men to hunt buffalo for food. During the week without our luggage I was able to borrow clothes from Beth. One of the missionaries let Joe wear some of his. We ate some strange food, including water-buffalo roast and green plantains cooked with onions and tomatoes that tasted like potatoes.

**Masai Hospitality** We were invited with four of the missionaries to visit a nearby Masai Village where the men and women were tall, slim and good looking and the whole village was neat and clean. We were served tea and "buns" in a hut where only the missionaries and Masai men were allowed—their women ate in a different hut. Before we ate, a man went around the room with a basin and a kettle and poured cold water on our hands—no towel, so the men wiped their hands on their shirts and we women dried ours on our denim skirts.

The large yeast rolls were not wrapped—a runner from the village had gone the day before to bring them especially for us and had run/walked for hours to and from the nearest general store—we felt obligated to eat them. I pinched out the inside to eat and surreptitiously put the rest in my pocket. I thought no one saw me but Beth did and afterwards shamed me for not eating all of it. They served us rice from a large bowl in the center of the room. We helped ourselves with our hands, putting the serving into our small bowls then with our hands we formed balls of rice that we dipped into meat stew. After the meal we gathered under a big shade tree where the white men were given chairs and the white women were given stools. The Masai women sat on the ground with children gathered all around. They all sang as the men did a typical dance leaping high into the air.

**Tanzanian Village Church** On Sunday, Carter Geer, the missionary-in-charge, invited Joe and me to go with him to a village church (not Masai) where he was to preach. We gladly went. The little church was under large trees a few hundred yards from the village. As soon as we arrived there Carter rang the church bell—an automobile tire rim hanging from a tree that he struck with a metal bar. As we waited in the shade we presently heard singing in the distance. Carter told us to watch in the direction of the village. We saw a group of people walking towards the church, singing as they walked. The singing grew louder as they drew nearer and it was beautiful. When they reached the church they stopped singing and filed into the building. During the congregational singing we were startled by one woman suddenly ululating. I had read of that but never heard it before.

The "pews" were benches made of bricks plastered with mud, a row on each side of a narrow aisle. The windows were naked openings shaped like windows. The seats were all filled by adults except for young children on the two front pews but as more adults came in the children were unceremoniously pushed off. They sat on the floor in front of the pulpit facing the audience—about twenty of them. The song leader and Carter, when he got up to preach, stood there with little people all around their feet. During the preaching one of the children stood up, stepped gingerly over legs and feet of the other children and made his way outside. Soon another popped up and went out—then another and another. I thought of black popcorn popping! But none of that activity seemed to phase the speaker or song leader. After Carter preached with an interpreter one of the native men preached in Swahili. I was pleased that I understood Swahili words that were very similar to Shona words I had learned as a child and I understood the gist of what he was saying.

Our week was up and we left the mission very early to make the 500 mile trip to Dar es Salaam in one day. The road was paved but the huge potholes had to be avoided. Frequent road blocks with uniformed armed men stopped cars to collect "road tax." They certainly didn't seem to be using that money to keep up the roads! Carter carried his Tanzanian money in a suitcase because it took so many hundreds or thousands of shillings for every transaction. In Dar es Salaam we spent a night in what was supposed to be the town's best hotel. There was no hot water and no towels or soap—the beds did have clean sheets. We ate dinner in the hotel restaurant and had excellent service with good food, though the meat was too tough to chew.

That evening Carter drove us by the huge sports stadium built in the same style as stadiums in the U. S. with a seating capacity of 75,000. The night before it had been the scene of a thunderous music festival in which one of the performers was Bruce Springsteen.

The next day we went to the airport thinking we would be able to change our Tanzanian money back to U.S. dollars because we had not used any of it, but they said no. Instead they told us we were not allowed to get on the plane with any Tanzanian money. Carter had warned us that under no circumstances were we to argue with them about anything; if we did we would almost surely be put in prison and no telling when we would get out. He was not kidding. We gave our Tanzanian money to

Beth rather than give it back to them. We got by with that though they obviously didn't like it.

**A Shaky Departure** To our relief our luggage was waiting in storage for us to claim. Then we had to go through customs and immigration. Joe was ushered into a cubicle with a male and I was closeted with a female. The woman searched my hand bags—even under the bottom lining. Then she patted me down and I held my breath. I did not know the visa paper and return tickets would rattle when she patted my stomach, but they did. She said, "What is that?" With shaking hands I unpinned the fabric envelope, took it out and just barely pulled the papers so she could see the edge of airline tickets. I said, "It is our tickets to go home, I put them there to be safe because we have been traveling in the bush." With almost a smile she said, "That is very good!" I pinned them back in place and breathed again but I was shaking all over! I put my raincoat over my arm to hide some of the shaking, picked up my hand bags and went out. When we met Foy in Zimbabwe I told him about that experience. He said I had given the best reason possible for the papers being hidden—traveling in the bush with money or important papers was recognized as risky.

When I emerged from my cubicle Joe motioned me over to where he was standing at a high desk filling out Immigration papers. He noticed my shaking hands and asked, "Why are you shaking like that?" I leaned toward him and whispered, "I'll tell you when we get on the plane." But Joe was hard of hearing and said loudly, "What?" I tried whispering again a bit louder but he said loudly, "I can't hear you!" So I wrote it down on a scrap of paper! When we sat down on the plane I noticed everyone else on the plane was black and by then I was an untrusting soul so when Joe asked me what I was saying in the airport I told him I would tell him later. I wanted to be off that Tanzanian plane first!

**Zimbabwe** The Air Tanzania plane arrived safely in Zimbabwe. When the plane was taxi-ing to a stop at the Salisbury airport we saw Foy and Margaret on the flat, rooftop balcony from where people watched the planes land and take off. We spent that night in the Jameson Hotel—with hot water, soap and towels.

The next day was Sunday and we drove to WuyuWuyu where Foy had an appointment to preach in the church building that our father had built fifty-six years before. To get there we had to travel about 80 miles. Foy remembered the old road but there was a bridge out on that road and we had to make a long detour. Instead of reaching the church building at 11:00 a.m. we arrived there at 1:30 p.m. We were surprised to find people still there. They had had their communion service and a sermon and had been singing while they waited—they wanted to hear Foy preach. We had another communion service and then Foy preached.

**A Name Sake** While we stood talking to people after the service, an elderly woman came to me and said she was Noel's daughter. Noel had been our house servant and cook when I was nine and ten years old. His daughter told me she had married one of the school teachers. Their granddaughter now had a six-week-old baby that they had, at her request, named Sibelli (their way of saying Sybil). She said she remembered me and liked my name which she wanted her grandbaby to be called by. I was honored.

**Sights To See** We spent three weeks with Foy and Margaret and they took us on some interesting tours of the country including two nights in the Whange Game Park and a view of an almost dried up Victoria Falls because of six years of drought. We spent time in the Eastern Highlands that border on Mozambique and went to see the famous Bridal Veil Falls in the Chimanimani Mountains. Before leaving our hotel to see the falls, Margaret asked the desk clerk if it was safe to go in that direction because we had heard terrorists were still coming across the border from Mozambique. The clerk said seriously, "Well, some people went there yesterday and they came back!" So we went—and came back!

We visited several other interesting places as we headed south to Foy and Margaret's home in Bulawayo. Joe had read about Cecil John Rhodes and from me he had heard about John Sherriff, the stone mason who carved Rhodes' tomb out of solid granite. Foy let us use his pick-up-truck to visit Rhodes' Grave on Worlds View in the Matopo Hills not far from Bulawayo. While in Bulawayo I took Joe to see the place on Bamboo Road, where I had lived with my parents during the 1970s. There was almost no resemblance to the place I remembered; the front yard had been converted into a field of mealies (corn) and cabbage. Understandable; they couldn't eat flowers.

**South Africa** Then we flew to Johannesburg to visit with Alan and Verna Hadfield. Verna had urged her butcher to have on hand water-buffalo, crocodile, ostrich and kudu meat so she could cook some for her "American visitors." She asked him to grind what she thought would be too tough and made meatloaf or curry with it. Joe was pleased and enjoyed it all.

Kruger National Game Park was fairly near Johannesburg so Joe and I rented a car and drove there to see the animals and to spend a night in a Lodge within the park. When we turned off the main highway going to the Lodge we found ourselves on a rough, narrow, unpaved road. We were wondering if we had taken a wrong turn when we saw a handwritten sign, *"You are on the right road!"* After a short distance another sign said, *"Don't give up! It gets worse!"* then another, *"You will be glad if you keep going!"* By then we were laughing and watching for the next sign—and there were more. The road was horrible but when we reached the Lodge we could hardly believe our eyes. Before us were Spanish style cottages with Spanish tile roofs and a larger Office and Restaurant in the center. Bougainvillea bloomed around the doors and windows—picturesque and beautiful with a nearby large lake glistening in the sunshine. That evening we ate calamari for the first time and watched the moon rise over the lake.

Our evenings with Alan and Verna were a treat. During dinner Alan and I listened fascinated while Verna and Joe exchanged information from the depths of their amazing memories on any subject either of them raised. After a week we flew to Cape Town and checked into our hotel.

It was Saturday afternoon and I immediately phoned Tom Brown to ask directions to church to be prepared for Sunday. Tom said, "Where are you?" When I said that we had just checked into our hotel he said, "Don't unpack. No friend of ours is staying in a hotel. Go back down to the lobby and un-check! I'll be there in thirty minutes. You are coming to stay with us, don't argue, we have a room just for you."

We spent five delightful days with Tom and Georgina (Dodo), whom I had known in Bulawayo in the 1970s. In no time their exuberant personalities won over Joe's initial reticence at staying in their home and they showed us sights in and around Cape Town that we would not otherwise have seen. They took us to see Ann Gray (friend of Bulawayo days) who was in an out-of-town village for developmentally-challenged people. The residents lived in cottages and worked at whatever they were capable of doing. Ann was in charge of the "Milk House" where she oversaw the morning and evening electric machine-milking and tended the butter-making for sale in town. It was rote work that she could handle well and she chatted happily as she showed us her little cottage and the flowers she had planted around her door.

My good friend of boarding school days, Iris (Reynolds) Smith had moved from Salisbury to live in Cape Town near her daughter. She did the driving as we spent a talk-filled day with her. We went to the top of Table Mountain; we ate lunch on Fisherman's Wharf and had calamari again but cooked in a different way.

Joe and I had thought Table Mountain was the southernmost tip of Africa, but we learned that a place about 150 miles along the east coast from there was actually more south. The next day we drove to Cape Agulhas where the Indian and Atlantic Oceans meet. We walked to the tip of the peninsula, took pictures and spent the night in a nearby Inn—Joe had now been to the southernmost tip of Africa and he was content.

Back in Johannesburg we spent a few more days with Alan and Verna. Verna and I played games after dinner while Joe and Alan talked. The men went to bed leaving us playing and we didn't know when to stop—one night we went to bed at 5:00 in the morning! When our time was up Joe and I flew home from Johannesburg via Nairobi, Kenya and Amsterdam. At the Nairobi airport we were told we could deplane to get exercise or buy souvenirs but *only* within the terminal. Armed guards lined the way from the plane to the terminal and inside the terminal more soldiers patrolled. We were thankful to get back on the plane.

**Home Again** We arrived at the Cincinnati Airport at 9 p.m. November 23 and were greeted by Bud and Lucretia. The next day was Thanksgiving Day and we were exhausted. We rested at home then went for dinner at the only place we knew of that was open—Frish's in Lebanon. The dinner was good enough, especially since I didn't have to cook it, and the pumpkin pie was excellent.

I hurried to finish the bed-dolls and mount them in a sitting position on cloth covered circles of Styrofoam. We had Christmas with our Columbus children and recounted our adventures in Africa. On December 27 Joe and I drove to Alabama for a family get-together at Henry's house near Ardmore. All of my children were there with their families except Paul. All of the grand*daughters* were present and they were very pleased with their dolls. That evening we showed them a slideshow of our Africa trip.

At that time Robert was a Ford car salesman in Pulaski and Joe was ready to trade cars. With Robert's help he decided on a 1989 Crown Victoria. Joe had a headache and asked me to drive back to Henry's home from the dealership. At Henry's house I turned too sharply into the narrow driveway that had a deep ditch on each side and the *right* back wheel went down. Henry, Joe and I couldn't get it out but a neighbor from across the road came to help. He was a big man, weighing nearly 300 pounds. He stood on the *left* end of the back bumper, Henry and Joe pushed from the front and I gunned the motor in Reverse and we backed out! I felt very bad about misjudging my turn into the drive and could hardly wait for daylight to see if damage had been done to the undercarriage; it hadn't and I breathed easier.

**1989 Going And Coming** In January every afternoon after Robert got off work he and Dianne were cleaning and painting the interior of a house they had rented in Athens to be closer to his work in south Tennessee. One night on their way home about midnight, Dianne told Robert her head was hurting so badly she was desperate. He took her to the ER in Huntsville. She had suffered a brain aneurism. The specialist said if it sealed itself off as sometimes happened she should be o.k. but if it didn't—. Thank God it did, but she was kept in the hospital for three weeks. I offered to go down but Robert again asked me to wait and come when she went home and would need me more.

**Thorn In The Flesh** While waiting for time to go I was helping Joe clear brush and dead honey locust trees and honeysuckle vines along our nature trail. My boot caught in a vine and I landed against a felled honey locust tree that had long thorns protruding from the trunk. One of the thorns went into the calf of my leg and Joe had to pull my leg off of it before he could help me up. He said it had gone in about 2 inches—it felt more like 6! My ankle was twisted also but that pain was hardly noticeable compared to the intensity of the other. I wondered if I'd be able to walk the next day, and rejoiced that I could. A few days later I flew to Athens to spend two weeks helping Dianne.

When word came in April that Benjamin, Susan and family had moved from Oregon to Agoura, California, I was glad because, whether true or not, it somehow seemed nearer to Ohio!

**Remodeling Resumed** Joe and I had enjoyed the hiatus from remodeling but we were anxious to finish what we had begun. Our plans to redo the old kitchen consisted only of new cabinets and adding a bay window to enlarge the breakfast nook. Period. Somehow the bay window exploded into a 24'x12' full new kitchen and dining/sitting room extending along the whole end of the house, making a laundry/utility room out of the old kitchen and opening up the wall where the breakfast nook had been. Then Joe decided if we went that far we might as well go on up and add a 20-foot bedroom/studio/sitting room with a 12 foot closet and a 16 foot deck off the back of that! The plan for upgrading the back porch through which everyone came into the house turned into a Sun Room with windows all across the back. We divided off part of the original back porch to make a mud room behind the old kitchen-turned-laundry room, and put a back porch under the deck at the end of the new kitchen! Like I said, when Joe began something it invariably grew—and grew—and grew! Ever after that Scot teased us, asking if we were thinking about making another bay window somewhere!

**Remodeling century-plus old farmhouse.**

The first job of that huge project was to take down the big rock chimney on the outside of the old kitchen. As Joe knocked the rocks down, I hauled them in the wheelbarrow to the back for future use around flower beds. Immediately after that was done Joe and Dave Duncan, Bill Duncan's brother, began digging and laying the foundation for the addition. By then September was gone.

**Intermission** In October I flew south to attend the 50th Wedding Anniversary of Sara Faye's parents, Jamie and Celia Locke. Joe felt he needed to be home to keep his eye on the work. I stayed with Robert and Dianne in Athens and Nancy and children went with us to the Locke celebration in Franklin, Tennessee. Afterwards I went home with Nancy and flew from Birmingham to LAX where Maggie met me. After a week with her, I spent a week with Benjamin and Susan, who had just moved into a newly purchased home in Ontario. There I enjoyed feeling useful looking after the children while Susan job-hunted.

**Back To Building** Dave was a master-builder. He had had three heart operations and a transplanted kidney and was on disability, but he wanted to keep working and offered to help Joe with the building. By that time Joe recognized his need of help on the massive job he had outlined for himself. When he saw what a good job Dave did and how quickly he worked, he became Dave's helper instead of the other way around.

When I got home Joe and Dave had the sub-floor down, walls up and within a few days the roof was on. I horrified Joe by telling him the one window opening on the side of the new dining area was supposed to be a double window. Joe said, "It's too late to change it now." But Dave said, "No problem, I'll have it changed in no time!" and he did. Then he and his nephew Jeff propped up the old back porch roof and tore out everything under it down to the foundation. By the end of November they had a new back porch built that included a foyer and coat closet at the entrance.

One night during that time we had a fierce storm. A loud crash shook the house and we thought surely a tree had fallen on the house. We made a hurried tour looking in each room and out all of the doors and windows but didn't see anything. The next morning we saw that the top fifteen feet or so of the big old spruce tree by the kitchen porch had broken off. It had landed on top of a pile of old-porch debris in the back yard—what more could you ask?

**Making Haste Slowly** In January 1990 Dave resumed putting light gray vinyl siding on the whole house and hung windows in the new addition, but extreme cold weather arrived on the 15th and outside work ceased again. Towards the end of February Dave came back and finished the vinyl siding which unified the old house and the new addition. We thought it looked very nice with black shutters and the new Oxford Gray shingle roof. Late in March we were surprised with a big snow but by then the new addition was ready for insulation. I was relieved when Joe allowed a professional insulator to do the job and wonder of wonders, the man came when he said he would!

**Newell's Death** Meanwhile Newell was having a bad time with his feet and getting worse. I went once or twice every week to help them. Myrt didn't drive so I took her to the grocery store, changed their bed linens and did anything else I could to help. In June he got blood poisoning in his foot and his leg was amputated. He died June 26. Newell's visits to the farm had been sadly missed ever since his feet had kept him from coming, but in our visits with him and Myrt at their home, he had still been a joy to be with. Knowing he was gone left a great big void in my life and I could only imagine how much more so in Joe's.

**Here Some There Some** In July Jim Rader came to help Joe build the stairs for the deck at the back of the upstairs addition. Nothing straight and simple for Joe: he designed three short flights separated by two small landings and enclosed the oil tank and under-stairs with lattice. I planted clematis to vine on the lattice.

When the deck was done Joe built the little "country porch" outside of the foyer at the other end of the Sun Room. While he was working on that I was at the front of the house laying a rock walk from front door to the mail box. I heard a thud and "OHH!" from him and went to see what happened. He was sitting on the step holding his head, blood dripping across his hand. One of the corner posts had come loose and fallen and the sharp edge hit the top of his head. There was a gash on his crown that looked to me like it needed stitches. He held a towel on it while I took him to the nearest Urgent Care where the doctor put in five stitches. When Joe finished the porch, we painted it with many coats of white. It was the perfect entrance and I loved it!

**Myrt's Move** Myrt decided to move into a two-bedroom apartment in Twin Towers Retirement Home. I helped her find furniture to fit the apartment she had chosen. Among the things she was moving from her house was a wooden chair that was over fifty years old and had been painted many times. She wanted to use it for her desk chair and asked me to strip and refinish it. It took me two days to do it but it turned out well and she was happy—so I was happy. Everything was set for Myrt's traumatic move from the home where she had lived for so long. Bob, Merry and boys, Joe and I helped her with her final packing and the move into her apartment. Her adaptability at age 85 was amazing.

In early October a phone call from Bill Short informed us he would be in Columbus that weekend for a Language Professors Workshop. We had planned to go to Columbus that weekend for a wood-carving show in which Gary Denzler, Joe's nephew, would be showing some of his world class bird carvings, so we enjoyed a visit with Bill as we all admired Gary's work.

**Work, Work, Work** When Maggie came and helped us for six weeks it not only speeded up the work but added more fun to our days. She and I tore out walls between old and new kitchen addition and removed old rock wool insulation—itchy, dirty work! We moved unneeded lumber to the garage to get it out of the way, then as it was needed we moved it back in—so many times it became a joke! We helped Joe wire new areas and Maggie helped me find just the right light fixture for the new dining room—no small job.

The new walls and ceiling were ready for drywall and Joe agreed to have Bruce Duncan and his crew put it up, which they did in 4 days. The drywall finishers said they couldn't come until after January first so Bill Duncan volunteered to come and did it in evenings after his regular work. Floor covering for utility room and mud room and washer and dryer were chosen and installed. Joe agreed to have a plumber install the kitchen plumbing so he would not have to crawl around under the floor.

Kitchen cabinets were ordered to go with the cabinets we had brought from Columbus. Earlier Scot and his law partner had bought a house and remodeled it into office space and they were discarding the old kitchen cabinets that still looked like new. When Scot asked if we wanted them, of course we said we did and used them for more than half of our kitchen. With what we ordered and a counter top to unify them, we were all set, continuing our eclectic style! The cabinet people came and installed the cabinets and put on the counter top—but it was crooked. We registered our complaint with the company and asked them to wait until after the first of the year to fix it. A few months before we had decided to have a Fudge/Dewhirst Family Reunion between Christmas and New Year and there was still much to be done.

**Family Reunion Coming** When Maggie left December 10 we missed her every way we turned. We hired a college boy, Brian, to help. We could tell that there was not time to install floors so we had him vacuum the three-quarter inch plywood sub floors and apply cheap paint to settle the dust on that and on the unfinished walls.

During that time on one notable day, in the new addition Destry was installing light fixtures, the plumber was under the floor doing his work, the cabinet people were in the kitchen installing cabinets, Brian was painting the walls, Joe and I were cleaning windows, and every way I turned someone was asking, "Mrs. Dewhirst, do you want this here?" or "Mrs. Dewhirst, where do you want this to go?" I hardly knew whether I was coming or going, but I was operating on adrenalin. Every now and then when Joe said, "There's no way we'll get all of this done in time," I was able to assure him over and over, "We will and what we lack won't be noticed—just wait and see."

**A Breather** We went to Scot's for Christmas Eve dinner and spent the night—what a relief it was to get away from it all for that short time. Then Merry went home with us for two days to help me begin the cleaning up and moving things out of the Hub Room where they had all been piled while the work was going on. Paul, Janis and boys came and the next day Benjamin, Susan and kids arrived. Benjamin and Paul helped Joe hang doors in the mud room, they installed the microwave over the stove in the kitchen, carried endless boxes of stuff to the basement (out of sight out of mind) and put two coats of paint on the mudroom walls. Janis and Susan helped clean and put things in the new kitchen cabinets and helped me shop for groceries. While we were in the market it began snowing. When we came out we couldn't remember where the car was parked—we thought we would freeze to death before we found it and got our two carts full of groceries unloaded into it.

Weeks before I had cooked and put in the freezer three gallons of chicken stew, three and a half gallons of chili-con-carne, two gallons of B-B-Q—all frozen in quart or pint containers. I had precooked several pounds of bacon and sausage ready to warm in the skillet as needed. All hands helped get things shaped up for the crowd to be arriving December 30. How thankful we were for Merry's help and the two couples coming early and what fun we had working together!

**"Here They Come"** On the day we were expecting the next arrivals our work was about done but Benjamin said something was missing. He wanted it to look like Christmas. I told him where to find the decorations and he hastily spread them around the rooms to "give the place some

Christmas spirit," he said. He was putting away the boxes when someone called out, "A van's turning in the drive—it's Nancy and Raymond!" Broom, dust mop, and dust cloths were hastily stowed and I announced, "We're done! Now let's act like we've just been sitting around waiting for them to arrive!"

Joe and I had bought several sleeping bags at Big Lots and some extra blankets and those who came by car brought sleeping bags. We had a bedroom for each adult couple, Scot used a camp cot on the landing, big girls slept on Library floor, little girls slept on the floor in Joe's and my room and boys slept in a long line on the floor of the Sun Room. Merry, Bob and boys came for the days and evenings and went to his parents' house for the nights.

And we had four days of a wonderful, wonderful time. We missed Robert, Dianne and Bobby—she was not able to travel yet after back surgery.

**1991** After everyone left Joe and I began planning our next "to do" list even while we put away bedding, rearranged furniture and cleaned the house. As we worked we recounted memories, times with each individual and with all of the group. As we worked we talked of what a blessing the unfinished floor turned out to be in less stress for everyone as we looked at the coffee stains and grease spots and what fun we had had over the spills and the splatters.

We remembered:

- What joking and chatter went on over the sweatshirt paint signatures by all (a shirt for Joe and one for me) and how we enjoyed looking at every name on them and Erin's tiny footprint signature.
- How thankful we were for fast-drying paint that Paul, Janis and Susan had applied in the mudroom at those very last minutes.
- How thankful for the "pre-hung" doors so Joe could get the shower and toilet ready for use by the first arrivals—and laughing as we

thought of the first shower-takers having to scrape drywall plaster out of the shower stall.

- How Benjamin and Paul put the microwave/stove vent and hood in place even while Joe and Destry were getting the stove hooked up and the refrigerator moved in.
- How Merry began the cleaning and moving into the new kitchen with the job picked up and carried on by Janis and Susan. So much dust and so much stuff to be disposed of.
- How exciting it was Friday afternoon as we did the last minute rush jobs to hear someone call out, "A van is turning in—it's Nancy and Raymond!"
- How well the three bathrooms and two water heaters worked with everyone being thoughtful—if anyone missed out they were gracious enough not to complain.
- How on Saturday morning Scot arrived with all those delicious pastries.
- How exciting when Merry, Bob and boys arrived and some family members met each other for the first time.
- How thrilling when Henry, Jo Ann and Leslie arrived with our first great-grandchild, Erin, and how she won every heart.
- How coordinated all the women were in meal preparation and serving and how the frozen food supply kept us from spending hours in the kitchen.
- How all the children amused themselves interacting with each other so well.
- How cheerfully they all took to their sleeping bags on the floor.
- How every person, young and older, were so gracious and kind during the whole weekend in sometimes less than perfect conditions.
- How the very pinnacle of highpoints of the whole time had to have been our Sunday morning around the big table worshipping God together, remembering our Savior in the Communion, singing praises to Him and encouragement to each other.

- With a special thanks to Edward for making the early Sunday morning trip to the store because I accidentally picked up "Cran-grape juice" instead of plain grape juice and didn't realize it until that morning.
- How all participated, each in his/her own way from the youngest to the oldest.

My heart overflowed with joy and gratitude then and does now in remembering it all—to be so richly blessed.

**No Let Up** During the days that followed, Brian helped Joe run heat and A/C ducts to the new part, mend a hole in the culvert, patch a big sinkhole in the wall of the dam, clean and gravel the crawl space under the old kitchen. The cabinet men removed the crooked counter top and brought back and installed a straight one and mended the slit they had cut in the drywall to "make the crooked one fit!"—all time-consuming things that when done left a feeling of satisfaction.

**Parque Bargain** Ever the bargain-hunters, Joe and I had found a real bargain and bought enough tropical-oak parque to do the floors of the new addition—that whole 12'x24' length, plus the Sun Room, plus the upstairs long room that we called the Work Room or Guest Room, depending on our mood. Before gluing the parquet 12"x12" squares down, we laid 4'x8' sheets of quarter-inch luan plywood on top of the ¾ inch plywood sub floor. Joe said we needed to put lots of ¾ inch nails in the luan to keep the floor from squeaking so we did—hundreds of them. I helped him hammer nails—including my left thumb nail—but I got smart after that and used needle-nose pliers to hold the nail for the first blow of the hammer! The tongue and groove parquet squares were fitted and glued on top of that. It looked good!

Now we were ready to tackle the two fifteen by fifteen, side by side, hitherto untouched front rooms. Brian came during his spring break in April and helped us take out the 1970s shag carpet and padding—no small job. We had planned to put parquet floors in those rooms, too, but when we saw the old pine floors we decided with some patching and refinishing they would look better and more antique than the parquet. More of our eclectic look! We rented a sander and Joe did that hard job. He salvaged some pine flooring from the old back porch and used it to patch where the fireplace and sink had been in the original kitchen. In the double-door-wide opening between the two rooms he hung louvered folding doors. The room that had been a living room was designated as Joe's Library—it already had some bookshelves in it and his beloved wood-burning fireplace. What had been the dining room became my Music Room where the piano would be. Each room had a door opening to the other part of the house. Scot had given us two antique doors he found in his basement and they were perfect for those two doors: more eclectic.

I put three coats of polyurethane on the pine floors while Joe tended to leaks in the dam wall. Joe wanted natural finish woodwork in his library and I wanted painted white woodwork in the music room—we compromised by him doing natural and me doing white! Then we parqueted the Sun Room floor.

**The Dream** Lucretia volunteered to help me paper the Music Room, kitchen and dining area. I found beautiful pre-pasted blue striped-with-flowers wallpaper for the Music Room. It had so much paste on the back that after soaking it and getting it on the wall we still had paste oozing out of the seams. It was a messy job but it looked good. We were exhausted by the time we finished and that night I dreamed that it fell off during the night. When I woke next morning I hurried downstairs to see if it really had fallen and was thankful to find it still on the wall!

Joe was very busy outside during July so Brian and I parqueted the floor of the new 12'x20' room upstairs (including the closet). Brian used the electric saw to trim pieces as needed but he had to leave before we finished and I was not about to stop. I used the electric saw for the first time in my life and finished the job in time to get the room ready for Foy and Margaret's upcoming four day visit with two of their grandsons.

After that I was not afraid to use the electric saw when I needed to and I had added another skill to my list! We were ready for our guests when they arrived and Joe enjoyed fishing with them and teaching them to filet the fish they caught. We had fried fish for supper twice before they went home.

The summer passed swiftly and September was upon us when Maggie arrived to help me finish the big upstairs room. It was well-lighted with multiple windows and I planned to paint pictures there when I got caught up! We had already used it for a guest room but walls were not painted or papered, woodwork wasn't stained and polyurethaned and mini-blinds were not hung. Maggie and I were rushing to be ready for the coming of Foy, Margaret, Beth and Bill for a weekend while Maggie was still there—a reunion of the Short siblings. What fun we had! Maggie left soon afterwards to get herself settled in Prescott Valley, Arizona, where she had decided to make her retirement home.

**Last Room—Almost** One evening in October I was sitting with Joe watching the news when I decided to tear out the wallpaper in the old downstairs bathroom and put up the new paper I had recently found. That was the bathroom that was redone in 1983 when Joe and I were about to marry and after eight years of being the only bathroom it was in need of a facelift. Joe caught the fever and tore out the tile flooring and installed new, and built a half partition to hide the commode from kitchen view.

**Joe's Choice** When Joe said he wanted to pick his own wallpaper for his Library, I acquiesced with fear and trembling, but he surprised me when he picked a three-toned brown/beige with a fabric texture. We departed from our resolve to not paper together again and did the job with a minimum of animosity! He built a shelf around all four walls above the doors to hold some of his many books, and built-in his new desk across a corner. I stained all the wood and put polyurethane on it and for his birthday gave him a nice leather chair to go with the desk. When Joe saw how much the area rug I had picked for the Music Room helped the looks of it, he said he wanted to pick out a rug for the Library. I cringed again but again he surprised me with a choice that completed the room in a good way.

The last room was done and we heaved a huge sigh of relief. By then we had decided being retired did not guarantee a conventional life of leisure. We were just plain workaholics anyway so that kind of life would not have suited us.

**New Cookware** The more people we had for dinner the more I wished for some good cookware. So when Henry and Jo Ann, who demonstrated and sold Towncraft Cookware, said they could come to give a demonstration, I invited four couples. The meal was excellent and the evening was fun. Joe and I bought a medium sized set to replace the odds and ends we had been using. It was amazing how much easier it was to cook after that.

**Mason Church of Christ** Joe and I had attended Loveland church for several years and were happy there until suddenly the preacher was fired. There had been undercurrents there that we were not aware of. A new younger preacher was hired but he had such a dogmatic attitude about his opinions that we stopped going there and visited around at other churches looking for a better attitude toward the Bible and of members toward each other. In March 1991 we visited Mason Church of Christ and in that first visit we were sure we had found the place. We were cordially welcomed and invited into one of the two Senior Sunday morning Bible classes. There were 45-50 in that class and everyone we met seemed to be a kindred spirit. Many of the Seniors in those classes were residents of Mason Christian Village and we soon had many good friends among them. The attitude among the members was loving and the preaching every Sunday was a feast of good things from the Bible.

In the Sunday morning class, when they learned that Bennie Lee Fudge had been my husband and that I had been associated with The

C.E.I. Publishing Company, there were many who said they had grown up using *Use Your Bible Workbooks* in Sunday School. Two of the men who had been associated closely with Standard Publishing Company and Cincinnati Bible College were familiar with Bennie Lee's name and The C.E.I. Publishing Company.

Our class members met monthly for an evening pot-luck meal and various activities. In 1994 they asked me to be their Social Coordinator and Joe helped me with that for the next three years. I enjoyed planning the meals and programs and delegating to willing helpers. Various couples invited Joe and me to their homes for dinner, and many couples from our class were invited to dinner at our house. Twice we invited the whole class to our house for our monthly pot-luck meal. Both times we ended with gathering in the Library-Music Rooms and singing together in four part harmony. How they could sing!

The two Senior Classes had a friendly rivalry and each had an excellent teacher. On one occasion the teachers decided it would be interesting to have a combined review lesson on the order of "Jeopardy." They set up two lecterns at the front of the classroom with a bell on each one. Six contestants were asked to volunteer from each class. One of the teachers asked the question, the other kept score. If the contestant knew the answer he/she hit the bell and whoever hit their bell first was allowed to answer. I had not volunteered but at the last minute one of our six was absent and I found myself substituting.

First one side and then the other was ahead, then it was down to the last two contestants—I was one of them. My opponent knew her material as well as I did and it was a matter of who hit the bell first so I began forestalling the questioner, not waiting for him to finish the question before I hit the bell. After two or three of those times he said, "O.K. Sybil, I'm going to let you tell me what the next question is!" When the final question came, we were tied—excitement could be felt. The question was a multiple choice: "What was Samuel's home town: Pisgah, Ramah, Bethel or Gilgal?" I hit my bell thinking I knew the answer and said, "Pizgah" but that was wrong. The other side had won! Our teacher congratulated me for purposely giving the wrong answer so that the other lady could win because her class seemed to have a slight inferiority complex (perhaps they had heard that we called them "the old folks!") My teacher didn't believe me when I told him it was not on purpose!

**Christmas Trees** Robert and Dianne came for Thanksgiving and Dianne mentioned that they would like to get a Christmas tree. Robert thought he had talked her out of the idea and they left without it. Joe and I were barely back in the house when we saw them turn into the driveway and went out to see what they had forgotten. Robert sheepishly said, "We decided to come back and get a tree!" And Joe, in his usual generous way said, "Sure, you can have any tree you want." We went walking through the trees and Dianne picked one—but it was one of Joe's favorite blue spruce trees and he had thought she would pick a Scotch Pine! He tried to urge her toward a different tree but I saw that she really wanted that one and reminded him of his rash words. So he helped Robert cut it and tie it on top of their car.

It was time to put up a Christmas tree in our house and Joe wanted a five-foot Scotch Pine in the corner of his Library with multi colored lights and all of the many decorations from years past and lots of icicles. This time I wanted a three foot blue spruce on the table between the windows in my Music Room, with blue lights, blue balls with pearl garlands and no icicles. After some discussion I suggested we settle it by having two trees. "Why don't you put the kind you want in your Library and you decorate it just like you want to and I'll put the kind I want in the Music Room and decorate it to suit me!" I thought they were both perfect for their place. During the holidays our visitors enjoyed the novelty of "his" and "hers" Christmas trees and some even said they might do that themselves the next year.

**1992 This, That And All Kinds Of Other** For some time, as the mood struck him, when he had time, Joe had been writing short stories in longhand about his Army days during World War II, most of them about his time in the South Pacific. I had a Brother Typewriter with a sixteen-letter memory and volunteered to type his stories for him. During January and February I typed on Joe's stories and he kept on writing. It was a restful kind of work after what we had been doing for so long. We enjoyed our "new" house and played lots of Scrabble and read a lot and I even practiced some on the piano.

In March we decided to make a trip to visit our Katy children in Texas and do some other visiting along the way. We took an almost due west direction to spend a night with Vonnie and Gene in Pittsburg, Kansas; from there to see my Uncle Clarice (Daddy's brother) in Harper, Kansas; then to Denton, Texas to spend a few hours with Leroy Garrett and his wife, Ouida. In Katy we had a great time with Edward and Sara Faye for four nights. From there we headed home and saw our Alabama bunch briefly on the way.

In May/June we said "hello" to the Alabama kids on our way to Florida. We took Benji home with us and picked up Chris Fudge on the way back through Alabama. A few days after we got home Aaron and Joshua came for two weeks. We had a houseful of boys with never a dull moment.

Nancy, Tonya and Monica came for Chris but couldn't stay long. Benji went home by Amtrak and told me later it was a 36-hour adventure that he was ready to repeat at the first opportunity! Aaron and Joshua flew home and then we were back to just us.

An elaborate flower show called *Ameriflora* was held in Columbus. Scot invited us to come and bring Myrt and said he would take the day off. Myrt was not able to walk much and Scot pushed her around in a wheelchair so she could enjoy it all with us.

**"Hurricane"** For some time I had been acting as distribution center for used clothing and household goods that people wanted to donate to worthy causes. Joe and Grace had been good friends with Mary Lou and Dick Horn who had the connections to distribute to the needy in the city center and throughout the neighboring counties. Those were the days of CB radios and Mary Lou's CB name was "Hurricane" so she had become known by that name. I was a relatively small tributary to Hurricane's efforts but I sorted things that were brought to me; I boxed some to send to Verna Hadfield in Africa and took the rest to Hurricane.

Maggie came to visit on December 10th. While she was with us we helped Hurricane gift wrap 52 pairs of sox for nursing home folks who never had visitors and wouldn't get gifts otherwise. Hurricane had the knack of being able to wheedle things at a bargain—she had seen a pile of marked down sox in one of the supermarkets and asked the manager if she could have the whole bin full for less than half of what they were marked. She got them. Her daughter was an accomplished violinist who played with the Cincinnati Symphony Orchestra and she volunteered to play Christmas music in the nursing home to give the residents a treat. Maggie and I were proud to be a part of this lovely Christmas kindness.

Different friends at church and around home learned that I had channels to pass on usable things and my house became a clearing house as they emptied closets. One of the ladies at church worked for a school where she was manager of the lost and found department. After the prescribed time limit, it was her responsibility to get rid of what was unclaimed. She passed on to me backpacks, jackets, sweaters, lunch boxes, shoes, sports sox, caps and so forth. A wonderful thing about that lady, she always washed everything before giving it to me and I really appreciated that; if you have ever smelled weeks-old children's lost and found you would understand just how much! I sorted everything and a couple of full boxes went to Verna. So long as I labeled her boxes "Used Clothing" she didn't have to pay Customs on them.

**Family Gathering** We had another Fudge Dewhirst Family Reunion planned for December 24th-30th with some kids coming earlier and some later but all to be present for 26th and 27th except Edward's family and Janis and Benji. Having Maggie with us added to our pleasure, but there was sadness mixed with the joy of being together since Paul and Janis had divorced during the year. After the others left, Benjamin and family went to Alabama for a few days to visit special friends and kin.

**1993—Another Year Begun.** Benjamin and family returned from their Alabama visit. Weather was bad and children were restless so while Benjamin and I took Maggie to the airport, Joe and Susan made a fire in the Library fireplace with promise of a wiener/marshmallow roast. Joe enjoyed making fires in the fireplace and was tickled to have a wiener roast in his Library. The next day was another stay-in-the-house day so we took the kids to Dayton Air Force Museum—always a winner.

Myrt called me in March to come help her pack and prepare for the major apartment cleaning. All clothes, dishes, pots and pans, whatnots, everything but furniture, had to be packed in boxes and moved out into the hall while the apartment was thoroughly cleaned. The next week we put it all away again. That process was supposed to happen annually but Myrt kept her place so clean they allowed her to skip some years between the major cleanings and we were thankful for that.

**Doug's Month** April—welcome spring weather and beautiful flowers were back again. Paul made an overnight trip bringing Doug to stay for about a month. If there had been a way to put what Joe planned for that month into fast forward, we just might have done everything. As it was . . . but here's the list:

—move wood piles across the road, remodel milk house, clean up swimming area and daily keep it cleaned by weeding and raking sand, fix diving board, clear weeds and junk around tractor shed, clean weeds and grass off dam wall, clear and fix up three different underbrush areas, cut dead trees and dispose of them, clean up weeds from chicken-house foundation and stack loose rocks found there, catch night-crawlers every night and have a stand beside the road to sell bait to passing fishermen, have picnics every few days, go fishing early every morning and late evenings, go swimming whenever we get hot, haul up small boulders from around the farm to fix the rock garden by the driveway, go panning for gold in the ravines—all this besides regular mowing, trimming, and picking garden produce—and I'm sure there were more things on his list!

Doug enjoyed some excitement when we went to Columbus for the city's huge 4th of July fireworks display. It was reported that there were over 600,000 people there with a large part of downtown roped off against motor traffic. About 2/3 way through, an emergency weather warning came on loudspeakers telling everyone to go home as tornadoes were sighted headed our way. People hurried to their cars amid great excitement. Our fear was of getting separated in the crowd so we formed a chain—Bob led the way and we held tightly to the belt of the person in front of us. A day or so later the street where we and the mob had been walking to our cars, collapsed in a sinkhole and a car fell into it. Unknown to anyone, the underground had been washing away because of broken drains. It was horrifying to think what could have happened if that street had collapsed with hundreds of people, including us, on it.

Doug's time with us ended. We had fun while we worked and we worked hard, but when his month was up, there was still plenty to do. He probably thought Simon Legree had come back to life as twins and I was afraid he would never want to come back again. But as the future unfolded I was glad to see it didn't affect him that way.

**August 1, 1993** When we married Joe had said he would be happy if we could have just ten good years together. And here it had been ten good years since he said that—our tenth wedding anniversary. All our kids had combined their talents and efforts and produced an album of messages, every message so loving it made our hearts glow. We were amazed at all the poets, artists, tri-linguists, ingenious computer composers and meaningful writers of all kinds within our family group. What a treasure to have such children and to have the album they prepared. Joe and I found it almost unbelievable that ten years had gone by since we found each other—and what a full ten years they had been with never a dull moment.

**Here Some There Some** In August Scot moved from his house south of Columbus city center to a house in Victorian Village north of city center. His "new" house was built about 1890 and is so packed with antique Victorian ambiance that it thrills me every time I am in it. Joe and I were happy that he invited us on his moving day to help by being "receivers" at the new place while he dispersed from the old.

A less glamorous job on the farm took many weeks and more hard work. The culvert under the drive had to be repaired from the bottom up because a heavy truck had broken the big clay tile. Joe used all of his ingenuity to keep the drain open while alternating metal reinforcing rods with lots of cement to prevent future cave-ins. My job was to mix cement in the wheelbarrow and shovel it into places he pointed out while he held the reinforcements in place. Bill Duncan was interested in the process and said in his opinion there was no danger of it ever caving in again! While we were at it Joe and I built decorative rock sides from the water level to about 27 inches above drive level.

**1994** The Iwo Jima Survivors Association, of which Joe was a member, had a reunion in Wichita Falls, Texas in March. We decided to go to that and to add visits with Maggie in Prescott, Arizona and Bill in Abilene, Texas plus breakfast with Melanie, who was attending ACU in Abilene. From there we drove to Stephenville for a night with my cousins, Missy and her sister Marjy. We spent two nights with Edward and Sara Faye and as we made our way home had brief visits with our Alabama families. We had covered a lot of territory in a few short weeks.

Robert was graduating from University of Alabama Athens Extension in May and a trip south seemed appropriate and a good excuse for Joe to go fishing with Eldon in Florida. By the time we had the yard shaped up and things ready to leave for a few weeks, we were so tired we might have stayed at home if we hadn't enjoyed traveling so much.

Earlier Henry had completed work on his BA degree, like Robert, with night classes and computer work, but he opted not to attend formal graduation ceremonies. When Robert was ready for graduation he said after all that effort he wasn't about to miss out on the celebration! After the ceremony we enjoyed the President's Reception that followed for graduates and their families. Our car was loaded beforehand so we were ready to leave after having lunch with all our Alabama bunch at Cracker Barrel. By the time we reached Troy, Alabama, night was coming on and it looked so stormy we stopped at a motel. When the fierce storm hit we were glad we were not on the road. The next morning we found that a tree branch had landed on the windshield and cracked it but Joe decided it could wait until we got home to be replaced.

On the way home we stopped in Alabama for Monica. She was a joy to us and I was glad of her help in rescuing the flower beds from the weeds that had taken over in our absence. Nancy told me Monica needed new clothes for school and said, "but she's hard to fit and to please, so good luck shopping." Imagine a twelve-year-old being that! We shopped sales and had fun looking and she was thrilled to find things she needed, wanted and really liked. We would have liked to have kept her longer.

**Alaska** For some time Joe had been talking about going to Alaska and in July we finally took the trip with Bill and Betty Duncan. Scot's law partner's parents, Sam and Kay Artz, who lived near Dayton, were also in our travel group. We flew from Dayton to Chicago to Fairbanks. From there the next day we rode the scenic bubble-top train to Anchorage with a two night stop-over in Denali Park. The train's 35 miles per hour speed limit, we were told, was because the tracks were laid over unstable frozen tundra across that part of the country.

Our two days in Denali Park included a hair raising wild-life tour by bus up a mountain thousands of feet high on a winding road. It was so narrow it seemed at though the precipice side of the bus was practically hanging over the edge. Some curves were so sharp that the front end of the bus actually was sticking out over the edge of what the driver said was an eight hundred foot drop to the valley below. I insisted on Joe having the window seat "so he could see better!" Only official sight-seeing buses were allowed on that road and they met at designated spots only slightly wider than the road, practically rubbing sides with each other. The only wild animals we saw were mountain sheep too far away to tell what they looked like and the tail end of a moose sticking out from a large bush! At the top we were served hot chocolate and cookies while we admired the breathtaking view that was worth the breath-holding on the way up.

In Anchorage we spent a night in the historic Captain Cook Hotel then took a bus to Seward where we boarded a cruise ship and sailed through the Interior Passage winding among the Misty Isles. We went ashore for brief tours at Juneau, Skagway, Wrangell and Ketchikan. We were amazed at how the towns were built on narrow shelves on the sides of the mountains and how the mountains went on down into the depths of the ocean—the ship docked practically on the side of the street. At the foot of the Mendenhall Glacier we watched from the deck as icebergs chunked off the end of the Glacier into the bay, adding to the hundreds of various sized, eerily-green icebergs already floating around there.

A few days after we arrived home we drove to Columbus to tell our family about the Alaska trip and to pick up Benjamin, Susan and children who flew in for a three week visit.

**"Summer Time And The Living Is . . ." Busy** Four days after they arrived Benjamin, Aaron, Joshua and I went to Cincinnati Airport to meet Doug and David (Maria's son). Friday evening Susan volunteered to take care of the home crowd while Benjamin, Joe and I attended our Church Senior Class pot-luck. We left early to meet Paul and his wife, Maria at the airport. Saturday evening Joe and I volunteered to stay with all the kids while Benjamin, Susan, Paul and Maria went out to dinner. We rented a car for the weekend so we could all get to church. Our visitors wanted Joe and me to go out to dinner on Monday evening—our 11th wedding anniversary, but we told them we'd rather take a rain check and go out after they had all gone home: we didn't want to miss any visiting time.

Joe had built a diving board at the new swimming area and with the help of 16 willing hands cleared the overgrown banks to make a beach. In the house more willing hands, Paul and Benjamin leveled the refrigerator and washing machine and Benjamin papered the end wall in the laundry room that I had planned to do for some time. Tuesday noon we had a swimming party at the "beach" with hotdogs and brownies. Tuesday evening Benjamin and Susan saw Paul and Maria off at the Cincinnati Airport. Thursday evening Benjamin and I took David to the airport to go from Florida to Spain with his mother and two sisters. Saturday Benjamin, Rebekah and I took Susan to Columbus to fly home for her new job beginning Monday. The next Wednesday night Doug left from Cincinnati and early Thursday Joe and I took Benjamin, Aaron, Joshua and Rebekah to Columbus airport. In all we had made five Cincinnati airport trips and three Columbus ones and we didn't miss a plane!

But we came close on our last trip to Columbus, which began with heart-stopping stress. Joe had had a new battery installed in our car at Walmart to have confident driving, but Thursday morning at 4:00 a.m. when we were all loaded ready to leave, the car wouldn't start. We had no time for repairs so Joe called our good neighbor, Bud Whitacre, who let us use his car for the trip. Fortunately we had allowed an extra hour in our estimation and left home with none of that hour to spare. Joe was so shaky over it all that he asked Benjamin to drive and I was glad.

We found out later the battery installer had damaged the cable clamps. Joe went in to get the manager at Walmart "told" and I urged him to be polite, which he promised to do. I didn't want to hear it so I don't know what he said but the manager refunded everything Joe had paid! Joe went somewhere else for a new battery and we returned the Whitacre's car with many thanks. Their anniversary was approaching so that evening the four of us went out to dinner and celebrated. All was quiet on the home front once more.

The next day was "hurry, hurry clean-up" because my niece on Bennie Lee's side, Deanna (Waller), her husband Jimmy and 6 year old Steve were coming to spend the night. They were in the area to pick up their 8 year old Elizabeth from a Florida College Camp about ten miles from the farm. I knew they would want to see our remodeled house they had heard about, so I did some fast cleaning. I used the old "closet trick" upstairs—threw bedding into the small closet and crammed cots and sleeping bags into the big closet for the time being. They came and we had a great visit. It always did my heart good when friends or kin wanted to come for a visit of any length and Joe had long ago become happy over visitors.

Soon after Deanna's visit, Foy's daughter Ellen Baize said she would like to come with her son, Jonathan, for a week. It was our first lengthy visit with each other since she had married. Joe was fishing in Canada with Bill Duncan that week so the timing was perfect. Ellen was especially interested in the old days and pictures that I had from the 1920s and '30s. One day we went over to Indiana to look up the little town of Vevay where her research showed some kinfolks of the old days had lived and died. In a heavy drizzle Ellen examined gravestones and took down names and dates with great excitement.

In September our hearts grieved with Sara Faye and her mother over the passing of Sara Faye's father, Jamie Locke. We traveled to Franklin, Tennessee for the funeral. At Celia's request Edward was the speaker. We stayed in a motel and had short visits with all of Edward and Sara Faye's family and the Alabama families who came for the service. We didn't go on to Alabama that time.

Joe had gradually decreased the size of his garden but I still had plenty of produce to put up—15 quarts of beans, 20 quarts of tomatoes in the freezer, and canned 14 quarts of tomato sauce. Bill Duncan had five acres of sweet corn that he shared with us and all his family provided we picked our own. Besides what we ate fresh we used eight dozen ears to make cream style to freeze. In the corn picking process Joe and I lost each other in the corn field! We could hear each other calling but couldn't see over the tops of the corn and couldn't find the same row at the same time. Finally he told me to go all the way to the end where we left the car and he would do the same. We did go to the same end!

**Seeing Stars** Chris and Heather's wedding in Columbus was less than two weeks away when I was upstairs dressing in the bathroom and tripped on my trouser leg. I fell backwards into the empty tub hitting the back of my head on the grab bar. I saw stars and for a few moments I felt desperate because I was sitting in the tub with my legs hanging over the side. I couldn't decide how to get out of the tub and knew that Joe was downstairs and couldn't hear me call. I finally figured out I simply needed to get my legs into the tub, stand up and step out—I must have been more addled than I thought. He took me to our favorite Urgent Care place where my crown was mended with three stitches. The stitches were still there when we went to Columbus for the wedding on the 29th but I managed to comb my hair over the shaved place. I had found a royal blue two-piece shantung dress and Joe a black suit—happily for us, both were on clearance sale, which prevented Joe from objecting too strenuously. He thought he had "a perfectly suitable suit!" but it was old and I insisted that he owed it to his grandson to make a special effort for his wedding and he protested no more. It was a beautiful wedding and lavish reception. Our first church wedding of a grandchild.

**Christmas Tree Time Again** Soon after Thanksgiving, Scot and Merry came back to the farm to get their Christmas trees. We walked toward the lake looking at trees and Scot said he needed a really tall skinny one. In his usual generous way Joe said, "Pick out any tree you want!" Scot found a very tall blue spruce, slender enough to go in his entry hall tower area by the spiral stairs. Joe tried to talk him out of it because it was his "pride and joy" of all the trees. Somewhat grudgingly he gave in but when we went to Columbus for Christmas and saw the tree spectacularly decorated in its place by the stairs, Joe understood why it was the perfect choice and was proud of it.

Scot had invited us and Merry and Bob's family to his place for Christmas dinner. He insisted that Joe and I get there as early in the week as possible for more visiting time. It was always a pleasure to luxuriate in his Victorian house and I was able to help a little with the dinner preparation. Scot knew how to produce an excellent meal. After the other guests had gone and Joe wanted to read the paper, Scot and I played Scrabble, a perfect ending to a perfect evening.

**A 50ᵗʰ Anniversary** Foy and Margaret were married in 1944 and in 1994 their children gave them a 50ᵗʰ Anniversary Celebration in Athens. My brother Bill told us he would fly to Dayton the day after Christmas and go with us to Alabama so we made sure we were home in time to go meet him. But when we got home from Columbus we found a message from Bill on our answering machine saying he was flying stand-by and would arrive in Columbus—so back we went to Columbus!

The next morning we left the farm headed for Alabama in good time. We had gone about 300 miles down the road when I asked Joe if he had gotten the hanging clothes from the foyer closet. He said, "No—I forgot to get them but we can't go back now. You'll just have to go shopping!" So on our first morning Dianne and I set off for the Huntsville Mall to shop for a dress, leaving Joe and Bill reading. They were to go to McDonald's for lunch when they got hungry. We had just been in Penney's a few minutes when Robert called to say he was on his way to the ER; when he had gone home for lunch he found a message from Bobby saying Bill had his leg mashed between car bumpers and Bobby had taken Bill and Joe to the emergency room.

We rushed back as fast as we could, not knowing what, where or how badly Bill was injured. As we went through the square in Athens we met Robert going back to work. He said Bill's leg was being x-rayed but the doctor said it wasn't broken. He was on crutches for a few days and provided hilarious entertainment to family listeners as he recounted the event in a way only Bill was capable of doing.

The following day Joe, Bill and I drove to Nashville to meet Benjamin's plane. Maggie, Sharon and Jim, Vonnie and Gene—from Arizona, California and Kansas respectively, were there for the celebration, as were our Alabama bunch plus all of Foy's children and Beth with Pat and Pam from Tupelo.

Foy and Margaret's children had made arrangements to have the celebration at the Athens Bible School auditorium. We early arrivers saw at once that there was much to be done getting it ready. All hands pitched in and worked hard. Benjamin and Vonnie found their niche setting up and decorating the trellis backdrop behind the head table. They needed greenery which could be a problem in winter. Benjamin remembered the nearby cemetery and evergreen magnolia trees, so he and Vonnie went to unobtrusively get some greenery. As they went out the door I admonished them, "If the police come to see what you are doing, whatever you do, don't use your Fudge name; give Vonnie's name—they won't know Corsini!"

A host of friends from near and far attended the joyful event. After the general crowd was gone, family folks cleaned up then sent out for pizzas to enjoy as we visited until very late.

1994 had perhaps been one of the busiest years of all. On the other hand it seemed to us that all our years were busy with the next thing happening as fast as the last one ended.

**1995** The year had begun even as we returned home from Alabama taking Bill and Beth with us. We took Bill to Columbus the next day to catch his plane and Beth stayed with us for a week then flew home from Dayton. While she was there she and I played games, crocheted, talked and enjoyed having tea several times a day. To make tea time more interesting we used a different teapot from my collection each time. Sometimes Joe joined us but he was very busy and wasn't as enamored of hot tea as we were. He did join us for games in the evenings if there wasn't a ball game on TV!

**Iwo Jima 50ᵗʰ Anniversary** The U.S. had declared Iwo Jima "secured" in March, 1945 and fifty years later Joe and I were on the island for the 50ᵗʰ Anniversary ceremony. The Iwo Jima Survivors Association, in coordination with a similar group in Japan, had organized a memorial ceremony to take place on the island on March 14, 1995. As one of those survivors, Joe wanted to be there.

We flew to Los Angeles, then to Hawaii and from there to Guam where about half of the group of veterans and their families were staying while others were on Okinawa. On the day itself a plane from each island took us to Iwo Jima. Troop-carriers met our planes and young Marines escorted us and saw to our every need. It was touching to see how respectful and careful the young Marines were with us "old folks." As they helped us into the trucks they said to the veterans, "Thank you, sir, for what you did." When we were taken on a scenic tour around the island, Joe pointed out to me places he remembered and had written about in his book.

The ceremony and speeches were at the official memorial. Joe met in person Rosa Ogawa, the Japanese lady with whom he had been corresponding, the daughter of a Japanese naval official. She had translated letters between Joe and a Japanese veteran of the Iwo Jima battle who had been a prisoner of war, Yoshio Nakajima. During their correspondence before coming to Iwo Jima, Nakajima and Joe had agreed that based on their memories, Joe's platoon had been the one to whom Nakajima had surrendered. In 1995 they shook hands on Iwo Jima and talked through an interpreter.

After the ceremony lunch was served under a tent. That evening there was a "soiree" or reception in a large decorated hangar. U.S. Ambassador to Japan, Walter Mondale was among the celebrities and Joe wanted his autograph but had a terrible headache and watched the activities from his seat in a corner. He sent me to shake hands with Mondale and to tell him that Joe had been on the island during the battle. Mondale signed Joe's program then asked with interest what unit Joe was with, I said, "He landed in February with an Army Unit attached to the Marines." When he heard "Army" before I could say any more Mondale turned away. That obvious snub would have really upset Joe and I was glad he wasn't there. I had Mondale's autograph for him and never told him about the other.

**A Week With No Sunday?** On the way over we crossed the International Date Line and had no Sunday that week. I took communion emblems with us and Joe and I had our own little service in our hotel room though it was actually early Monday morning. At breakfast in conversation with a couple who spoke of missing Sunday services, Joe told them what we had done. They said had they known they certainly would have joined us. We left Guam at 5 p.m. Thursday and arrived back at the farm about 10:00

that same night—we had more hours on that Thursday than I know how to count!

**Patio-Picket Fence-Rose Arbor** Spring was fast approaching and we began work on the patio at the side of the house. The flower bed full of lily-of-the-valley along the side of the house had to be taken up and replanted elsewhere so Joe could replace the old basement window. The project was bigger than expected but Joe did a number one job of repairing the opening and improving the window-well outside of the new window. He leveled the patio area, spread sand, and we gathered flat rocks from anywhere on the farm that we could find them. I outlined the seating area with flower beds under the two shade trees and edged the flower beds with thin rocks standing on edge.

**Patio building.**

Scot had redone his back yard and offered us the old bricks from the paving if we wanted them. We did, and made three trips to Columbus to bring them home in our car trunk. There were not quite enough bricks for the whole sitting area so we made a 4'x 4' square of flat rocks in the center. The addition of metal patio furniture made the perfect outdoor sitting room under the trees. The finishing touch to my mind was the matching metal teacart in the center.

It was a whole summer's project. During that time we found picket fencing that Joe installed along the front and side of the patio. My day dream was coming true, now only lacking was a rose arbor across the rock walk that came from around the front of the house. I knew exactly what I wanted and on every trip to a garden center I looked for just the right arbor. I finally found the perfect one, Joe installed it and I wound a garland of red silk roses on it to complete my dream until the real ones could grow! It was October when we finally declared the patio done.

**The Horned Animal** Joe was back at the lake one day when I looked out the kitchen window and saw a big animal standing on the porch. It looked like a sheep but it was bigger than any sheep I had ever seen or imagined. If it was a sheep and if sheep ate things like goats did, I didn't want it to eat things on the porch. I went out to "Shoo!" it away but it wouldn't "shoo": it just stood there looking at me. We were having a staring contest when suddenly it snorted loudly and startled me. I backed to the door and hurried inside. It didn't come any farther so I got my camera and bravely made its picture so I could show Joe how big it was. When I told him about it I declared it had horns. He said when he got back from the lake there was a big sheep in the back yard that he chased away. He said it was a ewe and *didn't* have any horns! I assured him this one did have and it must have been a different animal. By the time the pictures were developed, to my disappointment, it had lost its horns!

**Passing Of A Friend** This year of trips and projects was not without its sadness. In July our good friend Maurice Barksdale died suddenly and we drove to Alabama for the funeral. I had known the devastation of losing a beloved husband and my heart ached for Donna and their children.

The year **1996** began with a January visit from Ann Gray, friend of my Bulawayo days in the 1970s. We had visited her in Cape Town in 1988. Her brother, Simon, who lived in England and worked for The World Bank, brought her to the States to see some of her friends from the old days. They arrived on Friday and much to Ann's excitement snow was deep on the ground and she and Simon enjoyed a snowball fight before they flew south.

**Florida Calls** As soon as weather permitted we tried to catch up outdoors, enjoying all the signs of coming spring but in March before it was warm enough for too much work, Bill Duncan and Joe decided it was time to go to Florida for a week of fishing with Eldon. Betty and I had no objection. Bill did all the driving and Joe was content with that. On Sunday afternoon the six of us drove north from Lake Placid to meet Paul and Maria, who drove south to an agreed upon Mall where we enjoyed a good two hour visit.

**Hawaii** Joe and Bill had decided it was the year to make our Hawaii trip and we began bookings early in the year. On June 9 we flew to Honolulu where we spent two days. At the beach Joe was disappointed in me because I wouldn't go out in the hot sun and walk on the hot sand; I preferred to sit in the shade and watch him. From Oahu we took a seven day cruise with daytime tours on the islands. Betty's daughter and son-in-law, Frenay and John, went with us. It was a magical, educational and fun trip enjoyed from beginning to end and we came home thinking of future trips to other parts of the world!

**Bustling Summer** We worked hard in the yard catching up and getting ready for Benjamin and family coming for three weeks in July. What a busy, full and happy three weeks that was. Josh's friend, Eric, came with them and on one of their exploration trips into the ravines they each brought to the house a granite boulder that was as big as they could carry. Joe allowed them to use his power drill to etch their initials on them. They were sad they couldn't take them home to California, but added them to my collection at the side of the patio as keepsakes for me.

**Finished patio, Spring 1996-97.**

We were thrilled in September when Edward and Sara Faye came for a week. Fall foliage was at its most spectacular. Edward wrote a devotional as he stood in the "cathedral" formed by brightly flaming orange, yellow and red sassafras and sumac. To Joe's great joy the article was published in a magazine. During their visit Joe persuaded Edward to go fishing with him on one occasion while Sara Faye and I went shopping, which he gladly did.

**Destructive Deer** Any visitors we had were excited when they saw deer crossing the field or side yard. Joe and I enjoyed seeing them, too, but when those beautiful deer crossed a field of sod their sharp hooves cut into the grass and left holes. When the sod was laid in a yard those holes had to be laboriously patched by hand, costing Bill extra man-hour expense. The deer rubbed velvet from their growing antlers on trees, destroying about 75 of the 100 little pines Joe and I had, by the sweat of our brows, set out a few years before. They also did major damage to larger spruce and pine trees. With Scot's legal help Joe obtained a "slaughter permit" making it legal to kill deer on the farm any time. He and Bill killed several over the next few years. The meat was processed, packaged and frozen and divided between our families.

**An Annual Tradition Begun** Beth had returned from Tanzania in 1994 and lived in Tupelo, Mississippi to be near her son Pat and wife Pam. Beth, Maggie and I were in constant contact and she kept asking us to come visit her. In the fall of 1996 Maggie and I drove to Tupelo for a long weekend. A tradition was begun. We called it "The Sisters Reunion" and I would challenge any gaggle of sisters to have a more enjoyable time with each other.

Foy and Margaret had retired from their life in Zimbabwe and settled in White House, Tennessee where their daughter Kay and family lived. White House was just barely off of Interstate 65, conveniently located for us to stop for tea or lunch with them on our trips to Alabama and Mississippi.

Sharon and Vonnie, Maggie's daughters, loved antiques and began flying to Ohio in the fall to join Maggie and me for a few days of antiquing at the many places around our area. The girls then flew home from Ohio while Maggie and I made our Mississippi trip—until Beth complained that they didn't come to see her, too. And so, beginning in the fall of 1999 Sharon and Vonnie joined us and our Mississippi trips took on a whole new dimension of joyful times spent with Beth. Our drives to and from Ohio were hours of talking, singing, joking and being a quartet of word-lovers, trying out as many seldom-used words as we could think of. We stopped at antique shops along the way and always had time for tea or lunch with Foy and Margaret and an overnight visit with my Alabama children. We even found plenty of antique shops around Tupelo to keep us happy on that score. We played games, talked, ate out and attended church together. These delightful annual visits continue to this day and are highly anticipated all year long. Joe usually stayed with Merry and Bob while I was gone.

**Sister Trip. (Seated) Sybil, Beth, and (standing) Maggie (center); Maggie's daughters Vonnie (left) and Sharon (right).**

Something unexpected always seemed to happen to keep our times from being monotonous. Once I had an infected nail removed from my big toe the day they arrived in Ohio so Maggie and I stayed home while Sharon and Vonnie antiqued. Never idle, Maggie made black peachskin sheath dresses for each of us—she cut and machine sewed while I, with my foot elevated, did the handwork. Another time we left Ohio just as a severe snow storm came blowing in and we had to take shelter in a cruddy little motel not far south of Cincinnati. Once when meeting their planes, I fell in the airport and made the trip with a black eye, skinned nose and puffy upper lip. And there was the time after visiting the little church in Mooresville, just south of Athens, where James Garfield preached before he became president, that we got lost in the adjoining wildlife refuge. We might still be wandering the maze of roads if a park ranger hadn't come along and showed us the way out.

**Myrt's Death** Myrt had been in fair health and had been able to stay in her apartment, but on January 14, 1997 she was taken to the hospital with severe breathing problems. She died a week later. She would have been 92 in March. Newell had died just short of his 90th birthday. They had both kept their sharp minds, long memories and wonderful sense of humor until they died. They had no children but they were "favorite uncle and aunt" to all of their nieces and nephews.

The retirement home where Myrt had been living since Newell's death naturally wanted her apartment cleared as soon as possible. Three of her nieces in Cincinnati had been very helpful to her and they, Scot, Merry, Joe and I met at her apartment to sort and pack and disperse all her things. At the end of the day all of our cars were completely loaded; furniture was to be picked up the next day. They asked me to donate to our good friend, "Hurricane" almost all of her cooking paraphernalia, most of her clothes and many other odds and ends that none of them wanted.

**A Gift To Grandchildren** Myrt's death was a reminder of the brevity of life and I was inspired to connect with my grandchildren in a special way. Through the years my time with grandchildren had been limited to brief visits with little time for deep, personal discussions. I decided to write a special letter to all of them as a gift from their grandmother to help them know me more intimately. I typed and addressed a copy to each of them individually:

*April, 1997*

*A GIFT FROM YOUR GRANDMA SYBIL.*

*Because of the circumstances of our lives our times together have been relatively few and brief. I want to be more to you than just a photo and a few brief memories from get-togethers, as important as those are. I want this letter* to you to be like one I wish I could have received from my grandmothers, whom I didn't know well. Though I didn't know either of them well, I do know they were hard working people who believed in God and His Word. Their values and ideals were passed on to my parents and for that I am thankful.

I want to give you a sense of what my life has been about, not so much what I have done or where I have been, but what I believe in. I pray that this statement of my simple beliefs may help you in some small way.

I believe in God and that the Bible is His inspired Word given through His Spirit-inspired servants and preserved by Him through the ages for our information and instruction.

I believe Jesus Christ is His Son; that He came to earth to live a sinless life and offer Himself as a sacrifice for the sins of mankind—including mine and yours.

I believe God accepted His death on the cross as atonement for my sins.

I believe in spite of my many mistakes He has promised to forgive me as I forgive others.

I believe because I was baptized into Christ in obedience to His command, that God now sees me through Christ, cleansed from sin by His blood.

I believe the Holy Spirit lives within me, guiding, strengthening, comforting, rebuking me, assuring me of God's promises, helping me to understand His Word.

I believe there is available to me as a child of God, a power through the Holy Spirit that I cannot even imagine—that I must never limit my God by my own limited knowledge and vision.

I believe when Jesus said He is the Living Bread and Water, among whatever else may be included in that, is the urgent necessity of my partaking of that spiritual food constantly: reading, thinking and meditating on His Word and by so doing I feed on Him even when I am not actually looking at the written words.

I believe God has promised me, as His child, a peace that passes understanding; that this does not mean the absence of trouble but that His presence will give me peace even in the midst of troubles.

I believe as someone said, "The peace of God is not automatic, it is practiced and learned; and when much practiced and well learned it becomes a part of our being." There may be times in our lives when it seems that God has forgotten us, but if we will just talk to Him in prayer and read His Word, searching for His Will, we will know that He is with us.

I believe God is everywhere, all the time, all powerful, all knowing. I believe He knows exactly where I am at any moment, what I am thinking, and how I am reacting to whatever is going on. I believe He is there not as a fault-finding accuser waiting to pounce, but as a loving Father ready to guide and help me go in the right direction. I believe the key for this is to have my will in complete surrender to His Will, making me want to do and be what He wants me to do and be. This attitude requires conscious effort and decision on my part and it becomes easier with practice until it is almost automatic.

I believe I should love and appreciate my country and respect its rulers. I believe the better citizens we are in the Kingdom of God, the better citizens we will be in our earthly country.

I believe as people of God we are only temporary pilgrims in this earthly life; that this is our training ground preparing us for the perfect country that is promised to all the faithful.

*I believe God's promise that if I seek first His kingdom and His righteousness, He will see to it that I have what is necessary to take care of this physical life. I also believe that what I think I need may not be what He knows I need. This belief helps me keep my priorities in order.*

*I believe God has provided beauty all around us, in each other, in nature and music and countless other ways, not only to give us enjoyment in this life, but also to help us better imagine what the beauties of eternal life will be in the glorious place He is preparing for those who love Him.*

*It is a joy, a privilege and a blessing to be your grandmother. You have gladdened my life. I pray God to keep you and bless you, that you will love Him and serve Him every day of your life.*

*You are my beloved grandchild*

**England, Ireland, Scotland** Since early in 1997 Joe and I had been preparing to visit England, Scotland and Ireland. We agreed that this time we should take a package tour to avoid all the complications of being on our own. As independent as he liked to be, in this case with his weakening condition it wasn't hard to convince him to let someone else do it.

In London for two days we were free to do as we pleased—we visited the Tower of London and learned that "Beefeaters" were more properly "Yeomen Wardens." They told us the actual beefeaters were the ravens who frequented the tower grounds and were fed a daily ration of beef. We saw up close Westminster Abbey, The Royal Albert Hall, St Paul's Cathedral, London Bridge, Houses of Parliament and Big Ben. We walked through Hyde Park, and from the side of the mall in front of Buckingham Palace we watched the cavalcade and the Changing Of The Guards.

Foy and Margaret's son, Harold, lived in London and he and his wife invited us to dinner. We had to ride the tube, which neither Joe nor I had ever done; fortunately Harold gave me instructions beforehand. He told me that when we bought our tickets and used them to go through the turn-stile, to be sure and pick them up on the other side of the stile because we would need them to get out when we arrived at our destination. Without that warning we would certainly not have picked them up and would still be riding that train under the streets of London—like "The Man Who Never Returned" is still riding ". . . 'neath the streets of Boston!"

Our tour bus guide was a 60-year-old man thoroughly versed in history and able to communicate it in a most interesting way. There were thirty-seven of us on the bus and a more congenial, cheerful group could not have been asked for. Our competent driver navigated the narrow streets between buildings where we held our breath expecting to scrape the sides, but never did. After London we visited south England, Salisbury, Stonehenge, and a castle in Cardiff, Wales where I saw a stained glass window with the name Lucretia on it.

We crossed the Irish Sea on a very large ferry. Joe and I both reveled in the beauty and history of Ireland. We visited the glass works in Waterford. At Blarney Castle my hip was giving me trouble so I didn't climb up the steep steps with Joe, but he saw the Blarney Stone—though he declared he didn't kiss it! We spent five nights in delightful inns in Ireland, the last one in Dublin.

On the ferry crossing to Liverpool I visited a restroom that didn't have air conditioning. The heat and strange odor in there were almost more than I could handle. When I rejoined Joe and the couple we had been visiting with, they looked at me and said, "You look green!" I felt green but thought a cup of tea might help. Sitting very still and sipping hot tea did the trick and I soon felt better. During the night in Liverpool Joe had breathing problems. Our tour guide called a doctor who came to our room, prescribed something for Joe and told him not to travel any more. At that point how could we obey that order?

In Scotland, we saw more castles and breathtaking scenery. We spent a night in Edinburgh but Joe didn't feel well and we skipped the Castle tour. As we traveled south in England we saw Winston Churchill's parents' old home and cemetery where they were buried, we saw some of Hadrian's Wall, and stopped in Coventry. While there I talked with our guide about the old saying I remembered from boarding school days, of "sending someone to Coventry." When a school mate displeased us we might "send her to Coventry" which meant no one spoke to her until the sentence was up. The guide said that Coventry was originally the official seat of English Royalty. After it was moved to London, when a member of the Royal family broke a law he/she could not be put in a regular prison in London so the offender was banished to Coventry to serve a period of solitary confinement—hence the saying. During our conversation I learned our guide was born in Salisbury, Rhodesia, where his parents had lived for a time.

We saw the ancient Cathedral in York, where in spite of fires and wars and rebuilding many times over, church services had been conducted on that spot since the 900s. We toured the Wedgwood factory and watched them making fine porcelain from the beginning with clay to the painted, glazed finish. I looked for a small piece within our price range but saw none and settled for a small ironstone teapot made in Denmark! We saw Shakespeare's home in Stratford-on-Avon. Our last night on the English tour was spent in Wolverhampton, the name of the place being its greatest attraction to me. During our lives Joe and I had read so much history and so many novels set in the countries we were visiting that we almost felt at home as we recognized names of towns and streets.

When we got back to Ohio we felt thoroughly steeped in history and antiquity but Joe was sick with bronchitis for three weeks.

**Melanie and Michael** Hurriedly working to leave the yard in good shape, we flew to Houston in early July for Melanie's wedding to Michael Simpson. Edward hospitably accommodated all family members in nearby Marriott Hotel. Robert and Dianne, Henry and Jo Ann, Leslie and Mike, Benjamin, Susan and kids joined Joe and me there. After the beautiful wedding Joe flew home and I stayed to drive with Sara Faye to Abilene for the wedding reception of Gina (Bill's daughter) and Jarod. They had been married a year and guests invited were those who would have been invited to their wedding if it had been other than before a Justice of the Peace. While there we also had some good visiting time with Bill and Beth.

Then I was back home just in time to go to Alabama for August 23rd wedding of Leslie to Mike Lucas in Madison. Joe wasn't feeling well enough to attend all of the events connected with it but was able to go to the ceremony—another beautiful wedding.

**Dodo Brown** After all our traveling, it was good to settle down again at home. We were thrilled to host Georgina ("Dodo") Brown for a week's visit. I had known her and Tom and grown to love them when I was in Bulawayo in the 1970s, and Joe and I had spent a week with them in Cape Town. Since then Tom had died and she was living with some of her children in Austin, Texas. Her wit and sense of humor with tales of her life in Scotland and Rhodesia kept us entertained and we were sorry when the week was up.

**Three Quarters Of A Century** It seemed utterly impossible to me that I had been living for three quarters of a century, but they tell me calendars don't lie. Earlier in the year my children had asked what I would like to have for my approaching 75th birthday. I said, "Oh, nothing in particular, perhaps just a little more attention than usual." I was floored in December when they informed me that on December 27th they were giving me a 75th Birthday Party in Athens and inviting my friends, young and old.

**Sybil's 75ᵗʰ birthday in Athens, Alabama.**
**(Left to right) Scot, Merry, Joe, Sybil, Paul, Robert,**
**Nancy, Henry, Benjamin, Edward.**

Merry and Scot drove down, Paul, Doug and Benji came from Florida, Benjamin and Susan from California, Edward and Sara Faye from Texas, Nancy and Raymond from Hayden, Alabama, Henry and Jo Ann from Madison, Alabama, Robert and Dianne from Athens—all eight children, six spouses and several grandchildren were there and many friends from near and far. It was held in the Donnelly House, an ante-bellum home used for such occasions. I was well and truly honored. Having Merry and Scot there to mingle with my other children made Joe and me doubly proud. Besides the joy of seeing all of our children together, having our Ohio children meet so many of my friends in my old hometown setting was added joy.

**1998** began and February 28th was fast approaching, the date for another wedding. This time it was Bobby and Connie getting married in Athens. Everything about the wedding was beautiful and all went well—another of the grandchildren was launched into wedded bliss.

**Engrave A Boulder** By now, Joe had finished writing his wartime stories and the conclusion of his writing left him wanting to memorialize in some way the three Army men of his platoon who had saved his life during combat. He decided to engrave their names on a large boulder he found near the lake. He hauled the boulder to his desired spot. But before that could be done he decided to add another lake just above the old one and bulldozing began. Joe's outdoor projects were like those indoors—once begun they grew and grew and grew. So his visions for doing things around that lake grew.

**The Mountain** Instead of the engraved boulder memorial he decided to have the earth from the new lake piled up to form a mountain that would be one-fifth the dimensions of Mount Suribachi on Iwo Jima and a flag would fly on at the top. The project became an obsession that consumed his mind and means for the next five years. During that time he was diagnosed with severe Post Traumatic Stress Disorder and consented to twice a week sessions with a counselor at the VA. The counselor was a good one who had seen combat in the Korean War and could relate to Joe's problems. He helped Joe and me tremendously but did not change Joe's mind about continuing work on the mountain.

**A G.I. Named Joe** Joe decided it was time to get a home computer so his completed stories could be put into it. We succeeded in putting the desk together but neither of us knew how to set up the computer. My brother Bill came for Christmas and volunteered to do that. I soon found myself typing Joe's stories into the computer's word processor. What he had begun in 1987 was declared done in 1997. He had written 101 stories for his book which he titled *A G.I. Named Joe.* The next step was to print it in manuscript form and submit it to publishers. One by one he received rejection slips and my heart ached for him.

But Merry and Scot had been resourceful. They invited Joe and me to Columbus to celebrate Joe's 80th birthday at Merry and Bob's house on April 4, 1998. There they surprised Joe with 50 hardback copies of his book. He was excited and pleased and very thankful to them for such a gift. It was just the right number for him to present a copy to each of the children and to his nephews and closest friends. Scot and Merry did not leave it at that. They carefully edited the book to be sure it would be suitable for the public and had it published on the internet, making it available in paperback through Amazon, Barnes and Noble and other bookstores.

That spring Joe had been diagnosed with prostate cancer. He refused surgery and opted to have hormone shots that would shrink the cancer for a time and hopefully prevent its spread, though the urologist warned him that his muscle mass would also shrink over time. And gradually that is what happened. The urologist had also warned Joe that the hormone shots he was taking would likely cause hot flashes—and they did, much to Joe's annoyance. But he kept a sense of humor about the hot flashes, saying they made him feel qualified to give both male and female viewpoints on any question!

**Grace's Side Of Family** Scot and Merry had invited their cousins, aunts and uncles on their mother's side of the family for a reunion on Saturday, June 27. They had decided the only time those family members ever saw each other was at funerals and they wanted to have a fun time together. They wanted it at the farm and while the two of them did the work for it, Joe worked on the yard and I worked in the house. The patio was to be the main seating area. That day the temperature was in the 90s but it was reasonably cool under the shade trees and any time someone wanted to cool off in the air conditioning they could go into the house. About 40 people came, many from long distances. The happy occasion was a real success.

**Celebrating Joe's Mountain** That July 4th Bill Duncan and his sons, Bruce and Destry, pooled resources for a supply of fireworks. All their families came to the farm and set up picnic tables near Joe's mountain in the wooded area between our house and Whitaces, whom we invited to join us for a picnic and fireworks show. Cars stopped on the road to watch and that pleased Joe and the men doing the fireworks.

**Fifteenth Anniversary** August the first was our fifteenth Wedding Anniversary and what a full fifteen years it had been. When we reminisced about those years, what we had done to the house and the grounds and all the trips we had taken, we wondered where the energy had come from. We rehearsed to each other what joy we had over our children, how privileged we each were to have such wonderful step-children. We recognized that we had become slower and less powerful of body but congratulated ourselves that our minds still worked reasonably well! Admittedly our fuses had become a little shorter but we could still laugh and have good times together and with others. And we agreed that we still felt young in our minds!

**Colorado Wedding** Then it was time for Jeremy's August wedding to Kristy Lang in Colorado, another beautiful wedding. Joe stayed home to oversee work on his mountain; he highly approved of Kristy from his impression of her at Melanie's wedding. I had never been to Colorado before and I enjoyed my time there immensely, sharing a room with Sara Faye's mother, Celia. While there I contacted my pen friend, Elsie Cleveland, a widow living in nearby Greely, Colorado, with whom I had been corresponding since 1979. We met over "brunch" at a Hardee's and talked for nearly two hours. During the time I was gone Merry went with Joe to Illinois overnight to find his cousin, Isabel, and visit family sites. They returned all aglow over their visit.

**Veteran Joe Honored** Later in August Ohio Veterans of World War II, Korea, Viet Nam, Desert Storm and peacetime veterans were honored in a special dedication ceremony on the Plaza in the State House grounds in Columbus. Two curved walls had been erected, one on each side of the Plaza. On those walls were permanently engraved letters written by veterans of those times—35 letters on each wall. Earlier in the year a request was sent out for submission of letters from veterans from which would be chosen the ones to be inscribed. About 1800 letters were sent in and the judges had a hard time choosing seventy of the most representative ones. Scot had asked Joe for copies of letters he wrote and he gave him three. One of the three, a letter to his sister, Margaret, was chosen to be on a wall. A book was compiled of all the most representative letters received in addition to the ones chosen for the walls.

The veterans and their family members who attended were greeted by the Governor in the newly renovated State House and honored with a reception. Scot planned and executed everything about our part in the ceremony so that all Joe and I had to do was be there and do as we were told. It was an inspiring ceremony and we deeply appreciated all that Scot did. Scot said in his working life he passed by those walls almost daily and often stopped to read the letters, proud that his father's was one of them. It did Joe untold good to hear him say that.

**Flagpole Feat** Joe's goal for Thanksgiving that year was to have a flag flying from the top of his mountain. To save money he cut the pole from a long tree, but such a pole was extremely heavy. He and I tried in vain to get it even started up the hill. Scot came about 11:00 a.m. for Thanksgiving Day and Joe soon had him out there trying to help do the job. The three of us struggled and succeeded in getting it part way up the mountain before I left them and went to see about Thanksgiving Dinner. I told them dinner would be ready about 2 o'clock but when that time came I could tell they were not ready to give up so dinner waited. They worked so hard I felt sorry for them and finally about 5:00 they gave up. Warmed over dinner was welcomed and eaten as though it were still good. That day had turned out to be nothing like anyone planned. A few days later Bill Duncan used his small tractor to set the pole in the hole Joe had prepared and Joe proudly raised his flag.

**Holiday Anticipation** We were expecting some of our children and grandchildren to come for a family gathering between Christmas and

New Year. In November I had prepared what I could ahead of time so we women could be as free as possible of the kitchen while they were with us: 12 pounds of ground beef made into chili, 15 pounds of beef and pork made into B-B-Q, 12 pounds of chicken breasts with lots of vegetables added made into chicken stew; all frozen in meal-size containers. I had made peanut butter fudge and chocolate fudge, dipped butter cookies in melted chocolate, chocolate-dipped Peanut Butter/Ritz Crackers and made two big roaster pans full of party mix. We were prepared for the crowd.

**Christmas In Columbus** With Joe feeling better since his VA visits, we enjoyed Christmas at Merry and Bob's with Scot and several of Bob's family. We spent a relaxing evening and night at Scot's and went home next day to be ready for as many of the Fudge families as could come. As it turned out, for many different reasons, Robert and Dianne were the only ones who came and we made the most of our time together. At least with all the food preparation and freezing we didn't have to cook and Mother Hubbard's Cupboard wouldn't be bare for a long while!

**A Difference** It was 1999 and in March Joe and I made a trip to Florida and a visit with Eldon and Dottie. The men went fishing as usual the first day. When they returned without any fish Dottie said, "So, the fish weren't biting today?" Eldon said, "We didn't even put hooks in the water. We sat in the boat and talked about the Bible and the Lord and salvation—and Joe brought it up!" Amazing because (Joe had told me) when he and Grace had begun going with Eldon and Dottie out west, Joe had specifically told Eldon, "No talk about religion, period." That was the way it had been through the years. Now that ban had been discarded by Joe and from then on our times with Eldon and Dottie were even happier than ever.

**A Near Miss** April often brought stormy weather and 1999 was no exception. A big storm with strong wind blew a branch (almost half of the tree) off of the more than 50-year-old cedar at the front of the house. It fell with a loud crash that shook the place. We opened the door to see that the big piece of tree had landed between the lamppost and front steps with no damage to either. The next day was beautiful and Joe went to work with his chainsaw. He cut wood while I wheel-barrowed the cut wood and dragged branches to the back. As I began the fourth wheelbarrow load, with excruciating pain my right hip gave way completely. That hip had bothered me for several years and I had been able to keep going but this time I had to quit.

**A Bad Decision** I went to an orthopedic surgeon who had an MRI made. It showed the hip joint had severe osteo-necrosis and a new joint would be necessary. However, the surgeon I had gone to would be gone on vacation until July, so in desperation I chose to use another surgeon in his group rather than wait on his return. June 26 my right hip joint was replaced. In the recovery room either too much blood thinner was given or I over-reacted to it and needed several units of blood. Evidently they thought my heart was acting up and I vaguely heard excited talk as an EKG was hooked up; but it didn't show anything amiss and I was sent home at the prescribed time. I couldn't walk without severe pain and we found out the replacement was 1½ inches too long. About a week after I got home I was roused in the night by what I thought was severe indigestion but Maggie called the doctor who said call 911 and go to ER. We did and after EKG again showed nothing, I was sent home the next day.

Maggie left and Nancy came. A night later I was wakened about midnight by what felt like a heavy sandbag landing on my chest. Nancy called 911 and we made another run to ER, Joe and Nancy following the ambulance in our car. About eight miles from home the ambulance had a blowout and came to a lurching, bumpy stop. My first thought was being thankful that the medic wasn't inserting the IV needle when the blowout happened! The driver radioed for a replacement and I was transferred to the other ambulance at 1:30 a.m. on the pitch dark country road.

Again EKG showed nothing wrong and the next day the doctor said I could go home. Nancy asked the doctor if repeated incidents didn't mean something was wrong but he said EKGs didn't show it and insurance would not let them do further tests unless the family insisted. So Nancy and her brothers had a phone conference and she requested an angiogram. Dr. Wayne, the cardiologist, found a 98% blockage in the right aorta and inserted a stent. No more heart problems!

But I still couldn't walk properly and hip pain continued. Other children Merry, Dianne, Paul, Scot, Janis, took turns coming to stay various amounts of time as they could until I was able to hobble around with a cane and make do. A built up shoe on my left foot compensated for the 1½ inch extra length of my right leg and at least then I could walk on a level. I changed to a different orthopedic surgeon whose tests showed severely pinched nerves in the elongated leg. He did surgery to relieve the worst and it helped. Then I began three times a week therapy for heart and hip and kept it up for five months. I still could walk only a short distance and ever since then that leg and hip have given me trouble. X-rays show the joint itself is good and I learned to live with the the pain and limited walking ability. One plus of having a longer leg—I could reach a higher shelf in my kitchen cabinets!

**Lincoln Town Car** Joe had been studying used car ads in the classifieds and had decided on a used Lincoln Town Car. Robert knew a friend in Alabama was planning to trade in his 1997 Lincoln so he connected them and Joe bought that car. Robert, Dianne, Billy Wayne and Marge came to Ohio in two cars and went home in one. As Joe planned, I became the owner of a Lincoln Town Car. When we walked out of the DMV, knowing that I would never have picked a car like that, Robert asked how I liked it. I jokingly said, "The only people who own Lincolns are elderly and rich!" and Robert responded, "Well, you qualify in one of those!" I really did like it and decided to enjoy it, praying it would last as long as I needed a car.

It was November and the year was flying! After our Mississippi trip in late October, Maggie stayed until after Christmas; Bill drove from Abilene, Texas to Tupelo to bring Beth to join us all for ten days on the farm. Joe was getting weaker and less able to handle stressful situations but he was still able to enjoy Beth, Maggie and Bill being there. He sat in his recliner reading but said he enjoyed hearing us sing as we worked the big jigsaw puzzle on the dining table. He joined in conversations, devotions and the games we played.

A letter from Bill summed up our time together. *"It is impossible to describe what a wonderful 10 days we had together at your house. Sybil and Joe. There is nothing like family. That is the way God made us, and that is the way he wants us to be—people who enjoy family togetherness in Christian fellowship. Thanks for the wonderful devotions. Thanks for the wonderful conversations. Thanks for the wonderful food. Thanks for the wonderful songs, walking in the mall, riding in the car, singing, working puzzles, watching birds through the window, and playing fun games. Most of all thank you for your wonderful hospitality that made your house glow with the warmth of the season. God bless you all with health and happiness. Love, Bill*

**The New Century** Great excitement reigned over the beginning of a new century. How many of us had wondered in our youth about the possibility of living to see such a thing as the year **2000**? Dire predictions didn't happen and soon we were accustomed to writing "2000."

We could all tell Joe was getting worse but he still walked to check on the state of the dam, especially after rains. He used his long-handled shovel as a support and to fill in holes he found made by groundhogs or other critters. He thought the severe pain in his shoulder and lower back was probably caused by that shoveling work, but in June his doctor ordered a bone scan that indicated the cancer was spreading out of the prostate to his shoulder and back. Joe seemed to accept the whole situation pretty well. He was able to keep mowing the yard with the riding mower and continued his walks to check on the lake, until one frightening day.

He announced he was walking back to the lake and I went about my housework. Two hours later, he had not returned and I was worried. I was about to go looking for him when a friend who had come to do some work for him arrived at my door. I told him the situation and Rick said he would go look for him. About twenty minutes later he came back and said he had found Joe sitting on the side of the ditch on the back road and was going to get him in the truck. Joe had fallen down in a muddy low place and couldn't get up so he had crawled to the road side where he thought someone would surely find him. He was covered from head to toe in mud and completely exhausted. A shower and clean clothes revived him somewhat but that was the last time he tried walking to the back.

**New Neighbors** Two years before, Bill Duncan had bought a couple of lots from Joe across the road from our house and had built a house on one of them. A young couple with two children bought that house. Another couple bought the other lot and began to build. All of the wife's brothers and in-laws, men and women, came on weekends to help them build. True to his habit Joe went across the road to introduce himself and watch the work. He made friends with the wife's father who was also a spectator and a South Pacific World War II veteran so he and Joe had plenty to talk about. He was a religious man and when Joe let slip a "cuss" word one day he told Joe that bad language was not used among them. Joe took his rebuke well and from then on they discussed various aspects of Bible subjects every time they were together. When the man found out Joe had never been immersed into Christ he asked him why. Others had tried talking to Joe about it but he always said he was baptized when he was a child and that closed the matter. Knowing how he felt I had kept silent on the subject. None of that had in the least dampened his enthusiasm for our daily Bible reading.

At this time our morning Bible reading was in the book of Acts. Always before, when we read about Saul of Tarsus being converted after being an avid persecutor of Christians, Joe would say, "I guess if God could forgive him for killing people he might forgive me for killing so many Japanese;" and my answer was always, "He has promised to forgive *all* sins, no exceptions, when we believe and obey Him." The story of Cornelius and his household once brought the comment from Joe, "Cornelius was a good man but he still needed to be baptized!" Many times through the years Joe had expressed belief in Jesus Christ as the Son of God and the Savior of mankind.

**Joe's Surrender** On a Saturday noon in late October Joe came for lunch after being with his friend across the road. He walked in and announced excitedly that he had decided he wanted to be immersed and trust in God's forgiveness. He asked me to call Edward and see if he would come to do the baptizing. I called Edward and the date of November 5th was set for him to come. We met him in Columbus on the 4th. Previously when Joe asked visiting men questions, it seemed to me he was only half listening while working on his answer at the same time, but this time I could tell that Joe was listening intently to Edward's answers to all of his many questions. When Edward felt it was time to call a halt before Joe was overloaded, he explained to Joe what he could expect in the baptismal service the next day and then changed the subject.

In the afternoon of Sunday November 5th Joe was baptized at the Mason church building. Edward officiated. Merry and Scot came for the service and several friends from our class at Mason church joined us. That night Joe went to bed saying, "I can hardly believe that I have actually done it—I am forgiven!" And that was the first thing he said on waking the next morning.

**Paul and Melonie** November 17 was the date of Paul's wedding to Melonie Menzies in Florida and I flew down for that happy occasion. I enjoyed time with Melonie's mother and many kin who attended the wedding. Joe stayed with Merry and Bob and I appreciated knowing he was in loving hands in Columbus.

**Pain Increase** With the new year of 2001 Joe's pain became worse. He spent most nights in his recliner but even there he couldn't rest much and walked around in the house, making frequent stops at the medicine cabinet to look for something to ease his pain. I was afraid he might take too much of something or the wrong thing so I stayed on the couch beside his recliner, getting up whenever he did to keep an eye on him. He found that Mineral Ice helped some and I rubbed it on his back and shoulders often. Sitting at our breakfast table leaning forward seemed to ease him some and there we played countless games of Rummikube or Yahtzee at all hours of day and night.

Robert's job required him to be in our part of Ohio in February and Dianne came to spend time with us while he was there. Bob came down from Columbus to spend a day with Joe. Their visits coincided and proved a godsend that week. When Bob arrived, Joe was having trouble breathing and his blood pressure was higher than usual. We decided it was time to see his doctor at the VA and I was thankful to have Bob do the driving and Dianne along for company. We waited more than five hours for the doctor to see Joe and during that time Bob and Dianne's presence helped to keep Joe calmed. The doctor gave him a prescription that we had filled at a pharmacy on the way home.

What a blessing it had been to have Bob and Dianne. When we got home Robert was there and Bob left for Columbus. We had had only vending machine snacks for lunch and no dinner so while I helped Joe get settled, Robert fried bacon and Dianne made biscuits and gravy and eggs. After that Robert and Dianne went to the grocery store in Blanchester to stock the refrigerator, then we sat with Joe trying to out-guess the Millionaire Questions on "Who Wants to Be a Millionaire?"

The next morning Robert still had a half day's work to do. While he was gone Dianne cleaned house and made a big pot of her ground beef and vegetable soup, one of her delicious specialties. I made Robert's favorite pie—lemon icebox. When Robert came in he vacuumed the whole place. What a blessing to have children visit! But by then we agreed that Joe was looking very gray and breathing hard. We didn't want to go 40 miles to the VA and wait for hours again so we went to the ER at Bethesda North Hospital just 20 miles away and he was given immediate attention. The doctor said it was one of three things, either congestive heart failure or infectious bronchitis or a severe asthmatic attack or some combination of the three. He consulted by phone with Joe's doctor at the VA and prescribed something for all three.

When we got home Joe went to bed (they had given him a light supper while he was in the ER). Robert, Dianne and I ate soup and pie. Joe was feeling better the next day and Robert and Dianne felt better about leaving.

**Joe's 83rd** The Columbus children came down to help us celebrate Joe's birthday and as always we had a joyful time with them. Joe was feeling fairly well and that helped everyone's feelings. Later in the month Nancy and Raymond were able to come for a few days. Nancy's job and other activities at home made it difficult for her to look for needed clothes so she wanted to spend one day shopping. We left Joe and Raymond with Arby's Roast Beef Sandwiches in the refrigerator to warm up for lunch. We assured them we would be back before dark to fix dinner. The expression "shopped till we dropped" summed up our day nicely. On our way home we picked up dinner from a Boston Market.

When we drove up the men were sitting on the patio and seemed surprised that we were "already home," quite a different greeting from what we were expecting. It seemed that they had talked almost non-stop all day. Raymond, a Navy veteran of the Viet Nam War and Joe, a veteran of World War II South Pacific, had many worldwide subjects to discuss. We told them dinner would be served in ten minutes—and it was, much to their surprise. Good old Boston Market!

By August Joe was having extreme pain. His oncologist said the cancer had spread into more bones. With Joe's consent the doctor admitted him to the hospital for three days to prepare for radiation. That three days would qualify his being sent to a nursing home to have continued radiation to help control the pain. I went to be with him in the nursing home every day. Scot, Merry and I were surprised and pleased that Joe seemed to be content to be there. He said he was glad that I could go home and get some sleep after being up with him for so many nights and he even urged me to leave him in time to be home before dark. He said he felt secure in the nursing home knowing they would give him needed medication and also it was easier to call on nurses for help without feeling sorry for them! Merry and Scot spent Saturdays and Sundays with him to give me time off to tend necessary chores and go to church.

We moved Joe to Mason Christian Village Assisted Living in October. I had already decided I would not go to Mississippi that fall but Sharon and Vonnie said they would come anyway to help me in any way they could and perhaps get in some antiquing. Maggie had married Roger Weaver in July and didn't want to leave him so soon. While the girls were there Joe enjoyed their daily visits and on Saturday they helped me get rid of useless stuff I had sorted and bagged out of the garage. We disposed of several car-trunk loads of old newspapers that had been stacked in the tractor shed because Joe kept thinking he would find a place to recycle them.

**A Cottage In The Village** Harrison and Muriel Crader were getting ready to go to Florida for their usual five months' stay and in November they offered to let me live in their cottage at Mason Christian Village while they were gone. I moved there in November. It was only a five-minute-walk from Joe and I could spend more of every day with him. Scot and Merry still alternated coming Saturdays and Sundays.

On Thanksgiving Day Joe was feeling fairly well. I asked him if he would like to go for a drive to the farm. He said he would but when I stopped the car at the farm house he asked why we were stopping and said he wanted to get "home."

Every day Joe wanted me to read the Bible to him and many times he asked me to sing his favorite hymns for him, among them *I Come To The Garden Alone, Onward Christian Soldiers, Trust And Obey* and *The Lord's My Shepherd.* We still played either Rumikube or Yatzee to keep him occupied until he was tired. In early December Merry and Scot urged me to take a week off and spend it with Edward and Sara Faye which I did. I phoned Joe every day and was back before Christmas.

On Christmas Day Joe suddenly became frantic with pain and was moved to the Nursing Wing to be given stronger medication. From then on I sat with him all day every week day and part days on Saturday and Sunday though Merry and Scot continued coming on those days, too. Every day I was thankful to the Craders for allowing me to use their cottage.

Alva and Juanita Sizemore were among our best friends in Ohio. They lived in an apartment in Mason Retirement Village but Alva's health had been failing and he was in the Nursing Wing at the same time as Joe. He died February 23$^{rd}$. Juanita wanted me to move into the apartment with her and I appreciated her invitation but felt I needed my own private time in the cottage after I left Joe for the night.

**Hospice Care** Hospice personnel began coming to tend Joe every day and some days he seemed more aware than others. When I read aloud to him or sang to him, even when he didn't seem aware, the nurses said they could tell he was less agitated. I became good friends with the Hospice R.N. who came two or three times a week. She said she wanted to become a chaplain and we had some interesting conversations along that line. I met her in a restaurant several months later and she told me she had accomplished that goal.

**Joe's Death** March 23, 2002 Joe died. On the 25$^{th}$ we had a memorial service in the Village Chapel where kinfolks and many friends assembled to honor him. Scot gave a wonderful Eulogy, Edward made the inspirational talk, Henry, Robert, Paul and Raymond each talked briefly about what he had meant to their families as step-father and Grandpa Joe to their children. Benjamin and Rebekah were there from California but Benjamin said, though he wanted to, he couldn't trust himself to speak. As many grandchildren as could come were there with their parents.

With Scot's permission I'm copying the Eulogy he wrote:

# Eulogy to Joseph Edward Dewhirst
## Born April 4, 1918-Died March 23, 2002

*(Delivered by his son, Scot Dewhirst on March 26, 2002 at his memorial service in the Chapel at Mason Christian Village.)*

*Joseph Edward Dewhirst was born on April 4, 1918 in Cincinnati, Ohio. He was a man of the 20th century, and he lived through the best and the worst of that century. His life was quite extraordinary in many ways, and very normal in others. He was fated to meet and marry two remarkable women . . . and he was married for over 50 years. As with many of our lives, his was often shaped by circumstances of fate.*

*His father died when he was 4, and he was raised by his mother, Minnie Pearl, and his older brother, Newell. He was just completing his service in the Army . . . and then December 7, 1941 happened . . . and we all know how his military service in the South Pacific affected the rest of his life.*

*Our father started from humble beginnings, he served his country bravely, he held a job, he bought a farm, he married twice, he fathered 2 children and then at the age of 65 he gained 6 more children, all who are here today, and he lived a life that many would describe as the American dream of the 20th century. He also filled most of the roles that our society had to offer. He was a son, a husband, a father and step-father, a brother, a grandfather, a great grandfather, a worker in industry, a friend, a neighbor, a hunter, a fisherman, a farmer, a soldier, a traveler, an author, a Christian . . . and I think that he would like me to add . . . a proud American.*

*As we all know, the last few years were a difficult time for him. He was a worker at heart, and he loved his farm. It was a sad time when he could no longer spend his days building his mountain, fishing in his lake, or strolling his farm. But these last few years were only a part of a life well lived.*

*We all have our own memories of Joseph Dewhirst. I ask you to grab those countless good memories, and hold on to them. That's what Merry, Bob and I have done, and on behalf of all of us, we would like to share a few of our memories.*

*We will remember the Dad who took us fishing and swimming, the one who loved to read a good book, the one who always had an opinion about everything and who wasn't afraid to tell you what it was . . . and the father who decided when Merry and I were little . . . that we needed to see "all" of our country . . . and we mean all of it. So, every summer he planned a vacation where we would travel to a different part of the country. By the time I was 16, we had traveled to 48 states and most of the Canadian provinces. We didn't have a lot of money then, but he somehow managed to pull it off in a pretty spectacular way—from Times Square to the Golden Gate Bridge we crisscrossed the country;*

*He took us deep sea fishing in the Florida keys, we caught Northern Pike in the French River of Northern Ontario, and we played in the Pacific Surf off the coast of California;*

*We toured the White House in the summer of 1963, and we wandered through the relics of history at the Smithsonian;*

*We stood on the rim of the Grand Canyon, we watched Old Faithful erupt at Yellowstone, we crawled through Carlsbad Caverns in New Mexico, and together we gazed at the majesties of the Great Smoky Mountains, the Canadian Rockies and the Grand Tetons;*

*Miami, Chicago, Dallas, New York, San Francisco, Los Angeles, Kansas City, Denver, New Orleans, Seattle, Toronto, Boston, Atlanta—he took us to all of those cities and many more;*

*Gettysburg, Little Big Horn, the pueblos of the Southwest, the swamps of the Everglades, the wilderness of Canada, and the arch in St. Louis—we were there;*

*We were stranded in a sandstorm in Texas, our car broke down in the mountains of Colorado, and we sweated in our "un" air conditioned station wagon as we drove across Death Valley;*

*We swam in the ocean off the coast of Maine, we camped among the buffalo in South Dakota, we had a great day of fun at Disneyland, and we gathered starfish at low tide in Oregon;*

*We listened to the Mormon Tabernacle Choir in Salt Lake City, and we stood in awe before the great masters at the Metropolitan Museum of Art in New York;*

*He showed us the best of our country, and the memories of all of those places and of our family time together will stay with us always. Thanks Dad for all of those wonderful memories and for making them possible.*

*He was a learned man, but for the most part he taught himself about the world. He wanted his children to have what he didn't have—a solid family life, a safe world in which to grow-up, a college education, and through his quiet counsel he instilled in us the belief that we could achieve whatever we wanted if we worked for it. We thank him for that.*

*There is also a saying that you judge a man by the company that he keeps. If this is so, then without question my father's life was a soaring success—because of the two remarkable women that he married.*

*The first was my mother, Grace, and they were married for 34 years. My father described her best in his writings, and I quote him—"Grace's love, wisdom, dedication and indescribable courage salvaged me from the mental and physical ravages of my war."*

*The second amazing lady was Sybil, and she led him into a new and wonderful chapter of his life for 18 years. I again quote my dad—"Sybil whom I met in an unbelievable way, has been my salvation with her incredible love for me and our God."*

*Sybil, you have constantly demonstrated your love to our Dad in so many ways—you were his rock, his anchor, his caregiver, and you brought a multitude of new dimensions to his life, and we love you and thank you for that. Your life with him over the last 18 years is proof that life can just be starting when you reach your sixties—and wow did it take a new turn—with trips to Africa, the South Pacific, Europe, Alaska, Hawaii, and many places in between. The two of you also brought together a new extended family—the ultimate family of the 20th century—one that stretches from coast to coast from Ohio to Alabama to Florida to Texas and to California—a family who has come together today in Mason, Ohio to honor him.*

*So, our father's life was one that was well lived—with it ups and downs,—with its roadblocks and its many successes. We didn't always agree as often happens between fathers and sons, and we all know that he could be as stubborn as they come, but he was also as kind and generous as a person could be.*

*We will all remember him—as a tireless worker—as a committed and loving husband—as a wonderful provider for his family—as a father who encouraged his kids to shoot for the stars—as a man with countless stories—as one of the smartest people that I have ever met—as the author of "A G.I. NAMED JOE"—and as a good and kind man who was loved by his family. He will be missed by all of us.*

\*    \*    \*

After the memorial service the whole family went to the farm for a pot-luck meal and evening together. I was exhausted and numb feeling but having the children together was comforting. Listening to them share memories of their lives with Joe, some nostalgic, some even humorous, relieved pent up feelings in all of us. Then the Columbus folks went home that night. The Fudges spent two nights, some with me at Crader's cottage and the rest at the farm; with days spent together at the Crader cottage.

**Back To The Farm** Maggie had asked if I wanted her to come at once or to wait until I was ready to move back to the farm and I told her the latter plan would help me most. She and Roger came to help me move and then helped clean the cottage ready for the Craders' return on April 1. While sitting with Joe I had crocheted a lovely cream colored afghan for their guest bed as a token of appreciation. There was no way to adequately express how much it meant for me to be that close to Joe for those five months, nor how much I appreciated the generosity of our dear friends, Harrison and Muriel Crader.

**Arizona Visit** Maggie and Roger wanted me to come to Arizona as soon as possible so in June I went to spend a week with them. There had been wild fires around Prescott just before I arrived—they had seen the flames and smoke very clearly from their deck but fortunately the wind was blowing away from their hillside. Sunday afternoon we drove to the mountain nearby where the fire had swept through. To give some idea just how hot that fire had been, we saw along the upward winding road all wooden posts were burned flat to the ground and the metal guardrails had melted.

We went for a scenic drive up Canyon deChellie and spent a night in the lodge at the mouth of the canyon. Views were magnificent, breathtaking, spectacular and awe-inspiring. Navajo people inhabited the canyon during the summer, raised gardens and fruit trees and sold their produce and jewelry to tourists like us. Some of them climbed out every day and went to work in the surrounding areas of the uplands. During the winter they all lived "on top." We saw ruins along the ledges where ancient people had lived.

Our 550 mile round trip included panoramic views of endless miles of flat country with no trees, almost always mountains in the distance and rocky mesas across the desert with colored rocks and sands. We saw Hopi dwellings across the narrow tops of some of the mesas. Our road climbed from 5,000 feet to 7,000 feet, through mountains covered with scrubby cedars to pine-covered mountains. We passed through Flagstaff and back down to Prescott. It was great to be back in their hill-top home overlooking the town of Prescott in the valley. I told them we didn't have to drive anywhere away from their home to have it all.

**What Next?** Back on the farm because of my bad leg/hip I could not do much outside work so I began to sort through box after box of pictures collected over many years. I put them into chronological order and then into labeled albums. This was a job that engaged my mind and gave a sense of accomplishment.

**Five More Opinions** Robert and Dianne wanted me to see some other orthopedic surgeons about my hip and leg pain. Driving was no problem for me so I drove to Alabama and stayed with them while Dianne made appointments and took me to see four different surgeons all of whom said they couldn't do anything. Finally I went to a neurosurgeon, Dr. Joel Puckett in Huntsville. After studying the MRI he said he thought inflammation in the sacroiliac joint was causing the hip pain. He put a shot in the spot and for several months I had relief. That five weeks was the longest I had ever stayed with any of my grown children, and we didn't fuss a bit!

**Columbus And Katy** After Thanksgiving at Scot's with Merry, Bob and family, a night in Scot's guest suite and several games of Scrabble before bedtime, I drove home refreshed. In December, leaving my car at Scot's, I flew to Houston for three weeks with Edward and Sara Faye. From there to Myrtle Beach, South Carolina for a pleasant two weeks with Bill and Betty Duncan. It had turned very cold for Houston and because of the unusually cold weather in Myrtle Beach, Betty and I did less walking around shopping and spent more time in their condo doing a jigsaw puzzle. We enjoyed standing at their big window overlooking the ocean watching it snow on the beach—something they didn't see there very often.

I only had a wool blazer for a coat and dreaded going to Ohio where we heard it was extremely cold. Coats were almost non-existent in Myrtle Beach but I found a long sleeved, turtle-neck sweater to wear under my blazer. The morning I flew out of Myrtle Beach's little airport it was 19 degrees with an icy wind blowing and I was thankful for the sweater under my blazer. Scot met me in Columbus and after a night at his house with more Scrabble, I drove home next day.

**My 80th Year** How could it be **2003** already and time for my 80th birthday in a day or two! The year before, my children had asked what I wanted for my 80th birthday. I told them my wish was that each of them would come sometime during the year, whenever they could, for as long as they could, not necessarily all at the same time, though that would be O.K. too.

After a rainstorm in April, I was struggling to close the garage door when my feet slid out from under me and my shoulder hit hard against the corner edge of the door facing resulting in a torn rotator cuff. Surgery was recommended but I put it off and the pain was relieved periodically with a steroid injection; I didn't want surgery as long as it could be postponed.

Special to me were the weekends when either Merry or Scot came to the farm. In the evenings Merry and I played Boggle or Yahtzee as a rule. Scot and I spent more time with Scrabble games, playing until the wee hours and then sleeping late the next morning.

**Scrabble with Scot.**

The church had appointed a "Minister of Seniors" and called the Seniors group "Evergreen." We had monthly programs, sometimes pot-lucks, always enjoyable evenings with 75 to 100 fellow seniors. Lucretia and I went almost every month. Of course it was dark when we returned home so she brought along her overnight bag and slept at my house. We enjoyed each other's company and neither of us wanted to go into our dark house alone after being gone for the evening. When she didn't go, I had standing invitations to spend the night with either Juanita Sizemore or with the Craders and both were enjoyed.

July 4th weekend was a memorable "reunion" with some of my children. Edward and Sara Faye flew to Cincinnati, rented a car and arrived at 5 p.m. That same day Robert and Dianne drove up from Alabama and arrived at 6 p.m. We went to deSha's for dinner. Benjamin and Susan flew to Columbus, rented a car and arrived at deSha's at 8 p.m. to finish the meal with us. Friday was a wonderful visiting day. Saturday Scot, Merry and Bob came for a cook-out and visit. What joy! I was happy to call it my very best 80th birthday yet!

Robert and Dianne left Monday afternoon and Edward and Sara Faye left on Tuesday evening.

**Goodbye Milk House** Aaron arrived Monday evening and he, Benjamin and Susan stayed another two weeks. They wanted something to do and I suggested that we tear down the old milk house—a long time eye-sore. Bill Duncan saw Aaron carrying junk out to the tractor shed and said, "Why bother taking the junk out, just burn it too? With my tractor and loader I can mash it down in jig time ready to burn!" He did and then Aaron burned it—high adventure for him. He stood guard with the garden hose to wet down nearby trees so they wouldn't be scorched. The next time Scot came to the farm he said, "You have no idea how many times I thought about setting fire to it!"

**Social Months** You might say August, September and October were social months: Muriel and Harrison Crader came for dinner. The next week Ken Coyle and wife came to dinner. The Seniors went to Howard Pauley's house for outdoor pot luck in his spacious back yard. I fixed dinner for Laverne and Lois, veteran missionaries to China. Juanita came for an afternoon. The Evergreens had their annual Formal Gala which was a special evening attended by about 300 seniors.

In September Nancy and Raymond came for four wonderful days of great visiting. She wanted to shop at Goodwill and thrift stores and Raymond said he was very happy to spend time on our patio with a book.

John came by for a visit on the way to his home in Nashville, Tennessee. He ate lunch with me and afterwards pleasantly surprised me by asking if I'd like to play some games before he went on his way. He did that again another time before I left the farm. I doubt that he knew how much I enjoyed his company and appreciated his thoughtfulness.

In October Paul, Melonie, Chenese and Claudia (an exchange student) came for ten days. They helped me redo the front walk where a truck had run over and ruined part of it. Paul cut dead trees in the side yard and the girls hauled the wood to the back in the wheelbarrow and stacked it. And Melonie helped me clean out and organize the attic closet. Naturally we played games in the evenings. Then we took a day off work and enjoyed shopping at Value City before they went home.

In November Nancy and Raymond came again for four wonderful days. Benji came from Florida for Thanksgiving and I met him in Columbus. We had Thanksgiving at Merry and Bob's with Scot and all of Bob's family. We spent the night at Scot's house, and on to the farm overnight then took Benji to Columbus to catch his plane. I spent the night at Scot's again with more Scrabble and home the next day.

December was another full month. Our senior class pot-luck and program was a treat, then because Lucretia didn't go with me, I spent the night with Craders. A Christmas program was coming up at church in mid-December and I invited Scot and Merry to come for overnight and go with me to the program. One of the highest points to me of the outstanding program was the solo of *Oh Holy Night* sung by a male singer who put such feeling and expression in his rendition that it gave me chill bumps.

Robert came December 22$^{nd}$ and we left early next morning for Alabama. I visited Donna on the 24$^{th}$ and went to Henry's for Christmas Day then back to Robert's for the night. Monday 29$^{th}$ Henry took me to Ohio. The long rides with my sons were real treats, talking all the way.

All in all it had been a full and busy year and I declared my 80$^{th}$ year a resounding success.

**2004—Traveling And Trauma** My 81$^{st}$ birthday was marked with phone calls, cards and flowers from my wonderful children.

In March I enjoyed a special weekend in Columbus with my "local" children. On Saturday Scot went with me to see *The Passion*—the crucifixion movie. Sunday morning Merry and I attended a church service where we heard about the *Crucifixion* from a medical point of view. Sunday evening Merry and I went to a presentation in a Methodist church where a man dramatically recited from memory the entire book of John. It was impressive, amazing and inspirational.

Thanks to frequent flier miles Benjamin sent me airline tickets to attend Aaron's graduation with a BA from BIOLA University on May 29. Apricots were falling in Benjamin's back yard and I helped Susan make jam. I was back home for two weeks when thanks to Benjamin again I flew to California for Rebekah's high school graduation and spent two weeks with them. Maggie and Roger drove from Arizona for a weekend with Sharon and family in Santa Barbara and took me back with them to Arizona for ten days. I flew back to Columbus where Scot met me and hosted me for the night, complete with Scrabble, imagine! The next morning Merry rode to the farm with me and Scot came at noon for a great weekend.

During June Nancy and Raymond had moved into a better, bigger house on five acres a few miles east of Hanceville, Alabama. Monica's wedding to Blake McAvoy was scheduled for July 4$^{th}$ so they were in a tizzy trying to get settled and prepare for the wedding. I drove to Alabama for the occasion and stayed with Robert and Dianne. Monica was a beautiful bride and Robert did a great job officiating. Sad to say things did not work out for Monica and Blake and about eighteen months later they were divorced and she reverted to her maiden name.

My brother Bill came to the farm for a three day visit in mid-August and as always it was a joy to be with him. A Fudge family reunion was planned for Labor Day Weekend in Texas. I drove to Columbus, left my car with Scot while I flew to Houston and was met by Sara Faye. We all got together at Guadalupe River Resort for the third through the fifth of September. Not all of the Fudges were able to be there but we had a grand time together and too soon it ended. I stayed on at Edward's until the 13th.

Aaron and Liz's wedding in California was to take place on October 30. I flew west again to attend. Dianne had helped me find a suitable dress on my last trip to Alabama—I was afraid it might be "too fancy" because it had lots of sequins on the top, but it turned out to be just right in the circumstances since beads and sequins by then were turning up on about everything, including jeans.

It seemed to me I had been doing a lot of flying in 2004 and later in the month I was scheduled to fly to Orlando for Doug's wedding on November 26. Paul had already sent me a ticket for the flight but I didn't make it to Doug and Breck's wedding.

Joe's sister, Margaret, had died on November 3rd and Scot called to say the funeral would be on Tuesday the 7th. He said he and Merry would come by for me. Tuesday morning when I got up I didn't feel well and at 9:00 a.m. I called Scot to tell him I couldn't go—but he had already left. At that moment Paul called to talk but I told him I was feeling really bad and had to go lie down. I decided before I lay down I had better call 911 and unlock the porch door. I scribbled a note to tape on the door for Scot and Merry if they came by and for Lucretia in case she saw the ambulance and came to see about me. Paul called Scot, Scot called Robert, Lucretia saw the ambulance leaving, came to check on things and saw the note on the door. She tried to call Scot but couldn't reach him.

The ER doctor said there was a blood clot in my right leg and a piece of it had gone to my left lung causing pneumonia. I was in the ICU six days. Merry was with me the first night. Paul arrived the next morning and stayed until the following Monday morning. Since I was in ICU he couldn't stay in the room at night so he went to the farm to sleep. He was with me all day every day, quietly sitting in the corner, or beside my bed reading from the Bible at my request, or talking when I asked him to. Robert drove all night and arrived at 6:00 a.m. He stopped at the desk to get the lowdown from the nurse in charge. The doctor came while he was there and he was able to talk to him, so he was well informed when he came to my room. It was comforting to me to have two of my boys with me for most of that day. Robert went home in late afternoon.

After Robert left, Paul said he wished he were like Robert in knowing who to talk to and what to ask. I told him I only needed one Robert and I needed Paul just like he was—each one did me good in their own way. Maggie arrived on Sunday afternoon and I was moved to a regular room where she was able to stay in the room with me at night. Paul went home Monday morning. Maggie took me home the 21st but I was only there overnight when the next day severe chills hit me. She called 911 and it was back to the ER.

The doctor told Maggie my problem was either bacterial pneumonia in the other lung or blood infection. He told her to call my children to come and in the meantime rather than wait on a lab culture he began powerful antibiotic treatment that he said was the same thing needed for either one. He ordered an oxygen pump to re-inflate the collapsing lung and that mask and strong blowing in my face was an ordeal I hope never to need again, but I was thankful that it worked. I was again put in ICU. Maggie called Robert and that night he, Henry and Nancy drove all night. They walked in at 6:00 a.m. Maggie was with me all the time and Merry and Scot had come back at midnight and stayed until Saturday afternoon when the doctor said my condition was improving.

Finally in a regular room again, Maggie was able to stay with me all the time. Roger arrived the day before Thanksgiving and took us home. Beth and Bill arrived that same day and Maggie and Roger announced that Friday would be our Thanksgiving Day and they would prepare the dinner. It was a good one. Beth needed to be back to take her regular babies on Monday morning so she and Bill left Sunday morning.

Maggie and Roger needed to leave December the 4th and Nancy arrived that evening. She spent a week taking care of everything while I recuperated enough to travel. The drive to Alabama together was good and she dropped me off at Robert's house. I enjoyed Christmas there and spent some time with Henry's family. On Friday the 31st Nancy's family joined us and we all ate together at a catfish restaurant. Foy and Margaret's children were giving them a 60th Wedding Anniversary family celebration to which we had been invited. After lunch we went to congratulate them and thoroughly enjoyed seeing them all.

My children all begged me to move closer to them and we all prayed for guidance. Should I stay on the farm? Or should I move and if so, where? Dianne took time to drive around with me looking at apartment complexes in the area and getting their information but they were all much too expensive.

It was January 7, 2005 when Henry took me home. The night before I left I had called Beth and asked her if she really meant it when right after Joe died she had asked me why I didn't move to Tupelo? She said she truly did mean it and would go to the complex office the next morning to find out when a vacancy would be available and to ask the manager to send information to me.

**The Final Straw—Snow!** Back at the farm while waiting on the information I began going through drawers and closets, sorting and boxing things to be ready for whatever should develop. While that was going on a big snow came. One morning I took my walking stick and went to the mailbox. About half way there my foot slipped on a flagstone and I went down on my hands and knees with snow up to my chest. I tried waving cars down but two passed by without a look so I decided it was up to me. I struggled mightily and was finally able to get to my feet. It was hard for me to believe I was so infirm, but it strengthened my realization that as much as I loved the farm, I needed to move from there.

The information came from Tupelo and the office manager said a recently vacated and completely refurbished apartment would be ready February 1$^{st}$. I believed the Lord was answering my prayers for guidance. I conferred with Scot and Merry, who were not anxious for me to be so far from them but agreed that I needed to be off of the farm. The application was sent back with my signature and a check for the first month's rent. Sorting and packing continued in earnest. I cut pieces of green ribbon to tape on every piece of furniture that was to go with me and red pieces on what was to stay for Merry and Scot. They came one weekend with moving boxes and helped pack.

Doug was anxious for his wife Breck to see the farm before I moved. He wanted her to get a small taste of what he had talked so much about. They came for five days and Doug took her walking to places he especially wanted to show her. They also helped me no end—not the least was Breck pulling everything out of the attic closet; I had wondered how I would manage to crawl in there. They were wonderful company and I was sorry to see them leave.

**Moving Day Part One** Merry, Bob and Scot arranged for a van to move my things. The van was left at the back door to be loaded. The driver told us he would return to drive it away on February 5 and we agreed to have it loaded by then. On the morning of February 5 the director of Senior events from church brought five volunteer men to help. Scot, Merry and Bob and Bob's sister and their father were there. Robert had flown up on business then came to help and to drive me to Alabama. As the men carried things to the van, Scot and Robert placed them in the van while Merry and I directed the inside work to be sure the right things went and stayed.

When all was loaded in the van Robert and Scot locked it up and we heartily thanked the volunteers. The Ohio cars were loaded to their tops with things they wanted to take home with them. Robert packed my car with lamps and other delicate items until he declared not a thing more would go in. We told the Ohio family goodbye and headed south, worn and weary—and sad. I could well imagine how tired the ones left behind must have been. On the way when we stopped to eat, Robert told me that Dianne's mother was at their house and had bronchitis. They didn't want me to be exposed to that so Dianne had contacted Donna and I was to stay with her while we waited on the van to arrive in Tupelo.

As always Donna graciously received me and we had a relaxing week that I sorely needed before getting to the next phase of moving. Thus ended my twenty-two years of life on a farm in southwest Ohio. I would deeply miss my Ohio step-children and friends and the house that Joe and I remodeled and enjoyed together. But I looked forward to a completely different kind of life in Tupelo, Mississippi, praying the Lord would use me for good in whatever way he would see fit.

# PART VII

## MISSISSIPPI

# 2005–

**The Big Move** My week with Donna in Athens, while waiting for the moving van's delivery date in Tupelo, provided a much needed rest and transition time. We could have sat and talked endlessly, occasionally drinking hot tea, but she saw an opportunity for us to look through a stack of magazines she had saved. As we looked and commented I found ideas that would help me arrange and decorate my apartment with what I was bringing from the farm.

The day before delivery date I drove to Tupelo and spent the night in Beth's guest room. Early on February 12th, 2005 I was at my apartment door ready for the moving van that was bringing my earthly possessions from Ohio.

Henry, Jo Ann, Michael, Leslie, Anna, Robert, Dianne, Bobby and two men from Ephesus church, Raymond, Nancy, Monica, Blake and Chris were there in pick-up trucks and a U-Haul. The van was placed directly in front of the door so that the ramp reached from the bed of the van to the floor of my living room making it easier to unload. Strong men made light work of all the heavy things they moved as I told them where to put them. Meanwhile Dianne, Jo Ann, Leslie, Anna and Monica wiped cabinets and put things away for me, in kitchen, bedrooms, closets and bathrooms. I could not have asked for better help. The unpacking of the other jillion boxes would be done gradually over the next several weeks.

Beth had prepared a big pot of stew and invited everyone to her house at lunch time—a welcome break and rest before finishing the job. By dark that evening the van was emptied and gone and my Alabama children had departed with their loads, taking things they each wanted out of the surplus I purposely brought for them to divide. Some things I wasn't sure about would be dispensed later. The men placed where I wanted it the furniture I had chosen that would fit into my two-bedroom apartment, so I had no furniture moving to do.

For the next few nights I slept in Beth's guest room and worked all day at my place unpacking and putting away. Sometimes when I grew tired, I went to Beth's for a cup of tea and sat holding a baby or just watching babies play on the floor. Two weeks later I "celebrated" by having the 'flu and spent three days in the hospital. Robert, Henry and Jo Ann came at different times to check on me and to make sure my refrigerator and cupboards were stocked when I got home. Their two and a half hour drive to Tupelo compared to the eight hour drive to the farm in Ohio made all the difference. Nancy was able to come for a day and night after I got home.

My brother Bill came for a week in March. He slept at Beth's house and every day helped me unpack, sort and put away—mainly books. We enjoyed talking as we worked and were able to laugh when after he had carried load after load of books downstairs, I decided they belonged upstairs and he moved them back up without a word of complaint! By the end of his visit I called myself settled.

Leslie came for a Saturday visit in April, niece Genevieve from Montana and niece-in-law Donna Copeland from Georgia were doing a "kinfolk visit" through Alabama and came by for an afternoon. The month was rounded out one evening with ladies from church bringing a potluck dinner for us all to enjoy together. I felt as though I had been treated with a two month long "house warming."

**New Doctors** When I arrived in Tupelo my body was still recovering from the past November's illness and I still needed some repairs—my right shoulder was waiting for surgery for a twice-torn rotator cuff and my left hip joint needed replacing. Changing doctors when moving from one location to another was always a major adjustment, but this time, having a nephew who was a well qualified and established doctor in the renowned North Mississippi Medical Center in Tupelo, eased that change for me. I trusted his recommendations without reservation and was not disappointed in any of them.

Shoulder surgery was done in May in an outpatient procedure. Robert and Dianne were with me at the hospital and helped me settle at home afterwards. After Beth's babies were taken home every evening she came to prepare our supper and spend the night. I couldn't lie down in a bed and had to sleep in the recliner so I needed her help to get up and down and she slept on the couch. She was up at the crack of dawn, un-reclined the recliner so I could get in and out during the day, then went to tend to her babies. Merry and Bob came the day after I came home, brought in KFC lunch and we had a good four hour visit. Nancy came and spent a night and day. I was being spoiled with so much attention.

Since I couldn't do much else over the next three months of recuperation and therapy, I read or re-read nearly all of the books in my bookcases, downstairs and upstairs, hardback and paperback. Thanks to Pam taking me to doctor appointments and therapy during that time I enjoyed getting to know her better and learned my way around parts of Tupelo that I needed to know.

**Sisters Reunion** Soon it was November and time for our annual Sisters Reunion. Maggie, Sharon and Vonnie came for five days and what a joyful time we had, Vonnie and Sharon sleeping in Beth's guest room, Maggie in mine for three nights then we changed to Maggie at Beth's and Sharon and Vonnie at my house. Our days were divided between looking through antique stores and thrift shops, eating out and sitting around the kitchen table playing games. Our favorite game every year had become Bible Challenge, a Bible game on the order of Trivial Pursuit. Not satisfied with just looking at the answers, we recounted the Bible stories or if we couldn't tell the story from memory we looked it up and read it. Different card games furnished variety when we were running out of time but we never tired of Bible Challenge. That is pretty much the plan we have followed every year since then. Each year when we meet we look each other up and down and can tell that we are gradually aging but we don't talk about that—the joy and fun of being together never lessens.

**First Tupelo Thanksgiving** Three days after Maggie and the girls left, Benjamin arrived to spend five days. Then Paul and Melonie came for Thanksgiving week. They brought the turkey they had smoked ahead of time and Melonie prepared dinner for the Day including some of her favorite Jamaican dishes. On Thanksgiving Day Henry, Jo Ann, Lee, Robert, Dianne, Nancy, Raymond and Tonya all came with additions to the meal and in the afternoon Pat, Pam, Caleb and Rachel joined us for coffee and dessert.

All year my left hip had been almost unbearably painful. The doctor said the cause was osteo necrosis and replacement surgery was scheduled for January but we still had December to get through. Edward sent a plane ticket for me to spend three weeks with them. There I was lavishly pampered while loafing and reading books when they were otherwise occupied.

**Added Son And Daughter** It was already **2006** when I returned to Tupelo. Pat and Pam met me at the Tupelo airport—the first of many such meetings to take place in the following years. From my first day they had adopted me into their family and I felt that I had gained another son and daughter. Pam cooks the most delicious dinners at Easter, Thanksgiving and Christmas and if I am here during those times I am part of their family for the day. When Pat is not on duty at the hospital or on call, he takes us out to eat after church on Sundays.

**Convalescent Center** After the hip replacement surgery, by my own choice, I went to a convalescent home for recovery and therapy. Robert had looked over the available places in the area and chosen the one that seemed best to him. In my opinion he chose well. At the hospital he and Dianne, Henry and Nancy took turns being with me and monitoring my three day hospital stay. At the convalescent center Beth visited regularly and Pat and

Pam visited often to make sure all was going well. Five weeks later I was back in my apartment, reading books and continuing to recuperate. Pam took me to therapy sessions until I was able to drive myself.

By then it was May and my second year in Tupelo was well on its way. During Maggie's and my annual fall visits from Ohio we had attended church with Beth so it was natural for me to feel at home in the Lee Acres congregation surrounded by like-minded brothers and sisters in Christ. I made it my home church and was warmly welcomed.

**". . . a hundred fold . . ."** From childhood in an isolated foreign missionary family, my siblings and I felt the lack of grandparents, cousins, aunts and uncles. When I married a preacher and moved from one congregation to another, I felt again the lack of close family members. In every case, however, that lack was more than supplied by friendships with the church members. Everywhere I have lived I have experienced and cherished wonderful friendships. In Tupelo such friendships have developed and deepened—all of them precious to me. Everywhere I have lived there has always been one person that from our first meeting has been extra special—a soul mate—and my Tupelo experience has been no exception. I firmly believe the Lord has provided that special relationship for me. All of the friendships on their various levels have made me think about what Jesus said, *". . . there is no one who has left house or brothers or sisters or father or mother or wife or children or lands, for my sake and the gospel's, who shall not receive a hundredfold now in this time—houses and brothers and sisters and mothers and children . . . and in the age to come, eternal life . . ."* In all of my eighty-plus years I have not lacked loving and much loved "kinfolk" of that kind.

**Downsizing** From the ten room farm house to a two-bedroom apartment was downsizing in living quarters, but that was not the only downsizing I did when I moved to Mississippi. In Ohio my doctors had been twenty to thirty miles from home, the nearest mall nearly thirty miles away, supermarkets fifteen, and church about twenty-five miles each way.

In Tupelo my driving was reduced drastically—five minutes to Walmart, eight minutes to church, ten minutes to doctors and the big mall only eight miles away. Of course driving in town doesn't allow my car to get the good miles-per-gallon I had with the longer distances but time-saving is major.

**Projects** With a smaller house to keep and no yard work to do, I had time to do other things. I continued crocheting large afghans for every grandchild who married and baby afghans for each new great- grandchild and that kept me busy in the evenings for some time. In addition I began to see the possibility of having time to work on my long list of other projects. I had read all of my books and while still recuperating from hip surgery I was ready to tackle a day time project.

Thinking about that as I looked through a stitchery catalog, I saw a kit for a blue and white tea cozy in needle point. A long-time dream of mine had been to make a tea cozy and another to do needlepoint and I am partial to blue and white. With this kit I could kill three birds with one stone—tea cozy and needlepoint while enjoying blue and white. Weeks later, needlepoint done, I completed the tea cozy with matching blue fabric lined with batting, every stitch by hand. Project number one was done—now for the next on my list. At some point one of my children asked me how long it would take to do all I had on my list and I replied, "Fifteen years!" They asked, "What after that?" and I replied, "By then I will have added more to the list!"

For years I had wanted to do counted cross stitching, so my next evening project would be eight counted cross stitch pictures, approximately 12'x14', one for each of my children's houses. My choice for each would be what I thought best fit their personality and color scheme. As each was finished I had it stretched and framed under non-glare glass. I knew that cross stitched fabric was not supposed to be put under glass but I was protecting them from dust! That project took eighteen months to complete and was another one I thoroughly enjoyed doing.

**Counted cross stitch pictures crafted for each child.**

**Jeremiah** My new daytime project was to resurrect the long dormant workbook and teacher manual on Jeremiah that I had begun in 1971. In July of 2006 I pulled it from a back shelf and set myself to finish it during day time hours while I did the stitching in the evenings. It took six months to finish the Jeremiah project. Beth asked me to use it for a study in our Sunday morning ladies class and the ladies appeared interested all the way through, bless their hearts! The workbook style was popular in 1971 and by this time it was out of date so whether it is ever used by anyone else is unimportant to me. At least it is done and not just sitting unfinished on a shelf. I can testify that I learned a lot of Bible and Ancient History in the process.

The days, weeks and years were flying and I could see that my counted cross stitching project was taking too long. So after finishing the Jeremiah work I began stitching in the daytime as well as in the evenings. When that stitching project was finished, my evenings were occupied with the making of a long-dreamed-of crazy quilt. I had seen one in someone's home in 1948 and resolved to make one some day. When Joe and I cleared the farm house attic at the beginning of our remodeling, I found a box of neckties that he had saved (he never threw anything away!) My immediate thought then was, "crazy quilt!" Through the years in Ohio I added more of his ties to the collection and Scot and Bob handed over their discarded ties, too. But I never had time to begin the project. When I came to Mississippi I brought over a hundred neckties with me. In April 2008 I planned and actually began the crazy quilt. I had no pattern and made it up as I went, hand stitched throughout. For the next two years it was my consuming evening—and sometimes daytime—occupation.

**Revelation** In our Sunday morning ladies Bible class, for several years, every time we completed a study and talked about what to do next, someone said "I wish we would study Revelations." But that had not happened. When the subject came up again I volunteered to lead a study of Revelation. For the next seven months that occupied my every waking thought no matter what I was doing. Each week I prepared a lesson to hand out the next Sunday in addition to preparing the one we would study that Sunday. I typed them into my computer and printed a copy for each lady to take home. Leaning primarily on God's guidance, I gladly acknowledge five sources of human help: Bennie Lee had taught the book of Revelation so freely I had learned not to be afraid of it. Through the years I had read many explanations of the book and felt the approach he had used was the most true to Bible teaching. That explanation was laid out by four different men that I knew of in four different books written over nearly sixty years. I compiled my study using the Bible and gleanings from those four books: *More Than Conquerors* by William Hendricksen (1949), *Worthy Is The Lamb* by Ray Summers, (1951), *Revelation, An Introduction and Commentary* by Homer Hailey (1979) *Behold! The Revelation of Jesus Christ* by James E. Smith (2008). The ladies stuck with me throughout. We joked in class that if we didn't learn anything else about **Revelation** we would surely remember that the word is singular and never put an "s" on the end again!

All my adult life has been an inward struggle between feeling inadequate and at the same time strong and confident; especially true when standing (or sitting) before adults during the eleven years of ladies' class at Ephesus, in Africa in 1970s, and here in Tupelo. In spite of that the interested response and participation of ladies made me feel that the Lord was using me. When I studied for all those classes I knew what I wanted to say but in class my tongue wouldn't co-operate, so instead of lecturing I usually typed questions for them to do homework and then discuss in class. In my Tupelo classes on Jeremiah and Revelation I used the computer to print out what I wanted to say and then read it, adequate if not ideal in my mind. Children's classes through the years were different and my tongue worked better in them!

**More Handwork** When The Revelation project was completed I concentrated full time, days and evenings, on the crazy quilt. In April 2010 the last stitch was put into the quilt. I did not try to "quilt" the back to the front because I felt it would mar the effectiveness of the embroidery on all of the seams. Instead I "tied" the lining to the front from front to back so that the tie ends were on the lining side. It was òne project that to my mind turned out even better than my dream of it had been and I was proud to give it to my step-children. When I told them it was done I said I could not bring myself to trust it to the postal service so they would have to come to get it—and they did in October. Merry and Scot have promised that they will share the quilt, taking turns keeping it. I have seen them do that with other heirlooms and I know they will be happy with that arrangement.

During the quilt process my children asked if I would make one for each of them. I told them at two years per quilt that would be too much—but that I would make a single 14"x14" square for each of them in the same style, lined and tied in the same way—which I did. [By the way, there are enough neckties left over to make several more big quilts, so if you want to do that the ties are here for the taking!]

Throughout my Mississippi years I have crocheted a total of nine large afghans for grandchildren's wedding presents and twelve baby afghans for great-grandchildren as they arrived, not counting the ones done in Ohio.

Now that I have caught up with the demand I am crocheting extras of both to have on hand for future use.

Several years ago the ladies at church began a "Card Ministry" that went on for some time but gradually fizzled out. My physical limitations have kept me from volunteering on some projects at church but I decided I could be an "Encourager" by sending cards to shut-ins as well as to folks having birthdays and anniversaries. With the preparation of every card I pray a prayer for the receiver.

**Biological Family** Living just around the corner from Beth in our apartment complex has been a real blessing. After Beth retired from keeping babies, my children asked me if in my busy life I was neglecting Beth. I told them we talk to each other by phone at least once a day and sometimes more, we go to church together three times a week besides other church activities, drive to grocery store and hairdresser together every week, to doctor appointments whenever we have them, card shopping every few weeks, baby and bridal showers, occasional weddings. For several months we had a Thursday afternoon Bible reading and visitation time with two shut-in friends—I dropped Beth off at the home of one then went to see another in an assisted living apartment. Reviewing all this "togetherness," we concluded that Beth and I are practically joined at the hip!

Bill visited Beth and me three or four times a year until his sudden death in November, 2009—how we have missed knowing our "little brother" was in Texas and liable to appear at unexpected times. My time in Tupelo has been interspersed with visits of my children from Alabama, California, Florida, Ohio and Texas, along with their sending me airline tickets to fly to their homes for graduations or weddings or family reunions or just for visits, stays varying from two to six weeks. It has become a tradition for Nancy to come every Memorial Day weekend for a wonderful mother-daughter visit. I drive to Athens two or three times a year, taking turns spending nights with Robert/Dianne and Henry/Jo Ann and while there on Sunday mornings driving down to Hanceville to attend church with Nancy and Raymond, eat dinner with them and visit a while before driving back to Athens. And no trip to Athens would be complete without some time with my cherished friend, Donna.

**85th Birthday Bash** As hard as it was to believe, January 2008 heralded my 85th birthday. No argument on my part would deter my children from giving me a birthday party in Athens. It was held in the luxurious Founders Hall at Athens State University. My daughters, daughters-in-law and helpful ladies set everything up beautifully and with my sons, were floating hosts among the more than one hundred and three guests who signed the register. I floated, too—in a daze of joy at being so treated by my children and seeing and talking with so many seldom seen friends and kinfolk.

At my request, each of my children had brought their counted cross stitch picture and after the big crowd was gone the family looked at them together, I wanted each to know what the others had. We had a family supper then gathered in the lounge to sing and visit. Samuel Belo, one of our Filipino "boys," had come from Kentucky to celebrate with us and gave a touching tribute to Bennie Lee's memory and to what his time in our home had meant to him. Afterwards we all wished the Ohio folks could have stayed longer but they said they needed to head north that night.

Sybil's 85th birthday, 2008.

The next day was Sunday and that morning Edward spoke where Henry preaches. That evening we went to church where Robert preaches and heard him. Afterwards the family went to the nursing home to see Edith and sang for her, much to her joy. The next day Maggie and I saw Sharon off in Memphis and Beth and I were happy that Maggie could stay a few more days with us.

**In Loving Memory** On his birthday every October 6, and again in April every year since his tragic death in 1987 at the age of sixteen, I lovingly remember Eric and the happy times we shared.

The month of May always brings to mind Robert and Dianne's loss of Kristen Nichole in 1987. When that date came around in 2008 she would have been twenty-one and I felt inspired to write the following in her memory:

> **Butterfly On The Wing**
> *A butterfly on the wing*
> *Lightly flits among the flowers,*
> *Quickly it is gone from sight,*
> *But the eye is filled with its beauty.*
> *The touch of an angelic spirit*
> *Flutters into mortal life,*
> *Scarcely lingering,*
> *But hearts remember*
> *And cherish the brief encounter.*
> ~ by Sybil Dewhirst, May, 2008

In Loving Memory of Kristen Nichole Fudge Born & Died 5/24/87

**Ohio Visit** In September, 2008 my Ohio children sent me an airline ticket to visit them for two weeks. The first week I spent with Scot. While he was at work each day I worked on the crazy quilt sitting in the well-lighted corner of the breakfast nook in his beautiful kitchen, enjoying the overall feeling of Victorian ambiance that permeates his two and a half story house. Evenings were fun with Scrabble and talking about many things as we played. Saturday we took an interesting ramble through a huge antique mall. On Sunday Merry and I drove to Mason to attend church where I had been a member for fourteen years. The senior class I had attended was still meeting and about two thirds of the class was still made up of people I knew. It was like old home week. Merry and I ate lunch with friends in the Retirement Village Cafeteria then went to visit Lucretia who was in the hospital recovering from a broken hip.

Stormy weather was coming up and we hurried toward Columbus. The far-reaching effects of hurricane Ike were visible all the way. When we got to Columbus we found trees down in places and power off in many areas. I spent the second week at Merry's, working on the crazy quilt while they were at work and playing games in the evenings. One of the week's high points was the evening Merry and I went to dinner in the Southern Hotel Restaurant and then to the restored Great Southern Theater where the Columbus Jazz Band was playing, featuring music from Frank Sinatra and Sammy Davis, Jr. It was an evening to remember.

**Fudge Reunion** For several years the Fudge family had been having a reunion every two years, sometimes around the event of a family wedding and other times specifically a reunion. Plans were made well in advance for the 2009 reunion scheduled to take place at Gulf Shores, Alabama July 25-31. On the 24th I drove to Athens to ride with Robert and Dianne. A three story house on the beach had been rented for the occasion. It had many bedrooms and bathrooms and two very large gathering rooms with a kitchen at the end of each. Forty-two members of my Fudge tribe were able to be in the same house and what a wonderful time we had! During our time together there I realized that all of my children are Senior Citizens—which makes me a Senior-Senior Citizen!

**Maggie's 80ᵗʰ** In early August 2009 Roger surprised me with a phone call inviting me to Maggie's eightieth birthday party being given by her children and step-children. He said he would buy airline tickets for Beth and me to come. Beth said traveling was too hard for her but I told him I would be there with bells on. I could hardly believe my "little sister" was eighty years old. He said they would count on me staying for two weeks and who was I to argue? After a wonderful visit they took me to Phoenix to catch my plane home.

**How Could I Forget?** As I was going through security the agent asked if I realized my driver's license was expired. It had expired in January and I had not looked at it all year. It didn't affect my flight home and I resolved firmly to tend to it at the first possible moment. But fate was against me. I arrived home on Saturday. On Sunday my brakes began failing and I knew that would have to be a priority even before the license. But Monday was a holiday so Tuesday would be the first possible time for brake repairs. Early Tuesday morning all the way to the car dealership I prayed I would not be stopped for a license check. A piece had to be ordered for the brake repair so my car had to stay in the shop overnight. It was ready on Wednesday and as soon as I got it I made a bee-line to the DMV. I expected the examiner to notice the date with eight months expiration and to add a late fee but I was not about to call his attention to it. Nothing was said and I walked out with renewed legality and a resolve to watch my license dates from then on.

# CONCLUSION

It is now 2011 and life in Tupelo goes on with no end in sight of projects lined up—of which admittedly the writing of these memories has been the biggest job and the most difficult. My eighty-seven years so far have been divided into seven completely different lives in seven completely different parts of the world. Every place I have lived has been "the best" at that time, in location, in circumstances and the friends I have been blessed with. As long as the Lord allows me to live I look forward to whatever He may bring about in my life whether here or somewhere else. Whatever or wherever it is I pray that He will use me for His glory. I thank God for His Providence that placed me in the family that He did and I thank Him for memories to share and enjoy with you my children, grandchildren and great-grandchildren—memories I hope will be passed on from you to yours.

Edith Wharton expressed it well in her autobiography: "In spite of illness, in spite even of the arch-enemy sorrow, one can remain alive long past the usual date of disintegration if one is unafraid of change, insatiable in intellectual curiosity, interested in big things, and happy in small ones." These words ring true with me as I survey my life over these 8 decades—a life of many joys and some sorrows, of many changes and many challenges. But God has been faithful, my life is rich in memories, friends and family and my heart embraces the future in hope and joyful anticipation.